VOLUME

6

The New York Times

SUNDAY CROSSWORD OMNIBUS

Edited by
Eugene T. Maleska

ST. MARTIN'S GRIFFIN ❧ NEW YORK

VOLUME

(6)

The New York Times

SUNDAY CROSSWORD OMNIBUS

1 Please Think Twice! *by Bert H. Kruse*

ACROSS

1. Playwright Racine
5. Jazz form
10. Thank-you-___ (road bump)
14. Bellow
18. Farm unit
19. Meyerbeer product
20. "Kiss Me, Kate" co-writer Spewack
21. Sailor's saint
22. National League nine
24. S.A. capital
26. Some Swiss paintings
27. Galsworthy novel
29. Some yuks
30. Speaks tipsily
31. Eyelashes
32. Domino
33. Counterfeit
34. Frenchman's girlfriend
35. Like Smetana's Marie
39. British service-women in W.W. II
40. Great Lake
43. Yamamai's kin
44. Wave, in Pau
45. Flat fish
46. Piques at their peaks
47. Ancient Greek contest
48. Remick or Marvin
49. Super Bowl team: 1988
53. Shun
54. Acted as a figurehead
56. Blore and Porter
57. Hesitated
58. April 1 Abderites
59. Spain's Louvre
60. Army honchos
61. Most perspicacious
63. Oar fulcrum
64. Like the Sabbath
67. Turns rapidly, in Ayr
68. Rodgers and Hammerstein classic
71. Capital of medieval Armenia
72. Stuff to smelt
73. Mickey to avoid
74. Teen bane
75. Budge
76. Galba's "Go!"
77. Helen's abductor
81. Conductor Zubin ___

82. Forgives
84. Dispute, in Durango
85. Punchless punches
86. Snake eyes
87. Prophets
88. Rose oil
90. Sings à la Crosby
93. Apt anagram for notes
94. Cather's "___ Lady"
95. Locks
97. Memorable humorous poet
102. Pine
103. Valuable wood
104. Vienna's river, to Strauss
105. Learning
106. Campfire collection
107. Specks
108. Mothball
109. John L.'s widow

DOWN

1. Elbow
2. Old French coin
3. Rainbow
4. Jewelry item
5. Gaffe
6. Dueling pieces
7. Honey bunch
8. Neb.'s ex-Governor
9. Hobby
10. Tragedy by Euripides
11. Came to earth
12. Dalmatic's relative
13. Wild ducks
14. Scold
15. Actor Vidov
16. Oriental maid
17. Howard and Cey
20. Faith
23. Grads
25. Cardinal points
28. Omnium-gatherum
30. World's longest river
31. Deloul, e.g.
32. Kind of nest
33. More reasonable
35. Divulges
36. Edward or Norman
37. Undermine
38. Had a meal
39. Gobble
40. Prods
41. Root and branch
42. Midwest whitefish
45. Sparling
47. Nautical cry
49. Noted German sculptor: c.1440–1533

50. Fish-eating bird
51. Papal garment
52. Bill attachment
53. Take out
55. Christmases
57. El Greco's birthplace
59. Rec. player
60. Dark-colored goose
61. Unexcitable
62. ___-surface missiles
63. Awards named for Ms. Perry
65. Distinct parts
66. Money in Ankara
68. Developers' interests
69. Grandiose tales
70. Cluck of disapproval
73. Used artifice
75. Anagram for dyes et al.
77. Known, in Nantes
78. Without interference
79. Mortgage
80. Forays
81. Asian ornamental pine
83. Like a goner
87. Watergate figure
88. "___ needs a good memory": Quintillian
89. Brimless hat
90. Tobacco in the cheek
91. Carty of baseball
92. Subject of a Keats tragedy
93. Glaswegian, e.g.
94. ___ time (never)
96. Nigerian native
98. Last word in denials
99. Bill's partner
100. Biblical craft
101. Early Olds

Name Givers *by Victoria Black and Alex F. Black*

ACROSS

1. Who or which
5. November exhortation
9. June honoree
12. Record spinner
18. TV host Philbin
20. Burr role
22. Bring about
23. Sweaterman?
25. Posts for harbor houses
26. Banished Olympian
27. Soviet range
28. Like foo yong
29. Seine sights
30. English walled city
32. "The Morning Watch" writer
33. Surfeits
35. Arcade in ancient Athens
36. Pistil packin' papa?
39. Platters for 12 Across
41. Within: Comb. form
42. They take panes
44. Otherwise
45. "___ Heldenleben": Strauss
46. Trifle
47. Algerian seaport
48. Sheltered at sea
50. Places
51. Minnow man?
56. At the apex
57. The Dark Cont.
60. Cav. units
61. Aix-les-Bains attraction
62. Paternally related
64. Eddy in "Rose Marie"
66. Actress Van Doren
67. Oath taker
68. One of the Huxleys
69. Limnite and hematite
70. Tiny margin
71. ___ Moines
72. Celebrity
73. Man of war?
78. River in Corsica
79. Charged atoms
80. Antonym of c.c.
81. Greek underground: W.W. II
84. Sitcom alien
85. Showy lily
87. Apportioned
89. Mimic
91. Less than lg.
92. Highwayman?
95. Tether
97. "___ Sleep," Odets play
99. Pitchers' handles
100. Poacher's pitfall
101. H.S. subject
102. Pisa's river
103. Hellkite
105. Stem: Suffix
106. Winter melon
108. Porky patriot?
111. Two thousand pounds
112. Toothless
113. Factory
114. Dissimilar
115. Former chess champ
116. Monoski
117. City in S France

DOWN

1. Sticky sweet
2. Pagans
3. Consents concerning
4. Sesame
5. Wakefield's clergyman
6. Nuncupative
7. Rocky peaks
8. Terminate
9. N.Z. or Aussie W.W.I solder
10. Saws
11. Impugn
12. Underworld god
13. Dub
14. Quaestor's cousin
15. Superman's outfitter?
16. Bible book
17. Aye
19. One of the Carolinas
21. Bouts
24. Manumit
31. Clean energetically
32. Sellers' notices
33. Food from orchids
34. Cries of surprise
36. Bates and Badel
37. Zola heroine
38. Profound
40. Carnation variety
41. Hidden gunmen
43. Complain
47. Like Grendel
48. Shaking
49. Elegance
50. ___ Lang, Superboy's friend
52. Some penultimate words
53. Timothy and family
54. J. Baker and M. Hess
55. Deviating, as a storm-swept ship
57. Mixture
58. Leaflet, to a botanist
59. Motorman?
63. Actor Richard
65. Advice to Nanette
66. "And day's at the ___": Browning
67. Tasty
70. Polygamous group
74. Bad-news ball
75. Midday
76. Port near Cadiz
77. Jumped
82. Sanction
83. Resin ingredient
85. African whip
86. Many, many eras
87. Leave high and dry
88. Wynn and Sullivan
90. Is contrite
93. Yucatán's capital
94. Annul
95. Leftover dish
96. Ready for use
98. Raccoon's relative
100. Repelled a mugger
101. Author of "The High and the Mighty"
102. French violinist: 18th century
103. Jezebel's god
104. City near Padua
106. Alouette's neck
107. Chemical suffix
109. Superiors of sgts.
110. Diminutive suffix

3 Intrusions *by Ralph G. Beaman*

ACROSS

1. Add new insulation
6. P.O.W. camp
12. Genii
18. Entrance court
19. Myself, in Melun
20. Cather lass
21. Drug-related
23. A woman's cloak of yore
24. Fervent; strong
25. Skipjack
27. In any way
28. Conked out
29. Very, in music
32. Scale-song phrase
34. Tall Asiatic tree
35. Stick in one's ___
37. Exactly
39. Marker
41. "___ the season . . ."
42. Inventor of an early telescope
46. Roman magistrates
48. Reading room
51. Pinna
52. Refer (to)
53. Females, casually
54. Execrates
56. Deride
57. What to call a Spade
58. Solar deity
59. Fax relative
61. Fan
65. Baker or Bryant
67. "___ take arms . . .": Hamlet
69. Fouls up
71. ___-ground missile
72. Pines
74. Average
76. Father of "robots"
78. Some sighs
79. Cheeses
81. Calmed
83. Octo
84. Hard to get
86. Peruvian gold
87. Measure of film sharpness
89. Break
90. About the science of viniculture
92. Letters on a chasuble
93. Founded (on)
95. French I verb
96. Payment due
99. Land between Aram and Edom
101. "Network" director: 1976
103. Metrical feet
106. Canaveral grp.
108. Scrutinized
110. Branchlike
112. Cohort
114. Former
116. Schliemann and Carter
118. Two-___ (tandems)
120. Christmas-berries: Var.
121. Relative of dill and carrot
122. Conductor Ansermet
123. Gen. with G. Washington
124. Sandy tracts, in England

DOWN

1. Speedy
2. Of a people
3. Viennese park
4. Terriers
5. Denounce
6. ___ Canals
7. Iceberg feature
8. Infections caused by protozoans
9. Smooth: Comb. form
10. Church Society since 1714
11. In an icy manner
12. Genetic letters
13. Site of a fire god's smithy
14. Boxer Jake La___
15. Playlet
16. Worker with black alloy on metal
17. ___ à manger (dining rooms)
19. Postgrad degrees in public works
20. Alternately responsive, as verses
22. Third king of Judah
26. Assam export
30. Skiers' maneuvers
31. Assamese native
33. More embarrassed
36. Achieve
38. ___ all, folks!
40. Dixie tree
43. Child: Comb. form
44. A ___ (from boyhood, to Pliny)
45. First, in Berlin
47. "Vive ___!"
48. Evaluate
49. Title Macbeth held
50. Blood condition: Comb. form
55. This, to Pedro
56. Artifice
58. Polish manually
60. Old chest for valuables
62. Retinue
63. Moral code
64. Spill-wiper on TV
66. C.E.O.'s aide
68. George ___ Welles
70. Class with common attributes: Comb. form
73. Holy
75. Ancient Ethiopian capital
77. Part of N.E.A.
80. Means to ends
82. In a stupid way
83. O. Henry's Jimmy
84. Tall beer glass
85. Operation by an obstetrician
88. Bit
90. Abnormal swellings
91. Domesday Book money
92. Kibitz, in a way
94. Estonian river
97. ___ the belfry
98. African fly
100. She twice played Elizabeth I
102. "The Devil knows how ___": Coleridge
104. Palais social events
105. Nigerian native
107. Upbeats, in music
109. Roman day
111. U.S.C. rival
113. Victorian oath
115. Tough actor
117. Very long time
118. Quarter of four

4 Keeping Up with the Joneses *by Bette Sue Cohen*

ACROSS

1. Errand boy
6. Yankee backstop, once
11. Jewish month
15. Mirror reflection
20. Emulate Cicero
21. Starry hunter
22. Fly alone
23. Jaybirdlike
24. Where Mr. Jones lived?
27. Where Mr. Jones got engaged?
29. ___-de-France
30. Grievously
31. Hate
32. Mailer or Lear
34. Omit
35. Muslim ruler
36. Whirlpool
37. Typesetter's concern: Abbr.
40. Jane, to Peter
41. Late bloomer
42. Italian eight
43. Small hat
46. Fat
48. Where Mr. Jones's fiancée lived?
52. One of a Latin trio
53. Interstice
54. Motet anagram
56. One, in Köln
57. Companion of Aeneas
58. Carved pillar
59. Actress Garr
60. Designates
62. Michigan city
63. French painter
64. Where the Joneses were married?
67. Actress Jackson
68. Kind of wrestling
69. Neighbor of Ont.
70. Abundant
71. Lowly
72. "And ___ is to the living . . .": M.M. Dodge
75. Athenian lawgiver
76. Northern nation
78. New ___, Conn.
80. Hair style
81. "Thief" star
82. PAT preceders
85. Help
86. Where the Joneses had cocktails?
89. An Allen
91. Climbs, in a way
92. Cline classic
93. Appends
94. Lermontov's "___ of Our Time"
95. Laugh riot
96. Item in a chest
97. More timid
99. City SE of San Francisco
100. Sea eagle
101. Where Mrs. Jones threw her bridal bouquet?
105. ___ out (supplemented)
106. ___ Moines
107. Finn's neighbor
108. Broadcast
109. Prill or pyrite
111. Many ft.
112. Ring event
113. Begot
114. Brazilian dance
116. Peace in Israel
119. Gay ___
120. Impede
121. Underworld god
124. Where the Joneses go for Christmas?
126. Where the Joneses live?
129. Wear away
130. Penny ___
131. "Bubbles" author
132. Plunder
133. Golf great
134. Gist
135. Kilmer poem
136. Wing

DOWN

1. Asian desert
2. Spoken
3. Confront
4. Ordinal suffix
5. Della and Pee Wee
6. Rude
7. Was human
8. Ransack and rob
9. Poly's partner
10. Actress Alicia
11. "To make up a year / And ___": Emerson
12. Sorrow, in Sonora
13. Winglike
14. Cartoonist Chast
15. "Is there beauty ___?": Dostoyevsky
16. Wills of baseball
17. Actor Tamiroff
18. Japanese wooden clog
19. Actress Barbara
25. Kubrick film: 1962
26. Gong
28. Heel-___
32. Toot
35. Tennis great
36. Certain collars
37. Whey
38. Bad-tempered one
39. Where the Joneses spend their weekends?
41. Actor in "The Addams Family"
42. Bay window
43. Where the Joneses honeymooned?
44. TV role for Kate Jackson
45. Of the mail
47. Relief
49. Everlasting, poetically
50. Navigational system
51. Greek commune
54. Court call
57. Coeur d'___, Idaho
59. Workers' joyful letters
60. "There is ___ like an old . . ."
61. Solar disk
62. Skipped town
65. Visit
66. Imagist Doolittle
67. F.B.I. agents
69. Marjoram, e.g.
73. ___ Bernard
74. Colleen
75. Egyptian port
76. Actress Dee
77. Means' partner
78. Converted the chips
79. On land
81. Cryptographer
83. Mended
84. Headbands
86. Defeat decisively
87. Discontinue
88. Scottish hobo
89. Pinna
90. Quaker pronoun
92. Appropriate
96. Mental shock
97. Easy or Grub
98. Pay attention
99. "So Big" author
101. Inundated
102. Protection for locks
103. Ireland, to a Gael
104. Navigator's need
110. Singer Kitt
112. City SW of Algiers
113. Annual visitor
114. Elbe tributary
115. Plentiful
116. Females
117. Shofar, e.g.
118. Tub plant
119. Yearn
120. Legatee
121. Actor in "Family Plot"
122. As to
123. River of Charon
125. Camote
127. F.D.R.'s successor
128. Staff

ACROSS

1. Opposing teams
6. Vexed
11. Rockies crest
16. Space renter
17. Of ships
18. Misogynist's attitude
20. Ocean-loving snake?
22. Phantasm
24. Fall back
25. Form of currency
26. Meet the need
28. Squat, broad-mouthed jaw
29. In the center
31. Dutch export
33. Tattered
34. Silkworm
35. Showed nerve
37. Hazard
39. Make leather
40. Expresses joy
41. Dinner course
43. D.C. ballplayer, once
45. Fanatic
46. Bad breaks
48. Deck
49. Like Hume's tomes
50. Framed ursine goatees?
55. Stiffens
59. Indonesian islands
60. CMXXXVI ÷ IX
61. Rope
63. Balanced
64. "The ___ Sanction"
65. Reeking
67. Conference site: 1945
68. Put to the torch
69. Suffix with Boswell or Burns
71. Antarctic penguin
73. Through
74. Raccoon's cousin
76. Doubly stylish
78. Pass for a sports-loving beast?
81. Be unresolved
82. Darn it!
83. Roof section
84. Icy dessert
87. Poorly structured
90. Lost turgor
94. Suit fabric
95. Shopper's tote
96. Take to task
98. Show fear
99. ___'acte
100. Lahore garb
102. Alpine communication
104. Initiate
105. Role for Arnold Moss
106. Appointment
107. Pardon
109. Sesame
110. Judge
112. Wilbur's fleabag?
116. Jacket part
117. Acedia
118. Not as removed
119. Chemical compound
120. Cleric-poet
121. Launderette machine

DOWN

1. Like Australia or Hispaniola
2. Electees
3. Crows' cousins
4. Stage
5. Roil
6. Animate
7. Zodiacal animal
8. One of Frank's exes
9. Siberian tribesman
10. Londoner's lift
11. Give homework
12. Comeback
13. Devon river
14. Stock-market simians?
15. Portuguese resort
16. Unanimously
19. Fine-wooled sheep
20. Dashing fellow
21. Ohio city
23. Prepare turkey
27. Culture base
30. Mock
32. Spot or mark, in Madrid
36. Fleur-___
38. Prides' dens
40. Turns right
42. Fraternal fellow
44. Short-tempered
45. Fictional castle
47. Withdrew
49. Having teeth
50. True
51. Bellowing
52. Nary a soul
53. Bad dog
54. Satanic
55. Shire of "Rocky"
56. Philippine palm
57. Splice
58. ___ jury
62. Critic's blessing
65. Dim
66. Certain couturier's creations
70. Herpetological fruit?
72. S.A.T.'s
74. Municipal
75. Large American cat
77. Sow
79. Actor Keach
80. Marble
82. Codified
84. Commemorative slab
85. Baseball group
86. Altar-lights site
87. William's joint ruler
88. All-out
89. Church official
91. Tizzy
92. More spooky
93. Waggish
95. Shoemaking specialist
97. Require
100. Allen or Lawrence
101. Race: Comb. form
103. Measure of capacity
108. Bangkok native
111. Eastern observance
113. Boniface's domain
114. Emulate Slaney
115. Mine find

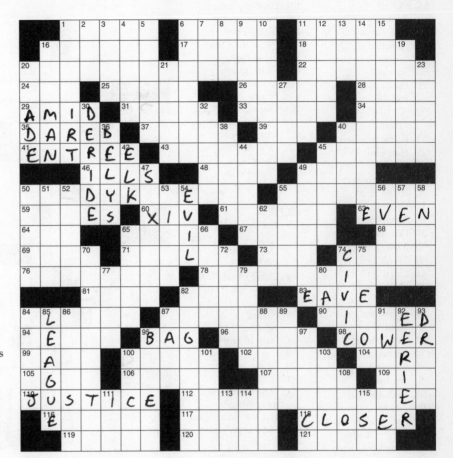

6 Type O' Foolery by Jim Page

ACROSS

1. Bear hug
6. Small shrimp
12. Signified
19. Marx's "____ Speaks!"
20. Hinders, in a way
21. Patrick Duffy, e.g.
22. N.I.H. toast to Perot?
24. Being produced
25. Harmony
26. Wired to Europe
27. Grand backers
30. Excite anew
33. Causing horripilation
37. Old campaigner
38. Claim
40. Tebaldi role
41. Quell
43. Univ. degs.
44. Yoko ____
45. Winter melon
47. Lauder, for one
48. U. of Chicago legend
50. Champ's dramatic account?
55. Soissons soul
56. Biotite
57. Bungo or Rob Roy
58. Pitcher catcher
59. Tough problem
61. Inventor Nikola ____
63. Hag
66. Jacks, e.g.
68. W.W. I craft gambling with turbulence?
72. Surreptitiousness
75. One cubic meter
76. Autocrats
79. Venezuelan writer
80. Psyche parts
83. "As You Like It" lass
85. Harper and Spike
87. "____ Heldenleben": Strauss
88. Congressional register?
92. Iowa city near Oskaloosa
93. Dian Fossey subject
95. Soprano role in "The Barber of Seville"
96. Patriotic org.
98. Conger
99. Make corporate changes
101. Glassmaker's oven
103. Icon feature
104. Big-bang letters
105. Indian "guitar"
106. Nematodes
109. Playwright Sean
111. Hardships
113. Corroborate
115. Certain footwear
118. Boxing, to Pincay?
123. Prepares for another challenge
124. More sanguine
125. Dale or Dwight
126. Darnels
127. Cheetahlike
128. First time out

DOWN

1. Thorax: Abbr.
2. Citizen of Vientiane
3. Discretion follower?
4. Shiny fishing lure
5. Elvis's gift from Ezra?
6. Basted
7. Arabian V.I.P.'s
8. Strip of stripes
9. Balm of Gilead
10. Eating leftover
11. Four pks.
12. Shady magnate's into apples?
13. Organic compound
14. "Ironweed" star
15. Caters to
16. Navy's C.I.A.
17. River to the Yangtze
18. Part of the U.K.
21. "Serpico" author
23. Gamboge or dammar
26. Thigh armor
27. Burst of energy
28. Yellow-tailed thornbill
29. View from the Vosges Mountains
31. Jambalaya base
32. Epps or Moreno
34. Cover a book again
35. Certain nuclide
36. Ingredients of perfumes
39. Ex-Philly Larry ____
42. '70s Highflying stk.?
46. ____ standstill
49. One of the Magi
51. Ruler division
52. Japanese seaweed
53. Advertising signs
54. Thrusting swords
57. Suffragette Carrie Chapman ____
60. Reduced, as goods
62. Syringa
64. Opp. of day
65. Do a bouncer's job
67. Bread for Wimsey?
69. Mann-Kramer sucker bet?
70. Part of a familiar palindrome
71. Gwyn or Quickly
72. Asparagus shoots
73. Capital of Taiwan
74. Screenwriter Lehman
77. Leases again
78. Moon goddess
81. Hades
82. Pix from movies
84. Bergman role in "Casablanca"
86. Like a pretzel
89. Bark in "Annie"
90. Draft status
91. Cowardly Lion portrayer
92. Obtained
94. Monks' adviser
97. Distant
100. Rebels
102. RNA sugar
103. Like some arguments
107. Angers
108. Hawk's home
110. Suffix with talk or form
112. Clarified butter in India
114. Calhoun of films
115. Opposite of sml.
116. Eastern Church chalice cover
117. Jeff Davis's govt.
118. Future grads.
119. Kind of fly
120. Collar
121. Wildebeest
122. Concorde, e.g.

9 *Celebrity Hilarity* by Jeanette K. Brill

ACROSS

1. Turkish title of respect
5. Israeli seaport
9. Watch part
13. Moist
17. Gravy container
18. Archibald ___ (Cary Grant)
20. "___ Grows in Brooklyn"
21. Jannings or Ludwig
22. Ex-President and his supporters?
24. Actress Sally's home construction?
26. Crowd feedback
27. Abzug or Spewack
29. Aegean island
30. Major follower
31. Benedict or Matthew
32. Dernier ___ (last word)
33. Profundity
36. Omni, for one
37. Future benedict
40. View amorously
41. Boston Celtic fan's favorite pastime?
45. Actress Gardner
47. Times of note
48. Therefore
49. English river
50. Former silver coin of Spain
51. Juan Carlos, e.g.
52. Tennis player Margaret's recreation area?
56. Ridge or rib
57. Cowboy hats
60. Share equally
61. Former First Family of Egypt
62. Capacious
63. Clearance sale, in Caen
64. Kitchen gadget
65. Walk cautiously
67. Layer
68. City or game
71. E.T., e.g.
72. Actor-dancer as composer?
74. S.E.C. member
75. Earlier Thailand
76. Scrutinize carefully
78. Stake of a sort
79. Daminozide
80. Tanning agent
81. Café pianist on tour?
85. Church part
86. Contemporary
88. TV backdrops
89. Lost color
90. Inst. at Troy, N.Y.
91. Resources
93. Chard
95. Attack
98. ___ Tshombe, Congolese statesman
99. Unsportsmanlike loser
103. First Chief Justice afoot?
105. Dinah's vacation?
107. "Judith" composer
108. Rose-colored dye
109. Expressing purpose
110. Mech.-eng. degree
111. What arroz is
112. Campus org.
113. One way to go
114. Relating to aircraft

DOWN

1. Israel's Eban
2. Increase in value
3. Hinged fastener
4. Decathlon participants
5. Alaskan native
6. Desist
7. Furor
8. Shield, in Savoie
9. Yet
10. "Don't ___ on me"
11. Lamprey
12. ___ Hat, Alta.
13. Confine
14. "Porgi ___," Mozart aria
15. Type of skirt
16. Entreaty
19. Lod deli tongue
20. Drifting about
23. Plaster backing
25. Scrawny animal
28. Danish composer: 1860–1939
31. Zeal
33. Activists
34. Wading bird
35. Golfer's musical instrument?
36. Watchful guardian
37. Santa Lucia, e.g.
38. Comedian's favorite diet food?
39. President of U.N. General Assembly: 1948–49
41. Look well on
42. Literary device
43. Sculpt
44. Screen
46. Welladay!
50. Copland composition
53. Spine
54. Cantab's rival
55. "M*A*S*H"-er and kin
56. Songstress Vikki
58. Freud's "___ und Tabu"
59. Anon
61. Perfumed bag
63. Hinder growth
64. Singer Page
65. Pravda source
66. Troy
67. Deneb is one
68. "Peanuts" character
69. Drudge
70. Like cups and pitchers
73. Egyptian cottons
76. More strident
77. Swindle
79. Execration
81. A dark brown
82. Back payment?
83. Sights on the Seine
84. Examine again
87. A participant in a bill-of-exchange transaction
89. Sense
91. Love-in-___ (garden plant)
92. Kind of boom
93. "___ Godunov," Pushkin play
94. Upright
95. Slightly open
96. Patola
97. Adjust for sound and sight
99. A flatfish
100. Bed of roses
101. Affirm
102. Item sent to a D.J.
104. Chinese statesman Wellington ___
106. Cut down

10 A Special Kind of Effort by Thomas W. Underhill

ACROSS

1. Stag or buck
5. Bracelet add-on
10. Trite
15. Lighter or tender
19. Prolific auth.
20. Bast fiber
21. Alleviates
22. Approximately
23. Jack London classic, with "The"
25. "___ Western Front"
27. Squeeze the tube
28. Like Times Square
30. Medicinal seeds
31. Wear away
33. Encouraged, as a team
36. Mubarak's predecessor
39. Mar
41. Lengthen
45. Scottish magpies
46. Facing a glacier
47. Wood sorrels
48. Brother
49. Killer whales
50. Author___ Congwen
51. Kennel adjunct
52. R.B.I., for one
53. Electrical unit
54. Author of the European Recovery Plan
59. Grant
60. Divides into three parts
62. Carols
63. Worshiper
65. Approaches
66. Italian poet
67. In wild confusion
68. Designer Cardin
70. Eton boy's mother
71. ". . . closer than ___": Proverbs
74. Berlin's "He's ___ Picker"
75. A. Conan Doyle work
78. Epoch
79. Autry or Kelly
80. The Greatest
81. Tax shelters, for short
82. Ski lift
83. Aim
84. Allen or MacMurray
85. Seraglio
87. Kissed by Henri
88. Certain
91. ___ chance! (good luck!)
92. Stair part

93. Records
95. Be behind
98. Dethroned Titan
101. Parts
103. Process of bone formation
107. Drug effect, sometimes
110. ___ Journal (financial daily)
112. Envelope wd.
113. ___ prosequi (court entry)
114. Hogan's cousin
115. Gaelic
116. Catch flies
117. Hydroxyl compounds
118. Jannings and Ludwig
119. Hammett's "The ___ Curse"

DOWN

1. Herb or weapon
2. Strong as ___
3. Attic
4. Pleads with
5. Set of beliefs
6. Hemmed and ___
7. "___ Blue?"
8. Brooklet
9. Docs
10. Further adventure
11. Stocking color
12. "___ was saying . . ."
13. Mr. Iacocca
14. Los ___ Unidos
15. Cramming, with "up"
16. Scraps
17. "Norma ___," Glaspell novel
18. Low digits
24. Harms
26. "___, you noblest English!": Shak.
29. Alternative to that
32. Fragrant compounds
34. Happens again
35. Zesty feelings
36. Variant
37. Drying structure
38. Evelyn Waugh novel: 1928
40. Ping follower
42. "___ Over"
43. Kind of union
44. Trencherman
46. Movie takes
47. Fanon
50. Arcane
52. Dart
54. Equipment

55. Growing out
56. Island or rabbit
57. Paris subway
58. Herd of stud horses
61. Suit fabric
64. He created "the sack"
66. Biblical king
67. Abreast the middle of a ship's side
68. Called, in a way
69. One of the Forsytes
70. Frays
71. Arabic demon
72. Delete
73. Scarcer
76. Poker Flat creator
77. Field of granular snow
82. Like some suits
84. By ___ starts (intermittently)
85. Ululate
86. Alaskan island
87. Actress Ekland
89. Seventh-___ stretch
90. Substantive
91. Daniel and Pat
94. Amusing

96. Spur wheel
97. Burros
98. First son of Eliz.
99. Biblical loyalist
100. Prefix with chord or meter
102. Noah's eldest
104. Antitoxins
105. Birthplace of Frederick II
106. "Nana" star: 1934
108. A ___ (yours, in Toulon)
109. U.N. arm
111. Spire ornament

11 Words on Parade by Charles E. Gersch

ACROSS

1. Ashen
5. Transparent fabrics
11. New Testament book
15. Cher's former partner
19. Old Irish war cry
21. Fold-up furniture
23. Easy existence
24. Shunned, in a big way
25. Franciscan Abbr.
26. "Ah! je ___ seule," Massenet aria
27. Composer Ned
29. Becomes sunny
30. Enforcement, figuratively
32. Expressions of inquiry
34. Commotion
36. "Do as I say, not ___"
37. "___ sow, . . ."
38. M.I.T., R.P.I. et al.
40. Lamb product
42. Nantes negative
43. ___ Lingus, Irish airline
45. "Holy" city?
47. Irish terriers, e.g.
50. Actor Hayakawa
53. Noted
55. Huarache, e.g.
59. Press on
60. Attacks flies
61. Fast plane
63. Fast's companion
64. "___ Blu, Dipinto di Blu"
65. Pismire
67. J.C. Oates book
69. Ireland, poetically
71. Silk from Assam
73. "We're off ___ the Wizard"
75. Coward's "To Step ___"
77. Vols' home
78. Popular Irish ballad
80. Like Croesus
82. Tree in an O'Neill title
84. Donate, in Dundee
85. ___ France, famed liner
86. Pastoral paths: Abbr.
88. Monoskis
90. Islands off the Irish coast
92. Lincolns' unpopular kin
94. Loire valley attraction
96. Ocellus
97. Prunelle flavoring
99. Engross
100. Ade's "___ Horne"
101. Word before mo
104. Synge or O'Casey work
106. Probe deeply
108. Late, in Lyon
112. Game-show group
115. Ex-astronaut on the Hill
117. Twice CCLI
118. Type of power
119. Start
121. "Ragged Dick" author
123. Son of Lamech
125. Latin I verb
126. "My Wild ___"
128. Vehicle for Molly Malone
131. Five-liners named for an Irish port
132. Wee hoarders of legend
133. Observed
134. Sch. groups
135. Bakers' needs
136. ". . . thrive as best ___" Shak.

DOWN

1. Jai-alai ball
2. Originates
3. River of Ireland
4. Cork-to-Kilkenny dir.
5. Health food also called bean curd
6. ___ potatoes (certain home fries)
7. Meat-and-vegetables combo
8. Former Indian P.M. Shastri
9. Historic Hungarian city
10. Fight ___ (avoid)
11. Tarkington's "The Magnificent ___"
12. First Family at Albany, once
13. Hear a case
14. Anti-child-abuse org.
15. Computer units
16. Acquire
17. ___-well (idler)
18. Heavily favored
20. "Gee whiz!"
22. Spaniard's greeting
28. ___ la Paix, Paris thoroughfare
31. Rib
33. Having tiny openings, as leaves
35. Modern music form
38. St. Patrick's land, for short
39. Move like a snake
41. "Certainly!"
44. Faulkner female
46. First word in Mass. motto
48. O'Flaherty product
49. Laugh in derision
50. Indefinitely, in legal lingo
51. The ___ Isle
52. Slates
54. A West African language
56. Heavy Irish tweed
57. Silly
58. Most suitable for Sprat
60. Bar seat
62. High and low phenomena
66. Norw. news service
68. Actor Gavin of "The Love Boat"
70. ___ canto
72. Llamas' locale
74. Out of ___ (disjointed)
76. Sliced off sharply
79. Scream
81. Followers of: Suffix
83. County in NW Ireland
87. Disgraceful
89. James Joyce collection of short stories
91. Right-hand page
93. The old ___ (Ireland)
95. "Not with ___ . . .": T.S. Eliot
96. Dutch commune
98. Energy unit
101. Loot
102. "Annie ___," 1838 song
103. Prompt
105. Where to find McCarthy, McKinley and McGrath
107. N.Y.U.'s hue
109. Tocsin
110. Helen Hunt Jackson novel
111. Ready for Morpheus
113. Big Bertha's birthplace
114. Oven for annealing glass
116. In recent days
118. Riza Pahlevi, once
120. Scenery changer
122. S. Korean president: 1948–60
124. Basics
127. Fall mo.
129. Environmental watchdog agcy.
130. Wheel spoke: Fr.

12 Reel Connections *by Bette Sue Cohen*

ACROSS

1. One of the Dioscuri
7. Bird of the night
12. Helen of Troy's mother
16. "___ Suspicion," 1943 film
21. Seek ambitiously
22. Nose: Comb. form
23. Concern on Wall St.
24. Ancient city of Egypt
25. CHOREOG-RAPHER
27. ASTRONOMER
29. "___ Cardboard Lover," 1942 film
30. Corrigenda
31. Sacred song
33. Malediction
34. Novelist Murdoch
35. Certain fighter
36. "Mondo ___," 1963 documentary
37. Gelada or pongo
40. Actress in "The Wedding Night"
41. Actress Patricia and actor Tom
42. Capitol Hill list
46. Used a treadle
48. Rich cake
49. Equipped with weapons
50. Defendants, in law
51. Hat adornments
52. CINEMA-TOGRAPHER
54. Mother of Eris
55. Added spirits
56. Carouse
57. Strip
58. Sherlock portrayer, often
59. Actor in "A Summer Place"
60. Capital of Lombardy
61. Coagulated part of milk
62. The March King and family
63. Tennis division
64. FARMER
67. "___ is . . . a refuge from home life": Shaw
68. Hole-___(ace)
70. Congrio, e.g.
71. Eminent
72. Made zzz's
73. LOCKSMITH
78. Scottish cap
81. Piscator
82. Jejune
83. Posts
84. Deli order
85. Rhea's role in "Cheers"
86. Go with the gale
87. Parsonage
88. Compare
89. Fourth-largest Great Lake
90. POULTRYMAN
93. "___ to my remains . . .": Dryden
94. Prepare flax
95. Texas longhorn
97. Author of "The Dynasts"
98. Girl in a calypso song
99. Ramate
101. Dance in a single file
102. Actor in "The Guardsman"
103. Wager
104. Gunfighter at the O.K. Corral
105. Standard
106. Flex
107. A Houston athlete
109. Uses a discus
110. Comedienne Anne and kin
112. Like a March hare
115. LIFEGUARD
117. REPORTER
120. Turned white
121. Puerto ___
122. Red dye
123. Intransitive verb
124. Segal's "Oliver's ___"
125. Stagehand
126. Takes five
127. Unit of electric current

DOWN

1. Singer Johnny
2. He wrote "Off the Court"
3. Boom
4. Sesame
5. Architectural fillet
6. Alters the text
7. Destine
8. "___ Up, Doc?": 1972 film
9. Director Wertmuller
10. Ref. book
11. Protection for a loafer
12. Famous racing site
13. Nice school
14. Condemn
15. Actress Harding
16. Brought into harmony
17. Fruitless
18. Blame
19. Wickedness
20. Arc. dweller
26. Was human
28. Squama
32. Capital of the Beaver State
35. Christie's "___ at End House"
36. Deloul, for one
37. Fameuse and pippin
38. Hairy covering
39. TEACHER
40. Komatik, e.g.
41. Roman Catholic devotion
42. Wept
43. MODEL
44. Rooftop sight
45. Money in Iran
47. Hemsley TV vehicle
48. Actress Feldshuh
49. Ward off
52. Canasta play
53. Magnum ___
54. ___ couture
56. Hot under the collar
58. Spoils
60. He may do some stripping
61. Zygote
62. Clogs or pumps
64. "She ___ Yellow Ribbon," 1949 film
65. College in Ore.
66. Carrot, briefly
67. Place for a bracelet
69. ___ prosequi
72. Trapper
73. More loyal
74. Screen
75. Blake of "Gunsmoke"
76. Dog in "Annie"
77. Señor's response
79. Meeting outline
80. When Grundy was born
81. Vinegary
82. Yearned
84. Heyerdahl's "Kon-___"
86. Precipitous
87. Actress-dancer Champion
88. Native of Riga
91. He commits grave crimes
92. Moll's companion
93. Large handkerchief or scarf
95. Kind of cat
96. Pulse
98. Saki
100. Lower
101. Drive-in waitress or waiter
102. Memorizes
105. Name in fashion
106. Suit
107. Premed subj.
108. Town WSW of Caen
109. BARBER
110. Muddle
111. Check
112. Spouse
113. Ripening agent
114. Streeter's "___ Mable"
115. Wife of Saturn
116. Work unit
118. Garden implement
119. Young seal

13 Sound Orthography *by Daniel Girardi*

ACROSS

1. ___ dixit
5. Actor Gulager
8. Turnery gear
13. Reflexive pronoun
15. Precarious spot
19. Ghastly
20. Norman Mailer book, with "The"
22. Small sandpipers
23. Bitter disagreement
24. Socagers, e.g.
26. Year in Alexius I Commenus's reign
27. Ancient wall word
28. Rhinoceros beetle
30. Mascara neighbor
31. Menilite is one
32. A son of Gad
33. Burt Lancaster role: 1960
37. Slightly tapering
39. City in Tuscany
40. Lunar plain
41. Long-beaked fish
42. Like many needs of the needy
43. Mother superior
45. Pisa divider
46. More pious
48. Opposite of saludos
49. Rapid movements in music
53. ". . . blue ribbons ___"
54. Book by President Carter
56. Diamond man
57. Sticks, e.g.
58. Ditty
59. Indian of N.M.
60. "Star Wars" role
61. Ordinal suffix
62. Actor who produced a director
67. Town west of 91 Down
68. Servant
70. Writer Gardner's namesakes
71. Rigorous
73. Sky bear
74. Sour ale
76. Folkways
77. German admiral
78. Uniform
79. Kind of battery
80. Gospel author
82. Benjamin Britten opera
84. Its symbol is a lion
87. Remunerates
88. Fraction
90. Nimble
91. Theda contemporary
92. Photog. abbr.
93. Slopes
96. Priest saying Mass, e.g.
99. Cato the Elder was one
101. Setting for a Christie classic
103. "Roxana" author
104. English poet-novelist: 1886–1967
105. Slant a certain way
106. Small springs
107. Inst. at Nashville
108. Arnold ___, memorable actor-puzzler

DOWN

1. Ship that brought Miss Liberty to the U.S.
2. Tijuana tender
3. Toil
4. Outflowing branch of a lake
5. Fidel's compadre
6. Scourge of serge
7. One-horned fish
8. Track circuits
9. Ibsen character
10. O'Neill play: 1920
11. Swingers of the 40's
12. Store fodder
13. Always, in Aachen
14. Throne of Israel contender: I Kgs. 16
15. Babiche
16. Doesn't heed
17. Circumspect
18. A suburb of Pittsburgh
20. Hoarfrost
21. Pope's crown
25. Explosive initials
29. Opening maneuver
31. Chimp's cousin
33. Gimlet ingredient
34. ___ van Delft, Dutch painter
35. Midget, in Marseille
36. Baseball's Mike or Tom
38. Stalker in a salt marsh
39. Agitated fits
42. Song popularized by Debby Boone
43. Idolize
44. Sevilla savants
45. Capp and Hirt
46. "Launching the Boat" painter
47. Explorer of N.M.: 16th century
48. Grieg dancer
50. Gaunt
51. Edmonton athlete on ice
52. Whacked
54. Bush's alma mater
55. Glyceride, e.g.
60. Life guard, at times
62. More sapient
63. Literary scraps
64. Superman portrayer
65. One who prods
66. Like street talk
69. Environs
71. Pump part
72. Notable periods
75. Belles-___
76. Impetus
77. Victim of 95 Down
79. Parthenope, for one
80. Emulates Jehu
81. G.I.'s, at times
82. Czech capital, to Czechs
83. Prowl after prey
84. Norman Bates's place
85. Kind of oven
86. Father of Remus
89. St. John follower
91. Gauguin's birthplace
93. Shoe widths for Bigfoot?
94. Military station
95. Hit signs
97. Montreal player
98. Accts.
100. Truncate
102. Chit

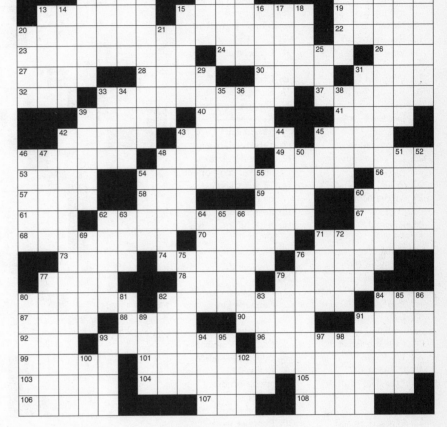

14 Triplets by Richard Silvestri

ACROSS

1. ___ Dhabi, emirate
4. Republican monogram
7. Hexahedra
12. Recon aircraft
17. Celebration conflagration
19. Cropped up
20. Bishop, for one
22. Clad
23. Beethoven's "___ solemnis"
24. Strike callers
25. It's not a moving picture
27. WKRP or WJM-TV
29. Model Macpherson et al.
30. Adorable
32. Give in
33. Visit
34. Drops in the morning
35. Marzipan ingredient
37. C.I.A. predecessor
38. Bucknell mascot
40. Clinch breaker
43. Evidence
45. Party pro
46. "The Haj" author
47. Agitate
48. Strike makers
52. Worked on soles
55. Marching-band glockenspiels
58. Property claim
59. Auditorium
60. One of the Jacksons
61. Makes airtight
62. Eight, in Ancona
63. Bass-baritone Scaria
64. Maxilla, e.g.
65. Makes eyes at
66. Canton's state
67. ___-majesty
68. Doctoral hurdles
70. A foe of Pan
71. Hold on to
72. "Dianetics" author Hubbard
73. Popular
75. Puppeteers Bil and Cora
77. Bodega quaff
79. Hibernia
80. ___ diagram, in symbolic logic
81. Ballet point
82. "Barbarella" director
84. Joy
87. Suitable position
90. Bro, e.g.

91. Tridents
93. "___ pro nobis"
95. Free throw's value
96. Objectives
98. Mortar ingredient
99. "___ Dei"
101. La. senator: 1948–87
105. Clumsy
107. Enmesh
108. Superlatively bad
110. Keyboard instrument
111. Tess, to Hardy
112. Clear the slate
113. Speaker component
114. "Ballet Class" painter
115. Postpone
116. Radical org. in the 60's
117. Thus far

DOWN

1. Demeaned
2. Canner's kin
3. "___ meet again!"
4. Little women
5. Pitcher Hershiser
6. Zoological stalks
7. Revived
8. Spoon-bender Geller
9. Bartlett relative
10. Repplier work
11. Otary
12. Packing a rod
13. Shed tears
14. Landed
15. Loving touch
16. Mono improved
18. Dossier
20. Yanks
21. Ruhr city
26. Seethe
28. Not so much
31. Store fodder
35. Droughty
36. Pickle type
38. Acknowledge applause
39. Sinister or ugly
41. Kind of mirror
42. Afore
44. Solidifies
45. Oater group
47. Narrate anew
48. Ball star
49. Choice word
50. Tightened the shoelaces
51. Busybodies
52. Cioppino leavings
53. M. Atget's companion

54. Author Lurie
55. Unoriginal
56. "The ___ of the Guard": G. & S.
57. Spread unchecked
60. "M*A*S*H" land
64. Knife man
69. Coaster
70. Keeps costs low
74. State flower of Tenn.
75. Units of loudness
76. Black cuckoo
78. Caviar
80. Court decisions
82. Schnitzel meat
83. Gave permission
84. Moist and chilly
85. Quality Ananias lacked
86. Fiduciary
87. Realm of Boreas
88. Adapted to rigors
89. Borgia or Siepi
90. Esther of "Good Times"
92. Pasch
94. Postulate
96. Secluded valleys

97. Stertorous sound
99. "Deutschland über ___"
100. Merriment
102. Portmanteau word
103. Blood state: Comb. form
104. Navratilova rival
106. Salacious
109. Calais-to-Paris dir.

15 First-Name Game by Peter Swift

ACROSS

1. Sailor, e.g.
4. Flirt with
8. Packs down lightly
13. Lister, e.g.
17. Tucked in
19. Writer Calderon
20. Brand new
22. Shankar, the sitarist
23. Dramatist de Vega
24. Mine, in Marne
25. Egypt's second president
26. Black cat, to some
27. Wine dregs
31. Pittsburgh athlete
32. Reno-to-Las Vegas dir.
33. English royal family
34. Misplace
35. Southern constellation
39. Command to Fido
40. Where the Miami flows
43. Shipshape
46. ___ over (collapses)
48. Some salad days
52. Low-cut shoes
54. Ticket-booth sign
55. Hiked, in a way
57. Word with jack or stick
58. Housebreaks
60. One of the Near Islands
62. Penny dreadful or shilling shocker
64. A marzo date
65. Clear
66. Certain tides
68. Greek letter
69. This, to Caesar
70. Fishes
77. Choler
78. Brazil's ___ Branco
79. Africa's largest city
80. ___ de la Cité
81. Year Claudius I died
82. Bon vivant
85. Atop
86. Western squatter
90. Annealing oven
92. Most crafty
94. A.L. member
96. Narrow groove
97. R. Wilbur's "Walking to ___"
99. Cartoonist Dean
100. ___ Blair (George Orwell)
102. ___-froid (calmness)
103. Supporting
105. Guys
107. Tear apart
109. Fun and games
113. Basinger of films
115. Fence in
119. Linear measures
124. Water body east of the Caspian
125. Cringe
126. Space
127. A Phillies' manager: 1987
128. Egg-shaped fruit
129. Lofty
130. Poet Lazarus
131. Lyricist Evans
132. Eucharistic rite
133. John Herzfeld TV film: 1987
134. Views
135. Lawyer's thing

DOWN

1. Arrests
2. Cancel a bombing mission
3. Plains Indian shelter
4. Most abject
5. Weapons manufacturers
6. A portmanteau word
7. They are often split
8. Heredity factors
9. Med.-sch. subject
10. Rumple
11. Attention getter
12. Cryptesthetic people
13. Validates a will
14. Debussy opus
15. Open
16. Paul McCartney band
18. Darkroom activity
21. Victorian expletive
28. U.N. agency
29. Ski wood
30. Clubs, e.g.
36. Juno, to Cato
37. Check
38. Furthermore
40. Elect
41. "Ben-___"
42. Cohan's "___ Popular Man"
44. Tabriz native
45. Auto court
47. Cleave
49. Diplomat Root
50. Rock bottom
51. Off-color
53. Scornful looks
56. Keep in custody
59. Runways
61. Take a powder
63. Scoops
67. Impertinent lass
70. Parts of wads
71. Mirador
72. River Quay
73. Dough
74. Flock
75. Boo-boo
76. Author's "jackpot"
83. Teases
84. Kind of caterpillar
87. Singing syllable
88. German article
89. Scandal sheet
91. Herpetologist's subject
93. Celebes, e.g.
95. Boring
98. Betsey ___ (Dickens character)
101. British movie theaters
104. End
106. Title Pinero had
108. TV adjunct
109. Sacred song
110. Trajan's courtyards
111. Furrows
112. Misjudged
114. Traditional customs
116. Edmonton hockey player
117. Slyly sarcastic
118. Kin of 21 Down
120. Actress Witherspoon
121. Enthusiastic
122. Fermented drink
123. Seward Peninsula city

16 Plus Factor by Louis Sabin

ACROSS

1. Diner staple
5. Gibe
10. Broadcasts
14. Secrete
19. Caravansary
20. Comicality
21. Warhol style
22. Where St. Paul was shipwrecked
23. In company
24. Papas or Bordoni
25. Water wheel
26. Actress Burstyn
27. Like a poor pickpocket?
30. Dogs, when riled
32. Mason's burden
33. Baum dog
34. Leo's pride
35. Cut
36. "Auld Lang ___"
37. Depend
38. Typeface
40. Fleet or Easy
42. Comfort
45. Thames boats
46. Short queries
47. ___ Islands, near the Shetlands
51. Lancelot's hair-raiser?
54. Houston pro
56. Took long steps
57. Gillette razor
58. Out of bed
60. Act up a storm
62. Asian weight
63. Drink lead-in
65. Culloden Moor wear
66. Securities expert
67. Some records, briefly
68. Nancy three-some
69. Inventor Howe
71. Prickle
73. Post or Balbo
75. Grain coats
76. Elected
77. Throng
78. Except for
81. Ream unit
82. Fraser of tennis
83. Rainbow
86. Tommie of baseball fame
87. Loser at Little Bighorn
89. Monkey's uncle?
91. Leyte neighbor
93. Wampum item
94. Hebrew measures
95. Command at West Point
96. Completed
97. Relay finisher
99. Welles of "Touch of Evil"
101. Gentle renters?
104. Critic
105. Nero's 1105
106. Fix loosened laces
108. Most exceptional
109. Do over
111. Vague and Zorina
112. First space travelers
113. Indonesian island
116. Choice words
117. Label designation
118. Suit or chute fabric
119. Navy noncom
122. Mischievous
124. Would-be Duses?
128. ___ acids
129. Halley novel
131. Bar-mitzvah reading matter
132. Any rich man
133. Boxlike sleighs
134. Swiftly
135. Boot out
136. A.L. batting king: 1954
137. Ringlet
138. D-day craft
139. School furniture
140. Shade of blue

DOWN

1. Greeting
2. Cuckoopint, e.g.
3. Emulated Kathleen Barne
4. Utilitarian style of design
5. Evasive
6. Article of virtu
7. Indication
8. Former Senator from Hawaii
9. Author of "Lee's Lieutenants"
10. Fine china
11. Trireme tool
12. Architectural curve?
13. Tourists, at times
14. Merganser
15. Starting five of Chamberlain, Bol, Ewing, et al?
16. Kegler's venue
17. Unyielding
18. Merchant guild
19. Cummerbund
21. Unity
28. Galsworthy novel
29. Long-stemmed palm
31. Run up a tab
37. Hindu tunes
38. Spring months
39. Talk-show invitee
40. Peale appeal
41. Triton
42. Brinker's blade
43. Surmounting
44. Turkish coins
48. Barbecue choice
49. "___ Psyche": Keats
50. Conger chaser
52. Post-spat activity
53. Nobelist after Wiesel
55. Zola's "La ___"
56. African wildcat
59. ___ Lederer (Ann Landers)
61. Elevenses cart
64. Actress Garr
66. Athens of America
70. Calvary soldier
72. Tool for Mrs. Wiggs
74. Vexes
75. Raised unreliable fish?
76. The mating game
77. Actress Berger
78. De Brunhoff elephant
79. Rocket stage
80. Jump away in sudden fear
81. Antithesis of surfeit
82. Italy's third largest city
83. Song by Tosti
84. Shoe strips
85. Peak
88. Places to pawn Stephen King's books?
90. A Muslim month
92. Venerate
95. Allergic response
98. Bauxite or galena
100. Kitty Hawk name
102. Bore
103. "Ah, woe!"
105. Dillon or Earp
107. Picked up the tab
110. Miss Piggy's pronoun
112. Powers
113. Modify to suit
114. Maholi or maki
115. Sheeplike
117. "Cheaters"
118. Nibble
119. Kind of servant
120. Shakespeare contemporary
121. Pelion's support
123. Setback
125. Noah's bird
126. Flag
127. Flagstad or Gluck
130. Make doilies

17 How to Achieve Happiness by Eugene T. Maleska

ACROSS

1. Start of a Stepquote
6. Noted conductor-composer
12. Singer Anita ___
17. Anno ___
18. Emend
19. Skipped over
21. Rife
22. Paradigms or paragons
23. Solve a "weighty" problem
24. Mellow
25. Kind of duck or sisal
27. Woodworkers' machines
29. On this side: Prefix
30. Seat in a bay window
32. Stepquote: Part III
34. Map abbr.
35. Like some bloomers
36. Zola and Berliner
38. One in a roll book
40. Kind of box
41. Chub
42. Insipid
44. Elman's teacher
45. Clandestine
46. Eagerly expecting
48. ___ Rabbit
49. Beau Brummell, e.g.
50. "___ Memorandum," Stepquote source
54. Subject of a long Frost poem
58. Plath work
59. Third person: It.
60. Light-amplification device
61. Old French coin
62. "___ Macabre"
63. Stepquote author
65. Independently
67. From ___ Z
68. Caesar's "I seize"
70. ___ Domingo
71. Inflections
72. Most abundant Atlantic Coast fish
74. Hurdles in Hollywood
76. Vendition condition
77. Joan or Marian
78. Hot spot for hops
79. "McGraw's boy"
82. Heart
83. Part of a lamp
85. Jelly ingredient
89. Courses for horses
90. Puccini opera: 1926

92. La ___, town in Spain ("The sunny spot")
94. Einstein's fourth dimension
95. Amazon estuary
96. Stepquote: part V
98. Red-ink entry
99. March 15 in Milano
100. Venus ___
102. In olden days
104. Hwy.
105. Jury panel
107. Screed
109. More reticulate
111. Crown protector
112. Scab, as after a burn
113. Regard highly
114. Purpose of a hansa
115. These make flights
116. End of Stepquote

DOWN

1. Grand; imposing
2. Elec. unit
3. Practical
4. Sicilian resort
5. Stepquote: Part II
6. Archbishop
7. Edit
8. Anne Baxter role: 1950
9. Perfume container
10. Nantucket native
11. Future fledgling
12. Left Bank headgear
13. Alternative to lagers
14. Baby sea otter
15. School
16. Diseur
17. First European to reach India by sea
20. Home of a sidewinder
21. Tore
26. Saroyan hero
28. "Some ___ meat. . . .": Burns
31. Certain ointments
33. Stepquote: Part IV
35. Existed
37. Recipe verb
39. Swarm, in Sedan
40. Presides
43. Losses of last letters
45. Preserve
47. Airs via video
48. Honeysuckle, e.g.
49. Ignominy
50. Choleric
51. Sheer fabric
52. Dickens villain
53. He's faithful to Homo sapiens

54. Dispatch
55. Intended
56. One of Sheridan's "Rivals"
57. McAuliffe's reply in 1944
58. Costa loser
60. Singer Cristy ___
64. Aromatic Himalayan plant
66. Ufficio ___, Italian mail center
69. Collier's access
73. Caucasian, to a Polynesian
74. Author Davidson ("Loose Change")
75. Signal after tattoo
77. Increase Mather was one
79. Reason
80. Plain
81. Arranged in thin plates
82. Radioactive minerals
83. Chorines: Slang
84. Give it ___ (attempt)

86. Divine messenger
87. "To a newspaperman a human being is ___ . . .": Fred Allen
88. Teacher, at times
90. Scot's cap
91. Hindu's "tree of the gods"
93. U.S. folk singer
95. A Shakespeare contemporary
97. Stepquote: Part VI
100. Stowe book
101. Relative of "Jaws": 1977
103. Caesura
106. "___ Stranger Here Myself," ultimate source of Stepquote
108. Hawaiian tuna
110. ___ Aviv

18 Heaven's Above! *by Warren W. Reich*

ACROSS

1. Jack preceder
5. Grimalkins
9. Italian coin of yore
14. Young pest
18. Bombay bigwig
19. Kauai greeting
21. Polynesian garment
22. Miff
23. His business is looking up
25. Unresolved
27. Actor Alan from Allestree
28. Tones down
30. Becloud
31. Chrysler cars of 1928–61
34. Grape variety
35. Assumes
39. Weapon for D'Artagnan
40. Luster
41. In a pacific way
42. Graduate-school hurdles
43. Sort of friend
45. By way of
46. One-stripe G.I.'s
47. Low blow
48. Had regrets
49. Guns an engine
50. Yes, to Nanette
51. Regardless of
55. Palmists' interests
56. Naval unit
58. Inclined
59. Hindu scripture
60. Soviet range
61. Ceramists' needs
62. "When the ___ breaks . . ."
63. Harasses
65. "Whom shall ___ . . .": Isa. 6:8
66. British sneaker
69. Befuddled
70. Elated
72. Be human
73. S. Korean soldiers
74. Actress-writer Chase
75. Time past
76. So long, in England
77. Half of MIV
78. The world over
82. Any rich man
83. Ornamental shrub
85. Laconian serf
86. Break one's word
87. More irascible
88. Noted name in polio research
89. River into Monterey Bay
90. Big A offshoot
91. Keglers' milieu
92. Macho type
93. Dreamily romantic
97. Like 93 Across
102. Domingo specialty
103. ___ nous
104. Part of a TV transmission
105. Parched
106. Obey a cheerleader
107. In a stupor
108. Combo
109. Gush forth

DOWN

1. Browning's "___ Lippo Lippi"
2. ___ Cruces, N.M.
3. Carpenter with six legs
4. Precooks
5. Stage name for Mr. Iskowitz
6. Fugard's "A Lesson From ___"
7. Collins and Mix
8. Haggard romance
9. Cool Italian dessert
10. French dynast
11. "The Angry Hills" author
12. Hideaway
13. Surpassed in audacity
14. City on the Weser
15. Inlet
16. "The Greatest"
17. ___ Borch, Dutch painter
20. More chichi
24. "Cybele" author
26. Backpacker
29. Once more
31. "A ruddy ___ manly blood": Emerson
32. Scolding
33. Phrase from "America the Beautiful"
34. Van Dine's Vance
35. Ha-ha
36. What Jimmy Stewart was in during 1937
37. Twist of fiction
38. Former name of Lake Malawi
40. Bathhouse of a sort
41. Air-show feature
43. Frustrates
44. Seed coverings
47. Victoria and Reichenbach
49. Saturn features
51. Lasso
52. "La Valse" composer
53. Apt anagram for notes
54. Veda adherent
55. Summa cum ___
57. Persea and poon
59. A thousand kilograms
61. Caricaturist Berger
62. Scottish offspring
63. "Viva Maria!" actress: 1965
64. Arc de Triomphe locale
65. Printer's roller
66. Weevil feature
67. Philosopher José ___ y Gasset
68. Cleans the slate
70. Not so fresh
71. English stargazer: 1868–1939
74. Beholden
76. Lilliputian hallmark
78. Condos
79. Expressed gratitude
80. Wife of Hercules
81. Phoenician name of Dido
82. Hold up
84. Like some modern music
86. Martinet
88. ___ Coeur (Paris landmark)
89. European finch
91. Figure-skating jump
92. "If I ___ Million," 1932 movie
93. Hawthorn
94. Vein yield
95. Wildcatter's quest
96. Genetic initials
98. Keeve
99. Opposite of nope
100. Afore
101. Kind of line

19 All Ears by Alfio Micci

ACROSS

1. Con game
5. Mighty mite in a computer
9. Withheld
13. Kitchen ender
17. Ancient Greek flask
18. Mozart portrayer in "Amadeus"
20. Structural bar
22. Center
23. Fleet V.I.P.'s
25. Movie star of the 30's
27. In a pleasant manner
28. Dated
30. Ideate
31. Dress material
32. Residue
33. Spare
34. Ess follower
35. Veranda
37. Dispatch
40. Approached
42. Fade-out
44. Kind of seal
46. Not so much
47. Honshu city
48. Fay of old flicks
49. Kirghiz range
50. Scamp
51. Reconnaissance groups
55. "___ of robins . . .": Kilmer
56. Cunégonde's creator
58. Suit material
59. Survives
60. Satiric twist
61. Henry IV's birthplace
62. States of pique
63. Student's action or electives
65. Folk-rock singer Jim
67. Certain barren area
70. Please, in Bonn
71. Fairy-tale title
73. "___ tu," Verdi aria
74. Composer Siegmeister
75. Hawthorne's "The Marble ___"
76. Cambodian neighbor
77. Godunov, e.g.
78. Itch
79. Christina Crawford book
83. Sanguine
84. Bypasses
86. Mignon lead-in
87. ___ capita
88. Table scraps
89. Group once ruled by J.E.H.
90. Descent
94. Beautiful woman
96. Full follower
98. Arlington, Va. structure
99. Alan Bates movie: 1966
101. Taking the lead
103. Fancy
104. Spanish commune
105. A hydrocarbon
106. Word with shoppe
107. Saucy
108. Modernists
109. Jane of fiction
110. "Camino ___," Williams play

DOWN

1. Syrup source
2. More lucid
3. "A grief without ___ . . .": Coleridge
4. Reconciles
5. Byron's "___ Harold's Pilgrimage"
6. Burly antecedent
7. "Now ___ me down . . ."
8. P.O. item
9. Affinity
10. London statue
11. Reduce
12. Actor Reed
13. Prickly: Comb. form
14. "And there's little ___ . . .": Kingsley
15. Tough trip
16. Rocket attachment
19. Chabrier favorite
21. Dormant state
24. Like lions or zebras
26. Elm's offering
29. Kin of P.D.Q.
33. Horne and Nyman
35. Nimble
36. Drenched
37. Delhi garb
38. Daredevil's trait
39. Famine's antithesis
40. Remote telecast
41. Very loud
42. Condemn
43. Small centipede
45. Morse-code signals
46. Actress Ullman
47. Scorching
49. Singer Baker
51. Rhone feeder
52. In ___ (having difficulty)
53. Attain
54. More loyal
55. Leaf-stem angles
57. Stale
59. Makes beloved
62. Patten's cousin
63. Mind
64. Mushroom caps
65. Finn and Sawyer, e.g.
66. Actor Santoni
67. Hell kite
68. Squirrel's nest
69. Lieutenant, to a private
71. Emulates Petruchio
72. Freeman's "R. ___"
75. Arm
77. Escamillo, for one
79. ___ Castle, historic Cuban fort
80. Sheds
81. Sweet syrup used in the East
82. First to come
83. Fashion's Oscar de la ___
85. Almond confection
87. Turpentine component
90. "Villa" composer
91. Spry
92. Town ENE of Lucknow, India
93. U.S. conductor-composer
94. Seek's companion
95. Lulu
96. Funeral sight
97. Palindromic name
98. Like heaven's gates
99. Monetary unit of 76 Across
100. Layer
102. Creator of Arthur Gordon Pym

Reverse Orders *by Jacques Liwer*

ACROSS

1. He played Mr. Chips
6. Joyous celebration
10. Barb of a feather
15. "Driving ___ Daisy," Uhry play
19. A symbol of purity
21. Elbe feeder
22. Major Joppolo's post
23. Region
24. Lively, to Solti
25. ENDURE YOURSELF!
28. Still burning
29. Loti contemporary
31. Hermes' mother
32. Mahoganylike wood
33. Sister of a padre, e.g.
34. ___-de-boeuf (a window)
35. Biblical sage: Prov. 30:1
37. Sleep, food, etc.
39. Divided
41. PORTRAY YOURSELF!
45. Painter George ___ Tour
47. One of the Joneses
48. Zinke player
53. Hunter's hideaway
56. Fellies
58. Felt eager
59. "Do not go gentle ___ . . .": Thomas
60. Most magnificent
63. SNUB YOURSELF!
66. Govt. man
67. Special kind of plane
69. What Bassanio pressed
70. Somber
71. ___ publica
72. Improper
74. ___ out (makes last)
76. Bellini's Norma, e.g.
79. Type of steam locomotive
81. PROMOTE YOURSELF!
85. One amok
88. Bone: Comb. form
89. Charles of the silents
90. Heath
94. Bath-to-London dir.
95. Wk. day
97. Boat cover
99. Greek letters
101. Muscat resident
102. UNDERSTAND YOURSELF!
107. Turncoat
109. ___ Nagy, Hungarian hero
110. Choreographer Ailey
111. Scene of Perry's victory
113. Loamy deposit
114. Pertaining to Gaius Julius
116. Certain Jayhawker
119. Polanski movie: 1980
120. OPPOSE YOURSELF!
128. Cowboy's cow catcher
131. Victor at Gettysburg
132. Reeking
133. Heraldic band
134. Flock member
135. SHAPE is part of it
138. ___ Beach, Fla. resort
140. Kafka heroine
142. Bani-___, ex-president of Iran
143. WELCOME YOURSELF!
147. Issued
149. Cartoonist Peter
150. Jubal's invention: Gen. 4:21
151. Biblical trader
152. Pribilof Islands, e.g.
153. Yellow-fever conqueror
154. "To a Steam Roller" poet
155. Actor Auberjonois
156. Monoskis

DOWN

1. One of the Websters
2. De Havilland or Hussey
3. To wit
4. Eureka!
5. Bye-bye
6. Hollow, as a pipe
7. "Iacta alea ___"
8. Work or play preceder
9. Verdi opera
10. Trujillo of the Dominican Republic
11. Nabokov novel
12. Gin poles
13. Biblical preposition
14. Manhattan section
15. Stomach
16. Incensed
17. Sans ___ (type style)
18. Leader before Mubarak
19. Lively dance
20. Disney character
26. Of a 24-hour period
27. "Mon ___," Tati film
30. He, in Napoli
36. Having secret meaning
38. British radio navigational aid
40. Livy's tongue
42. Swathe
43. Chilean mountains
44. "The Plague" author
45. Habit
46. Last stage of strategy, in chess
49. Exclamations
50. Within: Prefix
51. Bayard or Bucephalus
52. Statue with limitations
53. Edible fiber
54. Bedeck
55. Nightmares
57. Stallion
58. Toscanini
60. Kókon
61. Fret
62. Summer Olympic site: 1964
64. Copter cousin
65. City NE of Venice
68. Composer Janácek
73. Make happy
75. He wrote "Where the Money Was"
77. Photographer Morath
78. Nile end
80. A martial art
82. Eyepieces
83. Erect
84. TV's "Quantum ___"
85. Ward healer
86. Soul
87. Pic ___, Andorran mountain
91. Writers Levin and Wolfert
92. "___ Cradle": Vonnegut
93. Burrows of Broadway
96. Sexologist Havelock ___
98. Ajaccio and Algeciras
100. Heliacal
103. Rebecca, Benjamin and Adam
104. ___ Marie Saint of films
105. Because
106. ___ du Sahel, town in Mali
108. Buck book
112. Concluding part
115. Time periods
117. Sin
118. Small anchors
121. Gulch
122. River at Frankfurt
123. Tray
124. Push and shove
125. Sounded off
126. Rot-resistant woods
127. Cousin of wimpish
128. "Villa" composer
129. Informed
130. Catcher in the Rhine?
131. Cuban jazz artist Santamaria
136. Molecule part
137. Matador charger
139. Department in N France
141. City north of Des Moines
144. Israeli airport
145. Otology subject
146. Diva Merriman
148. Suffix for manor or baron

ACROSS

1. Highly seasoned fowl dish
6. Bamboo outrigger
13. "___ on Film"
17. Prohibits
21. Pleiades hunter
22. Containing a radioactive element
23. Whine
24. Irish island
25. "They must be crocuses"
27. Ballet bend
28. Sitarist Shankar
29. Quarter of four
30. Eras
31. Bone depressions
33. Spurred, with "on"
34. Nursery king
36. Revealing
37. American Revolution general
38. "... tomorrow is another day"
44. Tearful
45. River in Venezuela
46. Rumor
47. Wind sound
48. Ear: Pref.
51. Faction
52. Partake
53. Britain's emblem
55. Ancient Greek physician
57. "... but we must cultivate our garden"
60. Sudden burst of activity
63. J. Wilbrand's discovery
64. Think
65. Extinct people of Brazil
66. Dry table wine
68. Jai-alai ball
70. Actor Novello
71. Free-swimming aquatic life
73. Recluse
76. Entwiners
79. U.S. painter: 1871–1951
81. Mother-of-pearl
82. Gaucho's rope
83. Practice
86. Adriatic port
88. Controlled the water flow
92. "___ a Californian...": Frost
93. Comedian's foil
95. Coney
97. Hail!
98. In the thick of
100. Puppy cry
101. "Mine never shall be parted, bliss ___": Milton

104. "... yes I said, yes I will Yes"
106. Church officer
107. Squealers
109. ___ Sadat
111. Injury
112. Fed. benefit legislation: 1935
113. Ugandan exile
115. Into pieces
118. "West Side Story" girl
119. Helmet-shaped plant part
121. "I been there before"
124. Showed clemency
126. Certifying officer
127. Imitate an owl
128. "Tiny Alice" playwright
129. Richardson novel
130. R.I.P. notice
132. "___ Misérables"
135. ___ Horizonte, Brazilian city
136. Attorney's concern
137. "...now it's already Tennessee"
142. Former labor leader
143. Russian river
144. ___ often (repeatedly, to a fault)
145. Tots' hero
146. Zeus's wife
147. Trust with "on"
148. Car fuels: Brit.
149. Water mammal

DOWN

1. Where Dryden lived
2. ___ for one's money
3. Citrus fruit
4. Unruly throng
5. Helle's stepmother
6. Government concern
7. Comic Johnson
8. Soviet news agency
9. Geom. figure
10. We, in Roma
11. Explosive laughs
12. Ore. port
13. Attach
14. "The ___ Archipelago": Solzhenitsyn
15. Nobelist Wiesel
16. Shoe width
17. Gondolas
18. "Good night, Grace"
19. Prowl after prey
20. Sarcastic
26. Polynesian drum
32. Popular plastic
33. "___ bragh!"
34. Waxed, old style
35. Be in debt
36. Ky. college
37. Gazelle of Tibet

38. Braggart
39. Sedative
40. Pest
41. L.B.J.'s V.P
42. Madison Ave. come-on
43. Lamp-shade support
44. Growing in elevated areas
47. Calif. city
49. Domingo or Kraus
50. Humdingers
52. Plaice's place
54. Dancer Michio ___
56. At the vertex
58. Mezzo-soprano Jones
59. Philanthropic person
61. Less bland
62. Verse rhythm for Keats
67. Marco Polo was one
69. Sediment
72. Harmful fly
74. Within: Prefix
75. Actress in "Winterset"
77. French quisling
78. Lack of muscular coordination
80. Nineveh was its capital

83. Hoarfrosts
84. Ludwig and Jannings
85. "... people don't do such things"
87. "___ and the Rock": Wolfe
89. Biographer of Michelangelo, et al.
90. "___ fear to kindle your dislike": Shak.
91. Molelike mammal
94. Choose
96. Capek play
99. Kerry city
102. Weakly
103. French wave
105. Ray or beam
108. Pan-fry
110. "Chances ___," Mathis hit
114. Kind of sch.
116. Shore-dinner morsel
117. Nation of Minsk
118. Muscle: Pref.
120. Small interstice
121. Plain
122. Afr. horned mammals
123. Ecclesiastical court
124. State of Malaysia

125. West Point freshman
126. Twangy
129. Peel
130. Actor Kruger
131. Life sci.
132. Alfred ___ of stage fame
133. Patron of Tasso
134. Lead-role player
136. Mongrel
138. Universal-time initials
139. That woman
140. Service gp.
141. Ship's channel

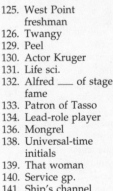

Fractured Phrases by Charles M. Deber

ACROSS

1. Scoundrel
4. Angels' headgear
9. ___ as the eye can see
14. Fixed or frozen follower
19. Fabulist George
20. Two-line verse
21. Beach
22. Weather, to a poet
23. Israeli airport
24. Tailor trousers
25. Pauline's problem
26. Exhausts
27. Silkworm
28. Routines
29. Frauds
30. Inclination
31. Get lost, after four
35. They may justify means
36. Total: Abbr.
37. Appraise
38. Bought time?
40. In particular
43. L.B.J. beagle
45. Diamond and Lagerlöf
48. W. S. Porter
49. Mata ___
50. Devour, after five
53. Penn and Tell, for short
54. Famed marbles
56. Map
58. Selves
59. Max and Buddy
60. Parboils
62. Newman and Revere
63. Bullfrog's sound
66. Right to the jaw, after four
68. "Dames ___," 1968 musical
69. Double features
70. "Mikrokosmos" composer
71. Stadium sounds
73. That, in Toulouse
74. Closefisted
75. Slightest
76. French vineyard
79. Broiled entree, after three
83. Land contract
85. Frightens
87. Eroded, as a river
88. America's Uncle
89. Warehouse function
90. From now on
94. West African country

96. "Tin ___," 1987 film
97. Osiris's wife
100. Specialization, after eleven
105. Christie's Miss ___
107. Novelist Sinclair
108. On one's toes
109. Afore
110. An Astaire
111. Shoe plate
112. Actress Verdugo
113. Operated
114. Frenzied
115. Lasagna or linguine
116. Flax fabric
117. 1 or 66, e.g.
118. Chest: Pref.
119. Skills, in Sevilla
120. Untidy
121. Word of assent

DOWN

1. Writer Carr
2. Cherish
3. Commemorates
4. Disappointments, after four
5. ". . . and pulled out ___"
6. Numbers game
7. Black Sea port
8. Sun. talk
9. Humane org.
10. Shaves a sheep
11. Style
12. Beard of grain
13. R.C., e.g.
14. Play parts
15. Deli specialties, after seven
16. Sea songstress
17. Correct a text
18. Exams
29. Hitler's architect
30. Freud contemporary
32. Arabian sultanate
33. Frome or Allen
34. Lioness or Lanchester
39. Yalie
40. At present
41. German physicist
42. Baseball's Sparky
44. Parachute strings, after four
46. Breed of cattle
47. Fur piece
49. Certain U.S. resident
50. Baby powder
51. Lasted
52. Mount in Tasmania
55. Dig
57. Wagtail's cousin
59. Dessert, after four

60. Caterpillar's hair
61. Greek portico
62. Leave, after seven
63. Half of DCC
64. American ostriches
65. Tin Man's plea in Oz film
67. Type of school
72. Prof. rank
75. Dud
76. Thanksgiving fruit
77. ___ U.S. Pat. Off.
78. Employ
80. Coal container
81. Bonnie's beau
82. Half: Pref.
84. City in Ohio
86. Length times width, e.g.
89. Melts
91. Like a small egg
92. Most mature
93. Will's contents
95. Net minder
97. Mohammed descendants
98. Former Egyptian president
99. Dunne or Castle

101. Tiny amounts
102. Queues
103. Speechify
104. M. Descartes
106. Walesa
111. Nos. man
112. Shade tree

23 *Headliners* by Ernst T. Theimer

ACROSS

1. Vista
6. Ready
10. Actor McKellen
13. Hillbilly's chaw
18. Northern N.D. town
19. Case
21. Largest Garden State city
22. Dan and Fred are somewhat amicable
24. Word-of-mouth bettor
25. Company V.I.P.
26. Masculine
27. Cutting tools
28. Russian peninsula
29. Conceive
31. Suffix with press or fail
32. Simon's "Plaza ___"
33. Shoe size
34. With William, singer Dinah props burning logs
39. Literary monogram
42. Eat
44. Gametes
45. Dock worker
46. Arabic letter
47. Periods
48. Drugstore cowboys
51. Wire measure
52. Blackboard
54. Stephen T. takes Harry to Plato, for one
58. To ___ (precisely)
59. Indian weight
62. Kind of virus
63. Declaim
64. Part of H.H.H.
66. Brigadier general's insignia
68. Vital fluid
70. One of the brass
71. Fastened
72. Presently
73. S.A. Indian
74. Foxy
75. Aleutian island
76. Former Giant great Mel joins Charles and George for emperor's favor
82. Public disorders
84. Bricklayer's burden
85. Wise legislators
86. Baseball Hall-of-Famer Rixey
90. Charged particle
91. Specific otary
93. Asian holiday
94. Moods

96. Opposite of ques.
97. William Allen needs Ted to make a Looking-Glass character
101. Poets' guides
102. Open a cage
104. Doze
105. Inform
107. Older
109. Eager
111. Three, in Berlin
112. Solmization syllables
113. Decorated anew
114. Why Morley, Glenn and Claude prefer snakes to lye
118. Emulates Cicero
119. Put up
120. Ham it up
121. Bushy legumes
122. Blue
123. Tinted
124. Thick

DOWN

1. Cagliari is its capital
2. Kind of horse race
3. Alienate
4. O.T. book
5. Montcalm and Wolfe, e.g.
6. Plunders
7. As to
8. Last Greek consonant
9. Nice hot time
10. West ___ (American archipelago)
11. Philippine timber tree
12. Napoleon's marshal's family
13. Currant pickers
14. Expect
15. Ned and Lou make harbor
16. Algonquian Indian
17. A soup base
20. M. Gide
21. Cold characteristic?
23. Operated
30. Simpletons
31. S.A. arrow poison
32. Go edgewise
35. Sacred
36. Finished
37. Marzipan base
38. Dim
40. Kind of pass
41. In a pleasant manner
43. Winding wind

49. Mire, in Ayr
50. Malayan skirts
53. The Elbe, to a Czech
55. "Vissi d'___," Puccini aria
56. ___ Paulo, Brazil
57. Kind of wine
59. Sun parlors
60. Maternal kinship
61. What James and evangelist Billy rarely were wont to do
65. Single
67. Closed
68. Swag
69. ___ Alamos
70. Graduation costume
72. Ermine in summer
77. "___ Wedding Journey": Howells
78. Egg cell after meiosis
79. Designer Cassini
80. "How use ___ breed a habit...": Shak.
81. Aye-aye, for one
83. Surgeon: Slang
87. Stance

88. Gifts
89. Taxpayer
92. Stock holdings
95. Officiated at Shea
98. Stabbed
99. Central points
100. Paved, in a way
103. E. Indian tree
106. Foot: Pref.
107. Welfare hotels
108. Architect Saarinen
109. Nile serpents
110. Spanish linear measure
111. Peace symbol
115. Roulette bet
116. Fingerlings
117. Soul, in Savoie

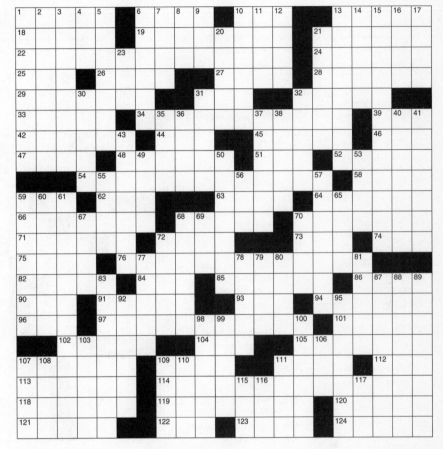

ACROSS

1. Title of courtesy, once
5. S.A. wood sorrel
8. French floor
13. Sudden tug
17. On the Indian
18. ___ de jambe (ballet movement)
20. Kind of renewal
21. "Big" or "Z," e.g.
22. "Death's Duel" author
24. Paint splashes
25. "___ we all?"
26. Conquistador Juan de ___
27. Sec. of State: 1977
29. English writer Arthur ___
30. Alley button
31. Haul into court once again
32. Franklin's father was born here
33. Voice of Tweetie Pie
35. Saloon where 50 Down bent an elbow
38. "A ___ the Misbegotten" (Robards vehicle)
43. Idi ___
45. Suffix with musket
46. "The Hungarian Rome"
48. "___ is sinking to-day": Ufford
49. Sloth, for one
50. "Return of the ___"
51. Meadow
52. Immerses
53. Scottish pudding
55. Whence comes take-home
58. Fran of "Kukla . . ."
59. ___ damnée (willing tool)
60. Made a path
61. Biblical shepherd
62. Prop finish
63. Tic
66. Monday-morning quarterbacking, e.g.
69. That is: Lat.
71. Charged particle
72. A eucalypt
74. Unbend
75. Extinct bird
76. ___ of paris
78. "Henry the Fifth, thy ___ invocate": Shak.
80. Aegean island
84. Calico ponies
85. Chinese dynasty
86. ___ Porsena
88. Gelderland city
89. Innuits, e.g.
91. Fancy
93. 650, to Cato
94. Expressions of disgust
95. Washington Square Players' vehicle by 8 Down
96. Tony role for Dewhurst: 1974
99. Invitation reqs.
102. Mother-of-pearl
103. Grown dearer in price
106. More underhanded
110. "___ Napoli": T. A. Daly
111. "Lest we lose our ___": Browning
112. Island off Venezuela
113. Amazon tributary
114. Super-model Campbell
116. Changed a menu selection
118. Powhatan, to John Rolfe
119. Customary drink
120. Some I.D.'s
121. Blood fluids
122. One Beatle
123. Rose element
124. J. F. K. visitor
125. Calls for silence

DOWN

1. Bowes, e.g.
2. Together
3. Working up old material again
4. Veronese neighbor
5. Gaucho's gold
6. Transported
7. Vehicle for Garbo
8. This E.G.O. arrived Oct. 16, 1888
9. Santa Fe or Oregon: Abbr.
10. Fermi focus
11. "The Thief" actor
12. Marks with scars
13. Time past
14. Hails
15. Numbered cloud
16. Etta ___
19. Tooth: Comb. form
21. Vehicle for Lunt: 1928
23. Venison
28. Handle a problem handily
34. The old bean
36. "Tears" poet
37. Forecaster
39. Town in Liberia or Italy
40. Bone hollows
41. Tear-jerkers
42. It curdles milk
43. Panatela residue
44. "Cara ___," 1954 song
47. Manta, e.g.
50. He and Hickey took the stage together
54. Chat idly
56. Alder tree: Scot.
57. Israeli city
58. Circa: Abbr.
61. Vehicle for Cohan: 1933
63. Fragment
64. Buff pumps
65. Mother of the Fates, to Plato
66. Roscoe: Abbr.
67. Monogram for Jesus
68. Rod
70. Pop
73. Hague's "___ Fables"
75. Danny's girl
77. Blend batter
78. F-J link
79. Pilgrimage to Mecca
81. Extends liability coverage
82. Poetic piece
83. French possessive
87. Dean and Edward
90. Card game
92. "And mine ___ one": Shak.
94. Adjective for Snow White
97. Cupcake toppers
98. Alum
100. "___ porridge hot . . ."
101. Weevil feature
104. German Republic's first president
105. Nothingness states
106. Upstart
107. Hyena, of the comics
108. Snow-blind?
109. Epochal
115. Lost lamb's call?
117. Q-U connection

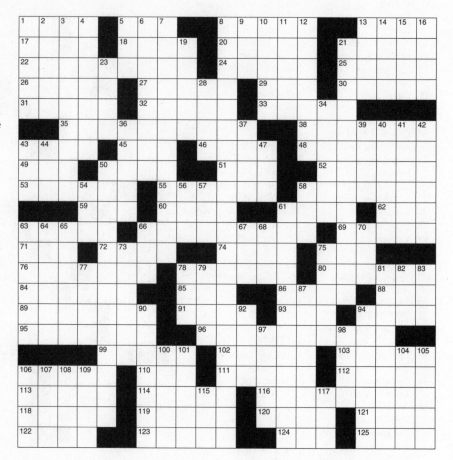

25 The In Crowd by Bette Sue Cohen

ACROSS

1. Riata
6. Respond to stimuli
11. Set the oven at 350 degrees
15. Franks' accompaniment
20. Fill with joy
21. Shout loudly
22. Actor in "Support Your Local Sheriff"
23. "Creatures that by a ___ nature teach": Shak.
24. Physicist born on March 14, 1879
26. Kentucky Derby winner: 1980
28. Fishing net
29. "___ a Kick Out of You"
30. Norwegian monetary unit
32. Chirp
33. Watched
34. Bustle
35. List of candidates
36. Seven-day cycle
37. Depth charge
38. Recording in writing
40. Deep-seated
44. Opined
49. Cayuga, Seneca, etc.
53. "Ben ___," 1959 film
54. Apportions
55. Actor in "Scarface": 1932
57. More profound
58. Wife of Zeus
59. For the most part
60. ___ Major
61. ___ on (trampled)
62. Gene Anthony Ray's role in "Fame"
63. A 1492 vessel
64. Outpatient facility
65. Bear
67. Bell-shaped flower
68. Archdiocese
69. Egghead
70. Interlace
72. Sharp-crested ridge
73. Condense
76. Architects' org.
77. Clothing
80. Moslem faith
81. Folding
84. Nurtured
85. Cut with an ax
88. Barrel part
89. Actress in "The Big Chill"
90. "Forever ___," Winsor novel
92. "Sliver" author
93. "___ you do?"
94. "Moonstruck" star
95. Got on one's feet
96. Carpenter's activity
97. Medicinal plant
98. Coquettes
100. "Thanks ___!"
101. "... there is ___ and a great man...": II Samuel
102. Wedding response
103. U.S. women's singles champion: 1979 and 1981
105. Interwove
107. River in southern Alberta
109. ___ to (adheres)
111. First ___
112. Emit smoke
113. Raid
115. D.C. group
117. West German river
121. Journalist-author Alexander
123. Brazilian seaport
124. Mascara recipient
125. Musical vamp
126. "Crisis" publisher: 1776–83
128. Pool V.I.P.
132. Label again
133. Singer James
134. Meantime
135. Newmar or Andrews
136. Test choice
137. Part of Y.W.C.A.
138. Prado display
139. Absquatulates

DOWN

1. Tenant's document
2. Bowling lane
3. Italic language
4. Spirited horse
5. "___ the ramparts..."
6. Checked
7. Catcher Howard
8. Hgt.
9. "Producer's Showcase" producer
10. Instant
11. Sired
12. Couer d'___, Idaho
13. Welles role
14. Flightless bird
15. Milwaukee team
16. Calif.'s motto
17. "I cannot tell ___"
18. Nutcracker's suite
19. Where to find a drip?
21. Depart!
25. Gaea's brood
27. O, e.g.
31. Prevailed uncontrollably
35. Is frugal
36. Nictitated
37. French president: 1954–59
39. Function
41. March movie
42. Sixth-largest continent
43. Sturdy wagon
44. Highway exits
45. May or Stritch
46. Carmel V.I.P.
47. Caffeine-rich nut
48. Flowing off gradually
50. Keep
51. "Brigadoon" lyricist
52. Footless animal
56. Black bird
58. Hayes or Traubel
60. Clothed
62. Enticed
64. Robbery or arson
65. Short plant stalk
66. "A Tramp Abroad" writer
67. More subdued
69. Hired assassin
71. Siestas
74. Leaf
75. A Queen
78. Costello's partner
79. Angered
80. Beloved of Tristram
82. Artery
83. A gun inventor
86. Show
87. Alar
89. Stylish
91. King Guzzle's kingdom
92. Actor Teeter
93. Hit musical of the 60's
94. "American Bandstand" host
95. Smooth
96. Made haste
98. ___ the breeze
99. Monetary unit of Ecuador
101. Correctly
103. Of adolescents
104. Activity for Sam Snead?
106. Two-wheeled carriage
108. Albee products
110. Outer coat enclosing the eyeball
113. Makes a pretense of
114. N.Y. city
116. Watering place
117. Wicked
118. Start of a Dickens title
119. Ade book: 1896
120. Annual Pasadena display
121. Queens stadium
122. "The ___ Baltimore," Wilson play
123. Leatherwings
126. Type of bus ticket: Abbr.
127. Thimblerig object
129. Division word
130. Marshal of France: 1804
131. Famed racecar driver's monogram

ACROSS

1. Splendor
5. City on the Ganges
10. Bundle of wheat
15. Luzon river
19. Culture medium
20. Like ___ (quickly)
21. Ham's affirmative
22. Tie
23. "___ want for Christmas . . ."
24. IHS: Isa. 59:20
26. Lode
27. Comet seen on Dec. 24
29. "The Glass Key" actor
30. Liberate
32. English horn
33. Memorable warship
35. Combed cotton
36. Farrier
39. Winold ___, painter of Indians
41. Trunk
42. Pablo Picasso's daughter
44. Short salutation
45. Waipahu's island
47. D-I links
50. Book by poet Ciardi
51. IHS: John 10:11
55. Papal name
56. Pre-Christmas activity
58. One + one to Burns
59. Attributes
61. London borough
63. Père Noel's affirmative
64. Caine role
65. Porter's "Kiss ___"
68. Bests in brainpower
71. Be imminent
72. Carroll's girl
73. New Guinea port
74. Mother of Samuel
76. Sheets, etc.
78. N.C. State's conference
79. Biblical verse
83. Yule ___
84. IHS: Luke 23:35
89. Verdi opus
90. Whoa!
92. ___ meridiem
93. S. A. armadillo
94. Warmhearted
96. Wintry floater
98. Share evenly
100. Certain Yemeni
101. "___ Along," Merrill musical
103. Perplexed
105. Start of Mont.'s motto
106. Adjective for "Metamorphoses"
108. "___ Rhythm"
109. Helter-skelter
114. Rudolf of opera
115. IHS: I Tim. 6:15
118. Biologist Metchnikoff
119. "Picnic" playwright
120. Cat Nation tribe
121. Slur over
122. Present
123. Hardy's "Pure Woman"
124. Delta preceder
125. Permanent place?
126. Concerning

DOWN

1. "I Kid You Not" author
2. Eye amorously
3. Algerian neighbor
4. IHS: Isa. 9:6
5. ___ Noster
6. Notable netman
7. Unit of heat
8. Trondheim loc.
9. Studios for Seurat
10. Nobel's compatriots
11. Wasted no time
12. "Spoon River" poet's monogram
13. Box-elder genus
14. Attack area for Graf
15. Unfavorable
16. IHS: John 6:35
17. Elevate
18. Bearded
25. Rich pastry
28. College room
31. Roman household deity
34. Desiccated
36. Hot tubs
37. Hodgepodge
38. Potpourri
40. ___ Camel, W.W. I plane
41. Article in common use
43. Lithe
44. Dream, to Dante
46. Kin of oho
48. Enter or arrive
49. Drenched the lawn
52. Naval C.I.A.
53. Case for pins
54. Plays
57. Open to all
60. IHS: Rev. 1:8
62. Ravines
63. See red?
65. They hum in Dec.
66. "Adam Bede" novelist
67. IHS: Rev. 17:14
69. Tortilla con carne
70. Flavor
71. Map within a map
75. Bobbsey twin
77. Hurry up!
78. Do something
80. French novelist
81. Adam's birthplace
82. Hindu garment
85. Directional letters
86. "Ye are the ___ the earth": Matt. 5:13
87. Apostolic letters
88. Thurmond of N.B.A. fame
91. Telethon call-ins
95. James ___ Jones
97. French friend
99. Peak of S. Colo.
101. Apochrypha book
102. Of the birds
104. Eliot's cruelest month
105. Comedian Ole
107. Ibsen's Helmer
108. Same: Lat.
110. Taro root
111. Ally of Sparta
112. Ski tow
113. Mother of Artemis
116. Flange
117. Suffix with pay or play

ACROSS

1. Holdups at sea?
6. Young salmon
10. Messy mass
14. Push-button predecessors
19. Make trouble
20. Sun-tan lotion ingredient
21. N.Y. college
22. Fisher in a whirl?
23. Soprano Mitchell
24. Brass instrument
25. Took a powder
26. Take off
27. Unemployed renter?
29. Lassie or Elsie?
31. Serpentine dagger
32. Little Red Book author
34. Delta collection
35. Flopsy and Mopsy
39. Resort near Lake Louise
41. Honey-loving deer at the rear?
46. Roman officials
47. Man of the people: Var.
49. Steve who took a dive
50. Haymaker
51. Bug
52. Leonine lingo
54. Manner of expression
55. My gosh, it's molding!
56. Amber, formerly
57. World lifter
59. Cinder chaser
60. Wimbledon forecaster?
62. Subject of sommeliers' argument?
64. All-purpose vehicle
65. Writer Levin
66. What some lords have?
73. Berlin's Christmas-eve dream?
80. ___ dixit
81. Emulate an ecdysiast
82. Unusual peep show?
83. Obscure
84. Happen again
86. Official stamp
87. Currier's colleague
88. Sordid
89. Copied painstakingly
91. David in the valley of Elah
93. "O ___ when we cry . . ." U.S. Navy Hymn
94. Twitch of a rabbit's nose?
96. Newscaster Leslie
97. Most serene
98. Sheepskin morocco
100. Elev.
101. HBO, e.g.
102. Computer bug's danger?
107. The good doctor?
113. African nation
114. Italian seaport
115. Operatic prince
116. Medic who monkeys around?
117. Upright
118. Cake decorator
119. Nearly gone goose
120. Saucy charmer
121. Necessary evils
122. Supplements, with "out"
123. Turns right
124. Choose

DOWN

1. W. African country
2. Made a hole-in-one
3. Versatile plane, for short
4. Styne song
5. More animated
6. Jargon
7. Grads
8. Toga
9. Venus de Milo's concern?
10. Mugger's forte?
11. Poet Ridge
12. "___ so near . . .": Job 41:16
13. Thoughtless remark?
14. Censors
15. Thought
16. Jewish month
17. "No evil deed ___ on"
18. Clairvoyant
28. Scraps of a sort
30. Blister
33. Actress Alicia
35. Odilon ___, French painter
36. Era of commercials?
37. "Carmen" composer
38. TV censor's signal
39. Prove false
40. U.S. playwright who's on his toes?
42. Visitor's quarters
43. Romantic interlude
44. Tot's favorite, after "choklit"
45. Dr. spelled out?
47. Spoon's elope-mate
48. Molls and dolls
51. Feels contrite
53. Ostriches, e.g.
56. Rosters
58. Rock debris
61. Jamaican export
63. Suffix with nectar
66. Circumference
67. The works, to Cato
68. Wild writer?
69. Two-spot
70. Mined matter
71. Iranian coins
72. What a bad will might do?
73. Part of Orville's machine?
74. German river
75. Cockney employer?
76. Girder
77. Angry look
78. Soil component
79. Lovers' meeting
85. Radial make-overs
88. Ravel preventer
90. Designing man
92. Shrew
93. "Greater love ___ no man . . ."
95. Hack
97. Nuclei of experts
99. N.Y. destination in a song
101. Hag
102. Coin opening
103. ___ colada
104. Wild goat
105. Unit of force
106. What Kilmer couldn't make
108. Pulitzer Prize author
109. Huge Russian lake
110. Gold cloth
111. "Beowulf" is one
112. Budget item

Book Country by John M. Samson

ACROSS

1. Italian violin
6. Engrossed
10. Biblical book
14. Swiss canton
19. Balzac's "___ Birotteau"
20. Take on
21. Bomb
22. Soap plant
23. SALINAS VALLEY
25. UKRAINE
27. Estranges
28. O'Casey's staff of life
29. Wilde's forte
30. What yeggs crack
34. Tubing joint
35. Potok novel, with "The"
39. XIII × IV
40. Olympics awards
45. Hard beds
47. Harpsichordist Landowska
49. Anticipated
50. Recoiled
51. Second after tau
53. Bloch's Bates
55. Dante's "La ___ Nuova"
56. Hollow out
57. Scraps for Fido
58. Baylor of basketball
59. Edmonton skater
60. Lofty verse
62. Thug
63. Utopia or Pianosa
64. Bungle
66. GUYANA
70. Uh-huh
71. Affidavit taker
73. Advance
74. Plunder
76. Try to find water
77. Columbia's team
78. Penrod's dog
79. Tot
82. "Jake's Thing" novelist
83. Kids' rocker
84. Big brown bird
85. Patchwork
86. Lesotho coins
88. Day's march
90. Niobe was one
92. Epistle
93. Ellington monogram
94. Bow ceremoniously
95. Cambridge coll.
97. The Hardy Boys, e.g.
99. Hebrew "T"
100. Mistle thrush
105. Flattery
111. GOPHER PRAIRIE
113. DEVONSHIRE
114. Mother's mother, e.g.
115. Turgenev's birthplace
116. Poet Sexton
117. Novelist Shaw
118. Dylan Thomas's homeland
119. Sweet pear
120. Corp V.I.P.'s
121. Big Brother, to Orwell

DOWN

1. Zoological suffix
2. Kind of ticket
3. Holly found in Dixie
4. British or U.S. poet
5. ALBANY
6. Scarlett's Butler
7. Man Friday
8. Fourth Estate
9. Decimal unit
10. P.M.
11. Erich Segal book
12. Corrida charger
13. Hammett hero
14. Incoherent one
15. Chinese border river
16. Matchless
17. Place of exile: 1814
18. Graphite
24. Swoon
26. Chinook
31. According to
32. DUBLIN
33. Phantom
35. Product-banning org.
36. Tee-hee
37. LONDON
38. Visit dreamland
41. Auld Clootie
42. YOKNAPA-TAWPHA COUNTY
43. Iron Age period
44. Turfs
46. Lost weekend
47. Kenosha loc.
48. Rival of Sparta
49. Team supporter
52. Trout or marble
54. Least
57. Grand Ole ___
59. Bones
61. Grim Grimm character
63. Anent
64. Ultimate goal
65. Bunkmate
67. Springe
68. Sea cow
69. Caulking material
72. Desirable quality
75. Driver's one-eighty
77. C.S.A. hero
78. Aberdeen's river
80. Swiss artist
81. French I verb
83. Austere
85. ROME
87. Waterloos
89. Author's assn.
91. Fla. city
96. Palpitate
97. Kilmer title
98. A Lyon river
99. Melodies
100. Merganser
101. Village in John 2:1
102. Coin of Teheran
103. Duck, to Doblin
104. First name in architecture
106. Fleming novel
107. Wrongful act
108. Amana's state
109. "Step" followers
110. Oahu avian
112. R. N.'s forte
113. Sir Launcelot du ___

Character Studies by John Greenman

ACROSS

1. Kind of check
5. Wave modifier
10. Cosmetician Max
16. Erwin of early TV
19. Ziti topping
20. Idolize
21. Rub with a rasp
22. Eschew
23. EL
25. GEE
27. Assist at a wedding: Slang
28. Eyes amorously
29. Divests of honors
31. "Lady" of song
32. Menial
34. Change timers
36. Contracts a cold
37. Not impetuous
39. Feel contrite
41. Raison d'___
43. Spotted piece
44. Expended effort
46. BEE
49. Midwinter malady
52. Autumns, in Avila
53. Kirk and Hartman
54. Yokum or Doubleday
55. Stats for Mike Greenwell
56. Authority
57. Piquant quaff
58. Sixty-thousandths of a min.
59. Bogus
60. Building wing
61. EX
64. These go from alpha to omega
65. Luge or pung
67. ___-do-well
68. Side petals
69. Supernatural spirits
70. Wars of the ___
72. Diagonal weave
74. Major appliance
75. With calm assurance
77. Soy or Roy
78. Cuban cat
79. Norman town
83. Most reasonable
84. ESS
88. Maneuverable, as a sailboat
89. Puccini's forte
90. Heart's-ease
91. Houston gridder
92. Fleet
94. Cheerleaders' calls
95. Kolo or merengue
96. Incense
97. Placid
98. Guido's note
99. VEE
101. Bedroom
102. Pages
104. ". . . 'E won't split on ___": Kipling
105. Sheep tender
106. Cooked beans, Mexican style
108. Egyptian dancing girl
110. Oleoresin
112. Roll top, e.g.
115. To no ___ (fruitlessly)
116. Graduates
118. Skating feats
120. Imitate
121. TEE
124. ZEE
127. Juillet-aout periods
128. Kitchen utensil
129. "___ You Glad You're You?"
130. Kind of jury
131. Actor Neill
132. Fondle
133. Circus areas
134. Comedian Mort

DOWN

1. Pay hike
2. KAY
3. Gelid
4. Laughton role: 1932
5. Last part
6. Most indolent
7. Use a divining rod
8. Constellation near Norma
9. Certain pewters
10. Oberon's subjects
11. Simmering
12. Jockeys' goads
13. N.M. art colony
14. Eccentric
15. Early Olds
16. JAY
17. Port on the Po
18. Not hardened
19. East Coast porgy
22. Felled, as a dragon
24. Concurs
26. Admitted
30. Infield coverage
33. Light gases
35. Come-on
37. Models
38. N. African bigwig
40. Evidence
42. Monarchs of yore
43. Blockhead
44. Forfeits
45. To any extent
46. More expansive
47. Matter-of-fact
48. Rotund
50. Tilts
51. Manipulates
53. Fla. exports
55. Textile fibers
57. Set of beliefs
58. "Night Court" actor
59. Eyetooth
62. Start
63. "Common Sense" man
64. Italian port
66. Laundromat items
69. Bowl at Jacksonville
71. Thessalian peak
72. More laconic
73. Undulatory
74. Less frequent
75. Kind of bull
76. EN
77. Swindler's scheme
78. Greek physician
80. EM
81. "Jezebel" popularizer
82. Money follower
83. Type of subject
84. Inclinations
85. Region of ancient Asia Minor
86. Carp pettily
87. Anxiety
90. Walked the floor
93. Pistol-packing
95. Run-down nightspot
96. Western resort
97. Strident
99. Lowers
100. Babbles
101. Unites firmly
103. Actors Estrada and Rhodes
105. Voodooist's activity
106. Wheezes
107. Patti LuPone role
108. Bring into agreement
109. Henry and Clare
111. Burdened
113. Turn rancid
114. Superman's alter ego
116. State
117. Moslem woman's garb
119. Placebos
122. "___ Horne," Ade book
123. Antipollution org.
125. "___ tu," Verdi aria
126. ___ Filippias, Greek town

ACROSS

1. Salami purveyor
5. Provoked
10. Ledge
15. Poznán natives
16. Sound-shield screens
17. Parents
19. Paar's light?
21. Supplication
23. Diminutive suffix
24. "There runs ___ by Merrow Down": Kipling
25. Begrudges
27. Educational org.
28. Sked. abbr.
29. Fashionable
30. Rubens' medium
31. Kind of flint
32. Tumult
34. Wreaths
36. African fox
37. Cheat
38. Speech sound
40. Well-groomed
42. Chinese city on the Wei
43. Hold for Ozzie?
45. Himalayan ointments
46. Optical network
49. Bergonzi, for one
51. Short song
52. Pertaining to the fibula
53. Harry's spouse
56. Kind of electricity
58. Soprano Frances: 1883–1952
59. Cozy
60. Type of suit
61. Color of Faye's dress?
63. ___ Lanka
64. Hector's protector
66. Talented
67. Fitted together
69. Orson or lima
70. In a somnolent way
72. Intimidate
73. Metropolis on the Missouri
75. Platform
76. Bristles
78. The Finnish language
81. Boggs of baseball
82. Contemporary persons
84. Hope's feline?
86. Twigs for grafting
88. Foal's dad
89. Descry

91. Michelangelo masterpiece
92. Fence picket
93. Wallace's transmitting device?
94. Obtuse
96. TV network north of the U.S.A.
97. Afflict
98. Aggregates
100. Young pheasant
101. Lorain's lake
102. Hairlike
104. Einstein's frock coat?
107. City ESE of Napoli
108. Snow leopard
109. Electrical unit of capacitance
110. Excavations
111. French heads
112. Out of

DOWN

1. Precept
2. Actress Sommer
3. Pope who was lionized?
4. Imam's faith
5. Slights
6. Pool game
7. Retired
8. Rocky crag
9. Feudal thrall
10. Mentally infirm
11. Execrates
12. Strays
13. Majors or Marvin
14. Olibanum for Sinatra?
15. Colonial Dutch landowner
17. Emend
18. Mug for Gertrude?
19. Actress Seberg's slacks?
20. Inland sea
22. Yin's partner
26. Pries into
29. Feeling, e.g.
31. Sullies
33. Condiments
35. Pertaining to rocks rich in silica
36. Handy one
37. Food: Pref.
39. Great quantity
41. Musical embellishment for 93 Down?
42. Italian evening
44. Celebrated or celebrity
46. Buys back

47. Writer Hobson
48. Illinois city
50. Auto race
52. Planet for a canine?
53. Bored
54. British nobles
55. Dulcet Tell?
57. Dye's partner
58. Hirt and Pacino
62. Take care
65. Mexican shawl
66. ___-de-camp
68. Smear
69. Salten book
71. Tablets
72. Yield, as land
74. Skirt spreaders
76. Famed French historian: 1842–1906
77. Hide securely
79. Parfait ingredient
80. ___ seat (enviable position)
82. A steam locomotive
83. Certain evergreen trees
85. Be silent, to Solti
86. Short gaiter
87. Dens

88. Workers' job actions
90. Lock of a type
93. Soprano in "One Night of Love"
95. Rod
98. A partner of there
99. Announcement of a kind
100. Liquid measure
101. Zaragoza's river
103. Cato's 151
105. Regret
106. Household spirit

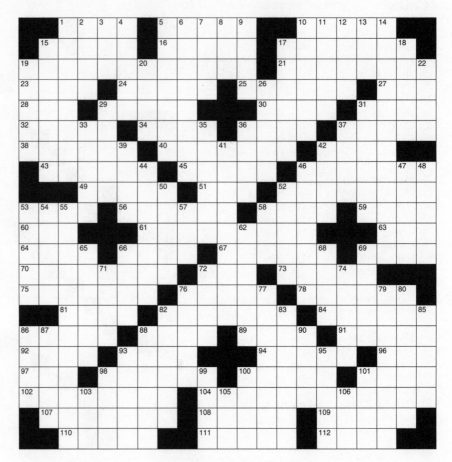

ACROSS

1. Wrinkled
7. Terse diner sign
11. Gen. ___ Arnold
14. Kind of plan
18. Former U.K. judicial writ
19. ___ cog (err)
21. Team's best pitcher
22. Boesky or Lendl
23. Memo to a gabby vintner
25. Use a death ray
26. Miles of films
27. Far out
28. Combiner with dyne or doxy
29. Arcane
31. Monogram of the 21st V.P.
32. Covert's cousin
34. Pollster's unit
36. Took the bait
37. Saison chaude
38. Sol of ours
39. A-U vowel connection
40. Nine-to-fiver
41. Rue ___ Paix
43. Memo to a sluggish walnut processor
50. Shebat, ___, Nisan
51. Opp. of WSW
53. Cinnabar, for one
54. One on the watch
56. Institute in Brooklyn
58. Kin of strathspeys
60. Cohan song: 1907
64. Effulge
66. Sartre novel
69. Word in Kan.'s motto
70. Kant's concern
71. Memo to a careless Bonn teller
74. ___ Downing Street
75. Small pikeperch
77. New Zealand's discoverer
78. Fatuous
80. Lacking a breastbone
82. "___ Kick Out of You"
84. Nary a soul
85. Came down in buckets
87. Durango demonstrative
88. Land-based newt
89. ___-Cynwyd, near Philadelphia
92. Memo to a waiting taxidermist

97. Riza Khan Pahlevi, e.g.
100. Bouquet
102. Alternative to hup
103. Like sushi
105. Guido's note
106. ___ Gulf, Aegean Sea inlet
107. Evince affection
110. ___-bel-Abbès, onetime Foreign Legion home
111. Afghan coin
112. Kind of shoe
114. Arabian kettledrum
116. Wynonna Judd's mom
118. Dark time, in ads
119. Israeli burp gun
120. Memo from a bored stripteaser
122. Acronym for an aircraft's ascent
123. Where Trevino got his start
124. AFB in Fla.
125. Auricles
126. "It ___ ancient Mariner"
127. Boundless: Abbr.
128. Garth, in "Ivanhoe"
129. Is written

DOWN

1. Supposed to be such
2. Keen
3. Memo to a lazy galena miner
4. Petri-dish filler
5. Siamese coins
6. Ike and Monty's bailiwick
7. Gravel ridge in a glacier
8. Found a perch
9. Antler subdivisions
10. Meadowsweet
11. Noisette
12. "___ of Identity," S. Holmes adventure
13. Squash, for one
14. Memo to a hasty seamstress
15. Warded off
16. ___ Trench
17. Thespian or thesmothete
20. Kind of pile
24. Where Alberich struck gold
30. TV network logo
33. L.B.J.'s birth month
35. Sourdough's sack

42. Prefix with tank or trust
44. Part of a golf club
45. A "Real McCoy"
46. Fresh crews
47. Bandleader-songwriter Jones
48. American news execs' org.
49. Name of cities in Ill., Kan., Ohio and Pa.
52. Whatnot
55. Former Brooklyn pitcher
56. Cue in group singing
57. Sitar solos
58. Out of the labor mkt.
59. Finland, to Sibelius
61. Memo to a U.S.M.A. recruit
62. "When the sheep ___ the fauld . . ."
63. John ___ Garner
65. Coated with tin-lead alloy

67. Metalworking tools: Var.
68. Conductor Ansermet
72. Yorkshire town
73. U.S. architects' org.
76. Memo to a dilatory chess player
79. Reactions to solar-plexus punches
81. "Yo te ___" (Avila avowal)
83. Kind of cross
86. Updike's "The Same ___"
89. African dog
90. Houseplants used medicinally
91. Lynn from Ky.
93. Disquiet
94. Put a play on again
95. Furbelow
96. Cabbage Patch dolls, e.g.
98. Homecoming V.I.P.'s
99. Some chemical compounds

101. Soft-drink tycoon Candler
104. Improvise
107. Defraud
108. A moon of Uranus
109. Houston and Coleridge: Abbr.
110. Rhone River augmenter
113. Dancing dress
115. "Oh, to ___ England . . .": Browning
117. Author Bontemps
121. Unfortunates of W.W. II

32 *Biblical Scions* by Jeanette K. Brill

ACROSS

1. Tick, e.g.
7. Succinct
12. Til
18. Pertaining to the nostrils
19. Nonterrestrial
20. Wild asses
22. Anna Mary Robertson
24. A 1914 Oriole who took wing
26. Lubricate
27. Caught sight of
28. Certain trucks
29. Buck's mate
30. ___-ha-Shanah
32. Brave who really could hammer
34. Connors or Wallace
35. Epithet of Athena
36. Lesions
37. Young tag-on
38. Subdued
39. Scorch
40. Angered
41. Even
42. Woodpeckers
43. Having paddles
45. Jet-engine housing
46. Type of pinafore
47. Open grating
50. Jester
53. Husband of Jezebel
57. Jack or Julie
58. Heddle's place
59. Naso of Rome
60. Mythical beast
61. Obloquy
62. Long Island troubadour
64. Manuel de ___, Spanish composer
65. No score
66. Garb for Lakmé
67. Canning equipment
68. Fine brushes
69. Düsseldorf donkey
70. Plans on reheating
72. Stop
73. One-eyed god
75. That ship
76. Doctrine
78. N.M.U. member
81. Island off Ireland
83. Iron-containing pigment
84. Daunting
88. Crazy Legs Hirsch
89. Dross
90. Errand boy: Slang
91. "Sting like ___": Ali
92. Claim on a property
93. Actor in "Hold Back the Dawn"
95. Grain for Vassar
96. Kind of dye
97. 1957 Nobelist in Literature
98. Shadows, to Jeanne
100. Bishopric
101. Bacharach's partner
103. U.S. novelist-poet
106. Conceal
107. Soul
108. Quiescent
109. Broke up a shutout
110. Part of a potpourri
111. Carolina river

DOWN

1. Certain cats and goats
2. Covered cart
3. Caspian's neighbor
4. ___ Tin Tin
5. State adjoining Ill.
6. Administrative division of Greece
7. Interfered
8. Carried away, as property
9. Perron parts
10. Down at the heels
11. Naval off.
12. Grew serious, with "up"
13. Captivate
14. Antipolio pioneer
15. Ripens
16. Matelot's milieu
17. Scholarly
21. O'Neill's Yank, e.g.
23. On land
25. Listens to
28. Glut
31. Netman from D.C.
33. Stage device
34. F. ___, Oscar winner in 1984
36. Mud eel
38. Country singer Bandy
41. Former Yankee pitcher
42. Tie
44. Medicinal plant
45. Game in "The Color of Money"
46. Follow surreptitiously
47. Take panes with one's work
48. Judges' garb
49. Habituate
50. Mulligrubs
51. Spots for slots
52. Type of grape
54. Handel's birthplace
55. "Deutschland über ___"
56. A sixth-day creation
58. Cambio in Calabria
62. Storage building
63. Hunky-dory; copacetic
64. Sow and hoe
66. Gyre
68. More discerning
71. River or Indian
74. Two watch-laps
76. Postponement
77. Breakfast fare
78. Hebrew word in the Psalms
79. Doolitle and namesakes
80. Small interstices
81. Referred (to)
82. Deserters
83. Dutch painter: 1638–1709
85. Disconcerted
86. Let go
87. Relaxing of international tensions
89. Heavy silk fabric in the Middle Ages
90. Significant first words
93. Show indecision
94. ABC's Arledge
97. Dear, in Italy
99. Shot or dragon preceder
102. Caesar's 700
103. Reverse of par
104. Olympic brat
105. Uno, due, ___

33 · Musical Creatures · by Kay Sullivan

ACROSS

1. Over again
5. Mil. weapon
9. Art-school subj.
13. Balin or Claire
16. "Kenilworth" heroine
19. City in Alaska
20. ___ gras
21. Tie down
22. British mothers
24. Ka ___, Hawaiian cape
25. Rossini opera, with "The"
28. Making braids
30. Young oyster
31. Folkways
32. Like some fires
34. Plus factor
36. More tender
37. Owns
38. Roof ornament
39. Director Peter
40. Needle holders
41. Schubert instrumental work, with "The"
47. Id relative
48. Berlin public square
49. Lamentable
50. Hindu god of love
51. Mussorgsky vocal composition
54. Silkworm
55. Kind of jury
56. Fathers of dauphins
57. Bavarian river
58. Medics, at times
60. Annapolis's river
63. Tennis stroke
64. Cousin of a smash
67. Excessively
68. Duelist's sword
69. Directional warning
72. Word history
77. Saint-Saëns zoological fantasy
82. "Two heads ___ than one": Heywood
83. Contralto Anderson
84. Dramatist James
85. Curmudgeon's word
86. Summer in Phila.
88. Black Hawk was one
89. Visionary plan
91. Fast-talking comedian
96. Piedmontese city
98. Portico
99. Light tans
100. Kind of coal or pump
102. Sibelius tone poem, with "The"
108. Brit. money
109. Philosopher who served as a sculptor
111. Certain tides
112. Rod "The ___" Stewart
113. Rimsky-Korsakov's "Flight of ___"
115. Aquarium fish
116. Puccini heroine
117. Luzon peak
118. Palindromic sheep
119. Patron saint of France
120. Genesis verb
121. Nonconformist
125. Lovely lasses
126. Diamond shape
127. Erstwhile campus cutup
128. Stravinsky opera
133. Vital statistic
134. ___ de veau
135. Indefinite time
136. Epitaph starter
137. School Wellington attended
138. Legal matter
139. Punty
140. Author S. S. Van ___
141. Autocrat
142. Sunder

DOWN

1. Kelep
2. Classic Japanese drama
3. Exhaust smoke, e.g.
4. Loser, proverbially
5. "___ Die," Gide work
6. Emulate Peter Funk
7. Kind of bass
8. Learn by heart
9. Phil the Fiddler's creator
10. Piles
11. "Unaccustomed ___ am . . ."
12. "For want of a nail ___ was lost"
13. Quacks
14. Invalid
15. Mozart's middle name
16. Others, to Ovid
17. Director Delbert
18. Peterman
23. Famed basso
26. Dye vessel
27. Brother of Eris
29. Trifle
33. Hazy purple
34. Intimidates
35. Lily of the West
36. Some photocopies, for short
40. Puckish
41. Weight allowance
42. Lasso
43. John Ford 1952 film, with "The"
44. Family name in "A Rage to Live"
45. Asian ruler
46. Makes edging
48. Indigent
49. Worldwide
52. Home of ouzo
53. Stubbornly willful
55. Corsican Pasquale
59. River in a Burns poem
60. Coterie
61. Biblical Hebrew measure
62. Change direction
63. Embankment
65. Get off the A
66. Moral standard
69. Kind of training
70. Basketball tourn.
71. ___ Kippur
73. Verily
74. Gerald Ford, by birth
75. Kind of plum, for short
76. Theoretic primordial source of all elements
78. Liszt and Prévost, e.g.
79. Foster
80. "Bake me a cake . . . ___ you can"
81. Bishopric
87. Predilection
89. Buddhist shrine
90. Doves' sounds
91. Buttinsky
92. Pituitary hormone: Abbr.
93. Corner overhead
94. Type of engine
95. Cut back underbrush again
97. ___ Pea, small comic character
98. White dwarfs
101. What a Scot wears under a kilt
103. "It Happened ___," early Colbert film
104. Fixations
105. Leave one's native land
106. Relative of a mesa
107. Mine entrance
109. Buck
110. Incited a criminal
114. Sub
115. Actress Garr
116. Scant
119. Dumb
120. Actor Gazzara
121. Munich's river
122. Hauling charge: Abbr.
123. Cuprite and tinstone
124. A daughter of Phoebe
125. Eponym of an Eastern state
126. Kind of table
129. Polloi leader
130. Refrain syllable
131. Nol of Cambodia
132. Result

34 *Seeing Double* by *Jim Page*

ACROSS

1. Olympics site: 1960
5. Coolidge from Nashville
9. Casca thrust
13. Boast
17. Son of Shem
18. ___ de Caldas, Braz.
19. Taurus neighbor
21. Kind of trumpet
22. Golfer Miller's dance is held in shaver's place?
24. Bolshoi's "Sleeping Beauty" looks fishy?
26. Irish river
27. Ibsen's "___ Gabler"
29. More jittery
30. Kind of bike
31. Rare object, sometimes
33. Customer
35. Group of eight
37. Threadlike
39. Shrine Bowl teams
43. Timid
47. Coe or Cram
48. Prof's protection
49. Nerve cell
50. Taken ___ (surprised)
52. Age; time: It.
54. CCC divided by C
55. Livestock
56. Sun-rooms
58. Sometimes they're shady
61. Oxford's emporium is hip?
63. Stocks, bonds, etc.
64. Flesh: Comb. form
65. Bull thrower
67. Simple sugars
68. Gets off the Yankee Clipper
71. Goober's cover causes misery for comics kids?
76. Lady ___ Lamb
77. A 1984 running mate
78. Hatred: It.
79. Eggs, to Ovid
80. Town in Norway
81. Journalize
82. Henley action
84. Galileo et al.
87. Slew
89. Miniature ornamental structure
91. Cubic meter
92. TV actress Garber
93. They sing so low
94. "Peyton Place" star
96. Yuletides
98. Alum
102. Harum-___
104. Actress Gallagher
106. Aisle-seat finder
109. Collection of Turners comes down on Ann and May?
111. Awed by leading man's pickup?
113. "___ boy!"
114. Chopin work
115. Flat sign
116. "The mind is like ___": Wilbur
117. Dawson's ex
118. Humdinger
119. Prune: Scot.
120. Dozes off

DOWN

1. Midianite king
2. Baltic island
3. Singer Nixon
4. Lock up
5. Composer Francesco Antonio ___
6. I, in Bonn
7. "___ to Handle," 1938 film
8. Ski resort
9. Quartz variety
10. Sticky sweet
11. Lend a hand
12. Excite
13. Anchor hoister
14. Mature
15. ___-Neisse Line
16. Simple card game
18. Before: Prefix
20. Koko's weapon
23. Manolete's concern
25. Hugo's "L'___ terrible"
28. Borrowed-money outlay causes imminent shortages?
32. Tranquilize
34. Texas city
36. Shackles are put on chain gangs?
38. Actress Chase
40. Litigant's activity
41. Wedges for wheels
42. Six, in Seville
43. Some: Sp.
44. Call at a deli counter
45. Dr. ___, "Buck Rogers" scientist
46. Don Pasquale's nephew
47. Sudan's ___ Mountians
48. Contemptible person's implements nurture fungi?
51. False gods
53. Hat material
57. Of a songbird suborder?
59. Prevaricates
60. Kind of current
62. Viscount's superior
63. R.A.F. promoter
66. Some Spanish murals
68. Cargo lifter
69. Clean the slate
70. A Ford aide
72. Tusked whale
73. Cut from a film
74. Scourge of serge
75. Theater section
76. Friday et al.
77. Trepidation
83. Get off one's high horse?
85. Large tank forces
86. Draws closer
88. ___ cassis (a liqueur)
90. Beyond doubt
92. Madrilène flavoring
93. "Homestead" artist
95. "Stuffed Shirts" author
97. Malt-drying ovens
99. Aired "The Honeymooners"
100. It's west of Curaçao
101. Open a bottle
102. P.M. of Japan: 1964–72
103. Jar or box: Abbr.
105. Danish weights
107. Fast jet
108. NASA space capsules
109. Terhune canine
110. Calembour
112. Wassail drink

Time After Time by Michael J. Parris

ACROSS

1. Reeking
5. Surly
10. Cote sound
13. Abominated
18. ___ Nostra
19. A hundred paise
20. ___ food
21. Sadat
22. Charlemagne (800)–Francis II (1806)
25. Lovelace's forte
26. Stages in lives of organisms
27. Legal claims
28. Parts of books
29. Viscid
30. Eucharist containers: Var.
31. Faint appearance
32. Early French monarchs
35. Ate elegantly
36. Loyalties
39. Wahines' dances
40. T'ai Tsu (1368)–Chuan glich-ti (1644)
42. Wawaskeesh
43. Agenda unit
44. Generic dog's name
45. Grafted: Her.
46. Norman town
47. Miss Piggy's pronoun
48. Paleolithic period
52. Brazilian state
53. Lamb or Bacon
55. Staggers
56. Neutralize
57. Chirp
58. Runs away
59. "___ d'Arthur": Tennyson
60. Animal tracks
62. Eat away
63. Agitates
66. Gripes
67. February 29
69. Gumshoe
70. Arrow poison
71. Tale
72. Tenor Shicoff
73. Whine
74. Eliot's "The Hollow ___"
75. When dinosaurs roamed the earth
79. Firth of Clyde island
80. Supposes
82. Fatuous
83. Plundered
84. "The Pumpkin ___," 1964 film
85. Coquette
86. Tracks relentlessly
87. ___ Zee Bridge, N.Y.
89. City on the Meuse
90. Located
94. ___ and a holler
95. A.H. 1 or A.D. 622
97. Mother-of-pearl
98. Pangolin's feast
99. Like a Cheviot
100. Innisfail
101. Hardwoods
102. What, in Weimar
103. Delirious one
104. Poop or orlop

DOWN

1. Folksinger Phil
2. Terhune novel
3. Cuba, e.g.
4. Reverie
5. Assemblages
6. Card game
7. Asian evergreen
8. Bog
9. Sensitivity
10. Numismatist's concern
11. Possessive pronoun
12. Violinist Bull
13. With pleasure
14. Consecrate by unction
15. Today, in a way
16. Tranquillity
17. Prohibitionists
20. Fast on one's feet
23. Mob actions
24. Kind of doubles
28. Shade of gray
30. Grape variety
31. "Beau ___," Wren work
32. Edge of cask
33. Auburn and Marmon
34. Ice Age
35. Biblical verb
36. Adder's armament
37. "___ Rhee," Civil War song
38. Kin of 46 Down
40. Center
41. Patricia and Tom of films
44. What time does
46. A votre ___! (Cheers!)
48. Court hearings
49. Ship's lowest deck
50. Indigent
51. Size of Bigfoot or Yeti?
52. Full of froth
54. Left Nod
56. Staghorn
58. Lehár or Schubert
59. Radio and TV
60. Be miserly
61. Anguished one
62. Saarinen's namesakes
63. Jacques's title in song
64. Anatomical tissues
65. Rise on a wave
67. Device used in microsurgery
68. Concerning
71. Red Sea republic
73. Foretold
75. Changes genetically
76. Houston eleven
77. Architect Jones
78. Like
79. Debate
81. Flavor, in Ferrara
83. Bustle; confusion
85. Edicts
86. Chemical compound
87. Lake ___, source of the Blue Nile
88. Cries of discovery
89. Irkutsk river
90. Hood's blade
91. Flag
92. ___ Blair (George Orwell)
93. Moist and chilly
95. Deviate from course
96. Pride of ex-Sen. Norris

36 Anagrams on Parade by John Greenman

ACROSS

1. "___ cold and starve a fever"
6. Perfume bottle
10. Kitchen utensil
15. C.S.A. troops
19. More mature
20. Con
21. Rub with rubber
22. Brainchild
23. PRECISE changes in letter sequence
27. Roosevelt or Teasdale
28. Churchillian sign
29. Zola novel
30. Rods' counterparts
31. Refusals
33. Murphy of movies
35. Flying saucer
37. Pig's digs
38. Kermit's kin
41. Two, of yore
42. Listing
44. ALTERED altered thrice
51. In the thick of
52. Windy City airport
53. Pindar's products
54. Prejudice
55. Hither's partner
56. Auspices
57. Norse deities
59. The King
60. Director Flaherty's "Man of ___"
61. Tuckered out
62. Actor Everett ___: 1909–65
63. PARSING into variations
69. Originates
70. "___ Irish Rose"
71. A grandson of Jacob
72. Fla. exports
73. Bridges
74. Barr. or sol.
75. ___ vous plaît
78. Hymn sign-off
79. Journalist Jacob
80. Basketry twig
82. Yea or nay
83. DIVERSE rearrangements
88. Unconscious states
89. Singer James et al.
90. Bouquet
91. Letters in danger
94. West role
95. Holding
96. Raw silk's hue
98. "Romola" writer
100. Island off SW Alaska
101. Galena, e.g.
102. Biography
106. RELAPSE into three other forms
112. "___ Misbehavin'"
113. Kind of bore or wave
114. Sapient
115. Mystery writer Hammond ___
116. Pastures
117. Rimes
118. "Zounds!"
119. Discombobulated

DOWN

1. Popinjays
2. Lamb's pen name
3. W. German river
4. Off one's rocker
5. Pendulum's path
6. Bud vessels
7. As to
8. Chowed down
9. Driver's permit: Abbr.
10. Spruce up a room
11. Cara or Castle
12. Havanan's house
13. Psychic power's inits.
14. Defendants: Law
15. Carty of baseball
16. Anthony and Clarissa
17. Rakish cap
18. Procacious
24. Anne Baxter role
25. Kind of ink
26. School for Simone
32. Explorer Johnson
33. Jug
34. Valley
35. Verbalize
36. Douglas and Oregon
38. Fracas
39. San ___, Italy
40. Tyr's father
41. Refrain syllables
42. Saying more
43. Scandal sheet
45. Ella and Josh
46. Tangible object
47. Red dye
48. Low couch or sofa
49. "Knots" author
50. Curves
56. N.Y. Indians
57. Mont Blanc's range
58. Original Olympics site
59. Crazy Legs Hirsch
60. "___ and Old Lace"
61. "Pleasure's ___ . . .": Byron
62. "No Exit" author
63. Caesar, e.g.
64. Time preceder
65. Marksman, e.g.
66. White water
67. Degrade
68. He wrote "Marius the Epicurean"
73. Twine fiber
74. Affectations
75. Middling
76. Inventory listing
77. Mother of Pollux
79. Ancient people of Gaul
80. Bone: Comb. form
81. Pew or perch
82. Noxious
84. Electrical units
85. Flame keepers of old Rome
86. "___ to You," Dexter-Paris tune of 1946
87. River near Nice
91. Flower element
92. Hardy, to Laurel
93. City S of Florence
95. "And every woe ___ can claim": Byron
96. Slipped up
97. Bee chaser
99. Fillies' fodder
100. "M*A*S*H" TV star
101. Thessalian peak
103. Fleming and Carmichael
104. Be on the lam
105. Pronoun for the Andrea Doria
107. Numerical ending
108. Brazil's ___ Branco
109. Ovine female
110. Equip a ship
111. Actress Zadora

(37) *Nota Bene: Scale Back* by *William Lutwiniak*

ACROSS

1. Dress trimming
6. Receded
11. Chest wood
16. Rambouillets
21. Pompeiian cover-up
22. Veiling
23. Genetic enzyme
24. Señor's mark
25. DO
28. Lazzarone
29. Durango dough
30. Swiss unit for watches
31. Org.
32. Young pilchard
34. Exist
35. Caught a bug
36. Debauchee
37. Spit curl
38. TI
43. Type of brandy
46. "Friends" role
47. Cavort
48. Foot, to Fabius
51. Uzbek, for one
52. Goalie's place
54. Muscovite
56. Singer Vaughan
58. LA
63. Josip Broz
64. Cast lead-in
65. Lake near Novgorod
66. Sniffs out
67. ___ State (Oklahoma)
69. Standoff
71. Galatea's love
72. Sky Harbor, e.g.
73. SOL
77. Tries very hard
81. Get around
82. Handel's forte
87. Asked for earnestly
88. "A linen stock ___ leg...": Shak.
90. Singer Lopez
91. Whilom
92. Roster
93. FA
96. Equalizes
98. Write a ticket
99. "Play ___ It Lays," 1972 film
100. Jeans material
101. Say "I do"
102. Grimace
104. A Yemeni capital
106. Sheep-ish?
107. MI
113. Menu
115. Dover domestic
116. Convex moldings
117. Light touch
120. Song from "South Pacific"
122. Insincerity
123. Extended family
124. Monterrey Ms.
125. Liqueur flavoring
126. RE
130. No way!
131. Classical ennead
132. Ben or Paul
133. English poet
134. Sheath, for one
135. Inscribed pillar
136. Gators' kin
137. Highway hazard

DOWN

1. Mexican dance
2. Wedding worker
3. Was selective
4. Hoagie
5. "Dulce et decorum ___ ..."
6. Savoie star
7. Fries' partner
8. Fair-haired chaps
9. Sand's "___ et lui"
10. "Agnus ___"
11. Coal-tar distillates
12. Attains a goal
13. Dragonfly
14. ___ rule (generally)
15. The Gray
16. Saddle features
17. Out of sight
18. Poet Havelock
19. "Lest we lose our ___": Browning
20. Goriot, par exemple
26. Somersaults
27. Spanish measures
33. Molecule member
35. ___ acid
38. Actress Sanford
39. Cathedral fixture
40. A Coward
41. The lower world
42. Mr. Chomsky
43. Assigns parts
44. To this point
45. Summer capital of the Raj
48. Carnera of boxing
49. Gourmand
50. Two-reel movie
52. French blueblood
53. Dizzy
54. Beethoven's "___ Solemnis"
55. Medic chaser
57. Surmounting
59. Depicted
60. Wearies
61. Bare
62. Water silk
67. Relating to life
68. Thereabouts
70. Chalet feature
71. Unanimously
72. "___ plan, a canal..."
74. Uneven
75. Playwright Garcia ___
76. Where Hamal twinkles
77. Guard, to a con
78. Treasure follower
79. Appraised
80. Netman Lendl
83. Make good
84. Actress Dunne
85. Of an element important in electricity
86. Frustrate, alternatively
88. Willow
89. Turner or Cole
90. Mighty one
93. Like some pockets
94. Chianti or Soave
95. He lost to Dwight
97. Comedic brothers
103. Draft status
104. ___ chance (may succeed)
105. "As the ___ a bird...": Blake
106. Beef cut
107. Stressful times
108. Lay blame
109. Colorful Coco
110. Pass up
111. Ootheca
112. Signs of spring
113. Rattan worker
114. Extant
117. Threefold
118. Expiate
119. Like many windows
120. Troupe
121. Beliefs
123. Author Heyerdahl
124. Street sign
127. Passé
128. Inst. in Henderson, Tenn.
129. Sales pitches

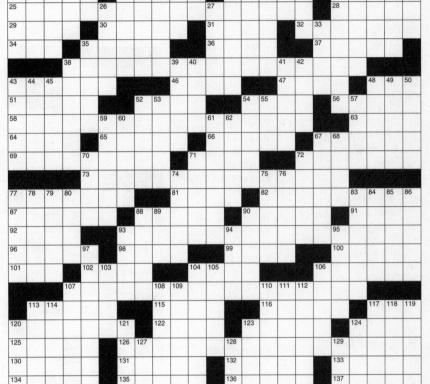

ACROSS

1. Kind of plan
9. Cloisonné
15. "¿Quién ___?"
19. Potential vitamin A
20. Lassie's family
22. Quahog
23. Unisex Shakespearean play?
25. Aleutian island
26. Nautical direction
27. Vic's radio wife
28. Zeus, to Cronus
29. Rooms at the top
31. Transformed
33. Snack
35. Swiss river
36. Souls
40. Eliot poem on the rewards of dieting?
44. Waters the garden
45. Truth, in Confucianism
46. Site of the patella
47. Pablo's uncle
48. Country song from a Gershwin musical?
54. Kind of price
56. Actress Rehan
57. "___ right with the world"
58. Diva Stevens
60. Theater part
61. Pillages
64. Olympic event
66. At full speed
69. Woolf work on the joy of housework?
72. Kepi part
73. "L' ___ c'est moi"
74. Norman and Walloon, e.g.
78. Traverse
80. Land in Eur.
82. Bank claim
83. Scandinavian coin
84. N.B.A. men
87. Fitzgerald's tale for tots?
92. Parseghian
93. Fervor
95. City in Neb.
96. "Ars gratia ___"
97. Updike work on cooking wild game?
101. ___ Pointe, Mich.
102. Blessing
103. City on the Oka
104. Guides
108. Unbranded calf, to cowboys
110. Alma-___, Kazakhstan city
112. Chip in a chip
113. Cartoonist Soglow
117. Alan or Robert
118. Freed-Brown film musical re commuters?
122. Match
123. Air: Comb. form
124. Went over again
125. Exam for a teen
126. Long-running show
127. "Hamlet" setting

DOWN

1. Recorded proceedings
2. Knightwear
3. Famed artist/ designer
4. Rake
5. Porter's "___ De-Lovely"
6. Stops
7. Former Indochinese kingdom
8. "Pagliacci" wife
9. Writer Umberto
10. Emulates Xanthippe
11. "Tennis, ___?"
12. Common bait
13. Tokyo before 1868
14. Rowan and Martin's show
15. Beetle or gem
16. Change
17. Glutton's activity
18. Cassowaries' kin
21. Conductor ___ Pekka Salonen
24. Like some tape
30. Estimates
31. Tabula ___
32. Relative of etc.
34. Tokyo drinks
36. Onward
37. ___ guerre
38. Russian log huts
39. Debussy's "La ___"
41. Straddler
42. One expanse
43. Grand Canal man
45. Cookbook Abbr.
49. Ohio/Mississippi city
50. Archeological site in India
51. Part of aka
52. Grain disease
53. Vienna, to Strauss
55. Franz or Kevin
59. Not so hard
62. "Common Sense" author
63. Dictionary Abbr.
64. Singer/actress Lenya
65. Italian exclamation
67. Flaherty South Seas film: 1926
68. Pointed instrument
70. Engage
71. Correct text
72. The life of a hobo
75. Mud hens
76. ___-Rivières, Quebec
77. Sixth follower
78. Cicatrix
79. Bowl-shaped antennas
81. Absolute
82. Trip tripper, for short
85. Lorelei's bailiwick
86. Prepared
88. Bagel topper
89. Hector's protector
90. Lincoln and Maxwell
91. ___-Magnon
94. Worshipful
98. Oscar winner of 1951
99. Three sea miles
100. Last syllable of a word
101. Hails
105. Japanese land unit
106. ___ nous
107. Lucy's TV pal
108. Northern nomad
109. Horned viper
111. Collections of sayings
113. Algerian port
114. Tex-Mex treat
115. Opera-house feature
116. Marcel's wave
119. Abner's father
120. Social followers
121. Cycle starter

ACROSS

1. Dade City's county
6. Long time
10. Plaudit
15. Fence's take
19. Certain voices
20. ___-ha-Shanah
21. Pine product
22. Strauss's "Die Frau ___ Schatten"
23. Landing places
24. Berlin product
25. Out of the way
26. Pedestal section
27. "Officious ___"
31. Actor Danson
32. Blind a falcon
33. Brachium's locale
34. Noon has two
35. Last exit
37. Abner's adjective
39. Solecist's contraction
41. Caboodle's mate
44. N.Y. Phil. output
45. "Armageddon ___!"
51. Pollen distributor
53. Tokyo, once
54. Febrero predecessor
55. Record the pace
56. The McCoy
58. An Arnaz
59. Contrite ones
61. Cytology inits.
62. Muezzin's God
64. Knish emporium
66. White-flag time
68. "Humus ___"
74. One of the Dryads
75. Equal, in Metz
76. Gunwale pin
79. Yard for Johann
82. Uncharged particle
84. Nautical raptors
88. Cameo's stone
89. Family name in baseball
91. Au revoir's kin
92. Bright signs
94. Aberdeen's river
95. "Universe ___"
100. Air: Comb. form
101. Snoopy's pair
102. Bartlett or Seckel
103. Churchill's letter
104. Islam's second city
107. Eureka!
108. Copy
110. ___ Comeau, Quebec town
114. Sideburn's neighbor
115. "Acrostic ___"
121. Exchange premium
123. Baited device
124. Trident part
125. Puff up
126. Leningrad's river
127. Just ___ in the bucket
128. Concert halls
129. Be gaga about
130. Migration
131. Not yet dry
132. Lather
133. Covers with frost

DOWN

1. Actress from Greece
2. Mrs. Roosevelt
3. Cubic meter
4. Dramatic tenor Franco ___
5. Tasmania's top peak
6. Pianist Schnabel
7. Dom DeLuise et al.
8. Theow's cousin
9. Dresser's "___ to the City"
10. Kindergarten pests
11. Hebrew R
12. Book by poet Ciardi
13. Word in a Caesar report
14. Upright
15. Earth layer
16. "Ament ___!"
17. Chilean landscape
18. Crystal-lined stone
28. Blabbed
29. Incan sun god
30. Kind of pro
36. Dog-show crasher
38. Aloof
40. "The Fourposter" as a 1966 musical
41. Lottolike game
42. Trav. papers, e.g.
43. Matador
45. Marine mammals
46. "The Sultan of Sulu" playwright
47. Eyeball section
48. Tribunal
49. K-O hookup
50. Where cows browse
51. Lingerie item
52. Reclusive fish
57. Off-schedule
59. Make parallel
60. Bambi's tail
63. Cape or Trader
65. Make do with
67. Say the same
69. Joyous hymn
70. Atelier
71. Incentive
72. Farrell or Jackson
73. Wayne film: 1953
77. Cleaning substance
78. Somerset river
79. Gen. Arnold
80. Violinist Bull
81. "Manon Lescaut ___"
83. Dakota Indians
85. Taught new software
86. Japanese drama
87. Whine tearfully
90. ___ nad Labem, Czech city
93. Reno-to-Las Vegas dir.
96. Bus or potent preceder
97. Snake: Comb. form
98. Sloped sheds
99. Soprano Renata
104. Intended
105. Gung-ho
106. Shilong's state
107. Skilled one
109. Entreaties
111. Forster's "___ With a View"
112. "___ do all . . .": Macbeth
113. Creator of the Moffats
116. Cancel
117. Patola, e.g.
118. Psyche's love
119. Singer Sayao
120. Construction piece
122. Acorn that made it

40 Step Quotes *by Charles M. Deber*

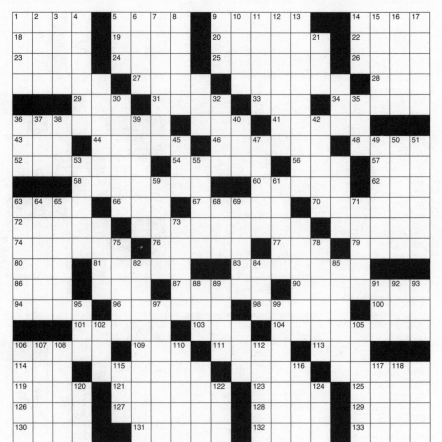

ACROSS

1. Commodity
5. Tender or hooker
9. "Sesame Street" grouch
14. Turkish chiefs
18. Arabian gulf
19. "___ la Douce"
20. Keyless
22. Cooked
23. Agalite
24. Grin broadly
25. Franchi or Mendes
26. Glissaded
27. What the passenger told the cabbie
28. Devoured
29. A.M.A. members
31. Fragrance
33. On a yacht, briefly
34. Kind of eclipse
36. Forerunner
41. Norwegian kings
43. Antique auto
44. Curtis and Bennett
46. Of the ribs
48. Too bad!
52. Beloit or Berea
54. Hebrew letter
56. Person Cinderella said was cruel
57. Can. province
58. Letter
60. Journalist Stewart
62. Volume of sayings
63. Ghislanzoni's great libretto
66. Cassowary
67. Kansas motto word
70. David, to Goliath
72. How the gradualist said he proceeds
74. Comedienne Kelly et al.
76. Shankar's ax
77. N.Y.C. subway line
79. Mtg.
80. ___ de France
81. Strasberg or Hayward
83. ___ Mauler (Dempsey)
86. ___ de veau
87. Undo
90. What perils test
94. Outside: Comb. form
96. Comedian Russell
98. Chalkboard
100. Fuss
101. Unisonally
103. What the politician was told to do
104. Scrutinizes
106. Commence
109. Queen Sophia's predecessor
111. Fledgling's abode
113. D-H connection
114. Possess
119. Parnassian number
121. Depict
123. Evangelist Roberts
125. Alt.
126. Indigo
127. Date
128. Wan
129. Ceramic piece
130. Reduce a sail
131. Judgment
132. Vegas machine
133. Takes a chair

DOWN

1. Escalator warning
2. Actress ___ Isaacs Menken
3. Depend
4. Construct a cipher
5. Child's cover-up
6. Cuprite and limnite
7. Loving
8. Domesticated
9. Alliance for Progress grp.
10. Hesse novel
11. Marine body
12. Rich Norman cheese
13. Barometer
14. Commercials
15. ___ Heights, in the Mideast
16. Singer Baker
17. Passover feast
21. Mean-spirited
30. Cheap cigar
32. What arroz is
35. Davis Cup team
36. Cinquefoil feature
37. New: Comb. form
38. Mountain pass
39. Part of Armstrong's statement
40. Surpass
42. Lowest female voices
45. "Erie Canal" mule
47. Keen
49. Abhor
50. Years, to Yves
51. Belle, Bart, and Brenda
53. Vaults
55. Slightest
59. Okla. oil center
61. The end, in Epernay
63. Aim high
64. Type of type
65. Hate
68. Penn. is one
69. Durations
71. "Where ___," 1969 Kanin film
73. Queues
75. Sleep, to Segovia
78. Feared fly
82. Cowardly
84. Loser to D.D.E.
85. What Levin called his heroines
88. In medias ___
89. Sixteenth Hebrew letter
91. Fond du ___, Wis.
92. N.Y. zone, at times
93. Distress call
95. Item for a shell
97. Punishment for sin
99. Actual
102. What the painters said they needed
105. Herons
106. Sub detector
107. Cord
108. Lennox or Potts
110. Extra charge
112. Halts
115. Grand ___, Evangeline's home
116. ___ Alto
117. LXIX × VIII
118. Ridge
120. Pixie
122. Beat for a P.O. man
124. Rent

41 *Our French Connection* by Joan P. Leemhorst

ACROSS

1. Cinch belt's cousin
5. Economist Smith
9. Sahara filling station
14. Shoot the breeze
17. C.I.O. partner
20. Canyon phenomenon
21. The Venerable ___
22. Gorge with a stream
23. Macrogametes
24. Kind of brother
25. Advice to Clouseau
28. Physiotherapist
30. Busy place, 4:00 P.M., London
31. Mexican standoff
32. Surroundings
34. Patriotic women's org.
35. Depletion
37. Witness
38. Indian foot soldier
40. Shelley subject
43. Stone pillar
45. Am. equivalent of a concierge
49. Diamond point
50. Locust
53. Collars
55. Moderate
56. Data fed to a computer
58. Eliminate malfunctions
59. Masonic doorkeeper
61. Operated
62. Immature, in a way
64. African plant
66. Conversation à deux
69. Harangue
71. Kyd work
74. Mingle
75. Allot
76. Embdem and quink
79. Age, as cheese
82. Interstices
85. Mun. official
86. Justification for existence
89. Australian bird
90. "Swanee" lyricist
94. Harness part
95. Provide new weapons
97. Aspersion
98. Vatican governing body
100. Wrists
102. Detroit action
104. Enamel work
108. Place
110. Uncover
112. Roman household god
113. Flies heavenward
115. One-tenth
118. Casino game
119. They call K's
121. Boite de ___ (nightclub)
122. Levantine garment
123. Glacé
124. Muddle with drink
126. Insinuating
128. Some N.Y.C. trains
129. Reared
130. Apologue
133. Negotiate
136. One needing an att.
137. Kin of a morganatic marriage
141. Originally called
143. Tells or sells
147. Beyond the megalopolis
148. Ambassador's stand-in
151. Taste
152. Suffix with verb
153. To love, in Paris
154. Robert (père) or Allan (fils)
155. Fustian
156. Nov. 1 group
157. Painter ___ Borch
158. Nervous
159. Sow chow
160. Purposes

DOWN

1. Conventicle group
2. Feel compassion
3. Strawberry's patch, once
4. Canapé
5. Antonym for adore
6. Profound
7. Wood-trimming tool
8. Dissolve
9. Tender
10. Part of a shandy
11. Pinnacle
12. At hand
13. Spots
14. Montague's son
15. ___-garde
16. Exceeds
17. Nonwindy side
18. Goatlike creature
19. Hugo's "Toute la ___"
26. Biggers hero
27. Give a leg up
29. Cancel
33. Give power to
36. A king of Judah
38. Long, slender cigar
39. Camaraderie
40. Unhinged
41. Top of a suit
42. ___ au rhum
44. Café au ___
46. Superior
47. French state
48. French director Clair
49. Puppeteer Baird
51. Dead end
52. Borodin's prince
54. Bristle
57. Chinese pagoda
60. Burgundy and Bordeaux, sometimes
63. Arrival at J.F.K.
65. Bacon bringers
67. Unit of elec. current
68. Tante, in Spain
70. Poetic contraction
72. First word of "Home, Sweet Home"
73. Sherry or Dubonnet, often
75. Singer Davis
77. Please the cordon bleu
78. "To ___ with Love"
80. Printemps follower
81. New Deal org.
83. Tried to equal or surpass
84. Big ___, Calif.
87. Peruvian plant
88. Slip or trip
91. ___ generis (unique)
92. "___ longa . . ."
93. Mayo and Yaqui
96. La Méditerranée, e.g.
97. Urbanity; tact
99. Shortly
101. Pocket bread
103. Bldg. material
104. Wodehouse's Drones ___
105. Brocaded fabric
106. Repugnance
107. Hibernia
109. Word feminizer
111. Was first
114. "A ___ time saves nine"
116. Belgian pilgrimage town, to a Parisian
117. Annapolis grad.
120. Up to now
122. Third letter
125. Type of hound
127. Fantasized
129. Kind of particle or ray
131. World-weary
132. Grease pencil
134. Wroth
135. Peg for Peete
136. Skim off grease
137. Kind of hall
138. Stage direction
139. Has dinner
140. Sports org.
142. Dutch cheese town
143. Mail rtes.
144. Persia, today
145. ___-Lease Act: 1941
146. Concordes
149. Thing, in law
150. Carte preceder

42 — Want Tibet? Peruve It! *by Jeanne Wilson*

ACROSS

1. A 1977 movie
7. "Batman," e.g.
9. "But war's ___ . . .": Cowper
14. Pollution problem
18. Chums
19. Shirley Temple's first
20. Thin layer
22. Famed hill near Dublin
23. Fusses
24. Custer's last major
25. "The guests ___ . . .": Coleridge
26. Time periods
27. With 65 Across, source of 40 and 87 Across
29. ___ B'rith
30. Rolling stock
32. Nap, in Nayarit
33. Sell or tell
35. Science that's on the rocks
36. Ticked off
38. ___ de plume (pen names)
39. Writer Calderon
40. Start of a quotation
49. Inductance unit
50. White bubbles
51. Covenant
52. Greek peak
53. College studies
54. Blame bearer in a song
55. Occur as a consequence
57. Understood
58. Also
59. Facility
60. Singer Laine
61. Schism
63. Imagoes
65. See 27 Across
68. Set back
71. Family of Portnoy's creator
73. City south of Moscow
74. Graf ___
76. Caviar
77. Mold
79. Expert
81. Salutation of a sort
82. Meerschaum
83. All atwitter
84. Dock support
85. A-F links
86. First: Comb. form
87. End of quotation
92. Wallet stuffers
93. She may wear a chador
94. Munster's pet
95. Divulges
99. Order from Hunter
101. Kind of license
105. He wrote "I Marry You"
106. Dish for a king?
107. Author of the quotation
109. Indigo
110. Obscure
112. Belém, Brazil
113. Dagger of yore
114. Canonical hour
115. Tso-lin of Manchuria and family
116. Balm
117. To be, to Bernadette
118. ___ bien!
119. Beginning
120. Canapés
121. Be zetetic

DOWN

1. Girasols
2. Spokes
3. Complete copy
4. Tax men
5. Token, sometimes
6. "Happy Days Are Here Again" composer
7. Landed estate
8. Call at a barn dance
9. Country-rock group
10. Parsley, e.g.
11. What one swallow doesn't make
12. La Bohème
13. Chem. ending
14. Bargain
15. Cuomo or Lanza
16. Chimp's cousin
17. Like long-winded orators
21. Essay
28. Pitiless
31. Simba's sound
34. Seaver and Sneva
35. Attendants on Aphrodite
37. "___ Dream": Wagner
39. Uncle of Joseph
40. "They went ___ way"
41. King of Judea
42. Celebrity's following
43. "Dog Day Afternoon" director
44. ___ Downs
45. Column style
46. Recondite matters
47. Calais-to-Rouen dir.
48. Sunbather's goal
54. Hawkeye's unit
55. Barkin of films
56. Patricia of films
57. "Fish Magic" painter
59. Major chaser
60. Parrot's mandible covering
62. G.H.W.B., e.g.
64. Steady Eddie of pitching fame
66. Home of the slave
67. Coward's "To Step ___"
69. Frosh teasers
70. Murrow's "___ Now"
72. Callahan-Roberts song
75. Basketball defense
77. Short noncom?
78. Cry of discovery
80. Start of a W.S. title
81. Opossum shrimp
82. Shams
84. Ottawa chief
85. Poison
86. "Is life ___?": Gilbert
88. "Mum's the ___": Cervantes
89. Settle
90. Inflatable life jacket
91. Seems
95. "___ Sleep," Odets play
96. Under full legal age
97. "Common Sense" author
98. Van Gogh slept here
99. Open, tartlike pastries
100. Islands off Sicily
102. Anne Sedgwick novel: 1911
103. Rhone feeder
104. Nerve
106. Radar action
107. Lozenge
108. Greek letter

43 Promises, Promises by Nancy Scandrett Ross

ACROSS

1. Dines late
5. Munch
10. Tribulations
14. Nedda's husband
15. Finery
18. Fainéant
20. Errors at Wimbledon
21. Pericles and Cicero
22. Actress Piper
24. Start of a verse
27. Singer Laine et al.
28. Stengel's wife
29. Composer ___ Hoffmann: Inits.
30. Suitable
31. Deadeye and Rackstraw
32. Bull fiddle
33. "Lakmé," e.g.
36. City NW of Leipzig
38. Harrow's rival
40. Institute in Brooklyn
41. Ross and Palmer
42. Mil. address
45. Endings for lobby and palm
47. Pearl Mosque site
48. Japanese salad plant
49. Verse: Part II
57. ___ Bell (Emily Brontë)
58. Shabby
59. The least bit
60. Popular apéritif
61. Greenish blue
62. Prospero's servant
64. Cautious
66. Greek Juno
67. Bowler or boater
68. Neighbor of Md.
69. Secular
70. Jeans fabric
71. Verse: Part III
78. "But is it ___?"
79. Composer Khachaturian
80. Bridge bid
81. Draft org.
82. Nettles
85. Streetcars
86. Command to Gabriel
88. Peep show
89. Euripides tragedy
90. Twofold
92. Curly coiffure
96. Syr. neighbor
97. Australian isl.
98. Louis challenger
99. J. F. Cooper subject
100. End of verse
107. Strict
108. Part of G.P.A.
109. Some women's fashions
110. Less well done
111. Ancient chipped stones
112. Tam-tams
113. Ayers and Hoad
114. Loamy deposit
115. Pulitzer Prize playwright: 1953

DOWN

1. Limoges item
2. Let go
3. Cores
4. Middling
5. Throngs
6. Cousins of hammer-heads
7. Guam's capital
8. Marshal Dillon
9. Drop heavily
10. One of the Flintstones
11. Anita or Alan of songdom
12. Jewish month
13. Soap operas
14. Arum lily
16. "De ___," Seneca essay
17. Postulate
19. Like breeze-kissed water
20. Reality
23. Adlai's running mate: 1956
25. Camper's shelter
26. Dep.
32. Greenish-yellow pear
33. E. Power Biggs' instrument
34. Henry's last Catherine
35. State of France
36. Lamarr of films
37. At the summit
39. Involuntary contractions
40. Kind of bull
41. Causing jolts
42. "... the rat that ___ malt"
43. Knight's weapon
44. Flattened at the poles
46. Metaphor's cousin
50. Trouble
51. Comprehend
52. Plants resembling spinach
53. Remote
54. Indehiscent fruits
55. Night's brightest star
56. Birds of passage
62. Mine entrances
63. Domicile: Abbr.
64. Soothes
65. Towel word
66. The bottom line, to Blass
69. Vicuña's cousin
70. Salesman's car, frequently
72. Appraise
73. Ontario Indian
74. Guardian's concern
75. "Dies ___"
76. Role in "King Lear"
77. Weary
82. Southern dish
83. Bacon portion
84. Advent
85. Seed coats
87. Banshee's activity
89. Actress Clarke of old films
90. Kneaded mixtures
91. Save
93. Projecting rim
94. American Beauties
95. Mel and Ed of baseball
97. Shea areas
98. Jalopy
99. Post used in air races
101. Parched
102. Teen detective of fiction
103. ___ Levi (Yves Montand)
104. Market
105. Chamber-music piece
106. O. Henry title word

Wise to the Words by Harold B. Counts

ACROSS

1. Van
5. Mary Janes
10. Calyx part
15. Lamb of pork fame
19. Being: Fr.
20. A manager of the Cards in 1990
21. Wing of a sort
22. Flows
23. Verdi product, full of froth?
25. Foolish, tree-climbing bird?
27. Subjugates
28. Alan, Cheryl and Diane
30. Glide nonchalantly
31. City in S. France
32. Latin teacher's command
33. Violinist Bull
34. Barbiturate
37. ___ Domingo
38. Sweeps under the rug
43. Kin of Tonys
44. Indecent planter?
46. Crooked
47. Impart
48. A concern of ecologists
49. Frost
50. River duck
51. Shaver
52. Obdurate bricklayers?
56. British shindig
57. Mouthpiece of a sort
59. Root used as a cleanser in Mexico
60. Egg box
61. Goes in with
62. Marsh bird
63. Groom
64. Bowling term
66. Caused by
67. Obstructs
70. Fleet St. product
71. Vague Donatello?
74. Skeet feat
75. Radiation dosages
76. G-men
77. Some votes
78. ___ qua non
79. Sèvres summer
80. Rash maitre d'?
84. Ky. college town
85. Justification
87. Avifauna
88. Half a decade
89. Bel Kaufman's "Love, ___": 1979

90. White wine, in 90 Down
91. Rex ___, film critic
92. He's got the goods
95. Move crabwise
96. Kin of floribundas
100. Emaciated hunting dog?
102. A short, thickset haddock?
104. Lotion ingredient
105. Finnish bath
106. Rich cake
107. Destiny, to Domenico
108. Tear
109. Co-Nobelist for Peace: 1978
110. Hairnet
111. Merganser

DOWN

1. ___-majesty
2. School 007 attended
3. Turkish river
4. Got off a 747
5. Hay; stubble
6. "High ___" 1959 song
7. Cuprite and limonite
8. Stray
9. Waxy substance
10. "___ Iwo Jima," 1949 film
11. Give the slip to
12. Places
13. Cover girl Carol ___
14. Postpones
15. Classroom item
16. A Prot.
17. "Child of the Sun"
18. Pale
24. Mythical beasts
26. Word on a Czech's check
29. Bohemian
32. Kind of line
34. Display in a toy shop
35. West Indian fetish
36. Unsubstantial ship?
37. Capital of Valais, Switzerland
38. Beldam
39. Suffixes used in medical terms
40. Moist cámise?
41. Sky: Comb. form
42. Airport tower
44. "Swinging ___," Haggard hit
45. Burn ___ in one's pocket

48. British guns
50. Basse ___, city in Guadeloupe
52. Filthy places
53. Having hair like Elsa
54. Friendship
55. City NNW of Gdansk
56. Rail for Susan Jaffe
58. Tender places
60. Tendrils
62. Like bubble baths
63. Supply food commercially
64. Throw about
65. Statue in the Duomo at Florence
66. Fuddy follower
68. Ringworm
69. Lieu
71. Gist
72. Loosen
73. European deer
76. Salad ingredient
78. Bon-voyage bashes
80. Despises
81. Bushy-tailed hoarder

82. Asian lake
83. Dresses
84. Dr. Spooner's "___ wenches"
86. Changed colors again
88. Wan
90. Where Duccio painted
91. Right-hand page
92. Ski lift
93. Cameo, for one
94. Soon
95. Ornament
96. Charger in Mexico City
97. Thailand, once
98. Varese's Palazzo d'___
99. Betoken
101. Chinese pagoda
103. Fashion

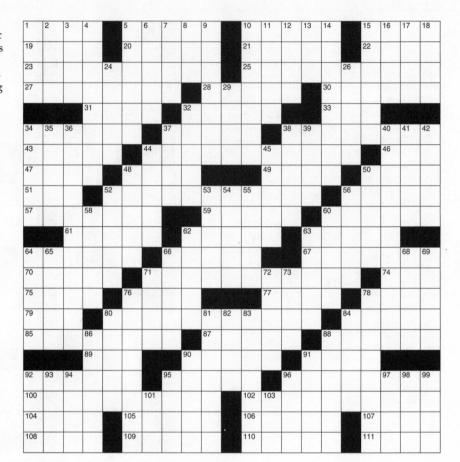

Svittles *by Phyllis Fehringer*

ACROSS

1. Supergiant in Scorpio
8. Put two and two together
15. Agreement
19. Arrowhead, e.g.
20. Bleach
21. Gate City of the West
23. Cassava grains
24. Dinner course, dressed up?
27. News nugget
28. "Get ___ the Church . . ."
30. Gaelic
31. Brazilian dance
32. Putting salt in one's coffee, e.g.
35. Lincoln's "Cap'n ___"
38. Tipples
40. Cowpoke's poker
41. Switch positions
44. Work
45. Make ___ in (progress)
47. Have the flu
48. ___ Lanka
49. Energy
50. Debussy's sea
51. Grilled fare gets splintered?
55. Like good news
57. Cliques
58. Apprizes
59. Free
60. Marathon winner: 1972 Olympics
61. A Borgia in-law
62. Donees
64. Ictus syllable
65. Jaeger
66. Bad Soden is one
69. Dame Myra ___
71. Hammett dog
73. Restaurants?
76. Yearn
77. Question
79. Ethyl's end
80. Spore clusters
81. Ears catch note of derision?
88. Capone nemesis
91. Calculator key
92. Featherweight champ: 1942–48
93. Burden
94. Lanyards
96. Put away
98. Pitcher Saberhagen
99. Bestow a right upon
101. Fined

104. Shutter parts
106. Washer's swasher
107. Reply to "Why?"
108. Inebriated vege-taters?
110. Chance
111. Macadam stickum
112. Lennon's "___ Do You Sleep?"
113. Kind of sided
114. German river and Hungarian city
115. Game of chance
116. Result of 8 Across
117. Cosmic times
119. Uke ridge
121. It opens sesame
122. Crude vessels?
124. Heart chambers
126. Medley
128. Arena for the Hawks
129. Sonora sandwich
133. Easter quarry fragment?
138. Unaffected
141. Flock of geese
142. Skier's turn
143. Put into law
144. Tolkien tree creatures
145. Squeeze out
146. Diapers, in Dover

DOWN

1. Oppositionist
2. Undiluted
3. Drink without moderation
4. Out on ___
5. One Grande
6. List extender
7. Grill counterfeits?
8. Kind of sphere?
9. God, in Genoa
10. Johnny's bandleader
11. Grand Exalted Ruler, e.g.
12. Go together
13. Intersection maneuver
14. Darius's subjects
15. Campaigner, for short
16. Nice souls in Iowa?
17. Chihuahua houses
18. Sadie of "Rain"
20. This, in Spain
22. Hair colors
25. Warmish
26. Achilles' killer
29. Aurora, in Greece
33. Attu canoe
34. Marine area

35. Diaskeuasts
36. Numismatic tails
37. Immovability
39. Decelerates
41. Finished
42. Ramses' river
43. Shake center, colored blue?
45. Kauai hi
46. Adriatic gulf
51. Act pts.
52. Gas: Comb. form
53. South African province
54. Choler
56. Madison Avenue come on
61. Heart track, initially
63. Candlestick Park info
65. Dirks of yore
66. Sarcastic remarks from the deli?
67. Cuzco country
68. Broadway play: 1985
69. Chest fastener
70. "___ homo"
72. Cigarette end

74. "Holiday ___" Crosby film
75. "Ad astra per ___"
78. Important ore of boron
82. Realm of Boreas
83. "Hell is ___": T. S. Eliot
84. Filbert
85. Kind of pudding
86. Narcotics
87. Reno raisers
89. Fabric for a filly?
90. "Make ___ Happy," 1960 song
95. Blackthorns
97. Principal's cousin
98. Kind of relief
99. One kind of maniac
100. Forage plant
102. Isaac's firstborn
103. Corium
104. Evens out
105. Fall tool
106. Desire, in this puzzle
108. Butter trees
109. Not ventro
115. Relations

118. Traffic stopper
120. Fax predecessor
122. Siberian city
123. Adhered
125. Colliery access
127. Whip lash
128. Huge hideosity
130. Esthetic course for freshmen
131. Calvados capital
132. Auto maker
134. Infantry gps.
135. Weber's "___ Freischutz"
136. Rhea's relative
137. Chisel
139. Literary oddments
140. Spigot

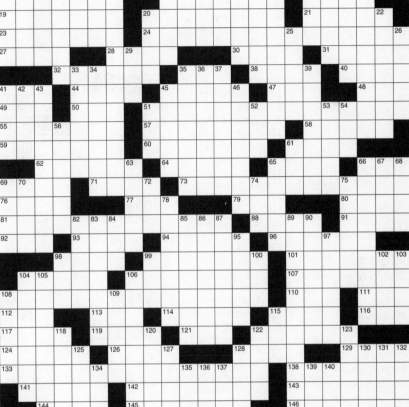

ACROSS

1. Gaiters
6. Zounds!
10. Duct
14. "___ Thirteen": Faulkner
19. Stash
20. Fifth-largest desert
21. A wife of Esau
22. "Kitchen" of Manhattan
23. "___ Grows in Brooklyn"
24. The color purple
26. Islamic devil
27. "___ on the Drina": Andric
29. Isak Dinesen book
31. Uncanny
32. Kobo and Burrows
33. Tessera
34. Leaf beets
37. Rich man in Luke 16, Vulgate version
39. Mountain ashes
43. Remedy
44. Frost book
48. Fermi or Caruso
51. Pluck
52. Was off base
53. Dactyl, e.g.
54. Demeter's dad
55. Hebrew letter
56. Employed busily
57. "The Seaman's Friend" author
58. Monarchy
60. Aerie components
61. Swimmer Weatherford
62. E. M. Forster novel
66. MX and Sickle
69. Herrick's creation
70. Dark period in a Koestler book
74. Give a hang
75. Many a "Brother Rat" character
76. In academia a 4.00, e.g.
78. Muslim messiahs
79. Levin or Wolfert
80. Criterion
81. Fulminate
82. Shell-game decoys
83. Graham Greene novel
86. Orange-neck goose
87. Soprano Resnik
88. Throws off
90. Books, to Zola
92. ___ Ifni, Morocco
94. Fed

95. Al-Qahirah, to Flaubert
97. Isaak Babel book
101. James Joyce book
105. Result of a wedge shot
106. Place to write letters
108. "Land of cotton"
109. Running: Comb. form
110. Cape of Chile
111. Large kangaroo
112. Moliére's "L' ___ des maris"
113. Tip
114. Of French rock music in the 60's
115. ___ Mawr
116. Passover feast

DOWN

1. Vamoose
2. It's often beaten
3. End of an E. Caldwell title
4. Deighton book
5. Be angry
6. Islands off Sicily
7. Overcharged
8. Author Prevost
9. Cube with 21 spots
10. Most ambiguous
11. Emulates Robert Giroux
12. Minute: Comb. form
13. A purloining
14. A rainbow followed this
15. New Testament book
16. She outwrestled Thor
17. Bankrupt Federal org.
18. She, to Soldati
25. Poet Service
28. Org. that audits
30. Springless mattress
32. Get around
34. Tab
35. Novelist Barbusse
36. Role in "Green Pastures"
38. It's worn on an obi
40. Fragrance
41. Kern's "___ But Me"
42. Kind of preview
45. Light: Comb. form
46. Inventive
47. City SE of San Jose
49. Pointed ends
50. ___ Peak, N.M.
51. Romany realm
56. Small part of an oz.

57. Thomas Mann novella
59. Bensalem is one
60. Gumshoe
61. Alice's cat
63. The Salt Palace, e.g.
64. Shoo!, in Dogpatch
65. Benedictine titles
66. Less amicable
67. "Daybreak" director
68. Fort in N.C.
71. Fainéant
72. Eeyore's creator
73. Squiggles
75. Homeland of 25 Down
76. Street urchin
77. Painter Mondrian
80. Container for coffee
81. Group anew
84. Supple
85. Estate
89. Scamper
90. "___ Liza Jane," 1916 song
91. Fleurs-de-lis
93. Antsy
94. Celebrity

96. Minor judge in Judges
97. Chances
98. Tittle-tattle
99. Bacchic shout
100. ___ Islands, off New Guinea
101. Gloomy
102. O.T. book
103. Ruffle
104. Melampus or Mopsus
107. "Charlotte's ___"

ACROSS

1. . . . "THE PALLID PROF" by J. B. Poquelin?
7. Men, e.g.
13. Seasoning herbs
19. An ointment
20. Of the moon
21. Ancient marketplaces
22. . . . "RIGHT? RIGHT!" by A. Loos?
23. Slender and sharp
24. Expand
25. Paradigm
26. . . . "GRAND IMAGES" by H. Gardner?
28. "The law is a ___": Dickens
29. Occupied
31. Convert into cash
32. Got a hole-in-one
33. Newspaper-publishing family
36. Part of Scotland
40. Year or frog preceder
43. Islet
45. Pronoun for the Andrea Doria
46. Medicinal root
48. . . . "O'ER THE LENT HERB" by P. Osborn?
53. Nicholas II & Ivan IV
54. World-weary
55. Lotion ingredient
56. Jockey's garb
58. Milieu for Levine
59. Effort
61. Blockheads, in Brest
63. Pasture
64. Cries of disgust
65. . . . "AVE, SALVADOR" by M. Stewart & J. Herman?
68. . . . "SAGAN'S TARS" by A. Miller?
71. Identical
72. ___ de plume
73. Hollow out
75. Cather's "One of ___"
76. Uncle in 36 Across
77. Organizational regulation
79. Generator's power output
81. Observant one
84. Bamboo lover of China
86. . . . "MOLDING MOLD" by E. Williams?
90. Harmonize
92. Norse poem
93. Mythical piper
94. Parts of joules
95. "More matter with ___ art": Shak.
96. Did some sowing
99. Fixations
101. Steal
103. F's forerunners
105. Job of TV's Teddy Z.
108. . . . "HOSTESS TO THE IMPECUNIOUS" by J. Gay?
114. Jockey, at times
116. Dwell
117. Frame braces
118. Plant also called germander
119. Ballerina McKerrow
120. Reference works
121. French ordnance
122. Book of prayers
123. Blush
124. Least forthright

DOWN

1. System of tenets
2. Spreads
3. Sleep, food, etc.
4. Carry on
5. Imperfective, as a verb
6. Maiden-name preceder
7. ___-de-mer (trepang)
8. Former Congolese prime minister
9. City on the Wabash
10. He lived 905 years
11. Upsets
12. Tantrums in public
13. Misfortune, in Hibernia
14. Spry
15. Guadalcanal, Malaita, et al.
16. New Persia
17. Lasting into the wee hours
18. Homophone for seize
20. Col. entrance exams
26. TV sound signal
27. Insecticide in disrepute
30. Niggardly
32. Asch's "The ___"
33. Pleasurable
34. A Lauder
35. Bat wood
37. Dorset town
38. Matches
39. Family of a memorable cartoonist
40. Lugworm
41. Signed up, as a G.I.
42. Humiliations
44. "The ___ Dogs," Burns poem
47. French connections
49. Actual
50. Israeli airline
51. Stir until foamy
52. Grade sch.
57. Land a haymaker
60. Like a skeleton
62. Relished
64. Public uproars in England
65. Hooked at the tip
66. Numskull
67. Oriental nurse
69. Scraggy
70. Intoned
71. Calyx segment
74. Byrd book
77. Interdict
78. Mineral resembling feldspar
80. Skinny follower
82. Brain specialist's rec.
83. T.L.C. givers
85. Trash-cans-on-Thames
87. Collegian's prerogative
88. Tricky drawback
89. Actress Markey
91. Living near the ground, as insects
97. Part of a journey
98. Human incarnation of a deity
100. Breakfast food
102. Hopper of Hollywood
103. Shakespearean forest
104. Food fish
105. Southwestern porridge
106. Chromosome constituents
107. Lovers' date
108. Trombone, to a jazzman
109. Half: Prefix
110. Those niñas
111. Rarely, old style
112. Toward the mouth
113. Raise a question
115. Gudrun's victim
118. Airgun ammo

ACROSS

1. ___ Alto
5. A step up
10. Fog's companion
14. Wetland
19. LXXVII × II
20. ___ nous
21. Dividing word
22. Air a view
23. Gatherers of honey for Georges?
25. A flier or fryer for Frédéric?
27. More glittering
28. "___ de Lune"
30. Soaks
31. An old story from Paul?
34. Fakes
36. Ampersands
37. Slanting
41. Charlie and clan
42. Drudge
44. Jr. high, e.g.
46. Town SE of Brussels
48. Resound
49. German state
50. Bull (transliteration from the Greek)
53. Jason's ship
54. Chi. airport code
55. A growler for Giacomo?
58. Actor Shackelford
59. Ready
61. Suffixes with attend and appear
62. Boring tools
64. Viking Ericson
65. Certain pitches
67. Fabricator
68. Pulpits
70. Safe place
71. Actress June from N.Y.C.
74. Residue
75. Footwear for Franz Peter?
79. Bk. notation
80. Type type, for short
82. Certain fishermen
83. Lament
84. Skin opening
85. Eatery
87. Mineo or Maglie
88. Custom
89. Polonius hid behind this
90. Extras
92. Bambi, for one
94. Municipal maps
95. A lure by Ludwig?
100. Protozoans
104. Loathed
105. Aquarium accessories
109. A watercolor by Wolfgang?
111. A few things for Franz to do?
113. Miscued
114. Certain entrance fee
115. Lincoln's late cousin
116. Start of Idaho's motto
117. Approaches
118. Spurry or henbit
119. ___ Carte, opera company
120. Enlist again: G.I. slang

DOWN

1. Chem. pollutants
2. Came to rest
3. Judy's girl
4. Projection
5. Gums
6. Ilka Chase's "___ We Cry"
7. Cubic meter
8. Before, to the Bard
9. Take back
10. Minor Prophet and namesakes
11. "___ Own Write," Lennon book
12. Attack
13. Apex
14. Every 30 days or so
15. Chevet
16. "Cherry-___" Herrick poem
17. Green bean
18. Coop group
24. Clips
26. Adherents
29. Inc. in the U.K.
32. New Zealand native
33. Uncouth person
34. Bake eggs
35. Applause for George?
38. Eggs: Lat.
39. A cove for Cole?
40. "The ___ Sanction," 1975 film
41. Field yield
42. Tempo
43. Example of 5 Down
44. Part of SST
45. Irritable
47. Stewart and Serling
49. Exterior boundary
50. Fire starters
51. Bronowski's "The ___ of Man"
52. Shore-dinner tidbit
55. What socks come in
56. More innocent
57. Oil, in Orléans
60. Favorite
63. Cheerful
65. Dolphins' former coach
66. Tag
68. Foray
69. Port for Pompey
71. Attention getter
72. Other women, to El Cid
73. Ayes' opposites
76. "Steppenwolf" author
77. Type of testimony
78. Sun. speech
81. Headed
84. One who babbles
86. Portrayer of many O'Neill protagonists
88. Teased
89. Cryptonym's cousin
91. Cardinal's quarters
92. Kind of line to sign
93. Woodward role in 1957
94. To a degree
96. Man in the van of a clan
97. "... Poker Flat" author
98. Impertinent
99. Cutting edge
100. Sitcom starring Sherman Hemsley
101. The man for all seasons
102. Biblical scribe
103. Humorist Arthur (Bugs) ___
106. Locale of Beauvais
107. Q-V connection
108. Octagonal sign
110. Observed
112. Wedding words

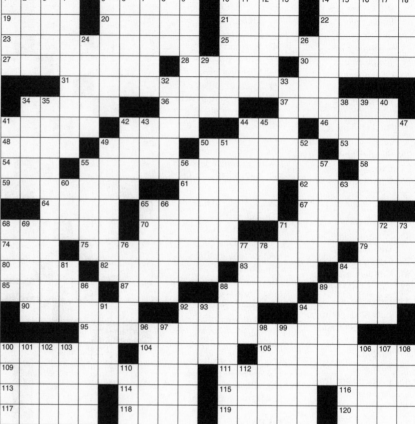

49 Skoal! by James E. Hinish, Jr.

ACROSS

1. A fruit for a spirit
6. Feel one's way
11. Clay or Webster
15. Sharpen a razor
20. Strong drink, for short
21. Glaswegian's great-grandchild
22. Man in the van of a clan
23. Italian philosopher 1866–1952
24. Certain turkeys
26. Deltas
28. Quarrel
29. Cerveza ingredient
30. Containers larger than six-packs
31. Without profit
32. "___ the Single Girl"
34. Necessity for a screwdriver
35. Cold ___
36. Vintner's vessel
39. NFL eleven
40. Elder (girl): Fr.
41. Wort ingredient
42. Utters, in Br'er Fox jargon
45. Heighten
47. Howe won here: 9/11/77
49. Monogram of Garfield's successor
50. Cover for the iris
51. Banshee sounds
52. ___ 'acte
53. Lewd material, for short
54. Common noun endings
55. Computer channels
56. Likeness
58. Singer Page
59. Burden
60. Deserve
61. British coins, for short
62. Bon ___ (cheap): Fr.
63. Hooper or Nielsen: Abbr.
64. Maugham book
68. ___ Vineyard
69. Harding's Secretary of Commerce
71. He summons: Lat.
72. Asiatic peninsula
73. ___ in bond
75. Plays a child's game
77. Beatty or Rorem
80. Lucy ___, the bride of Lammermoor
81. Complain
82. S.A. sorrels
83. Commercial Abbr.
84. Food and drink
85. Barbara's Oscar-winning role
86. Author of "Taras Bulba"

88. The Vaisyas, for one
89. Actress in "Tea and Sympathy"
90. Distinctive air
91. Hungarian wine
92. Hector, Hercules, et al.
93. Scotland's longest river
94. West Indies island chain
97. Beguiles
98. Simple sugar
99. Jigger
100. Wined and ___
101. Melkarth
102. French soul
103. Ursid
104. Four-time Wimbledon winner
105. Saki and family
107. Consents
110. Rickey ingredients
111. Sacred bird
112. Rudiments
116. Expire, à la Tennyson
118. Famed essayist and caricaturist
121. Fix the clocks again
122. Concerning
123. Costar in "The Seven Year Itch"
124. Forearm bones
125. Give an ___ (look after)
126. Brewer's need
127. Old Spanish sherry
128. Union general

DOWN

1. London taverns
2. Fabulist: Var.
3. ___ vitae
4. Gowdy and namesakes
5. N.T. book
6. Coburn's Pulitzer Prize play, with "The"
7. Summer TV fare
8. Mountain nymph
9. Seed holder
10. Draft or train endings
11. ___-jack, the Canada jay
12. "I ___ dream": M.L. King Jr.
13. Model ___ de la Fressange
14. Schnapps country: Abbr.
15. Stamp out
16. Kegs carrier
17. Newspaper section, for short
18. "Der Rosenkavalier" baron
19. Annoyance
22. Swapped

25. Home of Juárez
27. German firearm
30. Directs a ship's navigation
33. White-tailed birds
34. Lab items
35. Subject to 23 Across
36. Airplane's course
37. Rub with oil
38. "Coming ___": Burns
40. Saharan
41. Valuable vases
42. Kingston Trio hit: 1962
43. Singer Kitt
44. Kooks
46. Jillian and Sheridan
47. Poisons
48. Emulate Penelope
51. Ingredient of a barman's cubes
53. Cocktail ___
55. ___ Alaska
56. Newton or Hayes
57. ___ adagio (very slowly)
58. Coins of Belgrade
60. Prowl after prey
62. Drakes or harts
64. Wine is one
65. Kind of squash

66. Sharp; biting; cold
67. Affliction on skid row
68. Taj ___
70. Playful mammal
72. Genuine one
73. "___ the Future," 1985 movie
74. Family of a music-hall star
75. A treasurer of Nehemiah
76. Apparel at an "Animal House" orgy
78. Respect
79. Goddess, in Grenoble
81. Insert mark
83. Word on a Japanese freighter
85. Prevailing mania
86. Hopeless one
87. Approved
88. Rostropovich's instrument
90. Horrified
91. Prongs
92. Undertaker's purchase
95. Hard
96. Amuse

97. Jack or Josephus
99. Takes care of
101. Champagne feature
103. Assail
104. Nizer subject
105. Highball ingredient
106. Fla. cape
107. Israeli port
108. "Cabaret" costar
109. Kind of wine
110. Hyena created by Capp
113. ___ fide
114. Everett of TV and films
115. Widgeon
117. Stage freight?
118. Tequila country: Abbr.
119. Disciple's emotion
120. Strange, in Soho

ACROSS

1. Brief effort
5. Cassandra's gloomy prediction
9. Protrude, as the chin
12. Isaac Wise, e.g.
17. Attended
18. Utah ski resort
19. Allie's TV friend
20. Mrs. Irving Berlin
21. They can take a yoke
22. Ancien régime queen
24. Wall Street acronym
25. States firmly
26. NO CLOWNING, SIR!: 1988
29. U.S.A. LAST!: 1946
31. Early fig-leaf wearer
32. Face-stubble time
33. He dealt in pelts
34. Flower's Saturday-night special?
37. Most indolent
39. Operatic Eugene
43. Valor; virtue
44. D.A. WARM? LIAR!: 1937
46. Zilch
47. Low place
48. "You ___ mouthful!"
50. Whitewalls
52. Cole or Turner
53. Tolkien tree-giants
55. PACK BUNS, ED!: 1985
59. Keen
61. Loathed
63. Staring open-mouthed
64. Joined in a common cause
65. One quart, roughly
66. Cantankerous
67. MacLeod of "The Love Boat"
68. Kitchen gadget
70. "Common Sense" author
71. Marie von Trapp's title
74. Old Testament book
75. ONLY US, HANS!: 1983
77. Pitfall
78. The works
79. Gibbs of "227"
81. Large antelope
83. March 15, in Milano
84. Coral ridge

86. BLOBS OF RED!: 1976
90. O'Grady of song
92. Lord Mountbatten's wife
94. Previous
95. Stoppered the wine bottle
96. Coup ___
98. "___ We Got Fun?": 1921 song
99. Mason's burden
100. SEND LEE!: 1956
103. DUNCE SLAIN? YES!: 1989
109. Leaf angles
110. Compassionate
112. Play for time
113. Actor Julia from San Juan
114. "Giant" actor Sal ___
115. Plato topic
116. Jewish month
117. Pound or Stone
118. Forever, in poesy
119. Spider's parlor
120. Import tax
121. "Ich ___," Prince of Wales's motto

DOWN

1. Clumsy craft
2. Hirsch sitcom
3. Final word
4. Arnold or Tony
5. Weedy grass
6. Actor Vidov
7. Auricular
8. Flaherty film
9. Traffic tie-ups
10. Salt Lake City player
11. "Hello, sucker!" Guinan
12. Logic
13. Santa Anna's deposer
14. Tricolore hue
15. Spin a log
16. Part of M.I.T.
19. Abdul-Jabbar
23. Stowe's ice-crosser
27. Campus climbers
28. "The Art of Love" poet
30. Filched
33. In ___ (quickly)
34. Went white
35. Papas from Greece
36. SWELL ESTATE!: 1977
37. Put on cargo

38. Part of a daily dozen?
40. RUINS GIN? EEK!: 1980
41. Fuming
42. Well-known
44. Rheostat part
45. Ararat docker
49. Fall bloomer
51. Round of cheers
54. Fish catcher
56. "Mack the Knife" singer
57. Ecstasy's partner
58. Diamond corners
60. "Make my day" Eastwood
62. Iron or shovel preceder
64. Duelist Burr
66. Honkers' home
67. Festive affairs
68. Travelers' Midwest mecca
69. Propelled a gondola
70. Young hen
71. Plantation hand
72. Thompson or Hawkins

73. Looked through keyholes
75. Angels love these letters
76. Made dull
80. Taper off
82. Talk inanely
85. A crab on the roof?
87. Hoaxes
88. Ken ___ of "thirtysomething"
89. Cortices
91. Systematic
93. Wrestling hold
95. A bit nippy
97. Lopsided
100. Doe or Roe
101. Ramp sign
102. "___ kleine Nachtmusik"
103. Brahmin
104. Korean border river
105. Trollop
106. Hakenkreuzler
107. Smoke meat
108. Dash
111. Dander

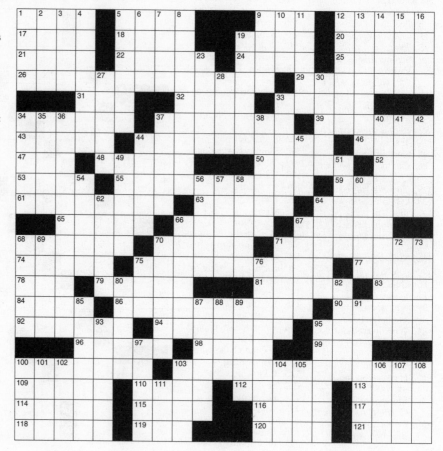

53 Show-How Session by Jim Page

ACROSS

1. Ibsen heroine
5. Part of NASA gets the gait
9. "___ c'est moi"
14. Bal. sheet worker
17. Jai ___
18. Gomorrah neighbor
19. Mason's concern
20. Attention-getting word
21. Pits turn into little arbiters
22. March along
23. Conjecture becomes embezzlement
25. Change a bulb
27. Certain taxes
29. ___ l'oeil
30. Tati's ta-ta
31. Russian area goes south
33. Stormy ___ (sea birds)
34. Nathan, to David
35. Tusked swine
37. Stupid guys become little cutups
39. N.Y.C. observes it
40. Soak flax
41. "To ___, to Greece, and into Noah's ark": Cowper
43. Bill-of-exchange signer
46. Intoxicating
48. Foxhole kin becomes illuminated
51. Batik expert
52. Restaurateur goes to a Jordanian peak
53. Entomb
54. Author goes to college
56. Time to irrigate
60. Bilbao visitor
62. Actress Claire
64. Silvertip
65. Kind of sauce
66. "Robust ___ alone is eternal": Gautier
67. Santa becomes less egotistical
70. Prefix with Raphaelite
72. Guido's high note
74. Depend (on)
75. Ade's "___ Horne"
76. Crab, lobster or shrimp
79. "Clair de lune" composer
81. "Streamers" playwright
83. Casked-wine process
84. Suffix from a trig function
85. Actress Raines
89. Bet becomes emporium gelt
91. Arabian prince
94. "...a sea of ___": Shak.
96. Safecracker
97. Forest humus
98. Blotter ltrs.
100. River duck
101. Eliel's son
103. Monogram of Garfield's successor
106. Pliant
108. Doughnut-shaped rolls
110. Computer buffs
112. Prepare a diamond
113. Oily resins
115. Fiendish
117. Cocktail becomes a coxswain
119. Lithe animal
121. "Wishing will make ___"
122. Attain justly
123. Pinguid
124. Whistle-blowing times
125. Baltic native
126. Concordes come to N.Y., N.J., etc.
127. Baseball Hall of Famer
128. WWI admiral
129. Mmes., in Mexico

DOWN

1. Petrarch's beloved, et al.
2. Wimbledon champ: 1959
3. Reptile becomes drowsy
4. Usher's beat
5. Bassanio's beloved
6. Hoopla
7. Col. Pickering portrayer
8. Charlatan of old
9. Dazed, miler becomes obsessed
10. Robt. ___
11. Twitches
12. Elephant boy turns into Arabian dad
13. Jousted
14. Foolish fancy
15. Colonized
16. Pardon
18. Social pos.
20. Suffix for comment
24. "...wherefore ___ Romeo?"
26. Reddish browns
28. Clocked
32. Leaflike plant part
33. ___ diem
36. Fish gets a cheer
38. Sault ___ Marie
42. Abruzzi town
44. Fastidious: Slang
45. Willy Loman's quest
47. Work units
48. Rock singer ___ Ford
49. Hardened
50. Football's Greasy, et al.
52. Mongol throng
55. Wind dir.
57. German navy V.I.P.: 1928–43
58. Mall becomes a warren
59. Power of the movies
61. Far from loquacious
63. Writer gets a connection
64. Looked good on
68. Philadelphia hockey player
69. Anderson's "High ___"
71. High-strung
73. Role in 20's Broadway hit
77. Emerged, as an article
78. Enthralled
80. Like movies, once
82. Swiss river port
86. ___ Alamos
87. Sleepy one becomes a woodsman
88. Perpendicular to the keel
90. Son of Odin
91. Punishes by fine
92. Bandicoot
93. Utensils on pencils
94. Tic-___-toe
95. Roman army units
99. Vagrants' area changes into children's line
102. Ancient ascetic
104. Awn
105. Ties
107. Like a quilt
109. Bar legally
111. Ballooners, e.g.
113. Odd number becomes the opposite
114. ___-majesté
116. ___ Antiqua
118. Philippine tree
120. Low digit

ACROSS

1. Parisian gangster
7. Cleanse thoroughly
12. Of an armbone
17. The Censor
21. Ameche-Verdon film: 1985
22. Department of France: 1815–1975
23. Daughter of Tantalus
24. Words of understanding
25. Fast player with lots of clout
27. Outfielder, at times
29. "___ Not Unusual"
30. Shock
31. Lessen
33. ___ double take
34. Half of XIV
35. Ancient Celtic priest
37. Bivalve mollusk
41. Hammarskjold
44. Desires
46. Cast amorous glances
48. Vowel changes in verb forms
50. Battologize
52. One way for runners to score
55. Hanoi holiday
56. Garb
57. Pick up the tab
58. Valley
59. Get one's goat
60. Don
61. Religious composition
62. Germ cell
64. Mistake
65. A son of Seth
66. Criterion for Kelly
68. Carnegie ___ U.
69. Ump's relative
70. This can be acute
72. War god
73. "Lili ___"
74. Small land masses
76. Wept
78. Concerning this
79. Irritates
81. Contented sounds
82. Musical ennead
83. "___ Sleepy People"
86. Portion of bacon
87. Yogi Berra was one
90. In the distance
91. John or Sean
92. Stadium pentagon
94. Dispatch boat
95. Daily rat race.
96. Lettuce variety

97. Player in an old song
98. Gripper of sorts
99. Art of horsemanship
100. Laders' org.
101. Strike-calling umpire
104. Flower part
105. Swivel wheels
107. Water wheel
108. Looks over hastily
110. Crandall or Ennis
111. Come back in
113. More rational
115. Numero ___
116. Ship-shaped clock
117. Position properly
119. Will topic
122. Wood sorrel
125. What a pinch hitter will do
129. At the end, for 25 Across
132. Declare positively
133. Baseball's Pee Wee
134. Standards
135. Nicotinic acid
136. Opposite of raves
137. T.N. Page's "___ Chan"
138. Dutch jurist Huig de ___: 1583–1645
139. Mystery awards

DOWN

1. Start of "Hamlet"
2. Larboard
3. Galatea's lover
4. ___ a plea
5. Jack or Tim
6. Sap
7. Dutch boat
8. Bulb's cousin
9. Mountain nymph
10. "Born in the ___"
11. Instructed again
12. Still bright
13. Gay tune
14. "Drake" poet
15. Broadcasting syst.
16. Unlike some scrawls
17. Homopterous insect
18. Rowan
19. Peg for Peete
20. Above, poetically
26. French critic-historian: 19th century
28. Outcry, in Rouen
32. Spleen
36. Turn
38. Wire
39. Where to see Rickey Henderson

40. Hunter beloved by Eos
41. Layette item
42. Bring into harmony
43. Hit or walk
44. Caution
45. Raid
47. Fogies
49. "Tristram Shandy" author
51. Branco and Mayo
53. Penury
54. Egypt–Syr. once
57. Bridge charges
59. Norse chieftain
61. Certain NCO's
62. Unfailing
63. Entreated
64. Montmartre chapeau
67. Rear
68. ___ nostrum (the Mediterranean)
70. Standish's stand-in
71. ___-do-well
73. "The evil that ___ . . .": Shak.
75. Title in colonial India

76. Scoter
77. Songwriter Harold
78. Ski jumper ___ Bulau
79. Lebanon language
80. Situated at the foundation
81. Styx ferryman
82. Water nymphs
84. Falsify
85. Severe trial
88. Roman helmets
89. Eye layer
90. American cartoonist
92. "___ porridge hot . . ."
93. Author Stanislaw ___
95. Needlefishes
97. Small agricultural enterprise
98. Gymnast's activity
99. Chorus reject
101. Star in Cygnus
102. Emphatic negative
103. Kind of bunt
104. Watercourse
106. Domingo, et al.
109. Most adorable

112. Olympic athlete Johnson
114. Kind of rocket
118. Opposite of a win
120. Foolish person
121. Geraint's wife
122. Grampus
123. French leather
124. Sothern and Harding
125. Breach
126. Eggs, to Ovid
127. Derek vehicle
128. Earl Grey, for one
130. Correlative
131. Kind of rule

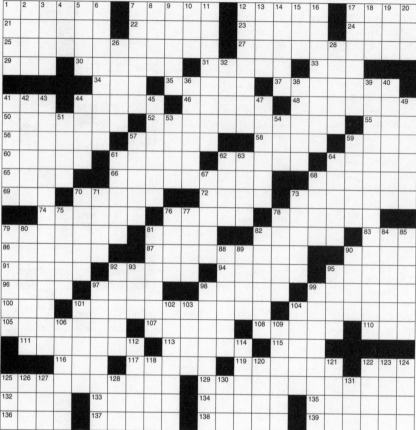

55 Versified Versions by Norman S. Wizer

ACROSS

1. Young salmon
5. Medieval estate
9. She loved Narcissus
13. British service-woman of W.W.I
17. Woodwind
18. Up and about
20. Porch
21. Earth goddess
22. Vulgar group avoided argument
26. "Die Fledermaus" maid
27. African timber tree
28. Annoy
29. Retiree's nest egg
31. Reconnoiters
32. Plants used for raising nap
33. Active chemical substance
37. Choreographer Tommy
38. H.H.H.'s state
39. Four couples expect big argument
46. French violinist: 18th century
47. Behold: Lat.
48. Precipitation in Dundee
49. Baseball stats.
50. Commanded
51. Solitary
53. Rabbit fur
55. Lighter and tender
56. Easter lead-in
57. ___ Nevada
59. Platitude
60. Intelligent men find fault with falsehoods
65. "Popo" author: 1980
66. Archer's goal
67. Mama or Peggy
68. Bury
69. Bog
70. Vents
71. Sir, in Madrid
74. S. state
75. Curve
76. Mantle
78. Take aliment
79. Silly people bilk fat relative
86. Rex or Donna
87. Broadway muggers?
88. Kitchen appliance
89. Orbs
93. Daffy Duck, e.g.
95. Cagers' gp.
96. Emulate Gulliver
97. Comportment
99. More experienced
103. Assistant held up sober young man
106. Orison finis
107. Leases
108. Moor plant
109. Portent
110. Dry run
111. Tokyo drink
112. To live, to Livy
113. Proceed

DOWN

1. Negri of silents
2. Retired
3. English poet laureate: 1715–18
4. Car stopper
5. Partner of wide
6. Fabulist: Var.
7. Okla. Indians
8. Preachy
9. Cultural characteristics
10. Betty of songdom
11. In what way
12. Allowing for contingencies
13. They cross warps
14. Mountain ridge
15. "...makes Jack ___ boy"
16. Aqua and motor endings
19. Detour traffic
20. Sea duck
23. Chapeau for Corot
24. Went for the pitch
25. Revolutionary diplomat
30. Actress Alicia
32. Rhea or Cronus
33. Kind of estate
34. "___ kleine Nachtmusik"
35. Ripened
36. Score
38. Lunatic
40. Tennis coup
41. ___ de corps
42. Tumults
43. Calculators of sorts
44. A tenth part
45. Sinuous letters
51. French artist
52. Load
53. She was an O'Hara
54. Prado offering
55. Consecrate
56. Pries
57. Infrequent
58. Imperfect merchandise: Abbr.
59. Person exercising power
60. Twist
61. Pat needs this to maintain composure
62. Bristles
63. Gawked
64. Most frigid
69. Tiercel and cob
70. Copy
71. Assembly
72. Head of a tale
73. ___-do-well
76. Mariner's aid
77. Nonattender
78. Veto
80. Goofed
81. Antennae
82. Rings
83. Allayed
84. Time without end
85. Wealthy man
89. Hessen or Hamburg
90. Coach
91. A brother of Zeus
92. Happening
93. Philippine island
94. Byways
97. Moist and chilly
98. Outfits
100. British title
101. Whence the Pison flowed
102. Tear
104. Where cows browse
105. Scottish river

Possessive People *by Bernice Gordon*

ACROSS

1. Airport feature
5. Prosaic
9. Residue of grapes
13. "Evita" role
16. Squinch, e.g.
17. State in NE Brazil
18. Nymph of the hills
20. McQueen film, with "The"
21. Colette character
22. Agitated movement by a singer
24. Nursery-rhyme pet
25. Family of a U.S. inventor
27. Balsam-yielding tree
28. Some bridges
30. Ouse feeder
31. "___ Millions," O'Neill play
34. Caspian feeder
35. Cities in R.I. and the Isle of Wight
39. Holds up
41. Comic Ole
44. Eye docs
45. Arose
47. Exequy
48. G.I.'s devil-dodger
49. Certain Wall Street options
51. Increase stitches
53. Expels
56. Article of merchandise
57. Critical
59. Lady of Spain
60. Possessions
62. Rorem or Sparks
63. College officials
65. Robert of "Quincy, M.E."
67. Aqueous resting place
69. Detail
70. Bellini's Druidic priestess
72. Armbone
73. Guido di Pietro, or Fra ___
76. Golfer's 19th hole
77. Where Dresden china is made
81. Yoko Lennon, née ___
82. Dissolute
84. A lady's maid to Cleopatra
86. Words on a Wonderland cake
87. Fish dish
89. Marine hazards
90. Burton of "Roots"
92. Dregs
93. Amount of assessment
95. Extol
97. Polish river
99. Old-timer
100. Ridge on a mountain
101. Blowhard's output
103. First steps
105. Because
107. Disdainful look
109. Bruce of films
110. Thesmothetes
113. "___ company . . ."
115. Yehudi Menuhin's teacher
118. Fail to use
119. Coveted award for a playwright
123. Acidity
124. Houston school
125. Champ after Braddock
126. What to spend in Shiraz
127. Arp's art cult: 1916
128. Wapiti
129. School book
130. Refuse to grant
131. Light British carbine

DOWN

1. Fashion
2. Song for Sutherland
3. Transport for a pitcher
4. U.K. prince
5. Thuringian article
6. Scold vehemently
7. "___ With a View"
8. Chanteuse's specialty
9. Jan. and Aug.
10. Metric measure
11. Funny Foxx
12. Students at the U.S.M.A.
13. Great dog for an actor
14. Abode
15. Points of decline
17. Historic commune near Naples
19. Unit of force
20. Sunday statute
23. Creator of "Melencolia"
26. Greek cupid
29. De ___ (superfluous)
32. Founder of British India
33. Crowded quarters for a thespian
35. Like some stock certificates
36. Bring out
37. Transmitter for an entrepreneur
38. Kind of jerk
40. Backyard gossip
42. Slipped or tripped
43. Destitution
46. No-nos for a pianist-songwriter
50. Popular cartoonist
52. Org. founded in 1949
54. Paintings by a hot pianist
55. Inscribed stone slab
58. Input data
61. Banks of baseball
64. Pertaining to tissue
66. Celestial body
68. ___ metabolism
71. Arthur's coat
73. Close, to Keats
74. Damage to a screen star
75. Sky: Sp.
78. Feline in music
79. Kuwait ruler
80. Hangouts
81. ". . . ___ perfumed sea": Poe
83. ___ T'ung, Chinese emperor: 1908–12
85. Gardner and namesakes
88. Glut
91. Primers, e.g.
94. Fast period
96. Scarsdale, etc.
98. He reconstructed St. Paul's
101. English feudal tribute
102. Change text
104. Steps
106. Covering for a chimney
108. Miss O'Grady
110. Tender
111. The screen's Jannings
112. Turn around
114. Medical procedure
116. System of rules
117. Algerian port
120. Fort in N.J.
121. Superlative suffix
122. One of the Khans

59 Doin' the Twist *by Caroline G. Fitzgerald*

ACROSS

1. Lively frolic
5. More untidy
13. Bobby of nursery rhyme
20. Khayyám
21. L.A. suburb
22. Tax
23. Betty Botta
26. Climb aboard
27. Commotions
28. Pianist Dame Myra
29. Wreath, in Wahiawa
30. Crabtree of "Topsy"
32. Peer Gynt's mother
33. Lincoln bill
34. Attitudinize
35. Mollusk merchant
40. Lanchester from Lewisham
41. Harrison from Huyton
42. Tune for two
43. Achaean Aurora
44. Certain knit goods
46. "___ at the pane...": Browning
49. Elicits
54. Charge
55. Symbol of remembrance
58. Eliot's "Coker"
59. Whoopee!
60. Breeze
61. Bannister's distance
62. Horned viper
63. Obtuse
64. Peter Piper
70. Laughing stock
71. ___ Alamos
72. Toulouse-Lautrec's birthplace
73. Roguish
74. Uncouth one
75. Borodin's "Prince ___"
77. "The ___ Storm": P. White novel
79. Neal-Douglas Oscar vehicle
82. Wrong places to change horses
85. Commedia dell' ___
86. Labor leader George
88. Wave, in Huelva
89. ___ bene
91. Queen before Sophia
93. In the altogether
94. Sister Suzie
99. Invent a new word
101. Having a part of
102. Droop
103. Matisse or Bergson
104. Hostel
105. Escort
106. Burnsian "do not"
108. Pear-shaped
111. Caesar
115. She wrote "Gigi"
116. Catherine II was his widow
117. Pericles's philosophy prof
118. Concord
119. Bertrand and Lillian
120. Son of Ares and Aphrodite

DOWN

1. Defrauds
2. Neglect
3. Embossed, as a fabric
4. Recommendation
5. He needs no mike
6. Peppery
7. Some are martial
8. Garbo and Nissen
9. Showy
10. Become effete, in a way
11. Old French coins
12. Soak timber
13. Stuff into a hold
14. Like Richard III at the end of Act V
15. Priestly robes
16. Scourge in 1918
17. Rip or Renée
18. S-shaped lines
19. Spooky
24. The two
25. Theopholus or Theogenes
31. Tracts
33. "A ___ and a fly in a flue"
34. Aquino coin
35. The ego
36. Writer Wiesel
37. Kind of speech
38. Ball part
39. Gallery
45. Psychoanalyst Erikson
47. Guillaume's girlfriends
48. Lobster's feeler
50. N. Norwegian
51. Puck or Feste
52. Heyerdahl
53. Manner or method
56. Mont. motto metal
57. Compensate
60. First-rate
62. Bower
63. Firmament
64. Arkin-Moreno film: 1969
65. Barely made out
66. Ice field
67. Birthplace of 117 Across
68. Suffix with sheep or wolf
69. Kadiddle-hopper
70. Predicament
75. "___ soon shake your windows...": Dylan
76. Ramps
77. Superlative endings
78. Tithe portion
79. Short cannon, once
80. Wavy, in heraldry
81. Beautician, often
83. Early
84. "September ___," Chabas painting
87. Invigorate
90. Point-guard specialties
92. Absence of bad germs
94. Individual
95. "...our help ___ past"
96. Medieval merchant guilds
97. Neglect
98. Snick-a-___
99. Lake herring
100. Gibson garnish
105. Morsel
106. "___ et droit"
107. Seed covering
109. Mythological wine maker
110. Paid athletes
112. Farm layer
113. A metallic elem.
114. Part of R.S.V.P.

60 Faunae Business by Nancy Nicholson Joline

ACROSS

1. Ornamental stud
6. Betel palm
11. Designates
15. Painter Benjamin
19. More cunning
20. Ancient Greek populace
21. Willow
22. First Chinese dynasty
23. A work by barnyard collaborators?
26. Agenda component
27. Pay dirt
28. City in S. France
29. Giraffe's kin
30. Suffragist Lucy
31. King Mark's castle
34. Female swan
35. Steno's need
37. Strut
38. Apian darners?
40. Clairvoyant
41. Window glass
44. ___ Paulo, Brazil
45. Manor or tutor ending
46. Nicaraguan rebel
48. Keeps in office
53. In a frenzied state
57. Leftist clupeids?
60. Exclamation of relief
61. Greediness
63. A main street in Roma
64. Kipling's ___ Khan
65. Portable lodge of a certain shape
66. Famed conductor
68. ___ show (spectacle)
69. Wheel spokes
70. Flower stalk
72. Pyromaniac
75. ___ code
76. Lagomorph from Llangollen?
79. Congou and hyson
80. Glass gardens
82. "Two ___ People," 1938 tune
83. ". . . ___ of little faith?": Matt. 8:26
84. Some hosts, for short
87. Grouts
88. Poem by Byron
92. Equine political demand?
95. Howard and Russell
97. Long-legged shorebirds
99. Joplin work
100. Callas's style of singing
102. A king of Crete
103. Routine duty
105. ___ Nostra
106. Twitching
107. N.L. batting champ: 1966
108. Canine dental visit?
112. Stigma
113. Entreat
114. Stale
115. "Ici on ___ français"
116. Spanish painter
117. Editor's notation
118. Intuit
119. Ledger item

DOWN

1. Some neckwear
2. Nimbi
3. Freedom
4. Mouse-spotters' cry
5. Refrain syllable
6. Confound
7. Shays or Tyler
8. Cassowaries' cousins
9. Mountain pass
10. Slanting
11. Oberon's spouse
12. On a pinnacle
13. Vitus ___, Danish navigator
14. Affirmation
15. Plastered pachyderm?
16. Bars, legally
17. Home of St. Catherine
18. Emulated Petruchio
24. Former Hungarian prime minister
25. Twists
30. Bargain
32. Tea, in Tours
33. Rhine feeder
36. Some of Tony's kin
38. Withered
39. Norse Fates
41. Wilbur or Merrill
42. Singer Gibb
43. Utmost
46. Dernier ___
47. Toxophilites
49. Kind of trip
50. Marilyn's "Bus Stop" role
51. Opera's Stratas
52. Bonbons
53. Ark's landfall
54. Victor of Hollywood
55. Kitchen item
56. Marsupial motel?
58. Deteriorate
59. Author Levin
62. Parts of dols.
64. Hit letters
66. Joad and Kettle
67. Williams athlete
70. A whale
71. Hold tightly
72. Incite
73. Saws with the grain
74. Hampshire's home
76. Snatch forcibly
77. Indonesian island
78. Actress Arthur
81. A Dr. Kildare portrayer
85. Diadem for Di
86. Turf
88. Fond du ___, Wis.
89. Alias
90. Tenants
91. A, e.g.
92. Integrity, English style
93. Accompany
94. Rids the body of
95. Mediocre
96. Concavity of a joint
97. Accumulate
98. Dulls ender
100. Kipling poem
101. A Lauder
104. Vast
105. Soldo or solidus
108. Bohemian martyr
109. Due follower
110. He checks the bks.
111. Is down with

ACROSS

1. Delhi dress
5. Fem.'s opposite
9. Make amends
14. Trim
18. Ancient: Comb. form
19. Ogee, e.g.
20. Yclept
21. Swear
22. HAVING VERY COLD FEET
24. ___ CIRCUM-STANCES
26. Certain reeds
27. Send back
29. Some Yugoslavs
30. Play parts
31. Venus's island
32. Nubby yarn
33. Women-to-be
35. Lightweight silk
36. Daydreamer's food
37. A votre ___
38. ELVIS HIT
40. W.C.'s chickadee
43. Sale proviso
44. African republic
45. Colors
46. Here again
47. Mil. address
48. PLACE FOR FIVE-YEAR-OLDS
52. Divide into segments
53. Answers
55. Abodes
56. Switches
57. "Was-saw" connector
58. Temptress
59. Singer Te Kanawa is one
60. Ransacked
62. Cowboys' nightspots?
63. Bêtes noires
66. Loos or Baker
67. YANKEE SKIPPER, ONCE
69. Chemical ending
70. Inhabitants: Suffix
71. Obi, e.g.
72. Flags
73. Buzzy body
74. Doze
75. THE BIG HOUSE
79. "Santa ___," Italian song
80. Britches
81. Pineapples, in Peru
82. Agrippina, to Nero
83. Heart parts
85. Eye nerve
86. Tackle tidbit
87. Sense
88. Brewing
89. NYC components
93. RIGHT-HAND MEN
95. ACCIDENTAL
97. Maynard and Olin
98. Actress Taylor
99. Mother of Aeolus
100. Goalies' goals
101. Helper, for short
102. Reads meter
103. Shane portrayer
104. Logger's travois

DOWN

1. Actress Mia ___
2. Plenty
3. Begins anew
4. OCTOPUS ARM
5. Posts
6. Martial ___
7. ___-fi
8. Rialto pony, e.g.
9. Thimbleweed
10. Airport lineup
11. Leave out
12. Avant-gardist
13. Enlightens
14. Dialect
15. Of birds
16. Income, in France
17. Saharan tracts
18. Mil. rank
23. Computer units
25. Pianist Rubinstein
28. Biblical land
31. Date element, often
32. De Mille-Copland ballet
33. Quebec peninsula
34. STEPPED UP
35. Full nelsons, e.g.
36. Hall of Fame boxer
37. European coal basin
38. Elissa of old films
39. German pronoun
40. UPKEEP
41. Bank no.
42. Barely gets by
44. Laid booby traps
46. Jacket copy
48. '50s war zone
49. "Watch"-ed river?
50. Moscow's main street
51. Whomp up ___ of pottage
52. Sandbank
54. Skins
56. Emerson, Mencken, et al.
58. Raw fish dish
59. Hot and humid
60. Wet weather
61. Dividing word
62. Groundwork
63. Wild hogs
64. Walking ___ (ecstatic)
65. Bristle
67. Whines
68. Writer Asimov
71. Thesmothetes
73. Of the throat
75. Father: Comb. form
76. Is against
77. LaToya's brother
78. Monogram ingredient
79. TARDY STATE
80. "Remembrance of Things Past" author
82. Hamlisch, to pals
83. French girlfriends
84. Has a premiere
85. Frequently
86. Foretold
87. Writer-actress Chase
88. Karenina or Christie
89. Combo
90. Contribute
91. Weeded
92. Neb. and Mo., e.g.
94. Agcy. succeeded by the N.R.C.
96. Gun org.

ACROSS

1. Hawthorne's birthplace
6. Russian river
10. Artist Chagall
14. Comedian Mort
18. Miniver Cheevy's love
19. Glorifies
22. Aka Lamb
23. Medicinal plant
24. USUAL VACATION?
26. DOUBLES
28. Brando role in "I Remember Mama"
29. Qaddafi's gulf
30. Actress Hughes
32. Soupçons
33. Evita Peron, e.g.: Abbr.
34. A ___ minute
35. Match
36. Hardy's partner
37. Marcus Aurelius's M.D.
38. Brownish gray
39. Mexican's estate
40. Handled by food pros
43. AVENUE GOING EAST AND WEST
45. Angle or color preceder
48. Greek GQ man
49. Having ups and downs
51. Opie's Bee
52. British gun
53. Loblollies
54. Square
55. French wrinkles
56. "Borstal Boy" author
57. Degenerates
58. Actress Witherspoon
59. Haut monde
61. Quibbles
62. Tough wood
63. TOOL FOR A PAIR
66. Backpackers
67. Exit
69. French composer Erik
70. Map key
71. Least furnished
72. DISCIPLE OF ANANIAS
74. As written: Mus.
77. Position properly
78. Wilbur and Kunitz
80. Train for many N.Y. commuters
81. Tel ___

82. Narrowly defeated, with "out"
83. Some are wild
84. Brief joy rides
86. "To a rag and ___...": Kipling
87. "Twice-___ Tales"
88. ___ spumante
89. Home, for one
90. Carpenter's tool
91. Sappho creation
92. BIKINI, E.G.
95. Miss America, e.g.
96. Yawns
97. A tropical ray
98. Centennial choice for U.S. President
99. Dragonfly
101. Some Russian planes
102. Actress from Greece
103. Gibraltar, e.g.: Abbr.
106. Money in Santander
107. TV's Sawyer
109. European thrush
110. Erin, to a Gael
111. TRIKES' COUSINS
113. FLETCHER-SHAKESPEARE PLAY, WITH "THE"
116. A carny
117. Kin of etc.
118. Saunter
119. Bristly
120. Damascenes: Abbr.
121. Anderson or Fonteyn
122. Actress Armstrong
123. Mohawk months

DOWN

1. Cloaca
2. Author Turin
3. U.N.'s Trygve and kin
4. Opponent of Luther
5. Trident and Titan
6. Rembrandt's birthplace
7. Film day-player
8. Okinawan city
9. Jungfrau, e.g.
10. "Miracle team" of 1969
11. Provençal love song
12. Inlet
13. Rhythm maker
14. Tuaregs' region
15. Marble or Walker
16. Hailey best-seller
17. Bargain price
18. Pennines or Carpathians: Abbr.

20. Tropical armadillo
21. Cloying
25. Enticed
27. Emit violently
31. Summers, in Soissons
34. 61-'61 man
35. Obscene
36. Mortgages
37. Tunney and Kelly
38. KIND OF TRUCK
39. Jujube or loquat
40. Director of "It Happened One Night"
41. Goodbye, in Granada
42. CRITICS' SEATS
44. Baby soother
45. CONGRESSIONAL REQUIREMENT FOR AMENDMENTS
46. Former Spanish coins
47. Caravansaries
49. Dawns, poetically
50. Toward the mouth
52. Reno "natural"

54. Keep going effortlessly
55. Flycatcher
56. He makes good scents
58. Stallone feature
59. Estoy, ___, esta
60. Secular
61. Burns's prop
63. Drift
64. Bass-baritone Simon ___
65. Crazy
66. Will personae
68. Classic von Stroheim film
70. Radiation term
71. Offspring
73. Honorary degree
75. Prongs
76. Ward off
77. Aware of
78. Spreads
79. Auricular
81. Borders on
83. Willow twig
84. Clefts
85. ___-cake (child's game)

86. Top ratings
88. Challenged a ruling
89. Tangy
90. Support of kings
92. "La Plume de Ma ___"
93. Bovary or Lazarus
94. New Orleans eleven
95. Author of "The Makropoulos Secret"
96. Attic natives
98. Filberts
99. Loser to Truman
100. Tribe of Israel
102. Plays tug of war
103. Simple one
104. Lock
105. Actor Auberjonois
106. Series of book copies: Abbr.
107. Mite
108. Key
109. A double-reed
110. "___ Perpetua," motto of Idaho
112. Greek long e
114. Sphere
115. Modernist

63 Hasty Pudding *by Will Weng*

ACROSS

1. Up to now
6. Smeltery leavings
11. Sound seeking silence
14. Supplement
17. "Cheers" barkeeper
18. Slanting type
19. Absence of the skull
21. Lacking a key
22. Mexican's moola
23. Former N.Y. Senator
24. Start of an impetuous person's prayer, with 101 Across
27. Small whale
28. Quality of having limits
32. Jumbo cymbal
36. Red Queen's advice to Alice
41. Sign for Churchill
42. Writer James and family
44. "Can do" serviceman
45. Clump of ivy
46. Pious talk
47. Boston suburb
49. German river
50. ___ capita
51. Word after omni or mini
52. Taunt to an early motorist
54. Relative of a prom
55. Central American
58. Units of syllabic length
59. Jewish month
61. Armenia's capital
62. Ordinary
65. Impetuous guest's question
69. French head
70. "Twelfth Night" lass
72. Sty sound
73. Mexican O.K.'s
75. Little weak coffee
76. Chess pc.
77. Actress Sally
81. Wino
82. Word before rata
83. Merry sounds
85. Symbolic show-biz city
86. In a while
88. Hush-hush agcy.
89. Pina ___ (rum drink)
91. Sp. misses
92. Neighbor of Arg.
93. Impetuous motorist's sounds
96. Wires: Abbr.
97. Status honored in May
99. Private eye
101. Rest of 24 Across
110. Number-2 golf club
113. Brought under control
114. Relating to gulls
115. Shipment of fliers
116. Mall units
117. Worn away
118. Chang's twin
119. Opp. of NNW
120. Ruhr city
121. Famous golf cup

DOWN

1. Japanese P.M.: 1964–72
2. Swan genus
3. "Ae ___ Kiss," Burns poem
4. Word jugglings: Abbr.
5. Kind of pitcher
6. Particle, in Scotland
7. Memory or Drury
8. Syrian city, to the French
9. Tall veldt grazer
10. Nova ___
11. ___ leave it
12. Like a sachet
13. Lost-article checker
14. Black cuckoo
15. Cacophony
16. Hammarskjöld
17. Prefix for adroit
18. Freshwater fish
20. Solar disk
25. Passages
26. Foot part
29. Shifty
30. Cambodian coin
31. Prepare the table
32. Kind of plank
33. Type of arch
34. Eft
35. Impetuous person's advice
37. Asian partridge
38. Welty product
39. One of the tides
40. Dakota Indian
43. N.Y.C. artists' area
46. Brusque person's command
48. Home for a Viking
50. Study hard
51. Grill's partner
53. Cheer
54. Peddle
55. Eases
56. One of the Turners
57. Singleton
59. Mine access
60. Juan or Carlos
62. Plant
63. Swedish poet Hansson
64. Stays to the end
66. Minor prohibition
67. Sonora is one
68. Cavatina
71. NYC line
74. Followers: Suffix
76. Polish city
77. Ruler who fled: Jan. 16, 1979
78. Notable French artist-designer
79. Coin of Iran
80. Impertinence
82. Type of device on which a door swings
83. Dearie
84. A resin
86. ___, esse, fui . . .
87. Spanish treasure
88. Certain barriers
89. Some seines
90. Opposed
93. Pétain and Matisse
94. Husky-voiced
95. Bowler
98. Greet
100. Cautious
102. Uncles, in Toledo
103. Concerning
104. One of the ages
105. Boxing units: Abbr.
106. Walked on
107. Pheasant group
108. Special person
109. Mat. day
110. Former mlle.
111. Writer Fleming
112. Get Beat poetry

ACROSS

1. Not up
5. Mich. city
10. Shadow
14. Play players
18. TV's Anderson
19. Bread
20. Yes ___ (ultimatum words)
21. Palo ___
22. Start of a verse
24. Resins
25. Certain wader
26. Conceal, in a way
27. Verse, Part II
30. High peaks
31. Chimney lining
32. ___-Magnon
33. Plow part
36. Fasten anew
38. Intoned
42. Hang fire
43. Urge
45. "Burnt Norton" poet
47. Widow of 37 Down
48. Siamese measure
49. Chanteuse Horne
50. Indian otter
51. Amaze
52. Verse: Part III
59. End of a Pope title
60. Poi makings
61. Salt tree
62. Ones, to Burns
63. Squelched
64. Bad reviews
66. Queue
69. Gone up
70. Humor
74. Verse: Part IV
79. Bible book
80. Drops dropping
81. Pro ___ (proportionately)
82. Stat. for a slugger
83. Masefield heroine
84. Frenzied
87. Type of type, for short
88. End of a loaf
89. French forest
91. Mournful tunes
93. Deputized group
94. Adipose
95. Fr. companies
96. Semaphores on a RR
98. Verse: Part V
104. Dash water about
108. Shoshonean
109. Archibald of the N.B.A.
110. End of verse
112. Article
113. Bismarck's st.
114. Producer Hayward
115. Viaud's pen name
116. Ancient Asian
117. Ballerina's leap
118. Redacts
119. Tore

DOWN

1. Lily plant
2. Beethoven's birthplace
3. Ref. books
4. Steadfast one
5. Concentrate
6. Actor Jack
7. ___ de France
8. Carry or Cat
9. "Don't rock ___"
10. Resin used in perfumes
11. One of a Kipling trio
12. Edge along
13. Sullivan song, with "The"
14. Paper type
15. Russian range
16. Recipe direction
17. Related
19. L-Q connection
23. Heraldic wreath
28. Uplifting fellow?
29. Smell ___ (be suspicious)
31. Eastern inn
33. Mast appendage
34. Erica
35. Cordial flavoring
36. Mystical mark
37. One of the Fab Four
38. Half of CCVI
39. Thoroughly wreck
40. Accustom
41. "The Flea" poet
43. Hook's opposite
44. "___ Bad Boy"
46. Youths
51. Prepares a sting
53. Carter country
54. Sonata part
55. Put away
56. Titus, the conspirator
57. U. of Maine site
58. Actress Elissa ___
63. Inked
64. Michelangelo work
65. Record of a single year
66. African boss
67. "___ of the Jungle," early TV show
68. "I Let ___ Go Out..."
69. Journalist Jacob
71. Penates' partners
72. Derides
73. Roman magistrate
75. Scene of a G.W. coup
76. Noted loser
77. Essays
78. Easter finery
84. ___ B'rith
85. Puerto ___
86. Dec. visitor
88. Lodging places
90. Start of a Wolfe title
92. Equipped
93. Map out
96. Makes yarn
97. Elated
98. Caprice
99. Table d'___
100. Parroted
101. General Hampton
102. Coup d'___
103. Astronaut Slayton
104. Ella's forte
105. De ___ (too much)
106. Chap, in Córdoba
107. Wallace of silents
111. Yalie

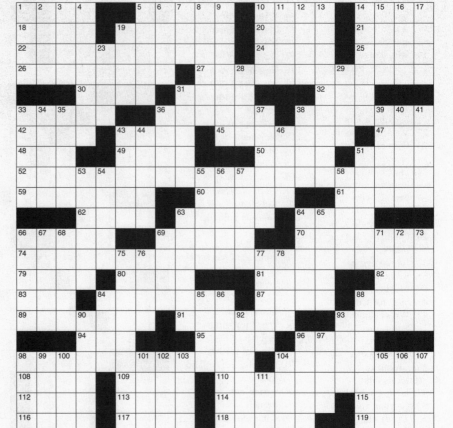

65 Kitchenware by Alfio Micci

ACROSS

1. Composer Bartók
5. Rcd. player
10. Extremely
16. ___-de-sac
19. Likeness
20. Hawkeye's friend
21. Heft
22. Jackie's second
23. PLATES
27. Moistens the bird
28. Mystic character
29. Total
30. Ollie's sidekick
31. Porker's pad
32. Health club
34. Cash
37. Short and very staccato: Mus.
39. Manipulators
41. Mouthward
43. Fight segments
46. CUPS
52. Attention getter
53. Family car
54. Jr.-to-be
55. Glacial ridges
56. Scuttlebutt
58. Nita of "A Sainted Devil"
60. Oil cartel
62. Dispatched
63. Expunged
65. Olive and castor
67. Guidonian note
68. BOWLS
77. Be human
78. Change for a five
79. Seek help from
80. Airplane runner
84. Kind of work or spirit
86. U.S. export
89. Actor Lloyd: 1902–85
90. Writer Tyler
91. Malaria Fever
93. Wolfish looks
95. Wimp's cousin
96. POTS
101. Titania's spouse
102. Composer Rota: 1911–79
103. Polonius hid behind one
104. Carries on
106. Harvest goddess
109. A North Caucasic language
110. Cry of triumph
113. Mind
115. Kind of cat
117. Biblical preposition
119. Of a poetic foot
121. PANS
126. Business Abbr.
127. Starry
128. Ms. Dinsmore
129. Road for Caesar
130. Fair grade
131. Live
132. Movie units
133. Action word

DOWN

1. Supports on ships
2. Prominence
3. Crummy
4. French novelist Claude
5. Blossoms
6. CB buff
7. Fragrant river?
8. Old Testament book
9. U. of Maine locale
10. "The ___ Dogs": Burns
11. Broody
12. Clears (of)
13. Arctic abodes
14. Foolish fancy
15. List ender
16. Asian language
17. Word with Major or Minor
18. Mortgage
24. "Demian" author
25. Fitted piece
26. Portuguese money
33. Harold of songdom
35. Work units
36. Bumpkin
38. Kind of artist
39. Greatest
40. Fountain order
42. Ladle's kin
44. Cannon of films
45. Noted muralist
46. Told all
47. Ruark novel: 1962
48. Musical subjects
49. Intrepidity
50. "Mood ___," 1931 song
51. Pincerlike claw
57. Legal thing
59. Half a fragrant oil
61. Incline
64. Music for two
66. Unsaturated alcohol
69. Large
70. Birthplace of Henry VIII's first wife
71. Indian or orange
72. Sue for payment
73. Jungle sights
74. Cove
75. Impolite look
76. Metal eye at the end of a lariat
80. Me. river
81. Bellpull
82. Logician's conclusion
83. Pays expenses
85. Bernstein's field
87. Bergman role
88. Jawaharlal ___ of India
92. Slave of yore
94. Herrings' kin
97. Long, long time
98. Display delight about
99. "Julius Caesar" setting
100. Water nymph
105. Conventicle participants
107. Pierce
108. Trite
110. Ebb
111. Scout, at times
112. Harsh
113. Auditory
114. Plant shoot
116. Lovely woman
118. Seine feeder
120. Twelfth-cen. date
122. Bern's stream
123. Downcast
124. Toby contents
125. Homophone for 124 Down

ACROSS

1. Nautical term
6. Sleight of hand
11. May or Charles
15. Pulverize
19. Cruel master
21. Mennonite
22. Arabian gulf
23. Carroll heroine
24. The indestructible Miss Bailey
27. Some art models
28. Terminate
29. Lunatic of old
30. Amorite king
31. Tun
32. Large European tree
33. Lab burners, once
34. Card-game leftovers
37. Burrowing rodent
42. More underhanded
43. Party of a sort
44. Monopolize
46. Wading bird
47. The lovable Mr. Holden
50. U.N. org.
51. Eastern Church monasteries
52. Scup
53. Swiss river
54. Brouhaha
55. QE1 or QE2
56. Like certain beaches
57. Fast
59. Fragment
60. Der ___ (Adenauer)
61. Russian communities
62. Rhodes of Africa
63. Famous evolutionist
64. Gentleman farmer's degree
65. Mork in tatters
68. Flavoring substance
69. Bury
71. Capital of Seine-Maritime
72. Set straight
73. N.Y.'s geographic center
74. The irrepressible Midler
76. High priest
79. Dahl or Francis
80. ___-et-un (gambling game)
81. Desiccated
82. Foie ___ (table delicacy)
83. Gardening tool
84. Indian princess
85. Do a framer's job
87. Icy
88. So
89. Ballad
90. Broadcast
91. Fox or jackal
92. Poetic contraction
93. The adorable Miss Pickford
96. Ancient Greek colony
97. Herb for McClanahan
98. Bonnie one
99. Common mosquito
100. Spread out
101. Sheathe
103. Nodded
104. "The pig was ___"
105. ___ de Calais
106. "Life is an ___ itself . . .": O. W. Holmes, Jr.
107. Quaid or Rodman
110. Cousin of kvass
113. Icy pinnacle
116. Miss Heming as a partner in crime
119. Period
120. Cordon ___ (top chef)
121. Edict in Odessa
122. One who sidesteps
123. Social attribute
124. Hall, in Hamburg
125. A concern of Whittier
126. Stood up

DOWN

1. Mont Blanc, e.g.
2. "I've ___ to London . . ."
3. Mild expletive
4. Airport Abbr.
5. Pinochle play
6. Expert
7. Verily
8. Encircled
9. St. John or St. Thomas
10. Bonos' baby
11. Members of a medieval sect
12. Juan's goodbye
13. Colonial Quaker
14. Siamese twin
15. Popeye's nemesis
16. Divest
17. The Red Baron, e.g.
18. Permissive word
20. Ocelli
23. Crown of flowers
25. Eastern potentate
26. Tendon
31. Curriculum ___
33. Poetic tribute
34. Bizarre
35. Tomlin shooting the rapids
36. Seek
37. Subject of Tennyson's "In Memoriam"
38. Serves
39. Hardy friend at Pikes Peak
40. Pebbly rubble
41. Speed
42. Gurth, in "Ivanhoe"
43. Thrash
45. Bridge whiz
47. Euphorbia
48. Poor
49. Poor man's mink
54. Circe, e.g.
56. Ess
57. Violin precursor
58. Small seeds of grapes
59. Debra of Hollywood
61. Bea Arthur role
62. Dracula, for one
63. Sere
65. Lorelei's river
66. Bee sound
67. Blusher
68. Satellite's path
70. Lacks
72. Sweet Rosie
73. Eurydice's beloved
74. Jag
75. Designator
77. Singer Kazan
78. "Ding-Dong! The Witch ___"
79. Actress Mary
80. Windmill parts
82. Columbus's hometown
84. Awaken
85. Frosty
86. Ages
87. Manxman, e.g.
89. Croats and Czechs
90. Postscript
91. Kind of audience
93. Etiolate
94. Quantity alongside a barn
95. Spooky
100. Rational
102. Excess of solar over lunar year
103. Nine: Comb. form
104. Diarize
106. ___ weed, rangeland plant
107. Mild expletive
108. Leisure
109. Hindu god
110. Actor ___ Ray
111. Residue
112. Raison d'___
113. Ready for action
114. Govt. agency
115. Fabled big bird
116. Network initials
117. Monogram of a musical Duke
118. Means of propulsion

ACROSS

1. Wrongly
6. Runs in neutral
11. A light: Slang
15. Collegian's pad
19. Saltarello, e.g.
20. Nantes's river
21. René's laughter
22. Fencing tool
23. CONSTITU-TIONALS?
26. Enclosed trucks
27. Hitchcock movie: 1964
28. Some amplifiers
29. Wraps up
31. Prima ballerina
32. Heredity factors
33. O.T. book
34. Summits, in Siena
36. Heretofore
38. Dike
42. Silly person
45. Watch over
47. Ranks of nobility
50. MORNING SHOWER-SHAVE RITUAL?
55. Morocco, to Marcel
56. Rim
57. Spanish river
58. Pintail ducks
59. Tex. shrine
60. Bridge expert Culbertson
61. Test photos
64. Backward
66. Plant also called avens
68. Abel Janszoon ___
69. Univ. in Dallas
70. J.F.K. Abbr.
72. Asian wild ass
76. Rama I's domain
78. "Iliad," for one
80. Ancient Greek geographer
81. Singer Tillis
84. Lasso
86. Slatterns
88. Dupe
89. Japanese sash
90. Limpid
91. BOGART TWIN FEATURE?
94. Lowered in social position
96. North Korean river
97. Ar chaser
98. Driving hazard
99. Insect's lower lip
105. Muscovite
107. Summit
110. City NE of Rome
111. Humorous
115. Stored away
118. Tropical bird
120. Zoroastrian sacred writings
121. Whip
122. HIRED GUN?
125. Commedia dell'___
126. Khayyám
127. Like some walls
128. Former county in Scotland
129. Kern's "Very ___, Eddie"
130. Rink feature
131. Mother-of-pearl
132. Bean and Shepard

DOWN

1. ___ a dozen
2. ___-arms (soldier)
3. Prefix for mission
4. Picturesque
5. Old-age infirmity
6. Chinese river
7. Condemn
8. Editor's concern
9. Utensil on a pencil
10. Moon goddess
11. Late governor of Conn.
12. West role
13. Vexed
14. Legal term for "middle"
15. Ardent
16. Oct.'s gem
17. Tear apart
18. Army meal
24. Poured
25. Church architect
30. COMPLETE NOBLEMAN?
35. Biblical patriarch
37. Welfare of the community
39. Short-tailed rodent
40. Author Ludwig
41. Glimpse
42. Skilled
43. Native-born Israeli
44. Aegean island
46. Dantès's creator
48. "To ___ and a bone...": Kipling
49. Men's house slippers
51. Impends ominously
52. Tarnish
53. Slacken
54. Suffix with journal
55. Loose robe
62. HONORABLY WON SWEET-HEART?
63. Escargots
65. Duplicate, for short
67. Actress in "Winterset"
71. A singing Boone
73. Measure
74. Muslim Satan
75. Functions
77. Murray and Marsh
79. Peculiar
81. Seed containers
82. Genesis man
83. Nursery-rhyme trio
85. Asian weight
87. Critic's disapproval
92. Chariot-of-fire prophet
93. Rumanian region now shared with the Ukraine
95. Restrained
100. Garb
101. "Lulu" composer
102. "___ the water shall float" (old English saying)
103. Quebec bay
104. Causing excessive pupil contraction
106. Perfumery compound
108. French wine region
109. Water swelling
112. Port city for Pompey
113. Harsh
114. Merits
115. Metal dross
116. Arum plant
117. Concerning
119. Not ever, to Blake
123. Droop
124. E.T.O. head

ACROSS

1. Ghana's capital
6. Reformer Jacob
10. Ancient fertility gods
15. Increases
19. Extensive
20. Atlanta arena
21. Burros
22. Station, in Paris
23. Ship's stern sail support
25. Display site
27. Eyelid problem
28. Sulky
29. Ending for hip or tip
30. Abrades
31. Gulf of Lions feeder
33. Afrikaner
34. Redness symbol
36. World-weary
39. Knave of Hearts' loot
41. Salt, in St. Lô
42. Pitcher
46. Enfold
47. "De ___," Seneca essay
50. Rod
51. Narrow channel
53. Dockers' org.
54. He calls K's
55. Did a preliminary survey
58. Douceur
59. Plummeted
61. Real, in Rouen
62. Vincent Lopez's theme song
63. Muslim Messiah
65. Monasteries
67. Anglo-Indian "first-rate"
69. Emulated Izaak Walton
70. Uncouth
71. The person summoned
72. Painter Andrea del ___
73. Deli hero
75. Grinder
76. Nimbi
79. Commedia dell' ___
80. Virginia of the lost colony
81. S. American wildcat
82. Its cap. is Bismarck
83. ___ alai
84. Sophomores at a Columbus col., e.g.
89. Call ___ day
90. Fourth book of the N.T.
91. British unskilled laborer
92. Dally
93. Queen's title: Abbr.
94. Seine
95. Car starters: Abbr.
97. Gosh!
98. Authority
100. Bore
102. Junior's col.-entrance exam
104. Lion's pride
105. Metal plate
108. Cousin of B.M.I.
111. Fairies
112. Picket
113. G.I.'s necessity
117. O. Henry product
120. Item on a Binet-Simon test
122. Japanese seaport
123. Pluck
124. Tabor
125. Metric measure
126. Weeps convulsively
127. Male and female
128. Simple sugars
129. Kin of blush

DOWN

1. Certain missiles, for short
2. Bk. reviewer
3. Snug
4. Demolition men
5. Humorist George
6. Kind of nose or candle
7. Turkish inn
8. Sec.
9. Pose
10. Stitches loosely
11. Eighth son of Jacob
12. Hebrew lyre
13. Actor Ayres
14. Pisa-to-Leghorn dir.
15. Related parrilinearly
16. June honorees
17. Minute amount
18. Stitches
24. Cpl. or sgt.
26. Petulance
29. ___ voce
32. Legatee
33. Popular diet item
34. He hit 358 home runs
35. Peace Nobelist Wiesel
36. Poker play
37. More unconvincing
38. Use
40. Hindu fire god
41. Stone pillar
43. Kind of tax
44. Slur over
45. Speedy
48. Amend
49. Lots of lots
51. Feed the furnace
52. Esteem
56. Western Hemisphere acronym
57. Printer's device
60. Shirt size
64. Nobelist in Chemistry: 1922
66. ___ d'être
67. Amassed
68. Western lizard
69. Units of capacitance
71. Trite
72. Twilled fabric
73. Mecca pilgrim
74. Borneo ape
75. Delicate purple
76. Scottish river
77. Gourmand
78. Ray
80. Comforter
81. Roe
85. Adventure tale
86. Ardors
87. Actress Martha
88. Widgeon
96. Car accessories
98. "She Didn't ___," 1931 song
99. Murky
101. Yellow dye
103. Bost. is one
104. Actress Dressler
106. Astringents
107. Kind of shirt
108. Inquiries
109. Begone!
110. Baseball's Georgia Peach
111. Entertainer Redd
112. O-T connectors
114. Bearing
115. "Utopia" author
116. Ace
118. College degrees
119. Dactyl, e.g.
120. Altar words
121. Concorde

69 Titular Titillation by Joy L. Wouk

ACROSS

1. Germany's Otto ___ Bismarck
4. Kind of prof.
8. Lewis's Timberlane
12. Excuse
16. Shaped
17. "___ Kick Out of You"
18. "Gypsy Love" composer
20. File
21. High cards
22. ___ Marmara
23. Old World lizard
24. Kitchen follower
25. Stone-Day collaboration?
29. Coarse silk
30. That, in Cannes
31. Inhibit
32. Tiny, in Scotland
33. "Auld Lang ___"
36. Besides
38. Elsa, e.g.
42. MacDonald-Graves collaboration?
46. Volcano crater
49. Asian weight
50. One of seven: Abbr.
51. Saharan ridges
52. Hamilton-Rice collaboration?
58. Sophia or Isabel
59. Actress Alicia
60. Wilder's "___ Town"
61. Keddah, e.g.
65. Warren-Kingsley collaboration?
72. North Sea feeder
73. Long time
74. "High ___": M. Anderson
75. One Muppet of two
76. Saint-Exupéry-Borodin collaboration? (with "The")
82. Russian mountains
87. Mouths
88. Arabian V.I.P.
89. Pokey dwellers
90. Wouk-Tolstoy collaboration? (with "The")
96. "___, Lover!," 1954 song
97. Henri's soul
98. ". . . Cupid ___ longer an archer": Shak.
99. Bearish period
102. Vedic god's thing

105. "___, That Kiss," 1931 song
107. Tristram's love
109. Conrad-Koestler collaboration?
115. Square column
116. ___ and sometimes Y
117. In a tumult
118. Use a musical fork
119. Rock star Billy ___
120. Town in Provence
121. ___ Sap, Cambodian lake
122. Galatea's lover
123. Prunes trees
124. ___ off (irate)
125. Hem
126. H.H.S. arm

DOWN

1. Empty space
2. Black Sea port
3. Retreats
4. Composer of "Happy Days Are Here Again"
5. Close an envelope
6. Follower of Zeno
7. Stiff fabric
8. Hammer part
9. Auspices
10. ___-al-Arab
11. Euphemism for "hell"
12. So-called, in Provence
13. Plaster holder
14. Tasso's patron
15. Mimic
16. Brewers' needs
17. Rainfall-chart lines
19. Basket fiber
26. Trouble, in Ayr
27. Orwell's school
28. Not in a whisper
34. Orderly
35. Hungarian city
37. Harem rooms
39. "___ Heidenleben": R. Strauss
40. Petition
41. Draft org.
42. Rivers in England and Ontario
43. Collect, as grain
44. World banking org.
45. King of Thebes
46. Corday's victim
47. Anoint, old style
48. Spry
53. ___-di-dah
54. H.S. subj.
55. Flavor

56. Rapa ___ (Easter Island)
57. Sea eagle
61. Threefold
62. Beatles' Starr
63. Suffix with form or reform
64. Equals
66. Moray
67. Japanese carp
68. Under one's control
69. Swab
70. Bungled
71. ___ Willie Winkle
77. Musical syllable
78. Pasternak girl
79. Body of African warriors
80. She wrote "Seven Women"
81. Having a skull
82. Hole maker
83. Trygve of the U.N.
84. Explosive letters
85. Nimitz and Byrd
86. "___ thee late a rosy wreath": Jonson
91. Group of eight
92. Fine

93. In a violent rage
94. Infant under one month
95. Price
99. Loafer
100. Persephone's love
101. Chromosome parts
103. Verona's river
104. Rhône feeder
106. A king of Judea
108. Ready for action
109. Multiseasonal pelter
110. Inner: Comb. form
111. Upon
112. Regretted
113. Trill or troll
114. Shoe part

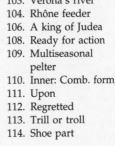

70 Writers Wronged by Bert H. Kruse

ACROSS

1. Agreed
6. Jam
10. Imprecates
15. Enforce
21. Papal cape
22. Loathsome one
23. Walking ___ (gleeful)
24. Planetarium
25. "Roar of the Bull" author?
27. "The Office Machine" author?
29. Purfles
30. Mortgage
31. "Mercure" composer
32. Choose
33. Comprehend
34. Dull surface
35. Holy Roman emperors
36. Bonnet item
37. Russian lake
40. Memorable stutterer
41. Hershfield's "___ the Agent"
42. Scads of money
43. Healer's org.
46. Sport of a sort
48. "Cooler in July" author?
51. Astronaut Shepard
52. Street shows
53. Composer-singer: 1936–73
55. Crooked
56. Impression
57. Jetson's dog
58. Thesaurus man
59. Helps a hood
60. Near the hip
61. Roman despot
62. Baldwin-Wallace locale
63. Reproductive cell
64. Kind of sale
65. Actress Joanne
66. "Too Hot to Handle" author?
68. More unruffled
69. Keaton or Baker
71. Fragrant loop
72. Nosed
73. Attentive
75. "Living with Elsa" author?
80. Dummy's pair
83. Dismays
84. Hyenas' homes
85. Day centers
86. Inhale
87. ___ a pig (obese)
88. Guillemot

89. Mythical hold-up man
90. Billiards immortal
91. Fire fodder
92. Pay to play
93. Like Harvard Yard's walls
94. King or Lombard
95. Site of the first Olympics
96. "The Onion Row" author?
98. Greyhound's small look-alike
99. Retreat
100. Tear
101. To be, in Paris
102. Irish assembly
103. Alpine road
104. ___ glance (instantly)
105. Roman shade
107. Painter of jockeys
108. Bustle
111. V.P. under G.R.F.
112. ___ nous
113. Straighten
114. Melville book
118. "The Apple of My Eye" author?
121. "Beaches" author?
123. Explosive containing TNT
124. Climbing plant
125. Commedia dell'___
126. Daunted
127. Dub again
128. Disclosed
129. Act
130. Lock

DOWN

1. Banter
2. Dies ___
3. Creator of the "Oz" books
4. Pipe elbows
5. Society gal
6. Better mannered
7. Shoelace tags
8. Witch
9. London's ___ Gardens
10. Gift
11. Not this one
12. Cuomo or Lanza
13. City NW of Marseille
14. Mrs., in Mexico
15. Vie
16. Emulates Demosthenes
17. Silkworm
18. Electric units

19. Native Canadian
20. Explorer of Australia
26. Gladdens
28. Unowned
31. Amen
34. San ___, Calif.
37. Ropelike piece
38. Hit man
39. "A Beer is a Beer" author?
41. "It's ___ day for the Irish"
42. Ex ___ (one-sided)
43. "Vatican Days" author?
44. Cope
45. Stag's weapon
47. Of aircraft
49. African republic
50. Jugs
51. Actress Renée of silents
53. Dante illustrator
54. Time, e.g.
58. Nonconformist
59. Shower time
60. S.A. Indian
62. Honorarium

63. Litigants
64. Rudiments
66. Lots
67. Trumpet sound
68. Teams of horses
70. Perfect types
73. Emulated the nursery wolf
74. Shoulder, in Sedan
75. Magna ___
76. Personnel director
77. Unimpaired
78. Dover delicacy
79. Backpack
81. Box elders, e.g.
82. Darling
84. Dueler's move
86. Hamlet
88. Makeup item
89. Reluctant
90. Salutes
93. Served in a hospital
94. ___ Kai-shek
96. Adjective for a morel
97. Principal mass of a tooth
98. Bet
100. Redeem

102. Set apart
105. Press, TV, etc.
106. Sadat
107. Plow inventor
108. Not in harmony
109. Title Christie held
110. Arabian gulf
114. To dare, in Durango
115. Confusing network
116. People
117. Track concerns
119. J. F .K. listing
120. Belli's deg.
121. Wander idly
122. Newt

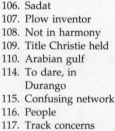

71 Combining Forms *by Robert H. Wolfe*

ACROSS

1. Spoil
6. Step on
11. Gator's relative
15. Unfurnished
19. One of the 400
20. Nomad
21. Amonasro's daughter
22. Alt.
23. Kind of accompaniment
25. Engender
27. Distant actor?
28. Around an attorney?
29. Comprehend
30. Collector from John Q.
32. Bell sound
33. Pinnacles
37. Decree by Hussein, e.g.
40. Santa's bane?
42. Total
43. Harness parts
44. A cause of mental and physical disturbances
45. Sea anemone or hydra
47. Shortened form, for short
48. One-tenth of a musician-comic?
50. Silica gem
54. Von Richthofen's title
56. Refuges of sorts
57. Concocted
58. Duffer's curving drive
59. In the center of
61. Hawaiian goose
62. King and Newton
63. Position Jackie Robinson usually played
65. Ling-Ling, e.g.
67. Head nun
68. Emerges
69. Diet
70. Championships
72. Octad in a gallon
73. Narrow opening
74. Corn or oat follower
76. Tennessee ___ Ford
79. Wise brush?
80. Very small country singer?
82. Mardi Gras, e.g.
83. Burdened
86. Talks back
87. Some small dogs, for short
88. Part of a barn
91. An amphibian
92. Phoenix's source of rebirth
93. Screenwriter Lehman
94. Mexican president: 1851–53
96. J. Wilbrand's discovery: 1863
97. Sault ___ Marie
98. Bad Christie character?
101. Deficiency of a designer?
109. European annual herbs
110. Earned 10%, perhaps
111. Lotion ingredient
112. Weight
113. Williams of "Happy Days"
114. Entirety
115. Units on space vehicles
116. J.F.K. sights
117. "Brigadoon" composer
118. Pledged

DOWN

1. A social grace
2. "Norma ___," Glaspell novel
3. Eur. country
4. Good reply to a dope pusher
5. Locks
6. Treasure follower
7. Columnist Barrett
8. Course for a horse
9. Kind of ton
10. Soviet committees
11. Cockney family in comics
12. Laughter, in Lyon
13. Balm or spice
14. Building burned by British: 1814
15. Initiated
16. Home of many Tlingits
17. Stated again
18. Leveled
24. Norma and Charlotte
26. Friendship
31. Supplied troops again
33. Jezebel's husband
34. Acronym for a sunscreen ingredient
35. Activity at a joyful reunion
36. Dry comic?
37. Like krypton
38. "Jailhouse ___," Presley hit
39. Coalition in 1941
40. Hammett figure
41. Slow flow
44. Rehan and Neilson
46. More than one actress?
49. A Darling dog
51. Harmless reptile of N.A.
52. Bullets, in poker
53. An end to motion
55. Yarborough's top cards
58. Marten
60. A.D.A. member
61. Dallas-to-Tulsa dir.
62. Thai temple
63. Enervates
64. Term for a worm
65. Bread, in Brest
66. Anagram for Sinatra
69. "In Like ___," 1967 Coburn film
70. Darnels
71. Escapees from a mythical box
73. Cousin of a hootamaganzy
74. Grill or grid
75. Sybarite's delight
77. Parts of La France
78. Port side when sailing south
81. Arcadian
84. Piers
85. Famines
87. Arranges beforehand
88. Man is one
89. Troupial
90. "___ is humble . . .": Cowper
93. Followers of zetas
95. Pochards
96. Probes
97. Type of stealer
99. Slapstick staples
100. Bridle hand
102. Comic Jay ___
103. ___ dixit
104. Accrete
105. Brumal blanket
106. "Tell ___ the Marines!"
107. ___ Islands (Attu et al.)
108. Slothful

Amadeus by Jack L. Steinhardt

ACROSS

1. West Coast nine
7. Juniper
12. He cameth before the refrigerator
18. Apply chrism
19. Intimidate
22. Comb. form for 12
23. Mozart's bride in 1782
25. Frittata, e.g.
26. A deadly sin
27. Unsubstantial
28. Mental inventions
30. Mansard borders
32. Diarized
34. Comes earlier than
38. Arithmetical sign
39. Incongruity
44. Outlying
45. Mecca for turiste
47. Dessert choice
48. Thought: Comb. form
49. Calcar
50. Italian town or gulf
52. Roman historian
53. Boxlike sleigh
54. Absquatulated
57. Alpha, beta and gamma
58. Man's slipper
59. Esculents
61. Bolt-head sides
62. Niblick sockets
63. Invocational figure
64. Rambler mfr.
65. Standoffish
67. Mathematically validated
70. Dike, Eunomia and Irene
72. Balloon cabin
75. Salieri, to Mozart
76. Kin of "By Jove!"
77. Rostrum
78. Lurch
80. Uniform
81. Pine cone
84. Grown-up chigger
85. Set of three
86. Sounds at a shower
87. Gula and cyma
89. Reserves
91. Stipulations in a contract
93. ___ the Impaler (15th-century Romanian prince)
94. Butter makers
96. Of a Mesolithic cultural stage
98. Conductor Walter
99. Rouen rooms

102. Harsh; bleak
103. Offensive odor
108. Radio's "___ the Magician"
109. Mozart opera: 1791
113. Tin and lead alloy
114. Racine tragedy: 1691
115. Home of Abraham
116. Velarium, e.g.
117. Teams of horses
118. Emulated Red Jacket

DOWN

1. S. American rodent
2. Shortly
3. Vietnamese monetary unit
4. Upheave
5. Importune
6. Dep.
7. Most comfortable
8. Tinker's target
9. ". . . ___-feather'd sleep": Milton
10. "We ___ the World"
11. Mortar-mixing tool
12. Mozart opera: 1781
13. Dermal blemish
14. Whence the Pison flowed
15. Deliquesce
16. Tops
17. Actor Pendleton
20. Certain fabrics
21. Where Perry triumphed
24. Wheel hub
29. Millet
31. Bolted
32. Film featuring Mozart's Piano Concerto No. 21
33. Nudnik or buttinsky
34. Buttress
35. "George White's Scandals," e.g.
36. Correct
37. Mozart opera: 1787
38. Through, for each
40. "Amadeus" director
41. Stop on ___
42. Demolish
43. Vacillates
46. Punty or mandrel
47. Short segment
51. Nautical chain
54. Spanish custard
55. Actor Cariou
56. Williams and Ralston
58. Crucifix
60. Chanteur Jacques ___
61. Plane curve

62. Nene cry
66. Chilean stream
67. Disturbed
68. Moon or Spoon
69. Unconcealed
71. U.S. satellite
73. French area, rich in coal
74. Permute
77. Apoidea member
79. Slighter
81. Mozart's birthplace: Jan. 27, 1756
82. Possessive adjective
83. Conducted
88. Sopherim
89. Phoebus
90. Suggest; volunteer
92. Whitman died here: 1892
93. Call on
95. Scottish philosopher: 1711–76
97. Wife of Tyndareus
98. Bobby Orr was one
99. Use maxilla and mandible
100. A "Shampoo" star
101. Oppositionist

102. Jamboree
104. Its chief town is Portoferraio
105. Illegality
106. Western Indian
107. Lacerate
108. Acct., often
110. Querying sounds
111. Use a ray gun
112. Between pi and sigma

ACROSS

1. Castile
5. Ontario tribesmen
10. N.Y.C. river
16. Piece of cake
17. Novelist Troyat
18. Birdman
20. CUPID
22. Hurdle
24. Farrell's knee bend
25. Peter and a Wolfe
26. "The Perfect Fool" composer
28. Prime-time time
29. Small "small"
30. Canary's cousin
31. Label anew
33. Athenian vowel
34. Asunder
36. Spruce
38. TV bee
39. Poor surfer
41. Voice
43. "Santa Claus Is Watching You" singer
45. Indeed
46. Rats!
48. They were: Lat.
49. Tower of Bombay
50. Alluded
54. Old age, of old
55. VIXEN
58. European capital
59. Oder tributary
61. In holiday spirits
62. Behold, to Brutus
63. Western lizard
64. DANCER
66. Jacky
67. Mild oath
69. Catcher Tony
70. Shelved
72. Convex moldings
73. Transient things
75. Marble
76. Abstruse
78. Ferric
79. Dr. Salk
81. John, in Cardiff
82. William Conrad role
84. Zingers
86. Ham
90. Swiss sledder
91. Bastes
92. Hang behind
94. Likely
95. "Artie" author
96. Tape over
98. Soft-palate projection
100. Divinity deg.
101. Letter opener
103. White poplar
105. Useful
106. A sister of Europa
107. Nov. 11 honoree
109. DASHER
112. Conspicuous
113. Propose
114. Mold
115. Where Virgil wrote the "Georgics"
116. Rating symbols
117. Focal points

DOWN

1. Suchlike
2. Third of thrice
3. French explorer in Colonial America
4. Modern medium
5. Dijon darlings
6. Resound
7. One of Eve's grandsons
8. White-tailed bird
9. Deep breath
10. COMET
11. Parsees' sacred writings
12. Cowboy's rope
13. Pomeranian's place
14. Lord Wimsey's alma mater
15. DONNER (popular variant of Donder)
16. Islamic leader
19. Charter car
20. Panel strip
21. "Sunny" composer
23. Psyched up
27. Praying figure
30. Brenda of comics
32. Belgian port
35. Copland ballet
37. Missionaries of Charity founder
38. Remedy
40. Pontifical cape
42. Lake in a cirque
44. RUDOLPH
45. Biography
47. Wobbling
49. Kind of cross
50. Roulette bet
51. Bar, to a barrister
52. BLITZEN
53. An aunt of Princess Beatrice
55. Swiss canton (former spelling)
56. Mites
57. Adapted to the desert
60. Mme., in Madrid
61. Male cat
65. Garment for Geraint
68. City in the Ruhr region
69. Keystone State's eponym
71. "Pacific" bird
72. Substance
74. "Santa Claus" star
75. Epigrams
77. Super Bowl XVIII site
79. Pink Panther, e.g.
80. PRANCER
82. Caliber
83. I.R.S. inquiries
84. Bristles
85. Deliverers
87. Even choices
88. Plenary
89. Fortification
91. E. Texas river
93. Abyss
97. Badgerlike mammal
99. Trammel of a sort
102. Reception room
104. Heroic verse
105. City in SE Turkey
106. Husband of Jezebel
108. Torn or Taylor
110. Sternward
111. Philosopher ___ Hsi

ACROSS

1. Rawboned person
6. Created
10. Textile city in N. France
16. But
19. Put to the test
20. "When I was ___ ...": W.S. Gilbert
21. Banana kin
23. Randan implement
24. Song for market tip that bombed?
26. Song for late Oct. 1929?
27. Southwest Indian
28. Tied
29. Pew accessory
31. Polanski film
32. Correspond
34. Influenced
35. Author of "The Fountainhead"
36. Debussy opus
38. Pincers
39. "I begin to smell ___": Cervantes
41. Located
42. Bach's "___ of Fugue"
44. Song for a broker's day?
49. Type of volcanic crater
50. Unbend
53. Value
54. Nobelist Wiesel
55. Gospel
58. ___ of Good Feeling: 1817–24
59. Kingly
60. Insincere language
61. Barley beard
62. Singer John
64. Arabian Sea gulf
65. Puts a new cover on a book
67. Sirius or Vega
68. Dr. Seuss's Thidwick
69. Cannonballed
70. Tokyo, formerly
71. "I Promessi ___," Manzoni novel
73. Swabbed
74. Hopeful plunger's song?
79. Brings forth
83. "___ Chan," T.N. Page story
84. Free electron
85. R.b.i. is one
89. Actress Irene from Greece
90. Bus station
92. Largest of the Galapagos
95. What esse means
96. Habituate
97. Film on bronze

99. Harold of Tin Pan Alley
100. Down Under lumberman
101. Wood shaper
102. Hit man or hero
104. Largest natural lake in Wales
105. Dürer's "Paumgartner ___"
106. Topple a tower
108. Palestine plant
109. Takeover song?
113. Slow mover
115. Refrain in old songs
116. Anti votes
117. Too
119. Cartouches
120. Dance
122. Bill
125. Pace
126. Attend Choate
128. Mercury's winged sandals
130. Clouseau's servant
131. Item stored in a buttery
132. Insider's song?
135. Bullish investor's song?
137. Kennel adjunct
138. Artificial
139. Actress Thompson
140. Longest modern note
141. Nationwide mil. instruction
142. Give the ___ (fire)
143. Very, in Lyon
144. More eccentric

DOWN

1. Barker's come-on
2. Desire fiercely
3. Did some ranch work
4. Eden's earldom
5. Set
6. Business tycoon
7. Outlander
8. Stunned
9. A biographer of Henry James
10. Everything
11. Snack-bar drink
12. Actress Stevens: 1934–70
13. French summers
14. Former D.C. team
15. Kinsman
16. Song for bluechip stocks?
17. Cafe patron
18. Dilo and dita
21. Henry Morgan was one
22. Antelope of E. Africa
25. Gumbos
30. Beethoven's "Für ___"

33. Carpenter's heavy beam
37. Wilbur concern
38. Balzac's "Le ___ Goriot"
39. Secret
40. Cambodia's monetary unit
41. Agitated states
42. Nile delta city
43. Ishmael's mother
44. Small herring
45. Hives
46. River in W. Africa
47. Manatee
48. Humerus neighbor
49. Aromatic resin
51. Rebelled
52. Faded
56. "___ d'arte," Puccini aria
57. Defective new auto
60. Ghanaian money
61. Consort of Pericles
63. Truncate
65. N.F.L. "zebras"
66. Danish weights
72. Placer material
73. Polynesian's supernatural force
74. Relative of a gore

75. Emulated Pearl White
76. Fast
77. Wintry
78. Weak-eyed worm hunter
79. Hoplite's weapon
80. Ling-Ling, for one
81. King of Siam's song for Wall St.?
82. What Aristophanes called "Area'chick"
85. Poles for some clowns
86. Silverheels role
87. Right-angled to a keel
88. "___ Promise": Maurois
90. Bender
91. Acuminate
93. "The Sheik of ___," 1921 song
94. Tree trunk
98. "Drake" poet
100. Summon, in a way
103. Dionysus specialty
104. Sac or city once sacked by Tatars
107. O.K. Corral figure
110. Emulated Red Jacket

111. Some of the Iroquoians
112. Without face value, as stocks
114. Dejection
115. Banish
117. Port city on Hokkaido
118. Soft palate
119. Confused struggle
120. Philippine Island
121. Occupation
122. Subdued
123. "The stag ___ ...": Scott
124. Shipworm
126. Catcher Tony
127. Harangue
129. Register
130. Wag
133. Badger
134. Avant-gardist
136. Oil-yielding tropical tree

75 Title Search by Nancy Scandrett Ross

ACROSS

1. Encourages a felon
6. Constantine slept here
11. Portrait sculpture
15. Printer's dot
16. Musical direction
17. "King ___ Road," 1965 song
19. Castro's predecessor
20. See 67 Across
23. Toothed: Comb. form
24. Maternally related
26. Yorkshire city
27. Month for lovers
28. C times XXXV
29. Zwei follower
30. Vesicle
31. Prefix for puncture
32. Ray
33. See 67 Across
38. Con
39. Suffix used by physicists
40. The 23rd Hebrew letter
41. "Fawlty Towers" star
42. Hypocritical talk
44. Melody
46. Spinning devices
47. Backward, nautically
50. Duroc's home
53. Tibetan monk
55. City on the Loire
58. Scrooge word
59. Wind of S. France
62. Ego
64. Former Spanish enclave in Morocco
65. Kind of sch.
67. Heart of the matter
69. Dispatch
70. Star's car
71. Greet
72. Dolt
74. Sign of triumph
75. Scaly crust
77. Buddies
79. Carrie or Louis
80. Playground time
82. Jazz dance
84. Ursula Andress film
86. Isinglass
87. Gun aimed at a bomber
89. Capp and Capone
91. Daisy ___ Scraggs
92. Mezzo Stevens
96. See 67 Across
101. Perfume measure
102. Bridle part
103. Wine experts' comb. form
104. Earthquake site: June 21, 1990
105. Grimace
106. Super serve
107. Base Gehrig covered
109. Some Renoir paintings
111. Thrice minus twice
112. See 67 Across
116. More drippy, as paste
118. A sister of Eunomia
119. Pupils' locales
120. Jubilant
121. Pipe part
122. Ethyl acetate, e.g.
123. Gulls

DOWN

1. Self-service restaurant
2. See 67 Across
3. Certain railways
4. Parisian head
5. Top-notch performer
6. Nonbeliever
7. Map abbr.
8. Sitter's feature
9. One of the Waughs
10. Least batty
11. Movie Messala
12. Sky sightings: Abbr.
13. P.O. item
14. See 67 Across
15. Outlaws
16. Paravane
18. Puts up
19. Pump, in Peru
21. Meadowlands team
22. Obloquy
25. Calla, e.g.
30. Kind of servant
33. Language of Helsinki
34. Motorists' org.
35. Like a street after sleet
36. Worker's rights org.
37. Part of Asia Minor
43. Branch
45. How madcaps act
46. Corolla part
47. Actor Walter and family
48. Of a Frankish people
49. See 67 Across
50. Narrow furrow
51. Joan Sutherland specialties
52. Gab
54. Ballerina Park
56. Writer of suspense tales
57. Teams
60. Olivia of the Met
61. Guided
63. Harbor sights
66. Human
68. Large cask
73. Ten: Comb. form
76. Centers of attention
78. Plumed hat
81. See 67 Across
83. Trading place: Abbr.
85. Big name in New Haven
86. Affected
87. Facing the pitcher
88. Pretentious
90. Brandy-based cocktail
91. Hoover Dam's lake
93. Satires' cousins
94. Tipsy
95. Eastern V.I.P.
97. Legal wrong
98. Nielsen or Uggams
99. Comes onstage
100. Bind tightly
107. Exquisite
108. Gossip tidbit
110. Sea in the W. Pacific
113. Permit
114. Fruit center
115. Expert ending
117. Carpet feature

76 Second Opinions *by Jeanette K. Brill*

ACROSS

1. Served perfectly
5. River in E. France
10. Part of a Latin paradigm
14. Competent
18. Rich fabric
19. Muster
20. Major Joppolo's post
21. Wampum item
22. Disco queen Summer?
24. Nicaraguan music makers?
26. Pledge
27. "Ici on ___ français"
29. Sham
30. Enameled metalware
31. Like Modigliani's "Reclining Nude"?
33. You're on one now!
36. Stair part
38. Old name of the Bulgarian port called Varna
42. "___-porridge hot . . ."
43. Obtuse
44. Fortunetelling card
46. City in E. Brazil
47. Violinist Kavafina
48. Int. group established in 1948
49. Song from "A Chorus Line"
50. Supercilious person
51. Orch. section
52. J.P.'s office?
58. Jewish month
59. Strict disciplinarian
61. Author of "The Making of a Surgeon"
62. Akin on the father's side
64. Upbeat, in music
65. Like some seals
66. Oneness
67. Least moist
69. Latin American dance music
70. Warehouse
73. Singer Stevens
74. Like a confirmed bachelor?
77. Nice article
78. Eager
79. Menuhin's title
80. Erwin or Symington
81. Diarist Anaïs ___
82. Fortify
83. Type of type
85. Rowdydow

87. Name in 1921 headlines
89. "X" math?
91. Play a higher card
92. German city on Belgium's border
93. Memo from rock singer Slick?
96. West Point mascot
97. Mite, e.g.
100. He doesn't like company
101. Clique
104. Gen. Jaruzelski and Lech Walesa?
106. Sock in the mouth?
109. Give forth
110. Baritone role in "I Pagliacci"
111. Sappho's Muse
112. Part of a pitchfork
113. Star in reverse?
114. Old Icelandic poetry
115. Sorrow
116. Kin of etc.

DOWN

1. Eisenhut, e.g.
2. Cavil
3. Arabian prince
4. Reduces in rank
5. Chancel seat
6. Win by ___ (inch ahead)
7. Writer Sarah ___ Jewett
8. ___ compos mentis
9. Goes by
10. Gustaf ___, former Swedish king
11. Painter of "Olympia"
12. Formicary denizen
13. Underwater projectile
14. Head of a convent
15. Brummell or Bridges
16. Cry from a crow's-nest
17. Edible corm of the taro
20. Stinging to the taste
23. Tosca's emotion
25. Valuable possession
28. Cries of triumph
32. Are they to the manor born?
33. Involuntary muscular contraction

34. Five: Comb. form
35. Like minoxidil?
36. Paine or Mather product
37. Reckless
39. Weekend libation?
40. One of Tirpitz's vessels
41. Buffalo man in a rink
43. Shelters for sheep
44. Not live
45. Shortly
50. "À votre ___!"
52. Sound of escaping steam
53. Components of monograms
54. Totally
55. Vikings
56. Faint light
57. Aunt, in Arles
60. Cornered
63. Encircle
65. This bore may cause excitement
66. Improper
67. Ibsen's forte

68. Competitor
69. Pique
70. Stage direction
71. In readiness
72. Companion of a mortise
75. Writer Singer
76. Archipelago unit
83. Dugouts
84. Arrange in degrees
85. Cornea irritant
86. Turned inside out
87. Dried tubers of orchids
88. Needle-shaped
90. Wading birds
91. Portuguese money of account
92. Glasgow or London
94. Impala's big cousin
95. Water wheel
96. Words to live by
97. Unoriginal person
98. Robin Cook novel
99. Finished parasailing
101. Pea or egg follower
102. "___ Really Me?": 1963 song

103. Suburb of Pittsburgh
105. School of whales
107. Relative of plata
108. Anguineous fish

ACROSS

1. Norwegian saint
5. Utter
10. World toter
15. Put away
19. Painter of "Aurora"
20. Trunk
21. ___ Vista, Mexican War battle site
22. Put an edge on
23. What are contracts?
25. If you pass the bar, what will it mean?
27. Birthplace of Columbus
28. Marner of Lapham
30. Pined
31. ___ Aires
33. Skid-row denizens
34. Cans, in Canterbury
35. Heraldic design
36. Presently
37. Kind of spoon
41. Dips
42. Which former female arbiter do you most admire?
45. Wine: Comb. form
46. Individualist
47. Mr. Flintstone
48. Bible book
49. Couple
50. Cahn-Styne product
51. Name at least one historic trial
55. Choreographer-director from Chicago
56. Cancels
58. Arab nobleman
59. Yosemite National Park river
60. A poplar
61. Takes off the cream
62. Pace
63. Tooth problem
65. Ill will
66. Out of the ordinary
69. Singer of "Stop the Music" fame
70. What is a talesman?
73. Refrain word
74. Arikaras
75. Kind of plane or dynamics
76. Grandmother of Timothy
77. Banking game
78. Lodge
79. What's equity?
83. Uses a kitchen appliance
84. Umpire's command
86. Kind of deck
87. Bits for Benji
88. Drenched
89. Horse follower
90. Be a witness
92. Where filets are often ruined
95. I.Q. tester
96. Spanish ice-skating figures
97. Define statutes
99. Name a prominent former court figure
104. Florence's river
105. Silly
106. Lustrous
107. Weaving need
108. Kind of drop
109. Lebanese tree
110. River and lake in Scotland
111. Crosses out

DOWN

1. Scepter's adjunct
2. Irish Neptune
3. Black bird
4. Nervous Nellie
5. Exec's brain, on occasion
6. Roads scholars
7. Silkworm
8. Apocryphal bk.
9. "The Barber of Seville" composer
10. Tasty mollusk
11. Helicons
12. "___ is more": Browning
13. Hill maker
14. Liner schedules
15. Chinese province
16. Go oystering
17. Erstwhile
18. Cull
24. Heredity determiners
26. Present
29. Party to
31. Prep cap
32. What exactly is a brief?
33. Emerson's middle name
34. Henry VIII was one
37. Sometimes it's ugly
38. Quitclaim is a deed, name some others
39. Rent
40. Over
41. Bank transaction
42. Originate
43. Soak flax or lumber
44. "The Golden Bowl" author
47. Heaters
49. African villages
51. Dutch genre painter
52. Dervish
53. Peaceful harmony
54. Convened anew
55. Our largest bone
57. "___ Irish Rose"
59. Biblical wall words
61. Game trail
62. Spring bloom
63. Brazilian Indian
64. Knockout of a place
65. Perk up a straightedge
67. Halt
68. Asian nation
70. Arrangement
71. Marry modestly
72. Costello or Groza
75. Puzzle variety
77. Damaged-goods rendition
79. Famed fabulist
80. "Faerie Queene" poet
81. Away
82. Cyrano's creator
83. Chopper part
85. Who starts the most suits?
89. City near Assisi
90. "Body all ___": O. Hammerstein
91. Dull sounds
92. Scholastic test, for short
93. Israeli port
94. Fish or pear
95. Finishing nail
96. Schenk or Harbach
98. One, in Paris
100. Cruise port, for short
101. Boston or Chicago team
102. Weeder
103. Bad ___, German spa

ACROSS

1. Rudimentary
6. Sacred choral piece
11. Scrooge's invectives
15. Scalawags
21. January, in Juárez
22. Massenet's forte
23. Petroleum cartel inits.
24. Shoulder-to-elbow bones
25. SILVER
28. Rubbed with rubber
29. Sinker
30. Inn's descendant
31. Robert Burns's one
33. Leaking radiator's sound
34. Self-important person
36. Nipa palm
38. Escorted anew
40. Convert into cipher
42. Ferrigno and Rawls
44. Two-toed sloth
46. Put down
47. Vega or Rigel
48. Preceders of xi's
51. KRYPTON
56. Discernment
58. ___ of iniquity
59. Brewer's need
60. Bireme gear
62. Depend (on)
63. Collapsed, with "in"
66. Oriental units of weight
68. Ring up
70. Greek goddesses of the seasons
71. Petri-dish contents
72. Ciro ___, 17th-century Italian painter
73. Bagel-like roll
74. Mortise's partner
75. Hero of "Giants in the Earth"
76. Classify
77. Intones
79. Woe
80. Undefiled
82. Pointillist's prop
83. Printing machine operators
86. Simone's school
87. Undeveloped state
88. Bloody Mary's daughter
89. Apt anagram of aye
90. Swizzles
91. La ___, Milano's opera house
92. Concede
94. Raison d' ___
95. Holmes's creator
96. Where Hercules slew the Hydra
97. Service club
98. Moral nature
99. Mil. truant
100. Dish list
101. Ear: Comb. form
102. Cariou or Deighton
103. Maligns
105. NEON
113. Celestial sphere
114. One of Manhattan's rivers
116. To's companion
117. Getz or Kenton
118. Positive
119. Ef, e.g.
121. ___ cum laude
124. Painting and poetry, e.g.
126. Oomph
127. Dutch or French follower
128. Catch in the act
130. University in Oxford, Ohio
132. Civil War general
134. Like a solarium
136. IRON
141. Mustard-family vegetable
142. Cannel
143. Cove
144. Take flight to unite
145. One of the Furies
146. Brontë's Jane
147. Idyllic spots
148. Actress Spacek

DOWN

1. ___ canto
2. Upward: Comb. form
3. Sentences
4. Mars: Comb. form
5. Doone of fiction
6. Super Bowl M.V.P.: 1990
7. Aperture: Abbr.
8. Rain cats and dogs
9. Boo-boo
10. Sapor
11. Kind of algebra
12. Eliot's cruelest mo.
13. "___ Rebel," 1962 tune
14. Bergman's "___ from a Marriage"
15. TV spy film of 1980
16. Computer-display pointers
17. ". . . the way of a man with ___": Proverbs
18. MERCURY
19. Fraternity V.I.P.
20. Caesar or Luckman
26. "___ in New York," 1935 song
27. Greece, to Greeks
32. Full
34. Hirt and Jolson
35. Trifle
37. Roast or roaster
39. Henna, e.g.
41. Preserves
43. Passover feast
45. End of a Poe title
49. Prussian cavalryman
50. Eye problem
52. Rubicund
53. COPPER
54. Disks for a dee-jay
55. Adz and awl
57. Perfume additives
61. Word with body and way
63. "Li'l Abner" cartoonist
64. Ripening device
65. PLATINUM
66. Coat with an alloy of tin and lead
67. Funnyman Johnson
68. Covered with evergreens
69. IODINE
70. Knock over a joint
72. Discomfits
73. Iraqi port
74. Doctor
76. Squirrel away
78. "¿___ Usted español?"
79. Beams
81. Herb of the lily family
83. Blueprint
84. A first name in architecture
85. Dundee denials
87. Oysters' hues
90. Seed planter
91. E.M.K. is one
93. Muddies the waters
94. Lab burners
95. Pedestal part
96. Diminish
97. Sand's "Elle et ___"
98. "Frae morn to ___ . . ."
100. Headcheese, e.g.
101. Social disintegration
102. Archway element
104. Maker of verses
106. Conditions
107. Grouse
108. Thespian Hagen
109. Woodchucks
110. Black gums
111. Bismuth, e.g.
112. Corded fabric
115. Hypnotic state
120. Borne by the wind
122. Singer Osmond
123. Better
125. Strongboxes
127. Double
129. Keep afloat
131. Inactive
133. When Yazdegerd III died
134. Mme., in Madrid
135. However, for short
137. Deface
138. Four-star off.
139. Periods of prosperity
140. Turhan ___, 40's film actor

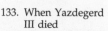

ACROSS

1. Suffix with gab or song
5. Beaver's structure
8. Strokes of fortune
13. "Status stripe" designer
18. Vilnius is its cap.
19. At all
21. Composition for eight
22. "___ in the Dark," 1964 film
23. Tommie of Gil Hodges's Mets
24. Celebration
25. Cowriter of "The Other Woman": 1983
26. Gibe
27. Start of a statesman's statement
31. Early car
32. Rivulets
33. Lettuce type
34. Anchovy sauce
36. Haw's companion
37. ___ the press (brand new)
41. City in SW Ga.
44. Felt one's way around
48. Statement: Part II
50. More difficult to find
51. Strauss's "___ Italien"
52. Mutt and Jeff, e.g.
53. Land map
54. African ruler
55. C.P.A.
57. Wrinkle
58. Bretons or Britons
59. Statement: Part III
61. Shadow
62. "Diary of ___ Housewife"
64. Heavy-weight
65. "Abbey ___," Beatles album
66. Ephthalite
67. ___ about (approximately)
68. Double this for a Chilean river
71. Something to break
72. Tree house
73. Statement: Part IV
75. Healing: Comb. form
78. Rousseau hero
80. Skin
81. Differently

82. Juan's 2 Down
83. Burt Reynolds's ex
84. ___ Jose
85. Solid rain
86. Statement: Part V
90. Some are stuffed
91. Combining form for 10 Down
92. Kind of band
93. Participate in a langlauf
94. Circle segments
95. Adherent
96. With 15 Down, quoter of statesman's statement
101. N.Y.P.D. order
103. End of statement
109. Capital of Baleares province, Spain
111. Arrowsmith's wife
112. Carry on
113. Baptism, e.g.
114. Ancient weapon
115. "Luncheon on the Grass" artist
116. Tokyo tipple
117. Legless creature
118. Let up
119. Tripura or Orissa
120. Charlie's comic brother
121. Go up against

DOWN

1. Walking shoes
2. Shell crew
3. Mosshorn, e.g.
4. Soothing word
5. Vilified
6. Disinclined
7. Distribute
8. Regains consciousness
9. Maple genus
10. Nihala or Nunki
11. Actress Copley
12. Awkward try
13. Furniture feature
14. Springsteen's "Born in the ___"
15. See 96 Across
16. Shape of a hogan
17. "Leave ___ Beaver"
20. Extend onself
28. "Half Magic" author
29. Horn emanations
30. Toddlers' perches
35. Emulated Jessica
38. Out ___ (no longer available)
39. Thrash or thresh

40. Oliver Stone product
42. Med. student's subject
43. Top-level business gps.
44. Super
45. Stallone role
46. Mythical hunter
47. Where Machu Picchu is
48. Spiked the punch
49. Language of Picasso
55. Niels Bohr's subject
56. Place of worship
57. Reason
58. Rob Reiner's dad
60. Server
61. "___ of Riley," former TV sitcom
63. Humorist Sahl
67. Hero of the 1936 Olympics
68. Cotton packer
69. Atlas feature
70. He wrote "Night Music"
71. Braggart
72. Curtain fabric

74. Lunchmeat emporium
75. Little bit
76. Bonn expletives
77. "You Turned ___ on Me," 1936 song
79. Marquand's sleuth
80. Hopper and Turner
84. Hide the loot
85. Glow
87. Doomed area in a Chekhov play
88. ___ Bud, a Dickens heroine
89. Flatter, in a way
90. Evaded
93. Elegant
97. Fabulous fiddle
98. Potboiler's product
99. "___ Africa," 1985 Oscar winner
100. Penurious
101. Cathedral section
102. Haydn's nickname
104. Attorneys' degs.
105. Accomplishment
106. O'Neill's daughter
107. Worry

108. Author of "The Valachi Papers"
110. West of Hollywood

ACROSS

1. New Zealand native
6. J. F Cooper subject
11. Off the mark
16. Out of breath
17. Namibia's game preserve
19. Grow together
21. ___ million
22. Polluted waters at Port Said?
24. Draw forth
25. Bedouin's workout?
26. Start of a Hardy title
27. Lump of earth
28. Town near Steubenville, Ohio
29. Boot bottom
30. Corn or verse preceder
31. TV's Donahue
32. Bu. or pk.
34. To, to Burns
36. East Indian sailor
38. Yamamai's kin
39. N.L., M.V.P.: 1952
42. Pou ___ (vantage point)
45. Donne's geographical error?
49. Fairy-tale sign-off
51. Certain lodge members
52. Apt. house, e.g.
53. Lasso
54. Methuselah's claim to fame
56. Kindergartner
57. Coal scuttle
58. Alfonse's polite ami
59. Valentino?
65. He played Ashley
66. Violinist Bull
67. Moscow square
68. Toastmasters, for short
69. Sierra Nevada resort
70. Beersheba's region
72. Be philanthropic
74. ___ Yisrael (Palestine)
75. Title for an aged Islamic rancher?
79. Rembrandt's last name
80. Bentsen, for one
82. Function
83. Numbers each leaf or page
85. TV's Headroom
86. Swift Atl. plane
87. Decant
89. Cube root of eight
90. Opposite of wax
93. Cover story
97. He wrote "The Gremlins"
98. Noted Indian diplomat
99. Mideast mecca for star-gazers?
103. Trudges
105. Persian Gulf diet observers?
106. Orbital high point
107. Voted in
108. Tribute
109. Ind. hoopsters
110. Tire imprint
111. Natives of Ecbatana, e.g.
112. Some collars

DOWN

1. Philippine island
2. Artery disorder
3. Of a verse form
4. Coty or Clair
5. G. & S. princess
6. Fuel for a lorry
7. "___ to Be You," 1924 song
8. Leopold's codefendant
9. Bone: Comb. form
10. "___ in the Hat": Seuss
11. Needle-shaped
12. DCL doubled
13. "Not for these ___/ The song...": Wordsworth
14. Feeling, in Ferrara
15. Writer Germaine de ___
16. Sad
18. Wonderstruck
19. City on the Garonne
20. Ultimatum word
23. Tool for Bunyan
25. Common Muslim name
27. "Death on the Nile" author
31. Ill. coal city
32. Jackie's second
33. Impish
35. Noah's landfall
37. Where Arabian knights park their steeds?
38. Nanny has three
39. Saharan sights
40. Plus
41. Widmark's first film role
42. Radio annoyance
43. Grand ___ (Western range)
44. Chimp's cousin
46. Presently
47. Aardvark's diet
48. Peek
50. "Call me ___" (drowning Arab's cry?)
54. Tired, in poesy
55. A land of plenty
56. Terrible: Slang
59. Do tailoring
60. Granada gala
61. Navajo's home
62. Sch. before jr. high
63. Gator's kin
64. Comedian Jay
70. Nope
71. Estonian river
72. A.E.S. defeater
73. Son of Odin
76. D-day craft
77. Four-fifths of the atmosphere
78. Matronly ladies
81. Grand ___ Ruler (B.P.O.E. bigwig)
84. Winos
85. Threat
86. "Cheers," e.g.
87. Brief respites
88. Electrical unit
90. Finnegan's ___": Joyce
91. No longer a minor
92. More trendy
94. De ___ ("Green Pastures" role)
95. Balin or Claire
96. Alcott girl
97. Requiem
100. Mideast bread
101. Alas!
102. Scan the print
103. Tiff
104. Like crazy hombre
106. Rue Morgue murderer

81 Tom Swifties Redivivus by Mel Taub

ACROSS

1. John Webster's "The Duchess of ___"
6. Ethereal ring
10. Trims away
15. Silent Lillian or Dorothy
19. First victim's namesakes
20. Askew
21. Rage
22. Engaged in
23. "___?" asked Tom abstractly
25. "___," said Tom divertingly
27. Spaghetti wheat
28. Credulous
30. Raised strip
31. Falsify
32. Measures
34. Flatter, in a way
36. Massive
38. Notice
40. "___," said Tom initially
42. Signal flares
43. Eagle plus two
44. Exclusively
45. Precise point
46. Played a shrill instrument
47. "___," said Tom haltingly
50. "___," said Tom unsparingly
54. Wolf's kin
55. Barley beard
57. Underdone
58. ___ Friday
59. Tycoon Turner
60. Tire print
62. The revenuers
63. Wall Street figure
64. Levin or Lansky
67. "___," said Tom grandly
69. Avifauna
70. Pink-slipped
71. Word, in Nice
72. Priest, to Pedro
73. "___ pig's eye!"
74. Doughboys' successors
75. Smell ___
77. Creek
78. "That's a ___ on me!" said Tom freshly
82. "___," said Tom dramatically
86. "___," said Tom rhetorically
89. Gulf of Aqaba port
90. Dutch airline inits.
91. Roald or Arlene
92. Pallid
93. Mother Goose dieters
95. "___," said Tom ravenously
98. Adduce
99. Silent Pola
100. Early show
101. Sources of ruin
103. Exist
104. Kin of strep
106. Acerbic
108. Hearts
110. "___," said Tom playfully
113. "___," said Tom disarmingly
116. Brief note
117. A Reagan Attorney General
118. De Valera's republic
119. Make used to
120. Glut
121. Vermont town
122. Hire out
123. Trifled

DOWN

1. Fairy queen
2. "At once, ___, and yet a rose full-blown": Herrick
3. "___," said Tom gracefully
4. Coquettish
5. Progeny
6. Cloche, e.g.
7. King of comedy
8. Lake Erie city near Cleveland
9. Most favorable situations
10. Omega's predecessor
11. Magnetic one
12. ___ Alverio (Rita Moreno)
13. Run to seed
14. Complacent
15. Prepare fish
16. "___," said Tom automatically
17. Alley coup
18. Sweethearts
24. Encroached
26. Blunt refusal
29. "___," said Tom flatly
33. Sans others
35. Disney film: 1982
37. Employer
38. Grand in scope
39. Me. city
41. Mont. neighbor
42. Bench penalties
44. Weasel's kin
46. Iron: Pref.
48. Famous
49. Special cop
51. Citizen Tom
52. Algerian neighbor
53. Pipe elbows
56. Bewail
60. Powerful person
61. Actress Conn
63. Donnybrook
64. Wise trio
65. Stairwell sign
66. "___," said Tom privately
67. Maugham's ___ Nesbit
68. Aba wearer
69. Ryan or Tatum
71. Snack-bar drinks
73. Red-handed
76. "___," said Tom dolefully
79. "___," said Tom sagely
80. All in order
81. Irish river
83. Winglike
84. Somewhat tardy
85. Romans' 156
87. Pledge of unity
88. Apparel
93. Symbols of sluggishness
94. Xerxes's realm
95. City near Vesuvius
96. McGuffey work
97. ___ olde England
98. Melville's "Benito ___"
100. Russell, Ball and Lansbury
102. Kind of game for Nolan Ryan
105. Like a pussycat
107. Asunder
109. Kind of bet
111. Minuscule
112. Waco nickname
114. Peevish fit
115. He's often raised

ACROSS

1. An October birthstone
5. Valjean of "Les Misérables"
9. ___ button
14. Tailored
18. Enthusiastic review
19. Old card game
21. Statistic for Tyson
22. Noyes play
23. Take heart
25. The lady vanishes
27. "Downstairs" folk
28. Worsted-cloth strainer
30. Aspirations
31. Irish lake
32. Disguise
33. Lemon
34. Contemptibly small
37. Speaks childishly
38. Devilfishes
42. Cartoonist Peter and family
43. Night out
45. Easter treat
47. Explorer Ericson
48. Entertainer Eartha
49. Cribs
50. Moore of the movies
51. Cardiologist's chart: Abbr.
52. All gone
56. Plumbers' tubes
57. No place to skate
59. Winged
60. Inflicts
61. Sometimes it hurts
62. Dogs sans pedigree
63. Lake dwellers
64. Bronco busters
66. Eastern inn
67. "Agon" and "Serenade"
69. In harmony
70. Timeless
72. Luau instr.
74. Gaelic
75. Fang, in France
76. Actor Richard
77. Devil's walking-stick, e.g.
78. Year in Claudius I's reign
79. Abandoned bride
83. Roll along
84. Adams, Harding, Hayes or Taylor
86. Needed an eraser
87. Bureaus
88. People of NE India
89. Battery terminal
90. King Balak's land
91. South African township
94. Concert hall
95. Describing picnics
99. No room
101. Skip breakfast
103. Sandwich source
104. Hotel de___ (town hall, in Tours)
105. It was nothing to Nero
106. Hindu hero
107. Extremities
108. Disburdened
109. "___ of the Mind," Shepard play
110. Neuter, as a pet

DOWN

1. Globes
2. Peel
3. Affirm
4. Cut grass
5. He's on the spot
6. Emulate Duse
7. Moslem names
8. Town in Iceland
9. Something to keep
10. Cliff dwelling
11. Cole and Turner
12. German pronoun
13. Cheeses named for an English village
14. ". . . ___ little failed much": R.L.S.
15. Shankar specialty
16. Bibliographer's "same"
17. Place in space
20. Try again
24. Marx and Malden
26. Saudi Arabian town
29. Coleridge's "sacred river"
32. Please: Ger.
34. Maldives capital
35. Upright
36. Little left
37. Cabinetmaker's machine
38. Barrel spigot
39. Counting-out word
40. Green leaves
41. Hebrew letter
43. English letter
44. R.I.P. notices
46. Peach or Piggy
48. Emulates Mme. Defarge
50. Chemical compound
52. Make used to
53. Composer Gabriel: 1845–1924
54. Mongolian range
55. Montand's morning
56. Laborer, for short
58. Goddess who is no hawk
60. Stout's Nero
62. Center of activity
63. Former Defense Secretary
64. Asian weight
65. Roman patios
66. Affected ones
67. Run, as dye
68. Trapshooting variety
70. Veins' contents
71. Concur
73. Sniggles
75. "___ zeffiretto" ("The Marriage of Figaro" duet)
77. Strike three
79. Something plighted
80. Freshened
81. Gap, in Grenoble
82. "The Silver Bears" author
83. Landing place
85. Mother of Achilles
87. Chain gang
89. Astaire's sister
90. CCCLI tripled
91. Nigerian singer
92. Poet Wilfred
93. Barbarous
94. Watteau works
95. Sprinter or skier: Abbr.
96. Speak sharply
97. Projecting molding
98. Anthem's beginning
100. By way of
102. Aunt, in Acapulco

83 *Oyez! Oyez!* by Jack R. Harnes

ACROSS

1. ___ House, Washington D.C.
6. Onto
11. ___ veau (sweetbread)
16. Items in stacks
21. Small stream, in England
22. Split
23. Outward
24. Praying female figure
25. Set ___ (prepare to snare)
26. Union general
27. Diplomat Silas
28. Devilfish
29. Closet pest?
31. Superman?
33. Having droopy auricles
34. Facial bone
36. Subject of some roasts
37. Hardy heroine
38. Singer Callas
39. Arrow's little cousin
40. Vexed or rubbed
44. Bribed
45. Stuffs
46. Morning hrs.
47. Valhalla gods
50. What an arsonist sometimes does?
53. Stigma
54. Sing Sing warden-author
55. Rake
56. Bill's partner
57. Donizetti heroine
58. Russian sea
59. ". . . ___ away the sin . . .": John 1:29
61. Posture at bat
64. R.I.P. notice
65. Surveying instrument
67. Quaker in a grove
69. Menhaden
71. Whale constellation
72. Trick alternative
73. Boy singer of the 30's
74. Barge
77. Ritual meal
78. Famed former miler
82. Music halls
83. Strut
85. Nova ___
87. An armadillo
88. "Hamiltons"
89. Gibbon
90. Prado offering
91. Certain gaits
92. Conductor Jeffrey ___
93. Rossini's Figaro when depressed?
98. Kayo blows
99. Some RR's
100. Painters, e.g.
101. Crazy as ___
102. Author of "Tristram Shandy"
103. Summers, in Arles
104. Fold
105. Partner of aid
107. "To every thing there is ___ . . .": Eccl. 3:1
111. Made with pickets
112. Led
117. Mystery novel?
119. Moonshiner?
122. Fanon
123. Conjecture
124. Rejoice
125. Rhone tributary
126. Passé
127. Bone: Pref.
128. Type of angler
129. J'___ (I was, in Paris)
130. Curves
131. Vance of whodunits
132. Crystalline crust
133. Purposes

DOWN

1. Melee
2. Graph starter?
3. Anchor position
4. "___ war": F.D.R.
5. Parrots, e.g.,
6. Hordes
7. Handles
8. Of grandparents
9. Advise, in Yorkshire
10. Sap
11. Memorable sportswriter
12. Summer refresher
13. Brenda or Bart
14. Of Denmark: Comb. form
15. Toothless
16. Alley frequenters
17. Some exams
18. ___-arms (mounted soldier)
19. ___ nous
20. Bet
30. Talking horse of TV
32. Inserts on skirts
35. Domesday Book money
38. "Cape Martin" painter
39. Pythias's friend
40. Assyrian city
41. ___ pin drop
42. Egyptian dam
43. Fox hunt?
44. Thin porridge
45. Ashcan School painter
46. Whodunit factor
47. Theme
48. Union unit
50. Display of daring
51. Pairs
52. A Mendelssohn opus in E flat major
53. An Ivy League jewel?
59. Rollers in the 1790's
60. Oliver or Thomas
61. Ship's poles
62. Triter
63. Actress Verdugo
66. Rent
68. Bishopric
70. Gods, to Galba
72. Lachrymose
73. Beaten, in Brest
74. Soprano Lehmann
75. Beau ___
76. Polite blokes
77. Clupeid fishes
78. Element used in metallurgy
79. Acuminate
80. Ever, in poesy
81. Ballet
84. Blackthorns
86. English explorer
91. Games for would-be-millionaires
93. Engine
94. Establishment not requiring union membership
95. Advertising hoopla
96. Not aweather
97. The common plantain
100. Sows again
102. A Belgradian
104. Piece of fourth-class mail
105. Confuses
106. Swarthy, in Savoie
107. Home
108. Koran chapters
109. Les ___ Unis
110. Formal mall
111. Loren's married name
113. Jai-alai basket
114. Twitch
115. Weird
116. Garb
118. Disdainful interjection
120. Hedge that bars cattle
121. Finnish city or river

ACROSS

1. Actor Will
5. Old Dutch coins
10. Mechanical repetition
14. Proportion
19. Gallimaufry
20. Confused
21. Always
22. Etchers' needs
23. Size of type?
26. Tippy craft
27. Sailor's dread
28. Stowe book
29. Ride in a roadster
31. Theater award
32. Objectives
33. The Little ___ (nursery-tale character)
37. French clerics' titles
40. "A House ___ Home": P. Adler
42. O'Hare tenant
43. Heraldic fur
44. Tiff?
47. Most M.I.T. grads
48. Kin of a dalmatic
49. Immature egg
50. "___ some other name!": Juliet
51. Morse symbol
52. Poivre's partner
53. Superficial prettiness?
58. Roll up
59. Sterne's "___ Shandy"
61. Indian princess
62. Layman in a monastery
64. Inc.-tax pros
65. Small vessel for oil
66. Afflictions
67. Galahad's mother
69. Ind. town
70. Freshwater fish
74. Rhythmical cadence
75. Spread before a strut?
78. High priest
79. ___ up (confine)
80. Shad delicacy
81. "___ Triste": Sibelius
82. Scottish bonnet
83. Casca's time for action
85. Short laugh?
89. Mention for military honors
90. Lands a fish
92. Turns down
93. Football grip
94. Passionate
95. Decorates a cake
96. Indifferent
98. Some rabbits
100. Court celebrity
101. European buntings
105. Belief
108. Pintail duck?
111. Break a commandment
112. Testa's cousin
113. Dissonance
114. Smidgen
115. Carbonizes
116. Foundation
117. Unrefined
118. De ___ (unwanted)

DOWN

1. Objective
2. German river
3. "___ Kleine Nachtmusik": Mozart
4. Chanticleer
5. Author Runyon
6. Eared seal
7. Man, for one
8. Gumshoe
9. Pilchard
10. Gives power back to
11. "Metamorphoses" poet
12. Half a score
13. Work units
14. More risqué
15. Hold ___ to (compare favorably with)
16. "___ Men," 1987 film
17. Altar words
18. Simple sugar
24. Greek letters
25. Mail
30. School V.I.P.
32. Mine ceiling
34. Berra of baseball?
35. Surrounded
36. Snuggle
37. Command from Bligh
38. Farm machine
39. Weight allowance?
40. Moslem faith
41. Zenith
42. Bide ___ (stay awhile)
44. Trans-Atlantic
45. AZ city
46. Skilled
49. "Barefoot boy, with cheek ___": Whittier
54. Flynn or Fauntleroy
55. Actress Prentiss
56. Living ___ (cohabiting illegally)
57. From bad ___
58. Scram
60. Polish's partner
63. Henri's kindness
65. Czech dramatists Karel and Josef
67. Mark Twain's burial place
68. Schubert songs
69. Part of speech: Abbr.
70. Traverses
71. Baby-powder base
72. Like a pterodactyl
73. Eras
76. Port of entry in N. Spain
77. Ties
84. Santa, e.g.
85. Locus
86. Letter by Paul
87. Nape
88. Letting go
89. ___ a day (retires)
91. High-hats
93. Auden's "___ Stranger!"
96. Ankh, for one
97. Sioux
99. Strikebreaker
100. Sacred bull of Egypt
101. Taft's state
102. "Omnia vincit ___"
103. Defense org.
104. Kind of bean
105. U.S. agency: 1933–43
106. S. Korean president: 1988
107. Stowe girl
109. Altar in the sky
110. Hide ___ hair

85 Dropouts by Judson G. Trent

ACROSS

1. Rigel, e.g.
5. Trade
9. Bath, for one
12. Herald's cloak
18. Fine fabric
19. Kennedy relative
20. Auto
21. Lariats
22. Fabian's opinion of Cesario: Shak.
25. "By their ___ ye shall know them"
26. Third
27. Peter's ___ (old tax)
28. Saturate
29. Church niche
30. "When I was ___ . . ."
31. Twangy
33. Flings
36. Author St. Johns
37. Above all
41. Poilu's weapon
42. Sultry
44. Kind of soup
47. Invent facts
48. Sward
49. Wings, to Ovid
50. "I've ___ had!"
51. Horne from Brooklyn
52. Bigger pic
53. "___, said . . . Chaucer": Spenser
57. Folk-tale creatures
59. Auditors' concerns
61. Tempers
62. Painting style
63. It can be scanned
64. Po metropolis
65. Lorelei
67. Islamic Messiah
69. Rel. of a bracket
70. Hampered
73. Prepare to deplane
75. Loud confrontation
77. Mme., in Madrid
78. Estuaries
79. Kind of sax
81. Mother of Jabal and Jubal
82. Folding bed
83. Literary monogram
84. Decrees
86. Tommyrot
87. Yield
88. Early ascetics
90. Squash variety
92. Weighty works
93. Smudges
95. Rounded moldings
96. Overcrowd
98. Part of AFL-CIO
100. Shapes
102. Walked aimlessly
106. Stage
107. How the deathfires danced for the Ancient Mariner
109. James Webb's "___ of Honor"
110. Baby raccoon
111. Some tides
112. Fad
113. Spare
114. Vane dir.
115. Yawn
116. Foil

DOWN

1. Lath
2. Subdued
3. Acidity, to an M.D.
4. Iterate
5. Author Hite
6. Undulating
7. Azimuth
8. Populated
9. Kind of sheet
10. Tuileries, e.g.
11. Tennyson's wrecked seaman
12. Piscatorial sport
13. Service begun May 15, 1918
14. Geegaw
15. One of the Cook Islands
16. Seed, in tennis
17. Sociologist's deg.
19. Seraglio sections
23. Apices
24. Prosperity
30. Ta-ta, in Tours
32. Section of "Le Tartuffe"
33. Joshua's fellow spy
34. Coliseum
35. Fisherman's quarry
36. Far East nurses
38. Start of Stephano's song in "The Tempest"
39. Luxury craft
40. Barm
42. Type of arch
43. Pressure product
45. Actor Buddy
46. N.B.A. team
51. Jogger's cousin
53. As far as
54. Nerve: Pref.
55. Black of "Nashville"
56. Gershwin's "Of Thee ___"
58. Author Lofts
60. Dangerous mosquito
64. Resort lake in the West
65. Caterpillar hairs
66. On edge
67. Guillemot
68. Indigo sources
69. Attention getters
70. Gaseous element
71. Wear away
72. Trysts
74. Fast-food specialty
76. A Polynesian tongue
80. Endure
84. Free
85. Cloy
86. ___ around (cavorting)
87. Liken
89. In decline
91. Search carefully
92. Shadow
94. Spike
96. Kind of paper
97. Norma and Charlotte
98. ___ majesté
99. Belt
101. Shea stats.
102. Hazard for Strange
103. Cinch
104. Fringe
105. Endure, in Edinburgh
106. Singer Tillis
108. Pedagogue's org.

ACROSS

1. Concavity
5. Extemporize
10. Submerge
15. Declines
19. Blunderbore, e.g.
20. Tropical vine
21. Fluke larva
22. Ice field
23. Take a back seat
26. Driver's shout
27. Saki and Sand
28. Release
29. Potted
31. Interstices
32. Ah Sin creator
33. Dynamo parts
34. Half a score
35. Amiens's river
36. Unfruitful
37. Fenway foursome
40. Belaboring
42. Corn serving
45. Indonesian island
46. Pots' companions
47. "Topaz" author
48. European capital
49. Doak Walker's coll.
50. Flinch
51. Insipid
53. Plods
54. Most convenient
56. Disparage
57. Ticket type
58. Act as gofer
62. Sofa
64. Carry on
65. Went over again
68. Throbs
69. Awn
71. Emulated Pan
72. Swedish coin
73. Molted
74. Skirt length
75. Limerick poet
76. Manger
77. Sizzling
78. Be successful
82. Viking alphabet
83. "Boys Town" actor
85. Peace Nobelist: 1987
86. Light bed
87. Expel
89. Cupids
90. Beat
94. Fissured
95. Derogatory
96. Aurora ___
97. River in Xanadu
98. Borge will do this for laughs
101. Kind of market
102. Cave being
103. Strained
104. Unicorn fish
105. Asian festivals
106. "Solstice" author
107. Chipped in
108. Roman clan

DOWN

1. Dad
2. Girl watcher
3. It may be whooping
4. Convention orator
5. President of Mexico: 1946–52
6. Cubes
7. Neighbor of Burma
8. Bavarian river
9. Nightstand sight
10. Scriptural
11. Pussyfoot
12. Taro part
13. "___ Liza Jane"
14. Bands stand for them
15. Lacking vigor
16. Boast
17. Shipworm
18. Pips
24. Holiday happenings
25. Nobelist in Physics: 1938
30. Mountain lake
32. Kind of chestnut
33. Flavorful
35. Private rooms
36. Incinerate
37. Blowout
38. Soprano Gluck
39. Proclaim widely
40. Medieval guild
41. Protect
43. Filamentous plant
44. Rubicund
46. Rifle
48. Spreads
50. Dinner drinks
51. Mixture
52. Alfred of acting
53. P.G.A. winner 1949
55. Old hat
56. Rating symbol
57. Brown shade
59. Characteristic
60. Gazelles
61. Asian nation
62. Cummerbund
63. Repeat
66. Buffalo's county
67. Society entrants
69. Alfred of testing
70. Impatient
71. Excuses
74. Sonata movement
76. Jitterbug
78. Source
79. Mark and Dorothy
80. Wear away
81. Cardinal's cap
82. Logger's sport
84. Neb. tribe
86. Crooked
87. Rough sketch
88. Lunar trench
89. Tarsus
90. Aplomb
91. Dress design
92. Connection
93. Fussy couple?
95. Bagpipe player
96. Propensity
99. "Watchful" name
100. One with a clutch

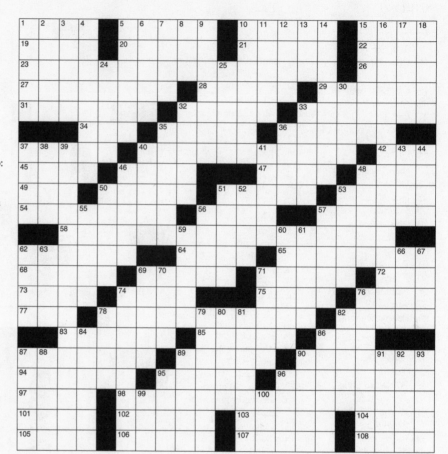

87 Celebritease by Shirley Soloway

ACROSS

1. City in Calif.
5. Rebuffs
10. Make merry
15. Chancel item
20. Noted research physician
21. Membranes
22. Writer Jong
23. Worsted
24. Shaking like ___
25. Guam's capital
26. Plump roasting fowl
27. Book by J. B. Cabell: 1937
28. Items in Liz's closet?
31. Made a bridge play
33. Ar chaser
34. Cousin of a wrymouth
35. "It ___ laugh": Pinero
36. Bouquet beauty
37. "___ for All Seasons"
39. Together: Mus. dir.
40. Tip
41. Party for Elke?
46. Ruffian
47. The Great Compromiser
51. Seething
52. S.E.C. member
53. Townsend ___: 1934
55. Clement people
58. Shea performer
59. Cassandra, e.g.
63. Medical suffix
65. Cavity in a cactus
66. Vow
68. Teresa has it?
70. Long looker
71. Straight or sharp follower
73. Some cats and dogs
75. Queen Elizabeth's Aussie vessel
76. Julius of songdom
79. Robin Hood's quaff
80. Accumulate
82. Herds of whales
84. Discontented one
86. Most spooky
90. Specify
92. Walter got set for a race?
96. Writer Wiesel
97. Milk curdler
98. Dot on a map
99. Highwayman
101. Nabokov book
102. "...lovely ___"
104. Towel designation
106. ___ generis
107. Western
109. Intertwine
110. Temperate
112. The ex-Mrs. Bono's hairdressers?
116. Queen of mystery
119. Ownership document
120. Always
121. Vocations
123. Private eye Peter
124. Jeanne or Cécile: Abbr.
125. Andress film
128. Strips a ship
129. Lorne's favorite side dish?
134. Concerning
135. Ryan or Tatum
137. Qum resident
138. Wrathful
139. Problem for Fido
140. Present occasion
141. Hebrew month
142. QE2, e.g.
143. Beeweed or starwort
144. Gallant mount
145. Tales or exploits
146. Aglets

DOWN

1. Song sounds
2. Minds
3. Clock face
4. Lowdown
5. Flower parts
6. Within the law
7. "When I was ___..."
8. Sheet of stamps
9. Ocean front
10. Emulate a diseur
11. One of the dryads
12. Bigwigs
13. He wrote "The Name of the Rose"
14. Japan's Feast of ___
15. Guarantee
16. Jack's favorite dessert?
17. Voyages
18. Jibe
19. Tall grass
20. Cloy
29. Foster
30. Seize power
32. Actress Charlotte
36. Chinese principle
37. "___ Blue?"
38. Blanc and Ferrer
39. Flooded
40. Christmas tree
41. Greek island
42. Voodoo
43. "Be prepared:" e.g.
44. Mata ___
45. Designer Cassini
46. Entire scope
48. Arrowsmith's first wife
49. City on the Rhône
50. River of Flanders
54. ___ credit
56. ___ de deux
57. Dudley Moore film
60. Pitcher
61. Trial's partner
62. One feared by xenophobes
64. Beehive's relative
67. Celeste in her nest?
69. Salted, as a noix
72. Sampler
74. Coleridge's "gentle thing"
77. Aug. 31 follower
78. How pongids behave
81. Wife of Tyndareus
82. Embden and Toulouse
83. Moffo and Moses
85. Lollygagged
87. Happify
88. Partisan
89. Shreds
90. Minute amount
91. Summer in St. Tropez
93. Snooped
94. Guided trip
95. Of the ear
100. Jughead
103. Famed Concord family: 19th century
105. Film segment
108. Spring mo.
111. Tax org.
113. Illusionist Doug
114. Keeps
115. Hot spot
117. Bandleader Lanin
118. Allow
119. Fought one-on-one
121. Suppers, in Sevilla
122. Catkin
123. Table prayer
124. Governing body of France
125. Ade medium
126. Despises
127. German reservoir
128. Lady of Spain
129. Actor Wilder
130. Fourth of HOMES
131. Pinza was one
132. Residue
133. Diva delivery
136. Negative word

ACROSS

1. Sticky stuff
6. Melville protagonist
10. Troy suffered one
15. Succeeded: Colloq.
16. Betel-nut producer
17. Ruined
19. Give oneself airs
21. Election results
23. Shoshone
24. Dozed
25. Shingle man
27. Venetian bigwig
28. Tropical tree
30. Inventor Howe
32. Perch
33. Rose's love
34. Divinity with a load on
36. Curtain on stage
38. Caboodle's pal
39. Wave lift
40. Dugong
42. African republic
44. Griffith Gaunt's creator
45. A Waugh
47. P.I. trees
48. Proverbially cheap item
49. Toy
54. Prisoners
58. Latin love
59. Bard's before
60. Veloz's dancing partner
62. Anger
63. Sayer's "The ___ Tailors"
64. Experimented
66. Actor John and family
67. Custard
68. Antarctic cape
69. Masticate
71. French born
72. Catch
73. Cook one's ___ (dash another's hopes)
75. Try to overcome insomnia
79. Foot part
80. El Paso's Vikki
81. Plant affliction
82. Emulate Kermit
84. Claims
87. Kind of firecracker
91. Fern part
92. Little, in Lothian
93. "Giant" ranch
95. Passover feast
96. Highlands girl
97. Hangs onto
99. Short smokes
101. Crème ___ crème
102. Up and ___ (Slang)
103. Knightly weapons
105. Subway item
107. Author Yutang
108. Apportion
110. ___ around (cutting capers)
113. Moe, e.g.
114. Charged particle
115. Testify
116. Bearded, botanically
117. Kind of house
118. Undermine

DOWN

1. Kneecap
2. Commotion
3. French cathedral city
4. Kind of fight
5. Kennedy and Barrymore
6. French artist
7. Name in a will
8. Thespian
9. Shaw's "___ and the Man"
10. Most dependable
11. Lifeless
12. Certain N.Y. time
13. Flesh-revealing photo
14. Attired
15. Undergo change
16. Gazing fixedly
18. Motor
19. Immature monarchs, e.g.
20. Homeric products
22. Beginning
26. Thwart
29. Ghastly
31. Indian tongue: Var.
35. Only
37. Villain
39. Pituitary location
41. Dry foe
43. "Taras Bulba" author
44. Incursions
46. Hold dear
48. Certain two-wheeled carriages
49. ___ arms
50. Kind of acid
51. Known, in Nice
52. Musical chord
53. Pay attention
54. Actress Leigh
55. Italian metropolis
56. Heaven: Pref.
57. Dispatches
61. Sally ___ (tea cake)
64. Eighteen-wheeler
65. Aristocratic
67. Aped a butterfly
69. Cell-producing gland
70. Student at times
74. Lollapalooza, to a flapper
76. Encourages
77. H.R.E. part
78. Regrets
80. Lauren Bacall vehicle
82. Cargo units
83. ___ stone (famous tablet)
84. Vocal approval
85. Dines at home
86. It was a Bearcat
88. Barbershop sweetheart
89. Fix brakes
90. German urge
91. Lie
92. Using a squab
94. Grate
97. W.W. II field marshal
98. Net
100. More reasonable
104. Whirl
106. Squash or melon
109. Cart or ball ending
111. Kind of luck
112. ___ and reel

89 Filmfest by Louis Sabin

ACROSS

1. Trial run
5. Italian cats
10. Least risky
16. Cast
17. Kin of auloi
18. Zenger, for one
20. Rainer's 1937 Oscar film
22. McLaglen's 1935 Oscar film, with "The"
24. George's lyricist
25. Squander
26. Pyle and Banks
28. Birthplace of Henry IV of France
29. Zing
30. Motherless calf
31. Less polished
32. George ___, baseball Hall of Famer
33. Marine mollusk
35. Carpenters' pins
36. Ranee's garb
37. Mature
38. Aplenty
39. Most uncommon
40. Scott role in a 1970 Oscar film
42. Some modern apts.
43. Humor
44. Medieval helmet
45. Babbled
46. "Platoon," e.g.
47. ___-do-well
48. Safari member
49. Tatum O'Neal's 1973 Oscar film
53. "Jamaica ___"
54. Actress Binnie
55. Crystalline amino acid
56. League of hoops
57. First name of three wives of Henry VIII
59. High points
60. Like Tithonus
61. Betimes
62. Soap plants
63. "Fatal Attraction" Oscar winner
64. Challenges anew
67. Some are racers
68. Knife expert
69. Oscar film: 1968
70. Casino employee
71. Tossed dish
72. More villainous
73. Gives access
74. Most stocky
77. Pyrrhuloxia or jacana
78. Subject of Amendment XVII
79. Pomanders
80. Former name of a Carib. island group
81. Bambi's aunt
82. "Moses" waterway
83. ___ distance (endure)
84. Mary Martin role: 1954
85. Appear afresh
87. George Burns's 1975 Oscar film, with "The"
91. Yukon vehicles
92. Teed off
93. Chooser's call
94. Magazine filler
95. Hosni's predecessor
96. Act

DOWN

1. Lemmon-MacLaine Oscar film
2. Work unit
3. Michigan region
4. Loren's 1961 Oscar film
5. Enters
6. Ebb
7. Sped
8. Asian holiday
9. His writing led to "Cabaret"
10. Slender rod
11. Palmer, et al.
12. Marching-band musician
13. Adam's grandson
14. Riv. boat
15. Modifying agent
16. "A Letter to ___ Wives"
19. Most genuine
20. Track info
21. Philistine deity
23. "I see but one ___ be clear": Stendahl
27. A sorry lot
30. Boot camp, e.g.
31. Less genial
32. Abdul-Jabbar of the Lakers
34. Metric unit
35. Edmond of "The Count of Monte Cristo"
36. Biting drama
38. Vandyke's kin
39. Prowls after prey
40. Lose one's grip
41. "Rocky" setting
42. Narrow opening
43. Clones
45. Serious risks
46. "Duck Soup" group
48. Specialized shoeworker
49. Kitchen tool
50. H. Fonda's 1981 Oscar film
51. Way overweight
52. Consumer spokesman
54. Incumbent
55. Parol
58. Panted
59. Charlotte ___, V.I.
60. Asian range
62. I. Bergman's 1956 Oscar film
63. Picks out
64. Thief
65. Stritch and May
66. Arliss's 1929 Oscar film
67. Bristlelike organs
68. Lurched
70. Most crowded
71. Japanese fare
73. Cratchit's book
74. Mack Sennett girl
75. Convinces otherwise
76. Cambridge cans
78. Suit material
79. ___ Rica
82. W. Beatty film
83. Eat, in a way
86. Brando film, with "The": 1950
88. Samovar
89. "All About ___"
90. Nectar collector

ACROSS

1. ___ Gan, Israeli city
6. Thrills for Domingo
10. In shape
13. Extreme sluggishness
19. Tony musical winner: 1980
20. Actor Mischa
21. Stir
22. One-celled organism
23. Dentist's office?
26. Underlying structure
27. Thai measure
28. Up to now
29. A Carter on TV
30. Swell
31. Garb
34. Poet who wrote "Opportunity"
35. A.L. Batting Champion: 1955
38. Mussolini's kin
39. Reason for marital breakup?
41. TV network
44. Rich dessert
45. Teeny-___
46. Lake in NW Italy
47. Become agitated
48. Upward curve of a ship's plank
49. Identical
50. Author Nin
51. ___ dixit
52. Jogger's complaint?
56. Lo-cal
57. Modernized
60. Baptism and confirmation
61. Kind of jury or larceny
62. Separated
63. Showed concern
64. Crude borax
65. Breakfast food in Dixie
66. Hall's musical partner
67. Type of periodical
68. Canary's trill
69. Tidal bores?
73. Everybody, in Bonn
74. Choice words
75. Crooner or cherry
76. Teachers' degs.
79. A.E.S. and H.S.T.
80. Yvette's sky
81. Rhône feeder
83. Commandment verb
85. Writer LeShan
86. "Equus"?
88. ___ counter

89. Actors Charlie and Martin
92. Cartoonist Gross
93. Ellington's "Mood ___"
94. Appraises
96. Nursery trio
97. Turkish title
99. Half a dance
100. "___ Fideles"
102. Square in an arena?
106. Learned
107. Craggy hill
108. ___ and anon
109. Speedily
110. Gore or gusset
111. Siamang
112. Melchior, by birth
113. "Ores" man

DOWN

1. What an ophthalmologist does
2. The Wright way?
3. Armed services
4. Pac.'s sister
5. Mai ___ (rum drink)
6. A wise herb?
7. Unseat
8. Rent
9. Qum native
10. Ribbed silk fabric
11. Pedestal object
12. Smart set
13. U.S.A.F. group
14. Muscat native
15. This is sometimes round
16. Clemens beauty?
17. R.I.P. notice
18. Risque
24. Bill and Louis
25. TV in England
32. Bank depositor's div.
33. Kind of deer
34. Dutch genre painter
35. Gold weights
36. Tall story?
37. Rover's restraint
39. Kind of truck
40. Rich
42. Inhuman
43. In a gentle way
45. Conjurer's rod
47. Chaplin's early films
49. Prune a tree, in Scotland
50. Verify
52. Crib toys
53. Salt Lake City team
54. Kitchen utensil
55. "Irresistibelle"

57. Marathoner's challenge
58. Released conditionally
59. Dentists?
61. Four noggins
63. Seasonal songs
64. Chinese secret society
66. Some are holy
67. Word on a biblical wall
69. Where cash might be stashed
70. "The ___" (Ore.'s motto)
71. Eng. foes' fast craft
72. Having tendrils
76. David Copperfield, e.g.
77. Refined grace
78. More potent
81. Type of bandage
82. Asserted without proof
83. Indonesian coin
84. Secreted
87. Displaced person
88. ___ Carlo Menotti

90. Nobelist in Literature: 1946
91. Nitrite, e.g.
94. Sitarist Shankar
95. S. Yemen seaport
96. L-Q connection
97. TV show starring Sherman Hemsley
98. Star of "American Gigolo"
101. N.Y. summer time
102. Greek letter
103. Actress Le Gallienne
104. Highlands headgear
105. Inst. in Troy, N.Y.

ACROSS

1. Singer Franklin
7. Burghoff role
12. Swedish explorer Hedin
16. Arrow-poison tree
20. Lewd one
21. Act, in a way
22. Wing: Comb. form
23. Part of TV
24. Herb's promise for kids?
27. Kemo ___
28. Acts dreamily
29. At ___ (free)
30. Takes forty winks
32. Chew the ___ (ponder)
33. Deficiency: Comb. form
34. NASA cart
35. Dill of the Bible
36. Honors
38. Jim Lawrence's advice to teetotalers?
44. Stadium surface
45. Diseases of rye
46. Orient expresser
47. Buffalo Bill
49. Upgraded trail
52. Tyke protector
54. Encapsulate
57. Sticky stuff
58. Shield border
59. More demure
63. Tops
65. Fake goldleaf
67. Agitate
68. Bonkers
69. Covered
70. Heap of stones
72. Part of the U.K.
74. All-purpose trk.
75. Fillings after drillings
77. Make a collar
79. Grandpa on "The Waltons"
81. More osseous
82. Start of Julius's phrase for a carpenter?
85. Cradle tenders
88. ___-do-well
89. Colima cover-up
90. Frightful
92. Thai's neighbor
94. Anil, e.g.
96. Challenger
97. Legal claim
98. Radiate
99. Prefix with chord or meter
101. Cabot Cove's Jessica
103. Cows, to Cowper
104. Ask repeatedly
105. Apex
106. Hoopster Manute
107. ___ Bacon products
110. Kind of bear
112. Brain passage
113. "The jig ___!"
115. Smell ___ (be suspicious)
116. Marina sights
121. Burbot
123. Harry's phrase for a goalie's crease?
128. Certain summaries
131. Kind of surgeon
132. Libation station potation
133. Smeltery pile
134. He wrote "The Brave Bulls"
135. Partner of Old Lace
137. Mouth, to a zoologist
140. Actress Massey
141. Feedbag filler
143. René's words for a lurker?
146. Soft cheese
147. Mixers' frozen assets
148. Tushington and Moreno
149. "Bridget Loves ___"
150. Koko's weapon
151. New Zealand parrots
152. About
153. Old lemons

DOWN

1. Thin silk for hoods
2. Change a shade
3. Parrot's activity
4. "...men have found a ___ love": Chesterton
5. TV's Ramsey et al.
6. Ham saver
7. Dub over
8. Arabian commander
9. Tintinnabular sound
10. To ___ (exactly)
11. Race a motor
12. Astringent
13. Last-word power
14. Notched, as a leaf
15. Horace's good news for a student?
16. Old musical syllables
17. France's wish for Marcel à la Neville?
18. Photo collection
19. Uses a gin
22. Gloat
25. Everest stat.
26. One with eagle eyes
31. A memorable Erwin
34. Actress in "Signore e Signori"
35. Hailing call
37. Fielder's boot
39. Most of the U.K.
40. Topple
41. Corn bread
42. Forte of a good hosp.
43. Kind of stick
48. Bush rival in 1988
50. Touched down
51. Galley mark
53. Gilead's lack
55. More contrite
56. Kilmer opus
59. Hunk
60. "Ecce ___," Titian painting
61. George's retail-failure admission?
62. Isole ___ (isles off Sicily)
64. Desert relief
66. Cartouche
69. T.R.'s advice to a strong mason?
70. Elm fruits
71. Thin pancake
73. Tackle
76. Opposite of hawed
78. Two, once
80. Species of wheat
83. Grant
84. Papal vestment
86. Flavoring for a Cannes cordial
87. Some NCO's
91. Sediment
92. Places
93. ___ above (better)
95. Author-lecturer Mills
97. Site of knights' fights
100. A certain fool
102. Flood
103. A tippy canoe?
104. Pod denizens
108. Author Bellow
109. Cometic path
111. Hoopla
114. Imposters
117. Wraths
118. Juliet or Cordelia
119. Shipbuilding peg
120. Tropical, herbaceous plants
122. U.S. flight org.
124. Moran and Gray
125. Lobo group
126. Most domestic
127. Minn.'s St. ___ College
128. Messy ones
129. Pine
130. Progeny
136. Exile isle
137. Leg part
138. Mal de ___
139. Algerian port
140. Angered
142. Bishopric
144. Between, in Bologna
145. Eng. title

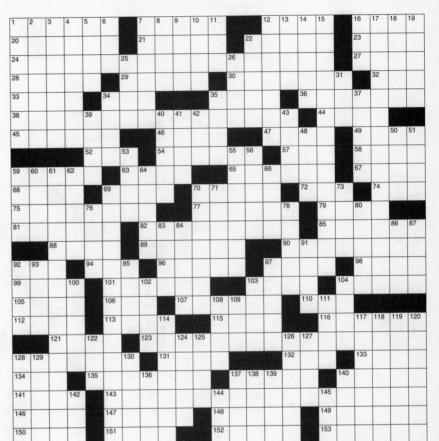

A- *by Donald V. Lee II*

ACROSS

1. Medicinal bark
7. While on the contrary
13. Finial
16. Music-industry acronym
19. Circus swing
20. Spanish city
21. Crumbly soil
22. Oil source
23. Hemingway title
25. Harden by heat
26. Harvest
27. Arrow poison
28. Eagles' nests
29. Of a religious festival
32. Basketball player
33. Pay attention
34. Settle by intervention
35. It comes in reams
36. South Pacific island group
37. Goneril's father
38. Level
40. Water from steam, e.g.
45. ___ de foie gras
46. Musical instruments
49. Diversion
50. Unexceptional
52. Former Raider QB
53. Liquid vessels
54. Small flasks
55. Thieves
56. Tolstoy et al.
57. Closely related
58. Greeted
60. Sicilian volcano
61. Sailor
62. Hurdy-gurdies
63. Brewer's yeast
66. Streetside pillars
70. Dried orchid tubers
72. Parsonage
73. Unfortunate event
75. Tenon's target
77. Suffers longing
78. Roil anew
79. Worker along the Thames
80. Flower parts
81. Dexterous
82. Spurious wing of a bird
83. Indulgent, in a way
85. Receives with approval
87. River islets
88. Couples
89. Roasting stick
91. Feel indignant
93. Elaborate meal
94. Grossly stupid
98. Restaurant order for two
100. Threaten
101. Bristlelike parts
102. French king
103. "Cavalleria" temptress
104. Cameraman
107. Early Christian pulpit
108. Carpentry need
109. Radiator adjunct
110. Resident of Haifa
111. Former Boston ace
112. City in Nev.
113. Landed properties
114. Discipline

DOWN

1. Radio interference
2. East Indian garment
3. Algerian cavalry soldier
4. Pyrexia
5. Demolish
6. Clown fish's home
7. Capital residents
8. Lifted with effort
9. Projecting rims
10. Shower
11. Lover on the run
12. Scheduled
13. Fortify
14. Budgerigar
15. Of the small intestines
16. Key work
17. Establish
18. Abele or aspen
24. Empties
30. Groovy
31. Fit to be surgically treated
34. Bad guy
36. Harnessed oxen
37. Weighted
39. Primitive family symbols
40. Qualified
41. Caucasian inhabitant
42. Part of N.A.A.C.P.
43. Ross and Rigg
44. Incensed
45. Solve grammatically
47. Close by
48. Ladies of Spain: Abbr.
51. Compass dir.
52. Brown ermines
54. Loud outcry
55. Range of view
57. Salmon or frog, e.g.
59. Household gods
61. Rove; ramble
64. Munitions depot
65. Untidy
67. Chew
68. Dravidian language
69. Former U.K. coin
70. Blaze and Brenda
71. Delineate
72. Marceau forte
73. Yugoslav town
74. Noun-forming suffix
76. Yacht race
77. Trails
79. Muscovite's land
80. Advantageous
82. Sideways
84. Complete failure
86. Precook
87. Gandhi's namesakes
89. Beats it
90. Irrational fear
92. Confine at the zoo
93. Doe or ewe
94. Weinberger et al.
95. Put back on the burner
96. Engraved pillars
97. European songbird
99. Armbones
100. Dissolve
105. Bryant or Loos
106. Hasty; reckless

93 Holiday RX's by Nancy Joline

ACROSS

1. Wilkes-___, Pa.
6. Jar of antiquity
13. Commotions
18. Sci-fi character
19. Headgear for a peer
20. Woodworking tool
21. Lady Mary Wortley Montagu's Rx?
24. Cartoonist Fisher
25. Israeli seaport
26. ___ off (angry)
27. Pacific islands
29. Diva Galli-Curci
31. Hotel ___ Invalides, Paris
32. Chit
34. S. Africa's ___ Paul Kruger
35. Consumer advocate
36. John Milton's Rx?
42. Let's assume
43. Brace
44. Opposite of sml.
45. Barnyard butter
46. Fade in the stretch
48. Change: Comb. form
51. Samples
54. John Fletcher's Rx?
58. Literary monogram
59. Former A. L. team
62. Like dark clouds
63. Midnight fluid
64. Cry of triumph
65. Sunny side of a mountain
66. Kind of jet
67. Trip segment
68. General at Gettysburg
70. River in E England
72. Gob
73. Attention getters
75. Cricket sides
77. Super-being
78. France of France
80. Me. city
81. Author of "Ulalume"
82. Tennyson's Rx?
84. Groups of three
86. Emulated Edwin Booth
87. Guidonian note
88. Pitch detector
89. Personal quirk
91. Kind of tax
93. Dance, in France
96. Sir Henry Wotton's Rx?
102. Carp
104. Honey, in prescriptions

105. Conquistador's booty
106. Rec. of brain waves
107. Picture
109. Calif. observatory
113. Abbr. in grammar
115. Director Flaherty's "Man of ___"
116. Nabokov lady
117. Byron's Rx?
121. Expunge
122. Jill or John of films
123. Part of a stage
124. Shoemakers' forms
125. States
126. Tower name

DOWN

1. Florida neighbors
2. City near San Francisco
3. Lip
4. Fix
5. Represent on the stage
6. Cause of eruptions
7. Stooge in charge
8. Imitates Polonius
9. Foursquare
10. Cousin of vague or flot
11. Bacon's Rx for becoming "a full man"?
12. F.A.A. airport serv.
13. French flatfoot
14. Spike the punch
15. Aleutian island
16. Carbolic acid
17. Kind of partner
21. Biggers' sleuth
22. Attach
23. Noon or midnight, e.g.
28. One of the "Little Women"
30. Rembrandt's birthplace
31. Base or hospital areas
33. Famed folk singer
37. Truck-stop sign
38. Indonesian island
39. Gaelic
40. Winery container
41. Correct
43. Musician's transition
47. Teraphim
49. Tony's relative
50. Pertaining to the open seas
52. Early 1900's school of painters
53. Poet-novelist May

54. Frat-party garb
55. D-day beach
56. Geometry verb
57. Perkins of the theater
60. Naturalist Edwin Way ___
61. Broadcast
64. Wonderland croquet ball
65. Menotti role
69. "___ Explain," Billie Holiday song
71. ___ up (paid)
74. "Sons and Lovers" hero
76. Sage of Greek myth
79. Work-break item
81. Bois de Boulogne, e.g.
82. Grand National or Iditarod
83. Gram or logic preceder
85. Screenwriter ___ Diamond
90. Chemical compounds

92. Film director Kurosawa
94. Odom or Post
95. Basswoods
96. Elec. unit
97. Stool pigeon
98. Site of cave temples in India
99. Israeli dance
100. Settle snugly
101. City in W Algeria
102. Cocktail accompaniment
103. Limericks man
108. They lived in Chichén Itzá
110. Harem rooms
111. A sloop has one
112. Inspires reverence in
114. Warlike Olympian
115. Tots
118. Pedro's aunt
119. Tolkien creature
120. ___ Filippo Lippi

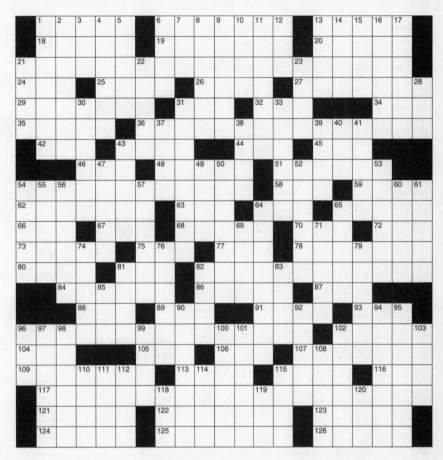

ACROSS

1. Washington city
7. Dart
12. Saint of Avila
18. Embodiment
19. Food mixture in a small mold
22. Conceive
23. Richard Strauss's flower pendant?
25. Washing utensil
26. Tatum or Ryan
27. Bakery worker
28. Verdi's philanderer?
30. Modified leaf
32. Used purchase
33. Sharklike fish
37. Cicatrix
39. Oater
44. Obeisance
45. One of the Dakotas
47. Sound from 46 Down
48. TV backdrop
49. "___ Old Cowhand"
50. Wagner's advice to Elsie the cow?
52. Service trucks
53. Sri Lankan seaport
56. Desert region
57. Scot's "own"
58. Henry James's forte
59. Pharynx tissues
61. Chubby rodents
63. Querulous
64. Area enframed by an arch
66. Muslim sacred book
68. Evaluate
71. Gone up
73. Billhooks
77. Midler or Davis
78. Thai language
79. Palmer's org.
81. Ocular pest
82. Olympic hawk
83. Wagnerian yuppie?
86. Harness part
87. Victory, in Berlin
88. Bitter vetch
89. Dialect
90. Locust
92. Attired
94. Played for a fool
95. Sire
97. Lagoon shapers
99. "___ is an island": Donne
100. Meyerbeer's bottom line?
104. River in Central Africa
105. Betel palm
110. Go back

111. Wagner's short-order cook?
115. Fielding novel
116. Fish sauce
117. Panay seaport
118. The woad plant
119. Indian antelope
120. Journalist James

DOWN

1. Poi source
2. Eden's earldom
3. Pomander
4. Great Barrier Island
5. Postman's pickup
6. Prince Valiant's son
7. Disconnected, as notes
8. Spicy stew of game
9. Gen. Bradley
10. Rect. figure
11. Pacific porgy
12. W Austrian native
13. Roman officials
14. M. Clair
15. Shrine Bowl team
16. Printer's direction
17. Baltic island
20. French painter: 1881–1955
21. Goddess of discord
24. Prevaricator
29. King Arthur's nephew
31. Her mate is ruff
32. South African coin
33. Porcelain
34. Proceeded toward a target, with "in"
35. Icon
36. Puccini's advice to his dallying heroine?
37. Treats a fever?
38. African river
40. Puccini's vacation activity in India?
41. Singer John
42. "Tears" poet
43. ___ Parker (busybody)
46. Ram's ma'am
47. Sharpens, with "up"
50. Rich source
51. Highlands Celt
54. Shiner
55. Receptacles for coal
58. A virus, for short
60. Worthless trifles
62. Drooping
63. Kong's first love
65. Opera trailer
67. Lollapalooza
68. Humble

69. Canary's relative
70. Do a conn job
72. Lyric poem
74. Put on
75. Fine cloth fiber
76. Fat: Comb. form
78. "___ the Flies," Golding novel
80. Japanese mountain
83. Entire; complete
84. Snake sound
85. Give courage
90. Turkish chief
91. Coterie
93. "Quality Street" playwright
94. Extreme
96. Cassowary's cousin
98. Rescind
99. Silent-screen star
100. Lobster pot
101. Blood: Comb. form
102. Arden and Queler
103. Lucy van ___, in "Peanuts"
104. Señorita's fingernails
106. Letters from Greece
107. Exude
108. A Gypsy language
109. Presently
112. Mos. and mos.
113. Call ___ day
114. Rifle range at Saint-Cyr

ACROSS

1. Early seafarer
4. Antic
9. Stonecrop
14. Decadent
20. Hail to Caesar!
21. Titania's man
23. Valor; virtue
24. Russian czar: 1645–76
25. Boozer
26. Nice
29. Nicer
31. Expect
32. Quarters and quavers
33. Capacious
34. Solos times eight
36. Shylock's pound
38. "G.W.T.W." group
41. "Lohengrin" role
42. Green cup
43. Stood up
44. Cowboy gear
46. Buck
50. Bias
51. Raiders' ex-coach
52. Netherlands township
55. Letter opener
56. Comic's forte
58. Interstices
59. Tangy
61. Tangier
63. Drag
64. Disconnects
66. To take off, at de Gaulle
67. Dash
68. Clears the slate
69. Libertine
70. Avoid bogey
73. Flat
77. Flatter
80. Forage plant
81. Take cover
82. OPEC members
85. Driving areas
86. He's unique, so to speak
87. Early astronaut
90. Hawks fly here
91. Better
96. Best
98. Diatonic spans
99. Flowering
100. Galba's successor
101. Court hindrance
102. Decreased?
103. Actress Burstyn
104. Churchman
106. More auspicious
107. Parts of carts
108. African pastureland
110. Southern Johnnies
114. Meese and Muskie
115. Nirvana
116. Sensitive plant
118. Former coin of Austria
119. Secret passers
121. Filling station for camels
122. Rainy
124. Rainier
130. Plumber's joint
131. Kind of price
132. Rough-edged
133. Rice, in China
134. W.C.'s chickadee
135. Japanese religion
136. "Dancers Resting" painter
137. Surfeits
138. Junk mail

DOWN

1. Pain in the neck
2. Declaration
3. Oxford lengths
4. Le ___ de Monte Cristo
5. Busy as ___
6. Five of trumps
7. "___ tu," "Ballo" aria
8. Turner
9. Madras dresses
10. Horace's "he was"
11. Phrontistery
12. All-purpose trk.
13. Most contemptible
14. Aristotelian element
15. Escape
16. Actor Parker
17. Outside: Comb. form
18. Shooting match for Jacques
19. W. Erhard's therapy
22. Stair post
27. Merit
28. Bridge site
30. Drat!
35. Scorch
36. Money for Monet
37. Opposite of brevis
38. Tenor Bergonzi
39. Javelin
40. Balance-sheet entry
43. Faye and Cooper
44. Less arcane
45. Holey roller
47. Harem room
48. Eye part
49. Recent
50. Struck
51. Disencumber
52. Young Athenian
53. Caller, in a way
54. Is comparable to
56. Pentateuch
57. Savings for sr. citizens
58. John Jacob
60. Of an armbone: Comb. form
61. Grappa's cousin
62. "Desire hath ___": Burton
65. Roberta or Bernadette
70. Simon acquaintance
71. In ___ (so to speak)
72. Oppose
74. Anyone that
75. Clinked
76. Brainstorms
77. Greek theater
78. Napa trailer
79. Over
82. Pine martens' kin
83. Poet who invented the dithyramb
84. Look ___ (respect)
87. TV hookups
88. Italian dynasty
89. Rhine tributary
91. French river
92. Pungent
93. Discontinues
94. Roof pointer
95. Annie and Monty
97. Reine's mate
100. Michigan car maker
103. Were
104. Hanger hangouts
105. Santa ___ Islands
107. Shake ___ (hurry)
108. Border stamp
109. Gives off
111. Dermal affliction
112. Folk song
113. Manners
115. Five in a row!
116. Karpov coups
117. Expert
118. Levees
119. Tibia's locale
120. Half a quarter gallon
121. Pelion supporter
123. Relative of a wheeze
124. What, in Weimar
125. Etna ejecta
126. Vail verb
127. Vein's glory
128. Strong ale
129. "___ Vidderne," long Ibsen poem

96 Sci-Fi Fantasies by John M. Samson

ACROSS

1. Milady
6. Epps of "Higher Learning"
10. Epic
14. Avow
19. Berries
20. Divergence
22. Roo's mom
23. Wells sequel to "Jude the Obscure"?
25. Garret
26. Genet play, with "The"
27. Bribed
28. "Storm" novelist
29. Maple fruit
32. Pianist Peterson
33. Trilled like a grasshopper
34. Old French coin
35. City on the Songka River
37. Drawing rooms
39. E. E. Smith cousin of "I Am a Camera"?
42. Manhandle
45. Bustle
46. S. C. river
47. Throw out
49. Holm or key
51. Fissure
53. Doggone!
54. Sprightly
55. Rose's enemy
56. Sacred
58. Hollandaise, e.g.
59. Zealous
60. Ende book that's hard to put down?
65. Robots
66. Fronton basket
67. Vidi, in English
68. Diva Marilyn
69. Rivera of stage fame
70. Beau Brummel
72. Lille's department
76. Slovene or Slovak
77. John Ridd's Lorna
78. Cable company
80. Resort of SW France
81. Idle hours
83. Tolkien book about the World Trade Center?
86. Bedouins
88. N.Y. city
89. Danube tributary
90. Singular
93. Walking on the Rue Royale
95. Of the number six
96. Nocturnal mammals
97. Novelist Jong
98. "Now I ___ down . . ."
100. Brick building
101. Pohl book about Fishburne?
106. Befuddle
107. Intrudes
108. Actress Shire
109. King salmons
110. Wilbur or Nemerov
111. Eleonora of "Cenere"
112. Sticky stuff

DOWN

1. Inner frame
2. Alas, to Arndt
3. Cutting tool
4. Aesopian characters
5. Mosque turrets
6. "Amores" poet
7. Bulk
8. "Exodus" hero
9. Part of a cell
10. Roman burial stone
11. Marksmen
12. Prod
13. "___ Veronica," Wells book
14. Activity in which camels may be executed
15. Adams book about the Nautilus?
16. Program in
17. Nimble
18. Rushed
21. Ballerina Alonso
24. ___ Dolorosa
28. Whoop
29. Up to now
30. Tolerate
31. City SW of Buenos Aires
32. Assault
33. Clepsydra, e.g.
35. Shakespearean drama
36. Stage org.
38. Gone up
40. Scoops for soups
41. Chilean poet
43. End of a Poe title
44. "Historia naturalis" author
48. "I conquered," to Caesar
50. S. C. summer time
52. Lem novel about Mike Tyson?
54. Danza's "Taxi" role
55. "Thou ___ lady": Kingsley
57. Wave on la mer
58. Sonnet unit
59. Postulate
60. King in "Peer Gynt"
61. Dike, Eunomia and Irene
62. Parroted
63. Hold back
64. Judge, in Judges
65. Some A. L. batters
69. Marine collective
70. Fussed over
71. Meat packers' union
73. "Werther," for one
74. Less manifold
75. Long unused
77. "La Dame aux camélias" playwright
78. Discharged
79. El Capitan locale
82. Evening gatherings
84. Cry to the hounds
85. Winter apple
87. Wrap of Juarez
90. Country, to Nietzsche
91. Rice field
92. Lyric poem
94. Embroidery loop
95. ___ Darya, Asian river
97. Author Wortman
98. Vientiane locale
99. "Comus" composer
101. Marceau character
102. Nashville col.
103. U.N. agency
104. Veto
105. Author Talese

ACROSS

1. Tiny Tim's problem
9. Water wheel
14. Hornbills
19. Like sandstone
20. Cheddar colorer, sometimes
22. To shine, in Sedan
23. Cross Word Puzzle
26. Filmdom terrier
27. ___-de-boeuf
28. Like J. Fred Muggs
29. Hindu's camel
30. Early Olds
31. Toothed bars
33. Suppresses
35. Encircled
39. Stratum
40. Cabbage
41. Perfumes
43. Slice of bacon
45. Again and again
49. "Welcome ___," Altman film
50. DeSoto or Hudson
51. Aleutian island
53. Divagate
54. This covers the world
57. French condiment
59. Scottish cap
61. Flagged down
63. Fannie or Ginnie follower
64. Essay
66. Club clubber
68. Cross Word Puzzle
73. To find, to a fra
74. Crusty entrees
75. Had a hero
76. Dance in 3/4 time
77. P.I.
78. Rating number
79. Poem's chapter
81. Foreshadow
82. G.I.'s need
85. Lisper's hurdle
87. Carbon particles
89. Anchorage
91. In the thick of
93. Honors
97. W.W. II hero Murphy
99. "___ and Sane Fourth" Masson
101. Grommet
102. Like zebras
105. Writer of ridicule
107. Prior, to Prior
108. Yak
109. Man in the van
111. Noah's eldest
113. Lagomorph
114. Cross Word Puzzle
118. Key
119. Lampooned
120. Escorted
121. Noblemen
122. Young bulls, in Yorkshire
123. Woven together

DOWN

1. Smiley's creator
2. Middle of a Stein line
3. Sheepskins
4. Actress Purviance
5. Wit or pick preceder
6. Mediterranean entrant
7. Craftier
8. Ongoing shows
9. Engine encl.
10. Cross Word Puzzle
11. Weapons for Lafitte
12. Sundries
13. Longfellow's bell town
14. Ma's doting
15. Oscar winner: 1985
16. Welsh onion
17. Dane's dollar
18. Fourth canonical hours
21. In some respect
24. Claudia ___ Johnson
25. Within: Comb. form
32. Author McFadden
34. A U.N. arm
36. Wooden clog
37. Genesis man
38. Deg. for a legal eagle
40. Lincoln Ctr. attraction
42. Spring break
44. Gammon
46. El Greco became one
47. Orator Edward
48. Kelly or Beatty
50. Indicator of pitch
52. No sirrees
54. Spirit, to the Sun King
55. April 15
56. Student, hopefully
58. Raison d'___
60. Elem. number
62. One, in Ayr
64. Spaniard's yearly income
65. Act listless
66. French cheese district
67. H. C. Andersen's birthplace

69. Sir Edmund P. Hillary, e.g.
70. "___ been had!"
71. Makes a choice
72. ___ gratias
76. Canaille
77. Hundred-___ shot
79. Apograph
80. To ___ (precisely)
83. Damsels
84. Curie title
86. Jazzman Kenton
88. Suffix with verb or herb
90. Wagoner's command
92. "Who ___ call Himself a man": Cummings
93. Glowed anew
94. Cinema's Little
95. Earthy; worldly
96. Headed the committee
98. Mark for removal
100. Garibaldi, e.g.
102. Cash substitute
103. The ones here
104. Winchester, for one
105. Face card?
106. Dovetail wedge
110. Dice throw
112. Colleague of suffragette Stanton
113. Hindu spring festival
115. Some coll. linemen
116. Hearths: Abbr.
117. Like sushi

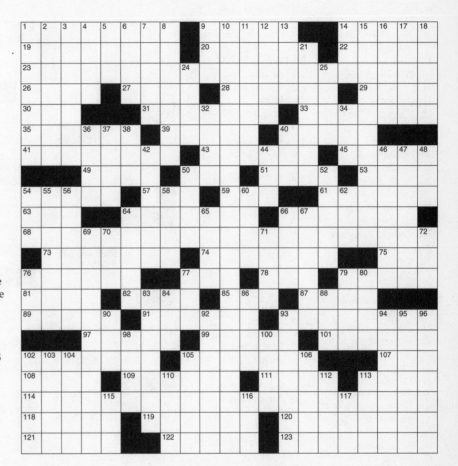

ACROSS

1. Ms. Picasso
7. Start of a famous speech of defiance
12. Dead Sea ___
18. Ethically neutral
19. Clarsach player
21. Capital of Taiwan
22. Effect
23. Herod ___ I
24. Mesh
25. Female goat
26. Mister, in Munich
28. Small snake
29. Gist
31. A drug, for short
32. Speech: Part II
36. River at Zaragoza
39. African antelope
40. Rio ___ Plata, S.A. estuary
41. Hebrew prophet
45. Struggles clumsily
48. Trellises
51. Quoits players
52. Arab garb
55. Large mackerels
56. Speech: Part III
61. Knock
62. Bantu language
63. Le jour de ___ (New Year's Day): Fr.
64. Eating place
68. Forbid
73. Panhandle
74. Pointer
78. Also not
79. Bargain word
83. ___ de guerre
84. In a foolish way
88. Speech: Part IV
93. Chaplains, to G.I.'s
95. N.J. river
96. W.W. II German cipher machine
99. Warning
100. Coiner?
101. Formicidae
103. Attu native
104. Actress Pitts
105. Crucifix
106. Trickle
108. "___ la Douce," 1963 movie
109. End of the speech
115. Activity during a riot
118. "Uhuru" author
119. Recesses
123. Skill, in Sedan
124. Remove by dissolving
125. Victors in Gaul
126. Wapiti's cousin
127. Contents of an onomasticon
128. One who attempts

DOWN

1. Salaried
2. Ordinance item, for short
3. Easy gait
4. Mouths
5. Papier ___
6. Kind of ego
7. Joker
8. Printers' mistakes
9. Silly
10. Tore
11. Psychic's claim
12. Bargain
13. Bel ___ (singing style)
14. Fix
15. Gemstone
16. Gangster Diamond
17. Schumann product
19. Conceal
20. Sri Lanka group
27. Student's new chance
30. Pass
32. Building promoters
33. Parts of a cent.
34. "___ Geordie," 1956 movie
35. ___ square (honest)
36. Salamander
37. Moral flaw
38. ___-ha-Shanah
42. Blackbird
43. Buccal
44. Mil. draft org.
46. Spanish baby girls
47. Hang loosely
49. Passage
50. "The Merry Widow" composer
52. Actress Alicia
53. Word of disdain
54. Witch bird
57. "Beauty ___ the eye . . ."
58. Had chits out
59. Eng. prof's degree
60. Skid-row denizen
64. Youngster's 2 Down
65. G.O.P. member
66. Lists of things to be done
67. Get one's goat
69. The Bee Gees, e.g.
70. Entity
71. Mountain pass
72. Rugby play
75. Motionless
76. "___ fan tutte," Mozart opera
77. Wife of King Latinus
80. Rotten
81. Newsy note
82. Jolson and Pacino
85. Paris-to-Senlis dir.
86. Sight from Taormina
87. Land in ancient Palestine
89. In a tumult
90. Mark or Mamie
91. Certain beards
92. I come in: Sp.
93. La___, Bolivia
94. Ga. neighbor
97. It's the word
98. ___ loss (puzzled)
100. Fish or war follower
102. Infield hit
105. Car-wash step
107. Israeli leader
110. Seine tributary
111. A Sudanese people
112. First author of the "Oz" books
113. Commedia dell'___
114. Clothing, informally
115. Roman household deity
116. Lyric poem
117. ___ Peak, Ariz.
120. Trifle
121. Moss Hart's "Act ___"
122. Ukr., once

99 Twinkle, Twinkle . . . *by John Greenman*

ACROSS

1. ". . . a tall ship and
   ___ steer her by":
   Masefield
5. Actor Hoffman
11. Little Iodine's
    creator
16. "___ moss-trooping
    Scot was he": Scott
19. U.S. columnist
20. Like some beds
21. Standoffish
22. Chinese dynasty
24. Very meager pay
26. Texas
28. Drain
29. Lowest points
30. Groups of three
32. Small change
33. On hand
35. Baseball pitch
36. Dennis and Duncan
37. Fatigue symptom
39. Turner of TNT
40. Fishing net
41. Binds
42. Daylight dimmers
44. Ratifies
45. Defaults
47. Half a score
50. Manned a shell
51. Military bigwig
54. Soft cheese
55. Residue
56. Hershiser et al.
57. Valhalla V.I.P.
58. Flunky
59. Effortlessness
60. French composer
61. Timber wolves
63. Nagged
65. Sell out
67. Rome's river
68. Mount ___, Jordan
69. Bard's "before"
70. Share top billing
73. Parish-Perkins tune:
    1934
77. Ukr., once
78. Sol.
79. Ft. soldiers
80. Mosquito
81. Became cheerful
83. Thusly: Colloq.
85. Tamar's half-
    brother
86. Swap
88. Fox terrier of films
92. Myrna's kinfolk
93. "___ a man with
    seven wives"
94. "A Rage to Live"
    author
95. Wan
96. A biol. sci.

97. Figurative signs of
    joy
100. Of ___
     (undistinguished)
101. Together: Comb.
     form
102. City: Ger.
103. Nitrous ___
     (laughing gas)
104. Melodic
105. Quotidian
107. Black tea
108. Fine, mod style
110. Natives: Suffix
111. Be calculating
113. Movable pointer
115. Some Italian
     singers
117. Bolivian city
118. Sword
119. ___ Sark, a Channel
     Islands ruler
120. Glasgow veto
123. A discarded title
     for "G.W.T.W."
125. "When ___ sang
     together . . .": Job
     38:7
128. Verb ending
129. Al ___ (chewy)
130. Author Welty
131. Activates anew
132. Sounds seeking
     silence
133. ___ down (scold)
134. Double dagger
135. Being, to Brutus

DOWN

1. Edison's middle
   name
2. Blue gems
3. Preschooler
4. Vent one's view
5. Scottish port
6. Relax
7. Fashionable
8. Shoelace ends
9. Cyprinoid fish
10. Young bird
11. A binary
    compound
12. Solo
13. Coloring agent
14. Former Brooklyn
    pitcher
15. "A pair ___ cross'd
    lovers . . .": Shak.
16. Accompany
17. G.I. publication
18. Poker pot
19. Spectral types
23. Scottish headland
25. Ovens
27. Isolated rocks
31. Washer cycle

34. Promise-breaker
35. Feel effects of a
    head blow
36. Dormer part
37. Habitat
38. Bow or Barton
40. Fuse ores
41. ___ Carlo Menotti
43. Dentist's deg.
44. State firmly
45. Brimmed headgear
46. Doric column edge
48. Sea ducks
49. Indigent person
51. Misrepresent as
    genuine
52. Goddess of peace
53. Prize eponym
54. Prevent
60. "___ Use Raising a
    Shout": Auden
61. Bed sheets, etc.
62. Nigerian V.I.P.'s
63. French nobleman
64. New Guinea
    people
66. "___ Born"
67. Commotion
68. Alaskan Indians
70. Maria of opera

71. Like some omelets
72. TV roles for Glaser
    and Soul
74. Plaint
75. Slowly, to Solti
76. Trumpet
82. Fervor
84. Part of i.e.
85. In the thick of
86. Bara of silents
87. Comedienne
    Martha
89. Meteors
90. Clipped
91. Poker payments
93. "Je dis," in English
94. Basketry twig
95. Swiss river
97. Take by surprise
98. Lariat loop
99. Urged
102. Carly or Paul
104. City SE of
     Cleveland
106. High hideaways
107. Ballet movements
108. Honshu seaport
109. Verdi works
111. Loudness unit
112. Irritable

113. Chili con ___
114. Whipper-snappers
115. Greek isle
116. Flaming
118. Remorseful one
119. "___ Dinah," 1958
     hit tune
121. Phoenician love
     goddess
122. Ar successor
124. Bizarre
126. Hawaiian syndicate
127. Vane dirs.

ACROSS

1. Arethusas, e.g.
7. Calif. white oak
11. Complete defeats
15. Carp-family member
19. Gone up
20. In ___ (bogged down)
21. Rung
22. Insect stage
23. With no sweat
25. Puccini heroine
26. Informed on
27. Glance askance
28. Anglo-Saxon dialect
30. Alabama commodity
31. Irregularly notched
32. Sets free
33. Plumbism
35. Uttered
36. Variegated chalcedony
37. Dobbin's fare
38. Foster's "De ___ Races"
42. Zambezi feeder
43. Kind of table
47. Arabian gazelles
48. Fen
49. Overwhelm
50. Plant angle
51. Suppose
52. Inborn
54. Prats
55. Unlikely
56. Sapience
57. Uses an exit
58. Paravane
59. Fling about
60. Overalls fabric
61. One of the Seven Wonders
63. Emulates Hirt
66. Expenses
68. Tomcat
70. Hirsute
71. Fabulist
72. Heisman, e.g.
74. Tantrums
76. Algonquian spirit
77. Huge land mass
78. Crowd response
79. Cringes with fear
80. Michelangelo, to Lorenzo
81. Greffier or chartulary
83. Opposite of 12 Down
84. Intersection
85. Cartel acronym
86. Gauntlets
87. Glyph
88. Maypop
92. S. European liquor
93. "G.W.T.W." locale
97. Age
98. Ruined photographs
100. Waiter's notes
101. Type of bean or horse
102. Devil's delight
103. Absolute
105. Tatting output
106. Actress-singer Carter
107. Bogus
108. Midday
109. January, in Ibiza
110. You are, in Mexico
111. Jack or Robert
112. Intuits

DOWN

1. Sibyl
2. Tree
3. Urticaria
4. French river or department
5. Dad's refuge
6. Daughters' mates
7. Declaimed violently
8. Stocks
9. Oner
10. Linguistics expert
11. Beaked
12. Alfresco
13. Shoe part
14. Cervantes or Velázquez
15. Melancholy
16. Nicolo of Cremona
17. Swiss district
18. Seasonal beverage
24. Abrading action
29. Chicago embrace?
34. Condescend
35. Runner or rhizome
36. Al ___, Cairo newspaper
38. Orange food
39. Neighborhoods
40. Of minute proportions
41. Indian tea
42. Largest of the Tremiti Islands
43. Raggedy Ann or Andy
44. Kidnapper, e.g.
45. Aspire
46. Type of gold or paradise
48. Roman Catholic title
49. Shapes
52. Numismatic unit
53. Amends
54. Fires; axes
56. Is indebted
58. Reactionary
60. Weak-minded, in Dixie
62. Gig implements
64. Siberian forest
65. Classified
67. Marksman
69. Like some lenses
70. Owls
71. Former monetary units of Riga
72. Poi base
73. Abie's beloved
74. Box chaser
75. Makeup applicator
76. Type of code
78. Assemble anew
80. Legal clauses
82. ___ gratia
83. Profitable holes
84. Awry
86. Nimbus
87. January birthstone
88. Streisand hit
89. Relating to bees
90. Bracket for candles
91. Peggy Lee hit
92. Puckers
93. Conch-shell blowing demigod
94. Male dreamboat
95. Aptly named novelist
96. Kingdom of Burgundy, once
99. Naut. detection apparatus
104. Part of a chord

101 *Craft-y Shenanigans* by Arthur S. Verdesca

ACROSS

1. Festoon
5. City in Egypt
10. Expression
14. "___ a horse with wings!": Shak.
18. Islamic judge
19. Be obtrusively conspicuous
20. Sacher or Linzer
21. Director Clair
22. Yonder
23. Chinese pleasure craft?
25. Old strongbox
26. Feed feasters
28. Eurasian region of Middle Ages
29. Good-for-nothing
31. Appeals
33. Remove TV broadcast
34. Surfeit
35. Adieu, in Bath
37. Some buoys
39. Lacrimator
42. Tires
45. Dummy
47. Psalm verse ender
49. "Twelfth Night" heroine
50. Hind
51. ___ Rapids, city in Minn.
53. Lesions
55. One-eyed god
56. Countertenor
58. Suitcase marker
60. Round
62. "___ Merrilies," Keats poem
63. Boa
65. Brief piece of writing
67. Cause: Fr.
69. Entanglement
70. Valor
71. "___ Get Started With You," 1936 song
72. Denmark's ___ Islands
73. Type of maid
74. Finder of the Holy Grail
77. Birthplace of Hippocrates
78. Quarrel
80. During
82. Soccer great
83. Actress Sommer
85. Daughter of David
87. He was Hutch on TV
88. Kid
89. Property claims
91. French pioneer in treating the mentally ill
93. British actor Roger ___
95. Giant jets
96. Clayware
98. Knob on a pipe organ
100. Check for Checkers
102. Canadian lake
103. Ovid's "you love"
105. 1965 U.S. Open winner
108. Stuck
111. Capital of Laconia
113. Exultant
115. River mouth
116. Don Giovanni, as a seaman?
119. Cry on a roller coaster
120. Bureau attachment
121. Was mistaken
122. N.Y. city
123. ___-majesty
124. Gainsay
125. Fume
126. Front cover of a book
127. Monoski, e.g.

DOWN

1. Hilum
2. Disk for sealing letters
3. Apothegm
4. Long-necked vessels?
5. Avers
6. Erwin of early TV
7. Penury
8. Indo-European
9. Set in order
10. President of France: 1954–59
11. Four in refrigerators
12. Fret
13. A-Q combo, in bridge
14. Handel specialty
15. Transport protectors?
16. Ever
17. Authentic
20. High order of angels
24. Nobelist in Literature: 1957
27. Site of Gray herd
30. Pole, e.g.
32. Shipboard psychiatry?
36. Wheezer's menace
38. Great Lakes vessel?
39. Slumber on a two-master?
40. Strange
41. Ratted
42. Land of Qum
43. Aïda or Radamés
44. Phrase for a disorderly sailer?
46. Japanese galley utensils?
48. Pt. of E.T.A.
52. Mother-of-pearl
54. Fur seal
57. Tom Joad, e.g.
58. Boil down
59. First name of a memorable loner
61. Horologe face
64. Alphabet: Abbr.
66. Hollywooders going steady
68. Photo
72. Book leaf
75. Landed
76. American Socialist: 1855–1926
77. Large seaweed
79. Friend, in Angers
81. Affaire d'honneur
84. Plea
86. Recorded anew
90. Fortune-teller
92. Miller protagonist
94. Italian gulf
95. Boat covers?
97. Polishing machine
99. Kind of car or maid
101. Bando of baseball
104. Orarion
106. ___ Levy, Cohan's first wife
107. "Tears" poet
108. Start of a kindergarten chant
109. "Divine Comedy" illustrator
110. Bell the cat
111. Ferret out
112. With, to Pierre
114. Quitclaim
117. Uno e due
118. Graze

102 The Anglo-Hebraic Way *by Bernard Meren*

ACROSS

1. Bushel's partner, in song
5. Dippy or dotty
9. Rec. measures
13. Packed away
19. Opposite of aweather
20. Turgenev's birthplace
21. Ham___ (emote)
22. Balzac
23. Kin of rhoncus in the bronchus
24. Yemeni capital
25. Hawaii's bird
26. Ulster town
27. S P A C E R
30. Avian midwives?
31. Auction chaser
32. Bro or sis
33. Murray and West
34. African antelope
35. S N I V E L
41. Street in a horror film
44. Eatery order
45. Long. sidekick
46. Famed muralist
47. Hindu Kush's locale
48. Pilasters
51. U.S. motor capital
52. "Vaya con___," 1953 song
54. Unsightly
55. Ululate
56. ___ cordiale
60. Readies an oven
62. D E V I L
64. Haw., once
65. Prefix for adroit
66. Sordino
67. Double DI
68. Hammett canine
70. Numbers' person
73. Lion's pad
75. S T R E S S E D
78. Comes in again
82. Vacuum tube
83. Breakout at high school
84. Leed's river
85. Deal-consummating word
87. Abbr. in a to-let ad
88. Pipe
89. Place to place tokens
90. Skater Babilonia and namesakes
92. Small whale
93. Arm of the Med.
94. L.B.J. beagle
95. S P O R T S

101. Mountain in Thessaly
104. Product of a Spanish pine
105. Philippine volcano
106. A Greek goddess of vengeance
107. Flock of turkeys
109. L E V E R
113. Greek
114. "Mary Magdalene" painter
115. Mopsus or Melampus
116. Greet
117. Metal balls used in pétanque
118. Egyptian solar deity
119. Radiator sound
120. Blast or carp precursor
121. Make jagged
122. Twerp's cousin
123. Being, in Barcelona
124. Haricot, for one

DOWN

1. Unit equivalent to 3.26 light years
2. Beetle type
3. Relish-tray item
4. Bewail, Irish style
5. A 1982 Oscar winner
6. Land fit for cultivation
7. Actress Rowlands
8. Opposite of apterous
9. Aural insensitivity
10. Audio systems
11. Castigated
12. Little sea pike
13. Kind of fir or cypress
14. Role for Todd or Silverheels
15. "___ of Old Smoky"
16. C A R E S
17. Composer Satie
18. Reps.' rivals
28. Fanon
29. Hit, old style
36. D. Arnaz's costar
37. Building wing
38. Badger's African cousin
39. Stumble
40. To use, to Nero
42. Rhythmic cadence
43. The Say Hey Kid
47. Menuhin's teacher
48. Polite interruption
49. Smoked salmon

50. D E N I M
51. Device for collecting plankton
53. Vessel with a long, sharp prow
56. Habituates
57. Thread: Comb. form
58. Bis
59. Fiat
61. Kind of master or hunter
63. Skip
68. State of lawlessness
69. Mil. banners
71. ___ colada
72. Copycat
74. A contemporary of Loti
76. Did the human thing
77. Top kick
78. Madcap
79. Haste, in Hanover
80. Calais entrée
81. Scoria from a volcano
86. Separate
88. Infatute

91. "Well-boiled icicles" man
92. Uppity one
93. Calumniate
95. Least furnished
96. Coil about
97. Hardest to find
98. Swimming, in heraldry
99. Gold look-alike
100. Star of "Bombshell"
102. Fence straddler
103. Aeschylus's "___ Against Thebes"
107. Physics Nobelist: 1944
108. Steinbeck character
109. Herring measure in Hereford
110. S. African fox
111. Check
112. "___ Funny That Way"

103 50 K's by Sandy Graf

ACROSS

1. Newsstand
6. Large brown bear
12. Flair
17. Klingon foe
21. Painter-writer Kokoschka
22. Anxiety, in Aix
23. King of Hollywood
24. Yemeni seaport
25. Destiny
26. N.Z. songbird
28. Composer Luigi ___
29. Russian river
30. Blackguards
32. Peon's mite
33. Fanatic
35. Yellow-fever mosquito
36. Sale sign
37. Cold-climate craft
39. Org. founded in 1915
42. Junket
43. Patch of land
44. Tarbell, e.g.
48. "Merry Mount" composer: 1934
50. Laughing jackasses
52. Philip Johnson's org.
53. Singer Baker
54. French physician-novelist: 1894–1961
56. Originator of Jellicle Cats
57. Richmond V.I.P. set
58. Recoil
59. Delirious
60. Primary locations
61. Actor Sam: 1891–1984
63. Calligraphers' needs
64. Catkin
65. Stick with these!
66. Whalebone
67. Compass pt.
68. "Either/Or" questioner
70. Hearth shelves
71. Massive mammals, for short
73. Standing start
74. Documentary film hero
75. Legendary victims of the Romans
77. De Mille epic with "The": 1927
81. ___ Cruces
84. Conjured up
85. Actress Hope or Jessica
86. Palindromic French quisling
87. Gasp
88. More pleasant
89. Signs on
90. Hairy herb
91. Luncheon follower
92. Post station in India
93. "Lili" film composer

94. Coronation gown
95. Buckwheat cereal
96. All-purpose trk.
97. Zorba's creator
99. Devilish
100. Betty Boop quality
102. Solar disk
103. Integument
105. Admiralty abbr.
106. Tarsus
107. Pastoral poem
108. Mr. Spock's father in "Star Trek"
109. Shrub of the rose family
112. "And giving ___ . . ."
113. Deep-seated
114. "Keystone" character
117. Part of 39 Across
118. Indian tobacco mixture
122. Skewer
124. Hindu discipline
125. Play the part
126. Aria for two
127. Mr. Kovacs
128. Jedi's furry friend
129. Advantages
130. Teeter
131. Bumpkin

DOWN

1. "The Mikado" executioner
2. Baroness Blixen, a.k.a.___ Dinesen
3. Gumbo basic
4. Danson role in "Cheers"
5. Eruption site: 1883
6. Beethoven trio, Op. 121a
7. Hardy one
8. Salaam preliminaries
9. Blue flag
10. Qty.
11. Memento
12. Russian beer
13. Bilbao boy
14. Nabokov title
15. Daunt: awe
16. Coconino County cutie
17. A Hawaiian
18. Iconoclast's target
19. "Splitsville," once
20. Clove hitch, e.g.
27. First president of Mali
31. Broadway gas
34. Listeners
36. Forth
37. Russian islands
38. Circus performers: Abbr.
39. Jeans' alternative
40. Screenwriters Garson and Michael

41. Sen. Bradley was one
43. Grosse ___, Mich.
44. Pondered
45. Gossip's delight
46. Noted French engineer
47. Poe-tic birds
49. N.Y.S.E. abbr.
50. Klemperer role
51. "Let independence ___ boast": Hopkinson
54. Carved gemstones
55. Baseball's Crab or Hoot
59. Bestowed abundantly
60. Founder of famed Academy
61. ___ Starker, famed cellist
62. Palo singer?
65. Yardstick
66. Bracelet, e.g.
68. Pittsburgh slugger, turned announcer
69. Tam-tams
70. Direct
72. Raise or increase sharply
74. Abounding with snow

75. Takeoff
76. Emulate Odom
77. Namesakes of 2 Down
78. Lifeless
79. Gold coin in Edam
80. Small racing vehicles
82. Key work
83. Places
85. Digestive enzyme
87. ___ de soie (cloth for dresses)
89. Filbert
90. Actor-folk singer from Vienna
93. City in Ill.
94. Noisy grasshoppers
95. "Cuckoo's Nest" builder
97. Cattle, in poesy
98. Handel's "___ the Priest"
99. Regimen
101. Ancient temple site
103. Female saint: Lat.
104. City on the Vistula
107. F.D.R. and D.D.E., e.g.
108. Swivets
109. Celestial terrier?
110. Till

111. Shakespearean baddie
112. End of vigil
113. Arrow poison
114. Quirk
115. Steinbeck protagonist
116. Strip off
119. N.Y.C. subway
120. Worn-out horse
121. Cloud, to Baudelaire
123. In favor of

104 Roman Infusion by June A. Boggs

ACROSS

1. Radio's "Our ___ Sunday"
4. Honored with entertainment
9. Hamper
14. Douglas Fairbanks Sr. role
19. A land in S.A.
20. Love feast
21. Houston gridder
22. Wild blue yonder
23. Gloaming
24. Type of sermon
27. Groom's milieu
29. Beat, in a way
30. Give forth
31. Baudelaire's "Les Fleurs du ___"
32. "B.C." character
33. Prepare
35. Corkers
37. Vehicle in a Monroe film
38. Cupidinous
40. Elmer Gantry's wife
41. "Family Ties" role
42. Span member
43. Compeer
45. Stem joint
47. Stem
49. Bond foe
53. "...Lord is ___ indeed": Luke 24:34
54. "Trust ___," 1934 song
55. Sign-language developer
56. Anadama or panettone
59. Roman attachment
63. Trifle
64. ___ were (seemingly)
65. Forward
66. Display pretentiously
67. Time piece
68. Roman magistrate
70. Drop-lid desks
72. Eureka!
73. "The Queen of the ___": Rice
75. Having color
77. Wood sorrels
78. Thrash
79. Harvard president: 1869–1909
80. He's often robbed
81. Scotch ingredient
82. Common contraction
83. Storied pachyderm
85. Frank Sinatra
88. Kind of box
90. He "loves mambo"
92. Confound it!
93. "... ___, tekel, upharsin"
94. State tree of Tex.
96. ___ Grande, city in Ariz.
99. Ebro and Segura
101. Muslim general
102. Part of a trident
103. Chorus syllables
105. TV's "Just the Ten ___"
107. Cur. unit
108. Put the kibosh on
109. Invent extender
111. Marijuana
113. Insincere show of sorrow
117. Grape, in Concordia
118. Shoptalk
119. "___ Work...": G. Will book
120. "... ___ that kills": Housman
121. Side of a triangle
122. "Home, Sweet Home" lyricist
123. Earl of Avon's family
124. Minuscular
125. Possessive pron.

DOWN

1. Company for Carson
2. Singer Franklin
3. Leslie-Burke song: 1935
4. Safe preceder
5. Type of moth
6. Oribi's hue
7. Majestic
8. Notorious marquis
9. Etna has one
10. Holey
11. Kin of a dalmatic
12. Nothing more than
13. Emergency treatment
14. Spice
15. Polo Grounds hero
16. Equilateral parallelogram
17. Co-Nobelist for Peace: 1907
18. Choice words
25. "___ Can Whistle," Sondheim musical
26. Chintzy ones
28. Grill item
34. Surpass
36. Caucho-producing tree
39. "___ Spiro, Spero" (S.C. motto)
42. Table for Tacitus
44. "...I am ___": Romeo
46. Mars and Venus, e.g.
48. Staggers
49. General's ___ camp
50. Written, e.g.
51. And not
52. Become publicly known
53. Sweeping
57. Thing, to Tiberius
58. Sepulcher
60. Independence Day
61. Remove husks
62. Worktable, in Etaples
66. "Old Dog Tray" composer
68. Vexillum, e.g.
69. Her mate is ruff
71. Marshy
74. High-minded
76. Gutta
78. Enunciation
80. Robed scythe carrier
84. Slugged
86. Of milk
87. Galley essential
88. Irish euphemism
89. Similitude
90. Kisser
91. Luanda resident
93. Rash
95. Became distant
97. "... the mountains of ___": Gen. 8:4
98. Brackish
100. More sophisticated
104. One more time
106. Layered coifs
108. Canvassers' concern
110. "Willard" creatures
112. Ethereal
114. Temporary beginner
115. Gazetteer letters
116. Financier's Fannie ___

105 Midway Mergers by Dorothy Smitonick

ACROSS

1. Site of the Taj Mahal
5. Nautical term
10. Greek letters
14. Dandelion, e.g.
18. Asian weight
19. Religious sayings
20. Modify to suit
21. Gudrun's king
22. Nurse joins Weld to get Porter phrase
26. Well versed
27. Sea duck
28. Palpates
29. Small change?
30. "___ the ramparts . . ."
31. ___ colada
32. Distant
33. Torsk
34. City SW of Buenos Aires
35. Sediment
37. Michael Jackson hit
40. Young Rooney backs N.M. town in quest for radio team
46. Asian lake or sea
47. Resident of: Suffix
48. Trouble
49. Idle
50. Order to Fido at historic site has a certain pop style
58. Footlike part
59. Fast fliers
60. Rib or pan
61. Soothes
62. Deg. for a cellist, e.g.
63. Spring mo.
64. Cpls.' bosses
65. Certain pipe
67. City in Bolivia
69. Fit to ___
70. Actor Majors
73. Tote bag on back of singer stirs up a form of business
77. Celebes ox
78. Title for Eliz. II
79. Panay native
80. Some ratites
81. Movie great gets behind bandleader in producing "Explorers"
89. Mouths
90. Gainsay
91. Iroquoian group
92. Hide ___ hair
93. Cousin of a twp.
94. Broadway musical since 1982
95. Folding bed
96. Book by Peter Evans
99. Bank deals
101. Ancient Roman port
103. Industrial Revolution inventions
105. Dickensian hypocrite combines with actress to create typing method
108. Guipure, e.g.
109. Glyceride, e.g.
110. Must for Pindar
111. On the briny
112. ___ War: 1899–1902
113. In a jiffy
114. Pravda founder
115. Kind

DOWN

1. Cockloft
2. Haggard
3. Shoals
4. Too
5. Southwestern promenade
6. Actor in "Fanny": 1961
7. Mild oath
8. Own, to Robert Burns
9. White wine
10. Rim
11. Wild goat of Nepal
12. Quick to learn
13. How goose-steppers march
14. Tout's subject
15. And others: Abbr.
16. Building additions
17. Cutting tool
20. ___ abet (be an accomplice)
23. Talk foolishly
24. Sheer fabric
25. Under, poetically
31. Hard puzzle
33. Serene
34. Racing sailboats
35. Shot, as of liquor
36. Concept: Comb. form
37. Atlanta baseball player
38. Wood trimmers
39. Colorist
40. Northern nomad
41. Escutcheon border
42. Simon ___ (elimination game)
43. Gloves for Gehrig and Berra
44. Beards of grain
45. At ___ for words
51. Ottoman Empire founder
52. Specialty of some sharks
53. Herb resembling spinach
54. Source of coconut oil
55. Actress Black
56. French painter Fernand ___
57. Subsequently
62. Twofold
64. This may be posted
65. Goof
66. Mary's TV friend
67. Fresh
68. Cadets' inst.
69. Certificates, in Durango
70. Gentle soul
71. Month after Av
72. Besides
73. A certain J.F.K. departure
74. Gab; yak
75. Robertson and Evans
76. Newcomer in January
82. Minneapolis suburb
83. British character actor and family
84. Any delicious drink
85. Scupper
86. A. J. Cronin's "The ___"
87. "___ wood" (superstitious statement)
88. Barbarians
93. "Star Wars" villain
95. Prickly pears
96. Unequal: Comb. form
97. Allude (to)
98. ". . . one of them ___ and grows old": Shak.
99. River in China
100. Head of a tale
101. Aware of
102. "Nana" star: 1934
103. Ill-tempered
104. Actresses Claire and Balin
105. Att.'s degree
106. G.I.'s hangout
107. Prefix with eminent

106 Labor Day Largess by Frances Hansen

ACROSS

1. Lille's department
5. Cause distaste
10. English estate feature
14. Arnaz, Sr. or Jr.
18. Thine, in 1 Across
19. Miss ___, J. R.'s mother
20. Sans assistance
22. Bow out gracefully
23. Baker's largess
25. Madison Ave. worker's largess
27. Hurdle, in a way
28. Shankar's instrument
30. The "Soviet Riviera"
31. Once again
32. Vladimir Ilyich Ulyanov
33. Blanch
34. What a choir requires
36. Alberta tourist center
37. Fondled
41. Gator's cousin
42. Assembly worker's largess
45. Medieval French poem
46. "Portnoy's Complaint" author
47. Yalie
48. Pacino and Hirt
49. Zilch
50. Org. founded in Bogotá: 1948
51. Roofer's largess
57. Temple or Rice II
58. Divided proportionately
60. Mrs. Ethan Frome
61. Silverweed
63. Sacked
64. Victoria ___
65. He played to the balcony
66. Bees do it
67. Ah Sin's creator
68. Set one's goal toward
71. Lt. Cable's love
72. Reaper's largess
75. Singer Sumac
76. Pilaster
77. "A Chorus Line" finale
78. Welsh-rabbit brew
79. Gist of the matter
80. Slave Turner
81. Washerwoman's largess

87. Beards grown by some farmers
88. Gladstone's political rival
90. Rich cake
91. Ankles
93. Part of a Racine product
94. Conclusion
95. Roast, in Reims
96. "... 'tis no sin for ___ labor ...": Shak.
99. Purim celebrates his destruction
100. Set free
104. Garment worker's largess
106. Corn farmer's largess
108. Memorable basso Pinza
109. Largest book size
110. Of a Great lake
111. Owlish comment
112. Silas Marner's apparatus
113. Beethoven's birthplace
114. Certain orgs.
115. ___ of Court, British bar group

DOWN

1. Part of N.R.A.
2. Kiowa's cousin
3. Columnist Barrett
4. Expedition
5. Stimulate the memory
6. Jostle rudely
7. Nag
8. German article
9. Diminishes
10. Lap dog's opposite number
11. Northern highway
12. Lot's refuge city
13. He may be tight
14. Throws down the gauntlet
15. Quiz
16. Kind of car at the bar
17. "___ boy!"
21. Steep slope
24. ___ consequence (trivial)
26. Heraldry bands
29. Dope
32. "___ Lazuli," Yeats poem
33. Bel ___ (mild cheese)
34. Bellowing

35. Electrician's largess
36. Did a cotton-pickin' job
37. Naos
38. Nurseryman's largess
39. Betimes
40. "Vaya con ___," 1953 hit
41. Riding whip
43. Fished for congers
44. Certain Hindu ascetics
49. Like hospital areas
51. Young salmon
52. Shopping-list notations
53. ___ Ike of comics
54. Hat materials
55. Complete: Comb. form
56. Plant aperture
59. Lariat
62. Wall St. acronym
64. Confronted
65. Rubbed the wrong way
66. Biblical mount
67. Vietnamese capital

68. "A flea and a fly in ___"
69. Man from Muscat
70. Pied Piper's entourage
71. Touch down
73. Mont. county
74. Observes Lent
79. Popular Mexican music
81. Ipso ___
82. Excused from duty
83. Secretary of State: 1929–33
84. Eugene O'Neill's daughter
85. Adornments for some surreys
86. Runners
89. Kidnapper's demand
92. Crown of Osiris
94. Oliver's wicked tutor
95. Continued in a musical-chairs game
96. The third man
97. Author de la Roche
98. Exchange premium

99. Heavenly headgear
100. Baseball stats
101. Presently
102. Black, poetically
103. N.Y. times
105. Alcoholic Roy
107. Kid ___, jazz trombonist

ACROSS

1. Plaster of paris
6. Thickness
9. Arrives
14. Heidi heights
18. Dresser
19. Gazetteer item
20. High crest
21. Not ___ in the world
22. Start of an Indians song
26. Indian film: 1975
27. Vegas lead-in
28. Netman Nastase
29. He minded the stoa
30. Hero tag-on
31. Suburb of Liège
32. Small kite
35. C. Moore beast of burden
38. Big Bertha's birthplace
40. Give another polishing
41. Kind of dancer
42. How's that again?
43. "Vissi d'___," Puccini aria
47. Banky of silents
51. Guitarist Paul
53. Tavern
54. More viscid
56. Gaga
60. With an ___ the ground
62. Famed chef
63. A Beery
64. ___ Vanilli (lip-sync group)
65. ___ vera (skin conditioner)
66. Red dyes
67. Fusses
69. Sea barrier
70. A Seoul G.I.
71. "___ Love You So," Humperdinck hit
72. ___ hit (single)
74. Put up
77. Brandy-based cocktail
81. Sally ___ cake
82. Ebenezer's word
83. Drug buster
85. Mart part
86. "___ Born"
89. This goes with something
90. Aka
92. Rubber tube
93. Squiffed
94. Less deceitful
95. Acts for
97. Sea snail
98. Weed
99. Kerouac's "Big ___"
101. Tameins' kin
102. Lake Indian
103. "My country, ___ . . ."
104. Surpass
106. Reddish hog
110. Captured
113. Biased
116. Conference city
117. Hot tub
120. ___ hepatica
121. Asian range
123. Memorable Belgian musician
125. Montpelier is its cap.
126. Indian film: 1969
133. Indian film: 1976
134. ___ barrel (in trouble)
135. "___ the Rose," book by Stark Young
136. Snake River flopper
137. More weird
138. Fringe benefit of a sort
139. Head lock?
140. ___ Moines
141. Indian princess

DOWN

1. Battleship part
2. Palindrome part
3. Vend
4. Cruise
5. Attire
6. Warm up an oven
7. Riga man
8. What a bore evokes
9. Ned of radio news
10. Hunter in the skies
11. Milano's subway
12. Kitchen tag-on
13. Far from altruistic
14. Throb
15. Insect stage
16. Do not rush in dressing
17. Seventh sons
18. Pot or double follower
19. Cold
21. ". . . lovely as ___": Kilmer
23. Sesame
24. Seep through
25. Long time
33. Indian comforter
34. Way out
36. Indian film: 1970
37. Haw preceder
38. Kind of market
39. Indian film: 1957
42. Venom
44. Get up
45. Rend
46. Mistypes
48. Abner's companion
49. Nonwinners at the track
50. Hun of Norse myth
52. "The ___," Indian film: 1956
53. Indian film: 1950
54. "___ Sleep," Odets play
55. Coarse fabric
56. Division word
57. "High" time
58. Lose color
59. Sommer from Berlin
61. "Thanks ___!"
66. Makeup
68. Mackerel's kin
73. Slyly sarcastic
75. Simplicity
76. Hill's partner
78. Continue
79. Once, once
80. Dakota Indians
84. Tears
86. ". . . ___ forgive those . . ."
87. Use a blender
88. Grant of "Being a Woman"
89. The libido
91. U.S.A.F., e.g.
94. Ichorous
96. Team
100. Western Indian
103. Bony fish
105. "Flintstones" child
107. Brown study
108. Supervise
109. Go at top speed
111. Word in the Kan. motto
112. Madeline from Boston
113. Buffet features
114. Hot spot
115. Waggish
116. Some do get the hang of it
117. Razor's edger
118. Pet ___
119. Tailor
121. Sentient
122. These give ade
124. Red ___ (night flight)
127. Sneak around
128. "Dial ___ Murder"
129. ___ tea
130. Mansard extension
131. Where Braves visit Mets
132. Little Big ___

ACROSS

1. Catamount
5. Color also called meadowlark
10. Inspiration for Blake
15. Zodiacal sign
18. Retired
19. Lip: Comb. form
20. Coeur d'___, Idaho
21. Inlet
22. Where Daniel was cast
24. Authorized
26. Twin of sorts
27. Ryan's daughter
29. Type of orange
30. Chew
33. Watchful guardian
34. A.U.S. or U.S.N.
35. Neglect
36. Shanks
37. Spotted racers
41. Quick, straight drink
42. Certain black-nosed rabbits
44. Wattlebird
45. Moisture of morning
46. A Margaret Mead subject
49. Soot or porn
50. Painter of American Indians
51. Site of 1952 Olympics
53. Brown feline from Africa
57. Actress Prentiss
58. Certain papers
60. Etchers' purchases
61. Vandal, e.g.
62. Slip-ups
64. Partita
65. Divisions of hockey games
66. "... draw thy breath ___": Hamlet
67. Whiner
68. Shoe part
69. ___ and end-all (whole)
70. Disasters
72. Alewife's kin
75. Yeast for Vassar
76. Franklin's mother
77. Ingredients of gimlets
79. Cohan's "___ Popular Man"
80. Airport info.
81. Conspirator
85. Hot, old style
87. Guitarists' arpeggios
89. Family in "Look Homeward, Angel"
90. Algonquian Indian spirit
91. Shake ___ (hie)
92. Old Spanish coin
93. Spotted cats
94. Emulate Lorelei
96. City at the foot of Mt. Etna
97. Avid
98. Grayish wildcat
100. Not absolved
105. Give ___ on the back
106. Turkish decree
107. Limerick starter
108. Otherwise
109. Insane
110. Diarist of the 17th century
111. Wader in the Everglades
112. Assess

DOWN

1. Expand, in a way
2. Honshu port
3. Alcott's "Little ___"
4. "... ___ in the house?"
5. Allot
6. An Oscar winner in 1986
7. Reed
8. Dog with two Tins on his tail
9. Panacea
10. Caused by touch
11. Intestinal obstruction
12. Microbe
13. Tolkien tree
14. ___ the wheel (devise unnecessarily)
15. Find
16. Knievel
17. Dict. published in England
21. Source of a perfume ingredient
23. Eyes the girls
25. One Eve had three
28. Pearl Mosque site
30. Err
31. Choreographer de Mille
32. Ounces
33. Peace Nobelist: 1987
34. Singer Cassidy
36. E. Indian herb roots
37. Certain moldings
38. Garfield lovers' emotion
39. Greeted
40. Sub detectors
43. Digression
47. "Green Pastures" role
48. Degs. for industrialists
50. Herbs liked by felines
52. Horseweed
54. ___ Ste. Marie
55. Less cordial
56. Peterman's purchase
57. Nice recreation area
59. Labor
61. An Attorney General under Reagan
62. Tippler
63. ___ time (singly)
64. Actress Dey
65. Wilbur product
67. A son of Priam
68. Dilutes
70. Sort
71. End of Mont.'s motto
73. Friendship
74. Secures by fitting into a groove
76. Incidental excursion
78. Frightened
81. Cigar tree, e.g.
82. Violent struggles
83. Physics Nobelist: 1944
84. Medial sounds
86. More irate
88. Guido's lowest note
90. Lodestone
92. Warbucks
93. Ville V.I.P.
94. Paper-mulberry bark
95. Mild oath
96. Snooze
97. Always
98. Fill too tightly
99. Ouse tributary
101. Modern lang.
102. Huge SE Asian fish
103. N.Y. time in winter
104. Duant

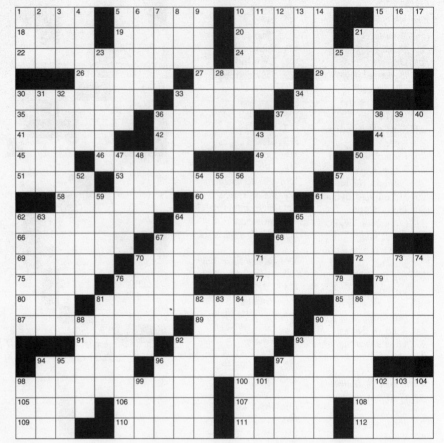

ACROSS

1. Make picots
4. Feigns
9. Over, in Ulm
13. Wire nail
17. Biblical verb
18. Sun: Pref.
19. Scruff
20. Flattens flats
22. "You're all litterbugs," said the janitor ___
24. "I'm on TV," said the chef ___
26. Muezzin's place
27. Kipling poem
29. "___ these truths . . ."
30. "I'm petrified," said the quarrier ___
31. Sky Whale
32. Rid Rover of insects
33. G. Burns role
34. Asp's cousin
35. Skier Jean Claude
36. "Forever" girl
39. "I'm in a rut," said the ditchdigger ___
41. Peace, in Pamplona
44. Calf meat
45. Yum-Yum, e.g.
46. Wagers
47. Game fish
48. The whole shebang
49. "Blast it!" said the dynamiter ___
53. Pound unit
54. "Alice" illustrator
56. Mrs. Will Durant
57. Ill-prepared
58. Rank-smelling
59. Topknot
60. Roman coins
62. Sky blue
64. Flat, in Italy
65. Kennedy compound, e.g.
67. Distort, in a way
68. "We need water," said the gardener ___
70. Slip
72. Exaction
73. See 85 Across
74. Dry, cold wind
75. TV ad award
76. Marmee's youngest
77. "No juice," said the electrician ___
81. Dallied
82. Like a Morse message
83. Nine: Pref.
84. "The ___ Sanction"

85. With 73 Across, an earth belt
87. With full force
88. "I'm all ears," said the corn farmer ___
92. "Viva ___," 1952 film
93. Savoy dance
94. Bassanio's friend
95. "It's permanent press," said the saleswoman ___
97. "Excuse my gear," said the truck driver ___
100. Salk's conquest
101. Bookbinding leather
102. Ex-Dodger
103. It, in Mexico
104. N.J. governor, once
105. Chevot
106. Grani or Bayard
107. "I ___," said the prophet, predictably

DOWN

1. Namely
2. ". . . ___ clock scholar"
3. "___ Wore Red," 1960 film
4. Scutum in the sky
5. "The Young Bugler" author
6. Math form
7. Wire measure
8. Hairy legume
9. Rude
10. Thai money
11. Finials
12. Dau, or bro
13. "Tight shorts," said the boxer ___
14. "I itch," said the barber ___
15. ". . . who lived in ___"
16. Singer Reese
17. G.I. awards
21. A Chaplin
23. Earlier
25. Harps (on)
28. Of the ear
31. Tenet
32. Simple song
34. Whalebone whale's food
35. Bell sound
36. Oahu drink
37. Dissolve
38. "I'm packing it in!" said the cotton picker ___
39. On a disk

40. Red as ___
41. "They escaped," said the pig man ___
42. A Johnson
43. Kind of suit
45. Half of MMXXIV
47. City in Crete
49. Stage direction
50. Singer Vaughan
51. A Castle
52. Cap projection
53. "Oklahoma!" hero
55. Perfumery ingredient
59. Quoter
60. Teed off
61. U.S.C. rival
62. Recorded proceedings
63. Kind of lens
64. Yearned
65. Col. Tibbet's mother
66. HOMES part
68. Knocked 'em dead
69. "Little Eyolf" dramatist
71. Wand

73. This gives you a sign
75. ___ goose (ruin)
77. Share
78. Boucher's teacher
79. Hindu land grant
80. Hidden marksmen
81. "Mittinata" composer
82. Braincases
84. Charged
85. Old card game
86. Polish city
87. Book of maps
88. Reichstag leader before Ebert
89. Fireplace, in Yorkshire
90. DeGaulle's birthplace
91. Spinner or weirdo
92. A code in the head?
93. Spill over
96. Altar above
98. Not gross
99. "___!" said the hansom driver rightly

ACROSS

1. File's partner
5. Kimonos
10. Water bottle
16. Shady spot
21. Bacchanalian cry
22. This can be grand
23. Deli-menu item
24. Varnish source
25. + 4
28. Ala. city
29. Couple
30. Plantation group
31. ¿Como ___ usted?
32. Jewish month
33. Spuds
35. Outlets for admen
36. Pair of pistols
38. Bounder
40. Wax-coated cheese
43. ___ capita
44. Give ___ on the back (praise)
48. Aunt, to Maria
51. Gorcey or Durocher
52. − 2
56. With regard to
58. Del. industrialist
60. ___ da capo
61. Flat straw hat
62. Soup scoop
64. Most confident
66. RR systems
67. Intact
68. + 998
70. Synthetic
73. Not frequent: Abbr.
74. Colorful shawl
75. Sound
77. Plant shoot
79. Tree toad
80. Yin kin
83. Fire residue
85. Crotchety one
87. Pungency
91. "... ___! the lark ...": Shak.
93. Grain sorghum
94. Peacock-feather spots
99. Look for prey
101. Imitate, in a way
103. − 3
107. Radiant
109. Tse-tung
110. Hunting dog
112. French wine region
113. ___ account (reprimand)
114. Fountain offering
116. Kerry county seat
118. ___ and terminer
119. − 1
122. Low island
124. Summertime in N.Y.C.
125. Ridicule
126. Gold: Pref.
127. Music halls
128. Broadcast
130. Boggs of baseball
132. Sly and nasty
135. Cold-weather wear
139. Indian term of respect
142. Eject, as in volcanic action: Var.
146. Fashionable
148. Diacritical mark
149. Novelist Karmer
150. + 58
153. Con man's targets
154. Prima ballerina
155. Sao ___, Brazil
156. Main man
157. "___ porridge hot ..."
158. Snakebird
159. European lindens
160. The Ohre, to Hans

DOWN

1. Contradict
2. Pastoral pipe in Palencia
3. Keep bases empty
4. German commander, W.W. II
5. Wand
6. Makes a choice
7. "I'll ___ for Christmas"
8. "Maid of Athens ___ part ...": Byron
9. ___ Koh, Afghan range
10. Religious mission
11. Air: Pref.
12. Bumpkin
13. Arabs' apparel
14. Nonwoven fabric
15. Intertwines
16. Groundwork
17. + 6
18. Artful
19. Madame Bovary
20. Nurture
26. Perfume ingredient
27. Gets one's bearings
34. Litigated
37. Sprang up
39. The March King
41. Eureka!
42. Involves in difficulties
43. Pliable
45. Course of action
46. Without principles
47. Nobelist Mother
48. Controversies
49. Dumbfounded
50. Fervency
52. Its capital is Lille
53. Actually existing: Lat.
54. Granite State flower
55. Town on the Adriatic
57. Kazan
59. "Canoe row a boat?" is one
63. Catch sight of
65. − 8
69. Jacob's substituted bride
71. Virginia follower
72. Tourist attraction
76. Some pineapples
78. High point
81. Cards raise this
82. Solecist's failing
84. Pulpits
86. Instr.
87. Typewriter device
88. Wild sheep of Asia
89. Hung loosely
90. + 28
92. South African enclosure
95. Reverberate
96. Oldest of the Bridges
97. Crescent-shaped figures
98. French composer: 1890–1962
100. Like George Apley
102. Chieftain, also called Rolf the Ganger
104. Coup d'___
105. M.P.H.
106. Found
108. Single-celled organism
111. Colorless, flammable liquid
115. Mass of ivy
117. Tombstone man
120. Made an estimate
121. One who cuddles
123. He wrote "The Hour Glass"
128. One and a half: Comb. form
129. Bend out of shape
131. Humiliate
133. Clumsy
134. The Furies of myth
136. Studio floodlight
137. Like very much
138. Sir, in Zaragoza
139. Meathead
140. Pea-plant petals
141. Israeli dance
143. "Pocket" bread
144. Calpurnia, to Caesar
145. Revise and correct
147. Statesman Cordell ___
151. Violinist Bull
152. Orion's beloved

ACROSS

1. "Rug" area?
6. Pledge
10. Catch flies
14. Fla. city
19. Eremite
20. Surfeit
21. Cook book
22. More developed
23. Very, to Verdi
24. O.K. Corral man
25. Mad as ___ hen
26. Old Testament book
27. Start of a four-line verse
31. Jose or Giovanni
32. Story start
33. Miscue
34. Hoffman from L.A.
38. Brahman, for one
40. Implore
41. Leb. neighbor
44. Pilasters
45. Arias
46. Speaker's place
47. Concerning
48. Second line of the verse
53. ___ day's wonder
54. Tropics topic
55. Half an aromatic oil
56. Netting for snaring
57. Fr. holy woman
58. Bearing
59. Manilow's "___ It Through the Rain"
60. Surgical tool
61. Skerry
62. Coin receivers
63. Nap
64. Computer component
67. Avignon's river
68. G & S executioner
69. Thrash
72. Inclined, as a ship
73. Lotto's kin
74. Whale
75. Marquand sleuth
76. Third line of the verse
80. "Ich ___," Prince of Wales' motto
81. Suffix with canon
82. Sow sound
83. Fanon
84. Admiral Benbow, e.g.
85. Hitch
86. Walk daintily
88. Knots
89. Top of the crop
91. Kan. senator
92. Pisan Mr.
93. Last line of the verse
101. Praying figure
102. Campaigns
103. German one
104. Wickerwork material
105. Patois
106. "Down with!" in Dieppe
107. "The Four Seasons" star
108. Actress Taylor
109. Is overly fond
110. Past due
111. Kind of processor
112. English hymnologist

DOWN

1. Blind part
2. Blackjack, in Soho
3. Faulkner character
4. Regan's father
5. Place for devout petitions
6. Arctic or Indian
7. "Sustineo ___" U.S.A.F. motto
8. African antelope
9. Mesmer's field
10. Like hen's teeth
11. Actor Mandel
12. Iowa State site
13. Assemblage
14. Stubborn
15. Mussolini's son-in-law
16. Like an adage
17. Their, in Tours
18. Radius's locale
28. Took the cake
29. Bankbook Abbr.
30. Worthless writing
34. Cockcrows
35. Without a scratch
36. "Platoon" director
37. Use the VCR
38. He wrote "Little Johnny Jones"
39. Landed
40. "Public Good" publisher: 1730
42. Inscribed pillar
43. Criticize harshly
45. Nectarous
46. Pairs
47. Unisonally
49. Yours of yore
50. Kyoto garments
51. Make merry
52. Tajo of the Met
58. Kind of millionaire
59. Novelist Karmel
60. Compare
61. Korean port
62. Paisley
63. Asher Lev's creator
64. Islamic prophet
65. Lard constituent
66. Free from illusion
67. Put a new label on
68. City on the Ashuelot
69. "Marching as ___": Baring-Gould
70. Under any circumstances
71. "The Loom of Years" poet
73. Like Congress
74. Smart
75. Pianist Hess
77. Shore from Tenn.
78. Far from musical
79. A moist Cheddar
85. Bouts
86. Chocolate ___
87. Under the weather
88. Captain's boat
90. Scope
91. Mr. Chips portrayer
92. Sam of golf
93. Beethoven's "Archduke," for one
94. Isla de Pinos site
95. Cylindrical structure
96. Chinese preceder
97. Prophet's words
98. Lollobrigida
99. Cad
100. An Algonquian
101. Antediluvian

114 *Sienna Tourist Stops?* by Maura B. Jacobson

ACROSS

1. Baker's aide
5. Flak sound
8. Laughing matter
12. Sell hot tickets
17. Meadow mouse
18. "If ___ a Hammer"
20. Colorful fish
21. Small drum
22. Actor Baldwin
23. Novelist de la Roche
24. Apiary sight
25. Rainier realm
26. Happy cloud
27. Signora on a camel?
30. Problems in the boot?
32. Count the pennies
33. Corrida contender
34. Mrs. Henry Wallace
35. Same old routine
36. Gael's land
40. Turn into
43. Sharp taste
45. Oriental nanny
47. Stephen Foster's "Old Uncle"
48. Antarctic cape
49. Ever so simple?
52. Short smoke
53. Matelot's milieu
54. Splinter group
56. Rita's Khan
57. Sizable
59. Licorice-tasting cordials
62. "Sail ___ Ship of State!"
63. Off a pedestal
65. Working woman's choice?
68. Bisector's results
69. Mouth piece
70. Fragrant plants
73. Actress LuPone
74. Rosary bead
75. News clipping
76. Fam. member
77. Ostrich look-alike
78. Italian obi?
84. Grant license to
86. Paver's pitch
87. Grigs
88. Anna of "Nana"
89. Edits TV goofs
90. Singles
92. High, in music
93. ___ for tat
94. Parlor piece
95. Go ___ (deteriorate)
98. How to keep the dottore away?
102. Second line of a nursery rhyme?

106. Familiar campus figure
108. Derivation
109. Zwei chaser
110. Breton brainstorm
111. Run in neutral
112. Shade of green
113. Algae extract
114. Parking lights
115. Give the elbow
116. Slyly disparaging
117. European blackbird
118. Grasshopper's critic
119. Whilom

DOWN

1. First czar of Russia
2. Muligrubs
3. "Uncle Vanya" role
4. Any sense organ
5. Part of a target-practice command
6. Copper: Pref.
7. Ocarina's kin
8. Andrew and Lyndon
9. Grand-scale
10. Goalie's successes
11. Union of the personal soul with God
12. 70 mph wind
13. Hors d'oeuvre item
14. Rhyme scheme
15. Math points
16. Malayan outrigger
19. A Dickens family
25. Rum cocktail
28. Chou ___
29. Dowdy one
31. Hotel amenity?
37. Not to be believed
38. King's tenure
39. Brink
40. The Crimson Tide, for short
41. Earl of Avon
42. Lampooned likeness
44. Brobdingnagian
46. Greeting from Michael Caine?
49. Impersonate
50. Hip follower?
51. Hilo howdy
55. Raison d'___
58. Very much
60. Table staple
61. Cannon salute
62. Comics cave man
63. Spume
64. Alas!
66. Outward images
67. Goddess of discord
68. Biblical villain

71. Cut a photo
72. Shoats' moms
73. Falstaff's henchman
74. Netherlands city
79. Think it through
80. "Oklahoma!" aunt
81. Cry of encouragement to Mary Lou
82. Fisherman's net
83. Digestive aid
85. Kind of cinch
89. Least timorous
91. Contrived
94. Sacred
96. Voice a view
97. Requiem
99. Daises
100. Fervor
101. Egg innards
102. Ward healers
103. Press
104. Sir, in Africa
105. Treasured
107. Iambic measures

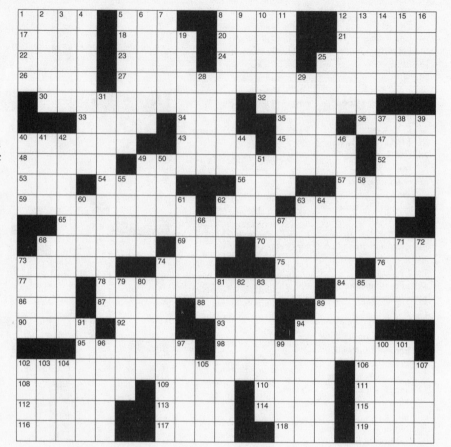

ACROSS

1. Spartan slaves
7. Health resort
10. R.N. specialty
13. Assagai
18. Kazoo's cousin
20. Conflict partly logomachical
22. Beside oneself
23. A 1939 song by 64 Down
25. Seed covering
26. Light amplifier
27. Con men
29. Use a swizzle stick
30. Nuisance
34. Press for payment
35. "Dinner ___," 1933 film
37. Afore
38. Professional standard
40. God of revelry
43. Made serious
45. A 1942 song by 64 Down
50. Twist out of shape
51. Metalworker
52. Will, the historian
53. Bring up a subject
56. Murrow's "___ Now"
59. Verse form
61. Vier preceder
62. ___ tai (rum drink)
65. Cure
67. Has to have
68. Be on the payroll
69. Opposite of dep.
70. Single-seeded fruit
71. Benefit
73. Poor grade
74. Hindu good spirit
76. Take a sip
78. ___ million
79. Sigmoid shape
80. Indigo
81. Theoretically
83. Habit
85. Prophetic
87. Lots and lots
89. Pianist's perch
92. Birthplace of Goliath
93. A 1972 song by 64 Down
97. Reproduce in kind
100. Shade of blue
101. Electrical rectifier
102. Once named
103. "Tender ___," 1983 film
107. Keydets' sch.
109. Avian crop
110. Bosnian
112. Metric weights
113. Do a double take
115. Runs in neutral
117. A 1929 song by 64 Down
124. Trombone section
125. Rustic
126. Stone Age tools
127. Belief
128. QB's measures
129. Modernist
130. Middle East waterway

DOWN

1. Glutton
2. Italian author
3. Youth
4. Symbol of royalty
5. Work the land
6. Sam or J. C.
7. Incision aftermath
8. Lap dog, for short
9. Schooner contents
10. Strong string
11. Milk: Pref.
12. "___ Wife," Kelly play
13. Mind the baby
14. Chief exec.
15. A 1933 song by 64 Down
16. Get-up
17. Brought up
19. In itself
21. Euphemistic expletive
24. Man of La Mancha
28. A 1946 song by 64 Down
30. Seat at St. Patrick's
31. Ordinal endings
32. Leveling wedge
33. Monkeys or trees
35. Houston athlete
36. Conveyance for skiers
39. Et follower
41. In the thick of
42. Shylock's practice
44. Wear away
46. A 1935 song by 64 Down
47. Literature Nobelist: 1929
48. Like llamas
49. Packed in the hold
54. Largest asteroid
55. Fatha of jazz
57. Clarifying words
58. Sawbuck
60. Robin of ballad fame

62. "Call Me ___," musical with songs by 64 Down
63. Coliseum
64. Subject of this puzzle, born May 11, 1888
66. Disconnect
72. Endured
75. Knot-tying location
77. Fencing piece
78. "Believe It ___"
82. Allays
84. Kind of boom
86. News bit
88. Scottish skiing surface
90. Olfactory datum
91. Mother of the Gemini
94. Donated
95. Cell dweller
96. Morning coat?
97. Declare firmly
98. Ride
99. Overly sentimental
104. Wrote a puzzle definition
105. Tittles
106. Superlative suffixes

108. Venous fluid for Venus
111. Venerable one
113. Gravure prefix
114. TV part
116. Fixed
118. Singer Whitcomb
119. Compass point
120. Disencumbered
121. "___ a Lovely Day Today," 1950 song by 64 Down
122. "When I Leave ___ World Behind," 1915 song by 64 Down
123. Half a Gabor

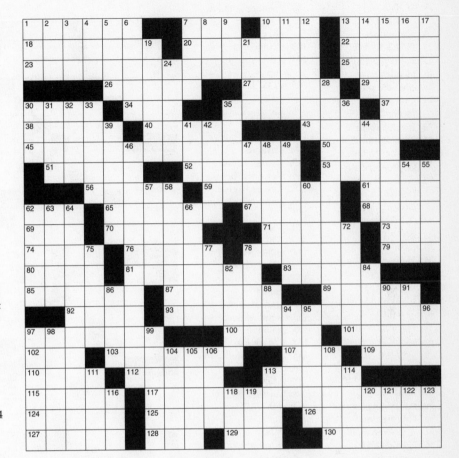

116 *Companion Piece* by Mary Virginia Orna

ACROSS

1. Contained
5. Summon
9. Flick's footstep
13. Pal of Porthos
18. Heathen
19. Melville novel
20. Creator of "Little Iodine"
22. Rumba relative
24. Director-dramatist
28. Cato's "to be"
29. Osprey's relative
30. Azimuth
31. Bernard ___ Haar, Dutch poet
32. "Call Me Madam" prototype
33. Also
34. Home-school orgs.
35. Francis, for one
36. Epicedia, e.g.
38. Rival of 87 Across
40. Teredo
41. Berlin products
43. Collar
46. "Stout-hearted ___"
47. Stomata
48. Actor-hero Murphy
49. Pop
50. Author-clergyman
56. Granny Smith, e.g.
57. "___-Bitsy Spider"
58. New Zealand beetle grubs
59. Turns rancid
60. Huff
61. Fable, e.g.
63. Mindanao municipality
64. Pilaster
65. Mark Antony's bodyguard
67. Decline
69. Certain berths
72. Expert
73. Australian-American singers
80. Essay
81. Oise cathedral town
82. Lothian slope
83. Market town of Normandy
84. Sculptor Nadelman
86. Metal containers
87. Radames's beloved
89. Faucet
90. Loath
92. East Coast fish delicacy
94. West Coast naturalist
96. Former N.Y.C. mayor
98. Presidentertainer
102. Rehan and Huxtable
103. On the ball
104. Adores, with "upon"
105. W.W. II scene of action
106. King, in Castilla
107. Fuses
108. Gods for Galba
109. Tenuous
113. Actress Louise
114. Stens and Brens
115. Author Bagnold
116. Diminutive suffix
117. Calcined
120. Society-page word
123. Actress O'Connor
124. OPEC member
125. Actor Pickens
126. Bridge champrima donna
131. Macadamized
132. Stendhal hero
133. A son of Adam
134. Cookie pan
135. Transmission parts
136. Auction
137. Affirmatives
138. Cry said with a sigh

DOWN

1. Horse-drawn vehicle
2. Goads
3. Halt
4. Genetic initials
5. Snakes often charmed
6. Last words
7. Body of knowledge
8. Birler's need
9. Silent-film star of "Forever Amber"
10. Picador
11. N.L. home-run champ: 1942
12. Scheme
13. Sigh, in Stuttgart
14. Motifs
15. Cods' relatives
16. Baron of "Der Rosenkavalier"
17. Jigger
18. Buonarroti masterpiece
21. Undivided
23. Hawaiian beverage
25. Where rhodopsin abounds
26. French operatic baritone: 1848–1923
27. Author of "Hatter's Castle"
34. Factory-adjusted
35. Vicious eel
37. Musicologist Taylor
39. Nobelist von Behring: 1901
40. Some babies
41. Nobel Peace Prize winner: 1984
42. Japanese veggies
43. Kind of ball game
44. Journalist St. Johns
45. Bistros
47. Exclusive rights
48. Hitchcock's "To Catch ___"
49. Seedy blueberries
50. Jacket part
51. "Rienzi" or "Jenufa"
52. Author Sinclair
53. Where to see "The Last Supper"
54. Go beyond
55. Rapidly
62. Not at home
63. Panel divider
66. Lampoons
68. Afore
70. Kid
71. Difficulties
72. Describing some cheeses
74. Salad green
75. Tangle; snare
76. Where the Lomani flows
77. Essential oil
78. Vicuña's relative
79. A companion to Doc
84. Dodge
85. SAC commander: 1948–61
88. Let up
90. Slightly open
91. TV's Barnaby Jones
92. Scram!
93. Judges' suites: Abbr.
94. Apportions
95. Shoshoneans
97. "Psychic Warfare . . ." author
99. Prussian cavalrymen
100. Mailer or Lear
101. Civet, e.g.
107. A Bette
108. Greek wreath component
109. Scythe shafts
110. "David and Lisa" star
111. Omits
112. Absolve
113. Word with cotta or firma
115. Muse or Dryad
117. Statute
118. Pile
119. Lagomorph
121. Inquiring interjections
122. Selves
124. Journey, for Juvenal
125. Comedian Mort
127. Ames and Begley
128. Pay dirt
129. Uraeus
130. Youth org.

117 Structural Works *by Joy L. Wouk*

ACROSS

1. Anthropologist Margaret
5. Comprehension
10. Old cries of contempt
14. Bust's opposite
18. Peak
19. QE2, e.g.
20. Sweet smelling
21. Taj Mahal site
22. Wilder novel
26. Turned's partner
27. Thrown skyward
28. What QB's wish to gain
29. North Sea feeder
30. G-men
32. Narwhal
33. Kaiser rel.
35. Glossy silk fabric
39. W. H. Hudson novel
45. Like knobs
46. Bog
48. Knead, formerly
49. Malayan boat
50. Vicki Baum novel
52. Writer Hammett
54. Riga native
55. Hautboy
56. Aquatic mammals
59. In the least
60. He wrote "The Hairy Ape"
62. Eats with others
64. "L.A. Law" actress
65. Walpole novel
70. Wheel projection
73. Church parts
74. Painter Andre: 1880–1954
78. Adjust oneself
80. Hammer targets
81. "Die Frau Schatten": R. Strauss
84. ___ time (pronto)
85. Sartre, e.g.
87. Tuchman work, with "The"
89. Tumult
90. Orleans-to-Paris dir.
91. Garment with short flaps
93. Tocsin
94. Remarque novel, with "The"
97. Goes back in thought
99. Suffragist's monogram
100. Rowan, e.g.
101. Ratio words
102. Snoop
105. Miss Hogg
107. Cloud type
109. Hudson port
114. Hawthorne novel, with "The"
118. As to
119. French ballot boxes
120. Street show
121. Garbo film: 1927
122. Tardy
123. Bar denizens
124. Large numbers
125. Deneb, e.g.

DOWN

1. N.T. starter
2. Second hearing
3. Iowa college town
4. Five-time Presidential candidate
5. Moved smoothly
6. Disencumber
7. Aberdeen ___ cattle
8. Ooze
9. Pertaining to obtaining
10. Typewriter part
11. Leghorn
12. As recently as
13. Learners
14. ___-relief
15. Monster
16. Utah city
17. Legendary Giant
20. Actor Davis et al.
23. Pleat again
24. Poets' temples
25. Doctrines
31. Disband troops
34. Small singing bird
35. Certain American
36. A 1961 Oscar winner
37. Radio's "___ With Judy"
38. Having prophetic power
39. Victory, in Aberdeen
40. Applelike fruit
41. Yukon neighbor
42. Mountain nymph
43. ___ prosequi
44. Quip
47. A Siouan
51. Composer of "The Planets"
53. Dispatch
56. Bank items
57. Piccadilly Circus figure
58. Business abbr.
61. Shoemakers' needs
62. Head
63. Done
66. Renter
67. Not so chubby
68. A New Hebrides island
69. Ripken, for one
70. Film maker Frank
71. Deborah of "Dynasty"
72. Rabat's country, to Marie
75. Sadat
76. Dull
77. Standards
79. Gists
81. Straight: Pref.
82. Garden tool
83. Sudanese people
86. Notorious
87. Wall painters' associates
88. Table, in Napoli
91. Radium discoverers
92. Hebrew measures
95. Theater award
96. Induces scratching
98. Stories in a maison
101. Grenoble's river
102. Singer Collins
103. Author Jaffe
104. Mongolian felt tent
106. Hair style
108. Of grapes
110. Some containers: Abbr.
111. "Thanks ___"
112. St. Petersburg's river
113. North Sea feeder
115. Bishopric
116. Explosive
117. Recent

118 *Anonymous Admonition* *by Jeanne Wilson*

ACROSS

1. Expressed by word of mouth
6. Muddle
10. Spring water, e.g.
18. Writer Calvino
19. "...I obeyed as ___": Gibbon
20. Beach baskers
23. Substitute
25. Horror film
26. Beat the incumbent
27. Boorish one
29. "Play ___ It Lays," 1972 film
30. Actress Talbot
31. Width for Big Foot?
32. Happy syllable
34. "Tristram Shandy" author and family
36. Galena and prill
37. Grenoble's river
39. Torrid
40. Gilbertian princess
43. Has-___(faded star)
46. "In vino ___"
49. Asps
53. Sharp-witted
55. A case for Cicero
56. Board a Concorde
58. Extravagantly ornate
60. Einstein's "The World ___ See It"
61. Express ways?
63. Summer quaff
64. Russian river
66. Civil War side
68. Map-in-a-map
69. Theme of this puzzle
73. "...from ___ dream of peace": Hunt
76. Swerves
77. Ancient Irish king
78. Jackie's second
81. "We are ___": Queen Victoria
84. Eureka!
86. QB Bradshaw was one
88. Neptune's scepter
89. Propose
91. One in a pool
92. Like some railways
93. Menu listings
95. The yoke is on them
96. Philosopher Lao-___
97. Cheerful, in Cherbourg
98. "Over the Rainbow" composer
100. Colorful fish
104. Gregorian plain songs, old style
108. Gender
109. Nabokov novel
112. Hearty's partner
113. Well, in Metz
114. Barbarian
116. French schools
118. "And the crack in the tea cup ___...": Auden
121. A Dionne, e.g.
123. Signs of middle age
124. Ruin
125. Mall unit
126. Sauce ___ (interest stimulator)
127. Sorbonne summers
128. Chemical compound

DOWN

1. Woven cotton fabric
2. In harmony
3. Rear
4. Ye ___ tea shoppe
5. Ex-pitcher Eddie and family
6. Chinese chairman
7. Some members of the Eng. gentry
8. Spirits
9. Beak
10. Kind of blonde
11. Antiquated
12. Bring together
13. Pumice, etc.
14. Links norms
15. Lizard of the western U.S.
16. Mammal of Afr. or Ind.
17. Odin led them
21. Neural network
22. Titles in Mex.
24. Form of address for an abbot: Abbr.
28. Theme definition
33. "...after the people ___": Proust
35. Subject of a Stein line
37. Division word
38. Time period
41. Force
42. Fabric decorations
43. ___ au rhum
44. Plant form
45. River at Chartres
47. Call ___ day
48. Interwoven series
50. Zesty feelings
51. Also ___ (losers)
52. Snicker chaser
54. Gear
57. Superlative suffix
59. Subject of a Keats ode
61. Dix and Bragg: Abbr.
62. Melville's captain
65. Destroy cells by certain antibodies
67. Result
69. A Gettysburg general
70. Approved, for short
71. They attack snacks
72. Inst. at Hanover, N.H.
73. Colonizer
74. British actress Diana ___
75. Diet follower
78. Author Haley
79. Tale by Chateaubriand
80. Ferrum
82. Les États-___
83. Patron of musicians
85. Bern's stream
87. College or collar
89. Boyfriend
90. Economics org.
94. Dangerous downpour
97. Web-footed sea bird
99. Cover story
100. Sounds of surprise
101. N.Y. Shakespeare Festival producer
102. ___ in the dark
103. Artist Matisse
105. Lafcadio ___, U.S. journalist-author
106. Tight topper
107. Perilous performance
109. Ration
110. Farm-machine name
111. Late bloomer
113. ___ Khan, Mongol conqueror
115. Secrete
117. Goes for
119. "Omoo" to "Typee": Abbr.
120. Suffix with Siam
122. "___ Knife," Beckett book

119 Razzle-Dazzle by Tom Mixon

ACROSS

1. Ale ingredient
5. Rostand or Rimbaud
10. As red as ___
15. Dingle
19. N.T. omission
20. Incite
21. Choleric
22. Footnote abbr.
23. Australia
27. Various
28. Earthen pots
29. Sartre novel
30. Burden
31. Athanasian or Nicene
32. Argot
33. "Journey into Fear" author
36. Musical upbeats
37. Point ___, Calif. cape
41. Hard to find
42. Tail-dragging nursery group
45. "___ Heldenleben": Strauss
46. Experts
48. Haggard queen
49. Dr. Seuss's "Hop on ___"
50. Literary initials
51. "___ Clear Day . . ."
52. Innsbruck thrills: 1976
59. Exist
60. Dessert wines
62. Speedily
63. American wildcat
65. Arty party
66. Yawning
67. Positioned for push-ups
68. Photog's copies
70. Coeur d' ___, Idaho
71. Scrutinies
74. Like some dicts.
75. Bugliosi best seller
78. Haw's opposite
79. Baby of opera
80. Itinerary info
81. DX ÷ V
82. Thesmothete
84. Corolla petal
85. Chapeaux for writer Jean
91. Hawk
92. Ouster; dislodgement
94. Maki or vari
95. Scholastic propositions
97. Rock attachment
98. Checks cagily
99. Jetty
100. Mister, in Monza
103. Yellowish green
104. Increase Mather was one
108. English actress's family treasures
111. A weather's opposite
112. An eye opener
113. Tubby
114. At the peak
115. Winter Palace resident
116. Agate and pica
117. Eminent
118. Hanging ends

DOWN

1. "The night ___ thousand eyes"
2. Work
3. Crocks
4. High follower
5. Disquiet
6. Looks too long
7. "Gadzooks!" relative
8. This comes short or long
9. Support
10. Random
11. Like E.M.K.'s "A"
12. Diner come-on
13. Biblical suffix
14. Like "Grease" characters
15. Weaken
16. Bedouin robes
17. Business
18. Icelandic saga
24. Lake in Ireland
25. Coleridge's "gentle thing"
26. Jerry-built
31. Angler's basket
32. Light fabric
33. Woolf's "___ of One's Own"
34. Unexpected gain
35. Rye coating
36. Gardener's bane
37. What to "give me"
38. Reitman film: 1986
39. Book, in Brescia
40. Start
43. Turkish empire founder
44. Modern frontier
47. Civil War battle
53. Came into being
54. Pub offering
55. Reaches
56. Czech
57. "Casablanca" costar
58. Examines minutely
61. Lug of a jug
64. U.S.N.A. graduate
66. At the ready
67. A larceny size
68. Homing device
69. Verdi princess
70. ". . . it is ___ of life": Proverbs 13:12
71. Workman, e.g.
72. Sierra ___
73. Transmits
76. Knight's shaft
77. Neutral colors
83. Cause an axle to break
85. U.F. student
86. Beg
87. Events for Phil Mahre
88. Broom for Twiggy?
89. "Each and All" poet
90. Up in arms, e.g.
93. Old French coin
96. Make sound
98. Task
99. Aplomb
100. Beat it!
101. What Pandora let loose
102. Mother of the Titans
103. Trap leader
104. Assemble
105. Jot
106. Portmanteau word
107. Three of these make a tbs.
109. Journalist-reformer Nellie
110. TV option

120 *Physicians' Findings* by Warren W. Reich

ACROSS

1. Part of the pinna
5. A savory jelly
10. Russian range
15. Reveal secrets
19. Mangle
20. Greek river
21. Generally valid
22. Mezzanine section
23. Unprepared
25. Sedate
27. Spates
28. Like lager
30. "Golden" songs
31. Film comic Roscoe
32. Aegean island
33. Sotto ___
34. Wielded
36. Indian police station
37. Left
41. Comminute
42. Susceptible
44. Dockers' org.
45. Troubles
46. Psychic
47. New Look man
48. Old Irish alphabet
49. Gelid
50. Obdurate
54. Thai coins
55. Broadcast
58. Billingsgate
59. Stitch
60. Pax, to Praxiteles
61. Catkin
62. Line on a letter
63. "Ay, ___ inch a king": Shak.
64. The Indian, for one
65. Idleness
68. Malayan palm
69. In flagrante delicto
71. "... to shining ___"
72. Cause for a lawsuit
73. Cannes evening
75. ___ fixe
76. Puchero, e.g.
77. Pindar product
78. Fatuitous
82. Parts of some hammers
83. Extremely old-fashioned
85. Rags-to-riches author
86. Electric catfish
87. Balanchine ballet
88. Hand measures
89. Monsieur's egg
90. First textbook
93. Kind of acid
94. Applauds
98. Excitable
100. Munificent
102. One of the Near Islands
103. Ariz.'s Mo or Stu
104. Small streets
105. Spanish demonstrative
106. Brit. decorations
107. Ill-natured
108. Arabian princes
109. Castle

DOWN

1. Swipe
2. Flat plinth
3. Adonis' killer
4. Boards a Pullman
5. Made amends
6. Injections
7. Darlings
8. Canaan follower
9. Of the founder of Thebes
10. Reveal
11. Haley book
12. Xiamen, formerly
13. Mae West role
14. Tall glass for beer
15. Cutlers' products
16. New Jersey city
17. "___ on Film"
18. Spots for bulbs
24. Gave a party for
26. Spanish hero
29. Jillian and Rutherford
32. Unkind kind of degree
33. "In ___ veritas"
34. Nick the golfer
35. Pusillanimous
36. Yonder
37. Insinuating
38. Parsimonious
39. Buck up
40. Super Bowl team: 1980
41. Trot or lope
42. Josh
43. What i.e. stands for
46. Like Rudolph's nose
48. Parched one's paradise
51. Dubbed
52. Voodoo fetish
53. Moslem law
54. Pressure: Comb. form
56. Upright
57. Actress Ralston
59. Both, in Bonn
61. Caustic
62. Heroic horse
63. Molder
64. Mirador
65. More bizarre
66. Adolescents
67. Veers away
68. Alphabet half
70. Low cards in pinochle
73. Flavorful
74. Algerian port
76. Mariner
78. German philosopher: 1770–1831
79. How the Niagara flows
80. Actor Rachins
81. Despicable
82. Comic Poundstone
84. Metrical foot
86. Pupils' delight
88. Whiff
89. Relative of sienna
90. Star in Ursa Major
91. Deteriorates
92. "Tell ___ the Marines!"
93. Jewish month
94. Hindu fire god
95. "Wishing will make ___"
96. "Take ___ your leader"
97. Neighbor of Wyo.
99. "___ mein holder Abendstern," Wagner aria
101. "___ no orator ...": Shak.

ACROSS

1. Schickele's Bach
4. Diva Lucine
9. Exactly vertical
14. Boxing refs' calls
18. Stead
19. Koran chapters
20. Kind of show
21. A lagomorph
22. Napoleon slept here: 1814
23. Pamphlet
24. Swelling in plant cells
25. Egyptian sun disk
26. Targets for Walter?
29. Lightweight champ Carlos: 1960's
31. Kremlin connection
32. B'way sign
33. High dwelling
35. Org. for Snead
38. Kind of basil
39. Sigma preceder
41. Antenna for singer Eddie?
44. Parts of dols.
46. Suppositions
48. Tito's real name
49. Loretta of "M*A*S*H"
50. "Casablanca" lady
53. Poison for Nero?
56. Luigi's "Enough!"
57. Attendance check
59. Suckling's output
60. Old French coin
61. Writer St. Johns
62. Muffin
64. Penultimate Greek letter
65. Swindles
69. Ball holder
70. Zhivago's portrayer
73. Medieval land tenure
75. O'Neill play: 1917
76. Will disclosures
78. Subvert
80. Type of buoy
81. "Oklahoma!" aunt
83. Jailbird
84. Went
86. What 1988 was
88. Phil the Fiddler's creator
91. What Michael uses to handle people?
93. Approximately
94. Aaron or Raymond
95. Dies
96. "___ Got Sixpence"
97. Actress Jillian
99. Fruit for Buster?

103. San Francisco's 49___
105. "___ World Turns"
109. Susan of "L.A. Law"
110. Hawley-___ Tariff Act
111. Denise of "The Garry Moore Show"
113. Wetlands
115. Kind of acid
117. Observers of a W.Va. legislator?
119. Schoenberg's "Moses and ___"
121. Shaw's phonetic spelling of "fish"
124. Fanon
125. Peak
126. "You're the pants on a ___ usher": Porter
127. Spring harbinger
128. Carter and Gwyn
129. Play re Sadie Thompson
130. Memorable jogger James
131. Southfork family name
132. "Why, thou ___ God . . .": Shak.
133. Stat for Saberhagen

DOWN

1. "___ Talk," 1959 film
2. Pre-election event
3. Summons for Dan?
4. Actor in "The Addams Family"
5. Group of crows
6. Berlin's "He's ___ Picker"
7. Speeds away
8. Brooke or Mary
9. G.R.F. was one
10. Terhune dog
11. British actress Mary
12. Learn by heart
13. Grin and ___
14. Bangkok native
15. Comedian Mickey's dupes?
16. Product of 51 Down
17. Member of Cong.
18. Nobelist Walesa and namesakes
27. PA sch.
28. Scand. nation
30. Asian festival
33. Sore
34. Hard wood
36. Spunk
37. Charleses' dog
40. British actress Wendy
42. Conventual superior
43. Jacob's brother's namesakes
45. Namibia, once: Abbr.
47. Ninth mo.
50. Steamed
51. Deposits
52. Wintry phenomenon
54. Korbut and others
55. Propitiatory bribe
56. Shepherdess of rhyme
58. One of the Dioscuri
60. Mr., in Milano
63. Adjust unsatisfactorily
65. Hindu queen
66. Houston player
67. Siphonaptera members
68. Iron: Comb. form
71. Grown-up pullet
72. Burden, to the Bard
74. ___ City, Calif.
77. Acidulous
79. Throw
82. Biggest part for Sue?
84. Dempsey challenger: 1923
85. Half of MCII
87. Jehoshaphat's predecessor
88. First four subheads
89. Attract
90. Fur for Redd?
91. ___ Bay, Yellow Sea inlet
92. Caused a rubber check
98. Drug cop
100. Theol. degree
101. Political exile
102. English cathedral town
104. Composer of "The Wiz"
106. Movie thriller in 1977
107. Lysander's love
108. City on the Ruhr
112. Maine town
114. Nuclear trial, for short
116. Chalcedony
117. Ex-Met director
118. Ridge
119. Sandy's only word
120. Jarry's "Ubu ___"
122. Kimono sash
123. Can

ACROSS

1. Historic Syrian city
7. Prague, to a Czech
12. Ballet's "Le ___ des Cygnes"
15. Penn pronoun
19. Curie's discovery
20. Ceremonial acts
21. Bodkin
22. Blessed
23. Busy Athenian's breakfast?
25. Dissimulation
27. Lake near a temple of Diana
28. Holiday greeting by Zorba?
30. Go lickety-split
32. Union unit
33. Grossly stupid
34. Mirror
37. Slumgullion
38. Actor Adler
41. Chaney
42. Squash
45. Son of an unc.
46. Fragrant evergreen
50. Budding classicist's statement about future plans?
56. Caucho yielder
57. Remainder
58. Lined up
59. Small constellation
60. Bourse
61. Resolution time for José
62. Guitar ridge
63. Vatican name
64. Wearing garments
65. "___ than none"?
70. Sinatra's cohorts
73. Tom's friend in "Typee"
74. Fork unit
75. Silk makers
79. Challenging
80. Li'l Abner's son
81. Was checkmated
82. Unfamiliar
84. Pig ___ poke
85. Song of the Aegean sailor?
88. Bit role
90. Auspices
91. Coptic Church title
92. Agcy. with an eagle
93. Accounts officer on a ship
95. Appearance
98. Induce
100. Mutiny inciter
102. Concerning
104. Son in "Desire Under the Elms"
106. Concurring words by Theocritus?
110. Spiked shield boss
114. Approached directly
115. Lettered composer?
117. Pow!
118. Ending for boff or pay
119. Expected
120. Conductor Fritz
121. ___-majesté
122. Male aoudad
123. Sumerian moon god
124. Safeguard

DOWN

1. "Man of ___," Flaherty film
2. Baikal or Peipus
3. Round cheese
4. Larks' cousins
5. Baby seal
6. City in Nebraska
7. O.T. book
8. Most abundant
9. "And jeers ___": F.P.A.
10. Bray
11. "While memory holds ___ ...": Shak.
12. Caribou herdsman
13. Wrong
14. Close tightly
15. "___ slaves who fear to speak": Lowell
16. Masters, as skills
17. "___ Dream," Wagnerian aria
18. Witness
24. "Wheels"
26. Pianist Rosalyn
29. A Pequod owner in "Moby-Dick"
31. Spanish, to Spanish
34. Spherical object
35. Lee J. Cobb role
36. Apply chrism, old style
37. "Tartan" producer Lesser
39. Elevate
40. "... ay, there's ___": Shak.
43. Catchall sentence ender
44. Author of "Hop-Frog"
45. L.A.-to-Reno dir.
47. Twofold
48. Ms. Nazimova
49. "The Third Man" director
51. M-1 rifle
52. Premature
53. Mars: Comb. form
54. TV-antenna device
55. Effortlessness
60. Tumblebug
62. Czars' jeweler
63. Calico pony
66. Egyptian god of artisans
67. Runagates
68. Kind of story
69. O'Hara's "From the ___"
70. "Blondie" cartoonist Young
71. Singer Cantrell
72. Saroyan's "My Name Is ___"
76. Turkey's President: 1938–50
77. Algae extracts
78. Kin of vibrissae
81. Blake's "The Book of ___"
82. Sad sound
83. Clumsy craft
85. Areas off fairways
86. Tyre monarch
87. A parent of a dzo
89. Embodiment
94. Eloquent speaker
95. Author Alcott
96. Surpass in firepower
97. Ottoman Empire founder
99. Jackal-headed god
100. Poilu's term for his foe
101. "Star Wars" director
103. One of a cap'n's aides
104. Region N of Afr.
105. Eric of movies
106. Small sailboat
107. Tissue layer
108. Costa loser
109. Dog buried in Hyde Park
111. Carte before the course
112. Fox or Rabbit
113. Story-time heavy
116. Stag attendees

123 *A Christmas Concert* by Walter Covell

ACROSS

1. Mother: Comb. form
6. Kind of tide
10. Pasturage
13. Seasonal ringers
19. Earthy oxide
20. Actor Jack
21. Pixie
22. Interstice
23. Mi re do re mi fa sol
26. Dec. 25 adjective
27. Shipworm
28. Paves anew
29. Bothers
30. River to the Baltic
31. "___ furtiva lagrima . . .": Donizetti aria
33. XXVII divided IX
34. Erector ___
35. Alter follower
36. La la si la do ti ti ti la si
43. With 50 Down, sol fa mi re do re mi do
47. Burdensome
48. Lessen
49. Squirrel's cache
50. Religious reformer of Bohemia
51. Hallowed woman: Fr.
52. Argentine river
53. Water wheel
54. The least bit
55. City in Morocco
56. ___ favorite
57. Student group
58. Maltreat
61. Scottish firth
62. Sniggles
63. Sol la sol mi sol la sol mi
66. Identical
70. Dodecanese island
71. Nestle
72. Heart chambers
73. Fervid
77. Arafat's org.
79. Byron's twilight
80. Manhandles
81. Marie Antoinette, e.g.
82. Former agcy. concerned with planes
83. Team of oxen
85. Sing like a bird
86. Mount of a Magus
87. Rock ___
89. With 118 Across, do re mi re do re mi re do sol sol sol sol

90. Do do sol do re sol
92. Rhea, to the Romans
93. Min. part
94. Coal size
95. Colonial bird
96. Like the Sahara
100. Twisted paper sweets-holders
105. Worlds, to René
107. Herbal beverage
109. Futile
110. Mi fa mi ri mi fa fi sol
112. Airborne team member
113. Pet name
114. One-time Korean president
115. Native of Mashhad
116. Passover feasts
117. East, in Essen
118. See 89 Across
119. Loudness units

DOWN

1. Saying
2. Yearned
3. "And ___ were shepherds . . .": J. S. Bach
4. Direct attention (to)
5. Crocus or gladiolus
6. Aye
7. Extreme
8. "In the ___ snow is glist'nin' "
9. Feelings
10. More suspicious
11. House additions
12. Labor org.
13. OSHA concern
14. Olympic hawk
15. Aerie
16. Carry
17. Having wings
18. Maglie and Bando
24. Rowdies
25. Dispenses with
29. Intrinsically
32. Ark maker in the Douay Bible
34. Bearcat maker
35. Lab heaters
36. Join freight cars
37. News organ?
38. Sweet treat
39. In the sack
40. Cleaning cloths
41. Other, to Pedro
42. Trotsky or Uris
43. New Year's Eve activity
44. Élève's milieu
45. Atoll material

46. ___ Kringle
50. See 43 Across
54. Danish-born reformer
55. Repel, with "off"
56. Feed-bag morsel
59. "Address to the ___ Guid": Burns
60. Actor Erwin
61. "___ entered in those wise men three"
63. Toper
64. Goals
65. Setting in "Brigadoon"
66. Lead players
67. Island off Venezuela
68. One-thousandth: Comb. form
69. Atelier stand
70. Emulated shepherds in a crèche
72. Accumulate
73. Ancient strong box
74. Interpret

75. Fast-stop site
76. Chemical endings
77. Sudden terror
78. Alan, Cheryl or Diane
82. Bistros
83. Channel north of the Isle of Wight
84. Beggars or lawyers
85. Elk
88. Repair a brick wall, in a way
89. Conquered
91. Organic compounds
95. Pale
96. Houston baseballer
97. Nobelist in Physics: 1930
98. Foolish
99. Arnaz and others
100. Food dish
101. Western Indian
102. Bark
103. Central point
104. Danish weights
105. Conductance units
106. Reverberate

108. Egyptian goddess of fertility
110. Abbott's first baseman
111. Col.'s command

ACROSS

1. Bit part
5. Parka piece
9. Intrigue
14. Whipper-snapper?
20. Blockheads
21. Ivy League school
22. Allan-___
23. Monte Carlo number
24. "Don't throw bouquets ___"
25. Nanny's carriage
26. Short ___ (little attention)
28. Pencil "helmet"
29. Greek letter
30. Film from a biblical phrase
33. Foiled the posse
35. Chili con ___
36. Naval off.
37. Jerky, e.g.
38. Ruins
39. Manual arts
41. Ex-constellation
42. Inventor of a sign language
43. Portly
44. Placed in a heavenly area
46. Consecrate
48. "___ Dei" (prayer)
50. "But ___ begin": J.F.K.
51. Orale
52. Cara or Papas
57. "... grow too ___ dream"
58. Sponsorship
59. Sugarless item
60. One leaving a will
62. Slipper
63. "Am" for two
64. Fine wool
66. Root and 21 Across
67. Three, at the Trevi
68. Houston org.
70. With "The," film from a biblical phrase
72. Writer Rand et al.
74. Abrogate
76. ___ of (addressing term)
77. Whilom
81. Film based on a biblical phrase
84. ___ Halaby (Jordan's Queen Noor)
86. Cry of pleasure
87. "...baked ___"
90. Actress North
91. Mideastern org.
92. Tally
94. Site of Stanford U.
96. Capek classic
97. Boat-bottom timber
98. Less apt to bolt
99. "___ Like I," Loos autobiography
100. Frequently
102. Wait on
103. Sultan's decree
104. In the attic, e.g.
106. Brief
108. Giant Hall of Famer
109. Hot box
113. Laugh, in Lyon
114. Condiment
115. "___ Way" Cahn-Van Heusen song
118. Prometheus's theft
119. "Life ___ jest...": Gay
120. Worthless talk
121. Flood
122. Film from a Donne phrase
127. Crock or trick ending
128. Overjoyed
129. Croaky
130. Call at sea
131. Power source
132. Ripped again
133. Gives forth
134. Sanction
135. No great shakes
136. Grand places?
137. Strikes out
138. In ___ (completely)
139. In business

DOWN

1. In a lather?
2. Film from a phrase in Gray's "Elegy..."
3. Film from a Burnsian phrase
4. Half a fly
5. - - -
6. Sculled
7. Norwegian saint
8. Show car
9. Rippling folds
10. Stuck
11. Cuts of beef
12. "What ___," 1939 film
13. Portside
14. Autry's hat
15. Indonesia's ___ Islands
16. Chicken Little's cry
17. Conforming
18. Old headstones
19. Cylindrical
27. Film from a biblical phrase
30. Meas. of revolutions
31. Second flyer
32. Donkey, e.g.
34. Sagacious
39. Film from a Julia Ward Howe phrase
40. Get even again
41. ___-Margaret
45. Satisfies
46. He wrote "Now We Are Six"
47. Lord or Sir, e.g.
48. Blood line
49. Forthwith
51. Stealthy
53. Bump, in poker
54. Numerical ending
55. ___-Turn (road sign)
56. Ending for 76
59. Fetch
61. Male and female
64. Average
65. Required: Abbr.
69. A moon of Uranus
70. Having strata
71. Ripken's cohorts
73. Flavor
75. Monogram of the author of "The Killers"
78. Film from a Daniel Webster quote
79. Film from a FitzGerald phrase
80. Voilà!
82. Omani money
83. Neath's opposite
85. Vino center
87. NW Argentine group
88. Fishwife's cousin
89. Man with 40 men
91. Nez ___ (American Indian)
93. Old round dances
95. Me-___ (coattails policy)
97. Doghouse
101. Ball prop
102. Like some birds
105. Electron tubes
106. Actress Holm
107. "___ bed..."
109. Bids
110. Bloomer girl?
111. Typos
112. Unit of force
114. Small thread
116. Bandleader Brown
117. Root word
120. Former N.Y.C. mayor
121. Raft
123. Remuda
124. Weeded
125. Big name in 126 Down
126. Where Ashtabula is
131. Japanese national park

125 *Iffy Answers* by Charles M. Deber

ACROSS

1. Resell tickets
6. Exposition
10. Jersey
15. W.W. II gen.
18. "Luck and Pluck" author
19. Suffix with major or kitchen
20. Splinter
21. Darling or Silver
22. ASK FOR IT
26. Hot tub
27. Rate of speed
28. QB Warren
29. Lawn item
30. A HA'PENNY WILL DO
35. Least cordial
38. Sahara area
39. Fla. county
40. Lenya of "The Threepenny Opera"
41. Former V.I.P. at the Met
43. Like some stadiums
44. Suffix with Finn or Lett
47. Do this, then reap
48. CAN SPRING BE FAR BEHIND?
51. Boy preceder
52. Workshops
55. Kalpa, to a Hindu
56. Eisenhower aide, in 1953
58. Excise, to a doctor
59. Use a Frisbee
61. Bluebloods
62. Peculate
64. LET HIM GO
67. Roman goddess of chastity
68. Came to rest
70. Israeli statesman
71. Blackish butterfly
73. Wakes
75. Penn., e.g.
76. Pets
79. Encolure
80. WEAR IT
84. Actress Joanne
85. Andress film: 1965
86. Actor from London
87. Xmas centerpiece
88. Certain fighter
90. Horn blower Al
91. Day, to Don Quixote
92. Entreated
93. YOU'LL BE A MAN, MY SON
101. Boredom
102. Greenish-blue color

103. Produce interest
104. In favor of
107. TRY TRY AGAIN
113. Dauphin's père
114. Straying
115. Courteous bloke
116. Undo
117. Bos. or N.Y.
118. Sitologists' subjects
119. Olden days
120. Categories

DOWN

1. Asserts
2. Sound on cobblestones
3. Orinoco contents
4. Was in charge
5. Set forth
6. Command to a canine
7. Bewildered
8. Suffix with Adam or Eden
9. Appear again
10. Argot
11. Skeet feat
12. Campus climber
13. Essex contemporary
14. Surpassed
15. Tempted
16. Producer-director Stanley ___
17. Ingress
20. Massé or carom
23. Mile on the water
24. World's most common name
25. Sadness
30. "O ___ we trust . . .": Tennyson
31. Outlet
32. Blue Moon of baseball
33. Domesticates
34. Start of a Yule hymn
35. Ingrid in "Casablanca"
36. Codger
37. 'TWERE WELL 'TWERE DONE QUICKLY
41. Whipping rod
42. Conforming
43. English poet
44. THIS MUST BE BELGIUM
45. Dutch genre painter
46. Medieval merchant guild
48. Like a homunculus
49. Stuffed pepper
50. Winds

51. Bhutanese, e.g.
53. Unit of distance
54. Keys
57. Movie role of 86 Across
59. Onward
60. Burns's Allen
62. Duplicate events
63. Pentateuch
65. Nobel novelist: 1946
66. List of runners
69. Check
72. Natives of San Juan: Abbr.
74. Goldbrick
77. Fulmar's kin
78. Impleaded
81. Duck, in Dresden
82. Study of causation
83. "___ Sorge," Sudermann novel
86. Headed a committee
88. Frisks
89. Whippersnapper
91. Couple
92. El Misti's locale
93. Oenologists' concerns
94. Sitting pretty

95. Not qualified
96. ___ bono?
97. Certain collars
98. ___-être (perhaps): Fr.
99. Amt. paid to an atty.
100. Dispatch
104. Anjou or Comice
105. Lie on the oars
106. Genethliacons
108. ___ Lanka
109. Three, in Torino
110. Sun ___-sen of China
111. Modernist
112. ___-Magnon

126 *Weekly Tabloid Editor's Dreams* by Bert H. Kruse

ACROSS

1. "___ Ike" button
6. A son of Jacob
10. Make sense
15. Flutters the sheets
16. Luster
17. Publication makeup
19. Ceremonies
20. Precocious Ivy Leaguer!
23. Alt.
24. Connery and Penn
26. New Orleans hoopla word
27. Buttons, for one
28. Writer Earl ___ Biggers
29. Borrowed
31. Alias
32. Bête ___
34. Stopped at a motel
36. Beat pounder
37. What a Mexican whistles
39. Cries of joy
40. Concorde bows to big birds!
43. Switches
44. Roh ___ Woo of the ROK
45. God, to Verdi
46. Certain gales
49. U.S. Open tennis champ: 1966
52. "Le ___ d'or"
54. Command at sea
55. ___ Mahal
58. Arduous
60. Thigh armor
62. Rollo's men
64. "Bus Stop" playwright
65. Egotist ties his knot!
68. Goddess of victory
69. Devil
71. Ivanhoe's love
72. Intensifying agent
74. Dolce ___ niente
75. Twin City suburb
77. Refrain start
79. Moved quickly
80. Karate ploy
82. Some Bx. trains
84. "Blame It on ___," 1984 film
85. Like deciduous trees
87. Snowman elected!
93. Globetrotters' home
94. Fall on Broadway
96. Crossette
97. Judicial attire
98. Kind of city
99. Pants maker of song
100. Actress Franklin

103. Budget concern
104. Nigerian city
105. "___ bleu!"
107. Cheryl Tiegs, e.g.
108. ___ time (never)
109. Vehicle made of ballpoints!
113. Inlet in SE Conn.
115. Yalta figure
116. Special collars
117. Steps for pairs
118. ___ the hills
119. Type of dancer
120. Aromatic compound

DOWN

1. Hospital person
2. Paris art palace lifted!
3. "Sliver" author Levin
4. Five-time Horse of the Year
5. Heart
6. ___ apso
7. Moray, e.g.
8. Kind of sign
9. Director Bergman
10. Valuable Nigerian tree
11. U.S. publisher
12. Great Lake being emptied!
13. U.S.A. draft program
14. Flag-waver
15. Wild pink catchfly
16. Like some Gospels
18. Insignificant ones
19. Excavate again
21. Fall tool
22. Keats feats
25. "___ would sink a navy . . .": Shak.
30. "Emerald Point ___," TV series
33. Endings for ball and harp
35. Understandings
38. Cato's "Go!"
39. Sharpen
41. In Hades
42. Pacify
43. Inured
47. Comedy title starter
48. Rained hard, in Yorkshire
49. French painter Delaunay
50. Blake's burns bright
51. Polished, in a way
53. One of five, for short
55. Threefold

56. Invited
57. Scoff
58. Dust-up
59. Ancient Thracians
61. Turkish inn
63. Gigantic citrus produced!
66. Variety of neck
67. Partner of hopes
70. Western capital auctioned!
73. Nosy one
76. Consider
78. They transfer property
80. Mazuma
81. Sports site
83. Put up with
85. Actress Carole
86. Composer Lecuona
88. Wane
89. Cuban province
90. One fostering a felon
91. Chang's game
92. Renaissance sword
93. Tore
94. Arrow part
95. Foo yong, for one

99. Checks over
101. Native of Muscat
102. Inventor Howe
106. Where Brunei is
110. Sidekick
111. Greek letter
112. Harding beat him
114. Rock star Adam ___

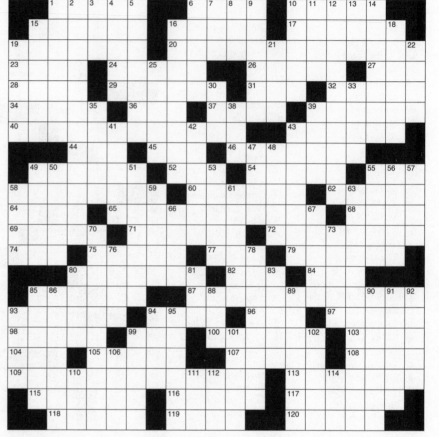

127 Greek Sandwiches by Kenneth Haxton

ACROSS

1. Obstinate person
4. Plagiarizes
9. Nessus, for one
14. Red alga
18. Lecture
20. Pillage; plunder
21. Black Sea port
22. Eldest of the Pleiades
23. Rapid rise
25. Dormant future shoots
27. Wives of Fatima's descendants
28. Automatic pistols
30. Formal avenue
31. Eucharistic dish
32. Kipling's "Soldiers ___"
33. Swiss river
35. Bodies of writing
37. Greek sea goddess
41. Prokofiev's lupine trapper
42. Okla. Siouans
43. Slyly sarcastic
44. F.D.R. measure
45. Actress Alicia
46. Most ceraceous
48. Naval assents
49. Bottom line
50. Actress Talmadge
53. Emulate Doré
55. Poet Hart ___
57. Flower parts
58. Stomach acidity
60. Curling teams
61. Great supply
66. Star-packed teams
68. Town in Ethiopia or Kenya
69. Type of estate
70. ___ fixe
71. Turkish city
72. Put out a candle
74. Conifers
79. Animal and plant lives of regions
80. Scapegoat
82. Species of Mexican yuccas
84. Soup or jacket preceder
85. A.P. rival
86. Uncle Milty
87. Greek goddess of victory
88. Terrier breed
90. Amour-propre
92. British general in the Seven Years War

95. "... ___ perfumed sea": Poe
96. Member of a Jewish sect
97. Competitor
98. Crownlet
101. "L'Heure Espagnole" composer
102. Ester of acid from cork
105. ___ Highway System
108. Origination of first life on earth
110. Causes (oneself) to go
111. Item on an alley
112. Blower on the proboscis
113. Rheo or thermo follower
114. Pushkin refusal
115. Laurel and Musial
116. Aquarium denizen
117. Compass dir.

DOWN

1. Sordini
2. Scold severely
3. Sousa march
4. June beetle
5. ___ Church, N.Z. sect
6. Eye part
7. Sis sibling
8. Systems that turn motors in time with generators
9. Streets, in Sonora
10. Growing out
11. Cole and Turner
12. Brownish gray
13. Sprinted
14. Mystery writer Eric
15. Part of Europe, once
16. Assistant
17. Make an incised mark
19. Defense discipline
24. Liquid measure
26. French pastry
29. Voltaire tragedy
32. Private student
33. Sand, to Chopin
34. Plant lice
35. Comic Jay
36. Poisonous
37. Haphazardly
38. Irrational
39. Boles
40. Furniture designer
41. Moccasin

43. Vanzetti's co-defendant
46. German woods
47. Early Mohammedan converts at Medina
51. Disdain
52. Disease with muscular spasms
54. Type of root
55. Condiment holder
56. Stair part
59. Roi's mate
61. Recording equipment
62. Largest S.A. country, to inhabitants
63. Lie snugly
64. King of England and Denmark
65. Brownie
67. Colonialist Cecil
68. Miss.'s ex-Governor
73. Last stage
74. Prodded
75. Pompey's way
76. Outer layers of cells of an embryo

77. Hair-raising
78. Antonio or Francisco
80. "To ___ not...": Hamlet
81. Crab-eating mongoose
83. Hissing
86. Indistinct
88. Group of 13 witches
89. Portuguese town
91. Arden, for one
92. Prowls after prey
93. Miss. delta town
94. Spanish painter Lo Spagnoletto
96. Fastener for a cloche
98. Lhasa native
99. Like a squid's discharge
100. Fits to
101. Punjabi potentate
102. Easily split rock
103. Pedro's aunts
104. Ferrara family name
106. Kin of aves.

107. Vietnam offensive
109. Caviar

ACROSS

1. Certain secants
7. Cried loudly
13. Border river in 104 Down
17. Prohibit
20. Charm
21. Each
22. Assert
23. Match king Kreuger
25. OPPOSED TO A BANNER SHARE
27. AWAY, SORROW!
29. Forum garb
30. European carp
31. Distort
33. Britain, poetically
34. Plow sole
35. Run, as a dye
37. DEDUCE A REFUSAL
38. Lay a lawn
41. Fondles
42. Suspicious
43. Foreign
44. Hedge shrubs
46. Hall in a casa
47. Son of Seth
48. Agnus ___
51. Atlas items
52. Ni
55. Flowerless plant
56. Speeds
57. Recess ramp
58. Capital of Guam
59. Apportion
60. Over
61. Marry in haste
62. Skipper's "Stop!"
63. European sea bream
64. Author Deighton
65. LOUGANIS'S CHARGED PARTICLE
67. Pipe repairman
68. Placid
71. Flightless bird
72. Race horse: Slang
73. Like fanatics
75. STREAKERS-TOP NOTES
78. Gypsy boy
81. Fragrant blooms
82. Australian tennis great
84. East Indian woody vines
85. Elephant's-ear
86. Basketry grass
87. European finch
88. Come up
89. Wreck completely
90. "Prince ___," R.L.S. work
91. SEAFOOD VENDOR'S STALL
93. Quarter___ (8:45)
94. Enemy
95. Executioner in "The Mikado"
96. Nominate, in Scotland
97. Crowds
98. Small napkin
100. Brainstorms
102. Very proper
103. Obtain
104. Supplements
107. Curl the lip
108. Solo
109. Appeared
110. Color
111. Imbibed
112. Turkish regiment
116. CONTRACT DEBT CHITS
118. HOW TO MAKE MEN TAT
122. Suffix with comment
123. Sisters
124. Navy engineering corpsman
125. Write symbols
126. Hurricane center
127. Ashen
128. Makes croutons
129. Soho cig

DOWN

1. Covenant
2. Melville novel
3. Respiratory organ
4. Esparto
5. Electrical unit
6. Hollywood hopefuls
7. Pressure units
8. Speedily
9. Accompanying
10. Wahine's wreath
11. Italian writer
12. More compact
13. Deviated from course
14. Own
15. Shelter
16. Franciscan nun
17. London attraction
18. To have: Fr.
19. Kept talking
24. City with lots of slots
26. Fall guys
28. Sprite: Fr.
32. Pitch
34. Small barracudas
35. Misrepresent
36. Page
37. Actress Massey
38. Helix
39. Overly frilly
40. BEEF ABOUT 3 A.M. RECORD PLAYING
42. Stocking run
43. Concerning
45. Barkley was one
46. Marsh bird
47. Epochs
48. PANNING THE COLD CUTS SHOP
49. Irregular
50. Bury
52. "___ Lucy"
53. Churchill's good will
54. Actor Richard
55. Blaze
57. David's weapon
59. Snug as a bug in___
61. British noble family
62. Rifleman, at times
63. Sanctify
66. ___ clock (six bells)
67. "The Old Wives' Tale" dramatist
69. Poetic Muse
70. Sake source
72. Grind one's teeth
73. IT CONSISTS OF 592 TCHASTS
74. Same
75. "Amores" poet
76. Conservatives
77. Pindar, for one
79. Bergamot or mandarin
80. Harass
82. Pervious
83. Tuscan river
85. Wells's "___-Bungay"
87. Roman cloak
88. Frighten: Dial.
89. The Velvet Fog
91. Problem on an icy road
92. Run away
93. SVELTE MONARCH
97. Mineral found in dried lake basins
98. Decorous
99. Unique person
100. Hostel
101. Hate
102. Home bases
104. Largest continent
105. Spaghetti al ___
106. Lure
107. Actress Spacek
108. Court decree
110. Albacore
111. Noted Socialist
112. Danish counties
113. Jump
114. Feed the kitty
115. Brain passage
117. Start of the Lord's Prayer
119. Modernist
120. Chinese pagoda
121. Common, in Hawaii

FURTHER CLUES

25 A-37 A
52 A-116 A
65 A-118 A
27 A-40 D
48 D-93 D
73 D-91 A

129 *Turning Phrases* by Jeanne Wilson

ACROSS

1. Fiery felony
6. ___ law (Germanic code)
11. Type of herring
16. Residue
19. Stiller's wife
20. Bandleader Louis
21. Enforcement powers
22. Watering hole?
23. Ait
24. "The Shield of Achilles" poet
25. Decathlete Johnson
26. Darn
27. Wrestling holds
29. Fernando's fast food
31. Is under new management
33. Yoko
34. Elec. units
37. Fill this puzzle
39. Quail
40. Syndicated columns?
44. Bury
45. Smith and Capp
46. Bucolic
47. Eschew
49. Tex. battle site
52. Memorable stutterer
53. "___ thee late a rosy wreath": Jonson
54. Halfway-like
57. Out of the race
59. Dublin or nothin'?
62. Cool quaff
63. Kind of frost
64. Aesopian finale
65. "My Fair Lady" lyricist
66. Wilbur works
68. Muslim wise man
69. Greek letters
70. Nod off
72. Scolded
73. Pseudologist
74. Stalemate
77. Hiked through campgrounds?
79. Librarians' clientele
81. Article
82. Physicist Bohr
83. Soviet sea
84. Merchandise
85. Group of badgers
86. Brilliance
88. Ens' followers
89. What Salk conquered
93. Beer foam?
98. Carry out
100. Wildebeest
101. Vend
102. Symbol of strength
104. He dyes for a living
105. Cartoon tiger
107. Dickens's Madame ___
110. Bern's river
111. Pepper pot ingredient
113. Capitol Hill body
116. Building projection
117. Racket
118. Kovacs
119. Depside is one
120. Arabian gazelle
121. Silly pair
122. Stormed
123. Facients
124. Après-ski drink

DOWN

1. ___ acids
2. Take umbrage
3. Jaundiced
4. Mine finds
5. Brussels-based org.
6. Bursts of energy
7. Indonesian island group
8. Palpebra
9. "___ a man who wasn't there"
10. Rummy game
11. Promenade
12. Green or jacket
13. What a pause does
14. Fit to ___
15. Advice to an inept gardener?
16. Agreement
17. Londoner's pantry
18. Mooring rope
28. Scots' negatives
30. Anthracite
32. Barrette
35. O. Henry
36. Swung around
38. Craft
41. "___ Camera"
42. Moths' meeting?
43. A.M.A. members
48. Muddied
49. Third king of Judah
50. Statistician's Abbr.
51. "I long for ___ . . .": Wordsworth
52. Discovery sounds
53. Mosque priest
54. Cathedral
55. Jewel thief's loot
56. German article
58. ___ Française (French national theater)
59. One-liners, e.g.
60. Jejune
61. Sixty minutes, in Siena
64. Dillon of "Gunsmoke"
67. Sounds from tack-sitters
68. Brinker of fiction
69. Spin a log
70. Agr. is one
71. Fall call
72. D.S. Freeman book
73. Abominate
75. Wrath
76. Ar's chaser
78. Attaching ropes
79. Churlish children
80. Porter's "DuBarry ___ Lady"
83. TV sitcom
86. Ferber or Millay
87. Gave reluctantly, with "up"
88. Make eyes at
89. Dressage maneuver
90. Soup ingredient
91. Ascertains
92. Here, in Haiti
94. Made a pact
95. Church officials
96. Vile
97. Lost muscle tone
99. ___ incognita
103. Singer Smith
106. Mediocre
108. Soho pad
109. Baltic island
112. Nesselrode, e.g.
114. Actress Christensen
115. Sun. discourse

130 Show-How Session by Randolph Ross

ACROSS

1. Strains the brain
6. Segovia's companion
12. Gerald Ford, by birth
18. Peer
19. Amusements
21. Notable Watergate figure
22. Eritrea's urethane riches
24. Believe; trust
25. Blue
26. Lucy lover
27. Produced milk
29. He wrote "The Sultan of Sulu"
30. Sinatra film: 1954
34. Auguries
37. Menace with reata
41. ___ Bator, Mongolia
43. Pile
44. Douse
45. Ending for scant or pant
46. Crandall and Webb
47. Pfc. superior
48. Arab garments
49. P.D.Q. realtive
51. Some radio buffs
53. Arias
54. Act like Mrs. Mitty
55. Country lass
57. Orange-red chalcedony
58. Beginning
60. More like Poe's midnight
62. Owing
64. New England eleven, familiarly
65. Owe a pony and a gun
68. Elide
70. Grammer of "Cheers"
71. Forsakes
75. Dealt
77. Word with miss or beer
78. Italian card game
79. Tatami
80. Dame Myra
81. S-shaped curves
83. A Bolger co-star in 1939
84. Skin
85. Lodge member
86. ___ Reekie (Edinburgh)

87. Author of "One Human Minute"
88. Core
91. Verb ending
92. Trim a photo
93. Act I—"On a secret mission"
95. Grassy plant
97. Explosive
99. ___ de deux
100. "...and take it for ___ worse": Cowley
102. Organic compound
104. Kimono sash
107. Webster or Clay
109. They span hybrid gestation
114. Italia's second largest city
115. Of ancient writing
116. Barton, e.g.
117. Took off
118. Jim Varney role
119. Silly ones

DOWN

1. Lee's men
2. Shade of blue
3. Coagulant
4. Winding of jazz fame
5. Luge lover
6. Tawdry
7. Application
8. Ending for a niña's name
9. "___ the season..."
10. Gris-gris
11. Stood for a second term
12. Movie whale
13. Dean and Downey
14. Revoke a legacy
15. Mexico's tourist expense
16. A tickbird
17. Finisher in "Wayne's World"
19. A gal. has eight
20. This could be a challenge to find
23. He went to town
28. W. Harrison's successor
29. Stout choices
31. Bathsheba's first mate
32. Profound
33. "___ Boot"
35. Capital of Campania

36. Gymnastics move
37. Article of food
38. Imprison
39. P.R. man's concern
40. N.J. township
42. ___-ran
50. Put this up or chase flies
51. Box for oolong
52. Cook up
53. Point of view
55. Corresponded
56. Aachen article
57. Mock
59. "Once ___ time..."
61. Stomach churners
62. "Casablanca" heroine et al.
63. Cylindrical seat
66. Protected, at sea
67. Soft food for invalids
68. Blackmailer's words
69. Place to hobnob all night in disguise

72. Muscat-eer?
73. Stupor: Comb. form
74. Painter of "The Feast of St. Nicholas"
75. Kojak and a Huxtable
76. Sullen
78. Soft and crumbling, as bricks
82. Hand warmer
83. A tribe of Israel
84. Favorites
86. Paint solvent
87. Auction unit
89. Flavor
90. Fish preparation
93. George Washington ___
94. Prepare another draft
96. Reach
98. He outranks the sarge
101. Walked on
103. G.E. subsidiary

104. Grimm character
105. A First Lady of the 50's
106. "Uh-huh"
107. An arm of the U.S. exec. branch
108. A Hope-Crosby location
110. Directional ending
111. Actress Charlotte
112. U.F.O. crew
113. Required

(131) Celebrity Headlines by Norman S. Wizer

ACROSS

1. Castle feature
5. Violin's predecessor
10. Girasols
15. Paraphernalia
19. "Othello" villain
20. Poetry muse
21. A Heep of literature
22. River at Rennes
23. Tallyho for dancer, pitcher, saxophonist, and actor
27. Conserve
28. Concealed obstacles
29. Ammonia derivative
30. Like Hume's tomes
32. Letter opener
33. Tahiti togs
35. Bower
39. White poplar
41. Handles roughly
42. The old grind for two actresses and two authors
50. Hemsley sitcom
51. Houston, to Warwick
52. Footpace
53. Type of vaccine
54. TV network's concern
56. Hooch or all-night flight
59. Clown in "Pagliacci"
60. Saturn attachment
62. Dispatch boat
63. Kitt from S.C.
64. Faulty cobbling for jockey, philosopher, runner, and TV actor
70. Humphrey's widow
71. Poet Lizette Woodworth ___
72. Centers; hubs
73. Structure on a predella
74. Lined with mother-of-pearl
75. Following the sun
80. Saul's uncle and grandfather
81. Tony Peña's glove
82. Abbreviated attribute
84. Arrow poison
85. Culinary blunder for actor, TV narrator, comedian, and essayist
91. Belgian river
92. This features Achilles wrath
93. Yoga position
94. Resembling
98. Cry of woe
99. Takes advantage of
102. Sky: Comb. form
103. Numbers game
105. Rats
110. Outdoor chore for author, singer, showman, and President
115. Stake
116. Acronym for an ex-treaty
117. Shade of green
118. Con
119. Inlets
120. Stand-in for Standish
121. Goren partner Helen ___
122. Use a scythe

DOWN

1. Wolverine st.
2. Locale of Diamond Head
3. Turkish titles
4. Pyramid, e.g.
5. Catherine de Medici was one
6. Subject to planation
7. Censor
8. Numerical suffixes
9. Advise
10. Increased faster
11. Vintner's gear
12. Broadcast
13. Billiard opening action
14. Andress film: 1965
15. Thingamajig
16. Sprite-ly
17. In conformity with
18. Harrison and Reed
24. G.I.'s devil-dodger
25. Brad and spad
26. Ankle: Comb. form
31. Gagne ___ (French breadwinner)
33. Hekzebiah Hawkins's daughter
34. Terrifies
35. From a distance
36. Hero in a Sanskrit epic
37. A Maverick of TV
38. Hawks fly here
40. PB&J alternative
41. Tie-breaking contest, e.g.
43. Loose overcoat
44. Bach's output
45. Common Latin phrase
46. Hebrew instruments
47. So much, to Verdi
48. One of Job's friends
49. Trondheim toast
55. Identifier
56. Croupier, e.g.
57. Enlarging gradually
58. Feasted
59. Goes from gate to runway
61. Effervescing device
63. Surpasses
64. Ade medium
65. Czech coin
66. Bizarre
67. Clear a tape
68. Right-hand page
69. Hawkeye
74. More refined
76. Madre's sisters
77. Quechuan
78. Element #10
79. Actress Rowlands
81. L. L'Amour's "The Haunted ___"
82. In the capacity of
83. Indic language
86. Parachute material
87. Explosive force
88. Make jubilant
89. Nightclubs
90. Thrash
94. Honeyed word
95. He may come from Qum
96. The Street Singer's theme
97. Rameau's "Les ___ galantes"
98. Winged ant
100. Franklin invented one
101. Support for Soyer
104. A Nobel Institute site
106. Ski lift
107. Clair de ___ (porcelain)
108. Spanish demonstrative
109. Corvette, for one
111. Hockey star Tikkanen
112. Electrical unit
113. Paper ball
114. Tease

132 Exterminate the Pests! by Kenneth Haxton

ACROSS

1. Plant of the nightshade family
7. Mexican fare
12. Instrumental silencer
16. ___ doble (corrida march)
20. Head garland
21. Cheerful
22. Son of Judah: Gen. 38:4
23. Tabriz location
24. Garden State borough
27. Factor in football
28. Pheasant brood
29. U.S. film critic-author
30. What Mollie Bloom said finally
31. Hero
33. Square-root signs
37. Postpone
39. TV's "I Married ___": 1987
40. Coeur d'___, Idaho
41. Norman town
44. Guanaco's descendant
46. Petty prince
50. Patrick Dennis's aunt
51. Thomson-Stein opera: 1947
54. Distrustful
55. Defective vision
57. Sambar, e.g.
58. Achilles' tissues
60. Seasoning for Bardot
61. Give orders
63. Oppenheim sleuth
65. Yesteryear
66. One of the Jackson Five
67. Black cuckoo
68. Yearn
70. Flowed to and fro
73. Panamanian province
75. ___ homo (religious picture)
77. Felis pardalis
80. Kind of physics
83. "Vaya con ___"
84. Snit
85. Sum of interest to Bohr
87. A son of Bilhah
88. Strauss's "Die ___ ohne Schatten"
89. High, in the French Alps
90. Know by cognition
91. Natives of Benin City
93. Type of print
95. Diet periods
97. Emulate Charles Carroll
99. Mrs. Sprat's fare
101. Steeplechase, e.g.
102. Diary abbr.
105. Honshu city
108. Rhythmic sequence
110. Auden's "The ___ of Anxiety"
111. Garage employee
114. Home of Irish kings
116. Spite
117. Fiber from a jute
119. Isherwood's treatise on philosophy: 1970
122. Prof's concoction
123. Photographer Adams et al.
125. Calif. resort
126. "Picnic" playwright
127. Struck a Philistine
128. Composer Janácek
130. Covered with frost
132. Twisted
134. French painter-lithographer
138. An S.S.R., once
140. Chadian town
141. Qualified
142. Augur
143. Dicey predicament
149. Baron Munchausen, e.g.
150. Turkish regiment
151. Oppositionists
152. Bowl-game locales
153. Optical device
154. A Yugoslav, once
155. Last word of Genesis
156. Mercutio's nemesis

DOWN

1. Make picots
2. "A Chorus Line" show-stopper
3. Staff
4. Nabokov opus
5. Bridge holding
6. The end
7. Number of Trevi coins
8. Ethereal
9. Checked the joint
10. Singular reflexive
11. Hordeolum
12. Cable-car V.I.P.
13. Coll.'s big sister
14. Like Kate in Act V
15. Anos openers
16. Featherlike
17. Hardscrabble
18. Nigerian singer
19. Unique fellow
25. Natives of Cardiff
26. Emulated Yorick
31. Rental document
32. Hurdles for would-be Ph.D's
33. Open shelter
34. Protein acid
35. U.S. election routine
36. Bungling
38. Having long, rounded grooves
42. Wineglass leftovers
43. City on the Oka
45. He played Gershwin
47. Historic 1974 event
48. Alpine crests
49. Tower used in air races
51. Films' M. Hulot
52. Cicero was one
53. Birler's footing
56. Titan who fathered Prometheus
59. Where Cain settled
62. Methuselah's father
64. Saps
66. Musical chord
69. S.A. country
71. Let out
72. New World rodent
74. Book appendixes
76. Desist
78. Jewish month
79. Like Marquand's Apley
81. "All ___ and Heaven Too"
82. Tall story
86. Sword-shaped, as a leaf
88. Ale vessel
92. Pouch-shaped
93. Persona non ___
94. Yevtushenko's "Babi ___"
96. ". . . ___ in the inn"
98. Vasco da ___
100. Pullulated
103. Sweet or split chaser
104. Enthralled
106. Muslim judge: Var.
107. ___ Islands, off Ireland
109. Perfume resin
111. Roman helmet
112. Cookout item
113. Moral precept
115. Pier of Hollywood: 1932–71
118. A star of "Dr. Strangelove"
120. Swerving
121. Dogma
124. John Philip's namesakes
127. In after-workout condition
129. Monument marker
131. Rhodes of Polo Grounds fame
133. Expect confidently
134. Like Bunyan's tales
135. N.Y. stage award
136. ___ Bator, Mongolia
137. Tower
139. Corvette or packet
143. Port on Huon Gulf
144. J.F.K. visitor
145. Collar part
146. Nancy Walker character
147. "Black gold"
148. Singer Cole

133 *Startling Statements* by Dorothea E. Shipp

ACROSS

1. State in E. India
7. Shaped like an oak leaf
12. Teddy, for example
18. Roll
19. Occasional TV fare
21. Small cavity
22. Regard
23. Type of cheese
24. Bigoted
25. Mr. Bumble's declaration in "Oliver Twist"
28. Chokes; stifles
29. Muscle protein
30. Custard dessert
31. One's companion
34. Former Ringling star
35. Burgeon
36. Relieve
38. Seat of Wayne Co., Utah
39. Begley and Lopat
40. Dweller in Hades
41. "Messe de Requiem" composer
42. Call-call answer
44. Kind of shooter
45. Business abbr.
46. Tree of C. America
47. According to Kipling, "The ___"
57. Hound's strong point
58. "But never ___ my love": Shak.
59. Amatory
61. Merry, to a Basque
62. Avian brood
63. Like a ghost
65. Granular snow
66. Lozenge
68. Repudiate
69. Shankar's instrument
70. Statement preceding 47 Across
74. Never, in Nürnberg
75. ___ polloi
76. Colorless
77. Kronborg Castle features
80. Syncope
82. Message medium
85. Monogram of a suffragette
88. Prop, e.g.
89. Orale
90. Actresses Bonet and Eilbacher
91. Fox hunter's goad
92. Year in the reign of Antoninus Pius
93. Anguish
94. Recoils
95. Has-been's place
96. Statement made by Alice
101. Screenwriter Lehman
103. Course participant
104. Offensive
106. Give a rendition of a poem
107. Suave British actor: 1906–72
108. Listen
109. Pertaining to a cenotaph
110. Makes sound again
111. First name of 107 Across

DOWN

1. Pay dirt
2. "Cyrano de Bergerac" playwright
3. Mexico's ___ of Tehuantepec
4. Escarpments
5. Closes a falcon's eyes
6. "Aeneid" starter
7. Lection
8. Forward a letter
9. Billy___, pop singer
10. Confessor's earful
11. Grub
12. Patten, e.g.
13. Retinue
14. Architect Saarinen
15. Impressive entries
16. U.N. arm
17. Just out
19. Flavorsome
20. Informal footwear
26. Muted trumpet sound
27. Lenard's "Winnie ___ Pooh"
28. Scheduled
32. Costello or Gossett
33. Hood's exit
35. Pahlavi was one
36. Told all to the fuzz
37. Dark purple
40. MacDonald branch, e.g.
41. Decree
42. Give a leg up to a yegg
43. Canada, once
44. Regretful
46. College of N.C.
47. Brilliance
48. This makes Rover no rover
49. Great Barrier Reef sight
50. Kind of orange
51. Dogfall, in wrestling
52. Curve of a ship's plank
53. Motilal or Jawaharlal
54. E.C. Bentley's sleuth
55. Vinegary: Comb. form
56. Type of engagement
57. Drain
60. Celtic Neptune
62. What this is
63. SST's, e.g.
64. Ashcan target
67. Heron's kin
68. Burlesque act
69. Tunisian port
71. A hit song of 1922
72. Do some piloting
73. Dazzles a disciple
77. Brit. raincoat
78. Shipment from Saudi Arabia
79. Loan
80. Hunger, to Henri
81. History
82. Watches
83. Glacial deposits
84. "Krapp's ___ Tape": Beckett
85. Family name of Princess Diana
86. Like sumo competitors
87. Sandy's remark
89. More like Arbuckle
90. Hampton of jazz
91. Japanese religion
93. ___ fagioli (Neapolitan dish)
94. Producer Sir Alexander
95. Emulate Katarina Witt
97. Do a plasterer's job
98. Nope's opposite
99. Scene of many a strike
100. Berlin's "He's ___ Picker"
101. Forage plant
102. Macerate
105. E.T.O. leader

134 Croakers *by Frances Hansen*

ACROSS

1. Prohibits
5. Hector's hometown
9. Contained
13. Tearful comedienne Pitts
17. One of the Waughs
18. Seductively beautiful woman
19. Bakery worker
20. Kin of 18 Across
21. "I'm alive," ___
23. "Eat your cookie," ___
25. Do a slow burn
26. Hinder
28. Texas border city
29. Horner's capture
30. Imitated Marceau
31. Oop's abode
32. Tote laboriously
35. Powerful beam
36. William Carlos Williams verse epic
40. Locomotive, e.g.
41. "Storm approaching!" ___
43. Aujourd' ___ (today, in Tours)
44. Chews the fat
45. Tennis units
46. Ben Hur's drag strip
47. Verlaine's birthplace
48. Ditty
49. "You mongrel," ___
53. First Viscount Templewood
54. In a seemly way
56. Like a road full of furrows
57. Elopement need, maybe
58. Lincoln bills
59. Linton Heathcliff's wife
60. Eunuch's milieu
61. Teed off
63. Henry Christophe's land
64. Mason's activity
67. Burlington's Bean
68. "Have a candy bar," ___
70. MacDowell's "___ Wild Rose"
71. Like Shangri-la's horizon
72. Usher's offering
73. Novello of "The Lodger"
74. Telegram's period
75. "The Sultan of Sulu" playwright
76. "I work in a lab," ___
80. Reagan's second Attorney General
81. Cardinal and scarlet tanager
83. Plea to a departing one
84. Squiffed
85. Butterfly's sashes
86. Lathered
87. Restrain
88. A Ladd from Huron
91. Brazilian novelist Jorge
92. Field game devised by Indians
96. "Fire's going out!" ___
98. "I'm dying," ___
100. Behind which Polonius hid
101. Nut for soft drinks
102. Church pledge
103. Tatum's dad
104. See 42 Down
105. Confederate
106. Mignon trailer
107. Fashion's Oscar ___ Renta

DOWN

1. Kin of tchus and pfuis
2. Turkish standard
3. Last mount Moses climbed
4. Krantz bestseller
5. Pole near a tepee
6. German industrial valley
7. Galena or bauxite
8. Aleichem's language
9. Underground water tank
10. Yearned
11. Villain's grimace
12. Mom's title
13. Buttons' replacer
14. La Scala harp
15. Gets the picture
16. Ruin
18. Caused to be arraigned
20. Assuaged, as one's conscience
22. "Oklahoma!" aunt
24. Not so untidy
27. That old ratite bird
30. East China Sea island
31. Gave a hoot
32. Discard as useless
33. Going to Jerusalem prop
34. "I teach," ___
35. "___ people go . . ." Exodus 5:1
36. Vought's comical Dink
37. "I let him in," ___
38. Bizarre
39. "My Day in Court" author
41. Loaf ends
42. With 104 Across, foul play
45. Emulate Fawn and Ollie
47. Exemplar
49. Number of "swans-a-swimming"
50. Wedding-gown aisle-sweeper
51. All together, in music
52. Moral precept
53. Made tracks
55. Pirouette
57. Rod of tennis
59. Untouchables, for one
60. Salome danced for him
61. Kind of bear
62. Molder
63. Gets wind of
64. Quay for the Robert E. Lee
65. Hangman's loop
66. Stared slack-jawed
68. Pays attention
69. Poker pot
72. Piercing
74. Coastal region
76. Female oracles
77. Like some vaudeville shows
78. Toward the mouth
79. Clever comeback
80. ___ Castle (Havana fort)
82. Of the north wind
84. "Filthy" money
86. Fragrance
87. Secrete
88. Fellow
89. Super-sandwich
90. Spain's longest river
91. Mil. truant
92. Man from Riga
93. Terrier type
94. Dr. Dolittle's Sophie, e.g.
95. Felix Unger's daughter
97. Trappist cheese
99. Whop

135 Borrowing from the Bard by Nancy Nicholson Joline

ACROSS

1. U. of New Mexico team
6. Baby-care item
10. Chevets
15. Kind of case or flight
19. "What's in ___?": Juliet
20. Pitcher Hershiser
21. Numbers game
22. Frogner Park locale
23. Actress Shire
24. Maginot, for one
25. Barrie title from "Julius Caesar"
27. Porter-Spewack title from "The Taming of the Shrew"
29. Major chaser
30. Copiers
31. Part of Q.E.D.
32. Enl. men
33. Roosevelt and Teasdale
35. W. Texas city
36. "O ___ Ben Jonson!"
38. New Haven, City of ___
39. "___ of the Mind," Shepard play
40. Does a diaskeuast's job
43. McGinniss title from "Macbeth"
48. Latin American dances
51. O'Neill play
53. Vagus, e.g.
54. Belgian resort town
55. Spanish liqueur
58. Gardener's tool
59. Bring up
60. Tossed off, as an exam
61. "___ Shelter," Rolling Stones hit
63. Paderewski
65. Capital of Turkey
67. Memorable Israeli political leader
68. Forsyth title, with "The," from "Julius Caesar"
72. Douglas Hyde's republic
73. George Eliot's weaver
75. Join a cause
76. Type size
78. Netman Nastase
79. Bryce Canyon locale
83. More comfortable
85. "Remember ___ wife": Luke 17:32
86. "___ 'em!"
87. Actress Jones of "L.A. Law"
89. Lewis or Weems
90. Ekberg and Loos
92. Maugham title from "Twelfth Night"
96. Pack fruit with the best on top
98. Clement
99. This may be floppy
101. Burbot
102. These are sometimes round
105. "___ la vista"
106. Distress
107. Sheet of ice asea
111. Moderate
112. Ten: Comb. form
113. Christie title from "Twelfth Night"
116. Kingsley title from "Twelfth Night"
118. Lombok neighbor
119. Miller's salesman
120. Like the White Rabbit
121. ___-Powell, Boy Scouts founder
122. Kind of rug
123. Tradition
124. Lean-to
125. Gather
126. Bath-towel word
127. Hordeola

DOWN

1. Potato pancake
2. Broadcasting
3. Model-airplane material
4. Lunts' comedy title from "Twelfth Night"
5. Place to caulk
6. "The Two Towers" author
7. Former president of Costa Rica
8. Mardi Gras follower
9. One of the Monty Python troupe
10. Municipal-council member
11. Writer of inferior verse
12. Census figs.
13. To be, in Brest
14. Kind of story
15. Some head coverings
16. Met bass-baritone
17. Calumnies
18. Fiber from a jute
26. Ulnae's neighbors
28. Way out
34. TV extra-terrestrial
35. Oldest street in L.A.
37. M.D.'s org.
39. Part of T.A.E.
41. Muralist Rivera
42. Ade's "Fables in ___"
44. "All the Things You ___," 1939 song
45. Betrayer; traitor
46. Lehár specialty
47. Nothing, in Nicaragua
48. Weaken
49. Plantae's counterpart
50. Edward Lear specialty
52. Undo
57. Lay doggo, in London
58. Teatime goody
60. Leacha title from "Henry VIII"
62. Palindromic word
64. "Eroica" key
66. Formerly named
69. ___ up (got smart): Slang
70. In reserve
71. Hwy.
73. Abbr. for a potpourri
74. Dogpatch denizens, e.g.
77. Ar chaser
80. Conduce
81. What an ampersand means
82. Annoying situations
84. In a risqué manner
88. Omissions
91. Sine qua ___
93. Issued
94. Tendon
95. Erhard's therapy
97. De Larrocha and Markova
100. Algiers native quarter
102. Singer Lou from Chicago
103. West Indian fetish
104. Sew loosely
105. Ibsen's Gabler
106. Freud contemporary
108. Air Force Chief of Staff: 1961–65
109. Indian or orange
110. Anglo-Saxon laborers
112. Tot
114. Bern's river
115. ___ fours
117. Arab's outer garment

136 *Pun Names* by Norma Steinberg

ACROSS

1. Caesar's partner
5. Skelton's script-writing spouse
9. End of a G. Eliot title
14. Soldat's hat
18. Di's ex
19. Dry
20. Emcee's opening word
22. Members of the peerage
24. French actress with chutzpah?
27. Jane Wyatt role in "Star Trek IV"
28. Record before showtime
29. Thwacks
30. ___ Gay; W.W. II bomber
32. Potter in "M*A*S*H"
33. Is human?
34. Sinuous
36. Maurois or Malraux
37. "Get lost!"
38. ___ standstill
40. Singles
41. Little charmer
42. Shaven
43. Espionage agent
45. Prying tool
47. "Crimes and Misdemeanors" director
48. Street weapon
49. Buddy
50. ___ seaman
51. Base runner's ploy
52. Of G.B.S.
55. Lovable evolutionist?
59. "But of course!"
61. Anagram for artisan
62. Roofing of a sort
64. Camus essay
65. Commit perjury
66. He wrote "John Brown's Body"
67. What 66 Across was
68. Integrity
70. Ghost of Christmas ___
71. Fearsome beasts
73. Strongman in a bar
76. Actress Lamarr
79. Internal obstruction
81. Tidy, in Ayr
82. Scandinavian kings
85. Governor of Guam
86. Palaver
88. Miss Kitty's business
90. Tartness
92. Turkey Day pie
95. Presidential Twinkle-Toes?
97. Matrons, in Madrid
98. A piece of resistance
100. Artificial: Abbr.
101. "___ the season..."
102. Caddis or crewel
103. Ballerina's rail
104. Pluto, to Plato
106. Opposite of ant.
107. One way to be in love
109. Bulwer-Lytton novel
110. Author of "The Counterfeiters"
111. Clairvoyance, for short
113. Functions
114. Corneous; callous
115. Artist's purchase
117. Dumbo's wings
120. Novel by Kathleen Coyle
121. Polite blokes
122. "En ___!"
123. Schleps
126. Kimbrough and Post
128. Muscular magazine editor?
131. Calif. county
132. Lacking a key
133. Mother Hubbard's quest
134. Neb. Indian
135. Asseverates
136. Fusty
137. Brings to court
138. Diminish

DOWN

1. Letters on a U.S.S.R. player's jersey
2. Chicago's airport
3. Prepare fare for an affair
4. Obsolescent receptacle?
5. O.K. Corral shootout participant
6. Helps with the dishes
7. "Winter of Artifice" writer
8. Author ___ Virginia Woolf
9. Speckles
10. Tall and thin
11. Parabases
12. Pinero's title
13. Tarkington opus
14. ___ Sutra
15. Pitcher's stat.
16. Leader in Mexican outerwear?
17. Like some sports
21. Sondheim's "___ the Clowns"
22. Bundle of cotton
23. Arty party
25. Vane point
26. Roadside stop
31. Miner's delight
35. Adored
36. "___ Lang Syne"
37. God riding a bull called Nandi
39. Red Deer's locale
41. Assure victory
42. Stock item
43. Master, in Madras
44. Kind of geometry
46. Joy Adamson's pet
47. Got off
48. Close
49. Pts. of a jigsaw puzzle
50. Change
51. Thin board
52. Area for a taffrail
53. Baba and Pasha
54. Gorbachev's refusal
56. Travis or Quaid
57. Expiate
58. Indian monkey
60. Not sotto voce
63. Hang out with
67. Sprightly dance
69. Clarinetist Jimmy of jazz
70. Madrid museum
72. "___ Goat-Boy": Barth
74. Apache chief
75. Prufrock's creator
76. Easter entrées
77. Mrs. Kovacs
78. Actor from Asti?
80. "Beau Geste" locale
81. Kind
83. Number for Hawaii
84. Toklas's companion
86. Ex-quarterback Bradshaw
87. T. Mann's "___ and His Dog"
89. ___ majesty
90. "Ma, He's Making Eyes ___," 1921 song
91. Jan.-to-Jan. periods
93. Embers
94. Lionel output
96. "___ cockhorse..."
99. Parisian airport
103. German cannon's name
104. Indian religion
105. Duly and truly, e.g.
106. Nickname Piaf had
107. Slip-ons
108. Sci-fi master
109. Nol of Cambodia
110. Mouthwash
112. Montenegrin, e.g.
114. "For ___ jolly..."
115. Sight from Buzzards Bay
116. Setting
118. Lariat
119. Attach, as a button
121. Places for workouts
122. Actress Rowlands
124. Yes votes
125. Koko's weapon
127. Moo
129. Salt pillar's husband
130. Singer Rawls

137 Bugaboos by Joy L. Wouk

ACROSS

1. Former Turkish official
6. European flatfish
9. Append
12. Sandal part
17. Anew
18. Bruce of N.F.L. fame
20. Oahu souvenirs
22. Sacramento's ARCO, e.g.
23. Plantation owner's enemies?
27. German measles
28. Ancient weight
29. ___ the finish
30. Spicy sausage
33. Grown-up grig
34. Katmandu native
36. Frowning elater?
40. Palpebras on the eyes
41. Goad
42. Ljubljana native
47. Arabian commander
48. Warm oneself pleasantly
51. Peruvian plant
53. Yearned
54. Lepidopteran structure?
60. Roman fountain
61. Newspaper sec.
62. Egg: Comb. form
63. Mandela's gp.
65. Soak flax
66. Hyde Park locusts?
74. At the age of: Lat. Abbr.
75. RR stop
76. Half of CCCII
77. Vishnu incarnation
78. Exaggerated comedy
81. Egyptian demagogue?
88. Small handbill
89. Botanist Gray
90. Ghazels
91. Latin I verb
92. Catherine or Josephine
95. Kettledrum
99. One's own: Comb. form
100. Future moth for Lot's wife
105. Site of Cromwell's first victory
109. Operate
110. Cuts short
111. Delicate
112. Japanese admiral and family
114. Lift ___ (make a slight effort)
116. Untrustworthy Puccini heroine?
123. Have ___ for news
124. Ego
125. Fencing cry
126. Historic Pueblo Indian village
127. Worthless item
128. Polka follower
129. Kind of storehouse: Abbr.
130. Gas used in TV tubes

DOWN

1. Larrigan's kin
2. Past
3. Posed
4. Struck
5. Eskimo jacket
6. Reynolds or Gibson
7. Lotion ingredient
8. Corrida ticket
9. Cakes' companion
10. Judge
11. Holy, to Dante
12. Bando of baseball
13. Follow
14. "At the Sign of the ___ Pédauque": A. France
15. Christie and Held
16. Glue
19. One of a pair of genes
21. Tendons
24. Insensible
25. Like corduroy
26. Jacket feature
30. Connacht county
31. A seventh-century Irish bishop who became a saint
32. Certain bank offerings: Abbr.
35. Vote to accept
36. Quahog
37. Sumerian god of wisdom
38. Rorschach item
39. French cashier's stamp
43. Man, to Brutus
44. First month, in Lima
45. At no time
46. Redacts
48. The Wrights: Abbr.
49. Pituitary hormones
50. New growths
52. Omani, e.g.
55. "___ gratia artis"
56. Peak
57. A pome caused her to leave home
58. About
59. Habituated
64. A Munster county
66. Blunder
67. Kingdom
68. Anchor position
69. S.A. rodent
70. Vestment
71. Tad's marble
72. TV role for Alvin Childress
73. Greek letter
79. Wax: Comb. form
80. Build
82. Copernicus's field: Abbr.
83. Scottish rope
84. Actress Montez
85. Co-Nobelist for Peace: 1978
86. Ludwig and Jannings
87. Core
93. Master, in India
94. Position
96. To look, to Miguel
97. Broad-faced banks
98. Star in Orion's belt
99. Neighbor of Syr.
101. Overacted
102. Miscellaneous assortment
103. Heed
104. Southern constellation
105. Family of a Portuguese navigator
106. Cheerful
107. Zeal
108. Former name of Lake Malawi
113. W.W. II battle site
115. Polish river
117. European gull
118. Newt
119. Bar need
120. Ending with penta or deca
121. Med. group
122. Thrash

138 *Searching Questions* by Jack L. Steinhardt

ACROSS

1. Short-legged horses
5. ___ Ababa
10. Drop heavily
14. Broadway's Jane
18. "___ the Great," E. Dumm cartoon
19. Early or late Crawford
20. Vibrant
21. Piece of Marilyn Mims
22. WHERE'S THE STATION?
24. WHERE'S THE SECOND?
26. He caused earthquakes
27. Unpleasant sound
29. Capricious indulgences
30. Month, in Milano
31. Pub drink
32. Skin or slick preceder
33. Cozened
36. Sheppard-Turpin guns
37. Elongated, as a spheroid
41. Month before Nisan
42. WHERE'S THE FINDING?
46. Like "cats" in the 40's
47. Rock group
48. Letters
49. Harness
50. Heraldic design
51. Kelep
52. WHERE'S THE ARIAN?
56. Scenic view
57. Swear anew
60. Viracocha worshiper
61. Iraqi neighbors
62. Kind of dropper
63. Ancient Greek city-state
64. Five of trumps
65. Grading systems
67. Amenhotep IV's god
68. Earlier bid
71. Construe
72. WHERE'S THE TILL?
74. Part of TNT
75. Stratum; level
76. Former Chinese leader
78. The life of Riley
79. A Sinatra
80. And the rest: Abbr.

81. WHERE'S THE SHOPPING?
85. Presage
86. Belittle
88. Designer Oscar de la ___
89. Usurp
90. It's between the U.S. and Eur.
91. Bourrée or forlana
92. Quality; nature
94. "I did but ___ little honey...": I Sam. 14:43
97. Twofold
98. Injured a joint
102. WHERE'S THE WAVE?
104. WHERE DO WE GET LACE?
106. Couple
107. Parts of pumps
108. Strand
109. Space on the face of a bird
110. Commits a bull
111. Kin of a hydria
112. One of the Dryads
113. Assyrian war god

DOWN

1. Quibble
2. Potpourri
3. Petitions
4. Intrigants
5. Footless ones
6. "An Essay upon Projects" author: 1697
7. Cockcrow
8. City in Peru
9. He practices pettifoggery
10. Flat double fold in cloth
11. Heeltap
12. Ab ___ (from the start)
13. Of necessity
14. Fishing fly
15. Battle of ___: July 3, 1940
16. Playwright Sir Arthur ___ Pinero
17. The Four ___, singing group
20. Reddening
23. Litigated
25. "Cats" libretto author
28. Paris's ___ Neuf
31. Roman burial stone
33. Senegal's capital
34. City NW of Trieste

35. WHERE'S THE PITCH?
36. Pack tightly
37. Dawber or Shriver
38. WHERE'S GREENWICH?
39. Beats, to Puccini
40. Flèche weapons
42. Ammonia derivatives
43. Sharp projections
44. Alcohol heaters
45. Falstaffian
50. Skin exfoliation
53. Runs amok
54. Table bay is one
55. Currants, e.g.
56. Javanese carriage
58. Four-time Wimbledon winner
59. Perpetually
61. Farm machine
63. Half a Samoan island's name: Var.
64. Cues in group singing
65. Commended for gallantry
66. Colligate

68. End of Mont.'s motto
69. Pelagic raptors
70. Cheerful
72. Bank abbr.
73. "Festina ___" ("Make haste slowly")
76. Of a lower social order
77. Triton
79. Mexican baker's product
81. Anon
82. Ancient Germanic people
83. Triclinium meal
84. Put a fence around
87. Teachers, at times
89. Swaddle
91. Reno roller
92. Rollick
93. "___ ed Euridice"
94. VCR insertion
95. In the distance
96. Rustle
97. Clay used as a pigment
98. Kin of a parvis
99. Ancient temple

100. Raw-silk shade
101. Sambar
103. Quo modo
105. Clock, in Köln

139 Bestiary by Stanley Glass

ACROSS

1. Girl in Maude Nugent's 1896 song
6. Poe's "gold bug"
12. Enticed via deception
19. Hysterias on Wall Street
20. Civil
21. Point in a certain space orbit
22. Vinegary
23. Raucous fan
24. "Johnny ___," Wyman movie
25. Unprized possession
27. Challenge to a surfer
28. Zenith's antithesis
29. Type of code
30. Homer's "homer"?
32. Cousin of an ophidiid
33. Prohibition
34. Ad infinitum
35. Thimblerig
37. A star of "Naughty Marietta"
38. Signoret film: 1967
40. Fannie ___ (Government issue)
41. Malevolence
44. Better prepared
47. College-credit unit
48. Knocked for a loop
52. Crimson Tide's archrival
53. Intuitive good judgment
56. Wrigley Field flora
57. Adorned
58. Gaelic
59. Colberteen, e.g.
60. Dawson or Deighton
61. Perambulates
62. Roe v. ___ (historic case)
63. Hawkeye's unit
64. Jerry's Anne
66. Within: Prefix
67. "The Way We ___"
68. Dignity
69. New Zealand statesman: 1878–1943
70. "Ich bin ___ Berliner"
71. Their job causes lots of interest
73. Swallow
74. Evil spirits
76. Geological periods
77. Bears witness
78. Chose
80. Bill's possible future
81. "Spandau . . ." author
82. Composer of "Le Roi d'Ys"
85. Rouget de ___ ("Marseillaise" composer)
87. Slice of bacon
88. Acquiesce
91. Mistress of 82 Down
92. Type of flycatcher
94. Metric thousand
95. Brownish photo
97. Hundredth of a peso
99. Certain whip
103. New England prep school
104. Come forth
105. Sheridan work, with "The"
106. Compensation
107. Blunt
108. What 2,000 pounds comes to
109. States
110. Out of bounds
111. Disseminate

DOWN

1. Protector of Joshua's spies: Var.
2. Silver center in N.Y.
3. Easy target
4. Less friendly
5. Ending for an inchoative verb
6. Celestial bodies
7. Lou Gehrig portrayer
8. Greeting on Maui
9. T.H. Benton's "Self-Portrait With ___"
10. Egyptian sun disk
11. Victoria's consort, to friends
12. Illegal blow
13. ". . . Mahagonny" is one
14. Propelled a gondola
15. Director-author Kazan
16. Immersed
17. Verily
18. Almost
19. Potential queen
26. Four-time Wimbledon winner
31. ___ Palmas
34. Correct
35. ___ célèbre
36. "The eyes are not ___": Eliot
37. Poetic twilight
39. Buenos ___
40. First telegrapher
42. Caesar's "myself"
43. Origin of a drive
44. Pollen source
45. Largest land mass
46. A source of mother-of-pearl
47. Swarms
49. Enlarges
50. Himalayan challenge
51. "The ___," Hardy's poetic drama
53. Actor Lafcadio ___
54. Informal garb
55. Facilitates
62. Evasive speech
63. A colleague of Danton
64. Casino game
65. Enthusiast
67. Habit
68. Travesty
69. Mentioned
71. Truncate
72. Fulfill a Hippocratic promise
75. Bovine comment
77. Airport area
79. Gambling cube
81. Striking
82. The house, to Pedro
83. Catkins
84. First baseball commissioner
86. Emulate S.C. in 1860
87. Home of the storied Mouse Tower
89. Producer of inertia
90. Machine for cleaning cotton
92. He prepares the way
93. Blessed ___
94. "Elephant Boy" co-director
95. Be frugal
96. N.A.A.C.P., e.g.
98. Guzzle
100. Part of N.A.
101. Rip along or rip
102. Plato's "Symposium" topic

ACROSS

1. Costume
6. Gown for Calpurnia
11. Harris or Silvers
15. Buddhist mound
20. Tex. shrine
21. Bane of grain
22. Site of St. Columba's abbey
23. Cicero's bread
24. Proper pistol handling
27. The skull reminded Hamlet that he ___
29. City RR's
30. Titillates
31. Requires
33. Main arteries
34. Loci
35. Composition theme
36. Compatriot
37. Gypsy husband
40. "Bali ___"
41. Eagle's nest
42. Soft cheese
43. Actor Torn
46. Beth preceder
48. Baghdad ruler more cantankerous
52. Three ___ match
53. Find another chair for
55. Months after Shebats
56. U.S.S.R. news agency
57. Rampart
58. Artist's stand
59. Modish
60. Right, in law
62. Poser
63. Manner
64. "Card game simple," says king of Siam
67. Angry
68. Gumshoe
69. Comedian Sahl
70. Heavy weights
71. Cease
72. Rock salt
75. Thong
76. Carpentry tools
78. Justified, as margins
80. Blue Jays or Cardinals
81. Shine
82. Fleur-de-___
85. Babbitt's creator
86. Bug the landlord
90. French seaport
92. Site of a knight's fights
93. Lifeless, old style

94. Electric catfish
95. Swift brute
96. Dairyman's anathema
97. Spades or clubs
98. Consecrate
100. Detroit headache
101. Macerate
102. Must be signed in ink
106. Within: Comb. form
107. Commercials
108. Cellini's skill
109. Common solecisms
110. Greek vowel
112. Lair
113. Periods of note
114. Spile
115. Kind of type
117. Trim anew
120. Stone pillar
121. Turn inside out
122. Mispickel or cinnabar
125. Stare at a certain seascape
127. Scales for singer Reese
130. "The Loved One" author
131. Bertolucci film
132. Emulate Zayak
133. Ribs of leaves
134. Weavers' reeds
135. Literary contest
136. Cut wood
137. Indulge in cabotinage

DOWN

1. Security
2. Jewish month
3. Browns
4. Japanese apricot
5. Dead Sea product
6. Giant redwood
7. Faith
8. Curved moldings
9. Acreage
10. An A.B.A. member
11. Certain tollgate employees
12. Lariat eye
13. Agnes, in Avila
14. Boston's Cardinal
15. Wire winder
16. Linger
17. Military force
18. Type size
19. Inquires
25. Collision
26. Preceders of febreros
28. Elis

32. Eastern potentate
35. Annealing over
36. Grain beard
37. Most attenuated
38. ___ of quinine
39. Licorice eaters' dentures
41. Speedily
42. Egghead
43. Worker indicating single lane, e.g.
44. Estuaries
45. Portable platform in a warehouse
47. Sense
49. Pakistani city
50. Dostoyevsky's "The ___"
51. Type of collar
54. Rarebit ingredient
57. More unpleasant
59. Coagulate
60. Electrical generator
61. Grate
62. Carriage
65. Bear witness
66. Rails
69. Kind of way
71. Grackle

73. Philippine idol
74. Minus
75. Sadr or Salm
76. Satisfy
77. C. P. Snow's title
78. Site of famed rock temples in India
79. Hidden
81. Grind
83. She signs "Liebestod"
84. Runner on a plant
86. Frequents
87. Priest's scarf
88. Meat entrée
89. Small birds
90. Seeded player's delight
91. Watercourse
97. Celestial being
98. Relied (on)
99. Mineral: Comb. form
100. Go to bed
102. Outcasts
103. Cathedral church of Rome
104. Small bottle

105. Extended a subscription
111. Lively
113. Melancholy poem
114. Office worker
115. Relative acquired
116. Egg-shaped
117. Tiers
118. Same, in Savoie
119. Guide for Holmes
120. Self-satisfied
121. Actress Chase
122. Paducah's river
123. Budget item
124. Gaelic
126. Biographer Winslow
128. Double curve
129. Muffin

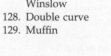

141 *Brief Encounter* by Betty Jorgensen

ACROSS

1. Town SW of Padua
5. Scrub
10. Moroccan capital
15. Hangars
20. Square columns
21. Creator of Truthful James
22. ___ Levant, French island
23. Divided country
24. WHAT HE WAS DOING
28. Three: Prefix
29. San ___, W. R. Hearst's castle
30. Sopranos Calve and Eames
31. Items thrown by Eris
32. Carry on
34. "___ we forget..."
35. Crisp topping
36. Bar Mitzvah, e.g. Ceremony
37. Kind of market
39. Lament
40. An act of suppression
44. WHAT HE SAW
49. Shamus
50. Stag's mate
51. Railroad stations
54. Home on a tor
55. Evans' mate
57. Bridle part
58. H. Clay, to A. Jackson
59. City on the Po
60. Dispatch boat
61. Desist
62. Mère's man
63. U.S. voters since 1920
64. Haze-smoke mixture
65. Pastors' homes
66. ___ shrew
67. Wagnerian earth goddess
68. Basso Italo ___
69. Filly's father
70. WHAT HE ASKED
79. Fixes the squeaks
80. Nine: Pref.
81. Dark-suit nemesis
82. Me, to Miss Piggy
83. "Oft in the ___ Night": T. Moore
86. Plied with potions
87. With 76 Down, Dino's big hit
89. Part of h.c.l.
90. Entire
91. Small nightclub
92. Emblem on a Greek flag
93. Street show
94. Nose-bag contents
95. Liquidated Russian: 1953
96. Prepare oysters
97. Apt. managers
98. Kind of virus
99. Forbid
100. WHAT SHE REPLIED
103. Ancestry
105. Unsubstantial
106. Bloch symphony
110. Seraglio rooms
111. Opium source
113. Great: Pref.
115. European tree
116. In disgrace
119. Bridal path
120. Cleanse the throat
122. Bonaparte's Marshal
123. WHAT HE SIGHED
127. Lustrous fiber
128. A.L. home run leader: 1944
129. Landed estate
130. Units of force
131. Ancient chariot
132. "Sing ___ songs for me": C. Rossetti
133. Oscar, e.g.
134. Germ

DOWN

1. Snare
2. Try hard
3. Chinese truth
4. They're often smoked
5. Impossible fancy
6. Bowling alleys
7. Rye disease
8. Abbr. on an envelope
9. O.T. book
10. Equatorial Guinea's Mbini, formerly
11. Grads
12. Procreated, biblical style
13. Sticky substances: Abbr.
14. Famed mummy
15. Doubting Thomas
16. Emulated Bugs Bunny
17. Of an epoch
18. Streeter's "___ Mable"
19. He directed "The Odd Couple"
20. Kind of turf
25. Easter blossoms
26. Pile up the leaves again
27. "Hotel" author
33. Cover with a rounded roof
35. Bobwhite
36. Kind of rocket
38. Bohemian
39. Calif. county
41. Notions
42. Racket
43. Hereditary factors
45. Kenyan rebel
46. To be, in the past
47. Member of largest Indian group in U.S.
48. French Prime Minister: 1847–48
51. Chauncey from N.Y.: 1834–1928
52. January, in Avila
53. Hidden
56. Half a fly
57. Continue a subscription
59. Commotions
60. One of a Latin I trio
61. Jeweler's weight unit
63. In a distorted way
64. Charger
65. Bearings
67. Caesar's early post
69. Vaudeville acts
71. Lazes
72. Pope: 795–816
73. Put in place (second spelling)
74. Kind of brace or bend
75. "Seward's Folly?"
76. See 87 Across
77. Also-ran
78. Buzzards' cousins
83. Side arm
84. Macbeth's title
85. Tiny amounts
86. June bug
87. For real
88. Pawn
89. Pranks
91. Inclinations
92. Circumspect
93. Mystical poem
95. Potassium supplier
96. Heists
97. An East African
99. Covered with morning moisture
101. Region of N. Europe
102. Ten o'clock scholar, e.g.
104. A sheep dog
107. Liquid used in perfumery
108. Worked on a ship
109. Chasm
111. Ancient people of Great Britain
112. Tessie ___, music-hall star
113. ___ Carta
114. Mistake
116. Discharge
117. Japanese female divers
118. Mobsters' exits
119. Concerning
120. Bite like beavers
121. Finishes
124. Longing
125. One of the Hoggs
126. By the ___

ACROSS

1. Neither fem. nor neut.
5. Thin-skinned area
9. Spring
13. Reporter's exclusive
18. Juárez water
19. Neophyte
20. Moon valley
21. Veil material
22. Actor Sean
23. Fail to include
24. Infix
25. Summer snake
26. Nobleman views oceanic wastes
30. Flowering shrub
32. August sign
33. County component
34. Vane reading
35. Auricles
36. Source of a syrup
39. It's W. of the Urals
41. Excavator overlooked secondary weather phenomenon
49. Ed or Leon
50. With full force
51. Greek Cupid
52. Biblical idol
54. Carmine
55. Old English bards
56. More dreadful
58. Foulard
59. NASA sites
60. Earthquake
62. Gourmand's joy
65. Virtuous relatives ran after insects
71. Gridiron gear
72. Selling places
73. Type of sch.
74. Prefix for form
75. "Aqui se ___ español"
77. Child's wear
79. "Major Barbara" auth.
82. Jeer
84. Funnyman Foxx
85. "___ by land . . ."
86. Donkey's cry
87. Ecclesiastical group dined on chicken
92. Earth: Pref.
93. Assuages
94. In two
95. Uraeus symbol
98. Early pulpit
101. Squids squirt it
102. Rubs out
103. Sedate singer remained vile

109. Careless hurrying
110. Clean a fluke
111. Yemeni, e.g.
112. English
115. Ethyl oxide
116. Slender candle
117. Ceremonial act
118. Galway's locale
119. Fabric joints
120. While preceder
121. Have to have
122. Mulligan

DOWN

1. Atlas page
2. A cause of grayness
3. Red from rays
4. Tenerife, Fuerteventura, etc.
5. Milkmaid's perch
6. Choir rendition
7. Rainbow
8. Distinction
9. Bar dance
10. Exile island
11. On the ball
12. Actor Armendariz: 1912–63
13. Tin
14. Chaws
15. Of yore
16. City on the Allegheny
17. Inherently
20. Do a lawn job
27. Hind
28. Terry or Glasgow
29. Washstand item
30. Truman's birthplace
31. Wicker's "___ to Die"
36. Sensitive plant
37. P.D.Q. kin
38. Penultimate Greek letters
40. Eve's genesis
42. Thane of Cawdor
43. Docs
44. Cork folks
45. Bellini opera
46. Carbohydrate ending
47. Glossy fabric
48. Sully
53. Tour segments
55. Stuff to the gills
57. Recite quickly
59. W.W. II craft
60. Sicilian street
61. Superlative suffix
63. Mideast gulf
64. Edinburgh beret
65. Engine sound

66. Three-time Olympic skating champion
67. Suspect's out
68. Brownish hue
69. Silent screen star Nita
70. One thing after another
76. Cartoon bark
77. Literary collections
78. He rose over Ty
79. Lube-job area
80. Wilkes' other half
81. Methods: Abbr.
83. Future finch
85. Honshu city
86. Gets around
88. Spectacular falls
89. Mausoleum
90. Tenant
91. ___ avis
95. Incinerator residue
96. One of 50
97. Turkish title
99. Sew with loose stitches
100. "Sesame Street" grouch
101. Ait

102. Declined
104. Piece of news
105. Undermines
106. Tall tale
107. ___-Lackawanna RR
108. Prom partner
113. Infuriation
114. Just on the market

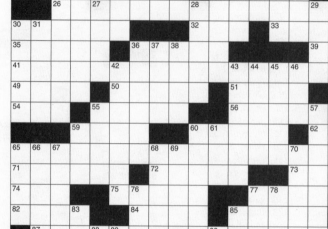

143 *Interlopers* by Virginia L. Yates

ACROSS

1. Propagates
5. Wood sorrels
9. Master beginner
13. Coincide
18. Nerd
19. ___ snuff (O.K.)
20. ___ Vista, city S. of San Diego
21. He wrote "Advise and Consent": 1959
22. "___ Want for Christmas . . ."
23. Cauda
24. Two-walled fortification
25. Stupid
26. Excitement over a national park?
30. Tours summers
31. Donatello specialty
32. British noble family
33. Wheat bristle
35. Check
37. ___ dieu (kneeling bench)
38. Charwoman's utensil
42. Member of the fold
46. Watergate evidence
50. Kind of therapy
51. Unusual bloke
52. Kálmán operetta
53. One of a nautical trio
55. "The Haj" author
56. "Hasta luego!"
58. Sugar daddy?
63. Tusked cetaceans
65. A, German
66. Wires
67. Endangered geese
68. Eng. start-up
69. Chestnut's kin
71. Blind ___
74. Malarial malady
75. Data and his ilk
79. Pei's winning work?
83. Of gold
84. Pro ___ (shared equally)
85. Emulate Julia Child
86. College sports org.
88. Hindu god
89. Creamy shade
91. Attar for 12 Down?
95. Wax-covered cheese
96. Like a trillium's leaves
98. ___-poly
99. Author Buscaglia
101. Resort of a sort
102. Man in a lodge
104. Cochise, for one
109. Beige
112. Under-the-counter ne'er-do-wells?
117. Gasconades
119. Extricate
120. Hip
121. Cinders of comics
122. Idaho senator: 1907–40
123. Like Redford
124. Rise high
125. Write Waugh
126. Hair-raising
127. Australian lake
128. With competence
129. "___ Fence Me In"

DOWN

1. Hangs in there
2. Little hooter
3. Author Cather
4. Avocet's kin
5. Lasts longer than
6. Ledger scanners, for short
7. Have ___ (tackle)
8. Without others
9. Sit at ___ of (be a disciple)
10. "Age of Anxiety" poet
11. Poles, Serbs, etc.
12. Welles role
13. Say more
14. Horticulturist's habitat?
15. Litter's smallest
16. Old tongue
17. Some are private
20. Attribute to
27. Away
28. Pianist Peter
29. Author Santha Rama ___
34. Inst. at Ogden, Utah
36. Darwin's ship
37. Esposito of the N.H.L.
38. Brighton sight
39. Jeopardy
40. Ammonia derivative
41. Items to count
42. Credit union's offer
43. "___ partridge in a . . ."
44. She wrote "My Life": 1975
45. Forest denizen's sweet?
47. Rubbish
48. Pierre's seraph
49. Gilt, e.g.
54. Moved in a curved course
57. Trim
59. Condescend
60. Uncover
61. Kind of tube or circle
62. Pelvic bones
64. Caper
69. Place to get pesetas
70. Necessitate
71. Hillside dugouts
72. Drudge
73. Hatchbacks, e.g.
74. NASA nods
76. Crocus or gladiolus
77. Aprile Millo, for one
78. Horn-swaggler's forte
80. Windbag
81. Hobgoblin's word
82. ___ 500 (event for Al Unser)
87. Depending on luck
90. Kennel sound
92. Author Caldwell
93. Grew swiftly
94. Arm bone
97. Pt. of Newfoundland
100. Saturn's spouse
102. Macho
103. John Lithgow, e.g.
105. Winning
106. Viola's kin
107. Reddy or Moody
108. Solar-lunar time differential
109. Refluxes
110. "Lizard of the Nile," for short
111. ___ avis
113. Grease job
114. Sub ___ (secretly)
115. Pommel
116. Useful Latin Abbr.
118. Retiring

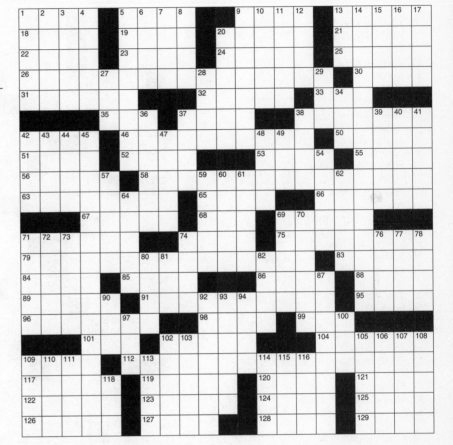

ACROSS

1. Disks for a deejay
5. Schwarzenegger and Stallone, e.g.
10. Track segment
15. Chem. room
18. Uninspired
19. Mexican horse-drawn cabs.
21. Bluster from de Bergerac
23. ___ Ghazi, Khan, Punjabi town
24. Frank Lloyd's fiscal views?
26. Elaine of Astolat's son
28. Hindu habiliments
29. Serve up
30. Larcenous rodent
31. Porcine
32. Actress Skipworth, et al.
35. Stop ___ dime
36. Jack's dance step?
41. Tuition
42. Norwegian river
44. Tartan wearers
45. Gainer or pike
46. A social sci.
47. Paucity
50. Utah ski center
52. ___ one's laurels (is content)
54. Gary's pocket money?
58. Floral scent
60. Breathing space?
63. Custer's last Major
64. Kinkajou
65. Actor Erwin
66. Addressed to Robert's family?
72. Attention
73. Mont ___, Alpine pass tunnel
76. Solothurn's river
77. Epicene
80. Violet perfume base
81. Horace's haymakers?
85. Related by marriage
87. Air trainee's aim
88. Cuisinier's creation
92. Ampersands
93. "___ corny as Kansas . . ."
95. Bando and Mineo
97. Body of poetry
98. Habitat
99. Helmut's dismissal?
104. Prefix with pay or plan
105. Hen and pen

107. Mardi Gras V.I.P.
108. Item widened in disdain
110. ___ mike (automatic pilot)
111. Home of Hercules' lion
113. Favoring (with "to")
114. Animus directed at Sam?
118. Actor O'Shea
120. Fraudulent
121. Wine cask
122. Glacial gravel ridges
123. Tina's ex
124. Red celestial body
125. Polk's predecessor
126. Nidus

DOWN

1. G.P.O. category
2. Woman of fashion
3. Vulturine S.A. hawk
4. Celery unit
5. Lord ___ of W.W. II
6. Capricious
7. Annina in "La Traviata"
8. Part of the U.K.
9. Slangy denials
10. Kindled
11. Word from Charlie Brown
12. Gray or blond preceder
13. Arctic menaces
14. Chinese linguine dish
15. Joseph's acres?
16. Fruit drink
17. Erstwhile Turkish honorific
20. Biblical comforter
22. Ayes' opposites
25. Type of hygiene
27. Tate display
30. About 36 pounds, in Pinsk
32. Post–W.W. II org. member
33. Re the new arrival
34. D.C. bigwig
37. Debris
38. Hoffman product
39. Aware of
40. Reflect
43. Roguish
46. Por ___ (therefore, in Toluca)
48. However, in short form
49. Kind of shell or sole
51. Demons of Arabic myth

53. Draw on
55. Modernist
56. Language of Isr.
57. One or another
59. Actor Calhoun
60. Fungal spore sacs
61. Repetition
62. Agnes's workout?
67. Excoriate
68. Epithet
69. Elizabethan letters
70. "___ spiro spero," S.C. motto
71. Piece of cake
74. First baseman and s.s.
75. Cinque follower
78. L-P filler
79. Contribution of a sort
81. Branch of a plant
82. Middling
83. Name of two Danish kings
84. People
86. Exactitude
89. Judge definitively
90. Mob goons
91. Düsseldorf donkey

92. Doughboys' gp.
94. Litterbug
96. Sound
99. Union general at Gettysburg
100. Golf's Champagne Tony
101. Put forth effort
102. Pie fancier
103. E.T.O. amphibian
106. Seed covering
109. Shakespeare's testy Athenian
111. TV science program
112. Mine entrance
113. Eddy gently
114. Twelfth-century starter
115. Satisfactory, to NASA
116. Chickadee's cousin
117. Napoleonic marshal
119. Meal leftover

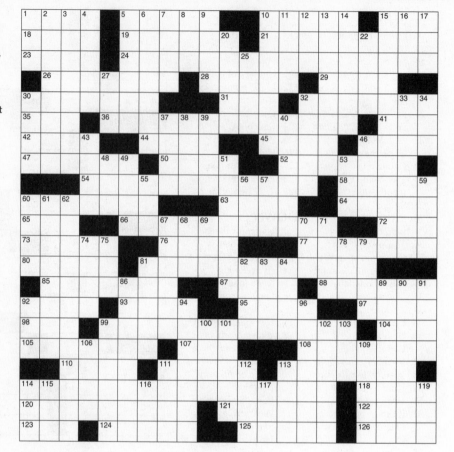

ACROSS

1. Fragrance
6. Jasper Johns medium
10. Ramble
14. "___ and Lovers": Lawrence
18. Bicycle parts
19. Dispassionate people
22. Lamb who wrote about a pig
23. Field of study
24. GOOD-TIME FELLOW'S SPREE, with "out": 1915
26. April 16, 1989, to 20 Down
28. Amonasro's daughter
29. Money-exchange allowances
30. Heart vessel
32. Drifts
33. Rose Bowl pts.
34. Camel's backbreaker?
35. Writer Bontemps
36. Pie edgings
37. UFO passenger
38. Renowned Canadian physician
39. Emulated Van Winkle
40. Kind of disk
43. HE KEEPS A FILLING STATION: 1914
45. Religious deg.
48. Terminates
49. Loves too fondly
51. God of love
52. Van Gogh's brother
53. Penal and Napoleonic
54. Juan and Eva
55. Wife of Osiris
56. Max, Buddy and Bugs
57. North Sea feeder
58. London's "White ___"
59. "Oro y ___," Mont.'s motto
61. Ancient Greek instrument
62. Syr. neighbor
63. LIFE OF RILEY: 1917
66. Il Duce's daughter and son-in-law
67. Whinnies
69. Jazz pianist Fatha
70. Butler or Morse
71. Sports palaces
72. DIVERSION: 1914
74. Forced emigrants: Abbr.
77. Old Athenian tunic
78. Poe's "___ in Paradise"
80. Aquatic flier
81. Bind with a ship's ropes
82. Great Lakes acronym
83. Beget
84. Del Rio film: 1928
87. Rock cavity's crystalline lining
88. Hot box
89. Zola novel
90. Comb: Comb. form
91. Gala in Galicia
92. Footlike part
93. Stage illumination
96. Gift for a third anniversary
97. Deserves
98. What a mantis does?
99. "Now the hungry lion ___": Shak.
100. Loudness
102. Old World lizard
103. Fencing defense
104. Links org.
107. Bagnold's "___ Blandish"
108. Staggering
110. Moon of Uranus
111. Prohibitionists
112. MISERY: 1918
114. HUSSEIN IN GOTHAM, with "A": 1957
117. Royal Indian
118. Scottish group
119. Catnap
120. Some are close
121. ___ St. Lawrence, G.B.S.'s home
122. Olden times
123. German river
124. Church council

DOWN

1. Garden pest
2. Hampton ___
3. Gumbo
4. Ott or Brooks
5. Nepalese, e.g.
6. Legendary Gaelic hero
7. Murrow's "See ___"
8. Clark Kent's girl
9. Mr., in Milano
10. Straight: Pref.
11. Olive genus
12. Department in E. France
13. "Once Upon a ___," 1959 musical
14. Most logical
15. Praying figure
16. Wimps' cousins
17. Puts into words
18. Ailurophobe's cry
20. SUBJECT OF THIS PUZZLE
21. Pelted
25. Plumed bird
27. What Mauna Loa can do
31. Undercooked
34. Laths
35. Pallid
36. TV ads honors
37. "___ moi le déluge"
38. Preminger or Bismarck
39. Groove
40. Nopal and saguaro
41. Shawms' successors
42. THIS DAY AND AGE: 1936
44. Hatching post
45. KLONDIKE EVENT: 1925
46. Poor boys
47. Capt's deck chief
49. Patron saint of France
50. Assns.
52. French philosopher: 1828–93
54. Ottoman title
55. Stagehands' union
56. Hitler's mistress
58. Dickens villain
60. Lascivious look
61. "___ of Athens"
63. Formal content of a culture
64. Paroxysm
65. Dutch artist Poortvliet
66. French Revolution song
68. Corroded
70. Pool person
71. Give thrust to
73. Like ___ of bricks
75. Phony gem
76. Supernumerary's weapon
77. Karate stroke
78. Shades
79. Vocal
81. Guitar's fingerboard ridges
83. One of Lyon's rivers
85. Court gp.
86. Hodgepodge
87. Anne Frank's book
89. Average state
91. Like the legendary Fosdick
93. Rural deities
94. ___ dixit
95. Cretans or Spartans
96. Scicolone on screen
97. Writ of execution
99. Two-time Oscar winner
100. May 8, 1945
101. Base for the Black Bears
103. Kind of ring
104. Home of the Cougars
105. Spun
106. Questions
107. Poet Teasdale
108. At a distance
109. Film maker Clair
110. Excited
111. Actress Cannon
113. U.N. arm
115. Captain on the ark, to Philippe
116. "___ Do I Love You?", 1927 song

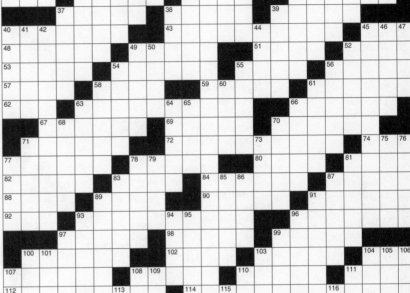

146 Dad's Day *by Nancy Ross*

ACROSS

1. Ares, in Rome
5. Ruth St. ___
10. Org.
15. Synthetic estrogen, for short
18. Parisian possessive
19. Wash out
20. Prefix for dactyl
21. Forwarded
22. Julian's father
24. Alan's father
26. Skylit courts
27. "L'Elisir d'amore" heroine
29. Dispossess
30. Editor's notation
31. Actor Keach
32. Schlep
33. Like some castles
36. Paul, in Pisa
37. Comes ashore
40. Laborers of yore
41. Margaret's father
43. Adlai's opponent
45. Part of C. in C.
46. Julia ___ Howe
47. Contrary: Abbr.
48. Chamber music piece
49. Benz product
50. Natalie's father
54. Sign
55. Wind flowers
57. Pontificate
58. Molts
59. Slogged
60. Night lights
61. Seed: Pref.
62. Acknowledged
63. Softly, to Solti
64. Saddle adjuncts
67. Gabby of westerns
68. Charlie's father
70. Tibetan gazelle
71. Western Indians
72. Comic Olsen
73. Blackbirds' habitat
74. Cut
75. N.H.L. goal
76. Carrie's father
81. Aspect
82. More like pelite
84. Glittery fabrics
85. Expunges
86. Pinza or Plishka
87. Criterion
88. Lord Rutherford's concern
89. Cranston of "The Shadow"
92. Chutzpah
93. Composer Frederic and Nicolas
97. Peter's father
99. Jane's father
102. Nitti's nemesis
103. Awaken rudely
104. Late 50's auto
105. Old Irish alphabet
106. Jap. Big Board
107. Displaces
108. Drives
109. Benefit

DOWN

1. Goya subject
2. "Thanks ___!"
3. Rhine tributary
4. Ominous
5. Judged
6. Surrealist Max
7. Negative prefix
8. Altar vow
9. Sam Houston was one
10. Pastel hue
11. Hardhearted
12. A grandson of Ham
13. Pitchblende, e.g.
14. Moorish capital
15. Marginal mark
16. Windups
17. ASAP in the OR
21. Frugal one
23. Concrete spreaders
25. Coeus or Crius
28. Gless's co-star
31. N.Y.C. restaurateur
32. Fiesta Bowl site
33. Mohammed's birthplace
34. Estogrul's son
35. Jamie's father
36. Urban oases
37. Twofold
38. Michael's father
39. Berlin's were blue
41. Loathed
42. Haley book
44. Billion years
46. Petered out
48. "___ is human"
50. Swellings
51. ___ home (out)
52. Sigurd's horse
53. "Lili" star
54. Spine
56. Gnu features
58. Operatives
60. Yes follower
61. Bullock
62. "The Profane Art" author
63. To grow dim, in Dijon
64. Flings
65. Alt's asset
66. Gluts
67. Attila, e.g.
68. Methods
69. Wedge: Pref.
74. Salon services
76. Large antelope
77. Unsettle
78. Shows off
79. Hunter and Richardson
80. Suppress
81. Potable's potency
83. "___ will is the wind's will": Longfellow
85. Antiknock fluids
87. Frangible
88. Like a country gentleman
89. Fast time
90. Citrus coolers
91. Store gds.
92. Cohort
94. Actress Swenson
95. Minot's loc.
96. Ditto
98. Tête holder
100. Maestro de Waart
101. Campus org.

(147) *Academe* by Barbara Lunder Gillis

ACROSS

1. Panier handle
5. Pen
8. Small containers for liquids
14. Rose fruits
18. Hit musical
19. Aunt, in Avila
20. Actor Oscar
22. Chinese nurse
23. Part of a typing exercise
26. ___ dixit
27. Gompers or Goldwyn
28. Berliner's 44 Down
29. Brood of pheasants
30. Tatter's output
31. Rhode Island's founder
34. Cava or contracta preceder
35. Fanfare
36. Alarm
38. Scrams
40. Carols
41. Innocent
42. Soil aggregate
43. Misfortune
44. Darling
46. Parrots
47. Norma or Charlotte
48. Troubles
50. Peace pipe
54. Lips
55. Converter
57. Epiphany trio
58. Eschews
60. Actress Pola
61. Postponed
63. Turkic or Mongolic language
65. Bill
67. Glance
68. ___ d'hotel
69. Architectural rib
70. Gentle as ___
72. Firth in Scotland
73. Tel ___
74. Small hand drum
76. Pout
77. Thesmothete
79. Pilaster
80. MOMA display
81. Small talk
85. Companion of file
86. Curve
87. High degree
88. Desdemona's detractor
89. Old Italian coin
92. "... ___ promise, serv'd no private end": Pope

94. Scatter
95. Smart, swift equines
96. "___ Three Lives": Philbrick
98. Half of a test name
100. Place
101. Privy to
102. Latin I word
103. Grows
106. Lifted an anchor
107. Broadway's Juliet: 1934
111. Dismounted
112. Military ornament
113. Operate
114. North Sea feeder
115. Affirmative votes
116. Separate seed
117. Color of a fez
118. Side dish

DOWN

1. Deeds
2. Capital of Okinawa
3. Glasses
4. Gentlemen just below knights
5. Allay
6. Obsession
7. Tibetan ox
8. Transplant expert
9. Aussie marsupials
10. "Coal-ition" initials
11. "Golden Treasury" item
12. Spritelike
13. Czech car
14. "___! happy land!"
15. Pierce
16. Inventor of first digital calculation
17. Nautical ropes
21. Chop
24. Ubangi feeder
25. Part of a basilica
32. Certain girders
33. Dangerous mosquito
34. Longfellow subject
35. Chemical compound
36. Resort
37. "Kindness"
39. Coast, in a way
42. Mount ___, Colo. peak
44. Surface for a Sabre
45. Devonshire seaport
49. Nimble
51. Like lager
52. Historic Hungarian city
53. Ocean flux
54. Havoc
56. Bond
58. Rose contemplator

59. Sliced or diced vegetables
62. River in Switzerland
63. Lackaday!
64. Of immediate interest
65. Woolen cap
66. ___ Longa
71. Paris subway
72. Jazzy Jelly Roll
75. Pique
76. Any sudden aid
78. NM town
81. False topazes
82. A Madison Ave. method
83. Ripen
84. Draw
89. Glide
90. Troupial
91. Baltic republic
92. Wallace work
93. Scholar's collar
94. Fly high
96. Clumsy
97. Hindu's brass water vessel
99. Palm leaf
101. Harry's successor

102. Olympian once imprisoned in a jar
104. Italian isle
105. Ruck
108. Pub request
109. Stray
110. Snooker stick

Ragtag Band by A. J. Santora

148

ACROSS

1. Next of skin?
5. Low life forms
12. Forgetful
19. Deed, in Dijon
20. Actors Edward and William
21. Make unfriendly
22. Colleen McCullough's music makers?
24. Family of Grant's first Veep
25. Fluffy fare
26. Shut up
28. Tinge
29. Fashion designer Simpson
31. Danza latina
32. Potent hallucinogen
33. Pants style
36. N.L. team
38. Three-pointed tooth
43. Entertain
44. Humbug
45. Beat it, Ringo!
46. Rock producer Brian ___
47. Soccer great
48. Candia
50. Abbot's aide
52. Folded, filled tortilla
53. R.E.O. middle
54. This bunch
55. Synthetic fabric
56. Of 60 Across
57. Lifeboats
59. Sofa
60. Back burner?
61. What this country singer needs?
66. Purpose
67. Clergyman
68. Handel handled this well
70. ___ deux (dance for two)
73. Burglar
74. Seasoning
75. Vandalize
76. Tract
77. Excitement
78. Poe's "___ in Paradise"
79. Satiate
80. Critic Reed
81. Chesterton's "___ Survey"
82. Dobbin gets hitched to it
83. Horse or car
84. Kind of clause
87. Where Bush whacked Dukakis

89. Wore
90. Singer Sumac
91. At the tip of one's lung?
93. A Jackson Secretary of War
95. Walk like Festus
97. Mythical beasts
100. Quartet members
103. Rooter for hockey's Oilers
105. Barn-dance song?
108. Proximity
109. End the reign of rain
110. Be next door to
111. In any case
112. Notched, as a leaf
113. Harmony, for short

DOWN

1. Boater or bowler
2. Reverberate
3. News bit
4. Practice
5. See eye to eye
6. One of the "M" boys of baseball
7. Pluto, e.g.
8. Sponsorship
9. Crosby was one
10. First ___ (above all else)
11. Krupp city
12. Lotion ingredient
13. Clement
14. Seaman's clock
15. Makes law
16. What Stan Getz has?
17. Suburban people?
18. "___ Magnifique," 1953 hit song
21. How to play polkas?
23. Call-in song
27. Darkness hrs.
30. Why the musical was R-rated?
32. Aggregate
33. Clothed in a fanon
34. Ms. Bloomer
35. Pouring out the whines
37. An hors d'oeuvre
39. Smooth out
40. Bad dog
41. Orejon, e.g.
42. Spot for a slot
48. Scold
49. Shorten a sail
50. Sidewalk brick
51. Pitcher Nolan
52. Jay Silverheels role

54. That bunch
55. Costa ___, San Jose native
56. Parlor set
58. Dutch cheese
59. Scenery of a sort
60. Like a smoothie
62. Manicure
63. Rictus
64. Actor Assante
65. Theater district
69. Acrylic fiber
70. Shave
71. Hawkish god
72. Erotic music maker?
73. Touched
74. Energy source
77. Tallahassee is its cap.
78. More complex
79. Laydowns, in bridge
81. In the style of
82. Glisten
83. Fake
85. Current unit
86. Big bird of myth
88. Stayed to the end of
92. Pear choices
94. Fiesta Bowl site

95. Singer Cantrell
96. "___ a Song Go . . ."
97. All-purpose trks.
98. Tweed twitter
99. Bandy words
101. Girl in a Kenny Rogers hit
102. Amaze
104. Kind of virus
106. Sinatra's coda?
107. Blah, blah, blah

ACROSS

1. Strident
6. Type of seaman
10. Seed oysters
15. Ethically neutral
21. Capital of Guam
22. Like some highways
23. College at Oxford
24. A source of potassium
25. Kafka novel, with "The"
26. This, in Taxco
27. German shepherd?
29. Pointer?
32. City on the Alabama
33. Steinbeck's Adam ___
34. Tee neighbor
35. Carriage
36. Razzias
38. Country singer Bandy
40. Like some toothpaste
42. Cowboy's buddy
43. Heaters
44. Twaddle
47. "Jagged Edge" actress
49. Siberian huskies?
53. ___ Canals
54. "A-Team" member
56. Composition
57. Potato state
58. Improvise, in jazz
59. Cardigan or Pembroke of Wales
61. Amanda Plummer role
63. Lammed out
64. Lures game
65. ___ dictus (otherwise called)
66. Court order
67. Verdure
70. Some are G.P.'s
71. Challenge a juror
73. The Scourge of God
75. An amino acid, for short
77. Boxers?
85. Salmon follower
86. Present; current
87. ___ foudre (French thunderbolt)
88. Pronto
91. Spend the summer
95. Admiral Maximilian von ___
97. Grain thresher
98. Another boxer?
100. ___ Cassin, Nobelist for Peace: 1968
101. Poker hand, also called kilter
102. Perfume ingredient
103. Placid
104. Fabled deliverer
106. Blanc's opposite
107. Bustle
109. De Maupassant
110. Boston bull
113. Firedog residue
115. West end
116. Salt's attention getter
117. Chinese isinglass
118. Bender
120. Low
121. "___ a Dolphin," 1957 film
123. Dale starter
124. Monogram of "Little Men" author
127. Pond protozoan
131. Laissez ___
133. Chow chow?
137. Afghans?
140. Emblem of Great Britain
141. Like neglected carpets or dryers
142. Black nightshades
143. Copacetic
144. Goatlike Roman deity
145. Single-celled organism
146. Unwrote
147. Actress Eve
148. Poker stake
149. Drum wire

DOWN

1. "... he ___ known my name"
2. Accede
3. Fulminates
4. Shapes up, in a way
5. Fifty percent
6. Antarctic penguin
7. Beat
8. Trajan's tongue
9. Impetuous ardor
10. Type of story
11. Chair
12. Televised
13. Famed Uri family
14. Garment size
15. Start of a child's song
16. Certain cat or dog
17. What towser has
18. Like Caesar's steak, perhaps
19. A Spanish liqueur
20. Dearth
28. Famed pantyhose peddler
30. Reddish brown
31. Ear part
37. Weapons
39. Holy Roman emperor: 962–73
41. Terriers?
42. Chemist's small container
43. Chewed on
44. ___ 91, source of 1 Down
45. Invited
46. Basketball defense
47. Pen
48. Old Roman cuirass
49. Actress Granville
50. Aswan's site
51. Notion, in Nimes
52. E.T.'s vehicle
53. Nape drape
55. Large marble
60. Surgical dressing
62. Seize
63. Graylag's cousin
64. Pug?
67. Frozen
68. Summer time in N.Y.C.
69. V.M.I. group
72. They start as elvers
74. Provoked
76. As ___ (generally)
78. Ship deserter
79. More gloomy
80. Having a flimsy texture
81. Not windward
82. Sprinkle
83. Repugnant
84. Nice ___ (prude)
88. Annapolis frosh
89. Eastern U.S. capital
90. Hussy
92. Ferruginous
93. Speak or fetch, e.g.
94. "Puppy Love" composer: 1959
96. Greek vowel
99. Hostelry
101. Voiced speech sound
104. Manhattan district
105. ___ kind (poker holding)
106. Canceled by NASA
108. Stunt person, e.g.
111. Like some wild animals
112. Outfits for baby
114. Rowdy
118. Stay until the end
119. Hawthorne character
121. Fonda was this in "Easy Rider"
122. Echo was one
123. Miao, e.g.
125. City in Nigeria
126. "... and ___ to steer her by": Masefield
127. Peak
128. Heath
129. Philanthropist Cornell
130. Secondary matters
132. Empress Ivanovna
134. Communications word
135. Shade trees
136. Irish President: 1938–45
138. A hallucinogen, for short
139. Methuselah, to Enoch

ACROSS

1. Breezy idiom
6. Ali Baba, e.g.
13. Strong dislike
19. Former federation in SE Asia
21. Steve Martin romp: 1987
22. College town east of L.A.
23. Start of message
26. Cherish
27. Plaines preceder
28. "Fiddler" matchmaker and namesakes
29. Einstein's birthplace
30. Down East
32. Summer in Noisy-le-Sec
33. ___ Islands, Blackbeard's base
37. Divided into areas
38. Baseball stat
39. B'way signs
43. "Hallelujah, I'm ___," Jolson film
44. Connection
45. Do some ushering
46. Whitman or Disney
47. More of message
53. Relative of et al.
54. Telephoned
55. Matriculate
56. E.T., e.g.
57. Quailed
59. Black eye
61. Same difference
62. He went over the wall
64. Character actress Parsons
66. Part of HEW
69. Actor Ed and family
71. Fritz, Carl or Rob
74. Mountain range in Russia
75. Smoke detector
76. Viking landfall
77. Sighs of satisfaction
79. More of message
84. "... Baked in ___"
85. World's longest river
86. Spooky-sounding lake
87. Columnist Barrett
88. Minister to
89. Ship-plank curve
90. Specified, as a date
92. Glyn or Wylie
94. Panay people
95. The original "golden boy"?

96. Claire of "Claudia"
97. Chief French naval base
100. Hot-pie ingredient
101. Reduced to a mean
106. End of message
110. Emulate Circe
111. Mother-of-pearl source
112. Silverware city in N.Y.
113. Moped about listlessly
114. Colorful spectral type
115. TV-tube element

DOWN

1. Struck hard, old style
2. Memorable Cowardly Lion
3. Winglike parts
4. Zilch, in Zaragoza
5. Plaster of paris mineral
6. "Comus" composer
7. ___ Reagan Jr.
8. Borden weapon
9. Villain, informally
10. Mean
11. Have ___ for news
12. A neighbor of Wyo.
13. Zest for food
14. Not a soul
15. "___ a Man," Ciardi book
16. Speck
17. Les Etats-___
18. Botanical pouch
20. Bastard wing
24. Estuary
25. Confrontation feature
30. Bop pioneer Thelonious
31. Singer Paul
33. Bunyan's Blue Ox
34. Touches on
35. Rabbit coop
36. Fifi's friend
37. Pizazz
38. Snappy comeback
39. Puffed up
40. "The Shadow" medium
41. Ancient, to poets
42. Songwriter Jule
44. Sri ___
45. Accent
48. Extreme
49. Western spread
50. Wahine's neckwear
51. Kind of tube or man

52. Somewhat like the Sears Tower
58. At ease
59. Oil-yielding tropical plant
60. Flit-fetcher of yesteryear
61. On the qui vive
63. In a wan way
65. Wipe out
66. Attacks with vigor
67. Skip the wedding march
68. Dined at home
70. Nandu's look-alike
72. Secretary of War: 1829–31
73. Nose: Pref.
75. Silly
76. Hitler's "___ Kampf"
78. Wound souvenir
80. "... leave no tern ___": Nash
81. St. Petersburg's river
82. God of war
83. Belligerent Greek god

90. Balm of ___
91. Commendable principles
92. January, in Trujillo
93. Voice box
94. Clover type
95. Possibly
96. "___ Got Five Dollars," 1931 song
97. Pueblo Indian
98. Vision: Comb. form
99. ___ the air (unsettled)
101. State firmly
102. Busy as ___
103. "___ Out of My Head," 1964 song
104. Taro root
105. Cannon of cinema
106. Fashion's whimsical line
107. Fun and games for 82 Down
108. Balderdash!
109. Bambi's aunt

(151) Career Changes by Judith Perry

ACROSS

1. Sew loosely
6. Gyrate
10. Iced
15. Choir member
19. Russian cooperative
20. Amonasro's daughter
21. Lured
22. Cross
23. Supply new weapons
24. Lowest high tide
25. Bitter
26. Designate
27. Candlemaker becomes mystery writer
30. Duck down
31. Sigma
32. Montague heir
33. Attention getter
34. Unit of land measure
35. Church tribunals
36. Nicholas II, e.g.
37. Give the once-over
41. Depreciate
44. Policeman becomes landscape painter
46. Courted danger
47. Honored
48. Actress Balin
49. Secular
50. Auto-racing name of fame
51. Stews
52. Literary monogram
53. "___ vincit amor"
54. Dutch commune
55. Poet Marianne ___
56. Help!
57. Haggard novel
58. Gymnast becomes singer
61. Doorkeeper becomes Broadway composer
66. Tote
67. Essay
68. Friendship
69. Author Ròlvaag
70. Slacken
73. Nitrous oxide; e.g.
74. Heath
75. Mountain mint
77. Actor Baldwin
78. Calendar abbr.
79. Iranian river
80. Well-mannered
81. Arrow maker becomes aerospace scientist
84. Upholstery material
85. Not gregarious
86. Marmalade ingredient
87. Sop
88. Louis ___ of the N.B.A.
89. Foot: Comb. form
90. City south of Florence
91. Crone
94. Gitche Gumee craft
97. Palace official becomes basketball star
100. At the summit
101. Appellation
102. Pernicious
103. Fate
104. Otherwise
105. Opponents
106. Kind of china
107. "___ Talking": Rivers-Meryman
108. ___-do-well
109. Voltaire was one
110. Discordia, to Demosthenes
111. Marsh plants

DOWN

1. Vt. granite center
2. Locations
3. Remains
4. Time period
5. Ranch worker becomes pollster
6. Sleep inducer
7. Flinders
8. Site of Hells Canyon
9. Calif. wine valley
10. Cordial welcome
11. French general, in-law of Napoleon
12. To the point, in law
13. Coconut fiber
14. Terminate
15. Pilgrim becomes golfer
16. Burden
17. Weighty volume
18. River to the Baltic
28. Eminent
29. Contemporaries of Hudsons
30. Formerly, once
34. Handle, to Hadrian
35. Strafe
36. Unsteady
37. Travelers' rests
38. Israeli statesman
39. Twice LXXVI
40. Mexican Indian
41. Condiment bottle
42. Indo-Aryan language
43. Site of the Krupp works
44. They come along for "deride"
45. Ocean pollutant
47. Face of a building
51. Pro
52. More spacious
53. Cry of amused surprise
55. Phiz
56. Disfigured
57. Le Carré character
59. Barrelmaker becomes rock musician
60. Now, now!
62. Greek letter
63. "___ With Love," Poitier film
64. Cream
65. Rent again
70. Indian prince
71. Greek underground in W.W. II
72. Exec's reminder
73. Kittiwake
74. Cultural
75. Sideshow pitchman becomes game-show host
76. Winglike structures
78. At a distance
79. Decisive experiment
80. Twain biographer
82. Beget
83. Latticework
84. Increases threefold
87. Islands off the Fla. coast
89. Florentine palace
90. Relish
91. Western local-color writer
92. Directed toward
93. Growls
94. City on the Orne
95. Tamarisk
96. Proboscis
97. Oenologist's interest
98. Cupbearer of the gods
99. Kent's girlfriend
101. Tiny amount

152 Senior-Class Ballot *by Nancy Nicholson Joline*

ACROSS

1. Papier-___
6. German grandma
9. Lhasa ___
13. U.S. Open golf champ: 1959
19. Profit
20. "Up to ___," Al Smith's autobiography
21. Becloud
22. Joint: Comb. form
23. Class Casanova
26. Grills
27. Yegg's diamonds
28. "...but the end is not ___": Matt. 24: 6
29. Alma mater of the 39th Pres.
30. U.S. dancer-choreographer: 1931–89
31. "The Jazz Singer" was one: 1927
34. Appropriate
35. Grip
38. Noted theater in Paris
39. Boy with the Best Physique
41. Ex-coach Parseghian
44. ___ nova
45. Oscars' kin
46. Joyce's ___ Livia Plurabelle
47. Angular border design
48. The law, to Mr. Bumble
49. Vast amount
50. Send to Coventry
51. Crossworder's Latin verb
52. Class Actress
56. Ecclesiastical vestment
57. Asseverate
61. Convenes
62. Sea-urchin features
63. Emitted
64. Cumberland, e.g.
65. Democritus or Dalton
66. Alarms
67. Site of ancient Olympics
69. Pedants
70. Ailurophiles' rewards
71. Teacher's Pet
75. Place for avions
76. Hybrid animal
77. Capital of the Maldives
78. Lincoln or Maxwell
81. Ligatures
82. Arabian sultanate
83. Allen or Lawrence
85. Snicker
87. "___ It," 1940 song
88. Class Clown
90. Extract forcibly
91. Bar where Hemingway hung out
93. Inlets
94. "Pathétique" or "Appassionata"
95. Type of phobia
97. Squeals
98. Actuary's concern
100. Upsilon follower
101. ___ Bueller, Broderick role
103. Big Woman on Campus
107. Used
108. Okla. Indian
109. Actress Alicia
110. Waste producer
111. Forsyth's "The ___ File"
112. Young salmon
113. Pili or macadamia
114. Weasel's kin

DOWN

1. Ontario neighbor
2. Guacamole items
3. Negligent
4. L.B.J. beagle
5. Guido note
6. Formerly
7. Doubtful
8. Wheat beard
9. Maltreaters
10. David Hare play
11. Iranian archeological site
12. Table scrap
13. Hack
14. "But he's an ___ knave": Shak.
15. Zeno, e.g.
16. Class Musician
17. A Gardner
18. Promising
24. Aneurin Bevan, familiarly
25. Ask
32. Aegean island
33. Concert follower
34. Non compos ___
35. Tristan da ___ Islands
36. Genus of flax
37. Dash
39. "Fear of Flying" author
40. Lively party
42. Most authentic
43. Certifies
45. Far from fresh
47. Shrine site in Portugal
49. Entangles
52. "...o'er ___ and hills": Wordsworth
53. Actor Bruce or Havers
54. Shelley's "Paradise of exiles"
55. Savory jelly
56. Famed English potter
57. Autocrats
58. Out of court
59. Class Athlete
60. Bird and Holmes
62. Fence straddler
65. Confuse
68. Suzanne from San Bruno
71. Karloff role
72. Norwegian kings
73. Comedian Jay
74. Crockett or Jones
76. "I never saw a ___": Dickinson
78. Most shoddy
79. Dilettante
80. Shopkeeper
83. Move like a snake
84. Pester
85. Jefferson's bill
86. North follower
88. Oregon and Santa Fe
89. Cicero, e.g.
92. Wall hanging
94. Bishopric
95. Hair style
96. Turned right
97. Pro ___
98. Japanese aborigine
99. Punkie
102. Kind of chest or dog
103. Bull
104. Kurosawa film: 1985
105. The ___, of rock fame
106. Dicer or skimmer

ACROSS

1. Drab; not stylish
6. Mirador
11. Fa-la connector
14. "From the Terrace" author
19. Suffered
20. Kowalski portrayer: 1947
21. Small case
22. Hemidemi-semiquavers
23. Kalmar-Ruby question
25. What "is" is
26. Pinch
27. Kind of guard
28. Banquet platform
29. A Capulet's question
32. Eyes and ears
34. Straggle
36. Testified
37. Dreamer
39. Question from Bugs
42. Tied the knot
43. Construe
44. Fry in butter
45. Part of a shandy
46. Russian C.I.A.
48. Site of Vance A.F.B.
49. Less populated
51. Agrippa's apparel
53. Part of M-G-M's motto
57. Capek play
58. Beatles movie: 1965
59. Ed Koch's former question
61. Wimbledon winner: 1987
63. Papa Bear of football
65. Cavatina
66. Arenaceous plant
67. Singer John
69. "Raving, ___, money-mad": B. R. Newton
71. Laves lightly
72. Wilde was one
74. Knock-knock question
78. Business abbr.
79. River in the Carolinas
82. Bony
84. Campus costumes
88. High praise
91. Shakespearean tinker
92. Meistersinger Hans
94. Hone
95. Veronese question
97. Surfeit
98. Past
99. ___ prosequi
100. Gouda's competitor
101. Kind of plate
104. Deneb or Mizar
105. "Sail ___ Union . . .": Longfellow
107. "Israfel" poet's monogram
108. Wasted time
109. Chanson de ___
110. Eliz II, for one
112. Part of a Gallic question
115. Glistened
117. Six bells on the midwatch
119. Sarah ___, Met soprano
120. In shipshape fashion
121. Jack Yellen's question
124. Juncture
125. Spline
128. Jacob's first wife and namesakes
129. Close by
130. Half-baked question?
134. A first name in fragrance
135. June heroes
136. Rock having roelike grains
137. Official language of India
138. Dutch genre painter
139. ___ Lanka
140. Like a bugbear
141. "___ by land . . ."

DOWN

1. Cockcrow
2. Eight, in Oaxaca
3. Routine question
4. Left in the lurch
5. A mi. = 1,760 ___
6. Fragrant root
7. Beams
8. Tavern
9. Tokyo, once
10. Depressed state
11. Printer's directive
12. Yours and mine
13. Drive of a kind
14. Ready for use
15. Question for Bossy
16. Relaxed
17. Used an auger
18. Questioned
20. Wild goose
21. Appraiser
24. Harem rooms
30. ___ nibs

31. It has seven vertebrae
33. Needlefish
34. So
35. Have status
37. Savage
38. Yearbook
39. Road to conflict
40. Furrow maker
41. "Absinthe" painter
44. Unhealthy looking
47. Carefree rover's activity
49. Hush!
50. Anjou or Comice
52. Physicians' org.
54. Juan's uncles
55. Anent
56. Some NCO's
59. Meteorological areas
60. Letters at Calvary
62. Mrs. B.'s question
64. O. Henry prod.
65. Itchy
68. Name in TV ratings
70. Capri, to Capriotes
73. Hyson and gunpowder

75. Endings for draft and employ
76. City pests
77. Classical geometer
79. Impignorate
80. A nymph pursued by Pan
81. Environmental subj.
83. Scat!
85. Question for Bennett Cerf
86. Void
87. Squirreled away
89. It has 21 dots
90. Senior
91. They wear fatuous smiles
93. Prefix for thesis
96. River in South Africa
101. Ten
102. Foofaraws
103. Pivot
104. Mukluk material
106. Colorful marine fish
109. Columbia, in a song
110. Most bashful
111. Embellished
113. Corrects

114. Zorro's mark
115. Mealtime prayer
116. Exec's car
117. Judicial writ
118. City in the Ruhr valley
120. Snappish
122. Rifle part
123. Ravine that is often dry
124. Cookery direction
126. "The Breeze ___," 1940 song
127. Letters for day six
131. Ad ___ committee
132. C.S.A. state
133. Cry of amused surprise

(154) Missed Connections by Jane S. Flowerree

ACROSS

1. Kin of kerplunk
6. Couple
10. Swashbuckler
15. Raiment
16. Drab shade
17. Tied in red tape in Mongolian center?
19. Tardy for shuttle in Orioles' home?
21. Neither oui nor non
23. Ale, in Aachen
24. Publish
25. "If ___ a Rich Man"
26. Actor Mineo
27. Rim
28. Bungled bus transfer in Ontario metropolis?
31. Central points
32. Shake a drink
34. Uno y uno
35. Lollapaloozas
36. W.W. II bomber
37. Ant. for ant.
38. A ratite
40. World-weary
41. Salamanders
42. Bright lights
43. Opposite of eso
44. Tar
45. Feral feline
47. ___ March to the Sea
50. Door hinge
54. Way off base
55. Papal name
56. Nanjing nursemaid
57. ___ Finklea, a k a Cyd Charisse
58. Evert's ex
59. Charges
60. Field yield
61. Cycle
62. Sow sound
63. Crooned
64. French president: 1954–59
65. Looseness
66. Preppy, e.g.
67. Independence
69. Ointment
70. Vichy resources
72. Needle feature
73. Kind of pie or board
74. Did lawn work
76. Sci-fi awards
78. ___ majesté
79. Juliette Low's gp.
82. Van Pelt and Ricardo
83. VCR button
84. Mo. in hiver
85. Juan Carlos's realm

87. Biblical well
88. Boarded wrong train in Pyrenees capital?
91. Bath residue
92. Fresh ___ daisy
93. Narc's prey
94. Composer Copland
95. Photographer Morath
96. Cramps a cowboy's style
98. Lost tour group in South Pacific site?
101. Marooned on monorail in Sunshine State mecca?
102. Cockney crony
103. Tibetan guide
104. Ketch tippers
105. Goad
106. Steel splint, in armor

DOWN

1. With decorum
2. Fogged in, in Pacific Northwest gateway?
3. British measures
4. Onassis nickname
5. Entice
6. Factories
7. ___ surface missiles
8. Campus climber
9. Electrical unit
10. Runs, in a way
11. Tierney title role: 1944
12. Stake
13. Inits. for Judith Anderson, e.g.
14. Dines at a restaurant
15. Convent head
16. Causing fear and anxiety
17. Type of mobility
18. Footprints
20. Corrosive
22. Director Kazan
25. Arrow poison
29. Cajoles
30. Missed connections in this puzzle
31. Overshot exit ramp in Dallas's sister city?
33. Well-to-do
36. Nice seasoning
39. Debatable
40. Hackmen
41. Hudson contemporary

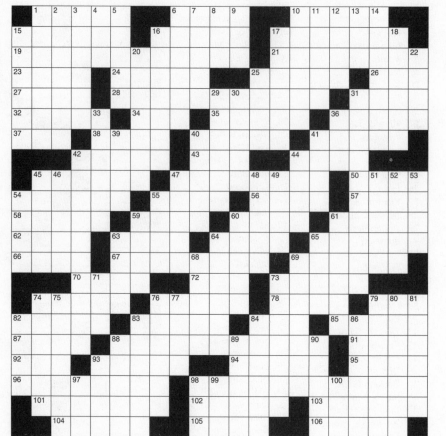

42. Late for the 7:58 in Gotham?
44. Cinch
45. Lt. Col. North, to friends
46. Duplicate
47. Mistimed excursion in S California locale?
48. Delbert Mann's 1955 Oscar winner
49. Old name of Xiamen
51. I.R.S. procedure
52. List of candidates
53. Divided, in heraldry
54. "Thanks ___!"
55. Confined
59. Counterfeit, in Paris
60. Cather's "Death ___ for the Archbishop"
61. Analyzes a sentence
63. King of the Meccans: 1953–64
64. South Dakota, the ___ State
65. Dregs
68. Israeli hot spot
69. Herringbone

71. Loser to D.D.E.
73. Without a doubt
74. Shore-dinner item
75. Cousteau's fld.
76. Capital of the Treasure State
77. D.O.D. div.
79. Some fancy dives
80. Mired in customs in Far East banking hub?
81. Light role on TV
82. Page
83. White water
84. Chipped
86. Awards
88. TV's "Trials of ___ O'Neill"
89. Milk: Comb. form
90. "___ of robins . . .": Kilmer
93. Dingle
97. ___ franc of W. Afr.
98. Mike's complement
99. Eg. and Syr., once
100. Contemporary of T.S.E.

155 Rare Aves by Jeanette K. Brill

ACROSS

1. Short haircuts
5. Perfume ingredient
10. Indian chief
15. Asian unit of weight
19. In ___ (going nowhere)
20. Ezra or Irving
21. Ham it up
22. University or playwright
23. He composed "Love Letters in the Sand"
25. "Best actor" Oscar winner: 1976
27. Nevertheless
28. Les femmes
30. Rota
31. Easy gait
32. Melancholy, to Milton
33. Gossip
34. Greek goddess of wisdom
37. "___ Keys to Baldpate"
38. Joshed
42. Greek letter
43. British lexicographer-author: 1894–1979
46. Wood sorrel
47. Ravens' strident cries
49. One of Pooh's friends
50. Stretches the budget
51. Gator's relative
52. Smell ___ (suspect)
53. U.S. poet who wrote "The Bridge"
57. Morley's "Kitty ___"
58. Bishop, e.g.
60. Had expectations
61. Rhythmical beat
62. Male duck
63. College in Lewiston, Me.
64. A man of morals
65. Gleam
66. Abbot's right-hand man
67. Deighton's "___ in Berlin"
69. It's used on a cue tip
70. Boston Celtics star
72. Goddess of discord
74. Elias or Gordie
75. Despina, in "Cosi fan tutte"
77. ___ rule (generally)
78. Attract
79. Quest of Indiana Jones
80. He painted "Old Battersea Bridge"
86. Actress Munson
87. Brought back into use
89. Parts of a horse's collar
90. Room for action
92. Author of "Battle Cry"
93. Shankar's instrument
94. Footnote abbr.
95. Excel on the track
98. "___ Laughing," 1967 film
99. Lengthen
103. Celebrity-roast host
105. Orioles' manager in 1970 Series win
107. Actress Sommer
108. He wrote "Hard Cash"
109. Crows, e.g.
110. Rock's partner
111. Device on a loom
112. Kirstie from Wichita
113. Velocity
114. Ko-Ko's dagger

DOWN

1. ___ California, peninsula in Mexico
2. German composer: 1895–1982
3. Loni's husband
4. Addison's writing partner
5. Gone con?
6. Neckpiece
7. Pawn
8. Tolkien creature
9. Modesty, in Madrid
10. Change the flower bed
11. Native ruler in Africa
12. Tittles
13. Ingested
14. If red, these may mislead
15. "Valse ___"
16. "___ She Sweet?": 1927 song
17. Behold, to Brutus
18. Oven used to anneal glass
24. Bombinate
26. One's strong point
29. Lewd look
32. Magazine for military stores
33. Miami's county
34. Chest for valuables
35. Twyla, the choreographer
36. Director of "The Big Sleep"
37. Censure
38. Used a tandem
39. N.B.A. player with the Sacramento Kings
40. What an élève attends
41. Cyprinoid fish
44. Steamed up
45. Coty or Cassin
48. Barren
51. Part of N.A.A.C.P.
53. Cod's kin
54. Bergère, e.g.
55. Revolving part on a machine
56. Imitation
57. Blend
59. Not curly, as hair
61. Hang fire
63. Finishing nails
64. Of hearing
65. Snipe's habitat
66. Performed diligently
67. Signs used in printing
68. Climbing plant
69. Carbonize
71. More despicable
73. Controlling influence
75. Type of spaghetti sauce
76. Cyclones play here
80. Large drinking bowl
81. Singer Houston
82. H. Broun's "Pieces of ___"
83. Turkish inns
84. Jostled
85. Marie Antoinette, for one
88. Changed, as leaves
91. Awards for mystery writers
93. Insinuating
94. "___ Seeing You"
95. River in central Europe
96. Ubangi feeder
97. The gate
98. Butcher shop: Fr.,
99. Coloratura Mills
100. Sight from Warwick Castle
101. Psychic affinity
102. Film director Kenton
104. Electrical unit
106. A founder of Dadaism

156 Kitchen-Garden Gossip *by Frances Hansen*

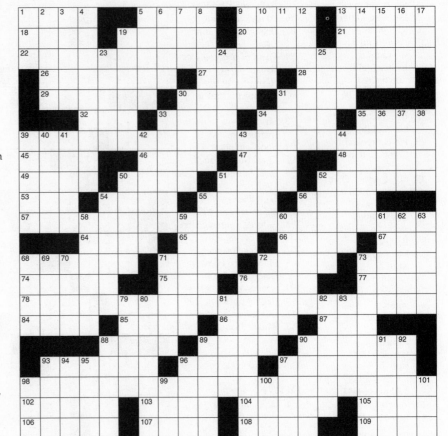

ACROSS

1. Wampum item
5. Hammerlock or half nelson
9. London cleaning woman
13. Degrade
18. Singer James
19. Caravansary
20. Let up
21. Insurgent
22. Why is the gardener so happy?
26. Catalogued
27. Entreaty
28. Quarterback Y. A.
29. "The ___ Green," E. Williams play
30. Ran in the laundry
31. Pull up stakes
32. Helmut's ice
33. Mister, in Malaysia
34. Writer Vidal
35. Movie mogul
39. How does that change the gardener's plans?
45. Portrayer of western villains
46. See 40 Down
47. Make tracks
48. Pahlevi's namesakes
49. Lilting melodies
50. Whitman or Wilbur
51. Aim
52. "___ Boat," Belafonte hit
53. Fish eggs
54. "Mens sana in corpore ___"
55. A sister of John Boy
56. Rubik of the cube craze
57. What kind of gift has he bought her?
64. Linguist Chomsky
65. Archibald of the N.B.A.
66. Psyche's lover
67. Day, in Durango
68. Woman warden
71. Actor Robert or Alan
72. In ___ (having trouble)
73. Treaty between nations
74. ___ con pollo (Spanish dish)
75. West of Hollywood
76. Small barracuda
77. Korea's Syngman
78. Do they plan a large family?

84. Winglike parts
85. Carries the day
86. ___ accompli
87. "Ich bin ___ Berliner": J.F.K.
88. Knife handle
89. Swindles
90. Fishing boats
93. Accomplice
96. Where to find Wailuku
97. Lop-eared dog
98. What do you see in their future?
102. Fashion designer Simpson
103. Author Ludwig
104. "Invisible Man" Claude
105. Singer Paul from Ottawa
106. Feasted one's eyes
107. One of a seagoing trio
108. Hunky trailer
109. Masher's grimace

DOWN

1. Big-A action
2. Moral precept
3. "___ clock scholar"
4. Does some woolgathering
5. Start of a toast
6. Toward the mouth
7. China's Zhou En-___
8. Showcases
9. Granted, as territory
10. Sounds of merriment
11. "___ live and breathe!"
12. Patch up a painting
13. Mountain ridge
14. Deliver one to the jaw
15. First shepherd
16. Withered
17. English cathedral town
19. NOW fights this bias
23. Toxic substance in a snake's fluid
24. Former queen of Italy
25. Cacomistle
30. Exploded
31. Bates's wayside stopover
33. ___ knowledge (Eden landmark)

34. Vast South American region
35. Key of Beethoven's Fifth
36. Marquis de Venosta's mistress
37. "Pictures ___ Exhibition"
38. Ponselle or Bonheur
39. "Do I ___ Waltz?"
40. With 46 Across, an "Untouchable"
41. First of the Cavalier poets
42. Unnamed person
43. Option
44. Praying figures
50. Other name of Lalitpur, Nepal
51. Garbo
52. Closet item
54. Grab some shut-eye
55. I.R.S. quarry
56. Printers' errors
58. Garb in regal garments
59. Falk-Arkin film, with "The"

60. Send back a manuscript
61. Gem State
62. "___ Easy," Sinatra favorite
63. Winner at Saratoga: 1777
68. Baby's first word, often
69. Russian inland sea
70. "___ Little Tenderness"
71. Catkin
72. Orbit point
73. Victoria of filmdom
76. Man of La Mancha, e.g.
79. Edgar or Emmy
80. Tennis score
81. Run ___ of (hit a snag)
82. French auto-racing locale
83. Tael
88. Put an edge on
89. "Cheers" waitress
90. Like a hedgehog
91. N.H. city
92. Quench one's thirst

93. Musical finale
94. "Hear ye!"
95. Golfer Irwin
96. "___ Leben," Wagner's autobiography
97. The pokey
98. Drinking spree
99. "Brother Rat" inst.
100. ___ Paulo, Brazil
101. Men's org. founded in 1889

157 *Look Sharp* by A. J. Santora

ACROSS

1. Muddle of nowhere?
5. Waist cincher
9. "... comes in like ___"
14. Fairway clump
19. "___ Named Sue"
20. Brawl
21. Wordsworth work
23. Plant used for making pipes
24. Complication
25. New Guinea, to Indonesians
26. Combat flight
27. Uncovered wagons
28. Start of Burma Shave Ad # I
31. Frat letter
33. Far East feast
34. Lizard called a fringefoot
35. Skater Brinker
36. TV alien
37. Part II of Ad # I
40. Assign (to)
42. ___ the Irish
45. Some awnings
46. Violinist Bull
47. Part of D.C.
48. Swindle
50. Heaviest U.S. President
54. High-gloss paint
57. "___ to Be You," 1924 song
59. Tractor-trailer
60. Have nixed emotions?
61. Start of Burma Shave Ad # II
67. John McGraw's wunderkind
68. More orderly
69. Without
70. Gdansk coins
71. Diagnostic aid
73. Sesame
74. Infant
75. ___ T'ung, last Chinese emperor
77. Long ago
78. Part II of Ad # II
81. Essence
85. "___ Irish Rose"
87. Irk
88. Actor McKellen
89. ___ precedent
90. Alphonse's companion
93. Shirt or coat preceder
94. White herons

97. Fled
98. Part III of Ad # II
103. A long time
104. Outstanding
105. Wirepuller
106. Keenness
107. Louis and Bill
109. It lessens
111. Legal claim
112. "___ Oncle," Tati film
113. Architect of Boston's John Hancock Bldg.
115. Viscous
117. Literary collection
121. Part III of Ad # I
125. Bishopric
126. "When I was ___...": Gilbert
127. Toronto's prov.
128. Harrison or Reed
129. Composer Delibes
130. Part IV of Ad # I
135. José's friend
137. Saloonkeeper's nemesis
139. Jibe
140. Innisfail
141. Inspected the joint
142. Petcock
143. Certain horses
144. French violinist: 18th century
145. Admittance
146. "___ Billie Joe"
147. Doctrines
148. Beatty film: 1981

DOWN

1. The Duke of ___, "Rigoletto" role
2. Units of resistance
3. Belt having 12 signs
4. Head set?
5. Peaceful
6. An anonym
7. Stitch line
8. Coop group
9. Smooth ___
10. Seek
11. Concerning
12. Available
13. Chess master Ivo ___
14. Boil down
15. Oldster's nest egg
16. Artistic quality
17. Group of eight
18. Flavor
20. A plum brandy
22. Astounding
29. From Santiago, e.g.
30. One of a class of amides

32. Moiety
38. Mote
39. Winner over T.E.D.
41. Actress Schneider
42. In a supple way
43. Groom's pal
44. Hosiery style
47. Playful tunes
49. Gentles
51. Smell ___ (suspect)
52. Anger
53. Kinski film
54. Gooey stuff
55. Kin of TNT
56. Perfume
58. Rules out
62. Turner's tool
63. "King of Hollywood"
64. Côte d'___, Riviera area
65. Anything extravagant
66. Styne products
72. Nobelist in Literature: 1923
74. What Jack did
75. Cheer
76. Strength

78. Prong
79. With head held higher
80. Style of film lighting
82. "Able was ___ saw Elba"
83. Lead off
84. Strong-scented Old World herb
86. Singing Tower sponsor
90. Verdon of "Damn Yankees"
91. Hey, sailor!
92. ___ curve, in math
93. Sexton or Nemerov
94. Shade of blue
95. Ruth and Gehrig, e.g.
96. Lower parts of duets
99. Kin of "The Emperor Jones" actor
100. His domain is lover's lane
101. Enclave
102. Pueblo dweller
108. Solti's title

109. "Baked in ___"
110. Do a scene over
114. It lingers on
116. Taken care of
117. A "Hellzapoppin" star and family
118. Cape Cod's ___ Bridge
119. Loosened
120. Dental compounds
121. Harness strap
122. Macho guy
123. Be alive
124. Ovum-to-be
126. Middle name of 20th U.S. President
131. Actor Andrews of TV
132. Delhi wear
133. Writers Betti and Moretti
134. Binge
136. Eur. tongue
138. Initials on army mail

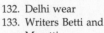

158 Spellbound by Randolph Ross

ACROSS

1. Muammar el-___ of Libya
8. Sheer; utter
13. Hula hoops, once
18. Idealists
20. Like a diorama
22. Actress Veronica from Philadelphia
23. Gunslinger's forte
24. Week, in Mexico
25. Love, in Roma
26. Powerful explosive
27. Fabulous finale
29. Mikhail of ballet
31. Colorless: Comb. form
32. George's lyricist
34. European wooden shoes
35. Egyptian king
39. Conjunction
40. W. Webster's gp.
43. Pyrite and pitchblende
44. Actress Beulah: 1892–1981
46. Where Jeanne d'Arc triumphed: 1429
49. Mid East ladies' rooms
50. Common code
52. Author Feodor
55. Film director Akira
57. Corresponded
59. Cereal fruit
60. Low digit
61. Touched down
62. Host of the 1992 summer Olympics
63. Cousin of Tony and Oscar
66. Philosopher Friedrich
71. Catch
72. They're bitten and banged
74. Anglo-Saxon money of account
75. Co-star of "Rocky III"
77. Type of minnow
78. Texas footballer
80. Deng ___, Chinese leader
85. Zbigniew of Carter's Administration
87. Squash variety
89. Myanmar group
90. "... fears that I may ___ be": Keats
91. Sergeant's "___ were!"
93. ___'acte (intermission)
94. Librarian's admonition
95. Recipe amt.
97. Philosophical writer Charles Louis de Secondat
101. Dormant
104. Ltd., in the U.S.A.
105. Tennyson poem
106. Philosopher-theologian Soren
110. "Se ___ español"
112. Wilde was one
115. As a friend: Fr.
116. English cloth measure, once used for tax purposes
118. Chief artery
120. Shore bird
121. Assented
122. Example
123. Awaits action
124. Namesakes of Actress Cannon
125. Poet Omar

DOWN

1. Egyptian village
2. ___ impasse
3. Biblical verb
4. Agr. is one at D.C.
5. Medics' assistants
6. King of Egypt: 1936–52
7. Graft, in a way
8. Wall and Fleet: Abbr.
9. "And ___ played on"
10. "Aeneid" starter
11. Nurtures
12. Nairobi native
13. Intone
14. Harold of "Ghostbusters"
15. In a frenzy
16. Zilch
17. Alt.
19. Namibia, once: Abbr.
21. German submarine film: 1981
28. Fancy wheels
30. Atrocities
31. Rodeo rope
33. Continue, as a subscription
35. Accepted
36. Language of Pakistan
37. Eye drop
38. Canyon mouth
40. Chinese cinnamon
41. Pressman's activity
42. A ___ apple
45. Rock stars, to some
47. ___ a conclusion (prejudges)
48. French spa
50. Leader before Hua
51. Author Wister
53. Of the ear
54. Eve's third
56. Make conventional
58. Wooden ship without an upper deck
63. Hardens
64. Passover staple
65. "And ___ to go ...": Frost
67. Perfect test scores
68. Actor Estrada
69. Shire of "Godfather III"
70. Arabian prince
73. Kind of bug
76. Film by 55 Across
77. Common lab tests
79. Synthetic material
80. Delete
81. False: Comb. form
82. Fire: Comb. form
83. Hoopster Archibald
84. Teacher, in India
86. Small bunch of flowers
88. Seashell often used as a horn
92. Little bit
96. Rang
98. Enclose a waterway
99. N.A. Indian language
100. Amounts
101. Carrying a weapon
102. Playlets
103. Li'l Abner's mother
106. Retain
107. "Picnic" playwright
108. Generate profits
109. Tabula ___
111. "___ Blue?": 1929 song
112. Vinous
113. Peruvian native
114. Rain cats and dogs
117. Begley and Bradley
119. Minstrel's song

Ditto by Ralph G. Beaman

ACROSS

1. Type of beer
5. Vainglory
9. At the stern
12. Rival of U.S.C.
16. Isle of Hawaii
17. Long narrative
19. Deadness symbol
21. Robards and Bateman
22. Part of a markka
23. Diarist's activity
24. Patriotic song words
27. ___ shrike of Madagascar
28. Monogram of T. Wolfe's eminent editor
29. Trifle
30. Kind of panel or year
31. Where Warden Lawes worked
32. Pipe elbow
33. Zero
36. One of Carmen's people
37. Was left on base
38. Vilipend
40. Multi-star 1963 movie
46. Spotted cat
48. River in N Chile
49. Mazuma
50. Use finger paints
51. Dowitcher
53. Sacred: Comb. form
55. Welkin
56. Tenon's mate
59. Tucker's partner
60. Strauss's "___ Italien"
62. Black tea
64. Phrase from a W.W. I song
68. Zoological suffix
69. Equality
70. Intention
71. Like certain seals
72. Side of a triangle
73. Actor Bruce et al.
75. Hampshire or Yorkshire
76. Curved inward
79. Medium is one
80. Broad sash
82. Varsity member's prize
86. "When ... marching ___!"
90. Retail sign
91. Formal order
92. Type of jet engine
93. Alphonse, to Gaston

94. ___ up (riled)
95. Composer of "The Seasons"
97. Scandinavian goddess of the future
99. An Afg. neighbor
102. One of the Hoggs of Tex.
103. An Asian capital
104. Doubled phrase in a novel ending
108. Fit for use
110. Fanfare
111. Lagging
112. Visit by a medic or clergyman
113. "The Wreck of the Mary ___"
114. ___ a time (singly)
115. For shame!
116. Swedish rug
117. Fr. holy women
118. Preadult person

DOWN

1. Electric wall receptacle
2. ___ about (date-setting phrase)
3. Contemptible one, to Cato
4. Mount ___, N.Y.C. exurb
5. Ta-ta
6. Designer Cassini
7. Labyrinth king
8. She wasn't hopeless
9. "Doe, ___ ..."
10. Loving
11. Add up
12. Biased in choice
13. Summoning, as sheep, in Ayr
14. D.C. panda
15. Water plant
16. Thin layer or plate
18. Force out of place
20. Critiques
21. Corbett, Jeffries or Braddock
25. Unpaid sitter
26. Words before tongs
31. "In Spain they say '___'"
34. Wight is one, Wong isn't
35. Thai language
37. Banned pesticide
39. Boor, in Brest
40. G. M. Cohan's ancestors
41. Hawaiian fish
42. Vocally

43. Do a farrier's job
44. Magic Johnson's team
45. Sylvan nymphs
47. Baker or Bryant
52. Chick's sound
54. "Rosmersholm" playwright
56. Do-re-mi
57. Province or city in NW Spain
58. Wood for railroad ties
59. City in Perm Oblast, U.S.S.R.
61. Goulash
62. A European capital
63. Small hooters
65. Neighbors of ulnae
66. Belgian painter: 1860–1949
67. "___, the gang's ..."
74. Given new quarters
75. Domain of Anna's boss
77. Sinatra-Minnelli show stopper
78. Of the heart
79. Gained a lap

81. Car's front shield
83. Papeete native
84. Neon is one
85. Impede progress
87. Schnapps
88. Opens hightops
89. "___ hooray!"
95. Bull and Nile, as gods
96. Win by ___ (narrowly outrace)
97. Gravestone, perhaps
98. Certain keynote
100. Monastery head
101. Sharp N.H. city?
103. Boniface
104. In a bad way
105. Interlaken's river
106. Lines on an A.A.A. map
107. "... I ___ wed"
109. Mandrel, e.g.

160 Rood Awakenings by Alfio Micci

ACROSS

1. A golf stroke
5. Aspirin target
9. Chest sound
13. Colorful fish
17. Pianist Gilels
18. Hitler's mistress
19. Particulars
21. ___ citato
22. Nick's spouse
23. Lofty sanctum
24. Jury
25. Pour forth
26. Tennyson title
28. Popular hymn, with "The"
30. Korea Bay feeder
31. Amphora
33. Liking, in Lyons
34. Ball game for 20
37. Do a double take
39. Freshwater turtle
44. Summons to court
45. Changed one's status
47. Indian of N.M.
48. Tolkien horse
49. ___ drop of a hat
50. Start of a tot's chant
51. Alternate movie shots
52. Problem in some concert halls
53. Life stories, briefly
54. Flock of quail
56. Seria or comique preceder
57. More uncertain
59. Stop, in Montréal
60. Rejects disdainfully
61. Wright wings
62. Focal point
63. Baker's aide
64. Mortarboard feature
67. City in Puerto Rico
68. Ariel's boss
72. Crockett's last stand
73. Heat and Jazz
74. Capital of 78 Across
75. Algerian port
76. City on the Adda
77. Sheltered at sea
78. Department of N France
79. Except
80. Getting ___ years
81. Suffer
84. Fonda or Rabbit
85. Uncalled for
87. Imprimeur's need
88. "When the Frost ___ the Punkin": Riley
89. Old verb ending
90. NASCAR event
91. A glove leather
94. Ill-tempered
99. De Mille epic of 1932, with "The"
105. U. of New Mexico athlete
106. City on the Po
107. Movement
108. Comment from Garfield
109. Bond's alma mater
110. Beethoven's "Für ___"
111. Source of a fragrant oil
112. Soprano Berger
113. ". . . ___ forgive those . . ."
114. Necklace unit
115. Level a Soho flat
116. Curious

DOWN

1. "Chariots of Fire" star
2. Parisian's "Help!"
3. Alpine snowfield
4. Become limp
5. Spinning
6. Choke's locale
7. Starling's N.Z. cousin
8. Sap
9. Comeback
10. "Thereby hangs ___"
11. Furnish
12. Crisis
13. Skater Protopopov
14. Quince
15. Etcher's need
16. Kind of bun
18. ___ Allah, Iranian religious leader
20. Calumniated
27. Mast chains
29. A Eur. country
32. "___ du lieber!"
34. Tamarack
35. Hi from Ho
36. Occurred to a person suddenly
38. Old letters
39. Yeti's homeland
40. With opposing aims
41. Meadowlands horse
42. Entomb
43. "___ a Stranger": Thompson
44. Between hic and hoc
45. Rail supports
46. Used the tub
49. "___ of Divorcement," 1932 Cukor film
54. Gators' kin
55. Old English money
56. Uncloses, in poesy
58. Role for Liz
59. "Judith" composer
60. Tea tidbit
62. Passageway
63. Position for a gymnast
64. Kite's weapon
65. Romberg's "One ___"
66. Berlin's "___ Salome"
67. Antae
68. Fares
69. Poet's inspiration
70. Fictional talking bird
71. Lulu
73. Photographer's need
74. One waiting in ambush
77. Record material
78. Forebear
82. Had a hankering
83. Hook: Comb. form
84. Memorable chanteuse
86. "___ Girls"
90. Mrs. Gorbachev
92. Laurie of songdom
93. Peas' spots
94. "Iacta ___ est"
95. Barflies
96. Medieval weapon
97. Tops
98. Maumee Bay feeder
100. Mezzo-soprano Petina
101. Feds
102. Deli purchase
103. Long, long periods
104. Intersection

161 *Wondrous Maze* by Timothy S. Lewis

ACROSS

1. French landscapist
6. Start of most of a passage by 66 Down
12. Lang syne
16. Kind of boat or train
21. Andean animal
22. Author Fallaci
23. Not fooled by
24. TV role for Sharon Gless
25. Stand-in for Standish
26. Bay west of Myanmar
27. Word on a coin
28. Four Holy Roman emperors
29. Yellowish brown pigment
31. "___ Evil," 1971 film
32. Entrance to 128 Across
34. Reflexive pronoun
36. Income from a tenant
38. Que. neighbor
39. Ethiopian prince
40. Alpine frock
43. Tomcat
44. Second passage: Part VI
46. Prefix with sphere
50. Aussie's warning cry
51. "On ___ Boat to China"
53. G. & S. character
57. Way out
58. O'Neill trees
59. Hexapods
61. Blue shoe material
62. ___-Lenape Indians
63. First U.N. Secretary General
64. Pakistani language
65. Squiggle or spiral
67. Boast
68. Humdrum
70. Humiliate
71. Hero of a 1922 play
72. River at Leeds
73. Maroons
74. ___ fide
75. Enzyme suffix
76. Turmoil
78. Inc., in Britain
79. Second passage: Part IV
81. Feverish
82. Rest
85. Court call
86. Josip Broz

87. Some kayakers
91. Exactly divisible by two
92. Singer Loretta ___
94. Pythias's pal
95. Blind spot
96. Crosby or cherry
97. Café au ___
98. St. Pierre and Miquelon
99. Child-advocacy org.
100. Tiff
101. Les ___-Unis
103. Chitchat
105. Krupp's milieu
106. A U.S. Open champ: 1968
107. Strait of Dover port
109. Radials on a Rolls
110. Web-footed beast
111. Half a tetrad
112. Second passage: Part II
114. Home of Johnny Reb
115. D.C. suburb
117. Hoppy drink
120. ___ Allen belt
121. Voltaire's forte
123. Wife of Henry II
128. Locale featured in this puzzle
131. Of a former Venetian ruler
134. Name in "The Raven"
135. Verve
136. Others, to Ovid
137. Used a pantograph
139. Admiral Andrea ___
140. Rude awakener
141. Musical epilogue
142. Regatta site
143. Sidled
144. Hemmed and ___
145. Earl of Avon
146. End of first passage
147. Movie units

DOWN

1. Skirmish
2. Partner of Stan
3. Writer Dotson ___
4. Straws in the wind
5. Like beachcombers or surfers
6. Criminal coterie
7. Provokes
8. The Mets or the Muses
9. With enthusiasm
10. Fatuous
11. First passage continued

12. Like wet cement
13. Record of one year's events
14. Counterfoil
15. Hoyden
16. Bats' hangouts
17. "Our Gang" author
18. Actress in "The Maltese Falcon"
19. String-quartet member
20. Ayes
30. Young friend of 66 Down
33. ___ 500
35. Gambols
37. Mesh; web
41. Iditarod terminus
42. ___ Plaines, Ill.
44. Second passage: Part V
45. End of second passage
46. Lends a hand
47. Apply muscle power
48. Lesser
49. Start of second passage

52. Event
54. Part of N.M.S.Q.T.
55. Revere
56. Less passé
59. Man of Ahvaz
60. Mr. in Madras
64. Wolf-pack member
66. Pen name of Charles Dodgson
69. Aardvark's dinner
70. In a preoccupied way
75. Some choir members
77. Mecca for cowboy poets
79. Second passage: Part III
80. Marksman, at times
82. Old fiddle
83. Señora Perón
84. Disciplinary
87. Sensitive one
88. A sibling of Cottontail
89. City near Boys Town
90. Filled
93. Bark

94. Get rid of
99. Propels a shot
102. Like some mirrors
104. Rustic
105. Tpk. or hwy.
108. Dueling trophy
110. Mint family member
113. Intertwine
116. Indigent one
117. Covered with water
118. Liza's sister
119. Furnish funds for
121. Slyly sarcastic
122. Composer Ned
124. Battery terminal
125. Norway, to the Norse
126. Bay window
127. Uses books
129. Engraver Gustave
130. Land owned absolutely
132. Scopes's supporter
133. Bottom of the barrel
138. FD&C Blue No. 2

ACROSS

1. Horned vipers
5. Alpine pinnacle
10. Title for Macbeth
15. Troon, e.g.
18. Use a bubble pipe
19. Madrid art museum
20. Student of Fauré
21. Cantina cash
23. Subject of this puzzle
25. "Can-Can" tune
27. Some playing marbles
28. Blackout while young F.A.S. sang
30. Woolly Andean
31. Had effect
32. Stops working
33. Pride of one in a pride
34. Bits of land
37. Ship to remember
38. Sevens and elevens
42. Chief buyers of performers' albums
43. "Anything Goes" tune
45. Neck warmer
46. Muslim chiefs
47. "___ Do It": 1928
48. State
49. Stuffy chap
50. Schisgal play
51. "Gay Divorce" tune
55. Light too bright for sight
56. Zetetic
58. Pouty looks
59. Kind of bullet
60. A prelate and a playwright
61. Seals, as pipe joints
62. Lake Volta is here
63. Triangular sail
65. Stupefy
66. Tricked
69. Where two become one
70. "The New Yorkers" tune
73. Violinist Kavafian
74. Move wearily
75. Unit of loudness
76. Roof segment
77. Shepard's "Fool for Love" won one: 1984
78. Lap pooch
79. "Red, Hot and Blue!" tune
83. Napoleonic general or red hog
84. Regular dates

86. Major Hoople's cries
87. Lighter fluid
88. Earsplitters
89. A.L. M.V.P.: 1960–61
90. Bender
91. Tar
94. Expand
95. Fragrant
99. Musical featuring "I Hate Men," "So in Love," etc.
101. "Born to Dance" tune
103. Dividing word
104. Cauthen or Pincay
105. Taffeta sound
106. "Fish Magic" artist
107. Long time
108. Motivates
109. Rorschachs, e.g.
110. Vocal impertinence

DOWN

1. Basics
2. Token taker
3. Chopin or Gomulka
4. Adds instruments to make a lusher sound
5. Victor's take
6. Missed a pop-up
7. "Peanuts" plaint
8. He wrote "The College Widow"
9. Pirate
10. Its rhyme scheme is ABaAabAB
11. Aureoles or glorioles
12. English Channel feeder
13. Ida. neighbor
14. Kind of shoe
15. Typewriter bar
16. Indiana birthplace of 23 Across
17. A ___ Able
22. She bear, in Barcelona
24. Dramatic designs
26. Barracks decoration
29. Médoc product
32. Gounod opera
33. Companionable, in Cheshire
34. Natives of Sic.
35. Musician's transition
36. Musical featuring "My Heart Belongs to Daddy"
37. Racing sailboat
38. Actress Patterson et al.

39. "Mexican Hayride" tune
40. River at Tours
41. Lyricist Carol Bayer ___
43. Petemen
44. Pluto, to Plato
47. Fabric for an amice
49. Sycamore
51. Gulf of Guinea feeder
52. Tickle
53. "___ This Earth," 1988 film
54. Because of
55. Cornucopia item
57. Shape manually
59. Pin inserted into a gunwale
61. Flood controller
62. Windfall
63. Finns' neighbors
64. Dole out
65. What some gentlemen prefer
67. Occipital protuberance
68. Dorothy, to Em
70. Is schneidered

71. Hautboys, e.g.
72. E. Indian timber trees
75. Brandy-based drinks
77. Shows verbal superiority
79. Language student's problem
80. Coryphaei
81. Grendel, in "Beowulf"
82. Most peacockish
83. Cynosure in Florence
85. Appends
87. Kiosks
89. Carpenter's ___ box
90. Possible cause of "seen us" trouble
91. Perform Christies
92. "___ kleine Nachtmusik": Mozart
93. Regarding
94. Dry spot except in a rainy season
95. William Hoffman play: 1985

96. Altman's "Welcome ___"
97. U.S. composer: 1874–1954
98. Fair marks
100. Little fox
102. Veneration

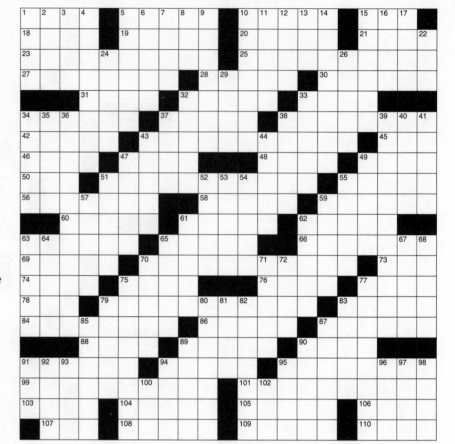

(163) Comments on Conjugality by Michael J. Parris

ACROSS

1. Andalusian port
6. Imarets
10. Disney's inventive mouse
14. Senegal's capital
19. U.S. rocket stage
20. What a swain presses
21. Niagara Falls sound
22. Evergreen shrub
23. Marriage, to Cicero
27. Flavorful
28. Lovelace's colleagues
29. Toils
30. Choler
31. Whirled
32. Satirist Freberg
33. "Marry'd in haste, ___": Congreve
42. Ivanhoe, e.g.
43. Opercula
44. Shower gift
45. Stole
46. Victorian expletive
47. She wrote "My Life": 1975
49. Tie material
50. Trifles
51. "Husband and wife ___": O. W. Holmes
58. Large wts.
59. Finished parasailing
60. Wrong
61. Fries quickly
62. Inverness uncles
63. Guidry or Darling
64. Other
65. Barrel parts
68. Rise on a wave
70. Chapeau ___ (a cocked hat)
71. Audit maker
74. What man and wife shouldn't have, according to Farquhar
78. Director Flaherty's "Man of ___"
79. Nothing
80. Cockle
81. Algerian port
82. "We'll ___ a cup o' kindness yet": Burns
83. Type of goat
85. Something real
87. End of a Stein line
88. "___ is born married": John Ray
93. Mr., in Munich
94. Watercourse
95. Lover of Tithonus
96. Stalactite locale
99. Islamic spirit
101. River of N Ecuador
106. Marriage, to Menander
109. Father of English empiricism
110. Frangipani, e.g.
111. Undiluted
112. Big cousin of a dik-dik
113. End of an O. Henry tale
114. Counting-out word
115. Record, as a wedding
116. Force units

DOWN

1. Margays and civets
2. Muslim title
3. Profound
4. Tout's dope
5. Kinshasa resident
6. Publisher
7. Streisand film: 1987
8. Pen point
9. Checked
10. Like honeymooners
11. Debatable
12. Dull-witted ones
13. Grads, not long ago
14. Orate
15. Certain Christian doctrinists
16. Ukrainian capital
17. Part of a French play
18. Thornbacks
24. Actor Calhoun
25. Husband and wife, e.g.
26. Bone: Comb. form
31. "Dum ___ Spero," S.C. motto
32. Incline
33. Gilly or democrat
34. Profs' concoctions
35. Fashion
36. Romola's creator
37. Shelters, in Savoie
38. Difficult journeys
39. Wolfpack member
40. Stir up
41. Bridge positions
42. The Shakers, e.g.
47. Annoy
48. Site of first Olympics
50. Swing around
52. Petruchio, e.g.
53. Valentine for moviegoers
54. "___ My Souvenirs," 1927 song
55. "Cielito ___," Spanish song
56. Oblique
57. Renaissance poet
62. Tied
64. Actian and Augustan
65. Groom's wear in yesteryear
66. Pentateuch
67. On the alert
68. Liners
69. Biblical spy
70. ___ retreat (flee)
71. Color: Comb. form
72. A.F.B. in N.H.
73. "Judith" composer
75. Walking ___ (happy)
76. Bedtime for a señora
77. Matador's foe
83. Frozen dessert
84. Horn-shaped structure
85. Montmartre money
86. Like S.T.C.'s Mariner
87. Used a cupel
89. Certain elongated snails
90. Cantankerous
91. Nullify
92. Sullen
96. Briton or Breton
97. Take ___ (say "I do")
98. Last of a Caesarean trio
99. Nephrite
100. Privy to
101. Kin of P.D.Q.
102. Depend (on)
103. Actor Dixon
104. Spanish movies
105. Auto pioneer
107. Dactyl or hallux
108. Poseidon's domain

ACROSS

1. It verges on Virgo
4. Skewed
8. Architectural recesses
13. Decamped
17. Portoferraio's island
19. Wife of King Latinus
20. Patch up a road
21. Vehicle for winter Olympics
22. She weds poet—gets lots of mail
25. "God's Little ___"
26. Southern constellation
27. Childish, in Chartres
28. Like Brown's walls
29. More reasonable
32. Joust standards
33. Elopes
34. The Red Cross needs it
35. Heart part
36. "___ Crazy"
37. "___ the ramparts . . ."
38. She weds novelist—OPEC applauds
43. Ubiquitous abbr.
46. Japanese foot covering
48. Casino cash-collector
49. City in Uruguay
50. Spanish river
51. Gin
53. Atlas aid
56. Wild guess
57. Raise ___ (create a commotion)
58. A Morrow medium
60. Señorita's snack
62. Parts of soft palates
64. Corolla petal
66. She weds boxing champ—plays in fast lane
70. Dental deg.
71. Alters a line
73. Stairway post
74. Huge star in Cygnus
76. Flightless birds
77. Consumer
79. Trite
82. Bits of marginalia
85. Observe carefully
86. Scurvy fighters
88. State founder
90. Oratorio part
91. Echidna's morsel

92. She weds ex-Surgeon General—elopes in roadster
96. T-bill payout
97. Netman Camporese
99. Sandy tracts in England
100. Like street talk
102. Irritate
104. Jams; pickles
107. Angler's casting plug
108. ___ lazuli (shade of blue)
109. Upright and grand
110. Aphorism
111. Arabian port
112. She weds former N.Y. mayor—turns down lights
117. The horror of Gomorrah
118. Auguries
119. Bows out
120. Tug's tow
121. Broadhorns
122. Rib
123. Apple or pear
124. When the French fry?

DOWN

1. Noted ecdysiast
2. "Spoon River" poet's monogram
3. Kabuki costume adornment
4. One cause of trysts
5. Bonnie bairn
6. Six-time N.L. home run leader
7. Cold wind from the Andes
8. Places for matériel
9. Kind of dollars
10. She knows roses
11. Wilson and Hines
12. Jrs.' elders
13. Taste in general
14. She elopes with explorer—smooth running assured
15. Swamp stalker
16. G. Cooper role
18. Everything, in Emden
19. These go to a higher court
23. Desert, in Diamante
24. Unc's mate
28. Relative of 15 Down
29. Dry cleaners' problems
30. N.Y. city

31. She weds actor—develops odd typing technique
32. Yeats and Keats
35. Conn. town
36. Small sphere
39. Troy, to Horner
40. Pallid
41. Singer John
42. Dirigible description: Abbr.
44. Group of three
45. Pine fruit
47. George's collaborator
50. Shield for Jeanne d'Arc
52. Dutch treat
54. FitzGerald's rhyme for "thou"
55. Scheherazade's stock in trade
59. Narrow-minded
61. Tara native
63. French oenophiles' delights
64. Tarkington's "In the ___"
65. Dud

67. Scipio, to Hannibal
68. Visorless cap
69. Gland: Comb. form
72. Suffix for Canton
75. Letter from Greece
78. Novelist Haggard's title
80. "___ moi le déluge"
81. Coins in Tirana
83. Trace
84. Bacchus attendant
87. Khartoum residents
89. Absentees at airports
92. Say Hey Willie
93. Boot camp's cousin
94. Ragtime dance
95. Kind of line
98. Monks, in Metz
101. Critic James and family
102. Wash. cape
103. Lowest point
104. Froth
105. "Adriana Lecouvreur" composer
106. Belasco portrayer: 1940

107. Runyon's $100
110. Brief gander
112. Little bit
113. Outside: Comb. form
114. Top gun
115. Pithy saying
116. Ram's dam

ACROSS

1. Stone paving block
5. Book of the Bible
9. Part of Montana's shoe
14. Sea dogs
18. Astronaut's milieu
20. White heron
21. Poet Garcia ___ of Spain
22. Primitive: Comb. form
23. Lait topper
24. The Summit in Houston
25. E.T., e.g.
26. Feeling contrite
27. Commotion
29. Franklin D. Roosevelt Museum site
32. Menlo Park name
33. Darling or Hiller
34. Actor O'Brien: 1915–85
35. Cynic
37. Modified, with "down"
40. Grocery item
41. New wine
42. Pluck
44. Jennifer O'Neill film: 1971
50. Bright
51. Gary Grimes in 44 Across
53. Jogs
54. Adjective for 69 Down
55. Introduction
57. Steeple adornment
58. Your, of yore
59. Aim high
60. Synthetic fabric
61. Tree of the rose family
62. N.Y.C. dept.
63. Not any, in law
65. Toronto's prov.
66. Part of N.B.
67. Sky enigma
68. Agency
70. Gives joy
73. Film or play that is the key to this puzzle
77. Teetotal
80. "___ of Endearment"
81. Hopped-up drink
82. Holier ___ thou
85. Two-cupped garment
86. "___ It Up," Little Richard hit
88. Spooks' den
89. Completed hang gliding
90. Make shipshape again
92. In a weird way
95. Southwestern stewpots
97. Hamlet's exclamation
98. Annoy
99. "___ . . . in infamy": F.D.R.
100. Dirk
101. Moth's glossa
103. He wrote "The Name of the Rose"
104. December messages?
108. Word with pin or fold
109. Jane or Zane
110. Zimbalist's teacher
111. Events at ovals
113. Finds a second renter
115. Idols
118. Allowed
120. Bind
121. T. Williams play
126. Tip givers at the Big A
129. Heavenly butter
130. "___ Male War Bride," 1949 film
131. Sky: Comb. form
133. Lustrous fiber
134. Recumbent
135. Outward
136. Dustin Hoffman title role: 1974
137. Swiftly
138. Mediocre
139. Real author of Baron Munchausen's tales
140. ___ fixe
141. Unique thing

DOWN

1. Schismatic group
2. Raison d'___
3. Shakespearean play
4. Pattern
5. A Cabinet dept.
6. Cheshire borough
7. "The ___," 1976 Polanski film
8. Status reached by Streep
9. Quahog
10. Actress Montez
11. Innisfail
12. Dice throw
13. Citrus fruits
14. Bull: Comb. form
15. Adjust precisely
16. Frog
17. Saw, in Siena
19. Superman portrayer
20. Emulate Horner
22. Pushes
28. Ancient Assyrian king
30. Talking bird
31. German reservoir dam
33. Cancel
35. Tops
36. Forage plant
38. Charms
39. Some ancient Greeks
40. Day after day
41. Saint-___, French port
43. Plant part
45. Benin native
46. Kyoodle
47. The Gorgons and Graces
48. German city on the Lippe
49. "Night Music" playwright
51. David Lean's milieu
52. Kid
56. Actor in "The Ghost Goes West"
58. Todd and Ritter of films
59. Isomeric
61. Certain Muslim
64. Capsize
68. French Republic personification
69. One of the seals
71. Menu item
72. Grief symbol
74. Ethereal
75. Rescue
76. Expert witness in a sanity trial
77. At right angles to a ship's length
78. City in S Netherlands
79. Wrapping material
83. A. Miller play
84. One's sibling's daughters
87. Game in "The Sting"
89. Taffrail's locale
91. Home of Aeneas
93. Part of T.G.I.F.
94. Attorneys' jargon
96. Suffer
98. Hopi village
100. More fitting
102. Kokoon
105. Undo
106. Shekels
107. Spurs
109. Third Reich secret police
112. Frightened
114. Ashley or Hobson
115. Mule's cousin
116. Goodbye, in Granada
117. Gland: Comb. form
119. Silly
121. Lamebrains
122. Service org.
123. Lines on maps: Abbr.
124. P.D.Q.
125. Vendition
126. Frisbee, e.g.
127. Sushi ingredient
128. Haruspex
132. Bangkok-to-Hanoi dir.

ACROSS

1. Ex-head of Japan
8. Town of the Big Red
14. San Diego wives, perhaps
20. "There is three ___ in this matter": W.S.
21. Gazed idly
22. Weaver bird, formerly
23. St. Louis runs
25. Maltreat
26. " 'Fraud!' ___ the maddened thousands"
27. Pop-ups, usually
28. Lou Piniella
29. Houston: No hits, no runs, no errors
33. Bull chaser
34. Neat as ___
35. Winning pennant: 1979
42. Imputes
47. Broke up or in
49. Belgian Congo, today
50. ". . . sin to prefer life ___": Juvenal
51. In order
52. Flourisher
54. St. Louis base of yore
56. Generation
57. Oakland players
58. "___ Grows in Brooklyn"
59. Miss Thompson
61. Power source
62. Diminutive
64. Painter Claude ___, né Gelée
66. Crinkly fabric
72. ". . . in the twinkling ___ eye": 1 Cor. 15:52
74. Kind of measure
76. Small bay
77. Coach's area in Kansas City
82. Enchantress
83. Chicago recruiter
85. Devoid of native minerals
86. Racing sled
87. Backslide
88. Source of igneous rock
89. More obtuse
91. Base security
92. Calif. pitching arms, slangily
94. Countertenor
95. Top pitcher
96. Squeeze-play sign in the Bronx
104. Four balls to a Torontonian
109. Silk, in Savoie
110. Kiel, e.g.
111. Tip of baseball
112. Feller and Garcia, for years
117. Raw material
118. Foiled by a Fisk throw
119. Eddy role
120. For this reason
121. Nevertheless
122. Individuals

DOWN

1. Kind of moth
2. Sharif et al.
3. Spar
4. It's quarry
5. Optic membrane: Comb. form
6. Haunt
7. Simile words
8. Deny
9. Canine, e.g.
10. Raise aloft
11. Joe Palooka's bride
12. This, in Tours
13. Ins and outs of tennis
14. Import
15. Dull
16. Home plate?
17. Debauchee
18. Hostess Maxwell
19. Spore
24. A Mo. patron?
28. ___ riot act
30. Tycoon, for one
31. Gluck works
32. Digger
33. Vent or view leader
36. Boston or ground follower
37. Old Testament book
38. ___ accompli
39. In play, as a ball
40. Tract
41. Pathogen
42. Facing Orel
43. Kind, in Calais
44. Odd job
45. Aftermath
46. Writer of suspense tales
47. Ramp alternative at a stadium
48. Detroit's batting-practice backstop
53. Employees
55. Wreath evergreen
57. Unisex gown of old Greece
60. Drysdale or Mattingly
61. Taradiddle
63. British hoods
65. Gimlet's larger cousin
67. Stocking fabric
68. Early Peruvian
69. Hill
70. "The Cat in the Hat" man
71. Feminine endings
73. Capp's Fearless fellow
75. Parish priest
77. City NW of Napoli
78. "Is it a hit ___ error?"
79. Peteman
80. Egyptian dancing girl
81. True, in Ayr
82. Minx
84. Confuse
86. Highly volatile fuel: Abbr.
90. Chicago-to-Detroit dir.
91. Get some shuteye
93. Pickpocket's prize
94. ". . . devotion is ___ love": Coleridge
97. "And this shall be ___ unto you": Luke 2:12
98. Netman Yannick's family
99. Exist
100. Family of a 1944 Nobelist in Chemistry
101. ___ a customer
102. San Rafael's county
103. Someone ___ (another's)
104. Banter
105. Poker payment
106. Manager of the ___
107. Help with the dishes
108. ___ breve (2/2 time)
112. Trainer's aid, often
113. Pt. of U.S.N.
114. Fitting
115. Devilkin
116. Tot's "little piggy"

167 *Table Talk* by Bert Rosenfield

ACROSS

1. ___ in a lifetime
5. Palm of the hand
9. "...as a wild bull in ___": Isa. 51:20
13. Street's boss
18. Okla. city
20. Make worse
22. Light-footed
23. Belgian moppets?
25. Actress Thomas
26. Leroy Anderson's "___ of the Ball"
27. Some legal writs
28. Where the Ambrosian Library is
29. Malefactor
31. Sole of a plow
33. Cosmetician Madeleine ___
34. Worker on a hill
35. Stolen sockeye?
39. "___ De-Lovely," 1936 Porter song
42. Thornburgh's predecessor
44. Kilauea effusion
45. Hoover Dam's lake
46. Hugh Johnson's org.
47. Highlands hillside
48. Like many U.K. drinks
51. Trans-central cord
54. One of the Aleutians
55. Baseball's Paul or Lloyd
56. Oriental restaurant cartel?
58. Pear variety
59. Have the miseries
60. "___ the Rear" (old song)
61. Bangladesh capital's former spelling
65. Undersized pickpocket?
70. He was TV sleuth Jones
71. Dahl or Francis
73. Make a selection
74. Fuzzy surfaces
76. Roughage fanatics?
79. Bowler's woe
81. Ridges between ice walls
85. "___ or five attend him": "Twelfth Night"
86. Simple wind instrument
88. Coiffeur's creation
89. Univ. degrees
90. Desdemona's handkerchief, e.g.
92. Shamrock land
93. London trolleys
94. Tic-toe connector
95. Beauty salon?
99. Creek
100. City in S France
102. Desert juniper
103. Tragi
105. Propounds
107. Guam's capital
109. Almost, to the Bard
110. Coalesce
111. Gorbachev in A.M. action?
117. "Gare Saint-Lazare" painter
118. Where concert musicians relax
119. Hindustani emperor: 16th century
120. Kitchen attraction
121. A York river
122. They sometimes bounce mgrs.
123. Ratio words

DOWN

1. Outlet for N.Y. horse players
2. Only, in Bonn
3. Driver's main course?
4. Gaul's chariot
5. De ___ of 92 Across
6. G.I.'s supervisors
7. Some coll. linemen
8. A Dadaist
9. Ducks
10. Ad ___ (to a sickening degree)
11. Chanson follower
12. Hardy protagonist
13. Material wealth
14. "Encore!"
15. What beefy waiters get?
16. Southwest stewpot
17. ___ tetra (aquarium favorite)
19. Slanting
21. Belligerent sea groups
24. Oil: Comb. form
29. Cobra's relative
30. Like argon
31. Laminated rock
32. Tool for Archimedes
33. Some propositions in logic
36. Make a fist
37. W.W. II India-Burma road
38. Marian, for one
40. ___ et quarante (Monte Carlo game)
41. Assyrian monarch
43. Thalassic expanse
48. ___ Jima
49. Timberlane of fiction
50. Prune
52. Dishes out
53. Jewish holiday eve
57. Antediluvian
58. Alberta park
59. Qty.
61. Touches gingerly
62. Spanish weight unit
63. Gambling spot for littlenecks?
64. Recent, to a geologist
66. Marathoner Allison ___
67. ___ facto
68. Kind of engine
69. Distress
72. Flees to a J.P.
75. Org. dating from 1897
77. Ambience
78. Fast-food magnate
79. Hindu outergarment
80. Spectrum producer
81. "___ Nell," Gershwin musical
82. Leftovers from a TV roast?
83. Come clean
84. Ponselle and Raisa
87. Incontrovertible
91. Catchwords
93. Wright or Brewer
95. Córdoba coin
96. Thought, to Pascal
97. Fortifies anew
98. Windmill impeller
101. "___ Eat Cake," 1933 musical
104. Harold ___, English political scientist: 1893–1950
105. Cougar
106. ___ about (circa)
107. Jason's ship
108. Spiritual mentor
112. Indonesia's ___ Islands
113. ___ de guerre
114. Diamond cutter's device
115. Basketball Hall-of-Famer Holman
116. Twelve doz.

168 "F.I.F.I.O." by Virginia Yates

ACROSS

1. Mecca trek
5. "Ars gratia ___"
10. Farmer's field: Abbr.
15. Kin of cock-and-bull stories
19. Actress McClurg
20. Jazz clarinetist Jimmie ___
21. Plain
22. Hornswoggle
23. Chauvinism in the fold?
25. Goat on a bender?
27. Occur
28. Gogol's "___ Bulba"
30. Appearance
31. Bother
34. Lab tube
35. Heat, at times
36. Culpabilities
37. English composer and family
38. Mediterranean flower
42. Provence city
43. Wild hogs' quartets?
45. Barker of the movies
46. Related
47. Profess
49. Lived
50. Year in the reign of Louis XII
51. Trick ending
52. Formal 1 Down parties?
56. A Koblenz river
57. Where boards are formed
60. Helm position
61. Rayon maker's solvent
63. "La Tulipe ___": Dumas
64. Acclaim
65. Xanthippe, e.g.
66. Flippers
68. Anonymous Richards
69. Clobber
71. Finish
72. Stable fables?
74. British medical org.
76. Irish river
77. Thunderstruck
79. Kind of resort
80. Minn. neighbor
81. Snooker stick
82. Cousin of a Cotswold?
86. Siepi, Hines et al.
87. Cop making a collar
90. Subleased
91. Out-of-the-way
92. Pouter's look
93. Song of praise
94. Extended a subscription
95. Apathetic
98. Ganef's job
99. Judges' seats
100. Nothing but bovines?
102. Lagomorph exes?
107. ___ many words
108. TV dragon
109. Earthen pot
110. Winter wind in Hawaii
111. Like Paul Pry
112. Deeds of paladins
113. A Simpson
114. Gurge

DOWN

1. Layer
2. Flap
3. Sine ___ (indefinitely)
4. Like a diadem
5. Monkeyshines
6. Drive out of bed
7. Suit for Belli
8. "Holiday ___," 1942 film
9. It has a tercet
10. Hepburn or Hepburn
11. Crow
12. Classic cars
13. "Ten thousand saw ___ a glance": Wordsworth
14. Hazard on Mont Blanc
15. Former U.A.W. head
16. Mull Island neighbor
17. Sound made by Big Ben
18. Kind of terrier
24. Off ramps
26. Result of a shaver's flub
29. Takeoff specialist
31. Mocha stone
32. Dithers
33. Colt on the loose?
34. Kind of car
35. Contrite one
37. "Life Is Just ___ of Cherries"
38. Fr. titles
39. Barnyard crone?
40. Number of Little Foys
41. Pearl Buck's "The ___": 1936
44. Little hooter
47. Like London in 1666
48. Field rodents
50. Bates ___ ("Psycho" locale)
53. It's sometimes saved
54. Mr. Oop
55. Slightest
56. Blackbird
58. Chunk, in Chelsea
59. Uris's "___ 18"
61. Lenten symbol
62. Coffer
64. Subject to planation
66. Siouan Indian
67. ___-propre (self-esteem)
69. Bias
70. Virtuous
72. Squint
73. Outlander
75. Schussed
77. "___ History": Toynbee
78. Word heard on a roller coaster
80. Praenomen sharer
83. Panegyrics
84. Homophone for seize
85. Kaffee
86. Put on the sidelines
88. Take on
89. Kind of bank
91. Tenant
93. Lapwing
94. Poker ploy
95. Castor, e.g.
96. Exclamation of dismay
97. Writer Macdonald
98. Salutation to a señor
99. French statesman: 1872–1950
101. Key, in Cannes
103. P.G.A. tourer
104. Angler's need
105. Type of table
106. Right to decide

ACROSS

1. Hamelin's problem
5. Mars, to Sophocles
9. "___ the Sheriff," 1974 tune
14. Galatea, originally
20. Remains in a tray
22. Security trouble
23. Beat the goalie
24. Infuse with oxygen
25. "Where Babies Come From"
27. Tangled stuff
29. Musical suite
30. Princess perturber
32. Actress ___ Dawn Chong
33. York symbol
34. Injure severely
36. ___ Stevens (TV's Peter Gunn)
38. Assent asea
39. CBer's licensed cousin
42. Kin of Micmacs
46. Fern grouping
50. Tax-deferred acct.
51. It multiplies by dividing
53. Bridge requirement
54. Took command
55. Garden spot
56. Perpetrate
57. "___ Lazy River"
58. Final checks for Karpov
61. Refrigerant
62. Character actor Benny
63. Sign on a staff
64. Earl ___ Hines, jazz pianist
65. Work on pumps
66. "___ live and breathe!"
67. Property talk
70. Egyp.-Syr. alliance: 1958–61
71. Shrove Tuesday follower
73. B.A. part
74. Not at all
75. Badger
77. Chevy's "Foul Play" co-star
79. Taxi riders
80. Fashionable
81. String beans
82. Path for Pluto
83. Cupola
84. Tag-team victories
87. Ziegfeld
88. Creative graduate course
91. "Gloria in Excelsis ___"
92. Skirted the basket
94. Trio of trios
95. Castor's slayer
96. Don ___ de la Vega (Zorro)
98. Grate glower
99. They pull in pushers
100. Examinee's T or F
101. Upolu native
102. Release
103. Toy-pistol ammo
104. Make tracks
106. Ascribe
107. Meditative discipline
108. Customary itinerary
113. Road ending
114. Prior to, to Prior
115. Czech. neighbor
116. A democrat is one
117. Bat Masterson's weapon
119. Italian bread?
120. Personification of reckless ambition
121. Anvil location
124. Decorative design
129. Aid an Italian town
134. Small role in "The Road to Morocco"
136. Kind of engine
137. Runs amok
138. Frankenstein's flunky
139. One of us
140. Unwavering
141. One year's record
142. Roric
143. Use the VCR

DOWN

1. Speak hoarsely
2. Hammett canine
3. Heyerdahl
4. Spanish muralist
5. Star in Aquila
6. Hudson contemporary
7. Dodge City lawman
8. Terrier type
9. Doctrine
10. Egyptian amulet
11. Malarkey
12. Former President of Nicaragua
13. Start for Ballesteros
14. Siberian sled dog
15. Sideboard display
16. Johnson of "Laugh-In"
17. Make doilies
18. All-purpose trk.
19. Profit chaser
21. Zip over the surface
26. "___ Mater," ancient hymn
28. Male mergansers
31. Served perfectly
35. Stained
37. Hosp. personnel
39. Dreadful place to hole up
40. Parts of irises
41. Way
42. Of religious rites
43. "...a man or ___?"
44. Hairdresser's union
45. Convoy constituent
47. French ruling family of yore
48. Strong brown paper
49. Gripper for the Gipper
52. Coal case
53. Sounds of hesitation
58. Cuban blade
59. Comte de la Fère
60. Spring phenomenon
61. Iron: Comb. form
63. Consecrated oil
64. "Little Shop of Horrors" storekeeper
65. Bookworm
67. Mooched
68. Gives power to
69. More or Mann
72. Anderson's "High ___"
76. Nile reptile
78. Light-amplification device
79. Nice piece of change
80. Monk or monkish
81. Less stocky
82. ___ about
83. "___ your fathers thus...?": Neh. 13:18
85. Undo
86. Squatter in 1889
87. Stand stock-still
89. Unsuitable
90. Feline sound
93. Sat in session
96. Weir
97. Limbs of the Devil
99. Sartre novel
101. Radio transmission
103. Gallant
104. Hit sign
105. Strobile
108. Embossed
109. "Den I wish ___ Dixie"
110. Saloonkeeper's nemesis
111. Sweat and tears, e.g.
112. Table linen
118. Imprint permanently
119. Actress Hartman
122. It turns litmus red
123. Fad
125. Lacking slack
126. Educator Willard
127. Use a harvester
128. What the "poor dog" had
129. Personals
130. Watch the baby
131. Visit
132. Madrid Mrs.
133. Icel. or Ire.
135. Heap of hay

170 Sound Effects by Arthur W. Palmer

ACROSS

1. "___ may look on a king": Heywood
5. High-school subj.
9. "Murder, ___ Said," 1962 film
12. Like a flapper's hair
18. Type of hit
19. "East of Eden" temptress
20. Loser to H.S.T.
21. "___ in the Sun"
22. Odd magazine?
25. Closed or open position, in golf
26. Mayan or Mundane
27. Suffix for Capri
28. Troy, to Ajax
29. Rameau's "Les ___ galantes"
30. Sheridan play, with "The"
33. Site of Phillips University
34. Town in N India
36. Annapolis freshmen
37. Gang of swans?
40. Org. for the rah-rah people
43. Certain wrench
44. "___ Foolish Things . . . ," 1935 song
45. Chinese warehouse
46. Black, in poesy
47. Distress letters
48. "Honi ___ . . ."
49. After a bit
50. Protracted
51. Former Scandinavian notables?
55. Concerning
56. What a hairline sometimes does
59. Like some beavers
60. Kind of box or joint
61. Wiped out
62. Turkish money
63. Minn. city
64. Wooden stand with a curved top
65. Doctrine
66. They're sometimes grand
67. Counterweight in a lab
68. Photos from Merthyr Tydfil?
72. A Siouan
73. ___ gin fizz
74. River at Bern
75. Wood, the boat builder

78. Saws with the grain
79. Lollapalooza
80. Assuage
82. He recruited Lafayette
84. Part of a TV set
85. Chemical flower?
87. Patten or huarache
88. A.B.A. members
90. To be, in Aix
91. Type of clause
92. Site of a Liza Doolittle triumph
94. Anatomical cavity
96. A verb for you
98. Cole Porter's "___ Clown"
99. Like betting partners' feelings?
101. Balance sheet for Amos?
105. "___ santé!"
106. This won't fill a filly
107. What Mr. America pumps
108. Pan-fry
109. "___ thou now O soul": Whitman
110. Strange need
111. Kind of house
112. Hundred-weights: Abbr.

DOWN

1. Tropical timber tree
2. Niña and her sisters
3. "Worm of the Nile"
4. Article printed daily
5. What Dana sailed before
6. Secular French clergyman
7. Part of TNT
8. Actions banned on many campuses
9. What to take a reverse in
10. Her lover drowned
11. Where the Pison flowed
12. Kind of relief
13. Action often taken on campus
14. Wishy-washy
15. Pops outlawed?
16. Lo! to Lucretius
17. Rick ___, talk-show host
18. Tibetan bearers
23. Antarctic sea
24. Adjust
31. Featherweight Attell
32. Dawson of football fame

33. Have an ___ (look after)
34. He makes vein efforts
35. Afire with ire
37. X's for Xanthippe
38. "Sweet ___! run softly . . .": Spenser
39. Revolver of a sort
41. Satisfied
42. Cats, goats or rabbits
44. A-one
46. May and Stritch
48. Tore
49. Smooth and connected, in music
51. Tenants
52. Summer refreshments
53. Boxing ploys
54. ___-tail (cirrus cloud)
56. Heads of certain colleges
57. Capricious
58. Egyptian manipulator?
60. Fen footing

62. Actress Ulric
63. Fabric texture
65. Like some vault locks
66. Skin
68. Agent
69. Punjabi princesses
70. Bogus
71. Perm term
75. Rover
76. Metrical feet
77. Quitclaim
80. Showed interest
81. Zeppelin, e.g.
82. "___ Kapital"
83. Ref. book
85. Paravanes
86. Mean
87. ". . . after they've ___ Paree"
89. ___-puissance (omnipotence): Fr.
92. ". . . more deadly than ___ dog's tooth": Shak.
93. Capital of Fiji
94. Espy
95. Dies ___
96. Like ___ of bricks

97. Declaim violently
100. Call at Wimbledon
102. Homophone for air
103. G.I.'s award
104. Nomologist's forte

(171) Brother Act by Michael A. Rampino

ACROSS

1. Co-author of a 1930 tariff act
6. Helot
10. Minstrel
14. One of Oberon's subjects
19. Singer Ronstadt
20. Cupid
21. Malarial malaise
22. Corbin's "L.A. Law" role
23. Dancer Dolin
24. Knee
25. Barrett or Jaffe
26. Lesions
27. Subjects of this puzzle
31. Sloth, e.g.
32. "How ___ the lady?": Shak.
33. Thee, in Tours
34. Panay native
37. Anguine fish
39. Type of jet engine
41. "Treasure Girl" song for Gertrude Lawrence: 1928
46. Secret society, Italian style
48. "Funny sheets"
50. Catapult
51. Classic introduced by Whiteman: 1924
53. Scotch admixture
54. The old sod
55. Sun. homily
56. British customs documents
60. Binaural
63. Bitter
67. Bond rating
68. Cynical song introduced by John Bubbles: 1935
75. Avant-gardist
76. Tin Pan Alley org.
77. "I beg ___ pardon now": R. Wilbur
79. Raised-letter printers
85. Function
87. Mother of Hermes
88. Den
89. Song introduced by Ginger Rogers in "Girl Crazy": 1930
95. Song AJ Jolson made famous
98. Playwright Ionesco
99. Of the skull
100. Estimated
102. Actress Merkel
103. Mariner's greeting
104. Pisa-to-Verona dir.
105. Monogram of House Speaker Mr. Sam
106. Abba of Israel
108. Rabble
110. Song introduced by Gertrude Lawrence in "Oh, Kay!": 1926
120. "A ___ Is a Sometime Thing": 1935
121. Tied
122. Clinton's canal
123. Haute-Savoie spa
124. Ancient Greek dialect
125. Hawk
126. Shade of green
127. Type of musical show
128. Malicious and sly
129. Salver
130. Mimicked
131. Coasters

DOWN

1. Scoria
2. Song in "Let 'Em Eat Cake": 1933
3. Upon
4. Fragrances
5. Chesapeake Bay island and sound
6. Grandiose tale
7. Edits
8. Musical composition
9. Fulfillment
10. Movie vamp
11. Expectant
12. Old Norse poem
13. Paucity
14. Vogue
15. Successively
16. Crucifix inscription
17. Nothing, in Nice
18. Start of a reply to Virginia
28. When it's warm in Chile
29. An equilateral parallelogram
30. Fair
34. Land measures
35. Gauguin's island paradise
36. Serai
38. Young men
40. Zilch
41. To venture, in Versailles
42. Head of the Sanhedrin
43. Painter Grabar
44. Yield
45. Varro and Vulgar
47. "Porgy and Bess," e.g.
48. Sorceress encountered by Odysseus
49. Order from Delbert Mann
52. Bear a lamb
57. Swiss river
58. Freshwater worm
59. Emporium event
61. Zwei preceder
62. Wallet fillers
64. Former N.Y.C. skyline letters
65. Endings for pant and scant
66. U.S. mil. award
69. Little corn grower
70. Soubise, e.g.
71. Chevet
72. Mandarin's residence
73. "___ Alive," Bee Gees hit
74. Man from Marietta
78. Willow: Fr.
79. Charles Laughton's wife
80. Gullets
81. Partiality
82. Department of NW France
83. Marsh growth
84. Inst. at Dallas
86. Apiece
90. Former name of Guyana: Abbr.
91. Extend a subscription
92. Alga causing fishy taste in water
93. Headache remedy
94. Temporary stops in journeys
96. Huxley's "Ape and ___"
97. Last word of Mo.'s motto
101. Scenarist Lehman
103. Roman's sacred shield
107. Anchor position
109. Chamfer
110. "Strike Up the Band" song: 1930
111. Where to watch Hawks
112. Bit part
113. "I loved you ___": Hamlet
114. Weblike tissue
115. Sole
116. Mind
117. Split
118. Whittier's "___ Muller"
119. Chemical suffixes
120. Minn. neighbor

172 *Plus Signs* by Jeanne Wilson

ACROSS

1. "The labor of ___ . . .": Milton
6. Holds court
10. Gait
14. Gorgons' mother
18. Humorist Myron ___
19. "___ to bury Caesar . . .": Shak.
21. O.T. book
22. On the summit
23. "Halt, salts!"
24. Yclept
25. Loupe
26. Wheys
27. With 4 Down, hand wave
29. Theater critic Barnes
31. With 14 Down, Hollywood's "cattle call" spot
33. Dictators
34. Peppard and pals
35. Actor Delon
36. Disgusts
38. Mortgage, e.g.
40. Cookies
43. "___ homo"
46. Model de la Fressange
47. Horn of a crescent moon
48. Philadelphia eleven
49. Eureka!
50. Ballerina Spessivtseva
51. Do over the bathroom
53. Rent
54. Chaste
56. Mauritian casualty
59. Actress Jones (Mrs. Addams on TV)
62. Dumbarton Oaks, e.g.
63. Get the lead out?
65. Monts ___, French range
66. Bet
67. With 47 Down, theme of this puzzle
70. Brazilian dance
74. Soprano Berger
76. Sacred: Comb. form
77. "There is ___ in love": I John 4:18
78. Prince Philip, e.g.
81. Very, very short time
82. Thrips, e.g.
83. ___ favor (Pablo's please)

84. R. Carson's "Silent ___"
87. Berry and Howard
89. Ref's decision
90. "Say good night, ___": G. Burns
93. Roscoe Coltrane's deputy
94. "___ Only Just Begun," P. Williams song
95. El ___, Tex.
96. Per ___ (yearly)
97. Himalayan sight?
98. Part of E.T.A.
100. Dine in a meadow
102. Goddess of peace
104. Birthmark
106. With 91 Down, glider's cushion
108. Wherewithal
109. With 95 Down, poultry preparer
112. Tony ___, Sinatra role
113. Allegation, in law
115. "All together, musicians!"
117. "Go fly ___!"
118. Spirit
119. Buttinsky
120. Historian Nevins
121. Pomme de ___ (potato)
122. Lear's loyal follower
123. Johnson of "Laugh-In"
124. An NCO
125. Made a boo-boo

DOWN

1. "For ___ and bells . . .": Lowell
2. Popular PBS program
3. "___ Day's Night," Beatles film
4. See 27 Across
5. Lure
6. Chantlike
7. Colombian Indian
8. Back-fence yowlers
9. Silvery fishes
10. One versed in disputation
11. Featherweight Attell
12. Moulin Rouge dance
13. Ford flop
14. See 31 Across
15. ". . . to be secluded ___ . . .": Donne
16. One-third of a 1970 film title

17. Kind of glass or lamp
20. Actress McClurg
28. Brand or Chamberlain
30. Worth
32. LEM's creator
37. Coryphaeus
39. D. W. Griffith product
41. Part of a hammerhead
42. Fast flier
43. ". . . a sparrow in the ___": Yeats
44. Treasure chaser
45. "___ diva," Bellini aria
47. See 67 Across
48. Architect Saarinen
50. Randolph Scott films
52. Cheryl ___ of "Charlie's Angels"
55. Frost's "The Road Not ___"
57. Spanish Main booty
58. Bravura
60. Welles and Bean

61. Browses
64. Homophone for use
67. Speak like a fishwife?
68. Placer material
69. J.F.K.'s favorite chair
71. "Gin a body ___ body": Burns
72. Supports
73. Robot Detoo in "Star Wars"
75. Proboscis
77. Capital of ancient Assyria
78. Schmaltz
79. N. Ireland Protestant
80. Kilmer subject
83. Tourn. won five times by J. Nicklaus
85. Hint at
86. "La Tulipe ___": Balzac
88. Showing clearly
91. See 106 Across
92. Mosque priest
94. Emulate Gorgeous George
95. See 109 Across

97. "Old ___," Disney film
98. Negates
99. Propel a triplane
101. Director of "Two Hundred Motels"
103. "Do I dare to ___ peach?": Eliot
105. Buzzing sound.
106. Long day's journey
107. What a dibble makes
110. To be, to Bernadette
111. Want
114. Autumn in N.Y.
116. Pitch

ACROSS

1. ___ Drive, near Salerno
7. Pure ___ driven snow
12. Frenzied
17. Lots of sailors?
21. Get back
22. Purplish red
23. Mennonite group
24. Director Kazan
25. Batman?
27. Book that's full of meaning?
29. Loot
30. "And the morne ___ outgrabe": Carroll
31. "My Antonia" character
33. Pays out
34. Lennon's widow
35. ___ a rail
37. Sting operators?
38. Comic Gilliam
41. Lesser of two ___
43. Fin units
44. Tin men?
48. Some guards
50. ___ dive (throw a fight)
52. Hereditary factor
53. Go cruising, in a way
54. Pluto, to Cleo
55. Poetry buff?
57. This may be a little Scottish
58. HIJKLMNO?
59. Correspond
60. Word to a refusenik
61. He wrote "The Chosen"
63. Epic finishes?
64. Playwright Howe
65. Style of pinafore
66. Author of "A Serendipiter's Journey"
67. Word after see and before Sea
68. Canines on the Concorde?
72. Chose chow
73. It has an eye, but it sees not
75. Synthetic fiber
76. Meager
77. Pretense
79. Material for mending a broken heart?
81. Family drs.
84. Ceremonial prayer
85. Baum barker
87. Seafood choice
88. "The Morning Watch" writer
89. Makes emends?
90. "If I ___," Beatles song
91. Roman ruins site in France
93. ___ Public (average person)
94. Touse or towse
95. Rogers's rye?
98. Bush's chief of staff
99. ___ cava (cor. part)
101. Former Met diva
102. Sphere to fear when pooling?
103. He has estranged feeling?
104. Tangles up
106. Maine river
107. Decide against the diner
109. Oregon or Santa Fe: Abbr.
110. Broadway musical: 1982
111. Snips once more
113. It's all in Rhine's mind
114. Pac-Man's home
117. Sharpens
118. Goddess who knew her oats
120. Lone Star sch.
124. Clip joint?
126. Work of a biased composer?
129. S. Grant beat him
130. Pass over
131. This is silly!
132. Taiwan brew
133. Close the eyes, in falconry
134. Stunned
135. Hilaire Germain Edgar ___
136. Hutch items

DOWN

1. Rainbows for Noah?
2. And now, a word from Morris
3. Pedro's 58 Across
4. K.D. of country music
5. Healthy
6. How herds of cattle arrive?
7. Explosive mixture
8. Of the kind mentioned
9. Reliable fund?
10. Loki raised her
11. Testy person?
12. Curtain material
13. Pierre's girlfriends
14. He comes in time
15. Blue ribbon
16. Deceitful sculptor?
17. Leader of 66
18. Buck character
19. Celtics' "33"
20. Simon does it
26. Pinched
28. Certain newspaper page
32. Have ___ to the ground
36. Mawkish
37. TV's Denise Huxtable
38. More dilatory
39. Aromatic tea
40. Country club?
41. Mideast bigwig
42. Commemorative stones
44. Passover repast
45. Search party near the Oval Office?
46. Cracked
47. Appeased thirst
49. "___ Tu," 1932 song
51. Pac. counterpart
52. Memorable, melodic Marvin
55. Parson's place
56. Place apart
59. Lord, for one
61. G.I.'s devil-dodger
62. Music to Manolete's ears
64. Woman's one-piece undergarment
65. Kirk's journey?
66. Rich gear?
68. Garb for a Stapleton?
69. Snitch
70. Kingston group
71. Ref. book
72. Lustrous gems
74. Part of Q.E.D.
76. Mount
77. Chop chops
78. Occult
80. Tell about being tardy?
82. He does the write thing
83. Hollywood P.S.?
85. Sees to
86. First name of a star on the bars
88. Par excellence
90. Maid, in France
91. Jargon
92. Ruhr roe
93. Member of a French dozen
95. Collected, as votes
96. Do a double take
97. Canine's neighbor
98. Twaddle
100. Poe maiden
103. Befuddled
105. Helper bringing a drink?
106. Leaked through
108. Penthouses on peaks
111. ___ Island
112. Rawboned person
114. Vigoda and Burrows
115. Chest sound
116. Native Canadian
117. Crackerjack
119. Mount ___, Colo.,
120. Calif. campus
121. Bender
122. Bonebreaker's cousin
123. Certain board members?
125. Abductors of the 70's: Abbr.
127. One, in Ayr
128. Ball of fire?

174 *Dearihful* by Frances Hansen

ACROSS

1. Top of the line
5. Indian symbol
10. Ophidian
13. Modern frontier
18. Solemn promise
19. Japanese seaport or dog
20. Defrost
22. Rink structures
23. Wound memento
24. Knight's weapon
25. Bathe
26. Some exams
27. Soapmaker's dearth?
29. Sommelier's dearth?
32. Very, in Vichy
33. Marabou
34. Cannel
35. Mitty or Cronkite
38. Weather satellite
39. Light foundation garment
43. Like ___ from the blue
44. Fishmonger's dearth?
46. Surrealist Salvador
47. Misplace
48. Singer Petina
49. Blundered
51. French co.
52. Forage plant
53. Orator's dearth?
57. Inquired
59. Imperturbable
61. Ways
62. Slaver
63. Bowling division
64. Loiter
65. "The ___ Madelon Claudet"
66. Burning
67. Guardian spirits
68. Contaminated
71. Model-airplane wood
72. Miniskirt maker's dearth?
75. Genetic inits.
76. Pizarro's gold
77. Max Sr. and Max Jr.
79. Les Etats ___
80. Feminist Carrie Chapman ___
81. Betsy whose work was saluted
83. Like Savalas
87. Mother-of-pearl
88. Distasteful
90. Utter inadvertently
91. Scraped one's shins
92. Israeli P.M. Eshkol: 1963–69
93. Chris of the courts
94. Cast a ballot
95. Tailor's dearth?
98. Census taker's dearth?
102. Aquarium fish
103. Addict
104. "Mule Train" singer
106. Guns a motor
107. Teheran resident
108. ___ Porsena
109. Computer key
110. Verve
111. Kind of committee
112. Bar drink
113. Vertiginous
114. First name in scat

DOWN

1. The ___ (Springsteen)
2. Every's companion
3. Linger
4. Choke
5. More like Wilt
6. Gives the nod to
7. Fork part
8. Bel Kaufman's "Love, ___"
9. Toscanini, notably
10. Least favorably
11. Its jaws give pause
12. Sandburg's "bucket of ashes"
13. Greek sculptor-architect
14. Let out conditionally
15. Gelling agent
16. Hibernian
17. Tee preceder
21. "... despise those ___ them" : Thucydides
28. Guitar feature
30. Unguis
31. Strong point
33. ___ table (dine)
35. Where they plug the leeks
36. Cancel a space flight
37. Dentist's dearth?
38. Change course
39. "The agony of de feet"
40. Railroad engineer's dearth?
41. Architect Gottlieb ___ Saarinen
42. Even-steven
44. Papal cape
45. All set
48. What "veni" means
50. Mild imprecation
53. Egyptian amulet
54. Praying figure
55. Large book size
56. Neighbor of Nev.
58. By and by
60. Spring bloomer
62. Naturalist Fossey et al.
64. Thick
65. This may be posted
66. Duelist Burr
67. TV moderator Moore
69. ___ nous
70. Passé
71. Irish king Brian ___
72. Vexatious
73. Two pints
74. Military group
78. From the beginning
80. Insouciant
82. Italian beachhead: Sept. 1943
84. Main side of a coin
85. Take to the hills
86. Jumped over the candlestick
87. Alliance acronym
89. Of sacred Hindu books
91. Seedy Manhattan area
93. Room for jugs and linens
94. S.A. country
95. Wimp's cousin
96. Greenland base
97. Russian ruler
98. Honey ___, Rose Kennedy's dad
99. Holler
100. Face shape
101. Annapolis inst.
102. Acapulco aunt
105. Cuckoo

175 First-Letter Fun *by Robert H. Wolfe*

ACROSS

1. Fellows
5. African republic
9. A machine load floating?
14. Dance for Miranda
19. Declare an oath?
20. Bear malice
21. Buccaneers of ___ Bay
22. Arrogate
23. Kind of bus
24. Part of a Presley autograph
25. Crucible
26. Lollobrigida and Manes
27. Wicked Arabian port?
30. Loyalty Islands port
31. First mate
32. Grounded Australian
33. Weed in a garden, e.g.
35. Bacon slices
39. River to the Rhine
41. Bemoan
44. Colette's "The ___ One"
45. Friable
48. Shingles, e.g.
50. Heaths for Heathcliff
51. "___ Aweigh"
54. Where the Crimson Tide rolls
55. A lump on a battery part?
56. Chou En-___
57. Paper measure
59. Elsa or Sylvester
60. Netherlands city
62. Timeless
65. Novel ending
66. Wee, in Dundee
69. Poetically close to a cob?
72. Dancer Eddie ___ Jr.
73. Slack part of a sail
74. Credos
75. An NCO
77. Kind of down
79. DL × IV
80. San Jose-to-Reno dir.
82. Freud contemporary
87. I.R.S. targets
90. Union or Victoria
92. Relaxed
93. Ouster
94. Seventh sign
95. Entertainer Luft
96. Elegant
98. "Like Niobe, ___ tears": Shak.
99. More suspicious
101. Most abashed
103. An objective of NOW
106. Bks. before publication
107. Sanctions
110. Bacon's place in a B.L.T. with vegetable?
116. Chivy
117. Swindles
118. Benison
119. In any way
120. "Cheyenne," for one
121. ___ de ballet
122. Toward the mouth
123. Scribes
124. Defense on a court
125. Skull protuberance
126. Danson and Knight
127. Assuage completely

DOWN

1. Priest of the East
2. Desirous
3. Cooked
4. Gurth, in "Ivanhoe"
5. Scarabaeid beetle
6. Actor Rhodes of "Daktari"
7. Do repent?
8. Jeans material
9. Aleutian island
10. More cautious
11. Accord
12. Homophone for spade
13. Computer in "2001"
14. Rio's mountain
15. Stage whisper from Elsie?
16. Actor in "The Good Earth"
17. Health food
18. Cathedral area
28. Supervise
29. Suppress
30. Tevye portrayer
34. Some wheys
35. Italia's capital
36. Hit like ___ of bricks
37. Word to a fly
38. Kind of triangle
40. To the left of a visit in an itinerary?
42. Broadway area
43. Antagonism
46. Kind of virus
47. Here, to Pierre
49. "Jalousie" composer: 1927
52. Kin of tombolos
53. Flesh: Comb. form
58. L-P connection
61. Light stroke
62. T. S. Eliot's "Sweeney ___"
63. Storehouse of a sort
64. Liq. methane for shipment
66. Small piece
67. Flaubert's "___ Bovary"
68. Sleeping with flowers?
70. Guernsey or Jersey
71. Objectives
73. Sight follower
76. An adjective for Sears Tower
78. Ebert and Siskel, e.g.
80. Beak
81. Preceder of easter
83. Porch adjuncts
84. Actress Singer
85. Puzzler's favorite Anglo-Saxon
86. Kind of admiral
88. Ayn and Sally
89. Coaster
91. Covered with terra cotta
97. Cleric
98. A beat in a musical direction?
100. Corrects texts
102. Puppeteer Lewis
104. "R.U.R." protagonist
105. Prior to a golfer's warning?
107. Over a toy?
108. Regan's father
109. Kind of show
111. Org.
112. Gun charge
113. Eye layer
114. Ten mills
115. Gaelic
117. B.S. part

Children's Hour by *John M. Samson*

ACROSS

1. Beam
6. Kura tributary
10. Piquant
14. Babushka
19. Upper house?
20. Hebrew letter
21. Twinge
22. Certain long bones
23. Irish breakfast? (Seuss)
26. Sesame
27. Ohio college town
28. Phoenician vessel
29. Pretoria's locale
31. Top of the world
33. French school
34. Pisa-to-Leghorn dir.
37. Vinegar: Comb. form
38. Provo plant
40. Diamond, actually
44. Associate
46. Mongoose's prey
47. Don Juan's kiss
48. Ace
50. Mideastern capital
53. Threesomes
55. Large moldings
56. Bring to terms
58. "A Sailor's Admiral" subject
59. Comber's comb
61. Patient helper
62. Mollycoddled
64. Holds
65. Come out
67. Deserts
69. Author Foley
72. Elk
74. Nobelist in Physics: 1912
75. Slouch
77. Abrades
79. Be a majority
83. Whiteness, in Palma
84. Little Red Hen, once
85. Bearded sheep
86. Reveal
88. Slugger Van Slyke
89. Weaken
90. Company lover
91. Warehoused
94. Radiance
96. "Echoi" composer
98. Pro ___
99. Like the oak leaf
101. Classified words
104. Ornamental pink
108. Play it again
110. AMEX overseer
113. Forbears
114. Nike's reveries? (Conford)
117. Frozen dessert
118. Novelist Hostovsky
119. Aye-aye's home
120. Wyeth model
121. Pleasure Island sounds
122. Headway
123. Sediment
124. Artemis gave him stardom

DOWN

1. Roman-fleuve
2. Round up
3. Domain
4. Tsk!
5. British marquee
6. Greek
7. Derby-winning filly: 1915
8. Peace Prize co-Nobelist: 1911
9. Ignominy
10. Talia Shire film: 1986
11. Ernst's eight
12. Brontë's trap? (White)
13. ". . . rosebuds while ___" Herrick
14. Beneath the Laptex's surface
15. Witty Cosby? (Nicholson)
16. Author Sewell
17. Indian prince
18. Intuit
24. Builder
25. Cape
30. Protestant org.
32. Actress Garber
34. Part of a rusty nail
35. Mexican state
36. Pepper missing? (Handford)
37. Dada daddy
39. Frenchman
41. Vereen's born? (Isadora)
42. Douay Bible book
43. Like prying Parker
45. Medical suffix
49. Teaching
50. Tennis great
51. Start of Mass.'s motto
52. Pleistocene Age
53. Asgard resident
54. Inroads
57. Inquisitive Carlin? (Rey)
60. Fox shelter
63. Type of truck
66. Drizzle
67. Actor Julia
68. Shady ones
70. Current unit
71. Penn, to Pennsylvania
73. Outfielder's error? (McClintock)
74. Genetic initials
76. Pakse's land
77. Nos. people
78. "Abou Ben Adhem" poet
80. Orsk's river
81. "The ___ My Fingers," Arnold hit
82. King of ancient Egypt
87. People of SW China
92. An antonym for restores
93. Morse "E"
95. Annelid
96. Jimmy Nelson's canine dummy
97. Gethsemane's locale
100. Showed partisanship
102. Caesuras
103. Seed: Comb. form
104. Judge Priest's creator
105. Livy's love
106. Abel's love
107. Brillant, as a color
109. Mirror, in a way
110. Sun: Comb. form
111. Therefore
112. Greenish blue
115. Ergate or kelep
116. ___ Borch, Dutch artist

177 Ooh, That Banana Peel! *by Lawrence M. Rheingold*

ACROSS

1. Start of a Stepquote
5. U.K. air arm
8. Agcy. dealing with nutrition, etc.
11. Clayey soil
15. Plant of the lily family
17. Styptic
19. Alpine snowfield
20. Anaglyph
21. The ___ Lewis Trio
22. Composer Rota
23. Jejune
24. Members of an I.R.A. wing
26. A Woody work: 1973
28. Pother
29. TV sales pitch
30. Tear, to Tacitus
31. "Aida" composer
32. By its very nature
36. Singer Reddy
37. Phone's dial letters at "7"
38. Blind cetacean
40. Reverie
41. Littoral flier
43. Actor Byrnes
44. Stepquote: Part III
46. Otiose
47. Townsmen
48. Partly open
52. Certain topsails
54. Grab
56. Hence
60. "The Way We ___"
61. Bagpiper
63. Due follower
64. Hen's pen
65. Whinny
67. Bruited
69. Tails
73. Shining examples
76. Nigerian native
78. Least messy
79. "___ go bragh"
80. Stepquote: Part V
83. Nil, in Nimes
84. Stephen and Phil
87. Latin trio starter
88. Another by 31 Across
92. City-bus route
94. Feral
96. Kind of seal
98. Smog or fog
99. Objective
101. Morman missionary elder
104. ___ fixe
105. Witnessed
106. ___ fatales
109. Fastens anew
110. Ten mills
111. Core of a canine
112. Regan's father
114. Stepquote: Part VII
116. He may be good or bad
119. "Dies ___"
120. Fragrant rootstock
122. Air: Comb. form
123. Jazz session
126. Indo-European
128. Unlike the distant future
131. Moon goddess
133. Drags one's feet
135. Lingerie item
136. Corrida cry
137. Limited
139. Penumbra
140. Gist
141. Part
143. Steels, in Savoie
144. Expiate
145. Weapon, to Ney
146. It's surrounded by glair
147. Bandleader from Barcelona
148. Seas, to Simone
149. Airport stat.
150. Society-page word
151. End of Stepquote

DOWN

1. Old German coin
2. Aaron's feats
3. Gaul's chariot
4. Stepquote: Part II
5. Skedaddled
6. Aka
7. Provided capital
8. Heavens
9. Exercise for a dentist?
10. Additionally
11. Sousa products
12. Juliet's emotion
13. Assail verbally
14. Appeared, as in a fog
16. Affirmative
18. Twilight times
19. Salon offerings
20. Audit maker
21. Invitation letters
25. Fortitude
27. Drench anew
30. Songlike
33. Shore sport
34. Strew hay
35. Sermonizer's desk
39. Ultra high resistances: Abbr.
42. Extreme
45. Stepquote: Part IV
48. Barley beard
49. Army vehicle
50. Oratorio part
51. Backslid
53. Hebrew prophet
55. Suffix with tank
56. Oddball
57. Euros, for short
58. Ibex or markhor
59. Make a choice
62. Uses logic
66. Stags
68. Actress Joanne
70. Saarinen
71. Lateen, e.g.
72. Macerate
74. Regimen
75. Geisha's case
77. "___ new world": Shak.
81. Cassowary's kin
82. Stepquote: Part VI
84. Contention
85. Sludge
86. Handyman
89. Of reproduction
90. Flood or spring
91. Chef's need
92. Fidel's pal
93. Counters game
95. Guam, to U.S.
97. However
100. Extravagantly theatrical play
102. Snickers
103. Flanders river
106. Nutria or marten
107. Venomous-snake genus
108. Arranged in rows
111. Shackles
113. Hyperbola
115. Stepquote: Part VIII
116. Ingests
117. Author of the Stepquote
118. Turn
121. Carry Nation target
123. Fancy cake
124. Noncombustible gases
125. Traipses
127. Passion
129. German President: 1919–25
130. Prom queen
132. Architect Jones
134. Ram's dam
138. U.S.A.F. body
140. Ginnie or Fannie ___
142. Skimp, with "out"

ACROSS

1. Chamfers
7. Lifts for skiers
12. Tach reading
15. "The Old Devils" author
19. Jolson song hit: 1920
20. Red dye
21. Baseball stat
22. "... for ___ of woman born": Shak.
23. Last Hawaiian queen
25. Rhine feeder
26. Chesterfield, e.g.
27. Long
28. Impaired gradually
29. Bay of Fundy attractions
31. Auspices
32. Alma-___, capital of Kazakhstan
33. Certain cocktails
35. Jot
36. NE N.J. city
37. La Scala's home
40. Medici protégé: 15th century
44. Brit. lexicon
45. Most venerable
48. Implement for catching a crab?
49. Bermuda ___
51. Broadway Joe
52. De Mille specialties
54. Gull-like predator
55. The Father of Microbiology
59. Boxer Griffith
62. Ky. fort
66. City in Provence
67. Cosmonaut Gagarin
68. Katmandu is its capital
69. Zola heroine
70. Haunt
71. Tennis term
73. Sora
74. Expiate
76. Gravesend goodbye
79. Little Iodine's creator
81. Erstwhile
82. Type of type
83. Small, round window
86. Seaport in Yemen
88. Nurse Maass
89. Lassos
93. White piano keys
97. "Artie" author
98. Of the number six
99. Conquistador's goal
100. Everglades lake
104. Croats' neighbors
106. Wickiup's cousin: Var.
108. Recorded proceedings
109. Co-Nobelist in Medicine: 1977
112. Tidbit for Hansel
113. Sacred image
114. Stone marten
116. Plenteous
117. Soil: Comb. form
118. Norman city
119. Mouths
120. Irish writer-teacher
124. Gould railroad
125. A.E.C. successor
126. Painter of waterlilies
127. "Dolce far ___"
128. German state
129. Comic-strip word
130. Bagnold and Markey
131. Scheduled

DOWN

1. Prophet rebuked by an ass
2. Dispossession
3. Odin's realm
4. Sculptor Nadelman
5. Singer Rawls
6. C. P. and Phoebe
7. Cancel, as a contract
8. Spanish dance
9. Botanist Gray
10. Japanese money of account
11. Stew
12. Computer product
13. Roman bigwig
14. Trumpeter Wynton ___
15. Photographer Adams
16. Cantonese chicken dish
17. Unbeliever
18. Monterey Bay city
24. "Hitchy ___," ragtime hit
30. Clock numeral
34. Slants
38. U.S.N. biggie
39. A 1963 Oscar winner
41. An anagram for nail
42. Don Marquis's cockroach
43. Like a certain bucket
46. Bed or home follower
47. "And ___ I plight thee..."
50. ___ uno
52. Flock member
53. Trifle
56. Neighbors of radii
57. Muse for Marceau
58. Hemingway's "The ___"
60. Secular
61. She, in Sedan
62. Knot in wood
63. Intl. alliance
64. Formation of words like "buzz" or "hiss"
65. Site of Kubla Khan's garden
72. Lanford Wilson's "Serenading ___"
75. Febrero preceder
77. Personal quirk
78. Imam's deity
79. As a result of this
80. Legal org.
84. Pedestal part
85. Aficionados
87. Japanese P.M.: 1982–87
90. To, to Sandy
91. Presumptuous
92. Sensualist
93. Marks
94. Indians of the Dakotas
95. Cornwell's pen name
96. Reversal
101. "East of Eden" protagonist
102. Won
103. George and T. S.
105. Under the influence
107. Intramolecular
110. Not working
111. Disaccustoms
115. Salinger girl
117. Ancient city near Argolis
121. Many, many moons
122. Violinist Kavafian
123. Soybean product

179 *It's Alimentary* by Gloria Evans

ACROSS

1. African republic or lake
5. Attempt
9. Caravel or coaster
13. Nephrite
17. Son, in Sonora
18. Greenhorns
20. Blue shade
21. Inky, poetically
22. Thyroid cartilage projection
24. Doctor Mirabilis
26. Athenian statesman
27. Fierce anger
29. Treeless plain
30. Kind of walk
31. ___ Taylor, memorable musicologist
32. Curdle
33. Saar ___, German territory
36. Many: Comb. form
37. Collected
41. Nuncupative
42. "Dream Children..." author
45. In the manner of
46. Widely prevalent
47. Baltic island
48. Seine land masses
49. Gyre
50. WNW's reciprocal
51. A bit at a time
55. Hustlers after rustlers
56. Ten-sided figures
59. "A Passage to India" director
60. They're often wild
61. Catherine de Médicis, e.g.
62. Organization for high-I.Q. folk
63. City of NW Turkey
64. Meager
66. Gallic girlfriend
67. Circular, towerlike fort
70. Implied
71. Chancy social engagement
73. ___ Gatos, Calif.
74. Actress Sommer
75. Scheme
77. Subject of Plato's Symposium
78. Steadfast
79. Highlands uncle
80. Tatterdemalions
84. An O'Neill
85. Spanish inns, English style

88. Kind of wrench
89. Province of SE China
90. Metropolitan thrush
91. Sub's "ears"
92. Mashhad money
94. "___ for tennis?"
97. Central Asian range
98. Pacific island group
102. Pretended disdain for the unattainable
104. Misleading clue
106. Sported
107. Needlework loop
108. Gannet
109. First-act finale in "La Boheme"
110. Home of Vance A.F.B.
111. Without
112. World's longest river
113. Emulates Dorcas

DOWN

1. Fellow
2. Coati's coat
3. "Momo" author: 1978
4. Residence
5. Pursue stealthily
6. Melville work
7. Some Dadaist works
8. N.B.A. stringbean
9. Cotterways
10. Companion of mighty
11. Frazil
12. Troubles
13. Patroness of France since 1922
14. Initial quartet
15. Kind of prize or post
16. Composer of "The Princess on the Pea"
19. "Black Beauty" author
20. One of a Dumas trio
23. Analyze verse
25. Dissipate
28. Plexus
31. Breed of hog
32. Milky
33. Used a gimlet
34. Originate
35. Yegg
36. ___-nest (hoax)
37. Effrontery
38. Scaramouch
39. Beethoven's "Für ___"
40. Jutlanders
42. Head over heels?

43. "Die Lorelei" poet
44. Climbing vine
49. Drench
52. Lacquer ingredient
53. Kingsley's "___ White"
54. Alleviated
55. Procacious
57. John Denver album
58. Essential part
60. Coercion
62. Its people were decorated for bravery: 1942
63. Long loaf of bread
64. Use a teapot
65. Majorca's capital
67. "Lower Manhattan" painter
68. Half sister of Liza
69. Ottoman dynasty founder
71. Quagmires
72. Put off
75. Old Testament book
76. Narrative poem by Byron
78. Tie fabrics

81. ___-tung, former Chinese leader
82. Bone below a humerus
83. Knacks
86. Doted on
87. Bell sound
89. "Age of Aquarius" musical
91. Komatiks
92. Indy 500 winner: 1986
93. One of the Horae
94. May Sarton's "___ Are Now"
95. High time
96. Cosmonaut Gagarin
97. Neat as ___
98. DXVII x III
99. Savage Island
100. Once more
101. York and Friday Abbr.
103. Celestial Altar
105. Ages and ages

180 Implanted Numbers by Ernst Theimer

ACROSS

1. Lyric poem
4. Bad days on Wall St.
7. Applied nutmeg
13. Reel
18. Strong dislike
20. Spanish loss in 1588
21. Tawed leather
22. Husband
23. Kite or eagle
24. *Ash*
25. *Customer group reveres*
27. Presided
29. Alley yowler
30. Followed a scent
31. Side issue
32. Stack role
33. Novelist Kingsley ___
36. Spanish currency
38. Louis XIV, e.g.
40. Gannet
42. Artist Shahn
43. Variety of gypsum
48. Young congers
49. S African fox
51. "Faith ___!" (*words by Faber*)
52. *Part of D.A.R.*
53. English poet laureate: 1790
54. Fleur de ___
56. Violinist Bull
57. Make lace
58. Actor Frobe
59. Capital of Sicily
61. Tourist attraction
63. Noted Russian-born artist-designer
64. Wear away
65. Nobelist in Physics: 1910
67. Thrash
71. Oblong eatery
73. Vehicle for Ben Hur
75. Slots spot
76. Ruby or river
79. Res followers
80. Luau instr.
81. Limit; restrict: Abbr.
82. *Stretch*
83. *Trainer*
86. Perry's creator
88. Create
89. Its capital is Jakarta
90. Assist
91. "Goodnight" girl
92. Cariou from Canada
93. Dishing out
96. Marshes
97. Bow or knot, in Lisboa
100. Pres. after J.A.G.
102. Popeye's tattoo
104. Motorists' gp.
107. Struck with fear
109. *Some boxing preliminaries*
113. *Lepidopterist's thought while chasing a butterfly?*
114. Maroon
116. Stone
117. Data for a computer
118. Like clothes after a diet
119. Extreme selfishness
120. "___ thou these great buildings?" Mark 13:2
121. "Gunsmoke" actor
122. ___ Moines
123. Singer Davis

DOWN

1. Convex molding
2. Jeans material
3. Gaelic
4. Grime
5. *Unusual occurrences*
6. Lip curl
7. Crusader foes
8. Babbles
9. Hinder
10. Broadway musical hit
11. Tokyo, once
12. "Pride and Prejudice" character
13. Leeward island
14. Ordinary looking
15. *Exhausted*
16. Siouan Indians
17. Alan and Cheryl
18. C.P.A.
19. Cambodian coin
26. Colza oil source
28. Medicinal-plants adept
31. *British P.M.: 1902–5*
33. Warned
34. Red planet
35. Officeholders
37. N.M. Indian
39. Avenaceous
40. *Butchery*
41. Manifest
42. The Bears of Waco
44. In conflict with
45. Asian holiday
46. Epoch
47. Q-U connection
48. Advantage
50. Shade tree
53. Partial paralysis
55. Nebraska neighbor
59. Contrition
60. Take heed
61. Bestowed liberally
62. Tries hard
66. Strong illumination
68. Tree exudation
69. *Deep*
70. Kind
72. A chemical compound
74. Half a bray
76. Half of MCCII
77. Eternity
78. Objective
80. Mineral found in dried lake basins
82. Bruce or Laura of acting fame
84. Sad
85. *Iroquoian Indian*
87. Cattlemen
88. Casino cube
94. Irregular strophe in a chanson de geste
95. Fireplaces
96. *Cargo*
97. Network
98. "A cottage in ___": Godley
99. *Poodle or Doberman*
101. Author Turin
103. Hooted, in a way
104. Pineapple
105. Tall story
106. On the Java
108. Hershfield's Homeless Hector, e.g.
109. Lucerne landmark
110. Heroic poetry
111. Get-up-and-go
112. Red-coated cheese
115. Hide ___ hair

ACROSS

1. Balm of Gilead
7. Berlin-to-Dresden dir.
10. ". . . ___ and hungry look": Shak.
15. Billiard shot
20. Popular uprising
21. Foxhole
22. Actress Thomas
23. Sharpness
25. Scrub
26. TV letters
27. Ponerology topics
28. Pine-tar product
29. Iranian sweet
32. Match king Kreuger
34. Home of N.Y.'s Blackbirds
35. ___ buco, Italian dish
36. Simon ___, St. John the Divine carver
37. Flash of light
39. Coal bed
40. Cassette
43. Gasthaus
44. Washington aspic
46. New York pasta
51. Lady Penelope Devereux
52. Succès d'estime
53. Monad
55. Family of Reagan's first Sec. of Treasury
59. He lived 912 years
60. ___ Tamid (synagogue lamp)
61. His Monday is our Sunday
63. Upon
65. Modernist
66. Pochette
68. Redacts
69. ___ ha-Shanah
70. Power proj. of 1933
71. Chilean grouse
75. Mulct
76. Crack
77. First American in orbit
78. Boundary
79. Actor Vidal
80. Some Princetonians
81. Foot form
82. Portion of a potion
83. Panamanian breakfast food
87. Hill inhabitant
88. Sock exchange
89. Fit for farming
90. Kin of bravo
91. "The Facts of Life" Charlotte
92. Bear, in Brest
93. Like Maine woods
94. ___ Dhabi, Eastern land
96. Lip
100. Wrong
102. Gaelic
103. Countrified character
105. Shocked
108. Illinois refresher
112. California seafood
116. Laconian clan
117. A Barrymore in "E.T."
118. Riyadh resident
119. Below, in Bonn
120. Peace-loving
122. Hero of Hindu epics
126. Constanta coin
127. Gazelle gait
128. New Mexican breads
132. Of a trunk in a trunk
134. Drug-culture leader in the 60's
136. King in I Kings
137. Anne Brontë's "The ___ of Wildfell Hall"
138. Record holder
139. Rousseau classic
140. Minor minor
141. Father of Spanish drama
142. Kirstie of "Cheers"
143. Khedive
144. Ethyl chaser
145. Ball-park offering

DOWN

1. Beak, in Bologna
2. Beijing baby sitters
3. Comedian Jay and family
4. Uzbek corn mix
5. "___ cara," Bellini aria
6. ___ Lazarus, "Miss Peach" cartoonist
7. Freshet
8. Husky's home ground
9. Whistler creation
10. Antarctic ice shelf
11. Pahoehoe, e.g.
12. "___ bragh"
13. Tennis term
14. Most prying
15. Massachusetts chew
16. The maples
17. Muffler menace
18. Frittata
19. Lackey
24. Musical notational sign
30. Please Nemesis
31. Suburb of Pittsburgh
33. Rose bowl
38. Concupiscence
39. Hart
41. Hockey's ___ Ross Trophy
42. Equine extremities
44. Sulawesi seaport
45. Hebrew letter
46. Some Brit. lords
47. Beatitudes verb
48. Whale: Comb. form
49. Court follower
50. Penitent's activity
54. Electees
56. Ayn Rand novel
57. Alternate locale for 128 Across
58. Afternoon fare on TV
61. Grenoble girlfriend
62. Okhotsk or Andaman
63. Plath work
64. Horse-drawn Indian vehicle
67. Golfer Woosnam
68. Lay or leather attachment
71. Level
72. Lass who got an A
73. Chanson topic
74. Preys for jays
75. Berg detachment
76. Kansas or Massachusetts cabbage
77. Fierce look
79. "___ a Rose": Friml
80. Ripken of the Orioles
82. New Jersey sinker
83. Inspiring intense fear
84. Punjabi princess
85. Featherweight boxer Attell
86. Tea V.I.P.
88. African antelope
89. I.R.S. collection time
94. Neighbor of Scorpius
95. Gautama
97. Sort of key
98. Actor Erwin
99. An Arab rep.
101. Two-syllable foot
102. Being, in France
104. Spadille, sometimes
106. ___ time (never)
107. One at Roanoke, e.g.
109. Like a quodlibet
110. Preclude
111. U.S. lexicographer-educator: 1869–1946
112. Casa units
113. Leaf area
114. Daphne turned into this tree
115. Involve necessarily
120. He's Hunter on TV
121. What aristarchs do
123. Encore
124. Shelly ___, jazz drummer
125. "There was ___ danced . . .": Shak.
127. Husband
129. Helmet border
130. Slumgullion
131. Start of Caesar's boast
133. Hill, to an Arab
135. Ratite bird

182 International Double Plays *by Mary M. Murdoch*

ACROSS

1. Fine horse
5. Freshwater fish
10. Trammel material
14. Soupçon
18. Agouti's cousin
19. ___ bell (seemed familiar)
20. Russian collective
22. Baltic island
23. Guiness-Davis film: 1959
25. "The Grass Harp" writer
27. Diminutive suffixes
28. Greek poet who rode a dolphin
30. The mind: Comb. form
31. Accountant's listing
34. Never ___ moment
35. Menlo Park family
39. Tryon novel, with "The"
40. Redford, e.g.
41. Dunderhead
42. Pompey's head
43. Agnes, in Acapulco
44. Garner-McQueen film: 1963
48. Chinese pagoda
49. News windups
50. Lineup on a fine report card
51. Foe of S. Grant
52. Argot
53. Erode
54. Book parts
56. Kind of consciousness or book
57. City NW of Waco
58. Stem cutters
60. Ripples
62. Chair worker
63. Goes off course
64. Hock and sack
65. Williwaw
67. Rome's Spanish ___
69. ___ of Good Hope
70. "Show Me ___ Go Home"
73. Santa's sounds
74. Kind of help
76. Straggle
78. Plump roasting fowl
79. Hematite and galena
80. Ardor
81. Amonasro's daughter
82. Japanese admiral et al.
83. Hyson, e.g.
84. Whimsy
88. Archibald of N.B.A. fame
89. Type of vb.
90. Miss Hogg of Tex.
91. Like some fruit
92. Dostoyevsky novel, with "The"
93. Made jottings
95. ___ means (certainly)
96. Family of an actor in the "Godfather" films
98. Witticism
99. Site of a 1431–43 council
100. Ky. college
101. Talents
105. Albany or Austin, e.g.
110. Major Hoople's "drat"
111. Framework
112. ___ Baleares, off España
113. Jazz singer Simone
114. Lacoste of tennis fame
115. Suburb of Paris
116. Leaning
117. Apprehend clearly

DOWN

1. Fitting
2. Stadium sound
3. Stich specialty
4. Lacking foundation
5. Pitcher Saberhagen and namesakes
6. Fads
7. A son of Seth
8. Vizier's superior
9. Sunday performer in Mexico
10. Belafonte hit
11. Cedric ___ (Little Lord Fauntleroy)
12. Floor
13. Haw's partner
14. Repeated musical passages
15. Auto of yore
16. Topic of an Emerson essay
17. Cohort of Larry and Curly
21. Constable and Turner paintings
24. Policeman, at times
26. Hubbub
29. Mystical mark
31. Bêtes ___
32. Of a Sicilian mount
33. Michael Redgrave film: 1946
34. Seaweeds
35. Disburdens
36. Walt Whitman poem
37. Shade
38. Part of a turbine
40. Noggins
44. Acuminate
45. They may be split
46. Takes effect
47. Greek resistance force of W.W. II
52. ___-banc (British motor coach)
54. Goddess of hope
55. Emulated Harvey Birch
56. Algonquians
59. Cucumbers
61. Open a soda bottle
62. Monastic symbol
64. "___ was one-and-twenty": Housman
65. Clupeid fishes
66. Amerinds of N.M.
67. "A ___ the Dark," 1964 film
68. See 9 Down
69. Farm mach.
70. True's partner
71. Ultra
72. Beginnings
74. Tightly sealed
75. Long series of woes
77. Screen part
82. Black pigment
84. Where Congress meets, with "the"
85. Long series of wanderings
86. Russian river
87. Coal region of central Europe
92. Arctic sight
94. Nylon constituent
95. Max, Buddy and Bugs
96. Part of a rose
97. "There's no music in ___ . . .": Ruskin
99. Orders
100. A Crosby-Hope destination
101. Antic
102. Ripen
103. Disallow
104. Mai ___ (rum drink)
106. Hissed reproof
107. Part of pewter
108. Up: Comb. form
109. Nomologist's forte

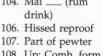

183 Iciest Cities *by Maura B. Jacobson*

ACROSS

1. Afflicted with ennui
6. W. Hoffman play: 1985
10. Dispatch
15. Con game
19. Hub of old Athens
20. Chess castle
21. Hawaiian porch
22. Poet Pound
23. Joseph's outerwear
26. Eshkol's successor
27. Weighed by lifting
28. N.Y.-N.J. river
29. Correctly reasoned
31. Rules to follow
33. San ___, Italian resort
35. Allergy symptom
36. Like a crazy hombre
40. Commit a gaffe at bridge
44. Battery terminal
46. Olympics host country in 1988: Abbr.
49. Coup d'___
50. Eaglet's birthplace
51. Cherish
53. Stay away from my door!
58. Units of work
59. Small planets
60. Elec. measures
61. Oil, watercolor, etc.
62. Fish with a net
63. Gucci of fashion
64. "Nightline" newsman
65. Ex-ember
67. Note left by a linksman
72. Peer Gynt's mother
73. Virginal
75. Qatar ruler
76. Applied oneself
78. ___ Julius Caesar
79. "I've Got ___ in Kalamazoo"
80. Storm or rainwear
84. End of an O'Neill title
85. Ferde Grofé opus
88. Nice
90. Outlander
91. Jason's vessel
92. Three times a day, in RX's
93. Arboretum specimens
95. Petty tyrant
97. Compass abbrs.
98. "The Rome of Hungary"
100. Wild guess
102. Toper
104. Indigenous
107. Poplars
111. Tenants' contracts
116. Lorelei Lee's creator
117. What to do after the soup course
120. Cambers
121. "Swan Lake" role
122. Capital of the Maldives
123. Another of the same
124. Part of A.D.
125. Now alternative
126. Scraps that Spot gets into
127. Lipizzan, e.g.

DOWN

1. One of the musical B's
2. Fairy-tale heavy
3. What the irate raise
4. Middle of Q.E.D.
5. Passé
6. Escort's offering
7. Go sky-high
8. Hebrides island
9. Read on the run
10. Skier's milieu
11. A daughter of Picasso
12. Rock producer Brian
13. Essex's title
14. Mess
15. Big rigs, for short
16. Plaid, for one
17. Song for Marilyn Mims
18. Crumbly soil
24. Incense emanation
25. Go headlong
30. Earth goddess
32. Tar's unit of distance
34. "___ Old Smoky"
36. Mother of Helen of Troy
37. Pawnees' neighbors
38. Bachelor's boast
39. Paravane
41. Have to have
42. Bobbles the ball
43. Actress Scala
45. Diamonds in Don Juan's deck
47. Bacchanalia
48. Thrift-shop transaction
52. Transude
54. Cobras' cousins
55. "Oh! ___ danced . . ."
56. Asian border river
57. Cato's 2550
61. Three-card games
63. Longest Swiss river
64. Well-recognized
65. Receive readily
66. "___ compare thee to a summer's day?": Shak.
68. Denies the truth of
69. Financial Fed
70. Decorate a lily
71. Large lizards
74. Capital of Elam
77. Nile dam
79. "Comus" composer
80. Tizzy
81. Terminer's partner
82. Slight advantage
83. Vintage cars
85. Fort
86. Section of Fez
87. Guido's high note
89. Goblet feature
94. Horse's home
96. Theda's colleague
99. Plaster of paris
101. Do tailoring
103. Works at the bar
104. Exile island
105. High time
106. Give over
108. Exec's reminder
109. Second caliph
110. Table staple
112. Mine access
113. Developer's interest
114. Borgia in-law
115. Not barefoot
118. "6 Rms ___ Vu," 1972 play
119. Aye

184 Sound Off by Charles M. Deber

ACROSS

1. Marries in haste
7. TV's Sharkey et al.
11. Period of power
14. Bistro
18. Discovered
19. Concern
20. Ex-coach Parseghian
21. Eye cheesecake
22. Texas trial?
24. Peruvian post?
26. Petulant
27. Half of CDXIV
29. Ravens' havens
30. Sillographers' creations
33. Kingdom east of Babylonia
34. Finished parasailing
36. Escapes notice
37. Glass in Colorado?
40. Up-to-date chap
43. Presses into grains
44. Meadowlands events
45. Travel plan
47. Rolling stones lack it
48. Domestic
49. Terra ___
50. Skelton's script-writing wife
51. Siouan
52. Bahamian baths?
55. Put one's feet down
56. Tommyrot
58. Certain buoys
59. Edicts
60. Lurch
61. Evian or Menton
62. Surface lusters
65. Fair-haired
67. Leslie King became one
68. Escamillo, e.g.
71. August, in Arles
72. Philippines beast?
76. Actress McClanahan
77. No-nukes group
78. Lechwe's cousin
79. City in S France
80. Jujube
81. Seat of fortitude?
83. Vouchers
85. Trances
86. U.S. draft agcy.
87. Nigerian objectives?
89. This is paid to heroes
90. Hot spot
91. Like the grapes of Aesop
92. Day, Duke and Hart
93. Y. A. Tittle was one
96. Strange
97. Fowl dish
98. Song of Norway?
101. Italian jet set?
106. Marble piece
107. A sign of summer
108. Punkies
109. Ocean current off Ecuador
110. Coop group
111. Objective
112. RR stops
113. Squealed

DOWN

1. Simple addition
2. ___ Salonga, "Miss Saigon" actress
3. Propel a randan
4. Has the chair
5. Stands the gaff
6. Eastern Church oraria
7. Pollock's kin
8. Working rule
9. Words of the wise
10. Woodland dweller or deity
11. He painted Helena Rubinstein
12. ___ Ben Canaan, of "Exodus"
13. Devil's-bones
14. Heavenly streaker
15. Turkish chiefs
16. Rove on the wing
17. Fish dish
19. Crooked or ironic
23. Gives the go-ahead
25. Pernod flavoring
28. Lacking reverence
30. Peale appeal
31. Former S.F. mayor
32. Arizona aristocrats?
34. Bryant, but not Gumbel
35. Actresses Olin and Nyman
37. Up
38. Two-cents plain item, once
39. Envelope wd.
40. Indian plays?
41. Third and fourth words of a soliloquy
42. Couples, but not Fred
44. Cup, in Caen
46. Part of the eye
48. Encolure
49. U.S.A.'s best customer
52. Uncool collegian
53. Still on the shelf
54. Above: Lat.
57. U.S. Skater David ___
59. Palpate
62. Wooden legs
63. Great Lakes acronym
64. Varro and Vulgar
65. Foundation
66. Advances
67. Polish or ploy
69. Power failure
70. Pee Wee and Jimmy of baseball
72. Bismuth or bullion
73. Set straight
74. One-billionth: Comb. form
75. Proverbial kingdom loser
80. Like some alleles
82. Cheongsam features
83. Au ___ (with it)
84. Bedrock
85. Flower's petals, collectively
88. ___ on (happenings)
89. Coal car, e.g.
90. Pommels
92. "___ Boot," 1981 film
93. Golly's cousin
94. Key
95. Baritone Opie
96. Birnam, in "Macbeth"
97. These: Fr.
99. P. N. Page's "In ___ Virginia"
100. Broadway's Cariou
102. West Pt. grads.
103. Coll. basketball tourney
104. N.Y.-to-Bos. dir.
105. Turf

185 *Out with You and You!* by June A. Boggs

ACROSS

1. Hog feed
5. Botswana boss
10. Honchos
16. Spread out
21. Claudia ___ Johnson
22. Carlos Saavedra ___, 1936 Nobelist for Peace
23. Attentive, in Lanark
24. ___ chose (a trifle)
25. Missing ring
27. Convertible
28. Poets Sexton and Marx
29. Persevered
30. Dickens clerk
32. Lower a spar
33. Wrinkles, to botanists
34. "...black as the ___ of night": Read
36. Philly's transit system
38. Rounders
41. Truncated trunk covering
45. Good times
48. Emulate Henry
49. Gas plant's family
50. Suffix with rend or vend
51. Sec.-largest planet
54. Out-and-out
56. ___ mind (remember)
58. Mother of Apollo
59. Calcutta cigarette
60. A Plummer from N.Y.C.
62. Auditions
65. Ai-ling and Mei-ling
67. Certain bottom lines
68. Showy plant
71. Politico Landon
72. Porcelain ware
73. Inspiration for W. C. Bryant
75. Prohibited
77. Vienna. to Hans
78. Kokoon
79. Thespian Thomas
81. No big theory connector
84. Galled
86. Master, in Mexico
87. Fetor
89. Cod cousin
90. Type of screw hook
92. Ploverlike bird of Asia
94. ___ vivant
95. Waterfront inn
96. Staff symbol
99. Skate blade
100. Draggletail
103. Be united
105. Ampersands
106. Aleutian island
108. Summit
111. Early TV sensation
112. Cato's 105 Across
113. Close, poetically
114. Page instrn.
115. Greeks' Greece
117. Still
118. Buzz off
122. Hawk aggressively
125. Senior member
126. ACTION is one
129. What some subscribers do
130. Gide's "___ Die"
132. Snorri Sturluson work
135. James Wright's predecessor
137. Constellation Grus
138. Ericaceous shrub
140. Muffled thud
142. "Landlord of New York"
143. Descry
144. Reunion in Dallas, e.g.
145. Force
146. Pothers
147. Carol starter
148. Chute material
149. Solomonic seasoning?

DOWN

1. Jet-speed unit
2. Fraternal baseball trio
3. Dwarf
4. Quintain
5. Beauty-shop comparative
6. Service person at Lackland base
7. Maid in Japan
8. Scruff
9. Measure
10. Linc. is one
11. "... ___ still a moment": Poe
12. Functioning continuously
13. Kitchen extension
14. Yell out
15. No. 9 on a menology
16. Austere
17. Dearth
18. Rush; charge
19. Cut ___ (transact)
20. Sycophants' oft-used words
26. Slight advantage
31. Bradley campus site
35. Puncheon
37. Pound, in Bayreuth
39. Collier's entry
40. Actress Kurtz
42. It precedes automne
43. From the ___ (long time)
44. ___ catechumens
45. Locale of Rainbow Bridge
46. Quince or pear
47. Dismiss pong's partner
51. Don't give a ___
52. Silvery white
53. Epithelium
55. Photographer Adams
57. Mardi Gras V.I.P.
59. Half a blunder
61. Disposed
63. Fla. cape
64. Fishing net
66. "___ vincit amor"
69. Haphazardly, with "miss"
70. He played in "Waiting for Godot"
72. Faithful
74. Headstall's kin
75. U.N.'s U ___
76. Acey-deucy
77. Particle
79. "Oklahoma!" star in 1955
80. Aggregate
82. Mountie's command
83. Mooch
85. Nouveau ___
88. Make mad
91. It's provided by 93 Down
93. O.R. personnel
94. Book-jacket item
95. Soul chaser: Abbr.
97. First name in "sleuthery"
98. Trilbies
100. Suppressed sob
101. Ill-kempt
102. Epic poetry
104. Fescennine
107. Sesame
109. Old times, old style
110. Lamb of pork fame
113. "Jeopardy" offerings
114. Forfend
116. Luanda native
118. Heretofore
119. Curule-chair occupants
120. Certain minstrel
121. Works clay
122. Predatory dolphins
123. Former Russian measure
124. Maternal kin
127. Lashes
128. Double this for a perfume
131. Lot
133. Lobster boat
134. A co-inventor of cordite
136. Cunctatious
138. "Bleak House" lass
139. Mischievous Olympian
141. Lifesaver of myth

186 Historic Day by Judith C. Dalton

ACROSS

1. Wellaway!
5. Oral-vaccine man
10. Mid pts.
14. Cartouche
18. Exuviate
19. Gross, in Granada
20. Restored bldg.
22. Middle East prince
23. Foolscap figure?
25. Mediators, occasionally?
27. Finnish poems
28. "Pippin" director
30. Gun org.
31. Greets intrusively
34. "___ diem"
35. Snow-sport conveyor
39. Large-eyed lemur
40. Glisten
41. Business deg.
42. Roman 502
43. Parched
44. Cad in charge?
48. Ending for differ or insist
49. May honorees
50. Samlet; skegger
51. Burden
52. Huff
53. Naval C.I.A.
54. Musical entrances?
58. Catchall term
59. Wine-and-nutmeg drink
61. Herbs, in Yorkshire
62. Noted U.S. surgeon: 1864–1943
63. Long successor on "Cheers"
64. Spelunking sites
65. Decrepit, in Dijon
67. Becomes wan
69. Finishes last
70. W.W. II tanks
73. Actress Raines
74. Nuptial cobblers?
77. Savanna
78. Skim over
79. Glitzy fabric
80. Moroccan coastal area
81. Wing: Comb. form
82. Poodle size
83. Container business?
87. Staffer
88. Baxter role in 1950
89. City in Peru
90. Waistcoats
91. Banks or Pyle
92. Seeds again
94. Bumps a Durant
95. What foes called

supporters of Mary Stuart
97. This, in Tours
98. Luck, in Livorno
99. Gratifies
100. Dermatologist, sometimes?
104. Minor augury?
109. Genuine
110. Maharashtra city
111. Object of Petrarch's affection
112. Variable star
113. Plant juices
114. Candid
115. City SSE of Dallas
116. Male only

DOWN

1. Elec. unit
2. Mauna ___
3. Eisenhut, e.g.
4. Controversial compounds
5. Pointer's best point
6. Butter in the sky
7. Sacks
8. Suffix for baby or old
9. "O short-liv'd pride! ___?" Shak.
10. Make crunchy
11. Succinct
12. Korea's Syngman ___
13. Micmac's cousin
14. Conductive substance
15. Scottish uncle
16. Address for Raleigh
17. Horace's "___ Poetica"
21. Tiered sleeping spots
24. Dancer Tamblyn
26. Due-process process
29. Mountain ashes, to Virgil
31. Cottonwoods
32. Cigar or crown
33. Illegal stratum?
34. Colette novel
35. Use finger paints
36. Equivalent cans in London?
37. Gable-top feature
38. Former quarterback Y.A. ___
40. Suit material
44. Flèche
45. Dred Scott decision Justice
46. Lumpy masses
47. Old cries of triumph

52. Red Cross supply
54. Bando and Mineo
55. Lake in SE Africa
56. Rapper in a courtroom
57. Dolly Varden, e.g.
60. Collect bit by bit
62. Nav. officers
64. Translating device
65. ___-Chu school of philosophy
66. High nest
67. What nudniks do
68. Room recess
69. Precarious perch
70. Lounge furniture
71. "He shall not ___ if he have his own": Shak.
72. Hindu garments
74. Asphalt, e.g.
75. Punjabi potentates
76. Trumpeter Al and family
81. Certain plastic tubes
83. Yearned
84. Exceeded limits
85. Lear's faithful companion

86. Actress Parsons
91. Fleuret's kin
93. Anagram for chase
94. Blackmore outlaw
95. Angelo ___, memorable educator
96. Rand's shrugger
98. Plug up
99. Daze
100. "___ a girl!"
101. La predecessor
102. Walker or Wightman
103. Dove sound
105. Golfer Baker-Finch
106. Pithy remark
107. Braun or Marie Saint
108. Henpeck

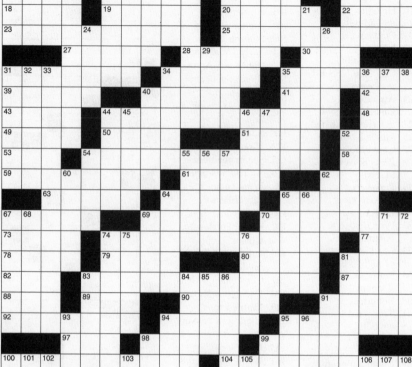

187 *The Battered Bard* by Ralph G. Beaman

ACROSS

1. Dadaist of note
4. Malefic
8. Shoreline peril
13. ___ Sec. of the Navy (F.D.R: 1913–20)
17. Old Ace of Spades
18. Family car
20. Cougar's color
21. Isinglass
22. Four ___ kind
23. Coded order to Adm. Nagumo: 12/2/41
27. Took the tube at Waikiki
29. Diet follower
30. Youngman quip
31. E.T.O. town
32. Riviera acquisition
34. Reveal or pretend
36. Honshu city N of Tokyo
37. "Japanese . . . swooped down on ___": Press: 12/8/41
40. Kind of bread
42. ___ du Diable
43. W.W. I poster man
44. Man with a Plan
50. ___ Island
52. Stack
53. ___ Flow
54. Mindanao's Tasadays, e.g.
57. June 6, 1944
59. Thief
63. Violinist Ughi
64. Thralls and helots
66. Snatch
68. Jawaharlal ___
69. Letter opener
71. Oklahoma and West Virginia
75. Bird or fruit
76. Longed
78. Chimney problem
79. Sedate
81. Fault
82. Kenya's capital
85. Get ready for the O.R.
87. Early penman's chore
89. Umpteen years
91. Requirement
93. Ships, to poets
94. Type of ship not in port: 12/7/41
99. Birchbark
102. Gene letters
103. Row
104. Memorable target: 12/7/41

106. Open-eyed
110. Bonheur and Ponselle
113. "Harper Valley ___"
114. River in Hesse
115. Infirm with age
117. Dweller in a Yemeni port
119. Pen
121. Army partner to Hickam Field
124. "___ on parle . . ."
125. Type of gas
126. Murrow's "___ Now"
127. Hints
128. Strategic port in W.W. II
129. Give it ___ (attempt)
130. Singer-actress Cara
131. Bristle
132. P.O. item

DOWN

1. Inge's "___ Roses"
2. Disproof
3. Site in the news: 12/7/41
4. Suffix for inchoative verbs
5. Kin of savannas
6. Ugandan exile Amin
7. Layers
8. Porticoes for Pericles
9. Visit habitually
10. Baruch's "My ___ Story"
11. Opposites
12. One of the Redgraves
13. "A miss is as good as ___"
14. Audit a course
15. Ancient name for a N European area
16. "Winner ___," 1975 film
19. TV network
24. Cain's "___ Pierce"
25. Ending for pant or scant
26. Plath work
28. Warred
33. Branch of mathematics
35. Ogre
38. Musicians Kipnis and Buketoff
39. Dance-drama of Japan
41. Apiece
45. Doohickey fancier
46. Scattered: Fr.

47. Mystery writer Foley
48. Joy ride
49. Noted Czech novelist
51. ___ alt. (druggist's "every other day")
54. Dey or Brownell Anthony
55. N.Y. city on the Mohawk
56. Newts
58. Derisive calls
60. End of a 7:58 A.M. alert: 12/7/41
61. General Rommel
62. Penitent's activity
65. End
67. Smidgens
70. Ice pinnacle
72. Actress Patterson
73. Old prospector
74. Address for a king
77. Active one
80. Otto, nove, ___
83. Stole
84. Lowdown
86. Examiner
88. Team jacket

90. Alarming person
92. Hades
94. Romanian city and county
95. Class comprising ants, flies, etc.
96. Pawl engager
97. ___-Magnon
98. Observations
100. Sandlot game
101. At a previous time
105. Shady business
107. Reboant
108. Put on the pan again
109. Finial
111. Salk contemporary
112. "Yesterday, December 7, 1941, ___ . . ."; F.D.R.
116. Italian town near Ancona
118. A.E.C. successor
120. Mount in Tasmania
122. Rocker Kiki ___
123. Snooker stick

ACROSS

1. Beatty film: 1981
5. Trek to Mecca
9. Behave
12. Cordwood measure
17. Frenzied
18. Penthouse?
19. Mrs., in Madrid
20. Tempting dangler
21. Child and Howe, grab, L.B.J. pet
24. Arabian group
25. ___ cantata (sung Mass)
26. A John
27. Like a wet hen
28. "___ Man Answers," Darin hit
31. Dregs
32. Torch
33. P.D.Q.
37. Parsons' homes
39. Swan's victim
40. Haggard novel
42. Mix
43. Performed one's work
44. Spanish blue, look at, young fox
47. Fight seg.
48. Soprano Gluck
49. Brief look
50. Classify
51. Prescribed amount
52. Mauna ___
53. He wrote "A Delicate Balance"
54. Green spaghetti sauce
56. Concert halls
57. Tools, riches, accompany, expand
62. Thespians' org.
63. Rainbow
64. Ethiopian prince
65. Topic, Magi gift, intone, range part, you and me
77. Beatles film: 1965
78. "And ___ with the setting moon": Tennyson
79. Entertainer Della
80. Numero ___
81. Mayan and Mundane
82. A ___ apple
83. Meadows
84. Reclined
85. Tate offering
86. Relative, joy, slip
90. ___ Delgada, E Azores
91. Equal

93. High dudgeon
94. Miller and Blyth
95. Aliens' transport
96. Add value to
98. Touch upon
99. Health clubs
101. Double curve
102. Luau food
103. Squirrel away
104. Puts a stop to
106. Emphasis
109. Center, classic car, put down, headland
114. Brunei's location
115. Washington bill
116. Having roof extensions
117. Flag
118. Canton dwellers
119. Koppel or Knight
120. Stowe book
121. Tangy

DOWN

1. "The ___ Quartet": Paul Scott
2. Big bird
3. U.S. currency
4. Hydroplane
5. Wiesbaden's state
6. Spaces
7. MIV halved
8. Wicked, shameless woman
9. Vanishing table item
10. Antigone's uncle
11. Mountain pool
12. Philippine island
13. Exchanges
14. Sea eagle
15. Dauphin's dad
16. Ands, in Nice
18. Dolts
20. Vie
22. Felt ill
23. Dodge
28. African antelope
29. Uncultivated
30. A kingdom
34. Walked triumphantly
35. Clinquant
36. Trial
38. Marmara, e.g.
39. "Network" director
40. Ray
41. Come up with, as an idea
44. Provençal love song
45. Goal, in Geesthacht
46. Once, once
49. Shine
51. Waterwitch

53. "Just ___ doch-an'-dorris": Lauder
54. Desiccate
55. Emulate Goya
58. Corn porridges
59. Cries of surprise
60. Smelting refuse
61. Except
65. Karloff film: 1940
66. Gentlemen, in München
67. Click beetle
68. Arafat
69. Lorelei's river
70. Ladder part
71. Van Gogh's "Room at ___"
72. ___-do-well
73. Binge
74. Nicety
75. Joins
76. Sub detectors
82. Emperor of Japan
84. McGrew's lady
87. Unnatural; stiff
88. Accustom
89. Matriculated
90. Meat pie
92. Ages

95. Greens dish
97. Volcanic peaks
98. Make up for
99. Thrust
100. Lost color
103. Boswell was one
105. Agitated state
106. Not pres.
107. Intimidate
108. Dernier ___
110. Musical acuity
111. Failed NOW goal
112. Title Drake held
113. Concorde, e.g.

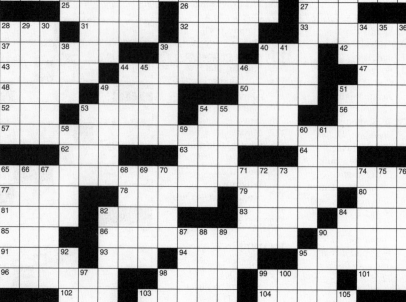

189 12 Christmas Gifts by Norma Steinberg

ACROSS

1. Early N.A. money
7. Board
12. Better
17. ___ facto
21. Director May
22. Conspirator against Peter III
23. A Montague
24. Pippin
25. Tundra hairdresser?
27. Wildebeest country?
29. Cat's-paw
30. Lie adjacent to
31. Lacks
33. Gather
34. Farm towers
36. Shorthander
37. Hack of baseball
38. Aspirin compound
41. Keep ___ on
42. Trumpeter from New Orleans
43. Grew tall and thin
47. Witnesses
49. Napoleon won here: 1796
50. Game divided into chukkers
51. "And ___ bed": Pepys
52. Street sign
53. Funny weasel?
57. Pi follower
58. Overturn
59. Turkish royal court
60. ___ E. Lee: Abbr.
61. Draw ___ on (aim at)
63. Indian matting
64. Tea treats
66. Glissade
68. Kind of knot
69. Map line: Abbr.
71. No longer ahead
73. Come to know
75. Breathe hard
77. Actress Arthur
78. "___ Remember," 1960 song
79. English dry-goods dealers
81. Beach find
85. Stallone's nickname
87. Dried grape
88. Immaculate
90. One on the payroll
92. Actor from Prague
94. Ouphs
95. Jean Kerr's "Lunch ___"
96. Blanches
97. Simulacrum
99. Reckless Olympian
100. Birds in the walls?
104. Grudge
105. Buzzing insects
107. Matches
108. Tie down securely
109. Cronyn and Tandy, often
110. In a natty way
112. Fellies
113. Highland lord
115. Hordeolum
116. Regions of shifting sands
117. Kern show
118. McMahon's drawn-out word
119. Brenda or Bart
121. Singer Baker
122. Miler Andersson
123. Crew cut's antithesis
127. Very early bird?
129. Buffalo celebration?
133. Hang around
134. Esposa de su padre
135. Cleo or Frankie
136. A star in Anaheim
137. Functions
138. Caught sight of
139. Enroll
140. Tripods

DOWN

1. Shrine Bowl team
2. ___ sax
3. B.L.T. option
4. Bolus
5. Prefix with corn
6. Chess pieces
7. Hoyden
8. Wake
9. Escutcheon stain
10. ___ Alamos
11. Twilight
12. Silvery
13. "___ Cane," Jacopetti film
14. Big birds
15. Society-page word
16. Handout
17. Manhattan and Roanoke
18. Pod contents
19. There are 100 in D.C.
20. Anomalous
26. Fragrant marsh shrubs
28. Role for Zimbalist Jr.
32. Spooky
34. Buffet features
35. ___ 500
36. Displayed
37. Bowler's problem
38. Circa
39. Correspondent of a sort
40. Song-and-dance cat?
43. Serious
44. Pack animals from Santa Monica?
45. Colorless, odorless gas
46. Early TV surname
48. Hold the deed on
49. Smallest amount
50. Nudge
53. Yearn
54. Perpetually
55. Innisfail
56. Jubal ___ of the C.S.A.
59. English Channel port
62. Lures
65. Thirteen witches
66. Ball of yarn
67. Page
68. En ___
70. Backcomb
72. Steinbeck siren
74. Short jackets
76. Foolishly affected
79. A Bond portrayer
80. Chief engineer on the Enterprise
81. Actor Bruce
82. Impart knowledge
83. Four balls
84. Prospectors' objectives
86. Cultured-milk product
87. Enjoys literature
89. San ___ Obispo
91. Washes out suds
93. Disorderly
95. Greets
96. Owl's shipmate
98. Inst. near Harvard
101. Bits of wit
102. Flash
103. Outrageous
104. Super
106. Straggles
109. Insert mark
111. Short wave
112. Like the Roman Forum
113. Sovereignty
114. Actress Marilu
117. Rhonchus
119. B'way hit signs
120. Metal used for trays
121. "___ sae weary . . .": Burns
122. ". . . ___ is in Heaven"
123. Donizetti's "___ Bolena"
124. Lahti resident
125. Surprise from Francis Marion
126. Fronton shouts
127. Actor Gulager
128. Lacuna
130. Golfer Woosnam
131. Quartet in "A Midsummer-Night's Dream"
132. Unit of luminous intensity

190 Pssst by John M. Samson

ACROSS

1. Stocking stuffer
6. Orange gem
11. "Cantique de Noél" composer
15. Colors
19. Doll up
20. Byword
21. Beach resort
22. Superior
23. Naos
24. Variable stars
25. "The World of Words" author
27. Those with telephonitis?
30. Cleanses
31. Thrills
32. Mother of Eos
34. "The Old Wives Tale" dramatist
35. Tannenbaum topper
38. Crush
39. Traveling salesmen
41. Trio from Oslo
42. Prefix for center
43. Gray and Moran
44. Puissant
48. Jumpy noblemen?
52. DII doubled
53. O.T. book
54. Sugarplum, e.g.
55. Fetch
56. Medicate
57. Self-image
58. Rustic
61. Elvis Presley hit
62. Confederate gen.
63. Poulettes?
66. Slow pacifist?
69. Linear measure
70. Puts away
71. Vaquero's relative
72. Radio plugs
73. Confines, in a way
74. About
75. Kind of tape
79. Society-page word
80. Mork's planet
81. Part of the holiday check-out snarl?
84. A sheepdog
86. Indian's protector
87. Under the weather
88. Female kangaroo
89. Firedogs
91. Admits
93. Rudolph's high beam
94. Come out
97. Lee in "Funny Face"
99. Range of NE Italy
100. Alert
102. Busy flautists
108. Spousal symbols
110. Swedish seaport
111. Preceder of 63 Across
112. Futile
113. Magpie
114. German river
115. TV's "___ Indiana"
116. Wrench
117. Very light brown
118. Soubrettes
119. Cob and pen

DOWN

1. Humane org.
2. Quarter
3. Dudley Do-Right's love
4. Job O. Henry had
5. "For want of ___ the shoe . . ."
6. Pony
7. Taos buildings
8. Opulent
9. Seaweed substance
10. Coconut, e.g.
11. Snowcapped peak
12. Magi headbands
13. In the arms of Morpheus
14. Peace Nobelist John R. ___: 1946
15. Superlative for Snow White
16. Fraternal club
17. Tannenbaum topper
18. Simpletons
26. Chastise
28. City in SW Idaho
29. Sequence
33. Dangled
35. 'Tis the season to be chary
36. Sif's husband
37. Solothurn's river
39. Wassail
40. Letter from Paul
42. Renaissance sword
43. D.W. Griffith films
45. Año nuevo time
46. Beersheba's locale
47. Gunwale pin
49. Denounce
50. Brooklyn's "field of dreams"
51. Irish islands
52. Two fortnights
56. Biblical seamstress
59. Swerved
60. Cut of beef
61. Blockhead
63. Coin for Père Noël
64. Copland ballet
65. Car of 1957
66. Basin in W China
67. Forage plant
68. Trifle
71. Sleighs, e.g.
73. Tip
74. Forty winks
76. Prank
77. Country Slaughter
78. S-curve
81. Joe Orton play
82. Wide ties or knots
83. "Matter of Fact" columnist
85. Wash
86. Plodding one
90. Peaceful
91. Peacock spots
92. Became friendly with "to"
93. Enoch, to Seth
94. Loaf
95. Lyric poem
96. Adjective for Loren
99. Observances
101. Eck!
103. Muslim scholar
104. Spanish shovel
105. Soprano Petina
106. Opposite of ja
107. Turns right
109. Miami inst.

191 Stick to It Iveness by Peter Gordon

ACROSS

1. Give ___ whirl (try)
4. Sahara sections
8. Wrong
13. Unbends
18. Buttonwood
20. Desiccate
21. More unctuous
23. Ron Nessen was one
25. Bug
26. Mentor of Luke Skywalker
27. Wizened
28. Setting for "Hogan's Heroes"
30. Scott Turow book
31. Parts of sonnets
34. Head swellers
35. Sydney-to-Lord Howe Island dir.
36. Puckerel
39. Avine activity
41. It has 32 men
45. Saw-toothed ridge
47. Bar slug
49. Actors Costner and Kline
50. Matthew, in Madrid
51. Clio and Edgar
53. Got the lead out
56. Europe's longest river
60. North Sea feeder
61. Any delicious drink
62. Draft initials
65. Coronet
67. Emulates Dennis Conner
70. Emulate Brian Boitano
71. Responsibility
73. They get cooked with vegetables
76. Run producer
77. Verso's opposite
79. Life-preserver stuffing
80. Coil or curl
82. Wino's ailment
83. Bing Crosby's birthplace
85. Jacob's-sword
87. Man
89. Shish-kebab holder
90. Lines of cliffs
92. Who's station
96. Nero's teacher
98. Tolerated
100. Caboose neighbor, perhaps
101. Phrase on many dietary foods
103. Like
105. "Kenilworth" heroine
106. Thematic letter herein
107. Send packing
110. "We yield our . . . ___ thy soft mercy": Shak.
112. Townshend ___: 1767
114. Ran-tans
116. Kinski role: 1979
117. Gimlet ingredient
121. U.S.A.F. Academy cadet
123. Flare, sometimes
126. Attain acclaim
127. Paid for a hand
128. Scone movers
129. A and B, e.g.
130. Nobelist in Literature: 1923
131. Erotic
132. Printemps follower

DOWN

1. Culp-Cosby series
2. Abecedarian
3. Eagled a par-three hole
4. There are two in mathematics
5. Antarctic arm of the Pacific
6. Addresses
7. Arcane matters
8. Parrot
9. Netman Wilander
10. Ticked off
11. Kind of whale
12. Cruel creditors
13. Gather, as oysters or logs
14. Step on it
15. Countertenor
16. Bad place to lie
17. Goddess of the moon
19. Botanist Gray and namesakes
22. Rent again
24. Site of rods and cones
29. Glaspell's "Norma ___"
32. Implant deeply
33. Like the top of Fuji
36. Distinctive doctrine
37. Woody's frequent co-star
38. Bushes' Millie, e.g.
40. Polynesian apparel
42. Steven's modifier
43. Some form-sheet data
44. Couch potato's meals, often
46. Gun a motor
48. Halloween option
52. Helps with the dishes
54. "___ Home," McCartney song
55. Sordor
57. Lille lily
58. Rubberneck
59. A Met score
62. Out of ___ (grumpy)
63. Jack Nasty
64. Horatio Alger book, e.g.
66. Jelly used as a garnish
68. Gets a circuit ahead in a race
69. Vaudeville performance
72. Family of "The Minister's Wooing" author
74. Rails
75. Monterrey Mrs.
78. Signs
81. Elbow grease
84. Calculus calculation
86. Damage
88. Predicament
90. Last of a familiar hebdomad
91. Part of a worm's body
93. Nipper's co.
94. Rick's pianist
95. Taste
97. Sabot's sound
99. Strips, in a way
100. Clarinet's large cousin
101. "You can ___ horse . . ."
102. Prom queen's date
104. Tenant
108. It's to the left of the Rive Droite
109. Seed coat
111. Actress Petrova
113. Narrow pew
114. Dates frequently
115. Don't dele
118. Dictator's phrase
119. Gold medalist Biondi
120. Ultimatum word
122. Croce's "___ Got a Name"
124. Kin of aves.
125. Like some stares

192 *Highly Proper* by Jim Page

ACROSS

1. Conger catcher
6. Honey of a drink?
10. Helen Mirren film: 1984
13. Actor Tamiroff
17. Shoot from ambush
18. Vince, to Gomer
19. Making iridescent
22. Bracing
23. Arboreal knots
24. Marksmen
25. Grantadvance
28. Oodles
29. Thundering
30. Shem's father, in Lourdes
31. "The Broken Jug" playwright
34. Protruding rock
37. Conditionsituation
42. Degree type
43. Magical conveyance
45. Quay
46. Actor Eisenberg
47. "The Morning Watch" author
48. Perspire
49. Fizzwater
50. Muslim cap
51. Card game
52. Teacher's org.
53. Erode
57. Chum
59. Disentangle, in football.
61. Stumbles
63. W. Hemisphere org.
64. Prefix for form
65. Checks
66. Sagatale
71. "Fickle and restless as ___": Heine
73. Pea petals
74. Scot's veto
75. "The Jolly Toper" artist
79. Lit up
80. U.S.N.A. part
81. Most sordid
84. Porcine parent
85. One less than septi-
86. Cistern
88. Korean boundary river
90. Davis in "The Hill"
92. Spy Penkovsky
93. Mouth: Comb. form
94. Bellow
96. Where to soul search
97. Free (of)
98. Pawpaw
101. ___ fixe

102. Bahamian resort
104. Sweep
105. Contaminate
107. "The Other Side of the Rainbow" author
109. Punchpoke
114. Call into question
117. Odd job
118. Its capital is Lyon
120. Me. storm
121. Toast start
122. Pioneer film producer: 1864–1948
123. Nitti's nemesis
124. Urban rails
125. Forward
126. A sister of Calliope

DOWN

1. Valuation: Abbr.
2. Enoch's cousin
3. Job
4. Peach peels
5. Happen again
6. Lathe spindle
7. Epochal
8. Earth: Comb. form
9. Removed grit
10. Pamper
11. Away from: Prefix
12. Vientiane's locale
13. Chem. compound
14. Cousincousin
15. Opposite of ext.
16. Booker T.'s group
18. Dagger of yore
20. Committeepanel
21. Catania citizens: Abbr.
26. Put to flight
27. Proboscis monkeys
32. Bargains
33. Ancient Athenian freeman
34. Prospect
35. Hoopster
36. Trailing
38. Rorschach, for one
39. Bacchanal cry
40. Adult doodlebugs
41. High ___
44. Zeta follower
47. Viperous
54. Pintquart
55. Fond du ___
56. Some Ghanaians
58. Expertise
60. Born
62. P.O.W. camp of W.W. II
64. Lifetime
67. See red?
68. Dockers' org.

69. Seafood?
70. She was Edna Garrett
71. Earhart
72. Veganova
76. Syrian President
77. Tours river
78. Borg, e.g.
79. Clipped
81. Dull
82. Soft breeze
83. Suffix for simple
87. A neighbor of Norma
89. "Henry ___ Little Secret," 1944 film
91. No rod sparer
95. Joined
96. Wife of Osiris
98. Ballerina Fracci
99. Hearth tools
100. Counties in Fla. and Ga.
103. Walk-ons?
106. They wrote in runes
108. Dresden duck
110. "Nearer, My God, to ___"
111. Cleft

112. Caffeine source
113. Stew
114. Crier's ntwk.
115. Weed killer
116. A semisolid
119. Amour-propre

193 Townspeople by Barbara Springer

ACROSS

1. One of the Canary Islands
6. Parrot
11. Kentucky Derby winner: 1955
16. Box
20. Argot
21. "Free Wheeling" auth.
22. A unit of weight
23. The Nile, as a god
24. Storm
25. "The Duino Elegies" poet
26. Israeli coin
27. Another, in Acapulco
28. Part of A.L.U.
29. Aerie resident
30. Dud
31. Sign of pleasure
32. Two-wheeled transport?
34. Carelessly constructed?
36. Regards
37. Germ
38. Seat for a judge
39. Sign language
43. Rocker John
46. Silenus, e.g.
49. Suffix for boy
52. Nev. neighbor
53. Fancy dive?
55. Cornhusker city
57. Packer
58. Means
60. Verve
61. More accurate
62. Fountain of Rome
63. Cut
64. Sincere
66. Part of Muslim prayers
67. Selfish one
69. Threads
70. Summons
72. Dallas-to-San Antonio dir.
75. Sharpen
76. Distinction
78. Kirghizian mountains
80. Certain railroads
81. A cotton fabric
83. Sentence
84. Dash
86. Gloriole
87. Trouble
90. Adlai's running mate: 1956
92. City W of Erfurt
96. A literary Bell
98. Eskimo knives
99. Send abroad
100. Impressions
101. Ballerina Shearer
102. Hair clasp?
104. Approximates
105. Org. for Spock
106. Coat rack
108. Make amends
109. Some carriers
111. Problematic
113. Indonesian islands
114. Prickly pear
115. Pasta request?
120. Brawl?
127. Selene's realm
128. Forgive
129. Cheeks like roses, e.g.
130. Light entertainment
131. Hillside near a loch
132. White poplar
133. Vapid
134. Grave
135. Color of raw silk
136. Troubles
137. Massenet opera
138. Stretch
139. Extremists, for short
140. Rendezvous
141. Publish
142. Lawn tool

DOWN

1. Father: Comb. form
2. Kind of salt or wit
3. Unwilling
4. Broadcaster's problem?
5. Quiz
6. Slough
7. Nearby, poetically
8. Arum lily
9. Out of line
10. Stimulate
11. Mounted
12. Hazard
13. Bouquet
14. Something stated
15. Fill-in
16. James Clavell novel
17. Hand game?
18. Eliot's "cruellest month"
19. Merry
20. Carson predecessor
29. Tree-of-life site
33. Swedish rug
34. Goo
35. Magnate
37. Fillet
39. I.R.S. employee
40. Volcanic crater
41. Otherwise
42. Strainer
43. Oust
44. Unique
45. Clunk
46. "___ Marner"
47. Nomadic Ethiopian
48. Roomy dress style
50. See 26 Across
51. Hector
54. Strapped
56. Painter Joan ___
58. Score for Steffi
59. Workbench adjunct
64. Judah Ben-___
65. Four seasons
68. Exude
69. Title for a Benedictine
71. Spicy dessert?
72. Plan
73. Aloha's cousin
74. Advertising medium?
76. Furze
77. Share
78. Box-elder genus
79. Hunger
82. Film ___
83. Question
84. Chief Justice: 1941–46
85. Tyrolean song
88. Roll up
89. Ice mass
90. Fair
91. English
93. Bullets, e.g.
94. Constellation Lepus
95. Org.
97. Relish
99. Famous last words
103. Exceptional
107. Magnetize
109. Slipper
110. Common connective
112. Meleager's father
113. Certify
114. Knack
115. Winsor's "Forever ___"
116. "Romancero gitano" poet
117. Interdict
118. Abrasive
119. McKinley's birthplace
120. Money of the Mid East
121. Native of Muscat
122. A sturdy chiffon
123. Spaded anew
124. Like Humpty Dumpty
125. Peripheral
126. Piercing
129. Lamebrain
134. Ecological org.

194 *All the Rage* by Stanley Glass

ACROSS

1. Medicinal plant
5. Recorded proceedings
9. Brazilian coffee
12. Big beetle
18. Kind of food or music
19. Where Qum is
20. French secular clergyman
22. A Roosevelt relative
23. Irate pop singer in Arkansas?
26. Recording process
27. Livy's language
28. Dig up
30. A crowd?
31. Sigma ___ (frat of songdom)
33. Trainer Dundee of boxing
35. City in Argentina
37. At a distance
38. Expense item
40. Poet ___ Manley Hopkins
42. Synthetic fabric
44. Pers. cards
45. Mt. Ida maiden
47. Street shows
49. "___ the Top": Porter
51. Actor Hardwicke
53. Affluent ex-Veep in Virginia?
57. Dash
60. Dash
61. Large sea duck
63. Fence material
67. The Bambino or Iron Horse
69. Mantua money
70. Labor gp.
71. World Series of Golf site
73. Snoopy one
74. Pen point
75. Handles clumsily
77. Grassy plains of Argentina
79. Trespasses
82. Lively horse
84. Its capital is Luanda
86. Stone lined with crystals
87. Singing Jackie in Pennsylvania?
89. Eyed wolfishly
93. Furious
94. Caveat ___
98. Dote on
99. The Greatest
101. Chilly time in Spain
104. Prewedding surprise
106. Nathan Hale's alma mater
107. Burrows' kin
109. Austrian essayist-editor
111. Lasorda's predecessor at L.A.
113. Rep.'s opponent
114. ___ cum laude
116. Dame Edith ___, English poet
118. Manet's "In ___"
120. Eventually
122. Ascetic family of Chief Justice in Carolina?
126. Start anew
127. Large kangaroo
128. "I remember Mama" role
129. Biblical pottage buyer
130. "___ Scared Stupid," 1991 film
131. QB's goals
132. Eddy-MacDonald number
133. Check

DOWN

1. Bat material
2. Trevanian's "The ___ Sanction"
3. Described in brief
4. "Lohengrin" heroine
5. Exposure outdoors
6. Shrinking one
7. George Hamilton acquirement
8. Sharp-cornered
9. Appraise
10. Metal structural unit
11. Opera by Von Weber
12. Summer time in Milwaukee
13. Miami's N.B.A. team
14. Omega's antithesis
15. Attractive 18th-century novelist in Connecticut?
16. Group of nine
17. Will or Ginger
21. Admission
24. School gp.
25. Nocturnal sawyers
29. Sanctified actor in Massachusetts?
31. Fang: Fr.
32. Epitaph starter
34. Period
36. Palindromic time
39. Ankles
41. Zeus, to Zeno
43. Modigliani's "The Rose ___"
46. Ref. book
48. Tussle
50. Fulminate
52. Staghorn ___
54. Matisse or Pétain
55. "___ Love," 1982 film
56. Weird
58. Durable columnist in California?
59. Balkan capital
62. Stonewall's boys
63. Drinks gingerly
64. S.A. border river
65. Depressed jazz notable in Massachusetts?
66. Yearns
68. Actor Leon ___: 1881–1951
72. Cowboy's loop
76. Egyptian king
78. Reduces
80. Notion
81. In want
83. Hawk's antithesis
85. Road base
88. Sty sound
90. Driver's exam
91. Author Gardner
92. Judge
95. Northern Connecticut town
96. Pained exclamations
97. Decorative altar structure
99. Esteem
100. Certain horseshoe throw
102. Swell the pot
103. Production measure
105. Vigorous
108. Marsh bird
110. Grassy area
112. Scand. nation
115. Iowa campus site
117. Psyche's beloved
119. Man's septet, to W.S.
121. Suffix with depend
123. New, in Nürnberg
124. Actress ___ Dawn Chong
125. Total

195 Spoonirizing by Cathy Millhauser

ACROSS

1. Type of jar
6. Rotisserie part
10. D.A.'s staff members
15. Program problem
18. Metrodome, for one
19. ___ incognita
21. Olympic slalom star: 1984
22. Paul Bunyan's cook
23. Driving hazard
24. Sounding like Niagara
25. Meccawee, e.g.
26. Soprano Souez
27. ___ polloi
28. Like an angry cleric?
32. Hymnist John Mason ___
34. Opel or Citroën
35. Massenet's "___ de Lahore"
36. Winemaking process
37. Like an angry perfumer?
40. Teenager's woe
42. Writer Bernstein
43. Battery part
45. Pacino and Hirt
46. Long tales
48. ". . . tomorrow ___ this petty pace . . ."
50. Over
52. Shed
53. Passover repast
54. Like angry Captain Kangaroo?
59. In any way
60. Beckett's "___ Knife"
62. Some are fine
63. If there should be
65. Woof's kin
68. What the angry clone was?
72. T.L.C. providers
73. Foolish fancies
75. Nixon nix, once
76. Anger, to Cato
78. Spot for a beret
79. Like angry Mr. Burns?
83. Ready at the bar
87. Singer James or Jones
88. Zwei preceder
89. Epicurean activity
91. Blackmore heroine
93. Artist Shahn
94. Florentine flower
96. Eight: Comb. form
97. Stats for Strawberry

98. Like an angry babe?
101. Makes a hook shot
103. Organic compound
105. Chassé, e.g.
106. "Tru" Tony winner
107. What the angry hangwoman was?
112. Skinny follower
115. Hawaiian island chain?
116. Author Segal
117. "An ___ Time of Hesitation": Moody
118. Actress in "Knots Landing"
120. Singer Kiki
121. Half note
122. Subject of a Cantor song
123. Red leader?
124. Uneven
125. Some lilies
126. "Ahem" alternative
127. Estaminets

DOWN

1. Couch potato's favorite show?
2. Woody's son
3. Like Skelton's angry wife?
4. Romberg's "___ Alone"
5. Violinist Milstein
6. Place for affairs?
7. Lima land
8. "Build it up with ___ steel . . ."
9. Defame
10. Latin I word
11. Dress accessory
12. Escutcheons
13. Vestige
14. Sevilla matrons
15. Like angry Ma Kettle?
16. Radius neighbor
17. Equipment
20. Valor; virtue
29. Korbut and Petrova
30. Astronaut Evans
31. Scenes; settings
33. Actress Brennan
36. Rhine tributary
37. Sphere starter
38. Emulated Yma Sumac
39. Varnish ingredients
41. "___ Down the Road," song from "The Wiz"
42. Vol. measures
44. U.S. wellness org.
47. Feudal slaves

49. Investigation
50. Angry states for Bumstead's boss?
51. Kind of inspection
55. Digs
56. Farrow's second
57. Parisian's donkey
58. Half of MCCCII
61. End of a Doris Day hit
64. Ethnic hairdos
65. Emulated Irons
66. Cicero, e.g.
67. Like angry Clara Bow?
69. Mule of songdom
70. "And miles to go before ___": Frost
71. Quant look
74. Rather like an ogre
77. Chekhov and Bruckner
80. Completed, in Caen
81. Certain saucers
82. According to
84. Like the angry clockmaker?
85. "Them" creatures
86. Player's org.

90. Famous fabulist
92. Admires
93. Ardent
94. Made available, as time
95. Make a dent
99. Abbr. on an overdrawn account
100. "Holy Mountain" in Greece
102. Peaceful
104. Weird
106. "Haystack at Giverny" painter
107. Actor Ray
108. ___ off (angry as a golfer?)
109. Plane type
110. Electric measures
111. Danish-American journalist-reformer
113. Concerning
114. Play-gun ammo
119. Munson of "G.W.T.W."

196 X-Cisions by Alfio Micci

ACROSS

1. Oklahoman
7. Juliet's family name
14. Nail or old plane
18. Uncompromising
19. Complete
20. Ignominy
21. Moundsman who begins a game?
23. River in central India
24. Rara follower
25. Dieppe donkeys
26. Cooked in a French oven
27. Easy gait
28. Garage worker: Abbr.
29. Growl
30. Pretty woman
31. Brass player
32. Seller's patter?
34. Disturb
35. "Tell ___ Sweeney!"
36. Gelid, in Granada
38. Lug of a jug
39. Chorister's big moment
40. A voice vote
41. Botanical interstices
44. Wreckage
47. Yule quaff, for short
49. Newsman Donaldson
50. Touring play?
52. Way from the heart
55. Hank or Phoebe of songdom
57. Paving material
58. Rascals
60. Sandbars
62. Longfellow's bell town
63. Certain utility conduits?
67. Shield border
68. A land was named for him
71. Haydn sobriquet
72. Motorists' org.
74. Halt
75. Thurify
76. Enjoying great popularity?
80. Witch bird
81. Call ___ day
82. Creator of Mrs. Tanqueray
83. Toward the center
85. Actress on "Murphy's Law"
87. Former Austrian Chancellor
89. Fool

91. If not
92. D.C. body
93. She wrote "Delta of Venus"
94. January store event?
98. Liqueur flavoring
100. ___ en scène (stage setting)
101. Rank above viscount
102. "Nightmare" street
105. Cavorted
106. "Look ___ hands!"
107. Capp's ___ the Hyena
108. Star in Serpens
109. Thin as ___
110. Certain undesirable passengers?
113. Galas
114. Joan of Arc triumphed here
115. Terse
116. Biographer Leon
117. Mountain chains
118. Racial; cultural

DOWN

1. Urbane
2. Courtier in "Hamlet"
3. Former Giant's family
4. In the: It.
5. Verdi opera
6. Of sovereignty
7. Mil. officers
8. Ryan's "Love Story" co-star
9. Sea bird
10. Remove stopple
11. Christine of Hollywood
12. ". . . ___ saw Elba"
13. Son of Odin
14. Miler's footwear?
15. Musical suite
16. Pardon
17. "For ___ me as light and life": Burns
18. Town in E Mexico
20. Lustrous mineral
22. Opera by Handel
27. Long, untapered cigars
29. U.K. stirs
30. Whittled
31. Golfer Sutton
32. Pedro's uncle
33. Vic's radio wife
34. Mielziner and Stafford
36. Overwrought
37. Compunction

39. Basso Cesare
41. Syria's President
42. Wakashan people of Vancouver Island
43. "___ I," 1924 Gershwin song
45. Tactical unit
46. "Arrivederci ___"
48. La-la lead-in
51. Cloak
53. Violent people
54. First Marxist President of Chile
56. Item for Rumpelstiltskin?
59. Hitch
61. Rig trucks
64. Sir, in India
65. Short ride
66. Regretful-sounding garment
69. Part of i.e.
70. Had a yen for
73. Author Rand
77. Piqued
78. Proboscis
79. "Seven Year Itch" actor

82. Spider in the kitchen
84. Part of a shandy
85. Gave a roast for
86. Liven
88. Abet's partner
90. Like Sue of songdom
92. Wine bottle
94. Doughnut: Slang
95. Meteorological line
96. Manipulate
97. Biblical landfall
99. Wrymouths' cousins
100. Twin crystal
102. Nicholas Gage book
103. Sammy Cahn creation
104. Neither fem. nor neut.
106. A spouse, in Savoie
107. Highland miss
108. Bard's stream
110. Morse recourse
111. Bambi's aunt
112. "___ bin ein Berliner"

197 *Fabulous Fifty-Sixer* by John Greenman

ACROSS

1. Heavyweight Max
5. Kind of lily
10. Harts
15. Addis ___, Ethiopia
20. Melville book
21. Anonym
22. Francis of "What's My Line?"
24. Festivals
25. Mythic coffer
27. Entertainer Kazan
28. First Family of Alaska in the 60's
29. Takes the helm
30. Craggy crests
32. Callowness
34. Serling of TV
35. Capita preceder
36. Trident prongs
38. Cays
39. Podded plant
41. Chisholm Trail town
43. What Nichols makes
44. Lets
46. Chg. for a loan
47. Perlman or Howard
48. Ms. Shire of "Rocky" films
49. Floating ice mass
50. One connected with: Suffix
53. Emulated Maxwell Perkins
55. Roger Clemens's team
57. Vanuatu's former name: Abbr.
59. Murmured fondly
60. Horehound and mad-dog
61. A Sedgwick
62. Enshrine
63. He fought Joe Gans
64. Avernus
65. Stowed cargo
67. Finally
68. Person from Ponca City
70. One of the Bears
71. Infant's garment
72. Certain airline initials
75. A courtroom procedure
80. Last year's jrs.
81. Satiated
83. Felt remorse
84. Cater basely
86. Birds' "thumbs"
87. "Robin ___," old Irish song
89. Absurdly eccentric
90. Hither
94. Tamarau's relative
95. Cabal
96. Nelson and Springfield
97. Spurn
98. Lead-pipe cinch
99. Dictionary compilation
102. Kitchen utensil
103. Fine lava
104. Unlatches a door, in poesy
105. Actress Taylor
106. Use a straw
107. Kyushu volcano
108. Betelgeuse's constellation
110. Scruffs
111. Prepare to braise
112. Napoleonic marshal
113. More reasonable
115. "Rosshalde" author
116. "Cara ___," 1954 song
117. Wood sorrel
119. Like a switch-hitter
122. Signet
124. Vandyke's relative
127. Tether
128. Dennis's Mame
130. Collusive behavior
132. Cat, in Catania
133. Admittedly
134. Simon's sporty slob
135. Newspaper section, for short
136. "There's no music in ___ . . .": Ruskin
137. Pressure units
138. Clayey rock
139. Eleven's numerals

DOWN

1. Conks
2. He loves: Lat.
3. Acquittal
4. Site for lots of bucks
5. Kissel and Opel
6. Yellowhammer St.
7. Leaned
8. Travail
9. Zither of yore
10. Mule "on the Erie Canal"
11. Conductor's aide
12. Arranges in rows
13. Chromosome parts
14. Impertinent one
15. Discriminator against older people
16. Deli favorites
17. "___ to the land of the dead": Auden
18. French lending institutions
19. African fox
23. Shoe-box ltrs.
26. Sent for
31. Elevating posts
33. Colleague of Paul, John and George
35. Brooch
37. Of a pelvic bone: Comb. form
39. Pawn's superior
40. Where Gideon defeated Midian
42. De la Mare poem
43. Observes Yom Kippur
44. Decorated anew
45. Manx tongue
48. Coloring agents
49. "Venerable" theologian
51. Young Durocs
52. More compendious
54. North Sea feeder
55. Awaits
56. Fortification
58. ___ noires (anathemas)
60. Dangerous Hawaiian shark
62. Concurring
64. Throng
65. Debussy opus
66. In the thick of
67. "Need ___ cry?": Burns
69. Indian, e.g.
70. Hawaiian island
72. Strikebreakers
73. ". . . pretty maids ___ row"
74. The March King's family
76. Muse of bridal songs
77. Cochise was one
78. Down at the heel
79. Uses a dabber
82. Drummers' cousins
85. "Ellie ___," post–Civil War hit
87. Auslander
88. Medics
89. Erases a chalkboard
91. Rationale
92. Soprano Sarah of the Met
93. Crazylegs Hirsch
95. Gourd
96. Bombay royalty members
97. Censure
99. Orléans's river
100. More lawnlike
101. Grosgrains, e.g.
102. Ms. Zadora
106. Andaman, for one
109. Wienie
110. Without gender
111. Mineral in quartz
113. Daub
114. Diminish
115. John Wayne film: 1953
116. Fen
118. City near Babylon's site
119. Kelp, for one
120. ___ chi (Oriental martial art)
121. Litter's smallest
123. Heroic poem
124. A "Pretty Woman" star
125. Fellow, in Madrid
126. Ids' relatives
129. Mag. group
131. The Lone Eagle's monogram

198 Crypt Teaser by Joel D. Lafargue

ACROSS

1. Strait outlet?
6. Ponderosa apparel
11. Librarian's device
16. What it costs nothing to be
17. Ho's partner
18. Creature with 14 legs
20. I AM A CAD, MA
22. Like Shelley's works
24. Davis's "Yes ___"
25. Hegel's forte
26. It carries a lot of weight
28. Hebrew Bible reading: Var.
29. Guitarist Lofgren
30. Work in a smokehouse
31. Flora and fauna
32. Avian chatterbox
33. Half of 11?
34. Daughters of Zeus and Themis
36. River to return as 33 Across?
37. He made a pile for Nabors
38. STONE'S DAD
41. Places for races
42. "___ Song Go . . ."
43. Exploits
44. Like Monday's child
45. Sudra and Vaisya
48. When overturned, is it a bucket seat?
49. Gets it all together
53. Quaker in a grove
54. UNSET
57. Chit
58. Landlocked country
59. Saarinen
60. Fit for the job
61. Evans or Carnegie
62. Navy's C.I.A.
63. DRAW A BOY
67. Paint-factory employee
68. Showy fan palms
70. The rite things to say
71. Beard erasers
72. Any time at all
73. Like a rugged bug?
74. Luigi's love
76. "The Kiss" sculptor
78. B. A. DONNA
84. TV's "Green ___"
85. "Stop, Pierre!"
86. This answer has three
87. Leandro's amorosa
88. Modernists
89. "___ Age," book by Comfort
90. Flavoring for a Cannes cordial
91. At a distance
92. Roscoe
93. A computer language
94. Huesca houses
96. French wines
97. Dub
99. FINGER
103. Shut tight
104. Don's January
105. Ups the ante
106. Cacophonous
107. Sole provider?
108. Team that's almost bare?

DOWN

1. Settings
2. King and Ladd
3. El ___, Heston role
4. This could a tale unfold
5. Tom cared about this voter?
6. Presided over
7. From this time
8. Amateur-sports gp.
9. Sgt.'s underling
10. Freud's appointments
11. Widened
12. Places of safety
13. Sped
14. Finial
15. MACARONI
16. Serpico on the screen
19. Rye grass
20. Heavy weight I'm lifting in N.D.?
21. Creature with a black-banded tail
23. Kind of poker
27. Etna feature
31. How Godiva rode!
32. It's for reel!
34. Moody tennis player?
35. Keats feats
36. Lass whom Cantor knew
37. Gretzky's stats
39. Developers' interests
40. Master, in Malaysia
44. Absquatulate
45. Close-fitting cap
46. Yoga squat
47. OLD PIES
48. On one's uppers
49. ___ sugar (lump for Castro?)
50. This and no more
51. He portrayed Chan after Oland
52. Litigious people
54. Felt silly?
55. Round figures
56. Shooting marbles
59. ___ effort
61. Dirty group out of Hollywood
63. Some tournaments
64. Hogged the conversation?
65. Fully grown
66. Italian magistrate
67. "___ Bulba"
69. Campus climbers
71. Wapner's wrap
73. Curled, as a Torah
74. St. Francis's bailiwick
75. Total wipeout
76. A to Z, for one
77. Where to paddle canoes?
78. Spacek's "___ Man"
79. Buck finisher
80. Ranger, before 1972
81. What de speeders pay?
82. Sumatran primates
83. From Oslo
89. "Deutschland uber ___"
90. Without ___ in the world
91. Dispatch vessel
93. Gudrun's mate
95. Tunisian city ('tain't photocopy!)
98. Honey-eating bird
100. Numero ___
101. It's east of Calif.
102. "As you sew, so shall you ___"

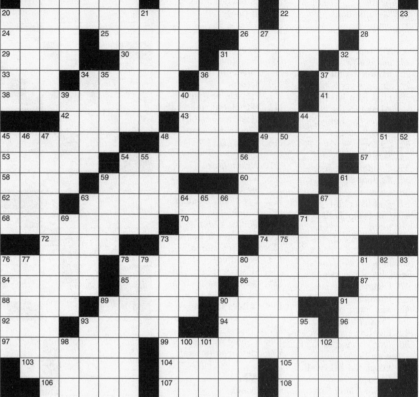

199 Gems by Joy L. Wouk

ACROSS

1. Part of a dart
6. Fuddy-duddies
11. Author of "Two Years Before the Mast"
15. Hari or Hale
18. Usher's milieu
19. A son of Midian: 1 Chr. 1:33
20. "Iliad," e.g.
21. Like Willie Winkie
22. Gaze with malicious pleasure
23. Sicilian code of silence
24. Primer dog
25. Altar on high
26. Blue Frost subject?
28. Keeve
29. Product of a lorimer
30. Infuriated
31. Most ironic
33. Yellowish-brown European?
37. Zodiacal sign
38. One of a Michelangelo trio
42. Prod
43. Begley and Asner
44. Red onlooker?
47. Victoria's consort
49. Actor Vidov
51. Old Faithful's activity
52. Let
53. Some putti
55. Kind
56. ___ Paulo, Brazil
57. Greek port
59. Labor leader Conboy: 1870–1928
61. Que. neighbor
62. Bluish-green chiefs of an armed forces branch?
68. With, to Cato
69. Titi or sapota
70. Truck-stop sights
71. Cover
72. Hasten
73. ___ Fair (N.Y. 1939 event)
74. First Indian ruler to embrace Buddhism
78. Grounds for belief
81. Sea east of the Caspian
82. Cheap: Slang
83. Yellowish-green, foolish oldsters?
85. Bern's river
87. Catholic tribunal
88. Incline
89. Number before sette
90. Deep-red gadfly?
93. Extents
96. Judge
97. Buffoon
100. Peer Gynt's mother
101. Bright-green municipal officials?
106. Eggs, to Caesar
107. Preside at tea
108. Oily hydrocarbon in petroleum
109. Pale yellow
110. Fall mo.
111. Of an epoch
112. Attentive one
113. Turn ___ new leaf
114. Lamb's dam
115. Sly
116. Heraldic borders
117. Of the kidneys

DOWN

1. Droops
2. Seed scars
3. Wet
4. Hullabaloo
5. Leash
6. Humbles
7. Irritable
8. Roof window
9. Group of eight
10. A Tai language
11. Ruins
12. Support, in Sedan
13. A queen of Thebes
14. Play part
15. Barter
16. Alpaca's habitat
17. Oenologist's concern
19. Abominable
27. Estuary
29. Limit
31. "Charlotte's ___": E. B. White
32. Glowing bit
33. Bedouin headband cord
34. Breakwater
35. ___ ghanouj (Middle Eastern salad)
36. City WNW of 57 Across
37. Drags along
39. That Menlo Park man
40. Lessee
41. Jargons
44. Blue-pencil wielders
45. Helices
46. New Orleans institution
48. Extract juice from
49. Suggest
50. Cotton to
53. Emend
54. One-horned fish
58. Hispanic-American
59. In a state of parvitude
60. Surrounded by
62. Believe in
63. Be tremulous
64. Diamond figure
65. Odd, in Oban
66. Limn
67. Classify
72. Gabler or Hopper
73. Dry watercourse
75. Payment for Charon
76. Forked-tailed hawk
77. Opera by Salieri
79. Dismal
80. Describing winds from the Orient
82. Cornered
84. Legal thing
85. French-built rockets
86. Stag adornment
90. She pulled a switch on a witch
91. Rub off
92. Earthquake feature
94. Soprano Kiri Te Kanawa, e.g.
95. Commonplace
96. "Abdul the Bulbul ___"
97. Region
98. Say it is so
99. Cathedral part
101. Dali's "Nostalgic ___"
102. Rant's partner
103. Appearance
104. Hebrew prophet
105. Colzie of the N.F.L.
107. "Treasure Island" character

ACROSS

1. Chip on chip on chip
6. Phonetic elision
10. Theater booth
14. Companion of Paul
19. De Valera
20. Type of space
21. Latin greetings
22. "Mother ___": Kipling
23. DOSTOYEVSKY NOVEL
26. Chief Etruscan god
27. Italy's golden age
28. New Orleans pro
29. Jewish village
30. Atlas was one
31. Phoenix's N.B.A. team
32. Weaver's reed
33. Valuable Brazilian tree
36. Author Mazo ___ Roche
37. Levant vessel
38. LEARNED MAN
41. Mire
42. DELIGHTED
45. ___ de Queiroz, Portuguese novelist
46. Property charge
47. Earth goddess
48. Otherwise
49. Ratite bird
50. Yerby's "A Rose for ___ Maria"
51. IN A POLYPHONIC WAY
55. Like a nobleman
56. WILL ROGERS'S HUMOR
58. Rich cake
59. Curved swords
60. Mus. mark
61. ___ Zagora, Bulgaria
62. Certain driver's warning
63. Climbing palm
66. Mme. Gorbachev
67. Kicker's nightmare
71. Detest
72. TARDINESS
74. Gullet
75. Hera's mate
76. Pants section
77. Obligation
78. Whodunit item
79. This might be slippery
80. Flats
84. His law relates to thermodynamics
85. Neighbor of Syr.
86. Fox hunter's shout
87. Soprano Berger
88. Impignorated
89. Spanish river
90. Cousins of 49 Across
91. Critter for Tex to tame
93. American cat
96. Like Daffy Duck
97. Excel
101. Crossbill's genus
102. "WHEN THE ___": RILEY
104. "Enigma Variations" composer
105. Photographer Morath
106. Tintinnabulate
107. Noted conductor from Genoa
108. Erect
109. Digitate
110. Wyes' predecessors
111. Ars' followers

DOWN

1. Parsees, e.g.
2. Wyndham Lewis novel
3. Fifi's friend
4. GUILT FEELING
5. Wrestler's ploy
6. Subject of a famed 1897 editorial
7. Tempted
8. Tell's canton
9. Antarctic waterway
10. Layers
11. Calcars
12. PIQUANT
13. "Iacta alea ___"
14. BEAT ___ (HIT FIRST)
15. FREEDOM FROM HARM
16. Prong
17. Monad
18. Phocid
24. Date preceder
25. Exerts traction on
29. Poor golf shot
32. Impertinent
33. Psalmic pause
34. Type of acid
35. Reinforced support
36. Costly
37. Maison section
38. Use antifreeze
39. FIRST ___: 264–41 B.C.
40. Caudal parts
42. Type of button
43. Baltic native
44. The Nile has one
47. English daisy
49. Baseball's Rookie of the Year: 1957
51. Certain luminary
52. Garret
53. Skoal, e.g.
54. Pianist Claudio from Chile
55. Austen character
57. Spanish deictic
59. Fuliginous
61. "À votre ___!"
62. Imitates Tinkerbell
63. FAIRY-TALE GIRL
64. White poplar
65. Tom, the General
66. Howard ___ in "The Fountainhead"
67. Type of law
68. Playwright Williams ("The Corn Is Green")
69. River or town in Ecuador
70. Soft fabric
72. Type of surgeon
73. Spanish port NE of Gibraltar
76. Sudden fright
78. CATTLEMEN
80. GAMBLING DEVICE
81. Transferred, as sovereignty, by death
82. Word on a penny
83. What Muses do
84. Keener from Kerry
88. A size of paper
89. Of Lamb's writings
90. Encomium
91. Wilderness Road traveler
92. Ladder steps
93. Pseudo butter
94. German city
95. OBLITERATE
96. Italian river
98. Newsmen Pappas and Seamans
99. Nest of pheasants
100. Compass dirs.
102. In good shape
103. Ice-hockey team

Do you want even MORE?

**Solve our daily, weekend and Sunday Magazine puzzles online,
FREE OF CHARGE for one month.**

Premium Crosswords offers access to over 2,000 New York Times crossword puzzles.*
This is an exclusive one-time offer.**

Plus you can:

❏ Play today's New York Times puzzle.

❏ Download puzzles to play online or print to solve offline.

❏ Play five years of daily & weekend puzzles (with solutions).

❏ Play both puzzles from the Sunday Magazine.

❏ Solve acrostics, Web-only puzzles and much more.

*Premium Crosswords subscription is $19.95 annually (as of 8/01). NYTimes.com reserves the right to change
these prices at anytime without notice. **You will be required to supply credit card information when registering for
the free 30-day period. After the free 30-day period you will be prompted to enroll as an annual Premium Crossword
subscriber. If you elect not to subscribe you will incur no charges. If you elect to become an annual subscriber, the
credit card supplied during registration will be charged. Your annual subscription will be automatically renewed
every year unless you cancel. We hope you enjoy your free 30 days of Premium Crosswords.

NYTimes.com/freepuzzles

1

```
JEAN  BEBOP   MAAM   ROAR
ACRE  OPERA   BELLA  ELMO
BUCCANEERS    EDIBLEBEAN
   KLEES  TOLET   LAUGHS
  SLURS   CILIA   MASK
 SHAM   AMIE   BARTERED
WAACS  GAMEOFCARDS   ERI
ONDE  SOLE   IRES   AGON
LEE  SMALLHORSES  EVADE
FRONTED   ERICS  CRANED
  FOOLS  PRADO   BRASS
SAGEST  THOLE   RESTFUL
TIRLS  SOONERSTATE  ANI
ORES  FINN   ACNE   STIR
ITE  CITYOFLIGHT  MEHTA
CONDONES  RINA    ADES
   ONES   SEERS  ATTAR
CROONS  STENO   ALOST
HITMUSICAL   ANTIQUECAR
ACHE  EBONY  DONAU  LORE
WOOD  DOTS   STORE  YOKO
```

2

```
THAT   VOTE   DAD   DEEJAY
REGIS  IRONSIDE    INDUCE
EARLOFCARDIGAN     STILTS
ATE  URALS  EGGY    ILES
CHESTER   AGEE   SATES
LESCHE  ANDERSDAHL   LPS
ENTO   GLASS   ELSE   EIN
 SOU  ORAN   ALEE   LOCI
  REGINALDGUPPY   ATOP
AFR  TRPS   EAUX   AGNATE
MOUNTIE  MAMIE  SWEARER
ALDOUS   ORES   HAIR  DES
LION   HENRYSHRAPNEL
GOLO  IONS   ORIG   EAM
ALF  SEGO   METED   APER
MED  JOHNMCADAM  HOPPLE
  ICANT   EARS   MANTRAP
GEOM   ARNO   BEAST   OME
CASABA  NICOLASCHAUVIN
ONETON  EDENTATE  PLANT
UNLIKE  TAL   SLED   ALES
```

3

```
REPAD   STALAG    DÆMONS
ATRIA  MOIMEME   ANTONIA
PHARMACOPŒIAL    MANTEEL
INTENSE   BONITO   ATALL
DIED  ASSAI  ADEER   ACLE
 CRAW   TOAT  LABEL   TIS
  LIPPERSHEY   ÆDILES
ATHENÆUM   EAR   ADVERT
SHES   DETESTS   SNEER
SAM  HORUS  STAT   ROOTER
ANITA  ORTO  ERRS  AIRTO
YEARNS  NORM  CAPEK   AHS
  EDAMS  SEDATED   VIII
 SCARCE   ORO   ACUTANCE
CÆSURA   ŒNOLOGICAL
IHS  BASED  ETRE    DEBT
MOAB  LUMET  IAMBI  NASA
PORED  RAMOUS   ABETTER
ONETIME  ARCHÆOLOGISTS
SEATERS  TOLLONS  ANISE
ERNEST   AWAYNE   DENES
```

4

```
GOFER  BERRA   ADAR  IMAGE
ORATE  ORION   SOLO  NAKED
BACHELORFLAT  PLAZASUITE
ILE  SORELY  ABHOR  NORMAN
    ELIDE  AMEER  EDDY
PTG  SIS  ASTER  OTTO  CAP
LARD  THELSHAPEDROOM  AMO
AREOLA  TOTEM  EINE  ABAS
STELE  TERI  NAMES  FLINT
MANET  GRANDHOTEL  GLENDA
ARM  MINN   RIFE   MENIAL
  ASLIFE  SOLON  SWEDEN
CANAAN  UPDO   CAAN    TDS
ASSIST  THEBALCONY  ETHAN
SHINS  CRAZY  ADDS  AHERO
HOOT  TOOL   SHIER  FRESNO
ERN  FROMTHETERRACE  EKED
DES  LAPP  AIRED   ORE  YDS
  BOUT  SIRED   SAMBA
SHALOM  PAREE  HAMPER  DIS
HOLIDAYINN   THEAPARTMENT
ERODE   ANTE   SILLS  HARRY
SNEAD   MEAT   TREES  ANNEX
```

5

```
  SIDES   IRATE   ARETE
 TENANT   NAVAL   SEXISM
BOASWAINSMATE   SPECTER
LAG   SCRIP   AVAIL  KORO
AMID  TULIP  RAGGY   ERIA
DARED  PERIL  TAN   GRINS
ENTREE  SENATOR  ZEALOT
  ILLS   TIER   DEEP
VANDYKEBEARS   TENSESUP
AROES  CIV  STRAND   SANE
LOO   FETID   YALTA   LIT
IANA  ADELIE  VIA   COATI
DRESSIER   OXSEATTICKET
  PEND   DRAT   EAVE
SORBET  MISMADE  WILTED
TWEED  BAG  SCOLD  COWER
ENTR  SAREE  YODEL   TIRO
LEAR  TRYST  REMIT   TIL
ARBITER   THIRDRATHOTEL
 SLEEVE  ENNUI  NEARER
  ESTER   DONNE   DRIER
```

6

```
CLASP  SEABOB    BESPOKE
HARPO  EMBARS   MONTANAN
TOYOURWEALTH   ABORNING
   ONENESS    CABLED
STANDS  REAROUSE   EERIE
POL  DIBS  MIMI   REPRESS
AMS  ONO   CASABA   SCOT
STAGG  WINNERSTALE   AME
MICA  CANOE   EAR   POSER
 TESLA  CRONE   OPENERS
  PITCHINGJENNIES
STEALTH   STERE   TSARS
PARRA  IDS   CELIA   LEES
EIN  CAPITOLTILL   PELLA
APES  ROSINA   SAR    EEL
RESTAFF  LEHR   HALO  TNT
SITAR  FILARIAE   OCASEY
  RIGORS    BEAROUT
LACESHOE   SPORTOFRINGS
RESTEELS  ROSIER   EVANS
GRASSES   SPEEDY   DEBUT
```

7

```
EBAN  SQUAD  PALP   STLO
FARO  QUITO  AMOR   BAHIA
THEFRUITEDPLANE      ARRET
STAREAT  GRAZE  ALTON
   INRE  REEVE  ALLOW
ATTLEE  SERGE  CLEARING
DAHL  SCISSORSALAD  NOL
DRESS  ALE   ARID   ATLI
USA  WESTWARDHOE  BEHAN
PIGMENTS  REALM  WERENT
   EADIE  MIR   PETIT
DOOMED  ELENI  FILTERED
ELFIN  AXIDENTALLY  OXO
BISE  ATTA   AGO   SAWIT
UGH  AWLORNOTHING  DELE
GOODDEAL  ORION  LADLED
   VOLES  AMICE  BANI
DEREK  FLANK   ANDCOLD
POLAR  BRIDGEOFSCYTHES
HERDS  RAVI  TRITE  ETAT
DAYO   OPEC  SEXES  DORS
```

8

```
MAHAN  COSTA  SHOVE  AMANA
ARADA  ALARM  HOVEL  LYRIC
IDOUBTIDDEEMITADISGRACE
DOLL  AREA  REVEL  HENLEY
REACTOR  VITAL  RARA
   TOT  COCA  APODI  NAM
WEREYOUTOCALLAVASEAVASE
ATE  ONINE  ORALES  ISSY
SHISH  TEA  SAGA  ARI  THIN
INDEEDIDNOTBEGIVENPAUSE
NOSTRIL  VAT  ACED  ONAIR
AET  MIEN  ONER  OSU
SWATS  CARR  END  OTTOMAN
WEREYOUTOCALLAVASEAVASE
ACRA  NRA  ALLY  ECO  LASSO
MOIS  MADAMA  ISTLE  SAN
IMVERYTOLERANTTHESEDAYS
SEE  ALORS  LOTI  TEE
STIR  PHOTO  TRELLIS
PATOIS  BLANC  CREE  IRAS
ITSNOTSOTOUGHIHAFMYVASE
ETAIN  ERUPT  EVADE  MEDIC
TARAS  POSSE  DETER  ARENT
```

9

```
AGHA  ACRE   STEM   DAMP
BOAT  LEACH  ATREE  EMIL
BUSHLEAGUE   FIELDSTONE
APPLAUSE  BELLA  ICARIA
   ETTE  ARNOLD  CRI
DEPTH  ARENA  FIANCE
OGLE  BIRDWATCHING  AVA
ERAS  ERGO  AIRE  REAL
REY  COURTYARD  COSTA
STETSONS  HALVE  SADATS
   ROOMY  SOLDE  PARER
TIPTOE  STRIA  LACROSSE
ALIEN  TUNESMITH  ALA
SIAM  SCAN  ANTE  ALAR
SUN  SHORTCIRCUIT  NAVE
   MODERN  OLEOS  FADED
   RPI  ASSETS  BEET
ASSAIL  MOISE  SOREHEAD
JAYWALKING  SHORELEAVE
ARNE  EOSIN  TELIC  MSEM
RICE  ROTC   WEST   AERO
```

10

```
MALE  CHARM  STALE  BOAT
ANON  RAMIE  EASES  ORSO
COFTHEWILD  QUIETONTHE
EXTRUDE  LITUP  ANISES
   ERODE  CHEEREDON
SADAT  SPOIL  ELONGATE
PIETS  STOSS  OCAS  FRA
ORCS  SHEN  RUN  STAT
REL  GEORGECMARSH  CEDE
TRISECTS  NOELS  ADORER
   NEARS  DANTE  ARIOT
PIERRE  MATER  ABROTHER
ARAG  THEVEYOFFEAR  ERA
GENE  ALI  IRAS  TBAR
END  FRED  HAREM  BAISE
DEFINITE  BONNE  RISER
   NOTESDOWN  TRAIL
CRONUS  ROLES  OSTOSIS
HUCINATION  THEWSTREET
ATTN  NOLLE  TEPEE  ERSE
SHAG  DIOLS  EMILS  DAIN
```

11

```
PALE  TOILES  ACTS  BONO
ERINGOBRAGH  MURPHYBED
LIFEOFRILEY  BOYCOTTED
OSF  SUIS  ROREM  CLEARS
TEETH  EHS  FUROR  ASIDO
ASYE  INSTS  ESSAY  NON
   AER  TOLEDO  PETS
SESSUE  EMINENT  SANDAL
IMPEL  SWATS  SST  LOOSE
NEL  ANT  THEM  HIBERNIA
ERIA  TOSEE  ASIDE  TENN
DANNYBOY  RICH  ELM  GIE
ILEDE  LNS  SLEDS  ARANS
EDSELS  CHATEAU  EYELET
   SLOE  ABSORB  DOC
SLO  DRAMA  DELVE  TARD
PANEL  GLENN  DII  SOLAR
OUTSET  ALGER  NOAH  AMO
IRISHROSE  WHEELBARROW
LIMERICKS  LEPRECHAUNS
SEEN  PTAS  YEASTS  IMAY
```

12

```
CASTOR  OWLET  LEDA  ABOVE
ASPIRE  RHINO  ECON  TANIS
SHALLWEDANCE  MOONSTRUCK
HER  ERRATA  PSALM  CURSE
   IRIS  PLANE  CANE
APE  STEN  NEALS  CALENDAR
PEDALED  TORTE  ARMED  REI
PLUMES  MOVIEMOVIE  HERA
LACED  REVEL  PEEL  BASIL
EGAN  MILAN  CURD  SOUSAS
SET  WILDHARVEST  AHOTEL
   INONE  EEL  NOTED
SNORED  THEGLASSKEY  TAM
ANGLER  ARID  MAILS  TOGO
CARLA  SCUD  MANSE  LIKEN
ERIE  THEEGGANDI  BEKIND
RET  STEER  HARDY  MATILDA
BRANCHED  CONGA  LUNT  LAY
   EARP  GAUGE  BEND
ASTRO  HURLS  MEARAS  MAD
ONTHEBEACH  THEFRONTPAGE
PALED  RICO  EOSIN  NEUTER
STORY  GRIP  RESTS  AMPERE
```

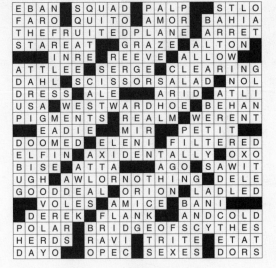

13

```
  I P S E   C L U       L A T H E  
  I T S E L F   T H I N I C E   A S H E N
R M I E S O F T H E N I G H T   P E E P S
I M B R O G L I O   T E N A N T S   M C I
M E N E     U A N G   O R A N   O P A L
E R I   L M E R G A N T R Y   T E R E T E
    S I E N A   M A R E     G A R S
  U N M E T   A B B E S S   A R N O
H O L I E R   A D I O S   A L L E G R O S
O N I T   Y N O T T H E B E S T   J I M
M A G S   A I R     S I A     S O L O
E T H   W A L T E R U S T O N   A N E T
R E T A I N E R   E R L E S   S E V E R E
  U R S A   A L E G A R   M O R E S
  S P E E     E V E N   S O L A R
S T M A R K   P T E R G R I M E S   M G M
P A Y S   P A R T   Y A R E   P O L A
E N L   E S C A R P S   V E N E R A T O R
E D I L E   T H E O R I E N T X P R E S S
D E F O E   S A S S O O N   U P T I L T
S E E P S     T S U     M O S S
```

14

```
A B U   G O P   C U B E S     A W A C S
B O N F I R E   A R O S E   P R E L A T E
A T T I R E D   M I S S A   U M P I R E S
S T I L L L I F E   C A L L L E T T E R S
E L L E S   C U T E   Y I E L D   S E E
D E W   A L M O N D   O S S   B I S O N
  R E F E R E E   S I G N S   P O L
  U R I S   R I L E   B O W L E R S
S C A L E D   B E L L L Y R E S   L I E N
H A L L   K A T E   S E A L S   O T T O
E M I L   B O N E     O G L E   O H I O
L E S E   O R A L S   S M E E   K E E P
L R O N   W E L L L I K E D   B A I R D S
S A N G R I A   E R I N   V E N N
  T O E   V A D I M   D E L I G H T
N I C H E   R E L   S P E A R S   O R A
O N E   G O A L S   S A N D   A G N U S
R U S S E L L L O N G   S K I L L L E S S
T R A M M E L   W O R S T   C E L E S T E
H E R O I N E   E R A S E   T W E E T E R
  D E G A S   D E F E R   S D S   Y E T
```

15

```
H A T   M A S H   T A M P S   P L O W
A B E D   E R M A   U N U S E D   R A V I
L O P E   A M O I   N A S S E R   O M E N
T R E V I N O G R A N T S T R A S B E R G
S T E E L E R   S S E   S T U A R T S
  L O S E   H Y D R A   S I T
O H I O   T R I M   K E E L S   T E E N S
P U M P S   S R O   R A I S E D   S L A P
T R A I N S   A T T U   N O V E L   I D I
  N E T   N E A P S   E T A   H I C
B O L G E R M I L L A N D B R A D B U R Y
I R E   R I O   C A I R O   I L E
L I V   S P O R T   U P O N   N E S T E R
L E E R   S L I E S T   V E T   S T R I A
S L E E P   A B N E R   E R I C   S A N G
  P R O   S T A Y S   R I V E
P A S T I M E   K I M   E N C L O S E
S T E I G E R C A M E R O N S E R L I N G
A R A L   G R O V E L   R O O M   E L I A
L I M E   A E R I A L   E M M A   R E D D
M A S S   D A D D Y   S E E S   R E S
```

16

```
  H A S H   S C O F F   S O W S   S T A S H
S E R A I   H U M O R   O P A R T   M A L T A
A L O N G   I R E N E   N O R I A   E L L E N
S L I G H T F I N G E R E D   G R O W L E R S
H O D   T O T O   M A N E   H E W   S Y N E
  R E L Y   A G A T E   S T R E E T
S O L A C E   P U N T S   E N S   F A R O E
K N I G H T M A R E   A S T R O   S T R O D E
A T R A   A R I S E N   E M O T E   T A E L
T O A S T   K I L T S   B R O K E R   E S T E
E P S   A L I A S   T H O R N   A V I A T O R
  B R A N S   C H O S E   S W A R M
B A R R I N G   S H E E T   N E A L E   A R C
A G E E   C U S T E R   O R A N G   S A M A R
B E A D   E P H A S   S N A P T O   D O N E
A N C H O R   O R S O N   B L A N D L O R D S
R A T E R   M C V   R E T I E   R A R E S T
  R E M A K E   V E R A S   M I C E
A L O R   O R S   S I Z E   S I L K   C P O
D E V I L I S H   P L E A D I N G L A D I E S
A M I N O   H O T E L   T O R A H   D I V E S
P U N G S   A P A C E   E V I C T   A V I L A
T R E S S   L S T S   D E S K S   Y A L E
```

17

```
  H A V E E   P R E V I N   B A K E R
  D O M I N I   R E V I S E   E L I D E D
R A M P A N T   I D E A L S   R E D U C E
A G E   B A H A M A   L A T H E S   C I S
C A R O L   E R A C L   N L A T   L A T E
E M I L E S   A T T E N D E E   M I T E R
D A C E   T A M E   A U E R   C O V E R T
  A T I P   B R E R   D U D E
  I N T E R O F F I C E   H I R E D M A N
A R I E L   C A I N O   L A S E R   E C U
D A N S E   O G D E N N A S H   A P A R T
A T O   C A P I O   S A N T O   T O N E S
M E N H A D E N   S C R E E N T E S T S
  A S I S   M A I D   O A S T
M E L O T T   C O R E   H A R P   A G A R
O V A L S   T U R A N D O T   S O L A N A
T I M E   P A R A   C E O R N   D E B I T
I D I   D E M I L O   O F Y O R E   R T E
V E N I R E   T I R A D E   N E T T I E R
E N A M E L   E S C H A R   E S T E E M
  T R A D E   S T A I R S   A T A L L
```

18

```
F L A P   C A T S   S C U D O   B R A T
R A N A   A L O H A   P A R E U   R I L E
A S T R O N O M E R   U P I N T H E A I R
  B A T E S   T A M E S   D I M
D E S O T O S   P I N O T   T A K E S O N
R A P I E R   S H E E N   S E R E N E L Y
O R A L S   F A I R W E A T H E R   V I A
P F C S   F O U L   R U E D   R E V S
O U I   R A I N O R S H I N E   L I N E S
F L O T I L L A   A T I L T   T A N T R A
  U R A L S   O V E N S   B O U G H
B E S E T S   I S E N D   S A N D S H O E
A T S E A   O N C L O U D N I N E   E R R
R O K S   I L K A   Y O R E   T A T A
D I I   U N D E R T H E S U N   D I V E S
O L E A N D E R   H E L O T   R E N E G E
T E S T I E R   S A B I N   S A L I N A S
  O T B   L A N E S   H E M A N
M O O N S T R U C K   S T A R R Y E Y E D
A R I A   E N T R E   A U D I O   S E R E
Y E L L   D A Z E D   B A N D   S P E W
```

19

```
SCAM  CHIP   KEPT    ETTE
OLPE  HULCE  IRAIL   CORE
REAR ADMIRALS NORMASHEARER
GENIALLY  PASSE   THINK
ORGANDY  ASH   LEAN
TEE  LANAI  SENDOFF
NEARED DISAPPEARANCE EARED
LESS  SETO   WRAY   ALAI
IMP SEARCHPARTIES ANEST
VOLTAIRE  SERGE  EXISTS
IRONY   PAU   SNITS
OPTING  CROCE  BADLANDS
BITTE THETHREEBEARS ERI
ELIE  FAUN   LAOS   TSAR
YEN MOMMIEDEAREST ROSY
IGNORES  FILET   PER
ORTS   FBI   LINEAGE
HOURI  HOUSE  PENTAGON
KINGOFHEARTS SPEARHEADING
IDEA  YESTE  TOLAN  OLDE
PERT  NEOS   EYRE   REAL
```

20

```
DONAT  FETE  RAMUS  MISS
GALAHAD ISER ADANO  AREA
ANIMATO STANDFASTHOWARD
LIVE  ANET  MAIA  TOON TIA
OEIL  AGUR  NEEDS  CLEFT
PLAYBALLLUCILLE  DELA
INDIANA  CORNETIST
BLIND  RIMS  ACHED  INTO
GRANDEST CUTGRASSGUNTER
NARC  STOL  SUIT  SAD RES
UNDUE  EKES  DRUID MIKADO
BLOWYOURHORNELENA
MANIAC  OSTEO  OGLE ERICA
ENE  TUE  TARP  ETAS  ARAB
DIGWELLESORSON APOSTATE
IMRE  ALVIN  ERIE  LOESS
CAESARIAN  TOPEKAN
TESS CROSSRIVERSJOAN
LASSO  MEADE  OLID  ORLE
EWE  NATO  VERO  OLGA SADR
HAILSTONEIRVING EMITTED
ARNO  ORGAN  ESAU SEALERY
REED  MOORE  RENE  SLEDS
```

21

```
SALMI  BATANGA  AGEE  BARS
ORION  URANOUS  PULE  ARAN
HUMBOLDTSGIFT PLIE RAVI
ONE  AGES  FOVEAE  EGGED
COLE  BARING  GREENE
GONEWITHTHEWIND  MOIST
APURE  HEARSAY  MOAN  OTO
SIDE  SHARE  LION  GALEN
CANDIDE  SPASM  OPINE
OTI  SOAVE  PELOTA  IVOR
NEKTON  EREMITE  ENLACERS
SLOAN  NACRE  REATA
REHEARSE  TRIESTE VALVED
IMET  STOOGE  HYRAX  AVE
MIDST  YIP  ORWOE ULYSSES
ELDER  RATS  ANWAR  HARM
SSA  AMIN  ASUNDER  MARIA
GALEA HUCKLEBERRYFINN
SPARED  NOTARY  HOOT
ALBEE  PAMELA  OBIT  LES
BELO  CASE  LIGHTINAUGUST
ABEL  URAL  ONCETOO SANTA
HERA  RELY  PETROLS  OTTER
```

22

```
CAD  HALOS  ASFAR  ASSET
ADE  EPODE  SHORE  CLIME
LOD  ALTER  PERIL  TIRES
ERI  RUTS  SCAMS  ASCENT
BECO MESEPARATED  ENDS
AMT  RATE  STALLED
NOTABLY  HER  SELMAS
OHENRY  HARI  TEARI  NTO
WMS  ELGIN  PLAN  EGOS
BAERS  SCALDS  PAULS
CROAK  UPPE  RCUT  ATSEA
CHINS  BARTOK  ROARS
CELA  NEAR  LEAST  CRU
LAM  BCHOP  DEED  SCARES
SENILE  SAM  STORAGE
ANYMORE  TOGO  MEN
ISIS  DIVISIONOFL  ABOR
MARPLE  UPTON  ATIP  ERE
ADELE  CLEAT  ELENA  RAN
MANIC  PASTA  LINEN  RTE
STETH  ARTES  MESSY  YES
```

23

```
SCENE  RIPE  IAN  BACCO
ALSEN  INSTANCE  NEWARK
RATHERFRIENDLY  ORALER
DIR  MALE  DIES  CRIMEA
IMAGINE  URE  SUITE
NINEE  SHORESAFIRE  RLS
INGEST  OVA  LADER  WAW
AGES  OGLERS  MIL  SLATE
EARLYREASONER  ATEE
SER  RNA  RANT  HUBERT
ONESTAR  BLOOD  GENERAL
LASHED  SOON  ONA  SLY
ATTU  OTTOSGOODWILL
RIOTS  HOD  SOLONS  EPPA
ION  ASEAL  TET  HUMORS
ANS  WHITEKNIGHT  MUSES
UNBAR  NOD  APPRISE
SENIOR  AVID  DREI  TES
REDONE  SAFERFORDRAINS
ORATES  PRESERVE  EMOTE
SOYAS  SAD  DYED  DENSE
```

24

```
MARM  OCA  ETAGE  YANK
ASEA  ROND  URBAN  MOVIE
JOHNDONNE  GLOBS  ARENT
ONATE  VANCE  MEE  RESET
RESUE  ECTON  BLANC
HARRYHOPES  MOONFOR
AMIN  EER  EGER  SOMEONE
SIN  JEDI  LEA  DIPSIN
HAGGIS  SALARY  ALLISON
AME  TROD  ABEL  ANE
SPASM  HINDSIGHT  IDEST
ION  YATE  THAW  MOA
PLASTER  GHOSTI ANDROS
PINTOS  HAN  LARS  EDE
ESKIMOS  IDEA  DCL  FIES
THEROPE  JOSIEHOGAN
RSVPS  NACRE  RISEN
SLIER  EEN  EDENS  ARUBA
NEGRO  NAOMI  REORDERED
INLAW  USUAL  SSNS  SERA
PAUL  PETAL  SST  TSTS
```

25

```
LASSO  REACT  BAKE  BEANS
ELATE  BELLOW  ELAM  RULEIN
ALBERTEINSTEIN  GENUINERISK
SEINE  IGET  KRONE  TWEET
EYED  TODO  SLATE  WEEK
CAN  NOTING  INGRAINED
RECKONED  FINGERLAKES  HUR
ALLOTS  RAFT  DEEPER  HERA
MAINLY  CANIS  TROD  LEROY
PINTA  CLINIC  STAND  TULIP
SEE  BRAIN  ENTWINE  ARETE
ABRIDGE  AIA  RAIMENT
ISLAM  LAPPING  BRED  HEW
STAVE  CLOSE  AMBER  LEVIN
HOWDO  CHER  STOOD  SAWING
ALOE  FLIRTS  ALOT  APRINCE
IDO  TRACYAUSTIN  THREADED
REDDEER  CLINGS  AID
REEK  FORAY  CONG  SAAR
SHANA  BELEM  LASH  INTRO
THOMASPAINE  MINNESOTAFATS
RETAG  ETTA  INTERIM  JULIE
FALSE  ASSN  GOYAS  FLEES
```

26

```
POMP  PATNA  SHEAF  ABRA
AGAR  ASHOT  WILCO  DRAW
ALLI  THEREDEEMER  VEIN
REINDEER  LADD  RELEASE
COR  MAINE  CARDED
SHOER  REISS  TORSO
PALOMA  SIRS  OAHU  EFGH
ASIF  GOODSHEPHERD  LEO
SHOPPING  TWA  TRAITS
EALING  OUI  ALFIE
MEKATE  OUTWITS  IMPEND
ALICE  LAE  HANNAH
LINENS  ACC  PASSAGES
LOG  THECHOSENONE  AIDA
STOP  ANTE  APAR  TENDER
FLAKE  SPLIT  ADENI
TAKEME  ATSEA  ORO
OVIDIAN  IGOT  PELLMELL
BING  LORDOFLORDS  ELIE
INGE  ERIES  ELIDE  GIFT
TESS  GAMMA  SALON  ASTO
```

27

```
MASTS  PARR  GLOB  DIALS
ACTUP  ALOE  IONA  EDDIE
LEONA  TUBA  FLED  LEAVE
IDLEROOMER  TAILBEARER
KRIS  MAO  SILT
RABBITS  BANFF  BEEHIND
EDILES  DEMAGOG  BRODIE
DAZER  RILE  ROAR  STYLE
OGEE  RESIN  ATLAS  ELLA
NETPROPHET  BESTCELLAR
UTE  IRA
GOODMANORS  WHITENIGHT
IPSE  STRIP  RAREE  BLUR
RECUR  SEAL  IVES  SEAMY
TRACED  SLINGER  HEARUS
HARETIC  STAHL  CALMEST
ROAN  HGT  CATV
SPIDERBYTE  WARDHEALER
LIBYA  BARI  IGOR  DRAPE
ONEND  ICER  NENE  GAMIN
TAXES  EKES  GEES  ELECT
```

28

```
AMATI  RAPT  ACTS  BASEL
CESAR  HIRE  FLOP  AMOLE
EASTOFEDEN  TARASBULBA
ALIENATES  SODABREAD
WIT  SAFES  ELL
CHOSEN  LII  MEDALS
PALLETS  WANDA  FORESAW
SHIED  PSI  NORMAN  VITA
CAVE  ORTS  ELGIN  OILER
EPOPEE  GOON  ISLAND
ERR  GREENMANSIONS  YES
NOTARY  LOAN  MARAUD
DOWSE  LIONS  DUKE  TYKE
AMIS  SEESAW  EMU  QUILT
LISENTE  ETAPE  MOURNER
LETTER  EKE  CONGEE
MIT  TEENS  TAV
SCREECHER  ADULATION
MAINSTREET  LORNADOONE
ENATE  OREL  ANNE  IRWIN
WALES  BOSC  CEOS  STATE
```

29

```
RAIN  TIDAL  FACTOR  STU
SAUCE  ADORE  ABRADE  SHUN
CITYRAILWAY  1000DOLLARS
USH  OGLES  STRIPS  EADIE
PEON  RESET  AILS  PATIENT
REPENT  ETRE  DOMINO
LABORED  WASPSCOUSIN  FLU
OTONOS  LISAS  ABNER  RBIS
SAYSO  CIDER  MSECS  FALSE
ELL  FORMERSPOUSE  GAMUTS
SLED  NEER  ALAE  GENIES
ROSES  TWILL  RANGE
POISED  BEAN  GATO  STLO
SANEST  CURVEINAROAD  YAR
OPERA  PANSY  OILER  RAPID
RAHS  DANCE  ANGER  SERENE
ELA  VICTORYSIGN  CHAMBER
LEAVES  APAL  HERDER
REFRIED  ALME  ELEMI  DESK
AVAIL  ALUMNI  AXELS  APE
LINKSDEVICE  ZEDINLONDON
ETES  OPENER  ARENT  PETIT
SAM  CARESS  RINGS  SAHL
```

30

```
DELI  IRATE  SHELF
POLES  GOBOS  REARERS
JACKOLANTERN  ENTREATY
ETTE  AROAD  ENVIES  NEA
ARR  SMART  OILS  SKIN
NOISE  LEIS  ASSE  STING
SONANT  SOIGNEE  SIAN
NELSON  NARDS  RETICLE
TENOR  LAY  PERONEAL
BESS  STATIC  ALDA  SNUG
LAW  ALICEBLUE  SRI
ARES  ABLE  NESTED  BEAN
SLEEPILY  COW  OMAHA
ESTRADE  SETAE  SUOMIC
WADE  MODERNS  BOBCAT
SLIPS  SIRE  EPSY  PIETA
PALE  MIKE  CRASS  CBC
AIL  TOTALS  POULT  ERIE
TRICHOID  PRINCEALBERT
SALERNO  OUNCE  FARAD
MINES  TETES  FROM
```

31

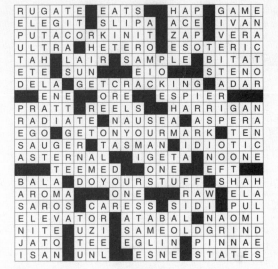

```
RUGATE  EATS   HAP  GAME
ELEGIT  SLIPA  ACE  IVAN
PUTACORKINIT   ZAP  VERA
ULTRA HETERO ESOTERIC
TAH LAIR SAMPLE  BITAT
ETE SUN  EIO    STENO
DELA GETCRACKING  ADAR
    ENE  ORE  ESPIER
PRATT REELS  HARRIGAN
RADIATE NAUSEA ASPERA
EGO GETONYOURMARK  TEN
SAUGER TASMAN  IDIOTIC
ASTERNAL IGETA  NOONE
    TEEMED ONE   EFT
BALA DOYOURSTUFF  SHAH
AROMA  ONE  RAW   ELA
SAROS CARESS SIDI PUL
ELEVATOR ATABAL NAOMI
NITE UZI SAMEOLDGRIND
JATO TEE EGLIN  PINNAE
ISAN UNL ESNE  STATES
```

32

```
ACARID TERSE  SESAME
NARINE ALIEN  ONAGERS
GRANDMAMOSES  BABERUTH
OIL  ESPIED SEMIS  DOE
ROSH HENRYAARON   MIKE
ALEA SORES STER  MUTED
SEAR IRED  TIED BORERS
    OARED  POD  TIER
GRILLE  COMEDIAN  AHAB
LONDON LOOM OVID  YALE
ABUSE BILLYJOEL  FALLA
ZERO SARI JARS SABLES
ESEL PRECOOKS  ARREST
    ODIN  SHE  DOGMA
SEAMAN ARAN HEME  HARD
ELROY SLAG GOFER  ABEE
LIEN WALTERABEL   MALT
AZO CAMUS OMBRES  SEE
HALDAVID ROBERTNATHAN
SECRETE ANIMA  ATREST
SCORED PETAL  PEEDEE
```

33

```
ANEW ICBM ANAT INA  AMY
NOME FOIE LASH MUMS LAE
THIEVINGMAGPIE PLAITING
SPAT MORES SMOLDERING
ASSET SORER HAS   EPI
WEIR ETUIS TROUTQUINTET
EGO PLATZ GRIEVOUS KAMA
SONGOFTHEFLEA ERI PETIT
    ROIS ROTT SEDATERS
SEVERN LOB  ADE  TOO
EPEE ONEWAY  ETYMOLOGY
THECARNIVALOFTHEANIMALS
AREBETTER MARIAN  AGEE
BAH EDT SAC   SCHEME
PATTERER  ASTI  STOA
ECRUS JET SWANOFTUONELA
STER SOCRATES NEAPS MOD
THEBUMBLEBEE TETRA MIMI
IBA EWE  DENIS  BEGAT
ICONOCLAST PERIS  PEAR
STREAKER THENIGHTINGALE
AGE TETE EONS HERE ETON
RES ROD DINE  TSAR REND
```

34

```
ROME  RITA  STAB   CROW
ELAM POCOS ARIES  AIDA
BARBERSHOP REDSNAPPER
ANNALEE HEDDA  TENSER
DIRT TBONE  CLIENT
OCTET FILAR  EASTS
UNHEROIC MILER TENURE
NEURON ABACK EVO   III
OXEN SOLARIA DEALINGS
STREETSMART HOLDINGS
SARC LASSO   OSES
DETRAINS PEANUTSHELL
CAROLINE FERRARO  ODIO
OVA NES ENTER  OARING
PISANS SCADS WALLETTE
STERE TERRI BASSI
MALONE NOELS  GRAD
SCARUM MEGAN  USHERER
LANDSCAPES STARSTRUCK
ATTA ETUDE TOLET ABAT
DORS ONER SNED  NAPS
```

35

```
OLID  GRUFF   COO HATED
COSA RUPEE SOUL  ANWAR
HOLYROMANEMPIRE  POESY
STADIUMS LIENS SPINES
ROPY PIXES  GLINT
CAPETS DINED FEALTIES
HULAS MINGDYNASTY  ELK
ITEM FIDO  ENTE  STLO
MOI OLDSTONEAGE  BAHIA
ESSAYIST REELS CANCEL
TWEET FLEES  MORTE
SPOORS ERODE FERMENTS
KICKS LEAPYEARDAY  TEC
INEE YARN  NEIL  PULE
MEN MESOZOICERA  ARRAN
PRESUMES INANE PREYED
EATER FLIRT  DOGS
TAPPAN LIEGE SITUATED
AHOOT YEAROFTHEHEGIRA
NACRE ANTS OVINE  ERIN
ASHES WAS RAVER  DECK
```

36

```
FEEDA VIAL RICER  REBS
OLDER ANTI ERASE  IDEA
PIERCESRECIPESPIECERS
SARA VEE  NANA  CONES
NOES EDDIE UFO   STY
FROGS TWAIN  ATILT
REDEALTRELATEDTREADLE
AMID OHARE  ODES  BIAS
YON EGIS AESIR  ELVIS
ARAN  ALLIN  SLOANE
SPARINGRASPINGPARINGS
ARISES ABIES  AROD
LIMES SPANS ATTY  SIL
AMEN RIIS OSIER  VOTE
DERIVESDEVISERREVISED
COMAS ETTAS  AROMA
SOS LIL ASSET  ECRU
ELIOT ATTU   ORE  LIFE
PLEASERLEAPERSREPEALS
AINT TIDAL WISE  INNES
LEAS HOARS EGAD  ATSEA
```

37

```
RUCHE EBBED CEDAR SHEEP
ASHES TULLE RNASE TILDE
SHORTFOROLIVEDRAB IDLER
PESO LIGNE ASSN SARDINE
ARE AILED ROUE TRESS
IMPERSONALPRONOUN
CASSIS ROSS ROMP PES
ASIAN CAGE MICA SARAH
SYMBOLFORALUMINUM TITO
TELE ILMEN NOSES BOOMER
STALEMATE ACIS AIRPORT
ANGELESORALAMOS
STRIVES ROVE ORATORIOS
CRAVED ONONE TRINI ERST
ROTA USASERVICEACADEMY
EVENS CITE ITAS DENIM
WED MOUE SANA FLEECY
CONTRACTIONFORIAM
CARTE CHAR OVOLI TAP
BALIHAI CANT TRIBE SRTA
ANISE SOUNDOFHESITATION
NEVER MUSES HOGAN DONNE
DRESS STELA CROCS SPEED
```

38

```
AMERICAN ENAMEL SABE
CAROTENE CANIDAE CLAM
TITUSANDROGYNOUS ATTU
ALEE SADE SON GARRETS
REMADE NOSH AARE
ANIMAS THEWAISTBAND
HOSES TAO KNEE TIO
EMBRACEABLEEWE ASKING
ADA ALLS RISE LOGE
DESPOILS LUGE AMAIN
ABROOMOFONESOWN
VISOR ETAT DIALECTS
SPAN AUST LIEN ORE
CAGERS THELASTRACCOON
ARA HEAT ORD ARTIS
RABBITDELUXE GROSSE
BOON OREL STEERS
LONGEAR ATA ANTE OTTO
ALDA SINGININTHETRAIN
PAIR PNEUMAT RETRACED
PSAT GREASE ELSINORE
```

39

```
PASCO AGES BRAVO SWAG
ALTOS ROSH RESIN OHNE
PIERS TUNE ASIDE DADO
ACREATUREWITHFINS TED
SEEL ARM ENS DEMISE
LIL AINT KIT MUS
SICKANDTIREDOFITALL
BEE YEDDO ENERO TIME
REAL DESI ATONERS DNA
ALLAH DELI TRUCE
STOPSMOKINGSOMUCH
ERATO EGAL THOLE
HOF NEUTRON ERNS ONYX
ALOU ADIEU NEONS DEE
PERSONIVETOLDTHISTO
ATM OES PEAR VEE
MEDINA AHA APE BAIE
EAR ISUSEDINBILLIARDS
AGIO SNARE TINE BLOAT
NEVA ADROP ODEA ADORE
TREK MOIST SUDS RIMES
```

40

```
WARE BOAT OSCAR AGAS
ADEN IRMA ATONAL DONE
TALC BEAM SERGIO SLID
CHYOU STEP PPENWO ATE
DRS ODOR SLG LUNAR
ANCESTOR NIT OLAFS
REO TONYS COSTAL ALAS
COLLEGE ALEPH STE ONT
EPISTLE ALSOP ANA
AIDA EMU ASTRA SMITER
STEPB ALLSTEPFO OTHER
PATSYS SITAR IRT SESS
ILE SUSAN MANASSA
RIS TEP ERASE METTLES
ECTO NIPSEY SLATE ADO
ASONE SID INSPECTS
START ENA NEST EFG
OWN EPLADD STEP ORDWI
NINE RENDER ORAL ELEV
ANIL ESCORT PALE TILE
REEF SENSE SLOT SITS
```

41

```
SASH ADAM OASIS RAP AFL
ECHO BEDE FLUME OVA LAY
CHERCHEZLAFEMME MASSEUR
TEASHOP TIE MISEENSCENE
DAR DRAIN NOTER
PEON MAB STELA SUPER
BASE ACACIA NABS BATE
INPUT DEBUG TILER RAN
LARVAL ALOE TETEATETE
TIRADE DRAMA ADMIX
METE GEESE RIPEN SPACES
ALD RAISONDETRE EMU
CAESAR TRACE REARM SLUR
CURIA CARPI RECALL
CLOISONNE SITE REVEAL
LAR SOARS TITHE MONTE
UMPS NUIT CAFTAN ICED
BESOT SNIDE ELS BRED
FABLE TREAT DEF
MESALLIANCE NEE RETAILS
EXURBAN CHARGEDAFFAIRES
SIP OSE AIMER ALDA RANT
STS TER ANTSY MAST ENDS
```

42

```
ORCA CAMP AGAME SMOG
PALS AGAR LAMINA TARA
ADOS RENO AREMET ERAS
LINESFROM BNAI TRAINS
SIESTA RETAIL GEOLOGY
SORE NOMS ERMA
THEONELLAMAHESAPRIEST
HENRY SUDS PACT OSSA
ARTS MAME ENSUE KNOWN
TOO EASE CLEO SPLIT
ADULTS THELAMA RECESS
ROTHS OREL SPEE ROE
SHAPE MAVEN SIRS PIPE
GAGA PILE BCDE ARCHI
THETWOLLLAMAHESABEAST
ONES RANI SPOT
IMPARTS FREEZE POETIC
CIARDI SLAW OGDENNASH
ANIL ARCANE PARA SNEE
NONE CHANGS ODOR ETRE
AMES ONSET DIPS SEEK
```

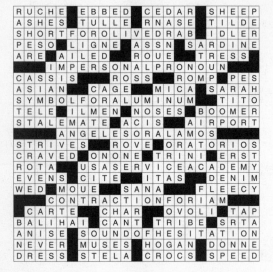

43

```
SUPS  CHAMP   WOES
CANIO REGALIA IDLER
FAULTS ORATORS LAURIE
ALCOHOLWONTPASSMYLIPS
CLEOS EDNA  ETA   APT
TARS BASS OPERA HALLE
ETON PRATT BETSYS
APO ISTS AGRA UDO
TOBACCOISPARTOFMYPAST
ELLIS MEAN RAP KIR
TEAL ARIEL CHARY HERA
HAT DEL LAIC DENIM
EXERCISEWILLSHAPEMEUP
ART ARAM SLAM SSS
GRATES TRAMS BLOW
RAREE MEDEA DUAL AFRO
ISR TAS CONN PILOT
THISDIETISTRULYMYLAST
SEVERE AVERAGE ALINES
RARER EOLITHS GONGS
LEWS LOESS INGE
```

44

```
LEAD SHOES SEPAL ELIA
ETRE TORRE ALULA RUNS
SOAPYOPERA NUTTYHATCH
ENSLAVES LADDS SASHAY
ALES PARSE OLE
DOWNER SANTO COVERSUP
OBIES DIRTYFARMER WRY
LEND SOOT HOAR TEAL
LAD STONYMASONS BEANO
SHYSTER AMOLE CARTON
JOINS SNIPE CURRY
SPARES DUETO ARRESTS
TIMES MUDDYTURTLE HIT
REMS FEDS NOES SINE
ETE HEADYWAITER BEREA
WARRANTY ORNIS PENTAD
ETC SOAVE REED
TRADER SIDLE TEAROSES
BONYSETTER STOCKYFISH
ALOE SAUNA TORTE FATO
REND SADAT SNOOD SMEW
```

45

```
ANTARES ADDEDUP PACT
NEOLITH ETIOLATE OMAHA
TAPIOCA SMOCKTURTLESOUP
ITEM METO ERSE SAMBA
BOOBOO ERI NIPS SPUR
ONS OPUS ADENT AIL SRI
VIM MER SLIVERANDONIONS
ELATING COTERIES WARNS
RELEASE SHORTER ESTE
TAKERS ARSIS SKUA SPA
HESS ASTA SEATINGPLACES
ACHE ASK ENE SORI
SCORNONTHECOB NESS PLUS
PEP ONUS ROPES STORED
BRET ENTITLE AMERCED
SLATS AGITATOR BECAUSE
SMASHEDPOTATOES LOT TAR
HOW LOP EGERS KENO SUM
EONS FRET ESS OILERS
ATRIA STEW OMNI TACO
SHARDBOILEDEGGS NATURAL
SKEIN TELEMARK ENACTED
ENTS EXTRUDE NAPKINS
```

46

```
SPATS EGAD VENT THESE
CACHE GOBI ADAH HELLS
ATREE AUBERGINE EBLIS
THEBRIDGE OUTOFAFRICA
EERIE ABES TILE
CHARDS DIVES ROWANS
HEAL NORTHOFBOSTON
ENRICO GRIT ERRED TOE
CRONUS YOD PLIED DANA
KINGSHIP TWIGS DEREK
APASSAGETOINDIA
ICBMS LYRIC NOONTIME
CARE CADET GPA MAHDIS
IRA CANON RAIL SHILLS
ENGLANDMADEME NENE
REGINA EMITS LIVRES
SIDI GMAN CAIRE
ODESSATALES DUBLINERS
DIVOT CROSSWORD DIXIE
DROME HORN EURO ECOLE
STEER YEYE BRYN SEDER
```

47

```
DONWAN BIPEDS BASILS
OLEATE SELENIC AGORAE
GEEGEE ACEROSE DILATE
MODEL ATHOUSANDCLONES
ASS INUSE REDEEM
ACED HEARSTS OSAN
LEAP AIT ESSA SENEGA
ONBORROWEDTHYME TSARS
BLASE ALOE SILKS MET
STAB ANES LEA FIES
HELLODALI ALLMYSUNS
SAME NOM CAVE OURS
EME BYLAW LOAD NOTER
PANDA THECORNICEGREEN
ATTUNE RUNE PAN ERGS
LESS PLANTED TICS
THIEVE ABCDE AGT
THEBEGGARSOPRAH RATER
RESIDE TIERODS BETONY
AMANDA ATLASES BALLES
MISSAL REDDEN SLIEST
```

48

```
PALO RISER MIST MARSH
CLIV ENTRE INTO OPINE
BIZETSBEES CHOPINSPAN
STARRIER CLAIR STEEPS
HINDEMITHSMYTH
SHAMS ANDS ASLOPE
CHANS PLOD SCH YVOIR
RING SAAR TAUROS ARGO
ORD PUCCINISPOOCH TED
PREPARE ANCES AUGERS
LEIF SLIDERS LIAR
ROSTRA HAVEN ALLYSON
ASH SCHUBERTSSHOE PTO
ITAL EELERS WEEP PORE
DINER SAL NORM ARRAS
ADDONS DEER PLATS
BEETHOVENSBAIT
AMEBAS HATED AERATORS
MOZARTSART LISZTSLIST
ERRED ANTE EDSEL ESTO
NEARS WEED DOYLY REUP
```

49

```
PEACH   GROPE   WHIG  STROP
USQUE   IEROE   THANE CROCE
BOURBONREDS     RIVERMOUTHS
SPAT  AGUA  CASES    ATCOST
      SEXAND VODKA DUCK
VAT RAMS AINEE  MASH     SEZ
ENHANCE  BRANDYWINE     CAA
CORNEA  WAILS     ENTR  PORN
TIONS  BANDS  IMAGE    PATTI
ONUS  RATE    SOVS   MARCHE
RTG  CAKESANDALE    MARTHAS
HOOVER   CITAT   MALAYA
BOTTLED  HOPSCOTCHES    NED
ASHTON  CARP   OCAS    MDSE
CHEER  FANNY  GOGOL    CASTE
KERR  AURA  TOKAY    HEROES
TAY  GRENADINES    DELUDES
OSE  SHOT  DINED  BAAL   AME
BEAR   LAVER    MUNROS
AGREES  LIMES   IBIS    ABCS
CROSSTHEBAR    MAXBEERBOHM
RESET   ANENT   EWELL  ULNAE
EYETO  MALT   XERES    MEADE
```

50

```
STAB   DOOM    JUT    RABBI
CAME   ALTA    KATE   ELLIN
OXEN   REINE   AMEX   AVERS
WINNINGCOLORS    ASSAULT
    EVE    FIVE    ASTOR
PISTIL  LAZIEST   ONEGIN
ARETE  WARADMIRAL   ZERO
LEA  SAIDA   TIRES    NAT
ENTS  SPENDABUCK    ACUTE
DETESTED  AGAPE   ALLIED
   LITER  CROSS   GAVIN
OPENER  PAINE   BARONESS
HOSEA  SUNNYSHALO   TRAP
ALL  MARLA   ELAND    IDI
REEF  BOLDFORBES   ROSIE
EDWINA  EARLIER   CORKED
   DETAT   AINT    HOD
NEEDLES  SUNDAYSILENCE
AXILS  KIND  STALL   RAUL
MINEO  EROS  ELUL    EZRA
ETERN   WEB   DUTY   DIEN
```

51

```
WIMP   LEDA    ROSE   RANSOM
ARIA   IRON    ITER   EROICA
RATIONALNUMBER    FAITHS
NEEDLE   TOPF  SAGEBRUSH
    LAGS   DIB   SIRI
SQUALL   BARRE   RECASTS
NOUNS  ACUTEANGLE    CHAN
ALIA  ECALE  ICES    HARE
BECKONING  ADAM   EMERGE
KANSAS   LEM   PROSPER
DIS  CULTUREDPEARL   CTS
EDIBLES  MIR   CROTCH
WELLED  SPAT  BOARSHEAD
LAVA  SPIN  BOLLS    IERI
ATEN  SMARTMONEY   URSAE
PERCALE  ELAND   ZIPPED
    VIAL   YIN   BENT
WISEACRES  DEAR   COARSE
ADESTE  PENETRATINGOIL
NECTAR  ERIN  ADIT    IONA
ESTERS  RAPS  NYSE    OMEN
```

52

```
AVEC   GETS    ALOHA  MELEE
RARA   IGOT    NEFUD  ALOST
CLARABOWANDARROWSMITH
ESSENES   RAIN   TRITONES
DEEDS      LIRA    SELE
    EPA   IRONS    DRAMAS
FULBRIGHTANDEARLYWYNN
ITER  THE     TREY    ARTE
NENES  AMOS  MAIL    BRAID
ARIELS  ANNIE   IAL
LINDAHUNTANDPECKINPAW
   TET   PAEAN   AMOUSE
RELAY  IDES  ACRE    PONTI
ATOM  ECOL   OLD     STER
HUGOBLACKANDBLUEBEARD
SIERRA   SCORE    LEA
    ITUP   EMIA    RASES
TEREBENE  RIEN   DORMANT
SPIDERMANANDBOYGEORGE
PETER  ELATE   APER   REEL
SEANS  TEPEE   GERE   TELE
```

53

```
LONA    PACE   LETAT    CPA
ALAI   SODOM   ALIBI   AHEM
UMPS   TROOP   PECULATION
REPLANT   TITHES   TROMPE
ADIEU   IBERIA    PETRELS
SON  BOAR  IMPS  EDT    RET
GAUL   ACCEPTOR    HEADY
LITTRENCH   DYER     HOR
INURN   ETON     DROUGHT
TURISTA  INA  BEAR    SOY
ART   ELFCENTERED     PRE
ELA  RELY  DOC    DECAPOD
DEBUSSY    RABE     AGING
INE   ELLA    MARTMONEY
AMEER   TROUBLES    YEGG
MOR  AKA  SMEE  EERO   CAA
ELASTIC    BAGELS   USERS
RESEED   ELEMIS   SATANIC
CREWDRIVER   OTTER   ITSO
EARN   OBESE   NOONS  LETT
STS    WANER   SPEE   SRAS
```

54

```
APACHE  SCOUR   ULNAR  CATO
COCOON  CORSE   NIOBE  ISEE
TRIPLETHREAT   FLYCATCHER
ITS   TRAUMA   ABATE    DOA
    VII   DRUID   SCALLOP
DAG  WANTS  OGLED   ABLAUTS
ITERATE  ONTHEDOUBLE   TET
ATTIRE   TREAT   DALE   RILE
PUTON  MOTET  SPORE   BONER
ENOS   SLIDERULE    MELLON
REF  ANGLE  ARES    MARLENE
ISLETS   CRIED    HEREOF
ABRADES   COOS   NONET   TWO
RASHER   HOMEGUARD    AFAR
ASTIN  PLATE  AVISO   GRIND
BIBB  DEER  CLEAT    MANEGE
ILA  DIAMONDHEAD    COROLLA
CASTERS   NORIA   SCANS  DEL
REENTER    SANER    UNO
NEF   ALIGN   ESTATE    OCA
GOTOBATFOR    INTHELONGRUN
AVER   REESE   NORMS  NIACIN
PANS   MARSE   GROOT  EDGARS
```

55

```
PARR  FEOD    ECHO   WAAC
OBOE  ASTIR   STOOP  ERDA
LEWDBROODESCHEWEDFEUD
ADELE PEARWOOD NETTLE
   IRA SCOUTS  TEASELS
REAGENT  TUNE  MINN
EIGHTAWAITGREATDEBATE
ANET  ECCE   SNA  RBIS
LED  LONE  LAPIN  BOATS
    LENT SIERRA CLICHE
WISEGUYSCRITICIZELIES
REEVES  TARGET  CASS
INTER MARSH  AIRS  DON
NCAR  ARC  CAPE   DINE
GEESEFLEECEOBESENIECE
    REED HAMS TOASTER
SPHERES  LISPER  NBA
TRAVEL DEMEANOR OLDER
AIDEDELAYEDSTAIDBLADE
AMEN  RENTS  SEDGE OMEN
TEST  SAKE   ESSE  WEND
```

56

```
RAMP   DRAB   MARC    CHE
ARCH   CEARA  OREAD  BLOB
GIGI   ARNOLDSEDDY  LAMB
EARLES TOLU  DENTURES
   AIRE  MARCO  TEREK
NEWPORTS DELAYS OLSEN
ODS  STOOD  RITE  PADRE
PUTS ADDON  VENTS  WARE
ACUTE DAMA ESTATE  NED
REGENTS ITO WATERBED
   ITEM NORMA  ULNA
ANGELICO  BAR  MEISSEN
ONO RAKISH IRAS  EATME
EELS REEFS  LEVAR  LEES
RATAL  LAUD NAREW  VET
ARETE HOTAIR STARTERS
   SINCE SNEER  DERN
SENATORS TWOS  ENESCO
OMIT WILDESOSCAR  ACOR
RICE LOUIS  RIALS DADA
ELK   TEXT  DENY  STEN
```

57

```
ERICA  RAND  ASH  SEATO
RADAR  ABIE  REE APACHE
AMELIAJBLOOMER  CARTER
PALOMAR  LORDRAGLAN
   ASE  BAER  OMOO
PERSONAGES  ESSE  FLIP
OBE  LILT  SLIER  SANE
LOSS NELLIEMELBA  ARNE
ELIA ORLE RICKY  ANGEL
DINMONTS MILTY ALDERS
   ULES DOTES  SPEW
BIPEDS TOURS SPECIALS
IDOLS TANTE OPEC  CHOP
TEEM JOHNHANCOCK  HARI
TATA ALOES ATOI   INE
SLAV ITER  RELETTERED
   ERLE  FLAT  ERN
MARIECURIE  ACCEDED
SAVIOR NICOLASCHAUVIN
EJECTS ICH  OTIC DRIER
NARKS  TAU  GASP SELMA
```

58

```
 HIGHS  SCALE  ROOM  PTAS
MOSAIC ERRING INRE  RARA
BILLCOLLECTOR CURTREPLY
ASEA TEETH ROSES  HOLIES
STS  PLACE SMUT  ROBINS
   GRANT NOISY SODOM
STRAINS ARTEXHIBIT  GAB
PRIZED PATTY  ELEC  PRIE
LACES RULES TREKS HOARD
ACHS DOPE  SOUPY  LANCES
TED IRAACCOUNT  CARTED
   ENDURE EFLAT GOSSIP
PSALMS SALLYFORTH  ETA
PASTES SCALY  OWES  DRAM
AREAS WHIRL PEONY BOISE
GIRL BAIT  LILTS  SABOTS
EST DONNYBROOK STRIDES
   WROTE REVUE SPREE
IDIOMS ACES SLOES  PSI
OCELOT SATIN APART SEED
WILLPOWER PEARLNECKLACE
LETA WENT ESPRIT HAILTO
SRAS NETS  TESTS  YIPES
```

59

```
ROMP  SHAGGIER  SHAFTOE
OMAR  TORRANCE  TOLLAGE
BITOBETTERBUTTERBUYER
STEPON STIRS HESS   LEI
   LOTTA ASE FIVE  POSE
SEASHORESHELLSELLER
ELSA REX  DUET  EOS
LISLE ATAP  CALLSFORTH
FEE ROSEMARY EAST  OHO
   AIR MILE ASP  SLOW
PECKOFPEPPERSPICKER
JOKE LOS  ALBI  SLY
APE IGOR EYEOFTHE  HUD
MIDSTREAMS  ARTE  MEANY
   OLA NOTA ENA  NUDE
SOLDIERSSHIRTSSEWER
COIN INON SAG  HENRI
INN BEAU DINNA  PEGTOP
SIGHINGSCISSORSSEIZER
COLETTE PETERIII  ZENO
ONENESS RUSSELLS  EROS
```

60

```
AGLET  ARECA  TABS  WEST
SLIER  DEMOS  ITEA  HSIA
COCKANDBULLSTORY  ITEM
ORE  ALES  OKAPI  STONE
TINTAGEL  PEN  NOTEPAD
SASHAY  SEWINGBEES
   SEER PANE SAO  IAL
   CONTRA  REELECTS
AMOK REDHERRINGS  PHEW
RAPACITY  CORSO  SHERE
ATENT  MEHTA  RAREE
RUNGS SCAPE  ARSONIST
AREA WELSHRABBIT  TEAS
TERRARIA  SLEEPY
OYE MCS  OATS  LARA
HORSEPOWER  BAKERS
AVOCETS RAG  BELCANTO
MINOS CHORE COSA  TIC
ALOU HOUNDSTOOTHCHECK
SLUR URGE  TRITE PARLE
SERT STET  SENSE ASSET
```

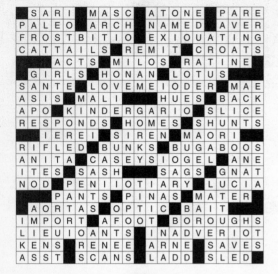

61

```
SARI  MASC  ATONE  PARE
PALEO ARCH  NAMED  AVER
FROSTBITIO  EXIOUATING
CATTAILS  REMIT  CROATS
    ACTS  MILOS  RATINE
GIRLS  HONAN  LOTUS
SANTE  LOVEMEIODER  MAE
ASIS  MALI  HUES  BACK
APO  KINDERGARIO  SLICE
RESPONDS  HOMES  SHUNTS
IEREI  SIREN  MAORI
RIFLED  BUNKS  BUGABOOS
ANITA  CASEYSIOGEL  ANE
ITES  SASH  SAGS  GNAT
NOD  PENIIIOTIARY  LUCIA
PANTS  PINAS  MATER
AORTAS  OPTIC  BAIT
IMPORT  AFOOT  BOROUGHS
LIEUIOANTS  INADVERIOT
KENS  RENEE  ARNE  SAVES
ASST  SCANS  LADD  SLED
```

62

```
SALEM  LENA  MARC  SAHL
MEDICI EXALTS ELIA ALOE
TWEEKSWITHPAY TBASEHITS
NELS  SIDRA  TRESA  TRACES
SRA  MILEA  BOUT  LAUREL
GALEN  TAUPE  FINCA
CATERED  TWAYSTREET  TRI
ADONIS  MOODY  AUNT  STEN
PINES  CORNY  PLIS  BEHAN
ROTS  CORA  ELECT  CAVILS
ASH  THANDEDSAW  HIKERS
EGRESS  SATIE  LEGEND
BAREST  TFACEDLIAR  STA
ORIENT  POETS  LIRR  AVIV
NOSED  OATS  SPINS  ABONE
TOLD  ASTI  PLATE  ROUTER
ODE  TPIECESUIT  CONTEST
GAPES  MANTA  HAYES
DARNER  MIGS  PAPAS  STR
PESETA  DIANE  OUZEL  EIRE
TWHEELERS  TNOBLEKINSMEN
GEEK  ETAL  STROLL  SETOSE
SYRS  DAME  BESS  MOONS
```

63

```
SOFAR  SLAGS  TST  ADD
MALONE  ITALIC  ACRANIA
ATONAL  DINERO  KEATING
LORDGIVEMEPATIENCE
SEI  FINITENESS
GONG  FASTERFASTER  VEE
AGEES  SEABEE  TOD  CANT
NEWTON  ELBE  PER  BUS
GETAHORSE  HOP  LATINO
MORAE  ADAR  ERIVAN
SOSO  WHENDOWEEAT  TETE
OLIVIA  OINK  SISIS
WATERY  KNT  STRUTHERS
SOT  PRO  HAHA  PEORIA
SOON  CIA  COLADA  SRTAS
URU  HONKHONKHONK  TELS
MOTHERHOOD  TEC
ANDIWANTITRIGHTNOW
MIDIRON  REINED  LARINE
MAILING  STORES  ERODED
ENG  SSE  ESSEN  RYDER
```

64

```
ABED  FLINT  TAIL  CAST
LONI  MOOLAH  ORNO  ALTO
ONCEONCRETE  LACS  RAIL
ENSHROUD  IBOUGHTABIRD
ALPS  SOOT  CRO
SHARE  RENAIL  CHANTED
PEND  SPUR  TSELIOT  ONO
RAI  LENA  NAIR  STUN
ITSPRICEISOONDIDLEARN
THELOCK  TAROS  ATLEE
ANES  SATON  PANS
BRAID  RISEN  INDULGE
WASNOTHIGHSOTHENIPAID
AMOS  RAIN  RATA  RBI
NAN  BERSERK  ITAL  HEEL
ARGONNE  DIRGES  POSSE
FAT  CIES  SGLS
WHATIOWEDONA  SPLATTER
HOPI  NATE  GRECIANERNE
ITEM  NDAK  LELAND  LOTI
MEDE  JETE  EDITS  SPED
```

65

```
BELA  PHONO  THRICE  CUL
ICON  RADAR  WEIGHT  ARI
BLUEHOMEHOTANDLICENSE
BASTES  RUNE  SUM  STAN
STY  SPA  MONEY  SECCO
USERS  ORAD  ROUNDS
BUTTERLOVINGHICANDEYE
AHEM  SEDAN  SOPH  OSAR
RUMOR  NALDI  OPEC  SENT
ERASED  OILS  ELA
DUSTSUGARGATORANDFISH
ERR  ONES  TURNTO
SKID  TEAM  GRAIN  NOLAN
ANNE  AGUE  OGLES  NERD
COFFEETOSSFLESHANDTEA
OBERON  NINO  ARRAS
RANTS  CERES  UDI  AHA
OBEY  HEP  UNTO  IAMBIC
TINSAUCESAMTAIANDCAKE
INC  ASTRAL  ELSIE  ITER
CEE  RESIDE  REELS  VERB
```

66

```
ABEAM  MAGIC  CAPE  BRAY
LEGREE  AMISH  ADEN  ALICE
PEARLYEVERLASTING  NUDES
END  DEMENT  SIHON  VAT
LIN  ETNAS  WIDOWS
HAMSTER  SLIER  FETE  HOG
AVOCET  SWEETWILLIAM  ILO
LAURAS  PORGY  AARE  STIR
LINER  SURFY  RAPID  PIECE
ALTE  MIRS  CECIL  DARWIN
MSA  RAGGEDROBIN  ORGEAT
INHUME  ROUEN  ORIENT
ONEIDA  BOUNCINGBET  ELI
ARLENE  VINGT  ARID  GRAS
SPADE  RANEE  REMAT  GELID
THUS  SONG  AIRED  CANINE
OER  BLUEEYEDMARY  AEOLIA
RUE  LASS  AEDES  SPLAYED
SLEEVE  ERRED  EAT
PAS  ENDIN  DENNIS  ALE
SERAC  CONFEDERATEVIOLET
EPOCH  BLEU  UKASE  EVADER
TACT  SAAL  METER  AROSE
```

67

```
AMISS  IDLES  GLIM   DORM
DANCE  LOIRE  RIRE   EPEE
INTENTIONALWALKS    VANS
MARNIE MASERS ENFOLDS
ETOILE    GENES  DEUT
    CIME  ERENOW    LEVEE
ASS   TEND   EARLDOMS
DAILYDOUBLE  MAROC  LIP
EBRO   SMEES  ALAMO  ELY
PROOFS ASTERN GEUM
TASMAN SMU  ETD  ONAGER
    SIAM  EPOPEE  STRABO
PAM  RIATA  DRABS  GULL
OBI  CLEAR  DOUBLEBOGIE
DECLASSE    YALU   ESS
SLEET  LABIUM  MICA
    ACME  TERNI  JOCOSE
STASHED TROGON AVESTA
LASH DESIGNATEDHITTER
ARTE  OMAR  IVIED  NAIRN
GOOD  CAGE  NACRE  ALANS
```

68

```
ACCRA  RIIS  BAALS  ADDS
BROAD  OMNI  ASSES  GARE
MIZZENMAST  SHOWWINDOW
STYE  CART  STER  RASPS
    RHONE  BOER  BEET
BLASE  TARTS  SEL  EWER
LAP  IRA  GAT  STRIA  ILA
UMP RECONNOITERED  TIP
FELL  VRAI  NOLA  MAHDI
FRIARIES  PUKKA  FISHED
    CRASS  CITEE  SARTO
HOAGIE  MOLAR  AUREOLES
ARTES  DARE  EYRA  NDAK
JAI OSUUNDERGRADS  ITA
JNO  NAVVY  LAG  HSM  NET
IGNS  GEE  SAYSO  EAGRE
    PSAT  MANE  PATEN
ASCAP  FAYS  PALE  AMMO
SHORTSTORY  IQQUESTION
KOBE  MOXIE  DRUM  STERE
SOBS  SEXES  OSES  TONER
```

69

```
    VON   ASST  CASS  PLEA
MADE  IGETA  LEHAR  RASP
ACES  SEAOF  AGAMA  ETTE
LUSTFORLIFEWITHFATHER
TUSSAH    CET   STIFLE
SMA  SYNE  TOO  LIONESS
    THEEGGANDICLAUDIUS
MAAR  TAEL   AFR   DUNES
ANGELSTREETSCENE
REINA    ANA   OUR  TRAP
ALLTHEKINGSMENINWHITE
TEES  EON   TOR   ERNIE
    LITTLEPRINCEIGOR
ALTAI  ORA  EMIR  CONS
WINDSOFWARANDPEACE
LETMEGO  AME  ISNO  SAG
    INDRAS  OOH  ISOLDE
HEARTOFDARKNESSATNOON
ANTA  AEIOU  ARIOT  TUNE
IDOL  DIGNE  TONLE  ACIS
LOPS    TEED  EDGE   PHS
```

70

```
JIBED  PACK  DAMNS  COERCE
ORALE  OGRE  ONAIR  ORRERY
SAULBELLOW  NORMANMAILER
HEMS  LIEN  SATIE  OPT  SEE
    MATTE  OTHOS  BEE
SEG  ATES  ABIE  POTS  AMA
TREATER  GEORGEADE  ALAN
RAREES  DARIN  AWRY  DENT
ASTRO  ROGET  ABETS  COXAL
NERO  BEREA  SPORE  GARAGE
DRU  ROBERTBURNS  SERENER
    DIANE  LEI  PRIED
HEEDFUL CHARLESLAMB  EMS
UPSETS  LAIRS  NOONS  DRAW
FATAS  MURRE  ATLAS  HOPPE
FUEL  ANTE  IVIED  CAROLE
ELIS  ESGARDNER  WHIPPET
DEN  RACE  ETRE  DAIL  ESS
    ATA  MANES  DEGAS
ADO  NAR  ENTRE  EVEN  OMOO
JAMESBALDWIN  GEORGESAND
AMATOL  LIANE  ARTE  FAZED
RENAME  BARED  DEED  TRESS
```

71

```
TAINT  TROMP  CROC  BARE
ASTOR  ROVER  AIDA  ELEV
CHAPERONAGE  PROPAGATE
TELESAVALAS  PERIMASON
    SEE    IRS    TINKLE
APEXES  IRADE  SOOT  ADO
HAMES  ANOXIA  POLYP
ABBR  DECIARNAZ  OPAL
BARON  ARKS  MADE  SLICE
    AMIDST  NENE  WAYNES
SECOND  PANDA  ABBESS
ARISES  FARE   TITLES
PINTS  SLIT  MEAL  ERNIE
SAGE  MINIPEARL  GALA
    LADEN  SASSES  PEKES
MOW  NEWT  AHSES  ERNEST
ARISTA  TNT  STE
MISMARPLE  OLIGCASSINI
MODESTIES  REPRESENTED
ALOE  HEFT  ANSON  TOTAL
LEMS  SSTS  LOEWE  SWORE
```

72

```
PADRES  CEDAR    ICEMAN
ANOINT  OVERAWE  DODECA
CONSTANZEWEBER  OMELET
ANGER  AIRY  FIGMENTS
    EAVES  ENTERED
PREDATES  PLUS  ANOMALY
REMOTE  TREVI  PIE  IDEO
OVEN  ORISTANO  LIVY
PUNG  FLED  RAYS  ROMEO
EDIBLES  PANES  HOSELS
ORANT  AMC  ALOOF
PROVEN  HORAE  GONDOLA
RIVAL  EGAD  BEAK  ROLL
EVEN  STROBILE  MITE
TERN  AHS  OGEES  SPARES
ARTICLE  VLAD  CHURNERS
    AZILIAN  BRUNO
CHAMBRES  GRIM  FETOR
CHANDU  DIEZAUBERFLOTE
PEWTER  ATHALIE  HEBRON
AWNING  SPANS  ORATED
```

```
SOAP  CREES   HARLEM
CINCH HENRI   AVIATOR
SAMCOOKESONG  LEAPOVER
PLIE NEROS HOLST  NINE
LIL  SERIN  RETAG  ETA
APART NEAT  MAYA  HODAD
THROAT STEVENS VERILY
     DRAT ERANT MINAR
REFERRED ELD  BATTLEAX
OSLO NEISSE  GALA  ECCE
UTA   TARANTIST    TAR
GOSH PENA  TABLED  TORI
EPHEMERA MIB ESOTERIC
   IRONY JONAS  EVAN
CANNON  RETORTS EMOTER
LUGER SEWS  DRAG  PRONE
ADE  ERASE  UVULA  STD
SIRS ABELE  UTILE  ASIA
STMARTIN  PARTOFACHURN
 SALIENT OFFER SHAPE
 NAPLES  STARS  HUBS
```

```
SCRAG MADE  AMIENS   YET
PROVE ALAD PLANTAIN OAR
IAPOLOGIZE  ILLGETBY UTE
EVEN KNEELER TESS  AGREE
LED  RAND  LAMER  PLIERS
   ARAT SITED  THEART
SUNRISESUNSET MAAR THAW
PRICE ELIE  EVANGEL ERA
REGAL CANT  ARISTA ELTON
ADEN RECASES STAR  MOOSE
TORE EDO  SPOSI  MOPPED
   IFIWEREARICHMAN
SPAWNS MARSE  ION  STAT
PAPAS STOP ISABELA TOBE
ENURE PATINA ROME  PINER
ADZ TORPEDO BALA  ALTAR
RAZE REED YOUBELONGTOME
 LAGGER DERRY  NOES
OVERLY MESAS  STEP  TAB
TEMPO PREP TALARIA CATO
ALE ONEALONE IMADREAMER
RUN MANNERED SADA  BREVE
UMT GATETO  TRES  ODDER
```

```
ABETS  ARLES   BUST
BULLET OTTAVA  OFTHE
BATISTA THEPENNYOPERA
ODON ENATE  LEEDS   FEB
MMMD DREI  CYST    ACU
BEAM FOURSAINTSINACTS
ANTI  IUM TAV  CLEESE
  CANT  AIR  GYROS
ASTERN STY  LAMA  BLOIS
BAH MISTRAL SELF  IFNI
ELEM STRIKETHREE  SEND
LIMO HAIL DULLARD  VEE
SCURF PALS  NYE  RECESS
  STOMP SHE  MICA
ACKACK  ALS MAE   RISE
THELITTLEKITTENS  DRAM
BIT  OENO  IRAN  MOUE
ACE FIRST  NUDES  ONCE
THELITTLEPIGS RUNNIER
 IRENE  IRISES ELATED
 STEM  ESTER  DUPES
```

```
ACED SAONE  AMAT  ABLE
LAME ENROL  ADANO  BEAD
PRIMADONNA  CONTRABAND
 PROMISE PARLE  PSEUDO
  TOLE  SHIFTLESS
SPHERE TREAD  ODESSUS
PEASE CRASS  TAROT  UBA
ANI   OAS   AND   SNOB
STR HITCHINGPOST  ADAR
MARTINET NOLEN  AGNATE
 ARSIS  EARED  UNITY
DRIEST SALSA ENTREPOT
RISE SINGLEMINDED  UNE
AVID  SIR   STU   NIN
MAN AGATE  MELEE  SACCO
ALGEBRA  COVER  AACHEN
 GRACENOTE  MULE
ACARID LONER  COTERIE
POLESAPART TOOTHPASTE
EMIT TONIO  ERATO  TINE
RATS EDDA  DOLOR  ETAL
```

```
OLAF SHEER  ATLAS  STOW
RENI TORSO  BUENA  HONE
BRIDGEBIDS  ABSTINENCE
 GENOA SILAS  LONGED
BUENOS WINOS  TINS
ENTE ANON  RUNCIBLE
LADES ARLINEJUDGE  OEN
ONER FRED   AMOS  DYAD
AIR SUITOFARMOR  FOSSE
NEGATES  AMEER  MERCED
 ABELE  SKIMS  TEMPO
CARIES SPITE  UNUSUAL
ARMEN STORYTELLER  TRA
REES AERO   LOIS  FARO
INN ACTORSGROUP  RICES
BATTERUP  POOP   ORTS
 ASOP  SENSE  ATTEST
PATIOS BINET  OCHOS
SCULPTURES ARTHURASHE
ARNO INANE  NITID  LOOM
TEAR CEDAR  DOONS  EXES
```

```
BASAL MOTET  BAHS SCAMPS
ENERO OPERA  OPEC HUMERI
LONERANGERSHORSE ERASED
 DONUT MOTEL  ANE  SISS
ASS ATAP  RELED  ENCODE
LOUS UNAU  LAY STAR  NUS
SUPERMANSPLANET INSIGHT
DEN  HOPS   OARS  RELY
CAVED TAELS PHONE  HORAE
AGAR FERRI  BIALY  TENON
PER  SORT CHANTS  GRIEF
PRISTINE EASEL PRESSMEN
ECOLE EMBRYO  LIAT   YEA
STIRS SCALA  GRANT  ETRE
DOYLE LERNA  LIONS  ETHOS
AWOL MENU   AURI   LEN
DEFAMES SIGNILLUMINATOR
ORB EAST FRO STAN  SURE
LETTER SUMMA  ARTS   PEP
DOOR NAB  MIAMI  MEADE
SUNLIT NUMBEREDGOLFCLUB
RADISH COAL  INLET ELOPE
ALECTO EYRE  EDENS SISSY
```

79

```
FEST  DAM  CASTS  GUCCI
LITH  EVER  OCTET  ASHOT
AGEE  FETE  MEARA  TAUNT
THEREAREATERRIBLE  REO
STREAMS  COS  ALEC
GEE  HOTOFF  PELHAM
GROPED  LOTOFLIESGOING
RARER  AUS  PALS  PLAT
EMIR  ACCT  CRIMP  CELTS
ABOUTTHE  TAIL  AMAD
TON  ROAD  HUN  ONOR  BIO
CAMP  NEST  WORLDAND
IATRY  EMILE  PELT  ELSE
OCHO  LONI  SAN  SLEET
THEWORSTOFITIS  SHIRTS
ASTERO  ONEMAN  SKI
ARCS  IST  WINSTON
APB  HALFOFTHEMARETRUE
PALMA  LEORA  RANT  RITE
SPEAR  MANET  SAKE  APOD
EASED  STATE  SYD  DEFY
```

80

```
MAORI  PILOT  AMISS
WINDED  ETOSHA  ACCRETE
ONEINA  THESEWAGECANAL
EDUCE  ARABICEXERCISES
FAR  CLOD  ADENA  SOLE
UNI  PHIL  AMT  TAE
LASCAR  ERI  SAUER  STO
OMANISANISLAND  AFTER
MASONS  CONDO  RIATA
AGE  TOT  HOD  GASTON
AWOLFINSHEIKSCLOTHING
LESLIE  OLE  RED  MCS
TAHOE  NEGEV  DONATE
ERETS  IMAMOLDCOWHAND
RYN  TEXAN  USE  FOLIOS
MAX  SST  POUR  TWO
WANE  ALIBI  DAHL  RAU
ADENPLANETARIUM  SLOGS
KUWAITWATCHERS  APOGEE
ELECTED  HOMAGE  PACERS
TREAD  MEDES  ETONS
```

81

```
MALFI  HALO  PARES  GISH
ABELS  ALOP  STORM  UPTO
BUTISITART  ITSOURTURN
DURUM  NAIF  RIDGE  LIE
STEPS  IMITATE  BULLY
ESPY  IOWNANRCA  FUSEES
PAR  ONLY  DOT  FIFED
ICANTGOON  ANOPENFRAME
COYOTE  AWN  RARE  GAL
TED  TREAD  IRS  BULL
MEYER  NICEPIANO  ORNIS
AXED  MOT  PADRE  IMA
GIS  ARAT  RIA  NEWONE
ITSALLANACT  BIGTALKER
ELATH  KLM  DAHL  WAN
SPRATS  NEVERMORE  CITE
NEGRI  MATINEE  BANES
ARE  STAPH  TART  CORES
ISAWHAMLET  DROPTHEGUN
LINE  MEESE  EIRE  INURE
SATE  ESSEX  RENT  TOYED
```

82

```
OPAL  JEAN  PANIC  TRIM
RAVE  OMBER  REACH  RADA
BREAKHOUSE  ORTHETIGER
SERVANTS  TAMIS  DREAMS
ERNE  BELIE  DUD
MEASLY  LISPS  SEABATS
ARNOS  AATTHEOPERA  HAM
LEIF  KITT  BINS  DEMI
ECG  INTHEFAMILY  PIPES
THINICE  ALATE  WREAKS
TRUTH  MUTTS  LOONS
TAMERS  SERAI  BALLETS
ATUNE  ONCEINALIFE  UKE
ERSE  CROC  GERE  TREE
LII  THEBARTERED  WHEEL
ACTRESS  ERRED  CHESTS
HOS  ANODE  MOAB
SOWETO  ODEUM  ALFRESCO
AWITHAVIEW  ATTIFFANYS
DELI  VILLE  NIHIL  RAMA
ENDS  EASED  ALIE  SPAY
```

83

```
BLAIR  AWARE  RISDE  TOMES
RITHE  RIVEN  ECTAD  ORANT
ATRAP  MEADE  DEANE  MANTA
WHITEMILLER  STRONGCLARK
LOPEARED  VOMER  TOASTEE
TESS  MARIA  DART
CHAFED  GOTAT  SATES  AMS
AESIR  BYRNESHOLMES  BLOT
LAWES  ROUE  COO  RITA
ARAL  TAKETH  STANCE  OBIT
HANDLEVEL  ASPEN  OLDWIFE
CETUS  TREAT  BREEN
LIGHTER  SEDER  BANNISTER
ODEA  SASHAY  SCOTIA  TATU
TENS  LAR  ARTE  LOPES
TATE  MOODYBARBOUR  ONERS
ELS  ROPES  ALOON  STERNE
ETES  PLEAT  ABET
ASEASON  PALED  DIRECTED
BUTLERSTORY  WOODSBREWER
ORALE  HUNCH  EXULT  ISERE
DATED  OSTEO  EELER  ETAIS
ESSES  PHILO  DRUSE  SAKES
```

84

```
GEER  DOITS  ROTE  RATIO
OLIO  ATSEA  EVER  ACIDS
ABNORMALCRAVING  CANOE
LEESHORE  DRED  SPIN
TONY  AIMS  REDHEN
ABBES  ISNOTA  AIRLINE
VAIR  OYSTERSPAWN  ENGS
ALB  OVULE  OBE  DIT
SEL  FEMALEPIGLET  FURL
TRISTRAM  RANEE  OBLATE
CPAS  CRUSE  WOES
ELAINE  PAOLI  STONECAT
LILT  AIRPLANEPART  ELI
MEW  ROE  VALSE  TAM
IDES  SUNKENFENCE  CITE
REELSIN  SPURNS  LACES
ARDENT  ICES  COOL
DOES  ASHE  ORTOLANS
CREDO  CAPTAINHOOKSMAN
COVET  ARIL  NOISE  IOTA
CHARS  BASE  GROSS  TROP
```

85

```
STAR  SWAP  SPA   TABARD
LACE  OHARE CAR   RIATAS
AMOSTDEV COWARD   FRUITS
TERTIARY  PENCE   IMBUE
    APSE  ALAD  NASAL
CASTS   ADELA   CHIEFLY
ARME  HUMID  LENTIL  LIE
LEA  ALAE  BEEN   LENA
ENL UNCHUNKIST  GNOMES
BALANCES  EASES  OPART
  METER  TURIN  SIREN
MAHDI  PAREN  RETARDED
UNBELT  SHINGMATCH  SRA
RIAS  ALTO   ADAH   COT
RLS UKASES HOOEY  CEDE
ESSENES  ACORN   TOMES
  BLOTS  TORI  CRAM
LABOR  TRIMS  TRAIPSED
PERIOD ABABINREELANDR
ASENSE KIT  NEAPS  RAGE
MEAGER ESE  GAPE   EPEE
```

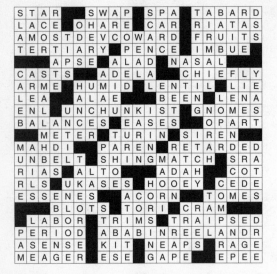

86

```
POCK ADLIB  WHELM   EBBS
OGRE LIANE  REDIA   FLOE
PLAYSECONDFIDDLE    FORE
PENNAMES  LETGO   STEWED
AREOLAS   HARTE   STATORS
    TEN  SOMME   BARREN
BASES  HARPINGUPON
ALOR PANS  URIS   OSLO
SMU WINCE  BLAND  SLOGS
HANDIEST  SLUR   ONEWAY
DANCEATTENDANCEON
SETTEE  RANT  REHASHED
ACHES BEARD PIPED  ORE
SHED MIDI  LEAR   CRIB
HOT RINGTHEBELL  RUNES
ROONEY  ARIAS  COT
DRUMOUT  AMORS  PULSATE
RIMATE  SNIDE  BOREALIS
ALPH TICKLETHEIVORIES
FLEA TROLL  TENSE  UNIE
TETS OATES  ANTED  GENS
```

87

```
LODI SLAPS  REVEL  ALTAR
SABIN TELAE ERICA  SERGE
ALEAF AGANA CAPON  SMIRE
TAYLORMADESUITS  TRUMPED
ESS  EEL  ISTO  TEAROSE
   AMAN  ADUE  CAREEN
SOMMERSHOWER GOON  CLAY
ABOIL  ALA PLAN SPARERS
MET SEERESS EMIA AREOLE
OATH WRIGHTSTUFF STARER
SHOOTER  RATTERS  HMAS
  LAROSA  ALE  ROLLUP
GAMS REPINER  EERIEST
DENOTE PIDGEONTOED ELIE
RENNET ISLE FOOTPAD ADA
ASATREE HERS SUI  OATER
MESH MILD CHERCROPPERS
  ELLERY DEED   EVER
CAREERS  GUNN  STE  SHE
DEMASTS GREENEBEANSALAD
ANENT ONEAL IRANI  IRATE
MANGE NONCE NISAN  LINER
ASTER STEED GESTS  TAGS
```

88

```
   PASTE   AHAB   SIEGE
 MADEIT  ARECA   UNDONE
PUTONTHESPITZ   RETURNS
UTE SLEPT  ROOFER  DOGE
PALM ELIAS ROOST   ABIE
ATLAS  SCRIM  KIT  SCEND
SEACOW  SENEGAL  READE
   ALEC  DAOS   TALK
MACBETHTHING  JAILEMUS
AMOR ERE YOLANDA   IRE
NINE TRIED LUNDS   FLAN
ANN GRINDUP  NEE   LAND
TOULOUSE  COUNTMERINOS
   INCH  CARR   SMUT
 CROAK  ALLEGES  PETARD
FROND SMA REATA  SEDER
LASS KEEPS  STUBS  DELA
ATEM LANCES STRAP  LIN
METEOUT LIPPIZANERING
 STOOGE ANION  DEPONE
  AWNED PENT   ERODE
```

89

```
 TEST  GATTI   SAFEST
 THROW OBOES   PRINTER
THEGOODEARTH   INFORMER
IRA  WASTE ERNIES   PAU
PEP DOGIE  CRUDER  KELL
SEALEMON  DOWELS  SAREE
RIPEN GALORE  RAREST
PATTON CONDOS  CATERTO
ARMET  PRATED  MOVIE
NEER BEATER PAPERMOON
INN BARNES SERINE  NBA
CATHERINE  APEXES  AGED
 EARLY  AMOLES  CLOSE
REDARES SNAKES  CUTLER
OLIVER  DEALER  SALAD
BASER LETSIN  BURLIEST
BIRD SENATE CASES  NWI
ENA REDSEA GOTHE   PAN
REEMERGE SUNSHINEBOYS
 SLEDGES IRATE  EVENS
  INSERT ANWAR  DEED
```

90

```
RAMAT SOLI FIT  TORPOR
EVITA AUER ADO  AMOEBA
FILLINGSTATION  FABRIC
RAI  YET NELL    NIFTY
ATTIRE  SILL   KALINE
CIANOS  STALEMATE  CBS
TORTE WEENY ORTA  STEW
SNY  SAME ANAIS   IPSE
  RUNNINGSTITCH  LITE
UPDATED  RITES   PETIT
PARTED  CARED   TINCAL
GRITS   OATES   MONTHLY
ROLL  CURRENTEVENTS
ALLE ANDOR  BING   MES
DEMS CIEL  SAONE  SHALT
EDA  HORSEPLAY  GEIGER
SHEENS  MILT   INDIGO
RATES   MICE  AGA  CAN
ADESTE ENGAGEMENTRING
VERSED TOR EVER   APACE
INSERT APE  DANE  MINER
```

91

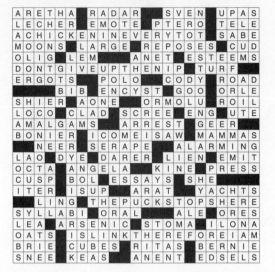

```
ARETHA  RADAR   SVEN    UPAS
LECHER  EMOTE   PTERO   TELE
ACHICKENINEVERYTOT      SABE
MOONS   LARGE   REPOSES CUD
OLIG  LEM   ANET  ESTEEMS
DONTGIVEUPTHENIP    TURF
ERGOTS  POLO  CODY   ROAD
BIB   ENCYST  GOO   ORLE
SHIER  AONE  ORMOLU  ROIL
LOCO  CLAD  SCREE  ENG  UTE
AMALGAMS   ARREST   GEER
BONIER  ICOMEISAW  MAMMAS
NEER   SERAPE   ALARMING
LAO  DYE  DARER  LIEN  EMIT
OCTA  ANGELA  KINE  PRESS
CUSP  BOL  ESSAYS  SHE
ITER  ISUP  ARAT  YACHTS
LING  THEPUCKSTOPSHERE
SYLLABI  ORAL  ALE  ORES
LEA  ARSENIC  STOMA  ILONA
OATS  ISLINKTHEREFOREIAM
BRIE  CUBES  RITAS  BERNIE
SNEE  KEAS  ANENT  EDSELS
```

92

```
SSSFRS  WHERES  EPI  SCP
TRPEZE  SEVILL  MRL  TRO
TOHVENDHVENOT  BKE  REP
INEE  ERIES  PENTECOSTL
CGER  MIND  MEDITE  PPER
TONG  LER  FLTTEN
CONDENSTION  PTE  ORGNS
PSTIME  ORDINRY  STBLER
BSINS  CNTEENS  STELERS
LEOS  LLIED  WELCOMED
ETN  SEMN  ROTS  BRM
LMPPOSTS  SLEPS  MNSE
DISSTER  MORTISE  PINES
RESTIR  RIVERMN  STMENS
DROIT  LUL  GRNDFTHERLY
CCEPTS  ITS  PIRS
SPIT  RESENT  FEST  CRSS
CHTEUBRIND  MENCE  SETE
ROI  LOL  CINEMTOGRPHER
MBO  NIL  GRILLE  ISRELI
SIN  ELY  ESTTES  CHSTEN
```

93

```
BARRE  AMPHORA  FLAPS
ALIEN  CORONET  LATHE
CHAMPAGNEANDACHICKEN
HAM  ACRE  TEED  OCEANIA
AMELITA  DES  IOU  OOM
NADER  FEASTANDREVELRY
SAY  STAY  LGE  RAM
DIE  TROPO  TASTES
TOBEDGOSOBER  TSE  NATS
OMINOUS  OIL  HAH  ADRET
GAS  LEG  MEADE  CAM  TAR
AHEMS  ONS  GOD  ANATOLE
SACO  POE  RINGINTHENEW
TRIADS  ACTED  ELA
EAR  TIC  HEAD  BAL
AWELLCHOSENBOOK  CAVIL
MEL  ORO  EEG  IMAGINE
PALOMAR  MASC  ARAN  ADA
SODAWATERTHEDAYAFTER
ERASE  IRELAND  APRON
LASTS  ASSERTS  SEARS
```

94

```
TACOMA  SCOOT  TERESA
AVATAR  TIMBALE  IDEATE
ROSEINLAVALIER  RINSER
ONEAL  ICER  GIGOLETTO
BRACT  RESALE
CHIMAERA  SCAR  WESTERN
HOMAGE  TETON  BAA  OLEO
IMAN  LOWANDGRIN  UTES
NEGOMBO  ERG  AIN  PROSE
ADENOIDS  VOLES  WHINEY
LUNETTE  ALKORAN
ASSESS  RISEN  SNAGGERS
BETTE  LAO  PGA  EYEGNAT
ARES  TOWNHOUSER  HAME
SIEG  ERS  IDIOM  ACACIA
ENROBED  USED  BEGETTER
ATOLLS  NOMAN
THEPROFIT  UELE  ARECA
REVERT  FRYINGDUTCHMAN
AMELIA  TARTARE  ILOILO
PASTEL  SASIN  RESTON
```

95

```
HAM  CAPER  SEDUM  EFFETE
AVE  OBERON  ARETE  ALEXIS
SOT  MEDITERRANEANRESORT
SWEETER  AWAIT  NOTES
LARGE  OCTETS  FLESH  CSA
ELSA  HOLE  AROSE  CHAPS
DOLLAR  SLANT  FLORES
EDE  DEAR  TIMING  AREOLAE
PIQUANT  MOROCCANSEAPORT
HAUL  SEPARATES  OTER
ELAN  ERASES  ROUE  PAR
BELOWPITCH  OVERPRAISE
ERS  HIDE  SAUDIS  TEES
ONER  CARPENTER  OMNI
LASVEGASHABITUE  SURPASS
OCTAVES  ABLOOM  OTHO  NET
IRONED  ELLEN  CLERIC
RIPER  AXLES  VELD  REBS
EDS  BLISS  MIMOSA  DUCAT
SPIES  OASIS  DRIZZLY
WASHINGTONSTATEPEAK  ELL
ASKING  EROSE  STAPLE  MAE
SHINTO  DEGAS  SATES  ADS
```

96

```
MADAM  OMAR  SAGA  SWEAR
ACINI  VARIATION  KANGA
THEINVISIBLEMAN  ATTIC
MAIDS  OILED  STEELE
SAMARA  OSCAR  CHIRRED
OBOLE  HANOI  SALONS
FIRSTLENSMAN  ROUGHUP
ADO  SANTEE  EVICT  ISLE
RENT  DRAT  BRISK  APHID
HOLY  SAUCE  ARDENT
THENEVERENDINGSTORY
DROIDS  CESTA  ISAW
HORNE  CHITA  DUDE  NORD
SLAV  DOONE  ROPERY  PAU
LEISURE  THETWOTOWERS
NOMADS  OLEAN  SIRET
SPECIAL  APIED  SENARY
TAPIRS  ERICA  LAYME
ADOBE  BLACKSTARRISING
ADDLE  IMPOSESON  TALIA
TYEES  POET  DUSE  EPOXY
```

97

```
LAMENESS  NORIA    TOCKS
ERODIBLE  ANATTO   LUIRE
COUNTRYRACEPERFECTBOX
ASTA  OEIL  SIMIAN  OONT
REO   RATCHES  STIFLES
RINGED  LAYER   MOOLA
ESSENCES  RASHER  OFTEN
TOLA  CAR  ATTU  ROVE
ATLAS  SEL  TAM  HAILED
MAE   ATTEMPT  BOUNCER
EXAMINERFORWORDHEADED
TROVARE  POTPIES   ATE
MINUET  TEC  TEN  CANTO
OMEN  AMMO  ESS  SOOT
BERTH  AMIDST  RESPECTS
AUDIE  ASAFE   EYELET
STRIPED  IRONIST   ERE
CHIN  LEADER  SHEM  HARE
REFERENCESOFHONOROVER
ISLET  SENTUP  NOTALONE
PEERS   STOTS   ENTWINED
```

98

```
PALOMA    WEARE    SCROLL
AMORAL  HARPIST  TAIPEI
IMPACT  AGRIPPA  ENGAGE
DOE  HERR  ASP  MEAT  LSD
HEREBYTHEWILLOF
EBRO  TORA  DELA  AMOS
FLOUNDERS   ESPALIERS
TOSSERS  ABA  SIERRAS
THENATIONANDWESHALL
RAP  SWAHILI  LAN
BRASSERIE  INTERDICT
BEG  INDICATOR  NOR
SPECIAL  NOM  INEPTLY
NOTLEAVESAVEONTHE
PADRES  RARITAN  ENIGMA
ALARM  MINT  ANTS  ALEUT
ZASU  ROOD  DRIP  IRMA
POINTOFBAYONETS
LOOTING  RUARK  GROTTOS
ADRESSE  ELUTE  LEGIONS
REDDEER  NAMES  ESSAYER
```

99

```
A*TO  DUSTIN  HATLO  A*K
ALSOP  UNMADE  ALOOF  TSIN
*VATIONWAGES  LONE*STATE
SAP  NADIRS  TRINES  CENTS
PRESENT  SLIDER  SANDYS
ACHE  TED  SEINE  GIRDS
BLINDS  AMENS  FAILS  TEN
OARED  FIVE*GENERAL  BRIE
DREGS  ORELS  ODIN  AIDE
EASE  IBERT  LOBOS  CARPED
RATON  TIBER  HOR  ERE
CO*  *SFELLONALABAMA  SSR
ANS  INF  AEDES  LITUP
LIKESO  AMNON  TRADE  ASTA
LOYS  IMET  OHARA  ASHEN
ANAT  *SINONESEYES  ASORT
SYN  STADT  OXIDE  ARIOSE
DAILY  BOHEA  AOK  OTES
SCHEME  CURSOR  SOPRANI
ORURO  RAPIER  DAMEOF  NAE
NOTINOUR*S  THEMORNING*S
ESCE  DENTE  EUDORA  RE*TS
SHS  DRESS  DIESIS  ESSE
```

100

```
RCHIDS  RBLE  RUTS  DACE
ARISEN  ARUT  STEP  IMAG
CNVENIENTLY  TSCA  SANG
LEER  NRTHUMBRIAN  CTTN
ERSE  LSES  LEADPISNING
SAID  AGATE  ATS
CAMPTWN  SHIRE  DRPLEAF
ARIELS  MARSH  FLD  AXIL
RECKN  CNNATURAL  BTTMS
RARE  WISDM  GES  TTER
TSS  DENIM  PHARS  TTS
CSTS  GIB  HAIRY  LIAR
TRPHY  CNNIPTINS  MANIT
ASIA  RAR  CWERS  PRTEGE
RECRDER  INDRS  CRSSRAD
PEC  GLVES  GRVE
PASSINFLWER  RAKI  TARA
EPCH  VEREXPSURES  RDER
PINT  EVIL  UNCNDITINAL
LACE  NELL  FAKE  NNTIDE
ENER  ERES  FRST  SENSES
```

101

```
SWAG  ASWAN   CAST   OFOR
CADI  STARE  TORTE  RENE
AFAR  SUNYACHTSEN  ARCA
REGALE  TATARY  WASTREL
REFERS  NEMO   CLOY
TATAS  NUNS  TEARGAS
IRKS  SIMP  SELAH  VIOLA
ROE  COON  SORES  ODIN
ALTO  DOGTAG  ORBED  MEG
NECKLET  SCRIP  RAISON
HITCH  ARETE  ICANT
FAEROE  METER  GALAHAD
KOS  SCRAP  AMIDST  PELE
ELKE  TAMAR  SOUL  RIB
LIENS  PINEL  REES  SSTS
POTTERY  STOP  LEASH
CREE   AMAS  PLAYER
ADHERED  SPARTA  ELATED
BOCA  LATEENLOVER  WHEE
CRAT  ERRED  OLEAN  LESE
DENY  REEK  RECTO  SLED
```

102

```
PECK  GAGA  TSPS  STOWED
ALEE  OREL  ITUP  HONORE
RALE  SANA  NENE  ANTRIM
STENOSBARSERIT  STORKS
EER  REL  MAES  TOPI
CRYLATEARIROHTUA  ELM
BLT  LAT  SERT  ASIA
ANTAE  DET  DIOS  UGLY
HOWL  ENTENTE  PREHEATS
EVILONETLEWD  TERR
MAL  MUTE  MII  ASTA  CPA
LAIR  ACCENTEDSEIP
REENTERS  TETRODE  ACNE
AIRE  SOLD  RMS  BRIAR
SLOT  TAIS  SEI  AEG
HER  BIGSPENDERSSENOH
OSSA  CONO  APO  ARA
RAFTER  CROWBARRETSIOR
ARGIVE  RENI  SEER  HAIL
BOULES  ATEN  SISS  ENDO
INDENT  NERD  ENTE  STEW
```

103

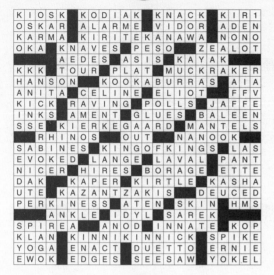

```
KIOSK  KODIAK  KNACK  KIR1
OSKAR  ALARME  VIDOR  ADEN
KARMA  KIRITEKANAWA  NONO
OKA  KNAVES  PESO  ZEALOT
AEDES  ASIS  KAYAK
KKK  TOUR  PLAT  MUCKRAKER
HANSON  KOOKABURRAS  AIA
ANITA  CELINE  ELIOT  FFV
KICK  RAVING  POLLS  JAFFE
INKS  AMENT  GLUES  BALEEN
SSE  KIERKEGAARD  MANTELS
RHINOS  OUT  NANOOK
SABINES  KINGOFKINGS  LAS
EVOKED  LANGE  LAVAL  PANT
NICER  HIRES  BORAGE  ETTE
DAK  KAPER  KIRTLE  KASHA
UTE  KAZANTZAKIS  DEUCED
PERKINESS  ATEN  SKIN  HMS
ANKLE  IDYL  SAREK
SPIREA  ANOD  INNATE  KOP
KLAN  KINNIKINNICK  SPIKE
YOGA  ENACT  DUETTO  ERNIE
EWOK  EDGES  SEESAW  YOKEL
```

104

```
GAL  FETED  CRAMP  ZORRO
URU  AGAPE  OILER  ETHER
EEN  IGNISANDBRIMSTONE
STABLE  CANED  EMIT  MAL
THOR  READY  LULUS  BUS
AVID  CLEO  ELYSE  MULE
EQUAL  NODE  ARREST
AURUMFINGER  RISEN
INME  EPEE  BREAD  ESQUE
DOIT  ASIT  SEND  FLAUNT
ERA  PRETOR  STIPOS  AHA
DAMNED  HUED  OCAS  DRUB
ELIOT  PETER  MALT  ITLL
BABAR  OLBLUEOCULI
BALLOT  PAPA  DRATS
MENE  PECAN  CASA  RIOS
AGA  PRONG  TRALA  OFUS
DOL  VETO  ORIAL  GANJAH
CROCODILELACRIMAE  UVA
ARGOT  MENAT  ANAIR  LEG
PAYNE  EDENS  TEENY  YRS
```

105

```
AGRA  ABEAM  ETAS  WEED
TAEL  LOGIA  ADAPT  ATLI
TUESDAYANDNIGHTINGALE
INFORMED  EIDER  FEELS
CTS  OER  PINA  FAR
COD  MORON  SILT  BAD
LOSALAMOSANDANDYHARDY
ARAL  ITE  WOE  LAZE
PLYMOUTHROCKNROLLOVER
PES  SSTS  ROAST  EASES
BMUS  APR  SGTS
BRIAR  SUCRE  ATEE  LEE
JOHNNYCASHANDCARRYALL
ANOA  HSM  ATI  EMUS
TEDLEWISANDCLARKGABLE
ORA  DENY  ERIES  NOR
VIL  CATS  COT  ARI
LOANS  OSTIA  MACHINES
LINDAHUNTANDPECKSNIFF
LACE  ESTER  ERATO  ASEA
BOER  SOON  LENIN  SORT
```

106

```
NORD  REPEL  MAZE  DESI
ATOI  ELLIE  ALONE  EXIT
TONSOFBUNS  SCADSOFADS
LEAPFROG  SITAR  CRIMEA
ANEW  LENIN  PALE
ALTOS  BANFF  CARESSED
CROC  HEAPSOFJEEPS  LAI
ROTH  ELI  ALS  ZERO
OAS  PILESOFTILES  OWLS
PRORATED  ZEENA  TANSY
FIRED  FALLS  ROMEO
SWARM  HARTE  AIMEDFOR
LIAT  STACKSOFFLAX  YMA
ANTA  ONE  ALE  MEAT
NAT  FLOODSOFSUDS  AWNS
DISRAELI  TORTE  TARSI
ACTE  FINIS  ROTI
AMANTO  HAMAN  RELEASED
BAGSOFRAGS  GOBSOFCOBS
EZIO  FOLIO  ERIAN  HOOT
LOOM  BONN  SYSTS  INNS
```

107

```
GESSO  PLY  COMES  ALPS
BUREAU  AREA  ARETE  ACARE
ONELITTLETWOLITTLETHREE
IWILLFIGHTNOMOREFOREVER
LAS  ILIE  ZENO  INE  ANS
ELANET  DASHER  ESSEN
REWAX  TOE  HUH  ARTE
VILMA  LES  BAR  ICKIER
INFATUATED  EARTO  CAESAR
NOAH  MILLI  ALOE  MADDERS
TODOS  DIKE  ROK  ANDI
ONEBASE  ERECTED  STINGER
LUNN  BAH  NARC  STORE
ASTARIS  ELSE  ALIAS  HOSE
STONED  TRUER  REPRESENTS
WINKLE  HOE  SUR  SARIS
ERIE  TIS  TOP  DUROC
TAKEN  SKEWED  GENEVA
SPA  SAL  ALAI  BREL  VER
TELLTHEMWILLIEBOYISHERE
RETURNOFAMANCALLEDHORSE
OVERA  SORED  EVEL  EERIER
PERK  TRESS  DES  RANEE
```

108

```
PUMA  ACORN  TIGER  LEO
ABED  LABIO  ALENE  COVE
DENOFLIONS  CERTIFI[CAT]ED
CLONE  TATUM  NAVEL
MASTI[CAT]E  ARGUS  SVCE
IGNORE  CRURA  CHEETAHS
SNORT  HIMALAYANS  IAO
DEW  SAMOA  SMUT  [CAT]LIN
OSLO  ABYSSINIAN  PAULA
EXTRAS  ACIDS  MARRER
BOOBOOS  SUITE  PERIODS
INPAIN  PULER  TOECAP
BEALL  [CAT]ASTROPHES  SHAD
BARM  SARA  LIMES  IMA
ETD  [CAT]ILINARIAN  CALID
RASGADOS  GANTS  MANITO
ALEG  DOBLA  MARGAYS
TEMPT  [CAT]ANIA  EAGER
JAGUARUNDI  UNVINDI[CAT]ED
APAT  IRADE  THERE  ELSE
MAD  PEPYS  EGRET  RATE
```

109

```
TWIST  TERSE  DODO   SPEY
EATON  SNIPE  OMNI   RUST
THEGAMEISUP   GLAD   EYAS
STYRIA LEHAR  ELA    MARU
    ALLY  ASNER  ELBOWED
OTS  PEAS  AUGER  LASS
HARM  WEEMS  NEPAL  ENE
ONEIN  APOS  SITUPS  NOT
SEPHARDIM  SERIE  DOOR
SPLEENY  STRAND  ANGLE
  ULAMA  STEAM  INCAN
OSSIP  PEANUT  PSYCHIC
LEEK  UNDID  GUYFAWKES
RIN  REPEAT  RANN  DORMS
ADO  STULM  RESIN  COLE
  NEAT  PRIER  PUNY  WON
SCORNED  ANNES  SETS
LIEU  SED  ANDES  TITLES
ALBS  ILES  INTHESPRING
ROOS  RICE  PANAY  PAVIA
OCTA  GRAB  SPARE  UPEND
```

110

```
AYES  TIBIA  DOES   BANG
LOVE  OTARU  ERNES  EROO
EYECLASHES   MADCHATTER
CONTESSA  TOOTS  RUTILE
    INTO  BRINE  HIRE
DICOTS  CLINI  MONARCHS
ATONE  BREAKCRANKS  RAP
MAPS  TREN  ETES  SOSO
ALT  CHARDBOILED  RECTO
SOILURES  ESSAY  MEEKER
  COLES  SISSY  SAHIB
SENATE  ATREE  AUDITORS
CLEMS  CHEATINGPAD  TEA
ADRY  SOAP  OOPS  ATAT
LEV  SPLITCHAIRS  DIODE
PRETTIER  LASSA  WORMED
  HUNT  TERSE  SIRS
ALPENA  TEMPI  CAPITATE
FIRSTCRATE   SPARECRIBS
ALAI  HEMEN  TRIER  IDAS
ROYS  VEST  SONES  PERE
```

111

```
TAT  SHAMS  UBER   BRAD
DOTH  HELIO  NAPE  RASES
SWEEPINGLY   CHILDISHLY
MINARET  BOOTS  WEHOLD
STONILY  CETUS  DEFLEA
  GOD  KRAIT  KILLY
AMBER  TRENCHANTLY  PAZ
VEAL  MAID  BETS  CERO
ALL  EXPLOSIVELY  CANTO
TENNIEL  ARIEL  UNSET
  FETID  CREST  AUREI
AZURE  PIANO  ENCLAVE
COLOR  WITHERINGLY  ERR
TOLL  ZONE  BORA  CLIO
AMY  POWERLESSLY  TOYED
  CODED  ENNEA  LOO
TORRID  AMAIN  MUSKILY
ZAPATA  STOMP  ANTONIO
IRONICALLY   ENGAGINGLY
POLIO  ROAN  SEESE  ELLO
KEAN  APSE  STEED  SEE
```

112

```
RANK  ROBES  CARAFE  BOWER
EVOE  OPERA  REUBEN  ANIME
BEHINDTHEFOURBALL   SELMA
UNITE  SOWERS  ESTA  IYYAR
TATERS  MEDIA  CASE
  LOUSE  EDAM  PER  APAT
TIA  LEO  NINEHILLSOFROME
INRE  DUPONT  ARIA  SAILOR
LADLE  SUREST  ELS  ENTIRE
TWOISLANDS  ERSATZ  OCCAS
SERAPE  SANE  CION  HYLA
  YANG  EMBER  COOT
SALT  HARK  MILO  OCELLI
PROWL  PARROT  SEVENHCLUB
AGLEAM  MAO  SETTER  RHONE
CALLTO  MALT  TEALEE  OYER
ELEVENGALLONHAT  CAY  DST
RIDE  AUR  ODEA  STREW
  WADE  SNIDE  PARKAS
SAHIB  SPUE  TONISH  TILDE
ILONA  SIXDOLLARQUESTION
MARKS  ETOILE  PAULO  HERO
PEASE  DARTER  TEILS  EGER
```

113

```
SCALP  OATH  SHAG   OCALA
LONER  CLOY  COMA  RIPER
ASSAI  EARP  AWET  NAHUM
THEREWASANIRISHTENOR
  DON  ONCE  ERROR
DUSTIN  CASTE  PRAY  ISR
ANTAE  SOLI  DAIS  ASTO
WHOPUTWHISKEYINHISTEA
NINE  HEAT  ILANG  TOILS
STE  MIEN  IMADE  LANCET
  PUNT  SLOTS  PILE
MODULE  RHONE  KOKO  TAN
ALIST  BEANO  CETE  MOTO
HESAIDITWASTHEONLYWAY
DIEN  ICAL  OINK  ORALE
INN  SNAG  MINCE  GNARLS
  CREAM  DOLE  SIG
THATHECOULDSINGHIGHC
ORANT  RUNS  EINE  OSIER
LINGO  ABAS  ALDA  RENEE
DOTES  LATE  FOOD  NEALE
```

114

```
ICER  ACK  JEST   SCALP
VOLE  IHAD  OPAH  TABOR
ALEC  MAZO  HIVE  MONACO
NINE  FLORENCEOFARABIA
  CAPRICORNS  SCRIMP
  TORO  ILO  RUT  EIRE
BECOME  TANG  AMAH  NED
ADARE  ASSISIASPIE  CIG
MER  SECT  ALY  LARGE
ANISETTES  ONO  FALLEN
  CARRARAMOTHERHOOD
HALVES  LIP  AROMATICS
PATTI  AVE  ITEM  BRO
EMU  CREMONASASH  ALLOW
TAR  EELS  STEN  BLEEPS
ONES  ALT  TIT  SOFA
  TOSSED  ANAPOLIDAY
PISAPORRIDGECOLD  PROF
ORIGIN  DREI  IDEE  IDLE
LODEN  AGAR  DIMS  POKE
SNIDE  MERL  ANT  ERST
```

115

```
HELOTS   SPA  TLC   SPEAR
OCARINA  COLDWAR   IRATE
GODBLESSAMERICA   TESTA
   LASER   ANTIS   STIR
PEST  DUN   ATEIGHT  ERE
ETHIC   COMUS   SOBERED
WHITECHRISTMAS    WARP
  SMITH  DURANT  BROACH
  SEEIT  RONDEAU   DREI
MAI  REMEDY  NEEDS  EARN
ARR  AKENE   AVAIL  DEE
DEVA  TASTE  ONEINA  ESS
ANIL  ONPAPER   DRESS
MANTIC   OCEANS   STOOL
  GATH  THESONGISENDED
INBREED   ETAIN   DIODE
NEE  MERCIES   VMI  CRAW
SERB  KILOS   REACT
IDLES  PUTTINONTHERITZ
SLIDE  PEASANT  EOLITHS
TENET  YDS   NEO  REDSEA
```

116

```
 HELD  CALL  CLOP   ATHOS
PAGAN  OMOO  HATLO  CHACHA
INGMARBERGMANTONCHEKHOV
ESSE  ERNE  ARC  TER  MESTA
TOO  PTAS  MULE  ODES
AMNERIS  BORER  TUNES  NAB
 MEN  PORES  AUDIE   SODA
LOUSIAMAYALCOTTONMATHER
APPLE  ITSY  HUHUS  SPOILS
PET  TALE  MATI   ANTA
EROS  WANE  UPPERS  ACE
LANACANTRELLAFITZGERALD
TRY  SENLIS  BRAE  STLO
ELIE  TINS  AIDA  TAP
AVERSE  SCROD  MUIR  BEAME
JAMESBUCHANANETTEFABRAY
ADAS  SHARP  DOTES  ETO
REY  MELTS  LARES  SLENDER
TINA  ARMS  ENID  ULE
ASHED  NEE  UNA  IRAN  SLIM
CHARLESHGORENATATEBALDI
TARRED  SOREL  SETH  SHEET
 GEARS  SELL  PROS  ALAS
```

117

```
MEAD  GRASP   PHOS   BOOM
ACME  LINER  OLENT  AGRA
THEBRIDGEOFSANLUISREY
TOSSED  UPCAST  YDS  EMS
   FEDS  UNIE   EMP
ALAMODE  GREENMANSIONS
NODAL  MORASS  ELT  PROA
GRANDHOTEL   DASHIELL
LETT  OBOE  SEALS  ATALL
ONEILL   PARTAKES  SEY
  CASTLEOFOTRANTO
CAM  STEEPLES   DERAIN
ADAPT  NAILS  OHNE  INNO
PARISIAN  PROUDTOWER
RIOT  NNE  COATEE  ALARM
ARCHOFTRIUMPH  REVERTS
  SBA  TREE  ISTO
PRY  IMA  CIRRUS  ALBANY
HOUSEOFTHESEVENGABLES
INRE  URNES  RAREE  LOVE
LATE  SOTS  SLEWS  STAR
```

118

```
PAROL  MESS  AQUAPURA
ITALO  ASON  SUNBATHERS
QUIDPROQUO  HAIRRAISER
UNSEAT  SLOB  ITAS  NITA
EEE  TRA  STERNES  ORES
 ISERE   HOT  IDA
BEEN  VERITAS  VIPERS
ACUTE  DATIVE  ENPLANE
BAROQUE  ASI  FASTLANES
ADE  URAL  SOUTH  INSET
  MINDYOURPSANDQS
ADEEP  SKEWS  BORU  ARI
NOTAMUSED  AHA  STEELER
TRIDENT  BROACH  STENO
SCENIC  ENTREES  OXEN
  TSE  GAI  ARLEN
OPAH  CHAUNTS  SEX  ADA
HALE  BIEN  GOTH  ECOLES
OPENSALANE  QUINTUPLET
SPARETIRES  UNDO  STORE
 PIQUANTE  ETES  ESTER
```

119

```
HOPS  POETE  ABEET  DALE
APOC  EGGON  IRATE  IBID
SUTHERLANDSMOTHERLAND
ASSORTED  OLLAS  NAUSEA
 ONUS  CREED  CANT
AMBLER  ARSES  ARGUELLO
RARE  BOPEEPSSHEEP  EIN
ONERS  SHE  POP  GBS
ONA  HAMILLSCAMELS  ARE
MADEIRAS  APACE  OCELOT
 SALON  AGAPE  PRONE
REPROS  ALENE  PERUSALS
ABR  HELTERSKELTER  GEE
DOE  ARR  CII  SOLON
ALA  GENETSBERETS  VEND
RIDDANCE  LEMUR  THESES
 ETTE  CASES  PIER
SIGNOR  CHLOR  MORALIST
CLAIREBLOOMSHEIRLOOMS
ALEE  ALARM  OBESE  ATOP
TSAR  TYPES  NOTED  DAGS
```

120

```
LOBE  ASPIC  URALS  BLAB
IRON  THETA  NOMIC  LOGE
FLATFOOTED  COOLHEADED
TORRENTS  MALTY  OLDIES
 ATES  TENOS  VOCE
PLIED  THANA  SINISTER
GRIND  THINSKINNED  ILA
AILS  SEER  DIOR  OGAM
ICY  HARDNOSED  BAHTS
TELEVISE  ABUSE  BASTE
 IRENE  AMENT  SERIF
EVERY  OCEAN  OTIOSITY
ARECA  REDHANDED  SEA
TORT  SOIR  IDEE  STEW
ODE  HAREBRAINED  PEENS
MEDIEVAL  ALGER  RAADS
 AGON  SPANS  OEUF
PRIMER  AMINO  ACCLAIMS
HOTBLOODED  BIGHEARTED
ATTU  UDALL  LANES  ESTA
DSOS  SURLY  EMIRS  ROOK
```

121

```
P D Q . A M A R A . P L U M B . T K O S
L I E U . S U R A S . R A R E E . H A R E
E L B A . T R A C T . E D E M A . A T E N
C L A Y P I D G E O N S . . O R T I Z . .
H O T L I N E . S R O . A E R I E . P G A
S W E E T . R H O . R A B B I T T E A R S
. . C T S . I F S . B R O Z . S W I T
I L S A . W O L F E S B A N E . B A S T A
R O L L C A L L . P O E S Y . S O U . .
A D E L A . G E M . P S I . R I P S O F F
T E E . S H A R I F . S O C A G E . I L E
E S T A T E S . S A P . N U N . E L L E R
. . C O N . F A R E D . L E A P Y E A R
A L G E R . K I D D G L O V E S . O R S O
B U R R . I R A E . I V E . A N N . .
C R A B B E A P P L E . E R S . A S T H E
D E Y . S M O O T . L O R . M A R S H E S
. F O L I C . . B Y R D W A T C H E R S
A R O N . G H O T I . O R A L E . A C M E
R O X Y . R O B I N . N E L L S . R A I N
F I X X . E W I N G . O W E S T . E R A
```

122

```
A L E P P O . P R A H A . L A C . T H E E
R A D I U M . R I T E S . A W L . H O L Y
A K A P P A C O F F E E . P R E T E N S E
N E M I . H A V E A H A P P Y N U Y E A R
. . T E A R . S T A T E . C R A S S . .
G L A S S . S T E W . L U T H E R . .
L O N . P E P O . N E P H . C E D E R
O M E G A T O L E A R N G R E E K . U L E
B A L A N C E . A R O W . A R A . S A L E
E N E R O . F R E T . P I U S . C L A D
. A L P H A L O A F I S B E T A . .
C L A N . T O B Y . T I N E . E R I A S
H A R D . A B E . L O S T . S T R N A G E
I N A . R H O R H O R H O Y O U R B O A T
C A M E O . E G I S . A B B A . N R A
. P U R S E R . L O O K . C A U S E .
. B L I G H . A B O U T . E B E N . .
Y O U T H E T A M O U T H F U L . U M B O
A C C O S T E D . S I G M A R O M B E R G
W H A M . O L A . U S U A L . R E I N E R
L E S E . R A M . N A N N A . E N S U R E
```

123

```
M A T R I . Y U L E . L E A . S A N T A S
O C H E R . E L A M . E L F . A R E O L A
T H E F I R S T N O W E L L . F E S T A L
T E R E D O . R E T A R S . P E S T E R S
O D E R . U N A . I I I . S E T . .
. . E G O . C O V E N T R Y C A R O L
D E C K T H E . O N E R O U S . A B A T E
A C O R N S . H U S S . S T E . N E G R O
N O R I A . R A P . F E Z . O D D S O N
C L A S S . I L L U S E . T A Y . .
E E L S . S I L E N T N I G H T . S A M E
. . K O S . C U D D L E . A T R I A
A R D E N T . P L O . E E N . M A U L S
R E I N E . C A A . S P A N . W A R B L E
C A M E L . A N D R O L L . W A S S A I L
A D E S T E F I D E L E S . O P S . .
. . S E C . P E A . A N I . A R I D
C O R N E T S . M O N D A S . T I S A N E
O T I O S E . W H I T E C H R I S T M A S
D O N D E R . H O N . R H E E . I R A N I
S E D E R S . O S T . S O N G . S O N E S
```

124

```
S P O T . H O D O . C A B A L . S A D I S T
O A F S . Y A L E . A D A L E . T R E N T E
A T M E . P R A M . S H R I F T . E R A S E R
P H I . T H E V O I C E O F T H E T U R T L E
E S C A P E D . C A R N E . E N S . M E A T
D O E S I N . T R A D E S . A R G O . E P E E
. F A T . S P H E R E D . A N O I N T . .
A G N U S . L E T U S . F A N O N . I R E N E
O L D T O . E G I S . G U M . T E S T A T O R
R O M E O . A R E . M E R I N O . E L I H U S
T R E . N A S A . L I T T L E F O X E S . .
A Y N S . R E P E A L . I N C A R E . E R S T
. A R I S E M Y L O V E . L I S A . O O H
I N A P I E . S H E R E E . P L O . S C O R E
P A L O A L T O . R U R . K E E L . T A M E R
A G I R L . O F T E N . S E R V E . I R A D E
. . S T O W E D . C O N C I S E . O T T .
O V E N . R I R E . F E N N E L . A L L T H E
F I R E . I S A . B I L G E . F R E S H E T
F O R W H O M T H E B E L L T O L L S . E R Y
E L A T E D . H O A R S E . A H O Y . A T O M
R E T O R E . E M I T S . F I A T . S O S O
S T A N D S . D E L E S . T O T O . O P E N
```

125

```
S C A L P . F A I R . S H I R T . D D E
A L G E R . E T T E . S L I V E R . R O N
Y O U D O N T S E E W H A T Y O U W A N T
S P A . P A C E . M O O N . . M O W E R
. Y O U H A V E N T G O T A P E N N Y .
I C I E S T . E R G . . D A D E . .
L O T T E . B I N G . D O M E D . I S H
S O W . W I N T E R C O M E S . A T T A
A T E L I E R S . E O N . S T A S S E N
. R E S E C T . F L I N G . E L I T E S
S T E A L . H E H O L L E R S . F A U N A
L O D G E D . P E R E S . A L P I N E .
A R O U S E S . S T N . C A R E S S E S
M A N E . T H E S H O E F I T S . D R U
S H E . C A I N E . . T R E E . P L A N E
. H I R T . D I A . P A R Y E D . .
Y O U C A N K E E P Y O U R H E A D .
E N N U I . . T E A L . E A R N . P R O
A T F I R S T Y O U D O N T S U C C E E D
R O I . E R R A N T . G E N T . E R A S E
S P T . D I E T S . . Y O R E . S O R T S
```

126

```
. I L I K E . L E V I . A D D U P .
. S N O R E S . S H E E N . F O R M A T
R I T U A L S . Y A L E G R A D A T T W O
E K E V . S E A N S . M A R D I . R E D
D E R R . O N L O A N . A K A . N O I R E
I N N E D . C O P . A I R E . W H O O P S
G E E S E B E A T S S T . S H U N T S .
. . T A E . D I O . E A S T E R S . .
S T O L L E . C O Q . L I E T O . T A J
T O I L S O M E . T U I L L E . N O R S E
I N G E . W E D S H I M S E L F . N I K E
F I E N D . R O W E N A . D E E P E N E R
F A R . E D I N A . T R A . D A R T E D
. K N E E I N G . E L S . R I O . .
L E A V E D . Y E T I T O S E N A T E .
H A R L E M . B O M B . E A R . R O B E S
I N N E R . S A M . B O N N I E . R E N T
E D E . S A C R E . M O D E L . A T N O
D I S P O S A B L E C A R . N I A N T I C
. S T A L I N . E T O N S . T A N G O S
. O L D A S . T A X I . . E S T E R .
```

127

```
μ L E ■ C R I B S ■ C N T τ R ■ A G A R
T A L K ■ H A R R Y ■ A N A P A ■ A M I A
E S C A L A T I O N ■ L A T E N T B U D S
S H A R I F A S ■ C O L T S ■ A L L E E ■
■ P A T E N ■ T H R E E ■ A A R E ■
■ L I T E R A T U R E S ■ A M φ T R I T E
P E T E R ■ O T O S ■ S N O D E ■ N R A
A N A ■ W A ξ E S T ■ A Y E S ■ S U M
C O N S T A N C E ■ E T C H ■ C R A N E
■ P η L S ■ A C O R ■ R I N K S
■ A B U N D A N C E ■ P O W E ρ U S U S
M U R R I ■ R E A L ■ I D E E
A D A N A ■ S ν F F ■ P I N E T R E E S
B ι S ■ B U T T ■ I S O T E S ■ P E A
U P I ■ B E R L E ■ N I K E ■ C A I R N
S E L F L O V E ■ R α B E R C R O M B Y
■ O E R A ■ H A S I D ■ R I V A L
T I A R A ■ R A V E L ■ S U B E R A T E
I N T E R S T A T E ■ A R χ G E N E S I S
β K E S ■ T E N π N ■ N O S E R ■ S T A T
N Y E T ■ S T A N S ■ T E T R A ■ S S E
```

128

```
P O L A R S ■ B A W L E D ■ Y A L U ■ B A R
A M U L E T ■ A P I E C E ■ A V E R ■ I V A R
C O N F L A G R A T I O N ■ W O E B E G O N E
T O G A ■ R O A C H ■ S K E W ■ A L B I O N
■ S L A D E ■ B L E E D ■ I N F E R N O
S O D ■ P E T S ■ L E E R Y ■ A L I E N
P R I V E T S ■ S A L A ■ E N O S ■ D E I
I N S E T S ■ I N D I F F E R E N T ■ F E R N
R A C E S ■ S L I D E ■ A G A N A ■ A L L O T
A T O P ■ E L O P E ■ A V A S T ■ B R A I S E
L E N ■ D I V E R S I O N ■ P L U M B E R
■ S E R E N E ■ E M U ■ G E E G E E
A D O R I N G ■ O V E R T O N E S ■ R O M
L I L A C S ■ L A V E R ■ O D A L S ■ T A R O
O T A T E ■ S E R I N ■ A R I S E ■ T O T A L
O T T O ■ S T A N D O F F I S H ■ T O N I N E
F O E ■ K O K O ■ L E E T ■ T H R O N G S
■ D O I L Y ■ I D E A S ■ P R I M ■ G E T
A D D E N D A ■ S N E E R ■ A L O N E
S E E M E D ■ T I N T ■ D R A N K ■ A L A I
I N C U R I O U S ■ E N T E R T A I N M E N T
A T O R ■ N U N S ■ S E A B E E ■ N O T A T E
■ E Y E ■ G R A Y ■ T O A S T S ■ G A S P E R
```

129

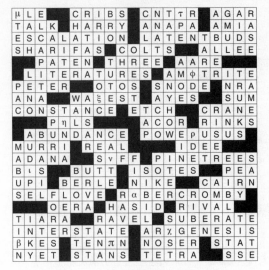

```
A R S O N ■ S A L I C ■ S P R A T ■ A S H
M E A R A ■ P R I M A ■ T E E T H ■ S P A
I S L E T ■ A U D E N ■ R A F E R ■ S E W
N E L S O N S ■ T A C O ■ R E O P E N S
O N O ■ A M P S ■ S O L V E ■ W I N C E
■ T W I C E S O L D T A L E S ■ I N T E R
■ A L S ■ R U R A L ■ S H U N
A L A M O ■ A T E S ■ I S E N T ■ M I D
S C R A T C H E D ■ J A M E S C H O I C E
A D E ■ H O A R ■ M O R A L ■ L E R N E R
■ P O E M S ■ H A K I M ■ B E T A S
D R O W S E ■ R A T E D ■ L I A R ■ T I E
P A S S E D T E N T S ■ B O R R O W E R S
T H E ■ N I E L S ■ A R A L ■ W A R E S
■ C E T E ■ E C L A T ■ O E S
P O L I O ■ H E A D O F T H E G L A S S
E X E C U T E ■ G N U ■ S E L L ■ O A K
S T A I N E R ■ R A G S ■ D E F A R G E
A A R ■ T R I P E ■ H O U S E ■ L E D G E
D I N ■ E R N I E ■ E S T E R ■ A R I E L
E L S ■ R A G E D ■ D O E R S ■ T O D D Y
```

130

```
R A C K S ■ G U I T A R ■ O M A H A N
E Q U A L ■ P A S T I M E S ■ R O D I N O
B U R I E D T R E A S U R E ■ C R E D I T
S A D ■ D E S I ■ L A C T A T E D
A D E ■ S U D D E N L Y ■ O M E N S
V E I L E D T H R E A T ■ U L A N ■ N A P
I M M E R S E ■ I E S ■ D E L S ■ C P L
A B A S ■ A S A P ■ C B E R S ■ S O L I
N A G ■ W E N C H ■ S A R D ■ O U T S E T
D R E A R I E R ■ I N D E B T ■ P A T S
■ C O N C E A L E D W E A P O N ■
O M I T ■ K E L S E Y ■ A B A N D O N S
T R A D E D ■ N E A R ■ S C O P A ■ M A T
H E S S ■ O G E E S ■ L A H R ■ P A R E
E L K ■ A U L D ■ L E M ■ E S S E N C E
O S E ■ C R O P ■ C O V E R T A C T I O N
S E D G E ■ V O L A T I L E ■ P A S
■ B E T T E R O R ■ E N O L ■ O B I
O R A T O R ■ C O V E R E D B R I D G E S
M I L A N O ■ H I E R A T I C ■ N U R S E
B O L T E D ■ E R N E S T ■ G E E S E
```

131

```
M O A T ■ R E B E C ■ O P A L S ■ G E A R
I A G O ■ E R A T O ■ U R I A H ■ I L L E
C A H M P I O N H U N T E R G E T Z F O X
H U S B A N D ■ S N A G S ■ A M I N E
■ D E E P ■ S I R S ■ S A R O N G S
A R B O R ■ A B E L E ■ P A W S
F A R M E R M I L L S W I L D E O A T E S
A M E N ■ A U N T ■ D A I S ■ S A L K
R A T I N G S ■ R E D E Y E ■ T O N I O
■ A L I A ■ A V I S O ■ E A R T H A
S H O E M A K E R K A N T F I X X S O U L
L A U R E N ■ R E E S E ■ F O C I
A L T A R ■ N A C R E D ■ W E S T I N G
N E R S ■ M I T T ■ Q U A L ■ I N E E
G R E E N E C O O K E B U R N S B A C O N
■ Y S E R ■ I L I A D ■ A S A N A
S I M I L A R ■ A L A S ■ U S E S
U R A N O ■ L O T T O ■ T A T T L E S
G A R D N E R W A T E R S R O S E B U S H
A N T E ■ S E A T O ■ O L I V E ■ A N T I
R I A S ■ A L D E N ■ S O B E L ■ R E A P
```

132

```
T O M A T O ■ T A C O S ■ M U T E ■ P A S O
A N A D E M ■ R I A N T ■ O N A N ■ I R A N
T E N A N E W J E R S E Y ■ T I M E ■ N I D E
A G E E ■ Y E S ■ L O V E R O N D E R
R A D I C A L S ■ D E F E R ■ D O R A
A L E N E ■ S T L O ■ L L A M A ■ S A T R A P
M A M E ■ T H E E R O F U S A L L ■ L E E R Y
A N O P I A ■ D E E R ■ T E N D O N S ■ S E L
D I C T A T E ■ S L A N E ■ A G O ■ T I T O
A N I ■ P I N E ■ T I D E D ■ D A R I E N
E C E E ■ O C E L O T ■ M E T A ■ D I O S
P E T ■ C U L A R W E I G H T ■ D A N
F R A U ■ H A U T ■ I N T U I T ■ E D O S
G L O S S Y ■ L E N T S ■ S I G N ■ F A T
R A C E ■ A P R ■ O S A K A ■ C A D E N C E
A G E ■ G R E A S E R ■ T A R A ■ M A L I C E
T O S S A ■ A P P T O V E D A N T A ■ E X A M
A N S E L S ■ T A H O E ■ I N G E ■ S M O T E
■ L E O S ■ R I M E D ■ E N T W I N E D
T O U L A U T R E C ■ R U S ■ L E R E
A B L E ■ S E E R ■ L I S H S I T U A T I O N
L I A R ■ A L A I ■ A N T I S ■ S T A D I A
L E N S ■ S E R B ■ E G Y P T ■ T Y B A L T
```

133

```
ORISSA   EROSE    STEPIN
ROSTER  SPECIAL  AREOLE
ESTEEM  PIMENTO  NARROW
 THELAWISAASSAIDIOT
DAMPS ACTIN   FLAN   ALL
UNUS  SWELL   SPELL  LOA
EDS  SHADE   FAURE  ADSUM
    PEA   INC   EBO
  ELEPHANTSAGENTLEMAN
SCENT TAINT   EROTICAL
ALAI  COVEY  ASHEN  NEVE
PASTILLE   SPURN  SITAR
  THEBULLOCKSBUTAFOOL
     NIE   HOI    WAN
MOATS FAINT  TELEX  SBA
AID  FANON  LISAS  SPUR
CLV  PAIN   KICKS  SHELF
  ACATMAYLOOKATAKING
ERNEST  LEARNER  RANCID
RECITE  SANDERS  ATTEND
STELAR   HEALS   GEORGE
```

134

```
BANS   TROY   CLAM    ZASU
ALEC  HOURI  ICER   SIREN
HEBREATHED  SHESNAPPED
SMOULDER  DETER   ELPASO
    PLUM  MIMED   CAVE
SCHLEP  LASER  PATERSON
CHEER  HETHUNDERED  HUI
RAPS  SETS   ITER   METZ
AIR  SHEMUTTERED  HOARE
PROPERLY  RUTTY  LADDER
   FIVES  CATHY  HAREM
PEEVED  HAITI  LEVELING
ORSON  HESNICKERED  TOA
LOST  SEAT   IVOR   STOP
ADE  SHERETORTED  MEESE
REDBIRDS  WRITE  LOADED
   OBIS  SOAPY  CURB
CHERYL  AMADO  LACROSSE
HEBELLOWED  SHECROAKED
ARRAS  KOLA  TITHE  RYAN
POOL   ALLY   ETTE  DELA
```

135

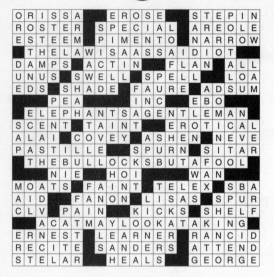

```
LOBOS   TALC   APSES   TEST
ANAME  OREL   LOTTO   OSLO
TALIA  LINE   DEARBRUTUS
KISSMEKATE   ETTE   APERS
ERAT  GIS   SARAS   ODESSA
   RARE    ELMS   ALIE
  EMENDS   FATALVISION
SALSAS  ILE   NERVE   SPA
ANIS  SHEARS  REAR  ACED
GIMME  IGNACE   ANKARA
 MEIR  DOGSOFWAR   EIRE
MARNER   ENLIST  ELITE
ILIE  UTAH  EASIER  LOTS
SIC   RENEE   TED  ANITAS
CAKESANDALE   DEACON
  MILD  DISC   LING
ROBINS  HASTA  AIL  FLOE
ABATE  DECI   SADCYPRESS
WESTWARDHO   BALI  LOMAN
LATE  BADEN  AREA  USAGE
SHED  AMASS  HERS  STYES
```

136

```
COCA   EDNA   FLOSS   KEPI
CHAS  ARID  LADIES  BARONS
CATHERINEDENERVE  AMANDA
PRETAPE  LICKS  ENOLA  COL
ERRS  SLINKY  ANDRE  SHOO
ATA  ONES  CUTIE  SHORN
SPY  LEVER  ALLEN  SHIV
PAL  ABLE  SLIDE  SHAVIAN
CHARLESDARLIN  NATURALLY
SINATRA  THATCH  LETE  LIE
BENET  POET  HONOR  PAST
DRAGONS   BOUNCER
HEDY  ILEUS  SNOD  OLAFS
ADA  TALK  SALOON  ACIDITY
MINCEMEAT  HERBERTHOOFER
SENORAS  ROAST  IMIT  TIS
YARN  BARRE  HADES  SYN
MADLY  LEILA  GIDE  ESP
USES  HORNY  CANVAS  EARS
LIV  GENTS  GARDE  CARRIES
EMILYS  HELENGURLEYBRAUN
SONOMA  ATONAL  BONE  OTOE
VOWS   STALE  SUES  WANE
```

137

```
PASHA   DAB   ADD   STRAP
AGAIN  ELIA  LEIS  ARENA
COTTONBALLWEEVILLAINS
   RUBELLA   MINA   INAT
SALAMI   EEL   NEPALESE
CLICKBEETLEBROWED
LIDS   NEEDLE   SLOVENE
AGA  BASK  OCA   PINED
MONARCHITECTURE  TREVI
  ROTO  OCI   ANC   RET
GRASSHOPPERAMBULATORS
AET   STA   CLI   RAMA
FARCE  SCARABBLEROUSER
FLIER   ASA   ODES   AMO
EMPRESS   TIMBAL   IDIO
  CATERPILLAROFSALT
GRANTHAM   RUN   ABORTS
AIRY   ITOS   AFINGER
MADAMBUTTERFLYBYNIGHT
ANOSE  SELF  SASA  ACOMA
STRAW   DOT   MAG  XENON
```

138

```
COBS  ADDIS   PLOP   COWL
ALEC  PEACH  ALIVE  ARIA
RIGHTOFWAY  BEFOREHAND
POSEIDON  SPLAT  FLINGS
   MESE  STOUT   OIL
DUPED  STENS   PROLATE
ADAR  AFTERTHEFACT  HEP
KISS  MAIL   TAME  SEME
ANT  INVARIANT  SCAPE
REPLEDGE  INCA  SAUDIS
  EAVES  POLIS  PEDRO
CURVES  ATEN  PREOFFER
INFER  INSTILLED  TRI
TIER  DENG   EASE  TINA
ETC  LEFTOFCENTER  OMEN
DETRACT   RENTA  WREST
  ATL  DANCE   SORT
TASTEA  BINAL  SPRAINED
AFTERSHOCK  OUTOFPLACE
PAIR  SOLES  SHORE  LORE
ERRS  EWER  ERATO  ASUR
```

139

```
ROSIE   SCARAB   ROPEDIN
PANICS  POLITE   APOLUNE
ACETIC  HOTTER   BELINDA
WHITEELEPHANT    BREAKER
NADIR  AREA   ILIAD   EEL
 BAN  EVER  CHEAT   EDDY
   GAMES   MAE   SPITE
READIER  HOUR   UPENDED
AUBURN  HORSESENSE   IVY
GRACED  ERSE  LACE   LEN
WALKS  WADE  MASH  MEARA
ESO   WERE   FACE  COATES
EIN  LOANSHARKS   INGEST
DAEMONS   ERAS   ATTESTS
   OPTED  ACT   SPEER
LALO   LISLE   BARD   BOW
AMA   PEWEE   KILO  SEPIA
CENTAVO  CATONINETALES
ANDOVER  EMREGE   RIVALS
STIPEND  DEADEN   ONETON
ASSERTS  ERRANT   STREW
```

140

```
GETUP  STOLA   PHIL   STUPA
ALAMO  ERGOT   IONA   PANIS
GUNETIQUETTE    KNEWYORICK
ELS  AMUSES  NEEDS   AORTAS
    SPOTS   LEMMA   ALLY
ROM HAI  AERIE  BRIE   RIP
ALEF  CALIPHORNERIER  ONA
RESEAT  ADARS   TASS   WALL
EASEL  CHIC   DROIT   MODEL
STYLE  LOOEASYANNA    IRATE
TEC  MORT   TONS   DESIST
  HALITE  STRAP  PLANES
EVENED  TEAM   GLOW    LIS
LEWIS  HARASSOWNER    BREST
LISTS  AMORT   RAAD   YAHOO
OLEO  SUIT   BLESS   RECALL
RET  PENCILVAINHERE   ENDO
ADS  ARTE  AINTS  ETA   DEN
    ERAS   STAKE   IONIC
RECLIP  STELE  INVERT   ORE
OGLEAHOMER    DELLAWEIGHER
WAUGH  LUNA   SKATE   VEINS
SLEYS  AGON   SAWED   EMOTE
```

141

```
ESTE   CLEAN   RABAT   SHEDS
ANTAE  HARTE   ILEDU   KOREA
STROLLINGTHROUGHTHEPARK
TRI  SIMEON  EMMAS   APPLES
RAVE  LEST   CRUST    RITE
OPENAIR   MOAN   ELIDING
  DREAMWALKING   TEC   DOE
DEPOTS  AERIE  AUTRY   REIN
ENEMY  TURIN   AVISO   CEASE
PERE  WOMEN   SMAZE   MANSES
ERD  ERDA   TAJO   SIRE
WOULDYOULIKETOTAKEAWALK
OILS  ENNE   LINT    MOI
STILLY  DOSED  THATS   COST
WHOLE  BOITE   CROSS   RAREE
OATS  BERIA   SHUCK   SUPERS
RNA  BAN   ILLWALKALONE
DESCENT   AIRY   AMERICA
  ODAS   POPPY  MEGA   SORB
FALLEN  AISLE  GARGLE   NEY
IMALWAYSCHASINGRAINBOWS
RAMIE  ETTEN   MANOR   DYNES
ESSED  NOSAD   AWARD   SEED
```

142

```
MASC   SHIN   LEAP   SCOOP
AGUA   TYRO   RILLE   TULLE
PENN  OMIT   EMBED   ADDER
BARONSEESBARRENSEAS
LAUREL  LEO   TOWN    NNE
ATRIA  MAPLE    EUR
MINERMISSEDMINORMIST
AMES  AMAIN   EROS   BAAL
RED  SCOPS   DIRER   TIE
   LABS   SEISM   EATING
CHASTEAUNTSCHASEDANTS
HELMET  MARTS   ELEM
UNI  HABLA   APRON   GBS
GIBE  REDD   ONEIF   BRAY
EIGHTFRIARSATEFRYERS
   GEO   EASES   APART
ASP  AMBO   INK   ERASES
STAIDBASSSTAYEDBASE
HASTE  SCALE   ARAB   SPIN
ETHER  TAPER   RITE   EIRE
SEAMS  ERST   NEED   STEW
```

143

```
SOWS   OCAS   TASK   AGREE
TWIT   UPTO   CHULA  DRURY
ALLI   TAIL   REDAN  DENSE
YELLOWSTONEFEVER   ETES
STATUE  EDENS   AWN
   TAB   PRIE   DUSTPAN
LAMB  REDHOTTAPE   CHEMO
ONER  SARI   NINA   URIS
ADIOS  GOLDDIGGERSMINE
NARWHALS   EINE   CABLES
  NENES   IGN   BEECH
ASABAT  AGUE   ANDROIDS
BLUERIBBONPRINT   AURIC
RATA  COOK   NCAA   SIVA
IVORY  ROSEBUDOIL   EDAM
SESSILE   ROLY   LEO
  SPA   MASON   APACHE
ECRU  BLACKMARKETSHEEP
BRAGS  UNTIE   ONTO   ELLA
BORAH  BLOND   SOAR   ALEC
SCARY  EYRE   ABLY   DONT
```

144

```
RECS   HEMEN   IRAIL   LAB
FLAT   ARANAS   GASCONADE
DERA  WRIGHTONTHEMONEY
GALAHAD   SARIS   FEED
PACKRAT  FAT   ALISONS
ONA  TWISTOFLEMMON   FEE
OTRA  CLAN   DIVE   ECON
DEARTH  ALTA   RESTSON
CHANGEOFHART   ATTAR
AIRHOLE   RENO   POTTO
STU  FORTHEBYRDS   EAR
CENIS  AARE   UNMANLY
IRONE  RIGHTSOFMANN
AFFINAL  SOLO   POTAGE
ANDS  IMAS   SALS   EPOS
ECE  SCUTTLEOFKOHL   PRE
FEMALES  REX   NOSTRIL
  IRON   NEMEA   PARTIAL
MALICETOWARDNUNN   MILO
COLLUSIVE   TIERCE  OSAR
IKE  MSTAR   TYLER   NEST
```

145

```
AROMA OILS   ROAM  SONS
SPOKES STOICS ELIA  AREA
CHARLIESNIGHT CENTENARY
AIDA AGIOS AORTA TRENDS
TDS STRAW ARNA CRUSTS
ALIEN OSLER SLEPT
COMPACT THEDENTIST THB
ABORTS DOTES EROS THEO
CODES PERONS ISIS BAERS
TEES FANG PLATA TRIGON
ISR EASYSTREET CIANOS
NEIGHS HINES SAMUEL
STADIA RECREATION DPS
CHITON TOONE TERN FRAP
HOMES SIRE RAMONA DRUSE
OVEN NANA CTENO FIESTA
PES FOOTLIGHTS LEATHER
EARNS PRAYS ROARS
VOLUME SEPS PARRY PGA
SERENA AREEL ARIEL DRYS
ADOGSLIFE KINGINNEWYORK
RANI CLAN SNOOZE SHAVES
AYOT YORE EGER SYNOD
```

146

```
MARS DENIS ASSOC DES
ALUI ERODE PTERO SENT
JOHNLENNON ROBERTALDA
ATRIUMS ADINA DIVEST
STET STACY TOTE
MOATED PAOLO DEBARKS
ESNES HARRYTRUMAN IKE
CMDR WARD OPP TRIO
CAR NATKINGCOLE TOKEN
ANEMONES ORATE SHEDS
WADED STARS SPORO
OWNED PIANO STIRRUPS
HAYES MARTINSHEEN GOA
UTES OLE PIES SLIT
NET EDDIEFISHER PHASE
SHALIER LAMES ERASES
BASS CANON ATOM
LAMONT CRUST CHOPINS
EDDYDUCHIN HENRYFONDA
BESS ROUST EDSEL OGAM
TSE BUMPS ROADS SAKE
```

147

```
ANSE STY CRUSES HIPS
CATS TIA HOMOLKA AMAH
THEQUICKBROWNFOX IPSE
SAMUEL EIS NIDE LACE
WILLIAMS VENA ECLAT
SCARE BEATSIT NOELS
PURE PED ILL IDOL
APES RAE AILS CALUMET
RIMS ADAPTER MAGI
SHUNS NEGRI TABLED
ALTAIC TAB EYE MAITRE
LIERNE ALAMB MORAY
AVIV TIMBREL MOUE
SENATOR ANTA ART CHAT
RANK ARC NTH IAGO
SOLDO BROKENO STRAW
ARABS ILED STANFORD
SITE INON AMO RAISES
HOVE KATHARINECORNELL
ALIT EPAULET RUN ELBE
YEAS THRESH RED SLAW
```

148

```
HEIR AMOEBAE AMNESIC
ACTE GARGANS ALIENATE
THEHORNBRIDS COLFAXES
OMELET SILENCED CAST
ADELE TANGO STP
CAPRI EXPOS TRICUSPID
AMUSE CANT DRUM ENO
PELE CRETE PRIOR TACO
ELI THESE RAYON SOLAR
DINGHIES DIVAN SUN
AGOODFIFECENTGUITAR
USE VICAR ORATORIO
PASDE FELON CHIVE MAR
AREA FEVER TOONE PALL
REX ALLI SHAY PINTO
ESCALATOR POLLS HADON
YMA LOBAR EATON
LIMP UNICORNS TENORS
ALBERTAN SKIPTOMYLUTE
NEARNESS CLEARUP ABUT
ATLEAST SERRATE SYNC
```

149

```
HARSH ABLE SPATS AMORAL
AGANA DUAL ORIEL BANANA
TRIAL ESTA BERLINCLERIC
HELPFULHINT SELMA TRASK
ESS MIEN RAIDS MOE
TUBED PARD GATS PAP
CLOSE BIGMENINTHEUSSR
SOO MRT OPUS IDAHO FAKE
CORGI AGNES BLEW TOLES
ALIAS WRIT GREENERY MDS
RECUSE ATTILA DOPA
FRAZIERBAERANDPATTERSON
ELLA ACTUAL COUPDE
PDQ ESTIVATE SPEE FLAIL
LOUIS RENE SKEET NEROL
EVEN STORK NOIR ADO GUY
BEANTOWNBALONEY ASHES
ERN AHOY AGAR SPREE
MOO BOYON AIRE LMA
AMEBA FAIRE TASTYRELISH
COZYBLANKETS LION LINTY
MORELS NEATO FAUN MONAD
ERASED ARDEN ANTE SNARE
```

150

```
SLANG ARABIAN ANIMUS
MALAYA ROXANNE POMONA
IHADPLANNEDTOBEPOETIC
TREASURE DES YENTES
ULM MAINE ETE
BAHAMA ZONED RBI SROS
ABUM LINK SEAT WALT
BUTIDRANKALITTLETODDY
ETC RANG ENROL ALIEN
SHRANK SHINER ALLONE
ESCAPEE ESTELLE
HEALTH ASNERS REINER
ALTAI ALARM MARS AHS
SOEXCUSEMYUNAESTHETIC
APIE NILE ERIE RONA
TEND SNY GIVEN ELINOR
ATI MIDAS INA
TOULON ALE AVERAGED
HAPPYNEWYEAREVERYBODY
ENTICE ABALONE ONEIDA
MOONED REDSTAR XENON
```

151

```
BASTE  SPIN   GLACE  ALTO
ARTEL  AIDA   LEDON  ROOD
REARM  NEAP   ACRID  NAME
RAYMONDCHANDLER  EIDER
ESS  ROMEO   AHEM    ARE
     ROTAS   TSAR  INSPECT
CHEAPEN   JOHNCONSTABLE
RISKED  FETED  INA   LAIC
UNSER   FRETS  RLS  OMNIA
EDE   MOORE   SOS    SHE
TINATURNER   COLEPORTER
  LUG   TRY   AMITY   OLE
REMIT  GAS   ERICA  BASIL
ALEC  AUG   ATREK  POLITE
JAMESFLETCHER   TABARET
ASOCIAL   RIND    BRIBE
   ORR  PEDI  SIENA   HAG
CANOE   WILTCHAMBERLAIN
ATOP  TITLE   EVIL  KARMA
ELSE  ANTIS   BONE  ENTER
NEER  DEIST   ERIS  REEDS
```

152

```
MACHE   OMA   APSO  CASPER
AVIAL   NOW   BLUR  ARTHRO
NORMANCONQUEST   BROILS
ICE    YET   ISNA   AILEY
TALKIE   MEET    CLENCH
ODEON   JERRYBUILT    ARA
BOSSA  TONYS  ANNA   FRET
ASS   MINT   SHUN    AMAT
   VIRGINIAHAM    STOLE
DECLARE  SITS   SPINES
EXHALED  GAP   ATOMIST
SCARES   ELIS   DIDACTS
PURRS   MOLLYCODDLE
ORLY   MULE   MALE    CAR
TIES   OMAN  STEVE  TEHEE
SAY   TOMFOLLERY   WREST
   HARRYS  RIAS   SONATA
AGORA   RATS   AGE    PHI
FERRIS  CATHERINEWHEEL
RESALE  OTOE   ANA   HASTE
ODESSA  PARR   NUT   OTTER
```

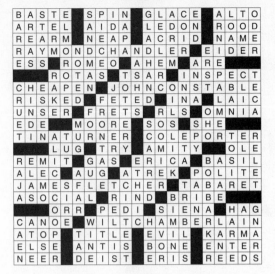

153

```
DOWDY   ORIEL   SOL   OHARA
ACHED   BRANDO  EYUI  NOTES
WHOSSORRYNOW  VERB  TWEAK
NOSE   DAIS   WHATSINANAME
  ORGANS   TRAIL   DEPOSED
FANTAST   WHATSUPDOC   WED
INFER   SAUTE   ALE    KGB
ENID  SPARSER  TOGA  ARTIS
RUR   HELP   HOWAMIDOING
CASH  HALAS  AIR  SANDWORT
ELTON   ROTTING   RINSES
  WIT   WHOSTHERE    INC
PEEDEE   OSSEOUS   GOWNS
ACCOLADE  SLY  SACHS  WHET
WHOISSILVIA   CLOY   AGO
NOLLE  EDAM  FASHION  STAR
ONO   EAP   ODLED   GESTE
SOV  PARLEZVOUS  GLEAMED
THREEAM   REESE   TRIMLY
AINTSHESWEET   SEAM  SLAT
LEAHS  NEAH  WHATSCOOKING
ESTEE  DADS  OOLITE  HINDI
STEEN   SRI   SCARY  ONEIF
```

154

```
   SPLAT    PAIR    BLADE
ATTIRE   OLIVE   ULANBAT
BALTIMEMARYL   PEUTETRE
BIER  PRINT  IWERE   SAL
EDGE  TONTOCANADA   FOCI
SLOSH  DOS  ONERS   STUKA
SYN   EMEU  JADED   NEWTS
   NEONS   EXO    SALT
OCELOT  SHERMANS    HASP
ALLWET  PIUS   AMAH  TULA
LLOYD  FEES  CROP   PEDAL
OINK  SANG  COTY   LAXITY
TEEN  AUTONOMY   CERATE
   EAUX    EYE    CHESS
MOWED   HUGOS   LESE   GSA
LUCYS  RESET  FEV   SPAIN
ESEK  RALAVELLARA    RING
ASA   DOPER   AARON   INGE
FENCESIN   AUCKLNEWZEAL
LOFLIDA  MATEY   SHERPA
GALES    PROD    TASSE
```

155

```
BOBS   ESTER   RAJAH   TAEL
ARUT   STONE   EMOTE   RICE
JFREDCOOTS   PETERFINCH
AFTERALL   ELLES   ROSTER
  LOPE   DREAR   DIRT
ATHENE   SEVEN   BANTERED
RHO   ERICPARTRIDGE   OCA
CAWS   ROO    EKES    CROC
ARAT   HARTCRANE   FOYLE
PRELATE   HOPED   PULSE
  DRAKE   BATES   AESOP
SHINE   PRIOR   FUNERAL
CHALK   LARRYBIRD   ERIS
HOWE   MAID    ASA    DRAW
ARK   JAMESWHISTLER   ONA
RESTORED   HAMES   LEEWAY
  URIS   SITAR   IBID
OUTRUN   ENTER   ELONGATE
DEANMARTIN   EARLWEAVER
ELKE   READE   TRIBE   ROLL
REED   ALLEY   SPEED   SNEE
```

156

```
BEAD   HOLD   CHAR   ABASE
ETTA   SERAI  EASE   REBEL
THEYVERAISEDHISCELERY
  INDEXED   PLEA   TITTLE
CORNIS   BLED    MOVE
  EIS   TUAN   GORE    CZAR
HECANMARRYACUTETOMATO
ELAM   NESS   HIE    RIZAS
AIRS   POET   GOAL  BANANA
ROE   SANO   ERIN    ERNO
ATWENTYFIVECARROTRING
NOAM   NATE   EROS    DIA
MATRON  ALDA  AJAM   PACT
ARROZ   MAE   SPET   RHEE
MAYBEAFEWRAPSCALLIONS
ALAE   WINS   FAIT    EIN
  HAFT   CONS    SMACKS
COHORT   MAUI   SPANIEL
JOYANDEVERLASTINGPEAS
ADELE   EMIL   RAINS   ANKA
GAZED   NINA   DORY   LEER
```

157

```
MAZE  SASH  ALION  DIVOT
ABOY MELEE SONNET ERICA
NODE IRIAN SORTIE CARTS
THISCREAMSLIKEA RHO  TET
UMA  HANS  ALF PARACHUTE
ASCRIBE  LUCKOF  TILTS
 OLE  DIST  RIPOFF  TAFT
ENAMEL ITHAD SEMI  RUE
PITYALLTHEMIGHTYCAESERS
OTT NEATER SANS  ZLOTYS
XRAY  TIL  BABE  HSUAN
YORE THEYPULLTHEIR GIST
 ABIES  RILE  IAN  SETA
GASTON POLO EGRETS  RAN
WHISKERSOUTWITHTWEEZERS
EON  OWED  SNAKE  ACUITY
NYES ABATER LIEN  MON
 IMPEI  RESINY  OMNIBUS
THEREISNO SEE  ALAD  ONT
REX  LEO OTHERSUBSTITUTE
AMIGO NATION AGREE ERIN
CASED SPIGOT ROANS ANET
ENTRY  ODETO  ISMS  REDS
```

158

```
QADDAFI  STARK  CRAZE
UTOPIANS THREED HAMEL
FASTDRAW SEMANA AMORE
TNT  MORAL BARYSHNIKOV
 LEUC  IRA  SABOTS
TUTANKHAMEN NOR  CIA
ORES  BONDI  ORLEANS
ODAS MORSE DOSTOEVSKI
KUROSAWA WROTE RAISIN
 TOE  ALIT  SPAIN
EMMY NIETZSCHE SNAG
NAILS ORAE  MRT
CUTLIP OILER XIAOPING
BRZEZINSKI ACORN SGAU
CEASETO ASYOU  ENTR
SSH  TSP MONTESQUIEU
 ASLEEP INC MAUD
KIERKEGAARD HABLA WIT
ENAMI ALNAGE MAINLINE
EGRET YESSED INSTANCE
PENDS DYANS KHAYYAM
```

159

```
 BOCK  POMP  AFT  UCLA
 LANIA ILIAD DOORNAIL
JASONS PENNI ENTERING
AMERICA"GODSHED  VANGA
MEP SOU SOLAR SING "
ELL NIL ROM  DIED
SLUR ITSAMADMAD"WORLD
JAGUAR LOA GELT SMEAR
 SNIPE HIERO  SKY
MORTISE BIB AUS BOHEA
OVERTHERE"SENDTHEWORD
OIDEA PAR END EARLESS
LEG  DERNS  SWINE
ADUNC SIZE OBI LETTER
HOMEAGAINHURRAH" SALE
 WRIT ION AMI  HET
HAYDN SKULD PAK IMA
HANOI ITISAFAR"BETTER
OPERABLE ECLAT BEHIND
SICKCALL DEARE ONEAT
TSK" RYA STES TEEN
```

160

```
BAFF  ACHE  RALE  OPAH
EMIL BRAUN ITEMS LOCO
NORA AERIE PANEL EMIT
†INGTHEBAR OLDRUGGED†
 YALU VASE GRE
LA†E REACT TERRAPIN
HALES †EDTHELINE TANO
AROD ATTHE ABCD †CUT
ECHO BIOS COVEY OPERA
CHANCIER ARRET SPURNS
 ELLS †ROAD ICER
TASSEL PONCE PROSPERO
ALAMO FIVES LAON ORAN
LODI ALEE AISNE SAVE
ONIN CARRYONES† PETER
NEEDLESS ENCRE ISON
 ETH RACE NAPA
AS†ASABEAR SIGNOFTHE†
LOBO TURIN TREND MEOW
ETON ELISE ORRIS ERNA
ASWE BEAD RASE NOSY
```

161

```
COROT MINEIS PAST GRAVY
LLAMA ORIANA ONTO ROSIE
ALDEN BENGAL UNUM OTTOS
SIENNA SEENO RABBITHOLE
HERSELF RENTAL ONT RAS
 DIRNDL GIB HYDOY
HEMI COOEY ASLOW YEOMAN
EXIT ELMS INSECTS SUEDE
LENI LIE URDU CURL CROW
PROSAIC ABASE ABIE AIRE
STRANDS BONA ASE WELTER
 LTD YSAIDALIC ILL
REPOSE LET TITO ESKIMOS
EVEN LYNN DAMON SCOTOMA
BING LAIT ILES PTA SPAT
ETATS PALAVER RUHR ASHE
CALAIS TYRES OTTER DYAD
 ILCER CSA RESTON
ALE VAN SATIRE ELEANOR
WONDERLAND DOGAL LENORE
ARDOR ALII TRACED DORIA
SNORE CODA HENLEY EDGED
HAWED EDEN EMOUSE REELS
```

162

```
ASPS SERAC THANE SPA
BLOW PRADO RAVEL PESO
COLEPORTER ILOVEPARIS
STEELIES SWOON VICUNA
 TOLD FAILS MANE
ISLETS MAINE NATURALS
TEENS YOURETHETOP BOA
AGAS LETS  AVER PRIG
LUV NIGHTANDDAY GLARE
SEEKING MOUES TRACER
 INGES LUTES GHANA
LATEEN BESOT ROPEDIN
ALTAR LOVEFORSALE ANI
PLOD SONE EAVE OBIE
POM ITSDELOVELY DUROC
STEADIES EGADS BUTANE
 DINS MARIS TOOT
SEADOG WIDEN AROMATIC
KISSMEKATE EASYTOLOVE
INTO RIDER SWISH KLEE
EON STIRS TESTS SASS
```

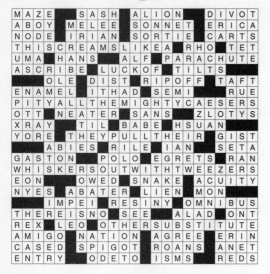

163

```
CADIZ  INNS  AMOS  DAKAR
ADENA  SUIT  ROAR  ERICA
THEFIRSTBONDOFSOCIETY
SAPOROUS  POETS  SLAVES
      IRE  SPUN  STAN
WEMAYREPENTATLEISURE
SAXON  LIDS  BROOM  BOA
EGAD  MEIR  REP  SOUS
COMETOLOOKALIKEATLAST
TNS  ALIT  AMISS  SAUTES
      EMES  RON  ELSE
STAVES  SCEND  BRAS  CPA
POWERTOHANGONEANOTHER
ARAN  NIL  OAST  ORAN
TAK  SCAPE  FACT  AROSE
SHEWHOISBORNHANDSOME
      HERR  RACE  EOS
CAVERN  JINNI  AGUARICO
EVILBUTANECESSARYEVIL
LOCKE  ODOR  NEAT  ELAND
TWIST  EENY  TAPE  DYNES
```

164

```
LEO    ALOP  APSES  FLED
ELBA  AMATA  RETAR  LUGE
EMILYPOSTMASTERS  ACRE
  LEPUS  PUERIL  IVIED
SOBERER  PENNONS  BOLTS
PLASMA  AORTA    GIRL
OER  OLIVEOYLWELLS  ETC
TABI  SLOT  SALTO  EBRO
SNARE  INSET  STAB  CAIN
  RADIO  NACHO  UVULAE
ALA  ANNEBOLEYNALI  LDS
REHEMS  NEWEL  DENEB
EMUS  USER  STALE  STETS
NOTE  LIMES  PENN  ARIA
ANT  MARYTUDORKOOP  INT
  OMAR  DENES  SLANGY
ANNOY  SCRAPES  CHUGGER
LAPIS  PIANOS  GNOME
ADEN  JULIETTELOWBEAME
VICE  OMENS  EXITS  SCOW
ARKS  TEASE  POME    ETE
```

165

```
SETT    ACTS  CLEAT  TARS
ETHER  EGRET  LORCA  PALAE
CREME  ARENA  ALIEN  RUING
TEMPEST  WARMMANSGEORGIA
  ALVA  WENDY    EDMOND
SNEERER  TONED  OLEO
MUST  GRIT  MANOFFORTYTWO
APT  COSTAR  TROTS  EARED
LEADIN  EPI  THINE  ASPIRE
ORLON  SORB  HRA  NUL  ONT
BENE  UFO  MEANS  PLEASES
  AMANFORALLSEASONS
ABSTAIN  TERMS  ALE  THAN
BRA  RIP  CIA  ALIT  REFIT
EERILY  OLLAS  FIE  PESTER
ADATE  SKEAN  TONGUE  ECO
MANSGREETINGS  NINE  GREY
  AUER  MEETS  SUBLETS
  BAALIM  LICIT  LASH
SUDDENLYLASTMAN  TOUTERS
ARIES  IWASA  URANO  RAMIE
PRONE  ECTAL  LENNY  APACE
SOSO  RASPE  IDEE    ONER
```

166

```
YOSHIDA  ITHACA  MADRES
UMPIRES  MOONED  ORIOLE
CARDINALPOINTS  MISUSE
CRIED  OUTS    REDHEAD
ASTRONOUGHTS  PEN
  APIN  PIRATEFLAF
ASCRIBES  STAVED  ZAIRE
TOHONOR  TIDY  THRIVER
BROWNBAG  AGE  THEATEAM
ATREE  SADIE  FUEL
TEENSY  LORRAIN  PLISSE
  OFAN  CUBIC  INLET
ROYALBOX  HAG  CUBSCOUT
ORELESS  LUGE  RELAPSE
MAGMA  DENSER  SAFENESS
ANGELWINGS  ALTO
  ACE  YANKEEGOHOME
JAYWALK  SOIE  CANAL
ONEILL  INDIANPITCHERS
STAPLE  CAUGHT  MOUNTIE
HEREAT  EVENSO  PERSONS
```

167

```
ONCE    VOLA  ANET  MASON
TULSA  AGGRAVATE  AGILE
BRUSSELSSPROUTS  MARLO
  BELLE  MISES  MILAN
MISDOER  SLADE  MONO
ANT  POACHEDSALMON  ITS
MEESE  LAVA  MEAD  NRA
BRAE  ICELESS  DIAMETER
ATKA  WANER  NOODLERING
  BOSC  AIL  STEPTO
DACCA  SHRIMPDIP  EBSEN
ARLENE  OPT  NAPS
BRANFLAKES  SPLIT  OSAR
SOMEFOUR  OCARINA  UPDO
ABS  PROP  ERIN  TRAMS
TAC  PEACHPRESERVE  RIA
ALES  RETEM  EARLETS
POSES  AGANA  ANEAR
UNITE  RUSSIANDRESSING
MONET  GREENROOM  AKBAR
AROMA  OUSE  UMPS  ISTO
```

168

```
HADJ  ARTIS  AGRIC  FIBS
EDIE  NOONE  CLEAR  ROOK
NOEWETURNS  TOOTENANNY
  EXIST  TARAS  VISAGE
AFFLICT  PIPET  RACE
GUILTS  ARNES  MUSKROSE
ARLES  BOARSOMES  LEX
TOLD  AVOW  WERE  MDVI
ERY  FOWLBALLS  MOSEL
SAWMILL  ALEE  ACETONE
NOIRE  ECLAT  SHREW
PADDLES  ROES  SHELLAC
OMEGA  PONYTALES  NHS
NORE  AWED  LAST  NDAK
CUE  SHEEPSKIN  BASSI
ARRESTER  RELET  REMOTE
  MOUE  PAEAN  RENEWED
TORPID  HEIST  BANCS
WHOLLYCOWS  SPLITHARES
INSO  OLLIE  CRUSE  KONA
NOSY  FEATS  HOMER  EDDY
```

169

```
RATS . ARES . ISHOT . STATUE
ASHES . LEAK . SCORE . AERATE
STORKSTORY . MATTEDMATTER
PARTITA . PEA . RAE . ROSE .
. MAIM . CRAIG . AYE . HAM
SACS . BRACKENBRACKET . IRA
AMOEBA . CARDS . LED . EDEN
COMMIT . UPA . MATES . FREON
RUBIN . CLEF . FATHA . RESOLE
ASI . CHATTELCHATTER . UAR
LENT . ARTS . NOHOW . HARASS
. GOLDIE . FARES . MODISH .
SCRAGS . ORBIT . DOME . PINS
FLO . SEMINALSEMINAR . DEO
RIMMED . MONET . IDAS . DIEGO
EMBER . NARCS . ANS . SAMOAN
EMIT . CAP . SCOOT . IMPUTE
ZEN . ROUTINEROUTING . STER
ERE . AUS . WAGON . CANE .
. LIRE . ATE . EAR . PATTERN
ASSISTASSISI . CAMELCAMEO
DIESEL . RIOTS . IGOR . HUMAN
STEADY . ANNAL . DEWY . TAPE
```

170

```
. ACAT . MATH . SHE . BOBBED
SMASH . ABRA . TED . APLACE
HARPERSBIZARRE . STANCE
ERA . OTE . ILION . INDES
RIVALS . ENID . MANDI
PLEBES . CYGENTRING . NCA
ALLEN . THESE . HONG . EBON
SOS . SOIT . LATER . LONG
. LAPPSOFMEMORY . ASTO
RECEDES . EAGER . MITER
ERASED . LIRAS . WINONA
CRISS . TENET . PARENTS
TARE . PRINTSOFWALES .
OTOE . RAMOS . AARE . GAR
RIPS . ONER . SALVE . DEANE
SCR . OXIDEDAISY . SANDAL
. ATTYS . ETRE . ESCAPE
ASCOT . SINUS . ARE . BEA
MUTUEL . PROPHETANDLOSS
AVOTRE . OAT . IRON . SAUTE
DAREST . TEE . PENT . CWTS
```

171

```
SMOOT . SERF . BARD . FAIRY
LINDA . AMOR . AGUE . ARNIE
ANTON . GENU . RONA . SORES
GEORGEANDIRAGERSHWIN .
. SIN . DOTH . TOI .
ATI . EELS . ION . OHSONICE
CAMORRA . COMICS . ONAGER
RHAPSODYINBLUE . SODA
EIRE . SER . TRANSIRES
STEREO . ACRID . AAA .
. ITAINTNECESSARILYSO
. NEO . ASCAP . DEATHS
EMBOSSERS . USE . MAIA
LAIR . EMBRACEABLEYOU
SWANSE . EUGENE . CRANIAL
ASSESSED . UNA . AHOY . NNE
. STR . EBAN . MOB .
. SOMEONETOWATCHOVERME
WOMAN . EVEN . ERIE . EVIAN
IONIC . SELL . NILE . REVUE
SNIDE . TRAY . APED . SLEDS
```

172

```
ANAGE . SITS . PACE . CETO
COHEN . ICOME . OBAD . ATOP
AVAST . NAMED . LENS . SERA
PARTING . CLIVE . CENTRAL
. DUCES . ATEAM . ALAIN
. REVOLTS . LIEN . SNAPS
ECCE . INES . CUSP . EAGLES
AHA . OLGA . RETILE . LET
VESTAL . DODO . CAROLYN
ESTATE . ERASE . DORE
STAKE . CROSSWORD . SAMBA
. ERNA . HIERO . NOFEAR
CONSORT . NSEC . INSECT
POR . SPRING . KENS . TKO
GRACIE . ENOS . WEVE . PASO
ANNUM . YETI . ARRIVAL
. GRAZE . IRENE . NEVUS
THERMAL . MEANS . CHICKEN
ROME . PLEA . TUTTI . AKITE
ELAN . PEST . ALLAN . TERRE
KENT . ARTE . SERG . ERRED
```

173

```
AMALFI . ASTHE . MANIC . GOBS
REGAIN . MUREX . AMISH . ELIA
COUNTDRACULA . DICTIONARY
SWAG . RATHS . MAREX . SPENDS
. ONO . THINAS . BEES
STU . EVILS . ONES . SOLDIERS
LINEMEN . TAKEA . GENE . SAIL
OSIRIS . METERREADER . SMA
WATER . TALLY . NYET . POTOK
ENES . TINA . TIER . TALESE
RED . JETSETTERS . ORDERED
. NEEDLE . ARNEL . SPARSE
CHARADE . TICKERTAPE . GPS
LITANY . TOTO . EELS . AGEE
EDITS . FELL . ARLES . JOHNQ
ADO . GINGERBREAD . SUNUNU
VENA . ALDA . EIGHT . ALIENEE
ENSNARLS . SACO . EATIN . TRL
. NINE . RECUTS . ESP
ARCADE . WHETS . CERES . UTEP
BARBERSHOP . PARTIALSCORE
ELEE . ELIDE . INANE . OOLONG
SEEL . DAZED . DEGAS . PLATES
```

174

```
BEST . TOTEM . ASP . SPACE
OATH . AKITA . THAW . CAGES
SCAR . LANCE . WASH . ORALS
SHYOFLYE . SHORTOFPORT
. TRES . STORK . COAL
WALTER . TIROS . CORSELET
ABOLT . OUTOFTROUT . DALI
LOSE . IRRA . ERRED . CIE
ERS . SCANTOFCANT . ASKED
STOCIAL . ROADS . DROOL
. FRAME . DALLY . SINOF
AFIRE . GENII . TAINTED
BALSA . WANTOFQUANT . RNA
ORO . BAERS . UNIS . CATT
ROSS . BAREOFHAIR . NACRE
UNSAVORY . BLURT . BARKED
. LEVI . EVERT . VOTE
. NEEDOFTWEED . FEWOFYOU
TETRA . USER . LAINE . REVS
IRANI . LARS . ENTER . ELAN
ADHOC . RYE . DIZZY . ELLA
```

175

```
LADS   CHAD   AWASH   SAMBA
AVOW   HATE   TAMPA   USURP
MINI   ARON   TRIAL   GINAS
ADENOFINIQUITY   TADINE
      EVE  EMU  EYESORE
RASHERS   AAR   DEPLORE
OTHER   CRISP   ROOFING
MOORS   ANCHORS   ALABAMA
ANODE   LAI   REAM   FELID
      EDE   ETERNAL   ETTE
SMA   ANEAROFCORN   FOY
SLAB   BELIEFS   SGT
EIDER   MMCC   NNE   ADLER
EVADERS   STATION   LOOSE
REMOVAL   LIBRA   LORNA
REFINED   ALL   LEERIER
REDDEST   ERA   MSS
ALLOWS   AHEADOFLETTUCE
TEASE   SCAMS   BOON   EVER
OATER   CORPS   ORAD   PENS
PRESS   INION   TEDS   SATE
```

176

```
SHAFT   ARAS   RACY   SCARF
AERIE   RESH   ACHE   ULNAE
GREENEGGSANDHAM   BENNE
ADA   TRIREME   TRANSVAAL
      EVEREST   LYCEE
SSW   ACET   SEGO   CARBON
COHORT   RAT   BESO
ONESPOT   BEIRUT   TRINES
TORI   RECONCILE   HALSEY
CREST   NURSE   SPOILT
HAS   EMERGE   REWARD   RAE
WAPITI   DALEN   SLUMP
CHAFES   OUTNUMBER   AMPO
PULLET   URIALS   LAYOPEN
ANDY   SAP   MISERY
STOWED   GLOW   FOSS   TEM
EROSE   FORSALE
CARNATION   REPRISE   SEC
OMITS   DREAMSOFVICTORY
BOMBE   EGON   TREE   HELGA
BRAYS   DENT   SILT   ORION
```

177

```
THES   RAF   FDA   MARL
HOSTA   ALUM   FIRN   CAMEO
RAMSEY   NINO   ARID   PROVOS
SLEEPER   ADO   CML   LACRIMA
VERDI   ESSENTIALLY   HELEN
PRS  SUSU  DREAM  ERNE  EDD
SHORT   IDLE   CITS
AJAR   RAFFES   SNATCH   ERGO
WERE   SKIRLER   TRE   COOP
NEIGH   NOISED   DRESSCOAT
PARADIGMS   ARO   NEATEST
ERIN   THESUBL   RIEN
FOSTERS   AMO   RIGOLETTO
CROSSTOWN   UNTAME   PRIVY
HAZE   AIM   SEVENTY   IDEE
EYED   FEMMES   RETIES   CENT
PULP   LEAR   OTHER
EGG  IRAE  ORRIS  AERI  GIG
ARYAN   PREDICTABLE   DIANA
TARRIES   BRA   OLE   STINTED
SHADOW   MEAT   ROLE   ACIERS
ATONE   ARME   YOLK   CUGAT
MERS   ETA   NEE   LOUS
```

178

```
BEVELS   TBARS   RPM   AMIS
AVALON   EOSIN   ERA   NONE
LILIUOKALANI   AAR   SOFA
ACHE   WORE   TIDES   EGIS
ATA   SOURS   IOTA   LODI
MILAN   POLLAIUOLO   OED
OLDEST   OAR   TRIANGLE
NAMATH   EPICS   SKUA
KEEUWENHOEK   EMILE
KNOX   ARLES   YURI   NEPAL
NANA   DEN   ALL   RAIL
ATONE   TATA   HATLO   ONCE
ROMAN   OEILDEBOEUF
ADEN   CLARA   RIATAS
NATURALS   ADE   SENARY
ORO   OKEECHOBEE   SERBS
TIPI   ACTA   YALOW   OAT
IKON   SABLE   RIFE   AGRO
CAEN   ORA   SEANOFAQLAIN
ERIE   NRC   MONET   NIENTE
SAAR   EEK   ENIDS   SLATED
```

179

```
CHAD   STAB   SHIP   JADE
HIJO   TYROS   ALICE   EBON
ADAMSAPPLE   ROGERBACON
PERICLES   WRATH   TUNDRA
CAKE   DEEMS   TURN
BASIN   MULTI   GARNERED
ORAL   CHARLESLAMB   ALA
RIFE   AERO   ILES   SPIN
ESE   PIECEMEAL   POSSE
DECAGONS   LEAN   DEUCES
REINE   MENSA   BURSA
SPARSE   AMIE   MARTELLO
TACIT   BLINDDATE   LOS
ELKE   PLOT   EROS   FIRM
EME   RAGAMUFFINS   OONA
PARADORS   ALLEN   HUNAN
DIVA   SONAR   RIAL
ANYONE   ALTAI   MARIANAS
SOURGRAPES   REDHERRING
WORE   BRIDE   SOLAN   DUET
ENID   SANS   NILE   SEWS
```

180

```
ODE   DNS   SPICED   SPOOL
AVERSION   ARMADA   ALUTA
CONSERVE   RAPTOR   BA2OD
CLIENT11ERATES   CHAIRED
TOM   TRACED   BYE   NESS
AMIS   PESETA   ROI
SOLAN   BEN   ALABASTER
ELVERS   ASSE   O4FATHERS
DOERS   PYE   LIS   OLE   TAT
GERT   PALERMO   RUINS
ERTE   ERODE   WAALS   TRIM
DINER   CHARIOT   RENO
DEE  MIS  UKE  CNF  DIS10D
CONDITI1R   ERLE   DEVISE
INDONESIA   AID   IRENE
LEN   DOLING   FENS
LACO   CAA   ANCHOR   AAA
ALARMED   LIGHTW8EVENTS
CA90OU   ENISLE   LAPIDATE
INPUT   LOOSER   EGOMANIA
SEEST   ARNESS   DES   MAC
```

181

```
BALSAM SSE ALEAN CAROM
EMEUTE PIT MARLO ACUMEN
CANCEL ABC EVILS RETENE
CHOCOLATEHERAN IVAN LIU
OSSO VERITY GLEAM SEAM
TAPE INN MOUSSEATTLE
MACARONIAGARA STELLA
PRESTIGE UNIT REGANS
SETH NER ASIAN ATOP NEO
KIT EMENDS ROSH TVA
PHEASANTIAGO FINE CHAP
GLENN METE OLEG COEDS
LAST DOSE GRANOLAPALMA
ANT BOUT ARABLE OLE
RAE OURS PINEY ABU SASS
ERRING ERSE RURALITY
AGHAST LEMONADECATUR
SALMONTEREY OBE DREW
ARAB UNTEN DOVISH RAMA
LEU STOT TOTRILLASVEGAS
AORTAL LEARY ASA TENANT
SLEEVE EMILE TOT ENCINA
ALLEY RULER ENE WIENER
```

182

```
ARAB BREAM MESH DRAM
PACA RANGA ARTEL AERO
THES EGOAT TRUMAN OTE
ETTES ARION NOO
NETLOSS ADULL EDISONS
OTHER BLOND ASS UT
INES THEGREATES E TAA
RE S AAAA ELEE CANT
EAT SPINES CLASS HICO
SNIPPERS PURLS CANER
VEERS WINES STORM
STEPS THE E THEWAYTO
HOHO HIRED SPRAWL ON
ORES ELAN AIDA ITOS
TEA RICIOUSNESS NATE
IRR IMA DRIED IDIOT
NOTATED BYALL PACINOS
MOT BASLE BEREA
ABILITIES STATE ITAL
EGAD CADRE ISLAS NINA
RENE ISSY ATILT KNOW
```

183

```
BORED ASIS SPEED SCAM
AGORA ROOK LANAI EZRA
CROATOMANICOLORS MEIR
HEFTED RAMAPO LOGICAL
DOS RENO RASH
LOCO RENEGE ANODE KOR
ETAT AERIE RREASURE
DONTKHMERANYMOOR ERGS
ASTEROIDS AMPS MEDIA
TRAWL ALDO KOPPEL
ASH IWENTGAULFINN ASE
CHASTE EMIR GOTAT
CAIUS AGAL SOUWESTER
ELMS GRANDKENYANSWEDE
PLEASANT ALIEN ARGO
TID TREES SATRAP NNES
EGER STAB SOT
ENDEMIC ALAMOS LEASES
LOOS SERBTHEMAYANDISH
BOWS ODILE MALE DITTO
ANNO NEVER ORTS STEED
```

184

```
ELOPES CPOS DAY CAFE
LEARNT WORRY ARA OGLE
LAREDOORDEAL LIMAMAIL
SULKY CCVII NESTS
SATIRES ELAN ALIT
ELUDES ASPENPANES MOD
RICES TROTS ITINERARY
MOSS MAID COTTA EDNA
OTO NASSAUSAUNAS TROD
NONSENSE NUNS FIATS
CAREEN SPA SHEENS
BLOND FORD TOREADOR
AOUT MANILAANIMAL RUE
SANE ELAND ALES DATE
INTESTINE CHITS COMAS
SSS LAGOSGOALS HOMAGE
KILN SOUR DORISES
GIANT WEIRD CAPON
OSLOSOLO NAPLESPLANES
SLAB LEO GNATS ELNINO
HENS END STNS RATTED
```

185

```
MAST BWANA CHIEFS SPLAY
ALTA LAMAS TENTIE PEUDE
COURTOFAPS RAGTOP ANNES
HUNGON HEEP REEF RUGAE
STEEDS SEPTA WASTRELS
THELEYSOFBROADWAY
UPS ORATE RUE ITION SAT
TOTAL BEARIN LETO BIRI
AMANDA READSFOR SOONGS
HEMS PHLOX ALF LIMOGES
GENTIAN TABU WIEN GNU
MARLO THEWHOLESHE IRATE
AMO ODOR HAKE PIGTAIL
COURSER BON BOTEL CLEF
RUNNER SLATTERN COHERE
ANDS ATTU APOGEE BERLE
ETS ANEAR PTO ELLAS YET
ENGELBERTPERDINCK
OVERSELL DOYEN AGENCY
RENEW IFIT EDDA ONEILL
CRANE AZALEA MOBILEALAA
ASTOR DETECT ARENA DINT
STEWS ADESTE NYLON SAGE
```

186

```
ALAS SABIN CTRS MESA
MOLT CRASO REHAB EMIR
PAPEREIGHT IRECUTTERS
RUNES FOSSE NRA
ACCOSTS CARPE SKILIFT
LORIS SHINE MBA DII
ARID STERRINGHEEL ENT
MOMS PARR LOAD SNIT
ONI SINGINGDOORS ETAL
SANGAREE YARBS CRILE
ALLEY CAVES CADUC
PALES LOSES SHERMANS
ELLA BRIDALSHOERS LEA
SCAN LAME IFNI PTER
TOY PANBROKERAGE AIDE
EVE ICA VESTS ERNIE
RERANKS DENTS PAPISTS
CET SORTE SATES
ITCHDOCTOR LITTLEOMEN
TRUE POONA LAURA NOVA
SAPS OPEN ENNIS STAG
```

187

```
ARP  EVIL   SHOAL  ASST
LEE  SEDAN  TAWNY  MICA
OFA  CLIMBMOUNTNIIITAKA
SURFED  ICIAN  ONELINER
STLO  TAN  LETON  SENDAI
OAHUISLAND   RYE    ILE
FLAGG  GEORGECMARSHALL
RHODE  HEAP   SCAPA
SUBTRIBE  DDAY  HEISTER
UTO  SERFS  GRAB  NEHRU
SIRS  BATTLESHIPS  KIWI
ACHED  SOOT  STAID  SIN
NAIROBI  PREP  SCRIBING
AEONS   NEED   KEELS
AIRCRAFTCARRIER  CANOE
RNA   OAR   USSARIZONA
ASTARE  ROSAS  PTA  EDER
DECREPIT  ADENI  CORRAL
SCHOFIELDBARRACKS  ICI
TEAR  SEEIT  CLUES  LAE
ATRY  IRENE  SETA   LTR
```

188

```
REDS  HADJ  ACT   STERE
AMOK  AERIE  SRA  CARROT
JULIASSEIZEHER  OMANIS
MISSA   ELTON   MAD
IFA  LEES  BURN  PRESTO
MANSES  LEDA  SHE  STIR
PLIED  AZULEYEKIT  RND
ALMA  GLIM  RATE  DOSE
LOA  ALBEE  PESTO  ODEA
AWLSWEALTHATTENDSWELL
AEA   ARC   RAS
THEMEMYRRHCHANTOVENUS
HELP  AHUSH  REESE  UNO
ERAS  ASIN  LEAS  LAIN
ART  KINGLEEERR  PONTA
PEER  IRE  ANNS  SAUCER
ENRICH  ABUT  SPAS  ESS
POI   STORE  HALTS
ACCENT  COREREOLAYNESS
BORNEO  ONE  EAVED  IRIS
SWISS   TED  DRED  TART
```

189

```
WAMPUM  TABLE  AMEND  IPSO
ELAINE  ORLOV  ROMEO  SEED
STYLINGMOOSE  GNUENGLAND
TOOL  ABUT  NEEDS  AMASS
SILOS  STENO  STAN
APC  ANEYE  HIRT  SPINDLED
BEHOLDS  LODI  POLO  SOTO
ONEWAY  PEEWEEERMINE  RHO
UPEND  DIVAN  ROBT  ABEAD
TAT  SCONES  SLIDE  GRANNY
LAT  OVERTAKEN  REALIZE
HEAVE  BEA  TRYTO
DRAPERS  DRIFTWOOD  SLY
RAISIN  CLEAN  EARNER  LOM
ELVES  HOUR  PALES  IMAGE
ATE  HEATINGDUCTS  ANIMUS
DORS  PITS  LASH  COSTARS
SNAPPILY  RIMS  THANE  STY
REGS  SUNNY  HERES
STARR  ANITA  ARNE  AFRO
CROWMAGNON  BISONTENNIAL
LOLL  MADRE  LAINE  MINNIE
USES  SPIED  ENTER  STANDS
```

190

```
SANTA  BALAS  ADAM  FLAG
PREEN  ADAGE  LIDO  AONE
CELLA  NOVAE  PARTRIDGE
CALLINGBIRDS  DETERGES
ELATES  THEA  PEELE
STAR  MASH  DRUMMERS
AHA  EPI  ERINS  POTENT
LORDSALEAPING  MIV  NEH
TREAT  BRING  DOSE  EGO
MOSSBACK  DONT  REL
FRENCHHENS  TURTLEDOVE
ROD  EATS  RANCHERO
ADS  PENS  CIRCA  VIDEO
NEE  ORK  LADIESWAITING
COLLIE  TOTEM  ILL  DOE
ANDIRONS  OWNS  NOSE
DEBUT  RUTA  CADORE
OPENEYED  PIPERSPIPING
GOLDRINGS  MALMO  THREE
IDLE  PIET  ALLER  EERIE
TEAR  ECRU  MAIDS  SWANS
```

191

```
ITA  ERGS  AMISS  THAWS
SYCAMORE  PARCH  OILIER
PRESSSECRETARY  NETTLE
YODA  SERE  STALAG  ONEL
SESTETS  EGOS  ENE
IMP  NESTING  CHESSSET
SIERRA  SNORT  KEVINS
MATEO  AWARDS  ERASED
VOLGA  YSER  NECTAR
SSS  TIARA  SAILS  SKATE
ONUS  SWISSSTEAKS  SNAG
RECTO  KAPOK  SPIRE  DTS
TACOMA  IRIS  STAFF
SKEWER  SCARPS  FIRST
SENECA  STOOD  BOXCAR
LESSSALT  SIMILAR  AMY
ESS  DUST  LIVESTO
ACTS  SPREES  TESS  LIME
DOOLIE  DISTRESSSIGNAL
ARRIVE  ANTED  TEACARTS
TYPES  YEATS  SEXY  ETE
```

192

```
EELER  MEAD  CAL  AKIM
SNIPE  SARGE  OPALIZING
TONIC  KNARS  SHOOTISTS
SECUREDLOANS  SCADS
AROAR  NOE  KLEIST
SCAR  UNITEDSTATES  NTH
CARPET  LEVEE  NED  AGEE
EGEST  SODA  TAJ  SKAT
NEA  ABLATE  PAL  UNPILE
ERRS  OAS  AERI  REINS
TOUCHINGSTORIES
AFAWN  ALAE  NAE  HALS
SMILED  NAV  BASEST  SOW
HEXA  VAT  YALU  OSSIE
OLEG  ORI  BLARE  INWARD
RID  CLASPEDHANDS  IDEE
NASSAU  OAR  TAINT
TORME  KNITTEDSOCKS
CHALLENGE  CHORE  RHONE
NOREASTER  HERES  SELIG
NESS  ELS  SEND  ERATO
```

193

```
PALMA  MACAW  SWAPS  SPAR
PATOIS ONASH  CARAT  HAPI
ATTACK RILKE  AGORA  OTRA
ARITH  EAGLET LEMON  GRIN
RICHARDSHAW   GERALDBUILT
       EYES   BUD    BANC
AMESLAN ELTON SATYR  ISH
CALIF  JOHNKNIFE     OMAHA
CASER  AVENUE ELAN   NICER
TREVI  DICED  HEARTY RAKA
       EGOIST DUDS   EVOKES
SSW  HONE GLORY ALAI ELS
CHINTZ DOOM   SCURRY
HALO EFFORT ESTES GOTHA
ELLIS ULUS EXPORT IDEAS
MOIRA ROBERTPIN   NEARS
AMA VALET ATONE MAILMAN
     MOOT  ARU   TUNA
ALBERTDENTE  DONALDBROOK
MOON REMIT SIMILE REVUE
BRAE ABELE INANE SEDATE
ECRU CARES MANON TAUTEN
RADS TRYST PRINT EDGER
```

194

```
ALOE ACTA RIO   CHAFER
SOUL IRAN ADDE  DELANO
HOTSPRINGSTEEN  TAPING
LATIN  UNEARTH  THREE
CHI ANGELO MORON AFAR
RENT GERARD NYLON IDS
OREAD  RAREES  YOURE
CEDRIC  RICHMONDALE
SCOOT  STREAK  EIDER
SPLITRAIL YANKEE LIRE
ILO AKRON PRIER NIB
PAWS LLANOS INFRINGES
STEED ANGOLA GEODE
ALTOONASSIS  LEERED
LIVID  EMPTOR  ADORE
ALI ENERO SHOWER YALE
DENS KRAUS ALSTON DEM
MAGNA SITWELL ABOAT
INTIME SPARTANBURGERS
REOPEN EURO NELS ESAU
ERNEST TDS DUET STEM
```

195

```
MASON SPIT ASSTS BUG
ARENA TERRA MAHRE OLE
SLEET AROAR ASIAN INA
HOI HOTUNDERTHECOLLAR
  NEALE AUTO LEROI
AGING INCENSED ACNE
CARL ANODE ALS SAGAS
CREEPSIN DONE LOSE
SEDER HOPPINGMAD EVER
  NOS ARTS INCASEOF
ARF BESIDEHIMSELF RNS
CHIMERAS VETO IRA
TETE ALLFIREDUP ONTAP
ETTA EINS FEASTING
DOONE BEN FIORE OCTA
RBIS UPINARMS SINKS
ESTER STEP MORSE
ATTHEENDOFHERROPE DIP
LEI ERICH ODEIN NOONE
DEE MINIM SUSIE INFRA
ODD SEGOS PSST CAFES
```

196

```
SOONER CAPULET SPAD
AUSTERE PLENARY SHAME
PARTINGSTITCHER PURNA
AVIS ANES ROTI CANTER
MEC GNAR PERI HORNIST
TAILSSALK JAR ITTO
FRIO EAR SOLO NAY
AREOLAS DEBRIS NOG
SAM SHOWEDROE AORTA
SNOW TAR IMPS SHOALS
ATRI MASSGAINS ORLE
DISNEY PAPA AAA STEW
CENSE HIDINGYRE ANI
ITA PINERO INWARDS
HAN RAAB ASS ELSE
CONG NIN SITEWHALE
ANISEED MISE EARL ELM
ROMPED MANO LENA ALYA
ARAIL SACKBEATDRIVERS
FETES ORLEANS LACONIC
EDEL SIERRAS ETHNIC
```

197

```
BAER CALLA STAGS ABABA
OMOO ALIAS ARLENE GALAS
PANDORASBO LAINIE EGANS
STEERS TORS INEPERIENCE
ROD PER TINES ISLES
PEA ENID FILMS RENTS
INT RON TALIA BERG AST
EDITED BOSTONREDSO NHEB
COOED MINTS EDIE ADORE
ERNE HADES LADED ATLAST
SOONER MAMA BOOTEE
SAS CROSSEAMINATION SRS
CLOYED RUED PANDER
ALULAE ADAIR WACKY HERE
BISON PLOT RICKS REPEL
SNAP LEICOGRAPHY PEELER
ASH OPES RENEE SIP ASO
ORION NAPES SEAR NEY
SANER HESSE MIA OCA
AMBIDETROUS SEAL GOATEE
LEASH AUNTIE PRICEFIING
GATTO INDEED OSCAR ROTO
AREST TORRS SHALE ONES
```

198

```
LACED CHAPS DATER
POLITE HEAVE ISOPOD
MACADAMIANUTS LYRICAL
ICAN LOGIC SCALE KRI
NILS CURE BIOTA MYNA
ONE HORAE SAONE GOMER
TOSSEDANDTURNED OVALS
ILETA USES FAIR
CASTES PAIL COLLECTS
ASPEN LOONEYTUNES IOU
LAOS EERO ABLE DALE
ONI OFFBROADWAY TONER
TALIPOTS IDOS RAZORS
EVER SNUG AMORE
RODIN RECKLESSABANDON
ACRES ARRET ESSES ERO
NEOS AGOOD ANIS AFAR
GAT ALGOL CASAS VINS
ENTITLE LUNATICFRINGE
SEALED ENERO RAISES
NOISY DOVER EXPOS
```

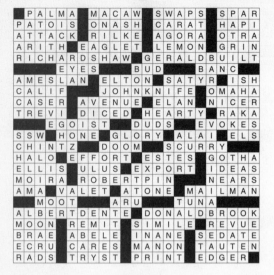

199

```
S H A F T   D O D O S   D A N A   S P Y
A I S L E   H E N O C H   E P I C   W E E
G L O A T   O M E R T A   S P O T   A R A
S A P P H I R E D M A N   T U B   S P U R
    E N R A G E D   W R I E S T
A M B E R L I N E R   L E O   P I E T A
G O A D   E D S   R U B Y S T A N D E R
A L B E R T   O L E G   S P U R T I N G
L E A S E   C U P I D S   I L K   S A O
    S A L O N I K A   S A R A   O N T
A Q U A M A R I N E C O M M A N D A N T S
C U M   T R E E   T R A I L E R S
C A P   H I E   W O R L D S   A S O K A
E V I D E N C E   A R A L   T W O B I T
P E R I D O T A R D S   A A R   R O T A
T R E N D   S E I   G A R N E T T L E R
    G A M U T S   A R B I T E R
Z A N Y   A S E   E M E R A L D E R M E N
O V A   P O U R   C E T A N E   M A I Z E
N O V   E R A L   H E E D E R   O V E R A
E W E   W I L Y   O R L E S   R E N A L
```

200

```
S T A C K   S L U R   L O G E   T I T U S
E A M O N   A E R O   A V E S   O M I N E
C R I M E A N D I S H M E N T   T I N I A
T R E C E N T O   S A I N T   S H T E T L
    T I T A N   S U N S   S L E Y
S A T I N E   D E L A   S A I C   D I T
E M B O G   P L E A S E D A S C H   E C A
L I E N   G A E A   E L S E   K I W I
A N A   C O N T R A T A L L Y   D U C A L
H O M E S W I T   T O R T E   S A B E R S
    S T A C   S T A R A   F O R E
R A T T A N   R A I S A   B L O C K E D T
A B H O R   N O N C T U A L I T Y   M A W
Z E U S   S E A T   D U T Y   C L U E
E L M   C T U R E D T I R E S   B O Y L E
L E B   H A R K   E R N A   P A W N E D
    E B R O   E M U S   B R O N C
O C E L O T   A L I S P   O U T S H I N E
L O X I A   F R O S T I S O N T H E K I N
E L G A R   I N G E   R I N G   E R E D E
O N E N D   T O E D   E X E S   E S S E S
```